D1505184

A Trading Nation

A TRADING NATION

**Canadian Trade Policy from
Colonialism to Globalization**

Michael Hart

UBCPress · Vancouver · Toronto

09 08 07 06 05 04 03 02   5 4 3 2 1

Printed in Canada on acid-free paper   ∞

National Library Cataloguing in Publication Data

Hart, Michael, 1944-
  A trading nation

  (Canada and international relations, ISSN 0847-0510; 16)
  Includes bibliographical references and index.
  ISBN 0-7748-0894-2 (bound); ISBN 0-7748-0895-0 (pbk)

1. Canada – Commercial policy. 2. Canada – Foreign economic relations.
3. International trade. I. Title.
HF1713.H372 2002   382′.0971   C2001-911707-8

Canadä

UBC Press gratefully acknowledges the financial support for our publishing program of the Government of Canada through the Book Publishing Industry Development Program (BPIDP), and of the Canada Council for the Arts, and the British Columbia Arts Council.

This book has been published with the help of a grant from the Humanities and Social Sciences Federation of Canada, using funds provided by the Social Sciences and Humanities Research Council of Canada.

UBC Press
The University of British Columbia
2029 West Mall
Vancouver, BC V6T 1Z2
(604) 822-5959 /Fax: (604) 822-6083
www.ubcpress.ca

CONTENTS

MAPS AND TABLES

PREFACE

This book was initially conceived more than a decade ago while I was on leave from the then Department of External Affairs and International Trade as an academic visitor at Carleton University, the University of Western Ontario, and the University of Ottawa. My teaching duties at these institutions, while pleasurable and rewarding, afforded me sufficient time to spend many happy hours at my computer, surrounded by stacks of books and papers and entertained by the mellow sounds of CBC-FM. One of the results was a good start on this book. I had hoped to complete it early in 1991. Upon my return to government, however, I found it impossible to find the blocks of uninterrupted time that a project such as this requires.

It was not until my return to Carleton at the end of 1995 that I found sufficient time and heightened motivation. In teaching trade policy to graduate and law students, it was disconcerting to realize that there existed no readily accessible work summarizing the main objectives, concepts, and events that had influenced the development of Canadian trade law and policy. Comprehensive accounts that do exist are now more than two generations old and are largely inaccessible to modern readers.

Most trade and economic policy is forged by practitioners in government within the framework of priorities and values set by cabinet ministers. While not unaware of the thinking of academic economists, political scientists, and independent commentators on issues of public policy, practitioners tend to base their advice to ministers on day-to-day experience, and their biases are toward the practical: towards what will work rather than what may be best. In considering what will work, they think in terms of negotiating experience, knowledge of international rules and practice, awareness of opinion in Canada, and the realities imposed by the political process. Ministers and cabinet are not often persuaded by theoretical and moral arguments about what is best for the country; they worry about what is doable. In preparing this book, however, I have taken a less involved, longer view that places issues into their broader setting.

I have relied largely on secondary sources, particularly for the material prior to the 1960s. For some of the chapters covering this period, there now exist excellent monographs based on careful archival studies, such as Ben Forster's *A Conjunction of Interests*. For other chapters, however, such studies are either non-existent or inadequate. There is a need for a thorough, archivally based modern history of Canadian trade policy. The pages that follow should help to delineate the themes and suggest the broad lines of inquiry, but they cannot fill in some of the missing detail that could be supplied by a more comprehensive study.

My selection of facts, events, and ideas represents a personal statement as to what is important. In making my choices I was, of course, guided by the ideas and principles that I believe to be important today and by my previous experience and training – those of a trade policy practitioner with a history background and with both a practical and theoretical appreciation of economics and politics.

Each generation must write its own history and explain its past in terms that speak to the present. In the area of public policy, knowledge of the past is indispensable to a thorough understanding of the present. The need to reinterpret and revisit the past is not a negative reflection on the insights of previous generations. It is simply a recognition that if we fail to write and rewrite our history, we will cling to static and dated portraits of ourselves and will reduce the past to caricatures rather than maintain it as living history. The alternative is that we will have to be satisfied with the work of foreign scholars and see ourselves and our place in the modern international trading system as others see us.

History does not divide well into distinct chronological periods, but all history must be written with such packaging in mind. It was not difficult to decide where to start. Where to stop was more problematic. In deference to my most recent responsibilities in government, however, I have deliberately chosen to confine any comments on the Uruguay Round of GATT negotiations and the North American Free Trade Agreement to those necessary to bring the story of Canadian trade policy to the middle of the 1990s. Each deserves a full-length study of its own. Together with the negotiation of the Canada-United States Free Trade Agreement, these negotiations mark a watershed in the development of Canadian trade policy. They are the culmination of a constant theme in Canada's trade policy as well as the beginning of a new set of challenges, also deserving of a full-length study. The end of the Uruguay Round thus appeared a good place to end this survey of the historical foundations of modern Canadian trade policy.

Nevertheless, I have added some thoughts on the main themes likely to dominate Canadian trade policy in the years ahead. Based on developments in the late 1990s and the opening years of the twenty-first century, the emergence of broad support for freer trade, hesitant steps toward governance of a much more integrated global economy, and efforts to deepen Canada-US linkages all point to both continuity and change in the political economy of Canadian trade policy. The tragic events of 11 September and their aftermath, however, have greatly concentrated the minds of governments in Canada and elsewhere, redirecting their priorities. It is too early to consider the full implications of these new developments, except to say that trade policy will remain critical for Canadians, even if its pursuit is likely to become more challenging.

ACKNOWLEDGMENTS

Modern governments are able to deploy a tremendous depth and breadth of expertise within their ranks, and volumes of high-quality material are prepared annually by anonymous civil servants for decision by senior officials, ministers, and cabinet. For twenty-two years, I was fortunate to have been privy to some of this excellent writing and the attendant discussion and debate. Such an atmosphere forms a unique and indispensable school for trade policy practitioners. I benefited greatly from the information and advice that this process generates. The "seminars" run by Simon Reisman during the Canada-US free trade negotiations proved particularly instructive. In preparing this study I have taken the liberty of reviewing and seeking inspiration from stacks of documents and memoranda. Indirectly, therefore, a great many friends and former colleagues have unwittingly contributed to this study, and I am grateful to them.

Over the past ten tears, many friends and colleagues have given generously of their time by reading and commenting on various drafts of the book, in whole or in part, and on previous books and papers that have provided much of its background. I would particularly like to thank Doug Arthur, Bob Bothwell, Dennis Browne, Laura Ritchie Dawson, Bill Dymond, Percy Eastham, Geza Feketekuty, Jonathan Fried, Hector Mackenzie, Chris Maule, Maureen Molot, Colin Robertson, Pierre Sauvé, Phil Stone, Chris Thomas, Brian Tomlin, and Gil Winham. Additionally, I would like to thank Derek Burney, Gerry Shannon, and John Weekes for their longstanding help and support. I would also like to thank those students who took my seminar on the history of Canadian trade policy at the Norman Paterson School at Carleton over the summers of 1998-2000. Their research papers and class discussion added importantly to the detail and arguments.

Three anonymous reviewers read the manuscript in full and provided important and useful insights and comments that helped to sharpen the arguments in the book.

The editorial and technical staff at UBC Press were, as usual, a tower of support and strength guiding me through the minefield of preparing a study of this length and breadth. Emily Andrew and Camilla Jenkins in Toronto were particularly indefatigable in their support and advice.

At home, my family not only forbore the usual boorishness of a preoccupied husband and father, but actively engaged on all fronts to help me get the text out the door in the best shape possible. My wife, Mary Virginia, pored over the manuscript time and again to find just the right word, phrase, or construction, agonized over extra commas or misplaced conjunctions, and generally ensured that the book said what I meant it to say, but better. My daughter Elinor did her own search for technical words, convoluted sentences, and obscure meanings. My son Edward injected a necessary note of levity and scepticism during the interminable lectures on the finer points of Canadian trade policy that have been known to mar family dinners. To all three I owe a great debt.

ABBREVIATIONS

AD	antidumping
APEC	Asia-Pacific Economic Cooperation
Benelux	Belgium, Netherlands, and Luxembourg
CAC	Canadian-American Committee
CAP	Common Agricultural Policy
CCTN	Canadian Coordinator for Trade Negotiations / Continuing Committee on Trade Negotiations
CDC	Canada Development Corporation
CET	Common External Tariff (EC)
CG-18	Consultative Group of Eighteen
CIDA	Canadian International Development Agency
CIT	Court of International Trade (US)
CITT	Canadian International Trade Tribunal
CMA	Canadian Manufacturers' Association
CTC	Canadian Trade Committee
CVD	countervailing duty
DISC	Domestic International Sales Corporation
DPSA	Defence Production Sharing Arrangements
DSU	Dispute Settlement Understanding
EC	European Community
ECM	European Common Market
ECSC	European Coal and Steel Community
EEA	European Economic Area
EEC	European Economic Community
EFTA	European Free Trade Agreement / Area
EPU	European Payments Union
EU	European Union
FAO	Food and Agriculture Organization
FCN	Friendship, Commerce, and Navigation (Treaties)
FDI	Foreign Direct Investment
FIRA	Foreign Investment Review Agency
FOGS	Functioning of the GATT System
FSC	Foreign Sales Corporation
FTA	free trade agreement / Canada-US Free Trade Agreement
FTAA	Free Trade Area of the Americas

GATS	General Agreement on Trade in Services
GATT	General Agreement on Tariffs and Trade
GNG	Group for Negotiations on Goods
GNS	Group for Negotiations on Services
GSP	general system of preferences
HS	Harmonized System of Tariff Nomenclature / Harmonized Commodity Coding and Description System
IBRD	International Bank for Reconstruction and Development (World Bank)
ICAO	International Civil Aviation Organization
IGA	International Grains Arrangement
ILO	International Labor Organization
IMF	International Monetary Fund
ITA	International Trade Administration
ITAC	International Trade Advisory Committee
ITC	Industry, Trade, and Commerce (Department, Canada)
ITO	International Trade Organization
ITU	International Telecommunications Union
IWA	International Wheat Agreement
LDC	less developed or developing country
LLDC	least developed country
MAI	Multilateral Agreement on Investment
MFA	Multifibre Agreement
MFN	most-favoured-nation
MTN	multilateral trade negotiations
NAFTA	North American Free Trade Agreement
NATO	North Atlantic Treaty Organization
NORAD	North American Air Defence Command
NTB	nontariff barrier
OECD	Organization for Economic Cooperation and Development
OEEC	Organization for European Economic Cooperation
OPEC	Organization of Petroleum Exporting Countries
OTC	Organization for Trade Cooperation
PPA	Private Planning Association / Protocol of Provisional Application
Prepcom	Preparatory Committee
QR	quantitative restriction
RTA	Reciprocal Trade Agreement (US)
RTAA	Reciprocal Trade Agreements Act (US)
SAGIT	Sectoral Advisory Group on International Trade
STR	Special Trade Representative / Special Representative for Trade Negotiations

TEA	Trade Expansion Act of 1962 (US)
TNC	Trade Negotiations Committee
TPRM	Trade Policy Review Mechanism
TRIMs	trade-related investment measures
TRIPs	trade-related intellectual property rights
UAW	United Auto Workers Union
UN	United Nations
UNCTAD	United Nations Conference on Trade and Development
UNESCO	United Nations Educational, Scientific, and Cultural Organization
UPU	Universal Postal Union
USITC	United States International Trade Commission
USTR	United States Trade Representative
VER	voluntary export restraint
WHO	World Health Organization
WTO	World Trade Organization

A Trading Nation

1 TRADE POLICY AND ECONOMIC DEVELOPMENT

The truth is that, historically, free trade is the exception and protectionism the rule.

— PAUL BAIROCH, ECONOMICS AND WORLD HISTORY

The streets of Quebec City are an unlikely place to find police in riot gear. First settled nearly four centuries ago, its old quarter normally evokes a romantic, old-world charm that attracts thousands of tourists annually. But not from 20 to 22 April 2001. That weekend, its visitors included the thirty-four democratically elected leaders of the Americas as well as an estimated 35,000 demonstrators determined to impress upon the leaders their disapproval of globalization, freer trade, and international trade negotiations. In order to avoid a repeat of the debacle that had marred the third ministerial meeting of the World Trade Organization in Seattle eighteen months earlier, the police relied on a temporary fence built around the perimeter of the conference site. Their strategy worked. The official meeting was able to pursue its task without incident.

The protestors, however, also succeeded. As has become increasingly common-place, television found the motley array of dissidents and their message more visually appealing and easier to report than the complex issues facing the leaders and their advisors. Unlike at Seattle, the leaders succeeded in adopting their communiqué and in giving renewed impetus to the quest for freer trade throughout the Americas. The protestors, not surprisingly, also claimed victory, and so the media reported. The goal of liberalizing international trade and investment and placing them on a more secure, rules-based footing seemed to be increasingly under attack, and the chances of ultimate success waning. Or was it?

Canadian antiglobalizers have been among the loudest voices protesting in Seattle, Quebec, Washington, Prague, and the many other places where leaders, trade ministers, or finance ministers gather to transact their business. Curiously, however, their claims and concerns have found but the faintest echo among most of their

Brian Gable, "Acronym Exhaustion," 17 April 2001.

fellow citizens. In the 2000 federal election, for example, Canadians gave the only party sympathetic to the claims of the protestors – the NDP – short shrift. For Canadians, the concerns of Seattle, Quebec, and elsewhere had been debated *ad nauseam* a decade earlier and proved wanting. Canadians had learned to accept that a country that derives an increasing share of its wealth from international commerce – the value of Canadian exports and imports of goods and services reached nearly 90 percent of the value of Canada's gross domestic product in the year 2000 – had much to gain from an open, well-ordered international economy. It was a lesson derived from more than two hundred years of experience, and driven home by the 1980s and 1990s. By the end of the 1990s, polling suggested that three out of four Canadians were satisfied that the international trade accords Canada had negotiated over the previous decades met their interests and concerns.[1]

The Trade Policy Challenge
Canadians could be forgiven, however, for not being familiar with the details of the charges and countercharges hurled across the fence in Quebec City. While not prepared to agree with most of the claims of the protestors, they did agree that the government should be more forthcoming in explaining the contours and purpose of international trade negotiations and their impact on Canadian and global developments. At the same time, governments could be forgiven for finding this a difficult task to discharge to the satisfaction of their critics.

Understanding the changes taking place in Canadian and global trade policy constitutes a challenge both to those who have a specialist interest and to those who have a general interest in gaining a better appreciation of Canadian trade policy and the issues involved. Stripped of its jargon and detail, however, trade policy is relatively straightforward. It is largely a matter of solving trade and investment problems within a framework of domestic and international rules as well as competing domestic and international political pressures. Ultimately, the solutions to these problems should increase national and global economic welfare. To achieve that end, governments pursue three basic objectives:

- improving access to foreign markets for competitive domestic producers and providers of goods, services, capital, and technology, by reducing or eliminating barriers to their exchange imposed by foreign governments
- maximizing national economic welfare by enhancing consumer and user access to competitive products at world prices, as a result of international competition and integration into the larger world economy
- establishing and preserving an effective, nondiscriminatory trade relations system based on transparency, due process, and the rule of law.

Market access is a business objective that seeks to maximize export, investment, and profit opportunities for domestic producers already able to compete on the international market; it has always enjoyed broad, popular support in the business community and elsewhere. Competition is an economic objective based on the ideas of neoclassical economics; it tends to raise suspicion and fear and can prove politically difficult to implement. An effective trade relations system is primarily a political and bureaucratic objective grounded in legal values; it also has enjoyed broad support because its successful pursuit provides the vehicle for fulfilling the other two.

By pursuing these three objectives, governments seek to influence directly the extent and nature of a country's foreign trade and indirectly a country's economic development. At its most basic, of course, trade is determined by the day-to-day decisions of individual consumers about what to buy, from whom, and at what price. Merchants, manufacturers, importers, and other private-sector firms respond to the cumulative impact of these decisions in their determinations about what to produce and supply. They, in turn, try to influence consumer decisions through advertising, product placement, and various other means. All of this takes place within a framework of laws and policies devised by governments to promote consumer safety, fair competition, environmental protection, and a host of other societal concerns and priorities. Trade policy instruments – tariffs, quotas, product standards, procurement preferences, and more – form an integral part of this framework of rules and regulations. Trade policy, trade relations, and trade negotiations are thus less about grand ideas and ideologies and more about the pragmatic working out of very specific problems within the contours of existing political and economic realities, informed by the decisions and experiences of the past.

For a trade-dependent economy like Canada, a well-balanced trade policy is a necessary but not a sufficient condition for growth and prosperity. To be effective, trade policy needs to be complemented by other government policies, ranging from fiscal and monetary policies to competition and industrial policies. Increasingly, the line between these various policy instruments has become blurred, adding to the challenges faced by governments in their design and implementation of appropriate policies.

Over the years, trade policy has been one of the primary instruments used by Canadian governments to guide economic development. Generally speaking, minor changes in the deployment of trade policy instruments will lead to minor changes in exports or imports or industrial activity, while major changes may lead to more substantial changes. Over the years, most changes have been small and incremental despite claims to the contrary. Cumulatively, however, trade policy has been one of the most important policy instruments influencing Canada's economic development.

Historically, the Canadian economy has been open, small, export-led, and resource-based. Canadians have been price takers, that is, their economic activity has been much influenced by external factors. Exports have been an important engine of growth and, until recently, have been concentrated in resource-based products. Canadian trade policy, on the other hand, long tended to work against rather than with these characteristics of the Canadian economy. It sought to insulate the economy from outside influences and to encourage the development of industries capable of replacing imported products. There was a high degree of conflict in Canada between those policies that encouraged resource exploitation for export and those that encouraged import-substitution manufacturing. In other words, trade policy was more than a matter of economics; it was also an intensely political issue. Protection through high tariffs became inextricably tied to nationhood, a connection that was not broken until the end of the 1980s when Canada finally entered into an unrestricted reciprocity agreement with the United States, and the federal government told Canada's uncompetitive manufacturing sector to either adjust to global competition or lose its markets.

Ultimately, trade policy decisions involve choosing whether or not to give certain groups or individuals in society advantages over society in general – choices that require some understanding of the economic and political costs and benefits involved. The study of trade policy thus combines the analytical tools of both economists and political scientists. Since most decisions rely heavily on precedent and rules, a thorough understanding of the issues also benefits from the insights of lawyers and historians.

In trade policy, decisions to favour a domestic group often involve discrimination against foreign producers by imposing a tariff, a quota, a procurement preference, a higher product standard, or some similar measure. For example, in the 1950s, the governments of industrialized countries concluded that domestic producers of textiles and clothing deserved a special degree of protection from foreign competitors – a decision that may have helped domestic producers, but discriminated against foreign producers and reduced economic welfare at home by increasing costs to consumers. Once domestic producers had become dependent on protection, they required more and more and developed a potent lobby dedicated to its maintenance. The choice then became not one of protecting one group in society at the expense of society in general but of breaking the spiral of protectionism by hurting one group (in the short term) while benefiting society in general. Most trade policy determinations essentially boil down to similar decisions to discriminate for or against the few.

Underlying most decisions to discriminate – whether domestically or internationally – is scepticism about the efficacy of markets and the price mechanism on the one hand, and faith in the beneficial effect of government regulation and controls on the other hand. Most of those decisions, however, are not based on economic concepts and analysis but on noneconomic instincts and biases. David Henderson, an economist with long experience in government, notes, "More than two centuries have passed since the publication of Adam Smith's great treatise, *The Wealth of Nations;* and trained economists are now well established, not just in universities and research institutes, but also in business enterprises, civil services, and the councils of presidents and prime ministers ... Yet DIYE [do-it-yourself economics] has not become a curiosity of the past ... Ideas and beliefs which owe nothing to recognized economics textbooks still retain their power to influence people and events."[2] He concludes that economics must be one of the few academic disciplines in which the professionals have failed to drive out the amateurs and in which "prescientific" notions continue successfully to influence serious opinion.

Because trade policy decisions often affect foreign interests, trade policy is an arm of diplomacy and may involve international negotiations and rule making. Again, the basic concepts in diplomacy and rule making are simple, even if they too have become the craft of professional experts. Negotiations involve making mutually satisfactory bargains by finding ways and means to satisfy often-conflicting objectives, while rule making concerns the establishment of precise standards that will govern future decisions, thus promoting predictability and stability. Years of negotiating and rule making have created a body of international rules that now limit the choices available to governments in deciding whether or not to favour one interest over another. The basic concept underlying these rules is the presumption that nondiscrimination is better than discrimination, whether domestically or internationally.

Trade policy can be divided into two branches – foreign and domestic. Foreign trade policy is concerned with access to foreign markets and the successful exploitation of those markets, while domestic trade policy is concerned with import competition on the domestic market. Ideally trade policy and international negotiations should seek to achieve a balance between foreign and domestic priorities, a balance that ensures gradual movement toward more open and more secure trading conditions in order to increase domestic and global economic welfare. In practice, however, these ideals are often tempered by political and other realities.

In order to make significant progress toward their foreign trade policy objectives in a negotiation, the partners need to frankly assess current practices and often be willing to make serious adjustments to their domestic policies. This is more likely to happen when the partners share a common view of the issues, when their economies are organized along similar lines, and when they are at approximately the same level of development. Trade-offs are less likely to be made when there is little ideological consensus, differing approaches to economic organization, and wide disparity in economic development among the players. Additionally, the greater the number of players involved, the more likely the benefits of more open access will be perceived as relatively diffuse and long term, while the payment may be seen as direct and painful, politically if not economically.

Inevitably, the question of sovereignty arises. Over the years, as nations have grown more interdependent and economic integration has intensified, the issues subject to international negotiations have expanded. Fifty years ago, trade negotiations principally revolved around tariff and quantitative restrictions, and the major concern was the extension of most-favoured-nation (MFN) treatment. Negotiators concerned themselves about what happened at the border and sought to end discrimination in the way countries treated foreign goods originating in different countries. Today, negotiations touch domestic laws and regulations and involve national treatment, that is, discrimination between national and foreign goods and services. Such negotiations can prove much more controversial.

Part of the problem, of course, is created by the rhetoric of politicians, when they suggest, erroneously, that *countries* trade with one another. Trade and production, however, are driven by the demand and imagination of *individuals* responding to market opportunities and desires. Government's role is to regulate the resulting flow of goods and services. Trade agreements do little more than reduce the scope for arbitrary and discriminatory regulations and for unproductive interference in market-based decisions. Concern about the impact of such agreements on sovereignty is perhaps overwrought and misplaced.

Indeed, it can be argued that every trade negotiation is an affirmation of sovereignty. The whole idea of entering into an international agreement is to impose the rule of law – one country agrees not to do some things and to do other things in particular ways, in return for other countries agreeing to do the same. The 1947 General Agreement on Tariffs and Trade (GATT) involved such commitments, as did the 1935 and 1938 bilateral trade agreements between Canada and the United States. In fact, these commitments strengthened Canada as a nation, because they made the country stronger economically and because trade and other matters came to be governed by agreed rules of international law, not by decisions made unilaterally in Brussels, Tokyo, or Washington.

It was a striking feature of the free-trade debate in Canada in the 1980s, for example, that the opponents of free trade were able to convince many Canadians that a bilateral trade agreement posed a special threat to sovereignty. Few questioned that Canada enjoyed a defence relationship of extreme importance and complexity with the United States, or that it should strike bilateral agreements on subjects as diverse as migratory species, water quality, extradition, and mutual legal assistance, but it was an article of faith that a bilateral *trade* agreement carried with it unacceptable risks of absorption.

As the forces of global integration continue to place pressures on domestically oriented producers, values, and institutions, more issues will become candidates for international negotiation, and an ever-wider array of special interests will feel threatened by such agreements. But if governments are to address today's problems and influence tomorrow's decisions, they must of necessity deal with the issues raised by the real world, including controversies that arise out of traditional domestic policy making. Governments cannot ignore the protectionist effect of trade-remedy legislation, ownership restrictions, cultural support programs, or agricultural supply management and still hope to negotiate useful agreements. As a result, trade negotiations require that governments confront entrenched domestic interests that are prepared to make emotional appeals to sovereignty.

A further limitation on what can be expected from trade negotiations is imposed by the conventions of international trade bargaining. Trade negotiations seek to increase economic welfare by reducing discrimination, removing barriers, and providing greater scope for the operation of market choices, unencumbered by artificial barriers imposed by governments. They assume that the order and stability flowing from clear rules and equitable dispute settlement provisions are to be preferred to the rule of power. In short, both economic and legal maxims suggest that international trade agreements are mutually beneficial.

But international bargaining is often pursued on the basis of pre-economic and pre-legal concepts. Negotiations are frequently viewed as a zero-sum game – every concession granted by one side must be matched by a concession from the other side. While negotiators know that the removal of barriers and the establishment of rules make sense, in their hearts they are convinced that they must also maximize export opportunities and minimize import competition to satisfy their political masters, who are responding to the noneconomic ideas of their publics. From time immemorial, politicians have accepted the mercantilist maxim that the strength of the nation requires a positive trade balance, an ability to do without imports, and the promotion of strategic advantage over all other nations. British economic journalist Martin Wolf has called this process "mercantilist bargaining" and has suggested that, perversely, politics dictates that it is only through mercantilist bargaining that progress can be made.[3]

One of the factors that promotes mercantilist bargaining is the reality of international trade. International trade theory teaches that reductions in trade barriers lead in most instances to a more efficient allocation of resources and to an increase in both national and global economic welfare. The gains realized are spread out thinly across the whole population, while the losses are concentrated among producers of the formerly protected goods and services and their employees. Beneficiaries of trade liberalization tend as a result to be much less vocal about their interests than potential losers, who are thus able to tilt the political balance against trade liberalization and require negotiators to demonstrate specific gains and losses in a mercantilist balance sheet.

Trade policy, therefore, involves the pursuit of some well-established principles of law and economics tempered by the realities of domestic and international politics. The constant interplay between principle and pragmatism is informed and influenced by the precedents of the past, which make the trade policy, laws, and practices of each country unique. Contemporary trade policy challenges can often be understood more clearly by examining their historical roots. Economic analysis may well demonstrate the fallacies of Europe's Common Agricultural Policy (CAP) or of Canada's system of supply management, but it will provide no more than a partial answer to those interested in negotiating solutions to the problems these programs pose for Europe's or Canada's trading partners. The historical origins of these policies also need to be studied. Understanding modern trade policy means grasping current political and economic circumstances as well as the historical development of the modern trade relations system and the place of Canada and its major trading partners in that system.

The Challenge of History

Canada has always been a trading nation. From earliest days, Canadians have relied for their livelihood on exports to bigger and wealthier markets. Those exports have been largely resource-based and often at very low stages of processing. Furs and fish, then wheat and forest products, and finally metals and minerals were sold on world markets in exchange for machinery, consumer goods, food, and other products not as readily or as cheaply available at home. Canada's colonial, imperial, Commonwealth, and sentimental ties to Britain and geographic ties to the United States ensured that the preponderance of the country's commercial relations would be with these two countries.

Much of Canada's trade policy, from its early pre-Confederation origins until well into the postwar era, was forged in reaction to policies pursued by these two world powers, policies typically adopted without any thought, positive or negative, about their possible impact on Canada. Throughout much of their history, Canadians sought a special place for their products in one or both of these two markets. Much of the history of Canadian trade policy, therefore, is a record of the changing priorities attached to commercial ties with one or the other. The quest for special status was complicated by the trade policy and attitudes in vogue in these two dominant powers as well as by noncommercial sentiments and considerations. The latter

"THE CREAKING OLD MILL"
Borrowing from Strube of the London Express, Dale again reverted to the theme of High Protection's effects. (Nov. 17, 1932.)

Arch Dale, "The Creaking Old Mill," 17 November 1932.

often flowed from the fact that Britain and the United States were major powers with worldwide interests, responsibilities, and influence, while Canada, rather self-consciously, worried about its self-image and identity. Only after the 1960s, with the decline in the United Kingdom's global economic role and the emergence of the United States as Canada's only major partner, did the government strike out across the Atlantic and Pacific in search of countervailing forces to the overwhelming influence of the United States.

For much of Canada's history, trade policy served as the basic building block in the country's industrial development. Tariffs and related instruments encouraged the growth of a domestic manufacturing sector, while trade negotiations provided access to foreign markets for Canada's resource producers. The result was a bifurcated industrial structure, a heavy reliance on foreign capital, and an increasing dependence on trade with the United States. Dissatisfaction with both the means and the result led in the 1970s to efforts to foster different trade and production patterns. Their impact, however, proved meagre at best. In a democratic market economy, a century of economic development is not quickly undone and the forces of geography, business judgment, and consumer preference are not easily overcome.

Canadians have historically found it hard to accept that a resource-based economy without secure markets for its products, coupled with an inefficient, import-substitution manufacturing sector, provided a poor basis for sustained growth and development. In the face of spreading protectionism in the United States and in Europe, however, it was difficult for a small, trade-dependent country either to find ways to reduce foreign barriers to its exports or to resist the siren call for protection from its own manufacturers. What might make economic sense now did not necessarily make political sense then. Nevertheless, Canada's dependence on outside markets made the autarchic impulse of nationalism increasingly untenable. If Canadians wanted to continue to benefit from international trade, the economy had to become both more diversified and more integrated into the emerging international economy, on the basis of a trade policy that would provide business with predictable and stable access to wider markets. To that end, trade policy in the 1980s and 1990s achieved a level of public attention and concern that had been absent for more than fifty years. Responding to wrenching changes in the domestic and global economies, the federal government pursued a range of bilateral, regional, and multilateral negotiations aimed at both encouraging and rewarding adjustment to these changes. The implementation of the Canada-US Free Trade Agreement in 1989, the North American Free Trade Agreement in 1994, and the World Trade Organization Agreement in 1995 completed the quests of more than a century of international negotiations while simultaneously mapping out the contours of future negotiations.

Trade policy had for centuries been organized on the basis of the measures governments use at the border to define and defend national markets and national producers. Over the past half-century, as a result of successful negotiations among nation-states, a rules-based international trade order has become a universally accepted part of both intellectual and intergovernmental discourse. By the 1990s, however, the success of that order in integrating national economies into a global economy posed a new series of challenges suggesting the need for both a new trade policy and a new regime capable of extending concepts of national governance to an increasingly integrated global economy.

The full impact and implication of the global economic changes that are driving the demand for a new paradigm are, of course, not yet fully understood. Understanding these challenges will require a greater appreciation of the road Canadians have travelled over the past century and a half. It is more than a cliché that those ignorant of the past are bound to repeat its mistakes. The past informs the present and makes it both more intelligible and easier to accept. With a firm understanding of the past and a realistic appreciation of the present, the challenges of the future are less daunting.

As we stand at the beginning of a new century, the salient features of the Canadian economy, when placed in their global context, suggest the need for urgent attention to a range of critical economic policy choices. Canadians now enjoy one of the highest standards of living in the world, while occupying the second-largest piece of global real estate with less than half of 1 percent of the world's population. Nevertheless, these features are in some ways liabilities as Canadians face the much more competitive and integrated global economy of the new century. If Canadians are to adapt their economy to the challenges of the new century, they will need to look again to trade and related economic policy choices. Making the right choices will require a clear understanding of the choices made in the past and of the influence these choices have exercised on Canada's economic development.[4]

The pages that follow treat an economic issue – trade – but they are not a contribution to the economic history of Canada as that subject is usually understood – the application of economic analysis to historical phenomena.[5] This study attempts to make a contribution to the history of ideas and public policy. It seeks to provide a better appreciation of the nature of Canadian trade policy and the contribution trade policy has made to Canada's current economy and its place in the global economy.

Much of the writing about these issues in Canada over the past few decades has been too much influenced by current political and economic ideas and values; governments, in making and implementing policy, react to contemporary pressures and realities on the basis of a rather limited series of choices. Governments do not have 20/20 hindsight, nor can they anticipate the views of later critics. When Prime Minister John A. Macdonald, for example, decided to pursue a National Policy, he was responding to the reality of a small and not very successful economy that had suffered the rebuff of first the United Kingdom and then the United States. He was looking for a policy mix that would help to develop the Canadian economy and at the same time create incentives for the United States to take Canadian reciprocity overtures seriously. Similarly, efforts by Liberal governments in the 1940s and 1950s to open the economy to greater competition and to enhance export opportunities reflected their continuing preoccupation with depression and global war. As Judith Goldstein points out in her study of the role of ideas and institutions in the evolution of American trade policy, "American trade policy has been very 'sticky'; the creation of rules and procedures to enforce a particular economic strategy at one point has acted as a constraint not only on current behavior but also on the range of options available to future entrepreneurs. In particular, laws have remained in force long after the economic conditions and political interests originally underpinning them have changed. Old statutes have constrained newer policies by giving standing to particular claims for protection from foreign goods. They have also affected the fundamental constitution of social interests."[6]

Generals often end up preparing for and fighting the previous war. Politicians similarly find themselves analyzing the last depression or renegotiating the last trade agreement. The gap between changing realities and the policy responses to them can sometimes be quite cavernous. While we will never be able to foretell the future, our ability to understand the present and to prepare for the future can be significantly enhanced by a better understanding of the past.

2 THE OLD MERCANTILISM

*To found a great empire for the sole purpose of raising up a people of customers
may at first sight appear a project fit only for a nation of shopkeepers. It is, however, a project altogether unfit for a nation of shopkeepers, but extremely fit for a
nation whose Government is influenced by shopkeepers.*

– ADAM SMITH, THE WEALTH OF NATIONS

Canada's beginnings lay in dashed hopes and broken dreams, its destiny in
unimagined wealth and promise. European adventurers, in search of gold and spices
and a new passage to the fabled treasures of the East, found instead a vast and
sparsely populated land of lakes and forests. They stayed to fish, hunt, trap, and
otherwise exploit its untold riches and thus bequeathed an even richer and longer-
lasting legacy than they had imagined in their wildest fantasies.

The commercial policy that initially nurtured and guided the development of
this wilderness of the North reflected the political organization and prevailing economic doctrines of the day. It was the king and his nobles who decided and adventurers and merchants who acted. Together they made an empire. Progress, however,
was painfully slow. The romantic schoolroom history familiar to generations of
North Americans obscures the fact that for more than a century after the first European contacts with the Americas, the territories that eventually became Canada
and the United States remained at the periphery of European civilization, of interest to no more than a few explorers and religious zealots. What economic and other
activities took place there were regarded as a net drain on the king's purse with little
prospect of long-term gain. In 1758, the last year of French rule in Canada, fewer
than 60,000 Europeans occupied a territory far larger than all of western Europe.
In order to survive they had to import some eight million livres worth of provisions and were able to export only two and a half million livres worth of fish, furs,
and lumber. Local taxes (mostly customs duties) made only a small dent in the
expense of maintaining local government and a military garrison.

The French and English courts found it hard to take the discoveries across the
Atlantic seriously. Between the pioneering voyages of Columbus and Cabot at the

end of the fifteenth century and the beginning of serious settlement early in the seventeenth century, developing the riches of the new lands was exceedingly low on the list of priorities of either government. Only sporadically did the French or English monarchs give any attention to the pleas of those interested in exploiting the potential of the Americas. If these enthusiasts had delivered on their promise of a new passage to the Orient, they might have found a more receptive audience. But they did not, and as a result found their monarchs and other aristocratic patrons preoccupied with more important matters, such as wars of conquest and aggrandizement, and domestic and international religious conflict. Even after the founding of permanent colonies under the sponsorship of various noble patrons and with the blessings of the king, the French court did not take New France seriously, converting it to a royal colony only in 1663. Until then the population and prospects were not sufficient to justify establishing a local government and settling the territory on a more organized basis. Farther down the coast, serious settlement by the English was only in its second generation.

Thus, while the Spanish and Portuguese courts sponsored thriving new empires in the southern part of the New World, the French and English courts were content to underwrite a few voyages of discovery and to encourage privateers to harry Spanish and Portuguese ships laden with the wealth of Central and South America. No similar riches had been found in the northern lands. Whatever the claims of France and England, each supported a minimum of activity to reinforce them. There was little incentive to do more. The voyages of Jacques Cartier in 1535 and 1541 into the Gulf of St. Lawrence and all the way to the confluence of the St. Lawrence and Ottawa Rivers showed little promise and were not followed by any serious effort to establish a permanent colony. Temporary settlements on the coasts of Newfoundland and Nova Scotia served the fishery but did not benefit from royal or even noble patronage and, without such support, had little hope of long-term success.

Not until early in the seventeenth century did the French and English make real but still hesitant efforts to gain more permanent beachheads along the North Atlantic coast. Their first forays consolidated the claims of French and English privateers who had successfully challenged the Spanish control of the West Indies and established small settlements on a number of Caribbean islands. The French followed with tentative steps farther north in various locations in Acadia along the Bay of Fundy in modern Nova Scotia, and along the St. Lawrence at Tadoussac, Quebec, and Montreal. At the same time, the English tried their luck at the headwaters of various rivers emptying into Chesapeake Bay and then farther north along Massachusetts Bay. Some of these early colonists came in search of wealth, while others sought to escape religious persecution and economic deprivation at home.

Few of these early settlements were immediately successful, but they began to suggest that there were other kinds of riches to be sought than gold and silver. The wealth of these new lands lay in fish, furs, tobacco, lumber, and other more humble commodities, which would become the basis for their gradual development.

Eventually, thriving colonies were established all along the eastern seaboard of what is now the United States and at strategic locations in Nova Scotia and Quebec. In each of these colonies, economic life followed the path of least resistance. The West Indies specialized in sugar plantations; the southern colonies, in rice and tobacco; the Mid-Atlantic colonies, in corn and other temperate-zone agricultural products. The northern colonies tried first to live on furs, fish, lumber, and shipbuilding, then turned gradually to wheat production as well as to manufacturing and shipping, despite colonial regulations forbidding such activities.

Canada's Earliest Industry: The Fishery

The rough fishermen of Brittany and England's west coast were the first to realize the real economic potential of the new lands.[1] John Cabot and his son Sebastian had described waters teeming with fish, a fact perhaps not unknown to some of the more adventurous fishermen of the time. Throughout the sixteenth century, increasingly large fleets of English, French, Spanish, and Portuguese fishing vessels harvested the vast wealth of the Grand Banks. Already in 1517, some hundred French and English vessels were known to have fished off the New-found-land, and by the late 1570s English merchant Anthony Parkhurst estimated that the Newfoundland fishery involved some four hundred ships from the English west coast and Brittany as well as from Spain and Portugal.[2] By the turn of the century these ships were almost exclusively French and English, as the Portuguese and Spanish concentrated all their dwindling resources farther south and relied on trade for their supplies of northern cod.

The Newfoundland fishery, however, was a European business rather than one based in the new lands. There were as yet no permanent settlements to support the fishery. It was a seasonal venture with ships setting sail in late winter, harvesting fish throughout the spring, and returning with their catch by late summer. Permanent settlements were considered out of the question because they would have exposed the settlers unnecessarily to the harsh winters and, perhaps more importantly, would have given them an advantage over the seasonal fishermen. Only gradually did the fishery lead to temporary settlements, and these were driven by technology rather than by a desire to found new homes and local businesses.

The Continental fishermen used a wet cure method for storing their catch: they dumped alternate layers of fish and salt into barrels and thus brought them home. The English, on the other hand, used a dry cure: they landed their fish on the shore and dried them in the sun, using a much lighter layer of salt. Dry-cured fish kept and tasted better and therefore commanded a higher price. The demands of the English method encouraged the establishment of seasonal settlements to which the fishermen could return year after year. The success of dry curing was particularly important for the English because salt was an expensive and imported commodity. The reduced need for salt was instrumental in reducing the cost of the final product. Continental fishermen had readier access to salt from the salt mines along the southern French and Portuguese coasts. Additionally, most of the English catch was not for home consumption but for export to southern, Catholic Europe, either through the home port of Bristol, through London, or directly. For the English, therefore, from earliest days, the Newfoundland fishery required contact with the land and comprised an important trade component; English merchants sold their fish in return for imports of sugar, spices, wines, fruits, and other products of the sunnier South or the Orient.

The fishery was a harsh business and soon proved so competitive that it required royal regulation. In keeping with prevailing views, monarchs, nobles, and merchants sought to give one group or another a monopoly either to catch or to sell the fish and thus both regulate the industry and increase national wealth. These monopolies proved practically impossible to enforce and did little more than encourage privateering and other extracurricular activities. The most serious competition to the Bristol-based dry-cure fishery on the Grand Banks came eventually from the Plymouth-based fishery off the coast of New England. That fishery was soon based in North America, with Plymouth and London merchants buying the catch from local fishermen. In addition, the French converted to dry-cure fishing and in the early seventeenth century began to use their settlements in Acadia to supply their fleet.

French and New England competition helped spur the Newfoundland fishery to progress gradually from a European venture into a colonial one. Early efforts at permanent settlement in 1583 and 1610 had not succeeded, but by the late seventeenth century, Newfoundland had evolved into a precarious colony pursuing the fishery and firmly entrenched in the British colonial system, dependent on the mother country for most of its needs but supplying both Britain and other colonies with fish. A brief interlude of French control slowed colonization, but with the return of Newfoundland and Acadia to British control under the Peace of Utrecht in 1713, Newfoundland became the mainstay of the North Atlantic fishery. By the middle of the eighteenth century, upward of 10,000 settlers called the colony home.

From Fish to Fur

Early in the evolution of the Newfoundland fishery, French and English fishermen began to make contacts with the Native inhabitants, if only to replenish their supplies of fresh water. It was not long before they began to trade some of their supplies for the furs worn by the Natives. Although initially the fishermen purchased the furs for their own use, they soon discovered that the supplies of furs appeared limitless and that they fetched a handsome price back home. Once hat makers discovered the superior quality of these furs, particularly beaver, a new industry was born. Even so, the potential of even this new trade took years to develop from its first feeble steps in the later sixteenth century to its heyday in the eighteenth century.

The French made the greatest effort to exploit the new fur resource to replace their dwindling supplies from Russia and Scandinavia. Unlike the fishery, the fur trade could not as readily be pursued exclusively from Europe. It required more organization and penetration of the interior. The fur trade's appeal, as well as continuing dreams of a passage through or around the inconvenient newly discovered land mass, convinced adventurers like Samuel de Champlain to establish permanent settlements in Canada. They were soon followed by priests eager to convert the Natives to Christianity. Priest and fur trader followed each other into the interior and began gradually to demystify the contours of the vast wilderness around the St. Lawrence drainage basin.

The early fur trade was exactly that. The Natives trapped the animals, cured their pelts, and then sold them to French, Scottish, English, and Dutch traders. Beaver pelts were the most desirable, particularly those that had been worn for at least a full season by the Natives, wearing off the long guard hairs and increasing the grease content. Natives, many of whom were quite familiar with barter among the tribes for furs and food, took to this new business with relish, eager to trade their cast-off winter clothing or spare pelts for knives, cooking pots, guns, alcohol, and other artifacts from the technologically more advanced Europeans. Once it was clear that the white men would continue to buy their furs, the Natives became shrewd traders, willing to travel hundreds of miles to obtain the best price.[3]

The English had missed out on the early fur trade by confining their northern activity to the fishery. Once the French had shown the way, English merchants wanted to get their share of the wealth, either from privateering, such as by the Kirke brothers who briefly held Quebec from 1629-32, or from exploiting their settlements in New England. The Dutch – and for a brief period, the Swedes – also took an active interest, organizing the trade along the Mohawk and Hudson Rivers and harvesting the area south of the St. Lawrence and the Great Lakes. As competition increased, agents no longer confined themselves to waiting for the Aboriginals to bring their pelts to the main trading posts – Tadoussac, Quebec, Montreal, and New Orange (Albany) – but ventured deeper and deeper into the interior to organize the trade, even if many Natives continued to bring their furs to the ports from which they could be exported to Europe.

These agents, as well as the merchants at the ports, were predominantly scoundrels and rascals, and the fur trade proved a very rough business. The nature and conduct of the trade did not add to the attraction of permanent settlement, which was already difficult enough given the harsh weather and difficult terrain of the northern colonies. But the fur trade, complemented by the continued search for a passage to the East and by the missionary activity of the Church, did encourage adventurers to wander farther into the interior and give Europeans a much more realistic picture of the new lands. These adventurers paved the way for the settlers who followed, established a more permanent and diversified economy, and required more sophisticated regulation of their political and economic affairs.[4]

By the end of the seventeenth century, most of the North American fur territory had been carved up between the English and the French. The English took over

New Holland in 1664, further developed the trade concentrated at Albany, and increased pressure on the French traders from the south. In 1670, with the help of the disaffected French traders Pierre Radisson and Médard des Groseilliers, the English also began to create competition in the northern and western reaches of the trade, after King Charles II gave a group of adventurers exclusive trading and property rights to the Hudson Bay drainage basin.

The Hudson's Bay Company was one of a long line of monopolies granted to French and English merchants and courtiers. But the success of these monopolies was undermined by the fact that there was always more than one outlet for and a dwindling supply of furs and shrinking demand for the pots, pans, rifles, and trinkets offered in exchange by the traders. Both the Natives and the traders exploited these factors and sold to the highest bidder rather than to those who had been granted the monopoly. This tendency, combined with export and import duties and the practice of delegating tax collection to the highest bidder, meant that few of these monopolies were profitable in the long term. Measured by modern commercial standards, the fur trade was a miserable failure. Neither the quantities of furs harvested and exported nor their value provided the basis for sound economic development. But despite the frequency of bankruptcy and failure, the fur trade, like the Atlantic fishery, proved an indispensable catalyst to the development of the northern colonies.

The French Regime

From its far-flung outposts along the St. Lawrence, the French court tried to control the fur trade of half the continent. With the exception of scattered farming and fishing settlements in Acadia and along the St. Lawrence, there were few long-term settlers. As a result, the French did not make much success of their North American colonies. The French fur traders may have been more adept at dealing with the Natives than their English counterparts, but the lack of permanent settlers coupled with excessive territorial ambitions doomed the French colonizing effort. The future lay with the English colonies along the Atlantic seaboard. By the middle of the eighteenth century, they had already surpassed more than one million in population, and the more adventurous settlers had begun to move farther inland. The Appalachian frontier had been breached, and the influx of settlers posed a continuous threat both to the French fur trade and to French territorial aspirations.

It was not long before political ambition had to adjust to economic reality: French claims had become both fantastic and unrealizable, and the French were soon reduced to a few island outposts. Already, in the 1713 Treaty of Utrecht, France had abandoned supremacy over the territories surrounding the St. Lawrence fishing grounds by ceding all claims to Acadia and Newfoundland to the British crown. France retained its claims, however, to the ill-defined territories of Canada and Louisiana as well as to the Caribbean sugar islands of Martinique and Guadeloupe.

Unlike the French colonies, the English colonies were growing at a rapid pace. From the outset, the English colonies welcomed agricultural settlers. The French colonies, on the other hand, existed largely to organize the fur trade. The little agriculture practised was strictly for local consumption. Large-scale settlements were at odds with the fur trade and were not encouraged beyond the lower St. Lawrence. Additionally, the British enclosure movement had created a steady supply of people driven off the land and willing to try their luck across the Atlantic. Finally, religious conflict in Britain, while sharp and bloody, as during the Civil War (1649-60), did not reach the levels of intolerance of Counter-Reformation France. The British crown was prepared to let dissenters move to the colonies and practise their various brands of Protestantism and even Catholicism. As a result, the expanding frontiers of the English colonies along the Atlantic seaboard were in constant conflict with French fur-trading interests in Canada and Louisiana (map 2.1).

Although the British government did not believe that its interests were at stake in these squabbles over fur and frontier lands far removed from the coast, the colonists believed these matters to be vital to their future. The rivalries among the colonial settlers were at first ancillary to the European conflicts but gradually increased in importance. Hostilities in America, resulting in the French and Indian War (1754-61), presaged the outbreak of what became known as the Seven Years' War in Europe.

For the British crown, the vast Canadian and Louisiana hinterland offered little of economic interest. As the French had discovered, these territories were expensive to govern, were not sufficiently populated to constitute a significant market for metropolitan merchants and manufacturers, and, other than furs, provided few raw materials that could not be found more cheaply and abundantly elsewhere. What interest Canada offered was strategic. If the French could be removed from North America and the Spanish claims reduced, the bickering among the various colonies would end, and France's mercantile and naval strength would be weakened to the advantage of the British.

Between 1756 and 1762, across Europe, in India, in Africa, in the West Indies, and in North America, the last of the European dynastic wars raged. Britain started off badly, losing both militarily and diplomatically, but in 1759 its superior naval and industrial strength began to turn the tide. By 1762, Britain stood supreme, having vanquished the navies and armies of France, Spain, and the Netherlands.

The British Succession
The dramatic victory of British general James Wolfe over his French opponent, the Marquis de Montcalm, on the Plains of Abraham on 13 September 1759, was just one skirmish in a global war. It was also not the first time that Quebec had fallen into English hands. A British conquest in 1629 had been readily overruled in the political and financial settlements that ended yet another of Europe's interminable dynastic squabbles. Louisbourg, the French fortress on Isle Royale (Cape Breton Island), had also been conquered in 1744 by New England militia and then handed

2.1   *North America, 1763*

back to the French. In 1763, at the negotiations leading to the Treaty of Paris, history nearly repeated itself as the English negotiators agonized over the choice of Quebec or Guadeloupe, a small but sugar-rich island in the Caribbean. Eventually, however, strategic considerations won out over economic ones, and, with the exception of the tiny islands of St. Pierre and Miquelon, the colonies around the St. Lawrence passed from French to British control. The French were prepared to abandon their dwindling fur trade and maintain no more than a toehold across the North

Atlantic for the benefit of the Breton fishermen. The British flag now flew from the Arctic Circle to the swamps of Georgia and from the Atlantic seaboard to the Mississippi River.

For most of the settlers in the vast lands of Canada, it was of little consequence who governed them. The number of English speakers was very small; most were Natives and French Canadians. The latter had found little to praise in the efforts of the French court, and many saw little significance in the passing of French rule. The fur traders were used to selling their skins to English, Scottish, and American traders at the outposts of the Hudson's Bay Company or at forts along the frontier. Whether they sold them at Detroit or at Montreal was of little moment. Many had ceased to be Europeans, and their outlook was increasingly North American. What distinguished the northern French-speaking colonies from their English-speaking New England counterparts was not attachment to either Britain or France, but the state of their economic, social, and political development. Additionally, the conflicts in the Indian lands had not been between the French and the English, but between the fur merchants of Montreal and the fur merchants of New York, and between those interested in the interior mainly for its furs and those interested in founding permanent settlements. As a result, rivalry between the thirteen colonies along the seaboard and the new colonies to the north remained unresolved.

The differences between the old and new British colonies were plainly apparent a generation later when the thirteen American colonies revolted and declared their independence. Though invited to participate, the Maritime and St. Lawrence colonies found they shared few of the grievances of their American cousins. The southern colonies had become economically self-sufficient and profitable, while the New England merchants, shipbuilders, and manufacturers had become formidable competitors of their cousins in England. For these colonists, the political and economic bonds to England had begun to chafe. With an end to hostilities with France and Spain, the colonists increasingly looked to their own situation and found it wanting. The northern colonies, on the other hand, had not yet developed to the same degree and continued to need the links to London: their thin population made more self-government unrealistic; Newfoundland relied on the English fishery; Nova Scotia depended on the British navy; and Quebec needed the London merchants. All three remained loyal to the Crown and continued to see their destiny as lying within the British colonial system.

Even a generation later, in the late eighteenth century, the northern colonies were a frontier and rural society, their leading citizens engaged in trade and shipbuilding. The bulk of the population farmed, lumbered, trapped, and fished. But as immigration began to pick up slowly after the turn of the century, economic development followed apace and the leading citizens in both the St. Lawrence and Maritime colonies began to develop clear views as to how imperial economic policy could be shaped to their benefit. In 1763, the northern colonies boasted some 60,000 Europeans. The population grew to 250,000 by 1800 with the influx of Loyalists from the American colonies, and reached one million by 1830. A population of a million people, even if unevenly distributed over more than a million square miles of land, required a much more developed economy and a more sophisticated commercial policy. The constraints of the old colonial system began to show. But whereas the American colonists had rebelled against the constraints of mercantilism practised for the benefit of the mother country and wanted to be quit of the colonial system, the northern colonies bemoaned the waning of mercantilism and sought to adapt the old system to their needs.

The Ferment of Ideas

The colonial system was the perfect expression of the economic theorists of the time – the mercantilists and physiocrats. Mercantilism was not an organized body of thought but rather the relatively coherent conclusions of men of affairs and letters in the seventeenth and eighteenth centuries reacting to events around them. It reflected the emergence of the nation-state as the principal form of political organization and advanced the doctrine of national self-sufficiency. It also advanced the view that men could shape their environment, culminating in the philosophical optimism of the eighteenth-century Enlightenment. By equating power and wealth, mercantilism provided a worldly rationale for Europe's restless, outward-looking search for new frontiers to conquer and new horizons to explore, and secularized the religious precept to spread the gospel. Mercantilism also provided an economic rationale to complement the political justification for the frequent dynastic wars of the eighteenth century.

Mercantilist thought justified extensive state regulation of a society's economic activities and fitted well with theories of absolute monarchy and with the practical control of affairs by concentrated groups such as the landed gentry or merchants. Mercantilism was also compatible with early notions of nationalism – the nationalism that sought to aggrandize the power of the nation-state as embodied by the sovereign, as opposed to later versions of nationalism that identified it with particular groups of people and their cultural values. Finally, mercantilist ideas reflected the continuing importance of the landed gentry and the growing importance of the merchant class, predating the emergence of a class of industrial entrepreneurs.[5]

Mercantilists believed that the purpose of economic policy was to increase the wealth of the nation-state. Espousing a static conception of wealth, they believed that whatever wealth or power was gained by one state was lost by another; trade was a form of warfare that had to be pursued with the same ruthlessness and dedication. Imports were a sign of national weakness, while exports denoted strength. The purpose of trade, therefore, was to create a surplus, particularly in the form of precious metals. The way to create such a surplus was to sell as much as possible and buy as little as possible or, more precisely, to sell things dearly and buy them cheaply. In order not to dissipate the gains from trade, the successful nation-state also maintained a favourable balance in "invisibles," for example, in shipping costs. Austrian thinker Philip von Hornick summed up these theories as follows:

> all commodities found in a country, which cannot be used in their natural state, should be worked up within the country; since the payment for manufacturing generally exceeds the value of the raw material ... the inhabitants of the country should make every effort to get along with their domestic products, to confine their luxury to these alone and to do without foreign products as far as possible ... such [imported] foreign commodities should ... be imported in unfinished form, and worked up within the country, thus earning the wages of manufacturing there ... opportunities should be sought night and day for selling the country's superfluous goods to these foreigners in manufactured form, so far as this is necessary, and for gold and silver ... except for important considerations, no importation should be allowed under any circumstances of commodities of which there is a sufficient supply of suitable quality at home; and in this matter neither sympathy nor compassion should be shown foreigners, be they friends, kinsfolk, allies, or enemies.[6]

Such theories underpinned mercantilist views concerning the purpose of colonies and the practical measures that guided the commercial policy of the seventeenth and eighteenth centuries. In order to develop and maintain a surplus, various regulatory instruments discouraged imports. If imports were necessary, they were to be imported at the lowest level of processing and shipped as much as possible in a nation's own ships. Domestic and imported raw materials were to be processed before exportation and finished goods again transported to their final destination in a nation's own ships. Various policy tools were used to achieve these results: high tariffs or even prohibitions on the importation of finished goods; duties and prohibitions on the exportation of raw materials; drawback or remission of duties if imported materials were further processed and then exported; navigation laws requiring that goods be carried in ships built, owned, and worked by a country's own nationals; subsidies or bounties encouraging domestic manufacturing; and monopolies to ensure that the economic rents stayed at home. The policy mix might have differed in England, France, Holland, Sweden, or Spain, but the end was the same – central governments ruthlessly stamped out economic activity that might undermine the accumulation of surpluses and increases in national wealth.

Colonies were seen as extensions of the nation-state, their purpose to supply the home country with raw materials that could be turned into finished goods for consumption at home and in the colonies. They were also regarded in terms of their contribution to the balance of power in the commercial rivalry between nation-states. Consistent with a strong belief in the efficacy of state control, colonial regulations required that the colonies trade only with the mother country, using ships built in the mother country or in the colony. Manufacturing was discouraged in the colonies as undermining the proper activity of the mother country and detracting from concentration on the exploitation of raw materials. Any trade by the colonies with other countries was to be pursued through the mother country. Trade among the colonies was rigidly controlled to prevent any erosion of mercantilist principles. Colonies were only beneficial if they were part of a closed and controlled economic system that ensured that colonial enterprise contributed to the power of the metropolis. Wrote English pamphleteer Sir Arthur Young in 1772:

> The wealth resulting from colonies ought certainly to arise from the cultivation of staple commodities; that is from the production of those articles which a mother-country must purchase of foreigners, if her own settlements did not yield them. The difference between purchasing a commodity of a foreign country, or of a colony, is immense: in the first case, it is paid for probably with cash; but in the latter, manufactures are exchanged for it; that is, the labour of our poor ... What a prodigious difference there is between paying to the French a million sterling for sugars, or exchanging a million's worth of our manufactures for the same commodity with our own colonists.[7]

There were, of course, other reasons to acquire colonies. If nothing else, they added to the prestige of the monarch and responded to the biblical injunction to evangelize the world. Rival versions of the gospel strengthened the urge to spread its message. More pragmatically, a whole catalogue of justifications was gradually developed – colonies were convenient destinations for the surplus population (including the more undesirable and criminal elements), and the merchant marine activity flowing from colonial trade served as a nursery for sailors. But, increasingly, it was the perceived economic value of colonies within a mercantilist system that drove their settlement and exploitation.[8]

The British Colonial System

The most developed and sophisticated of the various colonial systems of the eighteenth century was that of the British. Based initially on haphazard laws and administration, the system had been consolidated by the middle of the seventeenth century into a series of laws and regulations that fully embodied prevailing mercantilist ideas.

The Navigation Acts of 1651 and 1660 codified the generally accepted view and practice that all British trade should be carried in British-owned ships built in Britain or the colonies and worked by British sailors. The laws were commodity-specific and complemented commodity-specific tariffs and other rules including preferences, prohibitions, and exclusive fishing rights. Any loopholes in the system were quickly closed. The 1663 Staples Act, for example, required that all specified colonial trade be routed through Britain, be subject to British duties, and be transported to and from the colonies in British ships.

The importance of requiring that all trade take place in British ships can be readily appreciated from a brief survey of the role of the merchant marine and shipbuilding industry in the British economy and polity. In the middle of the eighteenth century, Britain's mercantile strength was around 500,000 tons. This capacity involved thousands of individual vessels ranging from small coastal cutters and sloops to large freighters of several hundred tons' capacity. Built of wood, most ships lasted no more than a dozen round-trips across the Atlantic, and even fewer around the Cape of Good Hope to India, before they had to be replaced. At any one time there were more than a thousand merchant ships under construction at home and in the colonies, requiring a large volume of high-quality lumber for the hulls, decks, spars, and masts.[9]

Complementing the merchant marine was the navy, considered the basis of British military strength from Elizabethan days. Better built and more extensively equipped, naval vessels required an active and experienced shipbuilding industry and a constant flow of sailors and officers, both provided by the large merchant marine. British economic and strategic considerations, therefore, revolved around the factors that kept the British navy strong, all regulated by the Navigation Laws. For Britain, shipping, trade, the colonies, and security were inextricably tied together.

The tariffs on goods entering the North American colonies were thus set in London and promoted imperial trade: the rate for goods of British origin, including from the colonies of the West Indies, was much lower than that for other goods. These mercantilist regulations ensured that British North America during the heyday of the first Empire remained a collection of disparate and separate colonies, their only commonality derived from British administration. The 1763 Treaty of Paris gave Britain control of some twenty-five separately identified possessions in North America, ranging from Jamaica in the West Indies to Newfoundland and Labrador in the North Atlantic. Britain was determined to forge these diverse possessions into a commercial empire through the rigorous application of mercantilist principles.

The End of the First Empire

Prior to the Treaty of Paris, the mercantilist system, anchored by tariffs and preferences, navigation acts, and bounties, had not been strictly enforced, but when it finally was, this enforcement led to revolt. King George III and his ministers had inherited a huge debt accumulated in a century of dynastic wars. That debt had to be serviced, and at the same time Parliament had to raise enough money to maintain a strong navy. The only substantive means to accomplish these goals lay in rigorous enforcement of the navigation and trade laws and an adjustment in these laws to increase revenues. In 1760, exports amounted to about £16 million and imports to about £11 million. The budget for that year called for expenditures of £15 million, an extraordinary sum when compared to the £7 million required the previous year and the £11.5 million spent in 1774 on the eve of the American Revolution. Raising such sums required extensive customs duties applied much more rigorously than had been the norm, either at home or in the colonies.[10]

The commodity-specific trade and navigation laws enumerated which commodities were taxed, which carried bounties, which had to be carried in British bottoms, which had to be shipped through British ports before they could be sold elsewhere, and which the colonists could not trade in at all. The fewer the goods enumerated, the more freedom the colonists had to conduct their trade as they saw fit. While the absence of these laws probably would not have greatly altered the patterns of trade, their existence had an important bearing on evolving attitudes. Where the laws did not fit reality, smuggling and privateering had for years provided an alternative. Though the number of enumerated goods rose steadily over the years, there was little difficulty until 1764, when the number doubled, and at the same time, the laws began to be more zealously enforced.

The system was attuned to colonies heavily dependent on the mother country and did not create major difficulties for the less developed and smaller colonies around the St. Lawrence and in the West Indies. When applied rigorously, however, the laws created resentment in the larger and more populated colonies along the Atlantic seaboard from Massachusetts to Georgia, particularly in New England. There, the most influential citizens were competitors of the London, Bristol, and Plymouth merchants. Colonial politicians and merchants – often the same people – resented rules that prevented them from seeking markets for themselves and from using their own ships. George III's advisors compounded this resentment by insisting that, as beneficiaries of the system, the colonists should make a larger contribution by paying consumption and other taxes itemized in the Sugar and Stamp Acts. Dissent focused on the imperial tax system and on the lack of colonial participation in decisions on what to tax and how to spend the revenue. Economic dissatisfaction complemented political discontent and gradually mounted, until in 1776 the radical elements in New England convinced their more conservative colleagues to the south to join them in revolt.

The novelty of the idea of rebellion combined with British ineptitude carried the day for the revolutionaries and reduced British holdings in North America by more than half in territory and by much more than half in economic strength. The northern colonies, despite repeated peaceful and military invitations to join the rebels, declined to participate and remained loyal. That loyalty, however, derived less from any great sense of patriotic attachment to the British crown than from a lack of grievance on the scale of that of the thirteen colonies. The merchant leaders of the northern colonies, while they did not hesitate to complain about the details of British rule, saw their destiny in continued mercantile links to London as the major outlet for their furs, fish, and lumber.

In addition, the political leaders of the northern colonies, particularly in Montreal and Quebec, were reluctant to join their commercial rivals. Twenty years of peace had demonstrated that the previous hostilities between French and English had been, as far as North America was concerned, less between two political dynasties in Europe and more between two commercial empires struggling for control of the interior. British administration of the interior by Indian agents had sharpened this rivalry and added to the conflict between fur trader and frontiersman.[11] In 1774, the British government sought to resolve the problem by returning the vast fur-trading regions beyond the Great Lakes to the administration of the governor of Quebec and his Montreal advisors. The Quebec Act, while adding to the resentment felt by the American colonists, also strengthened the conviction of the Montreal merchants that their destiny lay with Britain.

Similarly, the Halifax merchants saw their future as inextricably linked with the fortunes of the British navy. More than half of the population of Nova Scotia at the outbreak of the American Revolution had been born in New England but were resolutely British, especially following the expulsion of the Acadians in 1755. While some farmed and others fished, the economic mainstay of the colony lay in supplying the British navy with provisions. Again, there was little benefit in joining their cousins from New England in severing that connection.

With the loss of the rebellious thirteen colonies, Britain's American holdings were reduced to the West Indies and to what evolved over the next few years into the northern colonies of Newfoundland, Quebec, Nova Scotia, New Brunswick, and Prince Edward Island. In addition, the Hudson's Bay Company controlled the vast Hudson Bay drainage area, and small settlements had taken hold on Vancouver Island and around Puget Sound. These remaining northern colonies were now an even more disparate collection of individual settlements with little in common except British rule and the St. Lawrence waterway, which, from its headwaters in the Gulf of St. Lawrence, reached almost two thousand miles deep into the continent. The West Indies with its supplies of sugar and spices held much more promise. The northern colonies were regarded as the least important of Britain's far-flung possessions, and thus did not get much attention.

The unimportance of the northern colonies was plain to see in the peace negotiations with the newly independent Americans. The factors that had kept the northern colonies loyal were blithely ignored. The vast St. Lawrence drainage area was cut in two, with both merchants and Natives aghast to see the basis of their livelihood handed over to the dreaded frontiersmen and their drive to establish permanent settlements. New England fishermen were given the liberty to fish in British waters and to cure fish on unsettled shores, even if they could not land fish in British ports.

The Colonial System Redux

As if the American Revolution had not involved any commercial grievances, few adjustments were made in the commercial policy that would continue to guide the economic development of the remaining colonies. If anything, the conservative advisors of George III were determined to stiffen their administration of the system, convinced that it was not the laws but their lax administration that had allowed the colonists too much freedom and had encouraged rebellion. Their convictions were confirmed when the American rebellion was followed by the out-break of discontent in Ireland and not much later by the French Revolution. What was needed was a strong hand. Wrote colonial undersecretary William Knox: "It was better to have no colonies at all, than not to have them subservient to the mari-time strength and commercial interest of Great Britain."[12]

Thus the enforcement of the trade and navigation laws continued. Colonial trade had to be confined to British ships, had to be routed through British ports, and had to involve payment of British customs duties at the ports of entry. Each colony had its own commercial policy regime within the colonial system, and each was dis-couraged by that system to develop any links with the others or with the newly independent thirteen states to the south. In fact, imperial policy sought instead to encourage trade with the West Indies, allotting to the remaining northern colonies the role that had previously been assigned, with little success, to the New England colonies. It was a system that the northern merchants liked when it came to their exports of fish, fur, and lumber, but one that was regularly circumvented by the increasing numbers of settlers when it came to imports of foodstuffs and manufac-tures. Illegal trade with the Americans became an early mainstay of Canadian eco-nomic reality and nurtured two conflicting attitudes: support for British commercial policy that advanced the export interests of the mercantile elite, and a blind eye to the illegal import activities of the majority of the population. Tension between these two attitudes animated Canadian policy for the next two generations.

The Atlantic colonies looked to the sea and depended economically on fish, lum-ber, shipbuilding, and the carriage trade. Between the end of the American Revolu-tion and the middle of the nineteenth century, Newfoundland gradually evolved from a precarious land base for a largely nonresident fishery to a viable colony built around a resident fishery critically dependent on foreign markets for its economic survival. In 1825, with a population of 60,000, it finally gained official status as a colony, and by 1832, Newfoundland joined the other colonies in the right to a lim-ited level of representative government.

With their New England rivals now outside the British colonial system, Nova Scotians could count on improved markets for their exports but on reduced access to New England goods, except through smuggling. The influx of Loyalists in the closing decades of the century provided the various settlements with a larger popu-lation base and increased agricultural as well as timber activity. The gradual divi-sion of the Maritimes into four colonies – Nova Scotia, New Brunswick, Prince Edward Island, and, for a brief period, Cape Breton Island, helped stamp each re-gion with its own characteristics. New Brunswick became critically dependent on the timber trade and Prince Edward Island produced an agricultural surplus for export, while Nova Scotia continued primarily as a merchant entrepôt and fishery centre.

Quebec looked to the St. Lawrence system to export first furs and then timber products (lumber and potash), wheat, and flour, at the same time carrying on a lively illegal trade with the American states to the south. Until the influx of Loyalists in the 1780s and 1790s, Quebec was disinterested in permanent settlers except at the trading posts and along the upper St. Lawrence. Farmers played havoc with the fur trading system and with relations with the Natives, adding to the difficulties of governance and defence. The principal citizens were the merchants, and their business was to carry on the fur trade. The Loyalists, however, persevered and established settlements beyond the shores of the St. Lawrence system, opening up the interior to settlement and compromising the hunting and trapping that had been the mainstay of the economy. They cleared the forests and turned the sod, pushing the trappers and fur traders farther west, inadvertently replacing the fur staple with wheat and timber-based trade. In the opening decades of the nineteenth century, as population began to grow rapidly, on the basis of both natural growth and the arrival of Scottish, Irish, and American immigrants, a wheat economy began to develop. For a period of nearly a quarter-century, Quebec, or Lower Canada, exported a respectable quantity of wheat and flour before being surpassed by Upper Canada.

The Northwest continued to be a fur economy. As Loyalists began to settle the upper reaches of the St. Lawrence, and American frontiersmen settled the US Midwest, the fur trade moved farther west and north. Supply lines to Montreal became more and more tenuous, increasing the advantages of the Hudson's Bay Company and its dominance of the Rupert's Land fur trade.

The success of the American Revolution had spelled the end of the first colonial system. The American colonists had let their British political masters know in no uncertain terms that they resented paying taxes to a distant suzerain, particularly if they were given no voice in what the taxes should be and how they should be spent. There had to be some adjustment if similar tensions were not to recur. The answer lay in letting the colonists that remained loyal to the Crown pay for their own administration and impose the necessary taxes to do so. In 1778 the Declaratory Act established that the imperial customs duties collected in the colonies would be used to finance their own administration.

A generation later, the division of Quebec into Upper and Lower Canada by the Constitutional Act of 1791 brought with it not only adjustments in colonial administration but further recognition that the colonists had to have a greater role in managing and paying for their own affairs. From 1791, the assemblies of the two Canadas, as well as the other northern colonies, were given the right to keep the imperial customs duties to pay for local administration and to collect additional colonial duties as required. The Declaratory and Constitutional Acts provided the basis for the beginning of a made-in-Canada trade policy and ensured that, for generations to come, Canadian trade policy would be intimately associated with fiscal policy.

For the first half of the nineteenth century, the predominant interest in the colonies was to influence imperial policy in order to ensure that colonial fishermen,

Henry Byam Martin, "Gentlemen on Their Travels, Lake Simcoe," 1832.

farmers, lumbermen, but, above all, merchants enjoyed preferential status in the British market. It was still the only market that mattered. The new US market had not yet developed to the point that it offered an attractive alternative, while the markets of continental Europe remained largely untapped. The British market, however, was also of immense interest to Scandinavian, Russian, and American interests. Canadian producers felt that without preferences they would not be able to compete. Whether true or not, the perception of disadvantage acted as a powerful stimulant to Canadian colonial attitudes toward imperial policy. Canadian advocacy of the old colonial system, however, came at a time when that system was increasingly at odds with influential interests in the mother country.

Adam Smith and the Challenge to Mercantilism
Even as the advisors to King George III further consolidated the old mercantilist system, influential voices were being raised against it at home. It was a policy that had served its purpose but was now out of step with changing economic reality. Mercantilist trade and colonial policy had contributed to the consolidation of the nation-state and national economies. Trade between these national economies had further strengthened them and aided their industrial development. From the middle of the eighteenth century, trade and industrialization developed jointly to create a truly international economy by the middle of the nineteenth century. The industrial revolution added to the growth in world trade by diversifying the products

sold between nations. Traded goods expanded from luxuries and raw materials to include producer goods such as machinery and cloth. Although there was still not much trade in finished or consumer goods, growth in the industrial uses of metals and minerals as well as of agricultural goods further increased trade by adding to the demand for raw materials. Technological progress in transportation – the railway and steamship – and in communications – the telegraph – further facilitated increased international trade.[13]

These economic and technological breakthroughs added to the intellectual, political, and economic pressures on the old colonial system. Britain became the first to abandon mercantilist principles in favour of free trade, followed by Holland, France, Spain, and Portugal. This era of freer trade lasted until the end of the nineteenth century when it was overwhelmed not by the pressures of empire but by the new nationalism. Freer trade encouraged national unification in Germany and Italy and solidified it in Britain, France, and Holland. The resulting strong nationalist states then reintroduced more modern forms of protectionism at the end of the century. These European developments created the circumstances in which a native Canadian trade policy would develop and added to the forces leading to confederation of the diverse colonies in order to secure their independence within a new imperial system.

The earliest and most comprehensive challenge to mercantilism and its offspring, the old colonial system, came from Adam Smith and his contemporaries.[14] Published in the same year – 1776 – as the outbreak of the American Revolution, Smith's *Wealth of Nations* pointed out that producers were the main beneficiaries of mercantilism and that consumers were its main victims, a fact that holds as true for its more modern variants as for the mercantilism of the eighteenth century. Wrote Smith: "In the mercantilist system, the interest of the consumer is almost constantly sacrificed to that of the producer; and it seems to consider production, and not consumption, as the ultimate end and object of all industry and commerce."[15]

By turning the prevailing view of producers and consumers upside down, Smith provided the basis for modern economic analysis and, eventually, for changes in economic policy. He argued that the ultimate objective of economic activity is to satisfy consumption, and that it is the collective decisions of consumers that motivate people to produce. The interest of the consumer is to maximize choice and minimize cost, that is, to be able to choose from a wide variety of goods at the best possible price. Free competition to provide that choice should be the basis of policy.

Smith also challenged the mercantilist view of wealth and power and the relationship between them. For him, power was a means to an end, while for the mercantilist it was the end. For Smith, the end was increased national welfare. The pursuit of power was more likely to be at the expense of wealth, while the pursuit of wealth would ultimately increase the power of the nation.[16]

From the perspective of trade policy, the most important insight developed by Smith and his immediate successors was the benefit that derives from the division of labour, at both the national and international levels, complemented by the concept of comparative advantage as developed by David Ricardo. Smith argued that by specializing, individuals could produce more of what they were good at, sell the surplus, and use the profits to buy what they were less good at producing. They would thus be able to increase their wealth in two ways: as producers, they would become more efficient and more productive; as consumers, they would be able to satisfy more wants by choosing from a wider array of goods produced by other, more efficient producers, at a lower cost than they could achieve themselves. Ricardo refined the idea by emphasizing that it was not necessary for an individual to possess an absolute advantage; it was important to pursue one's comparative advantage. The same concepts explained the advantages to be derived from international trade. In Smith's words, "What is prudence in the conduct of every private family life, can scarcely be folly in that of a great kingdom. If a foreign country can supply us with a commodity cheaper than we ourselves can make it, better buy it of them with some part of the produce of our own industry, employed in a way in which we have some advantage."[17]

These modern economic ideas not only reflected the changing nature of economic activity in Britain in the period after 1760 but gradually began to influence a policy framework designed to nurture that activity. The policy shift took several generations and could not be fully realized until the restoration of relative political stability and peace. These conditions were achieved once the Congress of Vienna in 1815 brought an end to the convulsions unleashed by the American and French Revolutions.

The economic ideas of Smith and his immediate successors were influential first in the country that had given birth to them and that was, in terms of economic development and interest, best placed to implement them.[18] The growth in industry in Britain, fuelled by developments in technology, commerce, and business practices, provided a fertile ground for ideas that promoted specialization and a freer exchange of goods.[19] These concepts, however, were not unknown in the colonies by the 1820s and 1830s, and people of ideas and affairs began regularly to consider their application in a Canadian colonial setting. Among early students, advocates, and critics of these more advanced ideas can be counted John Rae, John Young, Francis and William Hincks, William Merritt, William Lyon Mackenzie, R.B. Sullivan, and Isaac Buchanan.[20] While their influence on the development of Canadian commercial policy varied, their ability to couch arguments for or against protection in more sophisticated terms began to influence political discussions in Canada and laid the foundation for the development of policy for the next fifty years.

More than anywhere else, Adam Smith's ideas about the benefits of a free exchange of goods and a minimum degree of government intervention in the economy took root in the American psyche. It was a set of beliefs tailor-made for a nation that was based on a revolt against taxation and government interference and that placed great stock in the myths of free Americans tilling the soil and sharing the fruits of their labour with one another. Subsequent adoption of protectionism thus had to be couched in terms that did not invalidate the fundamental tenets of the American Revolution. Alexander Hamilton's sophisticated concept of an industrial policy for an infant nation rested on the belief that the little guy needed to be protected from the rapacious policies of bigger, stronger nations like Great Britain. The protection of farmers and manufacturers in later years rested on the deeply held conviction that foreigners behaved unfairly. The antitrust laws adopted late in the nineteenth century again sought to protect the sterling qualities of the small, rugged individual American from the unprincipled behaviour of trusts and combines. Couched in economic language, the arguments were in fact political, rooted in the myths that had sustained the first revolution and then the development of a new kind of nation on American soil.[21]

The New Ideas Become Policy

The return to peace at the Congress of Vienna in 1815 marked the beginning of the end of the old colonial system. Britain was now clearly established as the principal global political and economic power. Its strength was derived from its industry and its navy, and not, as many influential members of society were beginning to recognize, from its imperial possessions. The energies released by peace, therefore, provided an opportunity for the government to review the basis of the Empire and the policies that held it together.

It did not take long for critics of the mercantile basis of the Empire to surface. The combined interests of merchants and industrialists had begun to crowd those of landowners and made an attack on the policies of the seventeenth and eighteenth centuries inevitable. Both manufacturers and intellectuals pointed to the costs of Empire, to the inadequacy of the system in promoting markets for surplus British production, to the additional costs of industrial inputs, and to the cost of feeding the urban masses. Political debate exposed the weaknesses of mercantilism and its adjunct, the old colonial system, and their inability to address the economic problems of rapid industrialization and urbanization.

Official attacks on the old system in the 1820s by the Board of Trade proved the turning point. The views of its chairman, William Huskisson, were decisive. To him, there was every reason to be more accessible to the Americans and the Scandinavians and to open up both British and colonial trade to all comers. He told the House of Commons in 1825, "An open trade, especially to a rich and thriving country, is infinitely more valuable than any monopoly, however exclusive, which the public power of the state may be able, either to enforce against its own colonial dominions, or to establish in its intercourse with other parts of the world." His assessment of Canadian attitudes toward such changes, however, was less perceptive. In the same speech, he noted, "I cannot doubt, that without any other encouragement than freedom of trade, and a lenient administration, these [Canadian] provinces will, henceforward, make the most rapid strides towards prosperity –

that connecting their prosperity with the liberal treatment of the mother country, they will neither look with envy at the growth of other states on the same continent, nor wish for the dissolution of old and the formation of new connexions."[22]

Not everyone agreed, and debate in Parliament, newspapers, and pamphlets was heated and uncompromising. Lord Stanley, a leading Tory spokesman, for example, made a stirring case for the old colonial system:

> Now, destroy this principal [sic] of protection, and I tell you in this place that you destroy the whole basis upon which your Colonial system rests ... It is by your Colonial system, based upon the principles of protection, that you have extended your arms – I do not mean your military arms, I mean your commercial arms – to every quarter and to every corner of the globe. It is to your Colonial system that you owe it that there is not a sea on which the flag of England does not float; that there is not a quarter of the world in which the language of England is not heard; that there is not a quarter of the globe, that there is no zone in either hemisphere, in which there are not thousands who recognize the sovereignty of Britain.[23]

The views of Huskisson, Richard Cobden, and other reformers, however, prevailed. Gradual and piecemeal changes in the Navigation and Tariff Acts over the next twenty years marked the end of the old regime and the transition to the new gospel of free trade. First to go were many of the absolute prohibitions on colonies trading outside the Empire. Instead, the reforms of 1825 introduced a general levy of 2.5 percent from all sources, duties of 7.5 to 15 percent on most nonimperial products, and duties as high as 20 to 30 percent on some products, effectively widening the margin of preferences enjoyed by the colonies in their exports to Britain (see table 2.1). The goods still prohibited were the staple products of various colonies such as sugar, rum, coffee, tea, and salted fish.[24]

The introduction of preferential rates of duty in favour of intra-imperial trade was at first much appreciated by the colonists. It allowed them to trade openly with the Americans but enjoy preferences in trade among themselves and, most important, with the mother country. But British interests saw little benefit in maintaining such preferences, and gradually these were attacked and reduced. The period from 1825 to 1849 was marked by frequent changes in direction as various factions carved out their views in a confusion of ever-changing statutes. Tariff, navigation, and other laws were in a constant state of flux as conflicting interests, imperial and colonial, sought to gain advantage. The trend, however, was clear. Free trade and nondiscrimination were in the ascendant. When the Corn Laws – the laws that regulated the importation and shipping of wheat and flour from the colonies – were repealed in 1846 in order to stave off the calamity of another famine in Ireland, one of the last vestiges of the commercial policy measures that had characterized the old colonial system disappeared. In 1849, the last of the Navigation Laws was repealed and for the next seventy years, Britain pursued a steadfast policy of free trade.[25]

Table 2.1

Duties on foreign imports in effect after 1825, Lower Canada

Commodity	Rate	Type
Barley	7d. per bushel	Imperial
Butter	15%	Imperial
Cheese	15%	Imperial
Flour (other than wheat)	2s. 6d. cwt	Colonial and imperial
General provisions	15%	Colonial and imperial
Glass and glassware	20%	Imperial
Hardware	15%	Imperial
Leaf tobacco	3½d. or 15%	Colonial and imperial
Leather manufactures	30%	Imperial
Linen	30%	Imperial
Livestock	10%	Imperial
Manufactured tobacco (not snuff)	Higher of 2d./lb. or 20%	Colonial and imperial
Oats	7d. per bushel	Imperial
Paper	15%	Imperial
Peas	7d. per bushel	Imperial
Wheat	1s. per bushel	Imperial
Wheat flour	5s. per barrel	Imperial

Note: d. = pence, s. = shilling, cwt. = hundredweight (112 lb.)
Source: O.J. McDiarmid, *Commercial Policy in the Canadian Economy* (Cambridge, MA: Harvard University Press, 1946), 40.

Canadian Staples Trade and the End of Mercantilism

Britain's gradual conversion to free trade spelled disaster for colonial farmers and merchants, whose whole existence depended, or so they maintained, on the colonial system. While the fur trade had gradually been reduced to a minor role in the colonial economy, fish, timber, and wheat had become the mainstays of colonial economic life. By the early 1830s, for example, exports from Upper and Lower Canada exceeded $4 million annually, half of them in timber and a quarter in grain and flour, with potash taking up the bulk of the rest. Newfoundland by this time exported close to $2 million in fish. The organization of both the production and trade of these staples depended critically on imperial trade and transportation policies.[26]

For the small but growing class of manufacturers, however, British free trade turned out to be a blessing in disguise. Manufacturing for local consumption had grown during the opening years of the century but remained secondary to imports from the more productive and thus competitive manufacturers in England and the United States. The release of the colonies from the strictures of British colonial policy, however, and the increasing ability of the colonial legislatures to set their own tariff policies, provided an outlet for growing protectionist sentiment, a sentiment that often as not dovetailed neatly with the growing revenue needs of each of the colonies. As long as the colonial administrations were dependent on customs duties for most of their revenue, there developed a happy coincidence between those seeking higher tariffs for protectionist ends and those prepared to raise them for fiscal reasons. At the same time, however, the colonial politicians had to maintain an adroit balance between the competing interests of import-sensitive local manufacturers, merchants, and export-oriented producers of staples. Early Canadian trade policy was dominated by attempts to reconcile sometimes conflicting and sometimes coincidentally concordant interests.[27]

The early Canadian economy was a classic example of a staples-driven economy. Indeed, the study of the early Canadian economy first gave rise to this theory of economic development. The pioneers in Canadian historical writing – Harold Innis, Frank Underhill, Adam Shortt, W.A. Mackintosh, Arthur Lower, Donald Creighton – all sharpened their skills analyzing the economic development of Canada. All focused on the influence of staples during Canada's early economic development.

According to the staples theory, the colonies needed a staple product to sell to the metropolitan country in return for some of the necessities of life, immigrants, and defence. While the colonies could be self-sufficient in the bare essentials – food, shelter, and clothing – luxuries had to be provided by the more sophisticated economy of the mother country. The presence of an abundant staple that could be easily exploited and was in great demand in the metropolitan country was essential to economic development. First fish, then furs, and later lumber and grain, dominated Canadian production and geared the development of Canada's productive capacity and infrastructure toward the export of staples at relatively low levels of processing.

Since staples are bulky, they need a cheap but reliable transportation system to take them out of the interior to the ocean ports from which they can be transported to the metropolitan country. The presence and then the further development of dependable transportation systems proved critical to Canada's economic development and tied transportation and tariff policy closely together.

Finally, the commercial policies of the metropolitan country ensured that the colonies would continue to concentrate on producing staples for export to the home country and to import their other requirements from it. Tariff and other policies discouraged the development of native industries to upgrade the staple before export or other more sophisticated economic activities.[28]

The fur trade had performed this function for the St. Lawrence colonies in the seventeenth and eighteenth centuries but gradually became peripheral to their interests and completely collapsed in 1821 when the Hudson's Bay Company took over the rights of the Montreal-based North West Company. From then on, the Hudson's Bay Company handled the fur trade exclusively from Churchill and

Pacific ports. While fur had waned as a staple by the early years of the nineteenth century, fish continued to be a major export commodity, critically important to Newfoundland, but also to some of the other settlements along the shores of the Gulf of St. Lawrence. For New Brunswick and Upper and Lower Canada, however, timber now became the main source of export earnings, once again largely in response to political and policy developments in Europe.

The British navy had long appreciated the quality of the large timbers available from the virgin forests of New Brunswick, and a modest export of these timbers had developed to supply the navy with spars and masts. Little was harvested for export to commercial markets in Britain, which continued to be dominated by the traditional Scandinavian and Russian timber trade. This situation changed in the early years of the nineteenth century with the disruption and blockade of the Baltic trade during the Napoleonic wars. British dealers scrambled to find alternative sources of supply and soon turned to the huge forests of British North America. Various merchants arrived in New Brunswick and Quebec to organize the harvest and transport of the giant pine logs or "sticks" to waiting ships.

Given the huge tracts of virgin forest, the merchants could resort to primitive means for harvesting the giant pines suitable for squaring and transporting to the river's edge. Fewer than one in ten of the trees proved suitable, but there were enough to ensure a steady supply for years to come. Once enough of the pine logs had accumulated on the shores of the Ottawa, St. Lawrence, or St. John Rivers, they were lashed together into huge rafts the size of modern football fields and several sticks high, and sailed down the river to Quebec or St. John to be loaded onto ocean-going ships. Once landed in England or Scotland, the logs were sawn into lumber and sold at retail.

Soon after the industry was properly organized by British-based factors, Canada became the principal supplier of the British market. By 1810, Canadian forests supplied two-thirds of the market, and the reopening of the Baltic thereafter did little to reverse the new pattern. The transportation advantages enjoyed by the Baltic states were more than offset by the imperial tariff structure. Between 1821 and 1840, Canadian timber paid a duty of only ten pence a load on entering British ports, compared to the fifty-five pence paid on Baltic timber, allowing Canadian timber to compete handsomely on the British market. The low tariff, combined with the popularity of Canadian white pine, meant that Canadian lumber dominated the British market by the 1840s. Potash, as an alternative to the lumber trade, provided farmers with cash from the lumber they cleared from the land.[29]

An unanticipated benefit of the timber trade was the opportunity for thousands of people to emigrate to the New World. Ships unloading their heavy bulk cargo of pine logs in British ports had cheap and abundant space for returning passengers, and the influx of Irish, Scottish, and English emigrants raised the population from 250,000 around 1800 to more than two million by mid-century. Most new arrivals found work either supplying the timber trade or adding to the growing number of farmers and farm workers in Upper Canada and the Eastern townships of Lower Canada. They further fuelled the growth of the fourth staple in Canada's economic development – wheat, referred to as corn in Britain. By the 1830s some one million acres in Upper Canada were under cultivation, producing close to a million bushels of wheat for export to Britain.[30]

Canadian wheat did not enjoy quite as distinct an advantage as timber because it had to compete not only with foreign wheat but also with domestic production. Additionally, wheat was not as stable and reliable a crop and was not as important in these early years as timber, or as it eventually became once the vast lands of the West began to be exploited. Nevertheless, between 1815 and 1846, a series of Corn Laws geared to Canadian needs gave Canadian farmers and merchants an advantage in an increasingly ambitious trade.

The Corn Laws had always been an integral part of the colonial system, but with the passage of the Canadian Corn Law of 1815, an additional level of incentive was added for the benefit of British North America. The Corn Laws were structured so as to reward, first of all, British farmers, then colonial farmers, and then all other suppliers. If the British harvest was abundant, all non-British grain was embargoed. If the British harvest was meagre, the duty on foreign grain was low and the market available to foreign suppliers. A sliding scale, based on average prices, addressed circumstances when the British harvest was middling to fair. After 1815, Canadian wheat could be imported once the domestic price reached sixty-seven shillings a quarter, while other wheat was embargoed until the domestic price reached eighty shillings a quarter. After 1825, Canadian wheat could be imported at any time but paid a duty of five shillings a quarter if the price was below sixty-seven shillings, and only six pence if it was above this level. Foreign, i.e., American, wheat paid four times this amount. Various additional incentives encouraged the importation of American wheat into the Canadas to be ground into flour for export, encouraging the development of both the milling and the transportation industries.[31]

Getting wheat or wheat flour to seaports for export to Britain at a competitive price required a more sophisticated transportation system than that required for timber. In the absence of roads, rivers provided the only reliable routes, but rapids and cataracts entailed frequent loading and unloading and relatively small vessels. Making the rivers more navigable required major capital investments in canals and locks around the rapids. The first major canal system built to transport grain from the interior to the sea was the Erie Canal in New York, completed in 1825. By starting at the eastern end of Lake Erie, the canal bypassed the cataracts and falls in the Niagara River and provided a sheltered passage to the Mohawk and Hudson Rivers and from there to New York. It soon ensured New York's future as the principal port and trading centre along the Atlantic seaboard.

The success of the Erie Canal severely undermined the role of Montreal. While within a few years the Welland, Rideau, and Lachine canals made it possible to make a continuous voyage from Lakes Huron and Erie and the rivers that they

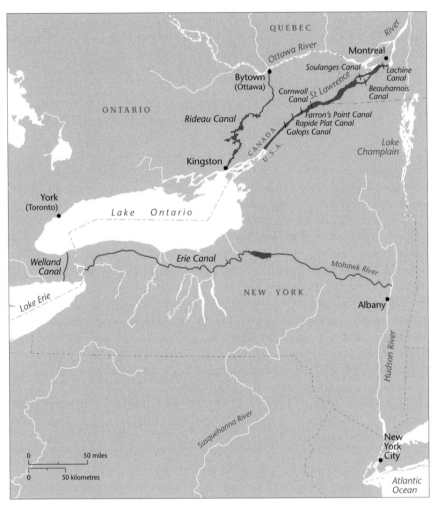

2.2   *Canals, 1840s*

drained all the way to Montreal – via Lake Ontario to Kingston and then to Ottawa – the route was long and could only accommodate small vessels (map 2.2). The result was that the advantage of shipping from Canada provided by the Corn Laws was largely erased by the extra cost of transportation.

To remedy the problem, Montreal merchants convinced the colonial legislature of the United Provinces to enlarge the Welland Canal and build larger locks around the cataracts in the St. Lawrence between Kingston and the Lachine Canal. To increase the incentive, the British Parliament agreed in 1843 that American wheat ground into flour in Canada and shipped from a Canadian port would enjoy the same preference as Canadian wheat. Completed in 1848, the first St. Lawrence Seaway met all expectations and reduced the cost of shipping from the farms around the Great Lakes to an Atlantic seaport from $15 a ton for New York to $10 a ton for Montreal. The extra distance from Montreal to London and other British ports reduced this advantage somewhat and underlined the continuing need for the advantage provided by the Corn Laws.[32]

Unfortunately, before the new route could be brought into operation, in 1846 Canadian farmers and merchants were presented with the startling news that the British Parliament had revoked the Corn Laws and severely reduced the preference on timber. The spectre of starvation in Ireland and the new doctrine of free trade had conspired to undo the careful plans of the colonials. The news proved a double blow. First, Canadian wheat and timber would no longer enjoy a preference; second, there would be insufficient traffic to generate an operating profit to help pay the huge costs incurred by the colonial legislature in constructing the canal.

The decision by the Peel Conservative government in Britain to repeal the last vestiges of the old colonial system and to rely on unilateral free trade made eminent sense for Great Britain. It was a pragmatic reaction to intellectual, political, and economic developments in Britain over the previous fifty years. Adam Smith's radical notion that free trade would lead to prosperity had by the middle of the nineteenth century become the basic tenet of economic orthodoxy. The reform movement of the 1830s, stimulated by Smith's fellow moral and political philosophers, had convinced the establishment of a need to accommodate more democracy, both at home and in the colonies. Most important, continued growth in British industry based on the factory system required imports of cheap food for the workers and cheap and abundant raw materials, as well as plentiful markets for British cloth and machinery. The old mercantilist colonial system had resulted in expensive raw materials, costly food, and limited markets. From 1846, secure in the strength of its industry, Britain threw open its doors to all suppliers of food and raw materials and sought to open as many markets as possible to the products of its factories.

The British North American colonies, however, relied on the preferential access they enjoyed to the British market under the colonial system. They could compete with their more efficient and productive American cousins and the more favourably located Scandinavians and Russians in supplying Britain with fish, timber, wheat, flour, and furs because they did not have to pay high duties. But once that preference was removed, all the disadvantages of a small economy with a slender population base strung out along several thousand miles of inland waterways and hinterland stood out in sharp relief. Investment in the St. Lawrence Seaway to carry goods to Montreal and on to the British market was for naught. Britain had abandoned the colonists.[33]

The Challenge to the Canadian Colonists
To the colonial merchants and farmers, the reversal in corn and timber policy between 1843 and 1846 appeared to be nothing less than imperial perfidy. Noted the

THE BRITISH LION IN 1850;
OR, THE EFFECTS OF FREE TRADE.

"The British Lion in 1850, or The Effects of Free Trade."

Tory *Morning Post* in London in 1849: "If, then, they have no hope of the injurious British law being repealed, who can wonder that a sense of self-preservation should turn them towards America? The duty of allegiance is indeed no light thing, but allegiance on the one hand implies ... protection on the other. If the British Government will not give protection, it is sheer tyranny to extort allegiance."[34] The *Quebec Gazette* was even sharper: "Our great ground of complaint is that British Acts of Parliament created the [timber] trade, causing capital to be invested in the trade, trusting to these acts, which by the uncertain character they now assume may ruin thousands. We never asked for protection: it was given on grounds of national policy."[35]

Unfortunately, none of the colonies could readily look to alternative markets: all were dependent on the export of a narrow range of staples; none had developed much native industry and thus needed export earnings to pay for the necessities of life; all were saddled with large debts because neither the colonial nor imperial duties had been sufficient to pay for various capital projects. To add insult to injury, the US Congress was in the process of adopting a policy opposite to that of Britain. It raised duties on Canadian and British goods while at the same time introducing a system of drawbacks to encourage Upper Canadian farmers to ship their grain to Britain through the Erie Canal and New York. For the northern colonies, the dilemma of 1846 called for urgent and immediate action if their economies were not to collapse. The depression of 1847-8 deepened the air of crisis and convinced many that they had to take steps to gain greater control of their own destiny.

Fortunately, the previous few decades had equipped the colonial legislatures with sufficient experience in managing their own affairs to make the situation less bleak

Table 2.2

Typical colonial duties, 1851

Article	Canada (%)	NS (%)	NB (%)	PEI (%)
Axes	12.5	6.5	1s. 6d.	5.0
Chains	2.5	6.5	1.0	Free
China	12.5	6.5	7.5	5.0
Coal oil	12.5	6.5	7.5	5.0
Cotton warp	12.5	6.5	1.0	5.0
Hardware	12.5	6.5	7.5	5.0
Leather manufactures	12.5	10.0	20.0	5.0
Linen	12.5	6.5	7.5	5.0
Machinery	12.5	6.5	7.5	5.0
Matches	12.5	6.5	7.5	5.0
Nails	12.5	6.5	7.5	5.0
Silk	12.5	6.5	7.5	5.0
Wheat flour, BNA & US[a]	Free BNA	Free BNA	Free BNA	Free BNA
Woollen manufactures	12.5	6.5	7.5	5.0

a Wheat imported from the United States and ground into flour in Canada enjoyed duty-free status.
Source: O.J. McDiarmid, *Commercial Policy in the Canadian Economy* (Cambridge, MA: Harvard University Press, 1946), 116-17.

than at first appeared. Since the Constitutional Act of 1791, the colonial legislatures of Upper and Lower Canada, New Brunswick, and Nova Scotia had enjoyed the right not only to keep the proceeds of the imperial customs duties but also to collect an additional colonial duty. As a result, the various colonial legislatures had developed and implemented a complex fiscal-commercial policy of their own.

The characteristics of this colonial policy included a mixture of fiscal and protective objectives – the primary purpose of the duties was to raise revenue, but farmers, merchants, and early industrialists quickly learned the value of protection and lobbied the legislatures to that effect. There were frequent adjustments in the rates as the legislatures juggled the competing interests of merchants, farmers, and manufacturers with their fiscal requirements. The policy combined imperial and colonial duties, with the imperial duties charged on all imports acting as a floor. On top of this, the colonists could add their own duty, paid not only by imports from abroad but also by imports from other North American colonies, with the exception of trade between the two Canadas. Until 1825, most imports from nonimperial sources, i.e., the United States, were prohibited, which encouraged a high level of smuggling. The subsequent introduction of preferences instead of prohibitions at least increased the chance that duties would be collected. Different rates of duty applied in different colonies.[36]

The details of colonial tariff making are not so interesting as the fact that the colonial legislatures had become actively involved in the making of fiscal and commercial policy. Varying interests in society were learning how to develop and present sophisticated arguments for and against protection and government involvement in related transportation policies. With the transfer to the colonial legislatures of full control over tariffs in 1846, tariff making became even more important and complex (see table 2.2 for some examples of rates of duty in effect in the four principal colonies in 1851).[37] The legislatures were beginning to articulate a quasi-autonomous commercial policy more attuned to the political and economic reality of each colony. Thus, while Britain's unilateral adoption of free trade may have been galling and frustrating, the colonies were not as unprepared for their future as contemporary complaints intimated. Nor was their trade as dependent on the British market as has been suggested. Trade with the American states, at first illegal and after 1825 permissible but at higher rates of duty than trade within the Empire, had by the 1840s become respectable. The colonies did have an alternative, to which they now turned.

3 RECIPROCITY AND PREFERENCES
EARLY NATIONHOOD

There is no policy more consistent with what we call the dark ages of the world than that of protection as a principle. There is no principle more consonant with the advance of human freedom, no principle more in accordance with the great prosperity that prevails in our time than absolute freedom of commerce.

– ALEXANDER MACKENZIE, PRIME MINISTER, 1873–8

Shall we not say Canada is for the Canadians and protect our markets for ourselves. Shall we not say if we have a short crop, our own people shall consume it and pay a fair price for it ... Let each manufacturer tell us what he wants and we will try to give him what he needs.

– SIR JOHN A. MACDONALD, PRIME MINISTER, 1867–73, 1878–91

As Canada stood on the threshold of nationhood, two centuries of colonialism had left a lasting legacy not only in the contours of the economy but also in attitudes toward government's role in shaping further economic development. The economy was indelibly stamped with the pattern of resource exploitation for export. For the next century, Canada continued to develop on this basis, exporting a relatively narrow range of resource-based products to foreign markets while protecting domestic manufacturers concentrating on the home market. At the same time, Canadians looked to governments for the policies and capital projects needed to realize further economic development. In the United States, private interests built the Erie Canal; in Canada, the colonial legislature in Kingston provided the funds for the Laurentian canals, setting a precedent for government involvement in capital projects that would continue in the years to come. The financing required for railroads, for example, would severely strain the fiscal resources of the colonies and complicate the making of future economic policy.

The critical importance of trade to the Canadian economy ensured that efforts to promote exports would figure prominently in the policies pursued by successive governments. Not convinced that Canadian producers could succeed in foreign markets strictly on their own merits, governments sought to find a privileged position for Canadian products in one of the two principal markets of the world economy: Great Britain and the United States. In Great Britain, the goal involved preferences; in the United States, it involved reciprocity. These twin goals would take turns over the next century in guiding Canada's approach to commercial policy. Overarching both, however, was an even stronger determination to extend protection to domestic producers. As Jack Young has written, "Between the late 1840s and

Confederation all the principal elements which were to play a part in the tariff history of Canada for the next century appeared."[1]

Conflicting Opinions

The first step taken in response to the crisis of 1846 in the United Provinces of Canada was to equalize the tariff rates for British and American goods. The Enabling Act of 1846 empowered the colonies to remove preferences and set their own general rates subject to review by the British Parliament. The general rate was set at 7.5 percent for goods from all sources, with some specified commodities assessed at higher rates. The legislatures of the Maritime colonies followed suit, but set the general rate at lower levels. All the schedules were relatively simple, with little room for more sophisticated tariff variations, such as low rates on industrial inputs and higher rates on intermediate and final goods. The general rate was raised several

Table 3.1

Average *ad valorem* rates of duty, Canada, 1841-58

Year	Imports (£000)	% of imports duty free	Average rate of duty (%)	
			On dutiable imports	On total imports
1841	2,694	5.4	8.9	8.4
1842	2,589	3.3	11.1	10.8
1843	2,421	0.6	10.1	10.0
1844	4,331	1.9	10.4	10.2
1845	4,191	1.4	10.9	10.7
1846	4,516	1.4	9.5	9.3
1847	3,610	2.1	11.7	11.5
1848	3,191	2.9	10.8	10.5
1849	3,003	9.0	16.3	14.8
1850	4,246	6.9	15.6	14.5
1851	5,359	7.9	14.9	13.8
1852	5,072	5.8	15.5	14.6
1853	7,995	5.6	13.6	12.9
1854	10,132	6.9	13.0	12.1
1855	9,022	28.8	13.7	9.8
1856	10,986	27.5	14.2	10.3
1857	9,658	31.5	14.5	10.0
1858	7,269	28.7	16.3	11.6

Source: O.J. McDiarmid, *Commercial Policy in the Canadian Economy* (Cambridge, MA: Harvard University Press, 1946), 76.

Table 3.2

Typical colonial duties, 1866

Article	Canada (%)	NS (%)	NB (%)	PEI (%)
Axes	15.0	10.0	15.5	10.0
Chains	15.0	5.0	4.0	Free
China	15.0	10.0	15.5	10.0
Cotton warp	15.0	10.0	4.0	10.0
Hardware	15.0	10.0	15.5	10.0
Leather manufactures	15.0	10.0	18.0	10.0
Linen	15.0	10.0	15.5	10.0
Machinery	15.0	10.0	15.5	10.0
Matches	15.0	10.0	18.0	12.5
Nails	15.0	10.0	15.5	10.0
Silk	15.0	10.0	15.5	10.0
Wheat flour, BNA & US[a]	Free BNA	Free BNA	Free	Free
Woollen manufactures	15.0	10.0	15.5	10.0

a   Wheat imported from the United States and ground into flour in Canada enjoyed duty-free status.
Source: O.J. McDiarmid, *Commercial Policy in the Canadian Economy* (Cambridge, MA: Harvard University Press, 1946), 116-17.

times over the next decade, but the revenue-raising character of the tariff in each colony clearly took precedence over its protective effect (see tables 3.1 and 3.2).[2]

While psychologically gratifying, penalizing British goods hardly made a satisfactory basis for long-term fiscal and commercial policy. A more fundamental and lasting solution was required. By 1847 economic conditions had deteriorated in the face of a severe depression, adding urgency to the debate. In response, various currents of opinion emerged among the colonists on an appropriate course of action, including: annexation to the United States, return to British preference, free trade, protectionism, and reciprocity.

An annexationist movement flourished briefly, largely concentrated among the Montreal merchants who reasoned that if you could not beat them, you should join them. The US economy had grown rapidly in the previous fifty years and presented an attractive alternative to those interested in commercial enterprise. The movement, however, did not resonate outside Montreal. It generated a lot of heated debate, but little came of it except perhaps to make reciprocity more attractive to both the Colonial Office in London and the more moderate elements in the colonies. The idea of annexation continued to echo in Canada every time economic conditions were bad and comparison with the US economy was unfavourable. Potential US interest in annexation provided a continuing spur, first to Confederation and later to the creation of a National Policy.[3]

Looking across the Atlantic, however, not everyone in the colonies was convinced that the free-trade movement in Britain would last. Powerful voices, particularly in the House of Lords, continued to be against it. If the colonists worked hard at adding their own voices, some reasoned, the policy could be reversed and the benefits of the colonial system restored.[4] While this alternative was attractive to many colonists, their prospects of success appeared increasingly dim. Additionally, a return to preferences would do little for the growing class of manufacturers and artisans who wanted protection from more competitive British and American producers, nor would it provide guarantees that there would not be continual changes in direction.

In fact, a significant number of influential colonists had imbibed the heady new brew of free trade and were convinced that it could do for Canada what it promised to do for Britain, an opinion held more strongly in the Maritime colonies than in the Canadas. In the colonial context, however, it should be understood that free trade did not mean the absence of duties; rather, it meant that duties would be neutral and applied strictly for revenue purposes. Markets would be open to all comers, and goods from any source would be assessed at the same rate. While attractive on the surface, this course of action ignored the fact that the difference between a revenue and a protective tariff is in most instances difficult to detect. Whatever its intent, a customs duty always has a protective effect. What made free trade work in Britain was increasing reliance on other sources of revenue, including land and consumption taxes. There was little appetite for such taxes in the colonies, making free trade an academic rather than realistic alternative.[5]

Just as some colonists had been swayed by the arguments of British free traders, others, particularly manufacturers and some farmers, were persuaded by the protectionist views of American and continental writers like Alexander Hamilton, Henry Carey, Horace Greeley, and Friedrich List. These colonists were convinced that the judicious application of tariffs would not only meet the colonies' fiscal requirements, but would also add to the growth of industry and employment and increase their economic self-sufficiency. This sentiment would gain greater currency as Canada gradually industrialized.[6]

Finally, there developed a view, particularly among the political elite, that the most promising course of action was to encourage reciprocity, both among the various North American colonies and between them and the United States. Reciprocity in this context had limited application; for most of its advocates, it meant free trade limited largely to natural products, that is, to resources in either their natural or partially processed form. Such reciprocity would allow the colonies to create an alternative to British preferences by providing new preferences either among themselves and/or to the United States for their traditional exports. It would also preserve continued scope for protecting manufacturers and raising revenues through the application of duties on manufactures.[7]

Opinion gradually coalesced around reciprocity as the most practical alternative. To the Colonial Office in London, the idea of the North American colonies working together toward the establishment of a customs union and then negotiating access for their staple products to the US market seemed a natural extension of Britain's own conversion to free trade. London officials perhaps imagined such a customs union in more grandiose terms than did the colonists, but both saw reciprocity with the United States as a welcome solution to the crisis of the 1840s. Efforts to that end, therefore, were soon set in train.

The First Search for Reciprocity

Early steps toward the establishment of intercolonial reciprocity or a customs union did not meet with success. Sporadically discussed and much favoured by the Colonial Office in the period leading up to Confederation, neither gained any real momentum until after the demise of US reciprocity in 1866. The ardour of the Maritime colonies for reciprocity cooled considerably when they realized that a full customs union would require them to raise their duties upon British and American imports to the level of the Canadas. As illustrated in tables 2.2 and 3.2, the duties in the Canadas were significantly higher than those in the three Maritime colonies and, given fiscal requirements, steadily increased during this period. While there were those in New Brunswick and to a lesser extent in Nova Scotia and Prince Edward Island who favoured more protection, many more found this too high a price to pay. Proposals to limit intercolonial reciprocity to natural products were at first dismissed but were agreed on in 1850 and extended as part of the larger package involving the United States. By 1856, free access was extended unilaterally to most resource products from all sources.[8]

Reciprocity with the United States soon became the only alternative that attracted sufficient support from a wide enough range of interests to be worth the pursuit. Promoted by Francis Hincks and William Hamilton Merritt, among the leading politicians in the Legislative Assembly of the United Provinces, as well as by the newly arrived Governor General, Lord Elgin, reciprocity became the main focus of commercial policy in the period 1849 to 1854. In their view, a reciprocity agreement would give the colonies free access to the US market for products traditionally sold on the British market but, at the same time, keep the colonies firmly within the British Empire. With the blessings of the Colonial Office in London, they pursued this objective with dogged zeal through two administrations in Washington, numerous shifts in the various colonial legislatures, several changes in colonial secretaries, and waning interest in the Canadas.

While annexation had some appeal in Washington, the benefits to the United States of a reciprocity agreement appeared less clear, particularly one limited to natural products, that is, to products of export interest to the Canadian colonies. From the outset, the colonies had made it clear that they had no interest in extending either free access or preferences to manufactures, that is, products of export interest to the United States. More fundamentally, however, Elgin had to address the policy preferences of a young nation that had become increasingly enamoured of protection as a principle. The American Revolution may have had its origins in a revolt against the tariff, but American legislators had not taken long to discover the importance of the tariff not only as a source of revenue but also as a tool of protection.

In the period immediately after the Revolution, American politicians had expressed their support for free trade, reciprocity, and equality, but the majority soon adopted economic nationalism as their guiding principle. For Alexander Hamilton, the first secretary of the treasury, the necessity of protection to build up infant industries had been the basis of his *Report on Manufactures,* the first full-length treatise setting out the contours of modern protectionism. For others, like Thomas Jefferson and John Adams, protection developed more slowly in response both to revenue needs and to the rebuffs suffered at the hands of Britain, Spain, France, and other trading nations. By 1816, protection was firmly ensconced as the basic creed of American trade policy. At that time, the duty on imports of manufactured goods averaged 35 percent, considerably higher than that in the Canadian colonies, Britain, France, or elsewhere.[9]

This first phase of protectionism reached its zenith with the Tariff of Abominations adopted by the US Congress in 1828, which raised rates to an average of 61.7 percent. While the worst excesses of this act were soon ameliorated, the overall incidence of duties on all imports still averaged 50.8 percent in the period 1829-31. In the years thereafter, the level of protection steadily declined to reach a low of 16.3 percent in the period 1857-61.[10] US political leaders had also tried their hand at trade negotiations, but with a singular lack of success. Their insistence on equality of treatment and strict reciprocity had made their task exceedingly difficult. More fundamentally, the Senate had yet to approve any trade treaty that did anything more than guarantee equal treatment in the American market. Exchanging tariff-cutting concessions remained unthinkable.[11]

Lord Elgin understood that he had his work cut out for him, but there was some justification for his optimism. The return of the low-tariff Democrats in 1844 had led to adoption of a new, lower tariff in 1846 as well as a series of measures placing customs administration on a more orderly basis. President James Polk's (1845-9) treasury secretary, Robert Walker, enjoyed a reputation as an intelligent and articulate spokesman for free trade on a par with Richard Cobden in Britain. His message to Congress advocating a tariff limited to the Republic's revenue needs had led to the reduction in rates in 1846.[12] These views had remained in vogue during the administration of Millard Fillmore (1850-3). Finally, President Franklin Pierce (1853-7) and his secretary of state, William Marcy, expressed their intent to British officials "to proceed, as long as they could gain the support of the country, in the direction of free trade."[13] Elgin had to find what it would take for both the administration and Congress to come on side, so that he could create a community of interest between Canada's goals and those of the United States.

The key for the United States lay in gaining access to the rich inshore fishing grounds off the East Coast, free navigation through the Great Lakes and Laurentian canals, and a tacit commitment not to raise the tariff on manufactures. The first of these US objectives created difficulties for the Maritime colonies, while the other two did not sit well in the Canadas. The timber and agricultural interests, however, succeeded in overcoming these objections, giving Elgin the wherewithal to negotiate.

It took Elgin five years to put the package together. By the mid-1850s, the combined concessions by the colonies on fishing and navigation rights brought the US administration reluctantly around. Unable to rely on President Pierce and Secretary of State Marcy to carry the day in Congress, Elgin assumed this task as well. Marcy had proven a worthy and competent protagonist of reciprocity, but the US administration was not sufficiently interested to squander any political capital on the issue. Despite this handicap, Elgin forged a senatorial majority by using artful bribes and entertainment effected through a confidential agent hired for the purpose, and by convincing Southern senators that reciprocity was superior to annexation. The latter, if successful, could bring up to six new free states into the union and upset the balance between North and South, delicate in the years leading up to the Civil War. Elgin managed to overcome opposition from protectionist interests in New England and the Midwest as well, and the treaty passed in 1854 to take effect at the beginning of 1855.[14]

The treaty negotiated by Elgin is a disarmingly simple document divided into seven articles. The first two involve the exchange of fishing rights off the East Coast and a mechanism for settling any disputes arising out of the exercise of those rights. Article IV bears on navigation rights on the Great Lakes and St. Lawrence River, while articles V through VII concern implementation of the agreement. Reciprocity is contained in article III, which reads: "It is agreed that the articles enumerated in the schedule hereunto annexed, being the growth and produce of the aforesaid British Colonies or of the United States, shall be admitted into each country respectively free of duty."[15] There then follows a list of twenty-eight products or groups of products, almost exclusively unprocessed raw materials, the exceptions being flour, lumber, rags, and preserved meat products. In effect, the Canadian and Maritime colonies had gained tariff-free access to the US market for their traditional exports in return for American access to the Atlantic inshore fishery and free navigation on the Great Lakes. That is the full extent of the agreement, but for the next fifty years, it would conjure up strong memories and images in Canada, particularly in the Maritimes.[16]

But the agreement was not to last. New England and Midwest manufacturing and farming interests continued to oppose it, and the colonists did everything possible to confirm them in their opinion. In 1856 the colonial legislatures put most of the products covered by the agreement onto the free list from all sources, thus eliminating the preferential treatment enjoyed by US exporters. In 1858 and again in 1859, the United Provinces of Canada decided to raise the tariff on manufactures (see below), despite a tacit understanding that they would refrain from creating greater obstacles to US nonreciprocity exports. British sympathies with the Confederacy and general Northern antipathy toward the colonies sealed the agreement's fate.[17] In the absence of low-tariff Southern Democrats, a Congress dominated by high-tariff Republicans voted to give the colonies notice of abrogation, and reciprocity ended on 17 March 1866, not to be revived again until 15 November 1935.

By the time the agreement was signed in 1854, the fears of 1846 had begun to recede and the colonists had begun to realize that their position was not as fragile as first feared. The 1850s were a decade of rapid growth. For most of those years the colonists enjoyed unprecedented prosperity, and their increasing self-confidence helped undo the shock of Britain's betrayal in 1846. Already in the late 1840s, shipments of both timber and grain had reached new highs and continued to grow, not only to Great Britain but also to the United States. In 1849, £314,000 out of a total of £1,327,000 in lumber exports went to the United States. Four years later, that is, before reciprocity and despite British free trade, lumber shipments had almost doubled to a total of £2,350,000 with £615,000 destined for the US market. The grain trade also flourished. In 1849, 3,645,000 bushels were exported; by 1853, exports had doubled to 6,597,000 bushels and reached 9,391,531 bushels in 1856.[18]

Railway construction helped to fuel the export-led boom of the 1850s. British, American, and some Canadian money, much of it guaranteed by the colonial legislatures, built a variety of rail lines that encouraged the shipment of Canadian grain and lumber to the United States, either for consumption there or for shipment overseas. By the end of the decade, 2,000 miles of track had been laid. The Grand Trunk and Great Western Railways provided a continuous service from the Ontario hinterland of Windsor, Sarnia, and London through Toronto and Kingston to Montreal, where it met lines to Maine and to the Maritimes.[19]

It is no wonder, therefore, that historians are divided on the economic effect of the Reciprocity Treaty. During the eleven years it was in force, the British North American colonies enjoyed steady growth, and many contemporaries were satisfied that the agreement was responsible. Trade increased (see table 3.3), particularly in products covered by the agreement, although trade figures must be interpreted with some caution because the absence of duties probably meant that the high level of smuggling in earlier years was now being replaced by legitimate trade. Additionally, a growing US economy provided a ready market for Canadian exports, and high US inflation during the Civil War helped to make Canadian goods more competitive. For these and other reasons, modern analysis has cast some doubt on the role of the agreement in underwriting the new prosperity. The fact that trade did not fall off much after the agreement's abrogation makes these arguments compelling.[20]

Nevertheless, trade between the colonies and the United States flourished, and the agreement grew in popularity. The staunch protectionist Isaac Buchanan was so impressed that he proposed the negotiation of a Canada-US *zollverein* or customs union, reasoning that high tariffs around North America would allow the development of infant industries, benefiting from a North American market but

Table 3.3

Canadian trade statistics, 1851-67 ($000)

	Imports into Canada				Exports from Canada			
	Reciprocity articles from		Nonreciprocity articles from		Reciprocity articles to		Nonreciprocity articles to	
Year	US	ROW	US	ROW	US	ROW	US	ROW
1851	1,039	355	7,325	12,713	3,860	7,188	212	1,704
1853	1,281	657	10,499	19,543	8,696	10,524	340	2,452
1855	7,726	649	13,102	14,608	16,508	6,652	228	1,536
1857	8,642	1,025	11,582	18,183	12,912	10,640	296	1,600
1859	7,106	1,424	10,487	14,538	13,625	8,455	297	725
1861	9,981	1,316	11,088	20,670	13,972	18,646	414	1,685
1863	12,339	1,667	10,770	21,188	17,573	16,608	2,477	2,689
1865	9,132	1,851	10,457	23,180	20,567	13,994	2,372	2,675
1867	6,114	1,925	14,159	36,852	22,051	16,108	3,533	3,278

Note: ROW = rest of world

Source: Adapted from Lawrence Officer and Lawrence Smith, "The Canadian-American Reciprocity Treaty of 1855 to 1866," *Journal of Economic History* 28, 4 (December 1968): 600.

protected from European competition.[21] Even a generation later, the agreement evoked fond memories. Sir Louis Davies of Prince Edward Island, Liberal minister of marine and fisheries from 1896 to 1901, summed up Maritime memories of reciprocity: "Since the Maritime provinces were peopled, there was never a decade when prosperity was so marked among all classes, when land rose in value so quickly, when the wharves were so lined with shipping, when the workmen had such steady employment, when the farmers had as good a market as between 1854 and 1866 when we had reciprocal trade with the United States of America."[22]

Whatever the economic impact of the agreement, it played a critical role in providing the colonies with an effective foreign commercial policy in the years immediately after the shock created by the end of the colonial system. It confirmed the value of the US market as an alternative to the British market; it suggested the possibility of a policy that promoted the export of resources but continued to protect manufactures; it provided a vehicle requiring cooperation and joint action among the disparate colonies; and it put paid to any notions of either annexation or a return to the old colonial system. In addition, the experience in the two decades after 1846 of wrestling with the twin problems of raising revenue and promoting economic development prepared many colonial politicians for more ambitious responsibilities. Finally, the success of the reciprocity experiment reverberated frequently in the further development of Canadian commercial policy.

Tariffs and Revenues

Throughout the 1850s, the colonial legislatures had to address a growing and pressing need for revenue. Not only did they have to service large debts – arising, for example, from the building of the Laurentian canals – but they also had to deal with growing operational costs as the colonies experienced rapid population growth. Between 1825 and 1851, the population had almost tripled, from 815,000 to 2.3 million.[23] Growth meant the building of new roads, railroads, and other public works. Although some infrastructure development was assumed by private interests, governments were involved in a variety of ways, including as guarantor of bonds. By the middle of the 1850s, the legislature of the United Provinces of Canada was spending close to £1 million. By the end of the decade, that figure had risen by half, with expenditures outstripping revenue by close to 50 percent.

The major sources of revenue were customs and excise duties. The legislators' desperate search for revenue was tailor-made for agricultural and manufacturing groups interested in protection. When these revenues declined, as they did in 1857-8 due to depressed economic conditions, circumstances almost dictated that ministers of finance and protectionist forces would find common ground.

As early as the 1840s, there had emerged a number of organized groups in the colonies actively promoting the protection of manufactures. The Tariff Reform Association in Montreal, the Association for the Promotion of Canadian Industry in the Toronto-Hamilton area, and similar groups in New Brunswick all succeeded in electing legislators who shared their sentiments and lobbied others to take account of their views. Most vocal among them was Isaac Buchanan, who from the repeal of the Corn Laws became a tireless crusader for more protection, invoking and promoting the views of List, Carey, Greeley, and other apostles of import substitution and national industrial strength. Most of these groups were allied with manufacturing interests, but with a growing population providing a reasonable domestic market, agricultural sentiment also developed in favour of protection. Already in the 1830s, for example, agricultural interests had succeeded, together with various manufacturing interests, in passing the protectionist American Intercourse Bill through the elected Legislative Assembly of Upper Canada, only to have it rejected by the appointed Legislative Council. The merchants who dominated the Council wanted preferences, not protection.[24]

These new, populist forces for protection came together in the legislature of the United Provinces in 1858-9 and produced the Cayley-Galt Tariff. Efforts by Inspector General William Cayley to meet unexpectedly high expenses arising out of the railway boom disposed him to raise the tariff significantly in 1858. The following year his successor, Alexander Galt, now styled finance minister, was faced with the unwelcome news that Cayley's estimates had been considerably below requirements. In order to get the revenue he needed, Galt had to come to terms with the protectionist overtures of Buchanan and his colleagues. The result was the first tariff schedule in Canadian history that was frankly structured not only to raise revenue but also to extend significant levels of protection. As Galt explained three years later, "The principle adopted in Canada had been that of admitting all raw materials free. The next class of articles were those which had received a certain amount of manufacture, but which could not be used until they had received a certain amount of remanufacture, and upon them a 10 percent duty was imposed; and upon articles manufactured the duty was 20 percent."[25]

While there were counterforces to the protectionist elements in society – various agricultural and commercial interests as well as the imperial watchdog in London and the trading interest represented by the Reciprocity Treaty – desperate fiscal straits had forced Galt's hand. Not only did he increase the overall rates in order to raise revenue, but he restructured the rates in order to increase the level of protection. As shown in table 3.4, a large number of primary and some intermediate products were added to the free list; for an equally large number of intermediate products, the rates were reduced from 15 to 10 percent, while the rates on most fully finished goods were increased from 15 to 20 percent or higher. This clever restructuring of the tariff was not lost on manufacturers. In Canada, it was welcomed as providing a much more effective level of protection, but British and American manufacturers cried foul. In Britain, they unsuccessfully petitioned Parliament to disallow the new tariff, and their failure confirmed the autonomy of colonial trade policy. In the

Table 3.4

The Cayley-Galt Tariff of 1858-9 (number of tariff items at various *ad valorem* rates)

Nominal tariff rate (%)	All items Before	After	Primary Before	After	Intermediate Before	After	Tertiary Before	After
0.0	97	113	56	75	26	35	15	3
2.5	55	–	10	–	35	–	10	–
5.0	15	–	–	–	9	–	6	–
10.0	–	57	–	1	–	50	–	6
15.0	184	1	10	–	24	1	150	–
20.0	2	175	–	–	–	8	2	167
25.0	–	4	–	–	–	–	–	4
30.0	–	3	–	–	–	–	–	3
Total	353	353	76	76	94	94	183	183
Average rate	8.54%	12.11%	2.30%	0.13%	5.24%	7.18%	12.81%	19.62%

Note: Excludes edibles (71 items), natural products (34), specific duties (27), and special items (settlers' effects).

Source: D.F. Barnett, "The Galt Tariff: Incidental or Effective Protection," *Canadian Journal of Economics* 9, 3 (August 1976): 393-5, tables 1-4. Reproduced with the permission of Blackwell Publishing.

United States, the new tariff hardened the opposition of New England manufacturers to the Reciprocity Treaty.

Galt fully appreciated the limits imposed on a finance minister whose main sources of revenue are excise and customs duties. If the rates are set too low, not enough revenue will come in. If the rates are set too high, however, the flow of trade will reduce – either because of smuggling or because consumers turn to domestic sources – to a point at which, again, there will not be enough revenue. Too much protection, therefore, is as inimical to revenue objectives as too little, a fine point not always appreciated by protectionist interests, but one that no finance minister of the period could afford to ignore. Galt also had to address the political reality of budget making. While he might not have liked the arguments of protectionists like Isaac Buchanan, he needed their support in the legislature if his budget was to gain approval. The increasing strength of protectionist sentiment was creating a political environment that further circumscribed a finance minister's room for manoeuvre.

Given the strength of free-trade sentiments in Britain and the continuing oversight of colonial policy exercised by Parliament, Galt insisted that his intent was purely to bolster his capacity to raise revenue, not to extend protection. He insisted years later, "Free Trade and Protection as abstract principles are both inapplicable to Canada from its situation and circumstances. My own views on this subject have refined, but have in no respect changed since 1859 ... The policy adopted then, and which to a large extent remains still, was properly known as Incidental Protection, though it might more appropriately have been termed Modified Free Trade."[26]

Galt went to great pains to deny what he had done, but his tariff effectively consummated the marriage between revenue needs and protection. From now on, no Canadian politician could fail to address this dual aspect of budget making. It would be another twenty-five years, however, before a third element was added: fiscal and trade policies eventually became the basis for the National Policy, forging an abiding alliance between protection and nationalism.

Confederation

The colonies' revenue needs, however, could not be satisfied solely through artful tinkering with the tariff. The colonies had reached a stage in their political and economic development that required a further step toward both self-government and economic union. By the beginning of the 1860s, the initial haphazard efforts at forging intercolonial reciprocity or economic union had become more pressing and more realistic. A number of factors contributed to the heightened urgency. Prominent among them was the growing public debt faced by each of the colonies as a result of the railway boom of the 1850s. Also contributing to their apprehension was growing sentiment in the United States against the Reciprocity Treaty. It had been signed in 1854 for an initial ten-year period, after which it could be abrogated on one year's notice. Efforts to that effect began promptly in 1864. While those first efforts were unsuccessful, the writing was clearly on the wall. Finally, the exercise of

tariff autonomy by each of the legislatures did little for their economic development and was not well received by the Colonial Office in London. Thus discussions
were initiated to establish a basis for greater political and economic union among
the Maritime and Canadian colonies.

It must be emphasized, however, that the fathers of Confederation were not intent on replicating on a more peaceful basis the American experiment of a century
earlier. They were not looking to establish an independent nation. Rather, they
sought to find the formula that would give the various colonies composing British
North America greater political and economic cohesion, while firmly within the
British Empire. There was no interest in cutting the ties to Britain's Parliament or
Queen; they clearly saw themselves as British subjects. Economic and commercial
policy considerations were central to their deliberations. In the words of Alfred
Dubuc, "Confederation had as its goal the creation of adequate institutions for the
pursuit of a centralized policy of long-term economic development."[27]

These considerations included the establishment of an economic union allowing
for the free circulation of goods throughout British North America, a stronger economic base to take on existing public debt as well as future public works, and a
stronger political and economic basis upon which to resist the continuing threat
posed by American notions of manifest destiny. American designs on the territories west of the Great Lakes remained robust, as did the allure of the American
economy to many Canadian settlers.[28] For most of the nineteenth century, Canada
was a second-best alternative for settlers, many of whom initially arrived in Canada
because of more restrictive US immigration policy but emigrated to the United
States at the first opportunity.[29] These considerations further underlined the importance of commercial policy in defining the terms of Confederation, as well as
the importance of finding the formula that would allow the colonies to enjoy access
to the American market without compromising their continued desire to be British
subjects.

For the Maritime colonies, the absence of reciprocity made Confederation much
less attractive. However, in the midst of the discussions, the US Congress finally
succeeded in abrogating the Reciprocity Treaty, to take effect 17 March 1866. Consequently, throughout the final Confederation debate, the need first to preserve and
then to renew reciprocity figured prominently. Several missions were sent to take
soundings in New York and Washington only to meet a solid negative front. There
was no interest in the United States in anything less than economic union.[30] In the
end, reciprocity did not matter and on 1 July 1867, New Brunswick, Nova Scotia,
Upper Canada, and Lower Canada joined together to form the new Dominion of
Canada. Prince Edward Island joined six years later, while Newfoundland preferred
to retain its colonial status for a further eighty-two years. By 1871, with the admis-
sion of Manitoba and British Columbia and the establishment of Canadian responsibility for the vast territories of the Hudson's Bay Company, Canada stretched
from sea to sea, the second-largest single piece of real estate in the world.[31]

Not convinced that the rebuffs by the Americans in 1865 and 1866 were genuine, Francis Hincks, finance minister in the first government of Prime Minister John A. Macdonald and a key figure in the 1854 negotiations, made efforts in 1869 and 1871 to rekindle interest in reciprocity. The importance of the US market had not diminished since abrogation of the treaty: 51 percent of Canada's exports went to the United States in 1870; only 38 percent went to Britain, and secure access remained a high priority. Hincks came home virtually empty-handed on both occasions. In 1871, a modest treaty was worked out that allowed US fishermen access to the East Coast fishery in return for free access to the US market for fish caught by Maritime fishermen, but the major goals were not achieved.[32]

The American rejection of Canada's overtures was particularly difficult for Hincks. Together with his brother the Rev. William Hincks, professor of natural science at the newly established University of Toronto, he had developed a sophisticated understanding of trade and economic issues and preached the virtues of free trade to an increasingly sceptical Toronto business establishment. While the merchants agreed with them, newly established manufacturers were not as sure.[33]

In 1874, the government of Alexander Mackenzie, not confident that the Conservatives (or Liberal-Conservatives as they were then) had made a convincing case, sent George Brown, editor of the *Toronto Globe* and an ardent admirer of the Americans, to make a further effort. Brown succeeded in concluding a reciprocity treaty with the administration of President Ulysses S. Grant, an agreement still largely limited to natural products but also including some manufactures and again extending fishing rights. The agreement was blessed by the Colonial Office in London but died in the US Senate. The president was not prepared to give it his whole-hearted support and, without such support, it could not gain passage.[34]

Thus on three occasions and to two different governments, either the American administration or the Senate made it clear to the new confederation that reciprocity on any terms other than commercial union was not acceptable. Canadian politicians, jealous of their new-found independence from Britain, and not about to exchange the Colonial Office for the State Department, insisted that it would be reciprocity plain and simple, or nothing.

American attitudes to reciprocity were conditioned as much by lack of interest in the Canadian market (or, more accurately, lack of concern about the level of protection and foreign competition) as by deep-seated convictions about the importance of protecting the American market. The Republicans who dominated American politics in the second half of the nineteenth century were dyed-in-the-wool protectionists and true believers in the manifest destiny of American industry. They had fully accepted the arguments of Alexander Hamilton and Henry Carey that the young republic needed to protect its infant industries and give them the guarantee of the home market. The predominant Republican on tariff matters for most of this period, Justin Morrill, opined during the 1857 tariff debate that "I am for ruling America for the benefit, first, of Americans, and for the 'rest of mankind' afterwards."[35] In that he echoed the views of Abraham Lincoln, soon to be president. In his view, "The abandonment of the protective policy ... must result in the increase of both useless labor, and idleness; and so, in pro[por]tion, must produce want and ruin among our people."[36]

Once firmly in control of Congress, Morrill and his colleagues passed a new tariff act every few years, adjusting individual tariffs, and steadily adding to their protectionist effect. Blessed with a large and growing economy and population base, the United States had little need for overseas markets and the lure of practising and preaching the most jingoistic version of mercantilism proved to be overpowering. Diplomatic historian J.L. Morison notes, "The keenness of American bargaining was sharpened by the national habit of regarding everything desired by Americans as natural right, and everything to be expected by the other side as an attempt to defraud the Union. Nothing that Machiavelli ever taught has proved half so helpful in the establishment of a great power, as the American capacity for turning rank greed into something savouring of righteousness."[37]

A similar retreat from freer trade had occurred in Europe. Britain's decision to adopt unilateral free trade was followed by efforts, initially successful, to extend the faith to other countries. With the conclusion of the Cobden-Chevalier Treaty with France in 1860, that policy seemed to have been crowned with success, and the system of most-favoured-nation (MFN) bilateral treaties negotiated by Britain and France ushered in over a decade of growth and prosperity in Europe that spilled across the Atlantic. By the mid-1870s, however, recession and then depression had convinced most European politicians to abandon their commitment to more open markets, and thus began the slow spiral of ever-increasing tariffs complemented by discriminatory quotas and exchange manipulation. Only Britain resisted the trend.[38]

American politicians were not influenced by the short-lived European enthusiasm for freer trade and the related institutional framework provided by the interlocking MFN agreements. Even after the initial appetite for trade liberalization had waned, European governments maintained their *système de traités,* which succeeded in acting as a brake on the return to protectionism. American politicians never accepted the benefits either of extending unconditional MFN treatment or of lowering trade barriers.[39] Occasional efforts by the State Department to negotiate reciprocal trade agreements were rebuffed by the Senate, as were efforts to provide the president with authority to negotiate tariff reductions.[40] Canadian politicians were also not much affected by European attitudes. As they pushed for a return to reciprocity and free trade in natural products, they saw no irony in increasing the range and height of tariffs on industrial products. Even while pursuing reciprocity, they had to address increasing pressure from domestic manufacturers, many of whom insisted that reciprocity was not for them. Growing conflict between an export-driven policy geared to the needs of staples production and an import-driven policy responsive to manufacturing interests was complicating the making of a coherent Canadian trade policy.[41] Export interests still dominated, but import-competing interests were catching up.

DAME COBDEN'S NEW PUPIL.

"Dame Cobden's New Pupil." Emperor Napoleon III learns his new ABCs from British apostle of free trade, Sir Richard Cobden, as Great Britain and France prepare to negotiate their first modern trade agreement.

Diverging Canadian and American objectives during this period also reflected differences in the economic development of the two nations. In the United States, the opening of the interior fuelled the growth of a large internal market and decreased interest in exports. In Canada, the opening of the interior stimulated the production of more and more staples for export. The success of US industrial development created surplus capital for investment in foreign markets, such as Canada; Canadian development of staples production created a continuing demand for foreign capital, including from the United States. Canada became a classic example of specialization through trade while the United States became a much more diversified economy and less dependent on trade. These fundamental differences help to

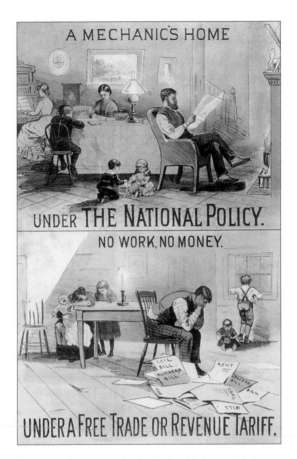

"A Mechanic's Home under the National Policy and under a Free Trade or Revenue Tariff, 1891." Throughout the 1880s, despite mounting evidence to the contrary, the popular press portrayed the benefits of the National Policy and the pitfalls of free trade or a revenue tariff.

explain the conflicting attitudes in Canada and the United States to the benefits of reciprocity.

The Development of a "National Policy"

Confederation came at a time when the colonies that made up British North America enjoyed continuing prosperity. The boom extended through the first government of Sir John A. Macdonald. Exports rose from $57 million in 1868 to $89 million in 1874, and a further 1,500 miles of railroad were constructed.[42] By the mid-1870s, however, the good times had come to an end. For the next twenty years, Canada experienced a period of unsettled economic conditions leading to hesitant growth and frequent recessions.[43] In these circumstances, the Parliament of Canada gradually forged a series of economic development policies that became known as the National Policy. Central to these initiatives was a high tariff deliberately set to induce industrialization, maintain employment, and attract population.

As John Dales has pointed out, Canadian politicians opted for a policy that emphasized aggregate growth rather than productivity, efficiency, and competitiveness. In that they succeeded. In the century that followed, Canada's population grew by a factor of six and the economy by a factor of at least fifty.[44] The nationalist basis of that policy, however, added a dimension that would complicate the adoption of more economically rewarding policies by future politicians. For Canada, protection through high tariffs became inextricably tied to nationhood, a connection that was not broken until the end of the 1980s when Canada finally entered into an unrestricted reciprocity agreement with the United States and the federal government told Canada's uncompetitive manufacturing sector either to adjust to global competition or to lose its markets.[45]

Macdonald mused about the virtues of high tariffs during his first administration, but he and his caucus did not fully seize on the potential of the tariff as a political issue until they were in opposition.[46] As a result, Confederation initially marked a step toward freer trade. Not only did it lead to a reduction in protection for Ontario and Quebec, but it created a larger common market, a point not lost on manufacturers, who immediately began to clamour for more protection. Rapid growth and rising incomes, however, allowed the first Macdonald government to pursue a tariff policy that was geared more to revenue than to protection.[47] The first tariff introduced by the Dominion government provided for free entry of natural products and many partially processed goods, 15 percent for manufactures, and high rates of over 30 percent for luxury goods. The overall incidence of that tariff was a little less than 20 percent. The basic rate was increased to 17.5 percent in 1874, raising the overall incidence of the tariff to over 20 percent.[48] While these rates are high by modern standards (the overall incidence of the Canadian tariff in 2000 was under 1 percent), the tariff was still the government's principal source of revenue.[49] It constituted around 60 percent of the federal government's revenue from Confederation until the introduction of the income tax in 1917 (see table 3.5). These high rates, however, despite their avowed revenue purpose, clearly had a protective effect. At the same time, while higher than European rates, they were still well below those in vogue south of the border. During most of the second half of the nineteenth century, the US tariff on dutiable imports averaged well over 40 percent, and average duties collected on all imports never fell below 20 percent.[50]

Macdonald's musings about the political advantages of further bolstering the protective effect of the tariff came to full flower in the 1878 election when he campaigned as the champion of a National Policy based on high levels of protection. For the first time, a leading Canadian politician linked tariff policy with Canada's

Table 3.5

Customs duties as a percentage of total revenue, 1866-1916 (Cdn$000)

Year		Customs duties	Excise taxes	Total revenue	Customs as % of total
1866	Canada	7,329	1,889	12,171	60
	NB	1,037	–	1,336	78
	NS	1,226	6	1,542	80
1868		8,600	3,000	13,700	63
1871		11,800	4,300	19,400	61
1876		12,800	5,600	22,600	57
1881		18,400	5,300	29,600	62
1886		19,400	5,800	33,500	58
1891		23,300	6,900	38,600	60
1896		19,800	7,900	36,600	54
1901		28,300	10,300	52,500	54
1906		46,100	14,000	80,100	58
1911		71,800	16,900	117,900	61
1916		99,000	26,000	172,000	58

Source: J.H. Perry, *Taxes, Tariffs and Subsidies: A History of Canadian Fiscal Development,* vol. 1 (Toronto: University of Toronto Press, 1955), 31, 72, 107.

national development.[51] Back in power, he wasted no time in putting his National Policy into effect. Its avowed purpose was to build the country and knit it together from east to west, a purpose that had become more crucial with the purchase of the North-West Territories from the Hudson's Bay Company and the addition of Manitoba to the Confederation in 1870, and the accession of British Columbia in 1871. Key policy initiatives included a railroad across the Prairies to Vancouver, immigration to populate the vast empty stretches between Ontario and British Columbia and create a more viable base for economic development, and high tariffs to develop import-substitution industries and to reduce emigration to the United States in search of industrial jobs. Introduced as separate responses to unique objectives, these policies gradually developed a rationale that wove their various elements together into what became the National Policy of folk memory.[52]

The National Policy was to some extent a Canadian version of, and response to, US convictions about manifest destiny. It provided a basis for consolidating the country and preventing its absorption into the United States. It reflected Canadian concern about irrepressible US attitudes toward expansion as well as envy of US success in developing a large continental economy. And it provided a basis for managing US expansionism by inviting US capital to invest in Canada on terms that would permit Canadian economic development and encourage Canadians to stay home, rather than moving to the new industrial centres of the US Northeast and Midwest.[53]

This broad conception of the National Policy, however, only developed over time and was not fully apparent in 1879. The tariff rates introduced in 1879, for example, were not radically different from those in existence since 1874. The basic rate was increased to 20 percent; duties on industrial goods and semi-finished goods were introduced at 10 to 20 percent, and some manufactures, such as textiles and machinery that were or could be made in Canada, were assigned rates above 20 percent. Luxury goods continued to attract very high rates. Due to the negative revenue effect of falling prices, a number of *ad valorem* rates were changed to specific rates.[54] The real changes in the tariff were structural. There were further splits in tariff classifications, and adjustments ensured that primary products attracted low rates, while finished products attracted high rates. The result was an increase in the effective rates of protection.[55]

Over the next decade, the structure and mixture of *ad valorem* and specific rates were gradually adjusted to take account of the growing sophistication of the Canadian economy. By 1887, when its basic structure was more or less complete, the overall incidence of the tariff on dutiable goods had risen to 30 percent. The initial change in 1879, however, was more in political rhetoric than in substance.

The National Policy nurtured industries that would experience trouble without protection, such as textiles and clothing, as well as basic industries with a future, which derived their comparative advantage from their proximity to Canada's storehouse of raw materials. The combination of inefficient import-substitution industries and export-oriented resource-based industries became the basic pattern of Canadian industrialization and would pose a continuing challenge to the making of Canadian trade policy for decades to come.

An important effect of changing the stated purpose of the tariff from revenue to protection was an effort to convince the Americans that two could play the protection game and that reciprocity was in the American interest. Macdonald told the House of Commons in March 1878:

> The welfare of Canada requires the adoption of a National Policy, which, by a judicious readjustment of the Tariff, will benefit and foster the agricultural, the mining, the manufacturing and other interests of the Dominion; that such a policy ... will prevent Canada from being made a sacrifice market ... and moving (as it ought to do) in the direction of reciprocity of tariffs with our neighbours, so far as the varied interests of Canada may demand, will greatly tend to procure for this country, eventually, a reciprocity of trade ... It is only by closing our doors, and by cutting them out of our markets, that they will open theirs to us ... it is only by closing the door that we can get anything.[56]

Macdonald and the Conservatives clearly saw the National Policy as the best way to attract Americans to the preferred course of reciprocity. Even in adopting protection as a principle, Macdonald saw it as a temporary expedient. His position was opposed by Mackenzie and the Liberal-Reform Party in the terms quoted at the beginning of this chapter. A revenue tariff might be necessary, but a protective tariff was an abomination. Even within the Conservative Party, not all agreed that high tariffs, except for revenue purposes, were the best answer. Dalton McCarthy, Conservative member of Parliament in the 1890s, decried the negative impact of high tariffs on competition. He added in a sour note:

> No doubt in the world the Conservative party were put out of power [in 1873] and by going in for the National Policy and taking the wind out of Mr. Mackenzie's sales [sic], we got into power. We became identified with the protective policy, and if Mr. Mackenzie had adopted a protective policy, we would have been free traders. I am willing to make this confession, that if Mr. Mackenzie had been a protectionist there would have been nothing left but for us to be free traders. But Mr. Mackenzie was either too honest or too earnest in his opinions to bend to the wave of public opinion and the result was that he was swept out of power and had only a corporal's guard to support him when the House met.[57]

Debate over the National Policy and its implementation also polarized attitudes within the Liberal Party. By making protection an integral part of Conservative policy, Macdonald forced the Liberals to adopt free trade and reciprocity as central to their approach. In reality, however, the party differences were more subtle. The Conservatives stood for what Alexander Galt a generation earlier had called incidental protection, and the Liberals opted for modified free trade. A pattern was thus set which endured until the 1950s – philosophically, the Conservatives stood for protection and the Liberals for free trade. The Conservatives put the accent on national economic development whereas the Liberals emphasized the benefits of greater continental integration. What they actually did in practice, of course, depended on electoral fortunes and opportunities.[58]

Industrialization and Economic Development

Protected or not, the Canadian economy had gradually increased its degree of self-sufficiency. A surprising range of industries were able to satisfy high percentages of Canadian needs as early as 1871 (see table 3.6). Few of these industries were export-oriented. Indeed, the degree of Canadian export orientation during this period can be easily exaggerated. In 1870, Canada exported less than 15 percent of its production and had reached only 17 percent by 1900. Most of that trade continued to consist of staples. What did change was the composition of Canadian trade and its direction, as well as the terms of trade.

As illustrated in table 3.7, the composition of Canadian exports changed substantially between 1870 and 1890. The old staples of timber and grain, which had been the mainstay of trade in the first half of the century, were gradually being

Table 3.6

Production and consumption in Canada, 1871

Industry	Value of production ($000)	Production as % of consumption and exports	Duty
Agriculture and machinery	2,685	95	15%
Boots and shoes	16,134	99	15%
Brewery products	2,141	95	15%
Carriages	4,849	99	15%
Cheese	1,602	99	3¢/lb.
Distillery products (whiskey)	4,093	97	80¢/gal.
Flour and meal	39,136	94	25¢/cwt.
Foundry products	893	79	Free
Furniture	3,581	97	15%
Machine manufactures	7,326	93	Free by Order-in-Council
Meats	3,800	88	1¢/lb.
Oil (coal, kerosene)	3,095	99	15%
Paper	1,072	82	15%
Rope, twine	770	95	15%
Saddlery, harness	2,465	95	15%
Soap, candles	1,324	95	15%
Stone and marble	1,088	97	15%
Tanneries (leather)	9,185	91	15%
Tobacco	2,435	98	12.5% & 2¢/lb.
Woollens	5,508	85	15%

Note: Duties applied since 1866, with the exception of the duty on tobacco, applied since 1870.
Source: O.J. McDiarmid, *Commercial Policy in the Canadian Economy* (Cambridge, MA: Harvard University Press, 1946), 148.

replaced by more sophisticated forest products and by meat and dairy products. Baltic competition began to make inroads into Canada's share of the British basic timber market following the end of imperial preferences. The United States for a time replaced the British market for timber, but in the closing decade of the century, pulp and pulpwood were becoming more important exports to the United States, while Britain became the main outlet for farm products. By then, metals and minerals had begun to assume their place as the staples of the future.

From 1840 to 1870, the rapid growth of the US economy had provided scope for a flourishing border trade. From 1870 to the close of the century, however, as the US economy became both more closed and more self-sufficient, Great Britain again became Canada's premier export market (table 3.8). The combination of a world-

Table 3.7

Five leading export and import items, 1870 and 1890 (value in current millions of dollars)

Exports			Imports		
Item	Value	%	Item	Value	%
1870					
Planks and boards	13	22.5	Woollens	11	13.0
Square timber	6	10.3	Cottons	9	10.7
Butter	3	5.2	Wheat	4	4.8
Codfish	2	3.7	Sugar	3	3.6
Cattle	2	3.4	Tea	3	3.6
Total five items	26	44.8	Total five items	30	35.3
1890					
Planks and boards	14	15.7	Wool and manufactures	11	9.8
Cheese	10	11.2	Coal	10	8.9
Cattle	9	10.1	Cotton and manufactures	8	7.1
Codfish	3	3.4	Sugar	6	5.4
Square timber	3	3.4	Rolling mill products	6	5.4
Total five items	39	43.8	Total five items	41	36.6

Source: O.J. Firestone, *Canada's Economic Development, 1867-1952* (London: Bowes and Bowes, 1958), table 55, 160.

wide glut in grains production, rising incomes in Britain, and the introduction of faster, refrigerated ocean transport induced Canadian farmers to turn to more remunerative dairy and horticultural products for export. Rapid industrialization in the United States, coupled with geographic proximity, allowed its producers to replace British manufacturers as the main suppliers of imported Canadian producer and consumer goods. Investment in miniature replica manufacturing facilities accentuated this trend. By 1887, the Canadian Manufacturers' Association could claim that there was not a single Ontario town of any consequence that did not boast at least one US branch plant.[59]

Between 1870 and 1900, as Canadian export prices rose by 10 percent, import prices declined by 26 percent, so that Canada's terms of trade – the relationship between the cost of imports and earnings from exports – rose steadily during this period. The growing productivity of British and US manufacturers had steadily driven relative import prices down; at the same time, US and British appetites for Canadian goods had driven relative export prices up. During the final quarter of the century, these changes helped to cushion the impact of recessions in Canada and contributed to a slow rise in Canadian living standards.[60]

Table 3.8

Canada's trade in goods with Great Britain, the United States, and the rest of the world, 1870-1901 (proportion of total)

Year[a]	Great Britain		United States		Rest of world	
	Imports	Exports[b]	Imports	Exports[b]	Imports	Exports[b]
1870[c]	57.1	37.9	32.2	50.0	10.7	12.1
1880	47.8	51.2	40.0	40.5	12.2	8.3
1886	40.6	47.4	44.8	43.6	14.6	9.0
1891	37.5	48.3	46.4	42.7	16.1	9.0
1896	31.4	57.3	51.4	34.5	17.2	8.2
1901	24.2	52.5	60.1	38.4	15.7	9.1

a Figures are for fiscal years ending 30 June for each year given.
b Domestic product only.
c Figures for Ontario, Quebec, New Brunswick, and Nova Scotia only.
Source: O.J. Firestone, "Development of Canada's Economy," in National Bureau of Economic Research, *Trends in the American Economy in the Nineteenth Century* (Princeton: Princeton University Press, 1960), 766, for 1870 and 1880; F.H. Leacy, *Historical Statistics of Canada*, 2nd ed. (Ottawa: Statistics Canada, 1983), series G389-400, for 1886-1901.

The National Policy accentuated these trends. The protection of domestic production encouraged both foreign and domestic investment in miniature replica manufacturing facilities. There was also a gradual shift toward the United States as a source both of capital and of producer and consumer goods through intercorporate linkages. British free trade and US protectionism, on the other hand, helped to tilt Canada's export orientation back to Britain. As shown in table 3.8, other markets continued to command very little attention from Canadian producers.

But even with the National Policy and the development of an increasing range of manufacturing industries, Canada remained small in population and rural in orientation. By 1881, the population was only 4.3 million, with more than half still on the farm. More importantly, Canadian economic development compared unfavourably with that south of the border, where growth in population and production far outpaced that of Canada. Emigration to the south continued; two million people left between 1881 and 1901. Small import-substitution industries may have been developing in the Windsor to Montreal corridor, largely based on American and British investment, but none promised sufficient growth to attract and keep the numbers of people necessary to increase the domestic market. The slow pace of development intensified criticism of the National Policy's high tariffs and renewed interest in reciprocity.

Unrestricted Reciprocity Enters the Fray

Given the perceived meagre results of the National Policy, the Liberals of the 1880s, inspired by the rhetoric and passion of Sir Richard Cartwright, Mackenzie's free-trade finance minister, decided to place their faith in unrestricted reciprocity.

Indeed, they adopted a much more radical version of reciprocity that would extend tariff-free trade not only to natural products but also to industrial goods. Support for the decision was not unanimous. Edward Blake, Liberal leader in the 1880s, decried the idea, and his writings after leaving office foreshadowed the nationalism of later generations of Liberals:

> The tendency, in Canada, of unrestricted free trade with the States, high duties being maintained against the United Kingdom, would be towards political union; and the more successful the plan the stronger the tendency, both by reason of the community of interests, the intermingling of population, the more intimate business and social connections, and the trade and fiscal relations, amounting to dependency, which it would create with the States, and of the greater isolation and divergency from Britain which it would produce; and also and especially through inconveniences experienced in the maintenance and apprehensions entertained as to the termination of the treaty.[61]

Despite Blake's denunciations, something akin to the modern concept of free trade had now entered Canadian politics for the first time. The introduction in the United States of the high McKinley Tariff of 1890 added to the calls in Canada for a more rational policy governing trade between the two countries. Unrestricted reciprocity, however, posed a grave political risk. By this time the close association between protection and nationhood could not be easily challenged without calling into question one's commitment to the future of Canada. Reciprocity, as it had been practised in 1854, was one thing; unrestricted reciprocity, at least to some observers, came perilously close to economic union and could pose a threat to the continued viability of Canada as a separate nation.[62]

In an effort to outflank the Liberals and respond to mounting criticism of high tariffs, Macdonald authorized one more try at old-fashioned reciprocity. In 1885 he had made quiet inquiries in the context of trying to resolve the perpetual problem of fishing rights off the east coast, but did not receive much encouragement.[63] The election of Democrat Grover Cleveland in 1884 on a low-tariff platform had provided some cause for optimism, but with the Republicans retaining control of Congress, Cleveland's ideas on tariff reform and reciprocity were doomed to failure.[64] Early in 1891 Macdonald tried once again. The Republicans were back in control of the White House and Secretary of State James G. Blaine, responding to growing export interests, had the previous year asked Congress for authority to pursue reciprocal free-trade agreements with "any nation of the American hemisphere" in an effort to find markets for American exports. The proposal never came to a vote; despite extensive popular support, the Senate Finance Committee refused to entertain such a broad mandate. Instead, it placed sugar and molasses on the free list, authorized penalty duties on other tropical products, and then invited countries to make concessions to avoid those same duties.[65] The policy met with some success in Latin America but was totally unsuited to Canadian circumstances.

Macdonald's 1891 inquiries, therefore, were not unrealistic. Nevertheless, they fell on deaf and somewhat frustrated ears. Never was a Canadian overture rebuffed more forcibly by the Americans than when Blaine summed up the confident, jingoistic attitude of late nineteenth-century Republicanism:

> Beyond the frontier, across the river, our neighbours chose another Government, another allegiance ... They do exactly as they have a right to do. I neither dispute their right nor envy their situation ... But I am opposed, teetotally opposed, to giving the Canadians the sentimental satisfaction of waving the British flag, paying British taxes, and enjoying the actual cash remuneration of American markets. They cannot have both at the same time. If they come to us they can have what we have, but it is an absolute wrong ... that they shall have exactly the same share of our markets and the same privileges of trade under our flag that we have. So far as I can help it, I do not mean that they shall be Canadians and Americans at the same time.[66]

With this snub, Macdonald knew his policy for the next election. The new leader of the Liberals, Wilfrid Laurier, had made the lowering of tariffs and unrestricted reciprocity key to his 1891 electoral platform; the Conservatives would rely on a burst of patriotism and the slogan "the Old Man, the Old Policy, the Old Flag." Macdonald now decided that even old-fashioned reciprocity would lead to economic and political union and declared, with the excess of rhetoric characteristic of politicians of all ages, "A British subject I was born; a British subject I will die." His Conservatives won and his wish to die a British subject was quickly granted. Exhausted by the campaign, he died on 6 June, three months after the election, to be followed by a succession of short-lived and less skilful leaders.

By the time of the 1891 election, central Canada had developed such a substantial manufacturing constituency dependent on the tariff that in popular discussion free trade was beginning to be seen as the challenger rather than as the presumed superior policy. Unsure of their ground, however, the manufacturers and Conservatives determined to strengthen their position by appeals to imperial sentiment and warnings of dire American intentions. Whipping up hostility to the United States was not difficult, given the popularity in the United States of pronouncements about American superiority and manifest destiny. Opposition to reciprocity or free trade with the United States had by now become inextricably linked with nationalism and anti-Americanism. Opponents successfully convinced many Canadians that there was a relationship between the tariff and Canada's development as a viable, independent nation, a theme that would be repeated in Canadian history time and again.[67]

The Liberals, somewhat chastened by their defeat, retreated from unrestricted reciprocity but upheld reciprocity in natural products and some manufactures as the key ingredient of their economic policy. They were given their chance in 1896. Sir Charles Tupper, the fourth successor to Macdonald, could not rally the old chieftain's

Table 3.9

Trade-weighted average rates of duty, United States, 1865-1909

Years	Tariff legislation	% of imports duty free	Equivalent *ad valorem* rate (%)	
			Dutiable imports	Total imports
1865-70	Act of 1864	8	48	44
1871-2	Act of 1870	8	43	38
1873-5	Act of 1872	27	39	27
1876-83	Act of 1872 repealed 1875	31	43	29
1884-90	Act of 1883	33	45	30
1891-4	McKinley Tariff	52	48	23
1895-7	Wilson-Gorman Tariff	49	41	21
1898-1909	Dingley Tariff	44	47	26

Source: Hugh McA. Pinchin, *The Regional Impact of the Canadian Tariff: A Study Prepared for the Economic Council of Canada* (Ottawa: Supply and Services, 1979), table 1-2. Reproduced with the permission of the Minister of Public Works and Government Services Canada, 2001. The findings of this Study are the personal responsibility of the author and, as such, have not been endorsed by Members of the Economic Council of Canada.

supporters, and the Liberals returned to power. Canada's nascent manufacturing interests might favour high tariffs, but there were more farmers, fishermen, miners, and lumbermen who were opposed. Laurier successfully appealed to those elements.

Once again, Canadians trooped to Washington to convince the powers that be, this time the second administration of Democrat Grover Cleveland, that a reciprocal trade agreement with Canada was in the interest of the United States. Again, events in the US capital gave some cause for optimism. Congress was rewriting the tariff and was preparing to include a new reciprocity provision at the request of President-elect William McKinley, sponsor of the Tariff Act of 1890.[68] This provision failed to provide the president with wide authority, but it did provide some room for negotiations by authorizing cuts of up to 20 percent on some products on which rates had recently been raised, subject, of course, to Senate approval.[69] At the same time, the Wilson-Gorman Tariff of 1894 had reduced tariffs on hundreds of items to an average of 41 percent, substantially lower than the punitive McKinley Tariff of 1890. As shown in table 3.9, the US tariff had continued its steady march upward in the years after the Civil War, reaching 48 percent with the McKinley Tariff. The Wilson-Gorman Tariff marked a significant, if temporary, retreat.

Since abrogation of the Reciprocity Treaty in 1866, Canadian politicians of every persuasion had made no fewer than six overtures to the United States to bring back reciprocity. Each had been rejected on the terms offered by Canada. Cleveland and his secretary of state, Richard Olney, gave a more sympathetic hearing than the

THE LATEST STYLE OF PULL-BACK AT OTTAWA.

"The Latest Style of Pull-Back at Ottawa," 8 April 1876. Free trade and reciprocity dominated political debate in Canada in the 1870s and 1880s and split the ranks of the Liberal Party.

Republicans but were equally blunt in their answer. It was still no. They were not prepared to engage in negotiations at the end of their term. More fatally, the Wilson-Gorman Tariff had eliminated the negotiating authority of the McKinley Act. Laurier had learned his lesson: there would be no more pilgrimages to Washington. The following year, 1897, President McKinley appointed a negotiator to pursue the limited new authority set out in the new, higher Dingley Tariff, but none of the resulting agreements were accepted by Congress.[70] No negotiations were initiated with Canada. Laurier's instincts had been correct. Reciprocity between Canada and the United States was dead in the water and it was time to look for alternatives.

The Renewal of Imperial Preferences
Ever-spiralling US tariffs, matched by continued increases in Canadian tariffs, had a direct impact on the volume, structure, and direction of Canada's trade. At Confederation, as a result of the Reciprocity Treaty of 1854 and the natural forces of geography, the United States had been Canada's principal trading partner. By the end of the century, Britain had replaced the United States as Canada's main export market, even though the United States continued to be the principal source of imports. In 1896, 57 percent of Canada's exports went to Britain and only 34 percent to the United States, largely natural products that attracted low rates of duty or were

eligible to receive drawbacks. In that same year, close to 90 percent of all Canadian exports consisted of unprocessed agricultural, forest, fish, and mineral products.[71]

W.S. Fielding, former Nova Scotia premier and Laurier's finance minister for the next fifteen years, decided he would make a virtue out of necessity. Reciprocity was dead and Britain had once again become Canada's premier market, as it had been during the heyday of imperial preferences. A new tariff structure would demonstrate that Canadian policy could be sensitive to these facts. It would also be sensitive to the views of affected parties; to this end Fielding and two cabinet colleagues toured the country and took its pulse. Laurier's choice of Fielding was a pragmatic one. Sir Richard Cartwright, finance minister in the last Liberal government, had been widely expected to be appointed, but there was some concern that his strong free-trade sentiments might lead to confrontation with the manufacturers. Cartwright was appointed to Trade and Commerce and responsibility for the tariff was given to Fielding, a relative newcomer to Ottawa and thus less identified with one point of view. Laurier had already learned that principle is one thing, and gaining and keeping office quite another.

Fielding's first budget in 1897 demonstrated the wisdom of Laurier's choice. Fielding revised the tariff structure and rates, with the overall effect being a slight reduction in protection. But he added a new twist. Imports from any country that offered Canadian goods rates equivalent to or lower than Canadian rates would benefit from a reduction of 12.5 percent from the most-favoured-nation rate. The upshot was that Fielding offered reciprocity to the world in the full knowledge that only Britain qualified. The move toward new imperial preferences had begun.

Fielding's decision to introduce preferences had been inspired by previous Conservative initiatives. Even before introducing the National Policy, Macdonald had toyed with the idea of imperial preferences, and in the 1880s Alexander Galt, Canada's first high commissioner to Britain, had pursued the issue with the Colonial Office to little avail. What distinguished Fielding's policy from that of the Conservatives, however, was that it was unilateral and freely offered. It did not require Britain to introduce tariffs on imports from other sources. In short, it was a made-in-Canada policy consistent with Liberal principles of free trade, although these principles had been much eroded by almost twenty years in opposition. Claimed Fielding in his budget address: "The evil of protection, like most other evils, is wide-reaching in its influences, and it has become so blended and interwoven with the business of Canada that if we should attempt to strike it down today, we should do harm not only to the protected interests, which have no claim on us, but to other interests which are not directly connected with the protected interests. It would be folly not to remember that we are dealing not with the protected manufacturer only, but that the interests of labour have to be considered as well as the interests of capital."[72]

The economic impact of the new tariff was marginal, but its political impact was immediate.[73] The Liberals had successfully captured the Conservative affinity for the imperial connection and had made it their own. The following year the preference was raised to 25 percent and confined to Empire goods. The other dominions were invited to follow suit, and overtures were made to Britain to cooperate in establishing a system of imperial preferences. Although Colonial Secretary Joseph Chamberlain favoured the idea, the British cabinet was not ready to betray Britain's faith in free trade. Some concerted missionary work by Canada and the other dominions would be required.[74]

Canada's two-tier tariff structure, however, brought with it some complications. Even though the country enjoyed a high degree of self-government, it had not yet achieved independence in treaty making and had inherited a number of obligations from British treaties. Canadian politicians had previously, but unsuccessfully, requested the Colonial Office to release Canada from these obligations. Canada was bound to extend its lowest rates to countries with which Britain had negotiated most-favoured-nation treaties. Germany and Belgium insisted on their rights, and the only solution was for Britain to renounce its MFN agreements – something Britain refused to do. Germany retaliated, and Fielding responded resourcefully by raising the rates for German goods (a very small sacrifice), raising the preference to one-third off the general rate, and offering to negotiate directly with others. Canada's lack of trade with the continent made Canadian interests clear, but Fielding's approach complicated British policy, a complication not fully resolved until the outbreak of war in 1914.

Canadian politicians had by now developed an intimate knowledge of tariff policy and of the clever ways customs rules could be used to meet political objectives. In the 1880s they had learned the joy of tinkering with the concept of valuation. The effective rate of a tariff could be substantially increased if customs officials were authorized to establish an arbitrary "fair market value" for goods in place of the declared value. Sparingly used at first, this kind of adjustment became one of the standard techniques Canadian governments would use in responding to producer complaints about foreign competition – a technique that proved much simpler than raising the rates. In 1904, reacting to charges that the US trusts were dumping excess production in Canada, Fielding introduced the first-ever antidumping duty. Customs officials were authorized to apply a temporary additional duty on dutiable goods being imported at less than their fair market value. Under Fielding, Canada also expanded the use of subsidies and bounties as an alternative to reducing the tariff, either on a general basis or for specific purposes. Canada thus established a reputation for administrative ingenuity by making full use of its tariff structure, a reputation that it would continue to enhance in the years to come.

In 1907, Fielding, reflecting the result of trade negotiations with smaller markets in Europe and Latin America, introduced a three-tier tariff: 1) the British preferential rate; 2) an intermediate rate for countries to which Canada owed most-favoured-nation obligations (either as heir to British treaties or newly negotiated agreements); and 3) a general rate for countries that discriminated against Canada, principally the United States and Germany. His creativity was by now being copied elsewhere. New Zealand and South Africa introduced imperial preferences in their tariff structures in 1903, and Australia followed suit in 1907. In 1909 the United States copied this technique, but, in keeping with its high-tariff sentiments, the Payne-Aldrich Tariff, rather than providing for reductions, added a surcharge for goods from countries that discriminated against the United States.

Fielding's inventiveness made him the real father of modern Canadian trade policy. Macdonald's National Policy had established the protective tariff as a policy instrument for inducing the growth of import-substitution industries, but Fielding, working closely with Minister of Trade and Commerce Richard Cartwright, made it into a sophisticated instrument of trade and industrial policy.[75] The objectives of turn-of-the-century Canadian tradecraft were three-fold:

- the protection of domestic manufacturing by means of the customs tariff and various related instruments such as valuation, classification, bounties, subsidies, and antidumping duties
- the encouragement of diversified exports through treaties and trade promotion (Canada introduced a Trade Commissioner Service in 1892)
- the encouragement of the export of primary products through the building of railways and other development policies requiring large government expenditures.

There was a high degree of tension or contradiction among these objectives, requiring dynamic and adroit management and frequent shifts of emphasis in continuing attempts to mollify champions of one element or another. These objectives remained, however, the basic orientation of Canadian trade policy for the next seventy-five years.[76]

Liberal improvements upon the basic strategy of the Conservatives endeared them to the manufacturers and kept them in power for fifteen years. Canadian manufacturers had by this time become staunch protectionists and the Canadian Manufacturers' Association stood out as a bastion of imperial jingoism. Exhorted its president, W.H. Rowley, at the 1910 annual meeting: "In season and out of season, in favour and out of favour, liked or disliked, I have always believed in protection, have always advocated it, and will always continue to do so. I have no politics other than protection, and I hope none of you have. If you have them, I think you should sink them for the good of the Association, for protection is the only politics the Association should recognize."[77]

Whatever Fielding's personal predilections, he had maintained and nurtured a popular policy. The Canadian economy was thriving. The uncertainty of the early years of Confederation had been replaced by a new confidence. Immigration was increasing dramatically, drawing on a much wider range of sources than in earlier years, and by 1911 Canada's population had reached 7.2 million. Urbanization was beginning in earnest, and the import-substitution industries were prospering, many as branch plants of American firms, which incidentally established an American

interest in continued high levels of protection in Canada. Since most of these manufacturers were not much interested in exporting, they were indifferent to the high
tariffs in vogue elsewhere. Some branch plants were even forbidden to export except to markets where they could take advantage of imperial preferences.

Despite the popularity of protection among manufacturers, there were other,
strongly held views against protection. New Brunswick Liberal member of Parliament A.H. Gillmor told the 1893 National Convention: "These industries are like
the fatted calf, always sucking, and they will never get weaned. These infants are
never ready to have their protective tariff taken off. You suggest a reduction of tariff
to them, and they will look so lean and miserable that you would pity them from
the bottom of your heart. But when they feel the tariff is safe for them, they swell to
enormous proportions, and display their carriages and footmen, and their eyes
stick out with fatness."[78]

That view was strongly shared by Western farmers. Maritimers who had seen
industrial development halt in the Atlantic region while Upper Canada (as they
continued to call Ontario) boomed, were also not enamoured of the tariff. Complaints to Ottawa increased as the Laurier years wore on. High tariffs in the United
States reduced the market opportunities for farmers and resource industries; high
tariffs in Canada increased costs, especially of farming, logging, and mining machinery and equipment. But even Western politicians were prepared to accept the
political virtue of a protective tariff. Clifford Sifton of Winnipeg wrote soon after
the introduction of Fielding's first budget:

> I not only would not retire from the Government because they refused to eliminate the
> principle of protection from the tariff but I would not remain in the Government if
> they did eliminate the principle of protection entirely from the tariff. I would consider
> that to so construct the tariff as to wantonly destroy the industries that have been built
> up under it would be utterly unjustifiable from any possible standpoint of reason. I
> may say that on principle I am a very strong free trader. I have been fed and educated
> on free trade doctrines, but doctrines do not always apply to facts. The people decided
> some eighteen years ago to have the protective policy and got it and have stood by it
> ever since, and the business of the country, to an extent that very few people imagine
> who have not made a study of it, has adapted itself to the tariff; and the introduction of
> a tariff from which the principle of protection would be entirely eliminated would be
> fraught with results that would be most disastrous ... I may say that upon a matter of
> this kind I do not take very much stock in abstract doctrines.[79]

The trade patterns of the late nineteenth and early twentieth centuries reflected
the results of moderate to high tariffs everywhere but in Britain. Trade was largely
concentrated in raw materials, machinery, and luxury goods. Trade in components,
intermediate goods, and nonluxury finished goods did not begin in earnest until
after the Second World War with the success of the multilateral attack on high

Table 3.10

Growth in the Canadian economy, 1900-13 (in millions of current dollars)

Item	1900	1905	1910	1913
Merchandise exports	156	205	281	443
Merchandise imports	177	264	429	655
Current account balance	−37	−87	−251	−408
Net long-term capital movement	+30	+110	+308	+542
Domestic investment	86	158	273	405
Capital employed in manufacturing	447	834	1,248	1,959
Steam railway mileage	17,656	20,487	24,731	29,304
Wheat acreage (000)	4,225	–	8,865	11,015
Terms of trade (1900 = 100)	100	103	114	111
Wholesale price index (1900 = 100)	100	113	125	133
Population (000)	5,322	5,992	6,917	7,527

Source: A.E. Safarian, *The Canadian Economy in the Great Depression* (Toronto: University of Toronto Press, 1959), table 1, 22.

tariffs, improvements in transportation and distribution networks, and the growth of multinational enterprises. Trade negotiations in this earlier period, therefore, concentrated on reducing barriers to trade in resources and agricultural goods.

By the early years of the new century, the National Policy, as adapted and made more sophisticated by Laurier and Fielding, was beginning to have the desired results. The tentative industrialization of the early years had given way to a rapidly growing industrial sector complemented by the beginning of the wheat boom on the Prairies. Canada's farm economy was still growing during this period because it was expanding the number of acres under cultivation, but the number of workers per farm was declining. At the same time, the urban and industrial economy was growing even more rapidly. As illustrated in table 3.10, the capital employed in manufacturing more than tripled in real terms between 1900 and 1913. By 1911, 42 percent of Canadians lived in towns and cities with populations of more than a thousand. Historians Robert Bothwell, Ian Drummond, and John English conclude that during this period, "Canada ... took part in a system of international specialization and division of labour which was shaped by her own tariffs, the tariffs of other countries, and her own advantages and disadvantages in production ... In the years between 1896 and 1914 the international division of labour was good for the dominion. Canada found new and buoyant markets for the things she could do well; the world economy supplied her with plenty of labour, capital funds, and the manufactures and raw materials which her growing and prosperous economy was eager to absorb."[80]

Reciprocity Once Again

In this generally satisfactory economic environment, reciprocity with the United States appeared to have been truly banished from Canadian trade policy thinking. An annoying fly in the ointment was Britain's continued attachment to free trade, but the tide there was also turning. Respectable opinion held that Britain should arm itself with a protective tariff aimed at Germany and the United States and other protectionist countries, and should develop a complete system of imperial preferences with the dominions. The Conservatives, under the sway of Joseph Chamberlain and his allies, agreed. The British electorate, however, decided in 1906 that they preferred cheap imports to colonial ties and returned the Liberals. Nevertheless, the dominions determined that time was on the side of the imperialists.

Into this comfortable situation, the Americans now threw a curve. President William Howard Taft, an old friend of Canada who regularly visited the country as he summered at his cottage on the St. Lawrence, felt uncomfortable about applying the punitive surcharges required by the 1909 Payne-Aldrich Tariff to Canada. Canada's tariff did discriminate against American goods, particularly after renewal of the 1893 Canada-France agreement in 1907 extended some intermediate rates to French goods. Canada continued to apply the highest rate to American goods despite the

Samuel Hunter, "Perfectly Satisfied," 15 April 1907. The British – and Canadian – ambassador to the United States, Viscount Bryce, contemplates new offers from Uncle Sam to re-open the Canada-US reciprocity debate.

fact that the French agreement was not an MFN treaty. Nevertheless, the American policy was not aimed at Canada but rather at Germany and other European protectionists, as well as Latin American nations. Taft may have been a Republican, but he also had some sympathy for American critics of the high-tariff policy set by Congress. Indeed, his proposed tariff schedule in 1909 had been substantially lower than what Congress had eventually produced. Finally, there were powerful American interests, particularly newspaper publishers, who wanted secure access to cheap Canadian pulpwood. For Taft, there were, therefore, strong reasons to resist State Department pressures to inflict the surcharge on Canadian goods.

Laurier might have given up on reciprocity, but he had not given up on good relations with the United States and, during the course of his fifteen years in office, he expended considerable effort on solving a number of problems in as amicable a manner as possible, including the Alaska boundary dispute and disagreements over Atlantic fishing rights. Periodic commercial negotiations that fell short of reciprocity, although not always successful, had also contributed to good relations. On this firm foundation discussions started on how to deal with the provocative terms of the Payne-Aldrich Tariff. The Canadian position was set out in great detail by Fielding in a long dispatch to James Bryce, the British ambassador in Washington. Fielding argued that the case for imposing the maximum rates was weak and in the end would be more harmful to American than Canadian interests.[81]

Fielding's case hit home. After a series of discussions between the two sides involving Fielding, the president, Governor General Lord Grey, and Ambassador Bryce, Canada made some face-saving concessions on thirteen products of export interest to the United States, and Taft was able to make a formal determination that Canada could continue to enjoy the normal tariff rate. But the American appetite had now been whetted for something more substantial.

Through an intermediary, the Rev. J.A. Macdonald, editor of the *Toronto Globe*, Taft proposed to Laurier that the two governments appoint plenipotentiaries and negotiate a reciprocity agreement that would end all discrimination. Taft's proposal was ambitious; he was prepared in effect to contemplate a comprehensive MFN agreement. By the end of March 1910, Laurier had accepted the invitation. After he and Fielding held exploratory discussions with American officials in Ottawa, Fielding was authorized to negotiate an agreement, although on a more limited scale than had originally been suggested by Taft. Fielding was to concentrate on reciprocity in natural products, extend the intermediate tariff to the United States in some cases, but maintain most of the cherished protective tariffs for the manufacturers. Laurier was confident that he was dealing from a position of strength. The pattern of trade and production that had developed over the previous generation reflected high levels of both US and Canadian protection. Canada had adjusted to American protectionism and a little bit more would make little difference. Nevertheless, a good agreement would be helpful and demonstrate that the Liberals were flexible and pragmatic.[82]

Laurier's acceptance, while a departure from a policy carefully developed and nurtured over a period of fifteen years, was not surprising. He and Fielding had pragmatically developed the National Policy, but at heart they were free traders, as the term was then understood. Now that the invitation had come from Washington, there was a real chance of success. Laurier was also not insensitive to the pleas of hardship expressed in western Canada. Realistically, however, the Canadian negotiating position was carefully crafted to respond to a variety of Canadian interests. Soon after he had accepted the American invitation, the strength of the antitariff lobby was demonstrated to Laurier during a Western tour and by a march by Prairie farmers on Ottawa. The strength of the pro-tariff lobby was taken for granted, although perhaps not sufficiently appreciated.

Over the course of several weeks, Fielding negotiated with American officials, periodically reporting his progress to Laurier. His task was somewhat complicated by Canada's continued lack of treaty-making authority: There was a painful exchange of letters with US secretary of state Philander Knox in which Canadian officials pointed out that Canada did not want a British plenipotentiary to negotiate on its behalf. To extricate Canada from this awkward problem, the two countries decided not to negotiate a treaty but rather to exchange letters constituting an agreement as to changes the two governments would make in their respective tariff and related laws. This sleight of hand also facilitated US approval by requiring simple majorities in both House and Senate rather than a two-thirds treaty ratification vote in the Senate.[83]

By the end of January 1911, the task was completed. A proud Fielding introduced the results to the House of Commons on 26 January. The package he had achieved was neither a treaty nor any other form of contractual agreement but a commitment by the two sides to secure the enactment of certain provisions. The arrangement consisted principally of four tariff schedules: Schedule A contained a free list comprising primary agricultural and resource products and a few manufactured goods; Schedule B contained a list of goods to be admitted at identical rates in both countries, consisting of further processed products of the goods listed in Schedule A, as well as a large list of manufactures such as automobiles and agricultural implements; Schedule C provided for reduced US tariffs on softwood lumber and shingles; and Schedule D lowered Canadian duties on coal.[84]

Fielding's announcement was greeted by cheers from the Liberals and a stunned silence in Conservative ranks. Conservative leader Robert Borden summed up the dark mood in his caucus in his diary: "the deepest dejection ... Many of our members were confident that the Government's proposals would appeal to the country and give it another term of office ... The western members were emphatic in their statement that not one of them would be re-elected in opposition to reciprocity ... I stemmed the tide as best I could, although I was under great discouragement. The difference of opinion which had developed seemed in itself to be a forerunner of disaster."[85]

Fielding had crafted a package that seemed to satisfy all interests. The US proposal for wide-ranging reciprocity had been firmly rejected.[86] In its place, he had negotiated an agreement that gave the Western farmers access for their products to the US market plus reduced rates on imported agricultural implements; that improved access for mineral and forest products; and that retained protection for Ontario manufacturers. With this agreement, the Liberals had protected the National Policy and married it to the original goal of reciprocity, combining the political appeal of both policies.

The confidence among Liberals, however, was short-lived. They had miscalculated the strength of protectionism among Canadian manufacturers. Warned by the interim package cobbled together in March 1910 to avoid imposition of the Payne-Aldrich surtax, they had begun to plot strategy and now immediately condemned the agreement as thinly disguised free trade. More critical to their case (given the weakness of their substantive position), they insisted that reciprocity in any form undermined the imperial connection and would harm Canadian independence of action. To nationalists like J.S. Ewart, Canada's independence hinged on its ability to make tariff policy free from British and American interference.[87] Again, debate on the trade policy merits of the agreement was overshadowed by appeals to patriotism and warnings about the imminent demise of the country. With all the power that they could muster, the manufacturers determined, in the words of former CPR president Sir William van Horne, "to bust the damned thing."[88]

Fielding did his best to put his case: "What we have done is no departure from the policy of Canada for forty years ... the historic policy of the Dominion from the first day of Confederation ... there was no difference of opinion as to the great importance and desirability of reestablishing reciprocal trade relations with the United States of America."[89] But the opposition case had nothing to do with trade and economic matters. It was successfully appealing to Canadian fears and emotions. Debate in the House dragged on. The government's case was not helped by pronouncements in Washington. During congressional hearings, Speaker-designate Champ Clark proclaimed his "hope to see the day when the American flag will float over every square foot of the British North American possessions, clear to the north pole."[90] President Taft further stirred fears when he declared that Canada stood at a parting of the ways. In April 1911, the US House of Representatives approved the package 268 to 89 and in July the US Senate, after abortive attempts to effect changes, did the same by a margin of 53 to 27. Even in victory, there was a sour note for the Liberals. The size of the margin added to the charges that the Americans had dark designs on Canada.

Without resolving the issue, a tired and disappointed Laurier adjourned Parliament in April to attend the coronation of King George V. In July, after several more weeks of desultory debate and without securing parliamentary passage of the agreement, he resolved to fight the issue in a general election on 21 September. By this time the momentum gained in the quick and successful negotiations had been lost and the government placed on the defensive. Disaffected Liberals, led by former cabinet minister Clifford Sifton, had joined the opposition, financed by a determined Toronto and Montreal business establishment.

Two campaigns were waged that summer. In Quebec, reciprocity hardly raised a ripple. There the issue was Laurier's decision to demonstrate his commitment to Empire by developing a Canadian navy. To Quebec Nationalists and their spokesman, Henri Bourassa, Laurier had sold out to the Empire, and the reciprocity agreement was no more than a smoke screen for the government's true intentions.[91] In Ontario, the naval decision was characterized as an inadequate substitute for contributing directly to the imperial navy, while the reciprocity agreement spelled the end of Canada. Even in the West and the Maritimes, where some saw the reciprocity agreement as a pitiful surrogate for the real thing, Laurier's imperial connections were considered suspect. The result was one of the meanest election campaigns in Canadian history. An unholy alliance between Borden Conservatives, disaffected Liberals, and Bourassa Nationalists focused on the common enemy for diametrically different reasons. Laurier rightly lamented: "I am branded in Quebec as a traitor to the French and in Ontario as a traitor to the English. In Quebec I am branded as a Jingo and in Ontario as a Separatist. In Quebec, I am attacked as an Imperialist and in Ontario as an anti-Imperialist. I am neither. I am a Canadian."[92]

The election results were decisive. The popular vote split was close – 51 percent for the Conservatives and 48 percent for the Liberals – but Borden could count on a solid parliamentary majority of 134 seats to the Liberals' 87. Laurier and Fielding went down to personal defeat. Reciprocity was dead for at least two generations, and the Conservative version of the National Policy was safe. Canada was no longer a nation of farmers and merchants; the manufacturing interests had shown their strength. For the next seventy years, no government would be prepared to confront their protectionist instincts. Only with a change in the views of business would bilateral free trade become politically acceptable.

The defeat of reciprocity also marked the triumph of central Canada over the peripheral regions. Confederation and the National Policy had together nurtured the wealth and dominance of central Canada. The reciprocity agreement of 1911 spoke to the ideals of the Western and Maritime provinces. Its defeat ensured the continued sectionalism of Canadian economic development and the political alienation of the periphery, whereas its victory might have meant a Canada in which the economic development of the periphery served its own needs rather than those of central Canada.

John Dafoe, the strong proreciprocity editor of the *Manitoba Free Press*, owned by the equally strongly antireciprocity former Liberal minister Clifford Sifton, concluded that Laurier had held office by placating various powerful interests at the expense of the general public, but "The moment he showed signs of putting real Liberal doctrine into effect, the interests combined and crushed him."[93] Herein lay

Laurier's political mistake. He forgot one of the rules that had kept him in power for fifteen years: satisfying the small but powerful business establishments in Toronto and Montreal. Since being elected in 1896, Fielding and his colleagues had regularly consulted with them and, as a result, had followed an astute if essentially protectionist tariff policy. By forgetting to take the views of the central Canadian business establishment sufficiently into account in reopening the issue of reciprocity, they had sealed their own downfall.

The West remained bitter about the defeat of reciprocity, which became part of Western folk memory. The Maritime provinces appeared less resentful, although there too convictions about the perfidy of central Canada became deeply ingrained. In immediate response, Western farmers organized an antitariff Progressive Party, which succeeded in complicating Canadian politics for the next twenty years. In the longer run, while Western alienation would not assure the success of its preference for free trade, it could act as a frequent spoiler for other policies. The political generation of the first half of the twentieth century had come to terms with one of the most decisive characteristics of Canadian politics: ideas count less than the gaining and holding of power. To achieve power, successful politicians have to astutely assess how to placate disparate regional interests across the country. In many situations, failure to act and to lead can bring greater rewards than firm action on one issue or another.

Viscount Bryce, the British ambassador to the United States during this period, who often assumed the task of representing Canadian interests, sardonically reflected a decade later on the nature of Canadian politics and the dominant role of commercial policy:

> Since 1867 the questions which have had the most constant interest for the bulk of the nation are ... those which belong to the sphere of commercial and industrial progress, the development of the material resources of the country ... – matters scarcely falling within the lines by which party opinion is divided, for the policy of *laissez-faire* has few adherents in a country which finds in governmental action or financial support to private enterprises the quickest means of carrying out every promising project ... The task of each party is to persuade the people that in this instance its plan promises quicker and larger results, and that it is fitter to be trusted with the work. Thus it happens that general political principles ... count for little in politics, though ancient habit requires them to be invoked. Each party tries to adapt itself from time to time to whatever practical issue may arise. Opportunism is inevitable, and the charge of inconsistency, though incessantly bandied to and fro, is lightly regarded ... In Canada ideas are not needed to make parties, for these can live by heredity ... The people show an abounding party spirit when an election day arrives. The constant party struggle keeps their interest alive. But party spirit, so far from being a measure of the volume of political thinking, may even be a substitute for thinking.[94]

One of those who had learned this lesson was Laurier's young labour minister, William Lyon Mackenzie King. When faced first with reciprocity (in 1935) and then free trade (in 1948), King would be even more cautious than was his normal wont. In his twenty-three years in power he proved to be a consummate politician, not in gaining friends and supporters but in avoiding enemies and detractors. To him no policy was often the best policy, and a decision delayed was a mistake avoided. Principle was not at issue. While he might have despised many of its members personally, he carefully nurtured a correct relationship with the central Canadian business establishment.

4 WAR, DEPRESSION, AND REVOLUTION

CANADIAN TRADE POLICY DRIFTS

Most significant and most regrettable ... is our unfriendly commercial relations with the Dominion of Canada, our nearest neighbour, our best customer, the country that should be our warmest friend and indeed, remains, I fully believe, at heart strongly attached to us notwithstanding the harsh and even boorish manner in which we have so long dealt with her. We have not only failed to attract Canada, but have alienated her; let us hope, not irrevocably.

– FRANK W. TAUSSIG, CHAIRMAN, US TARIFF COMMISSION, 1933

From 1896 to 1911, the Liberals had pursued a pragmatic trade policy, preaching moderation while practising deft, sophisticated, but modest adjustments in the National Policy of the Conservatives. By 1911, the Liberal tariff and associated practices provided as much protection as had been provided by the Conservatives, although often at lower nominal rates, due to the use of subsidies, drawbacks, and other administrative devices. The tariff had become not only the principal tool of fiscal policy, but also a sophisticated instrument of industrial policy.

The reciprocity agreement of 1911 would in no way have denied or undermined this basic orientation of the National Policy. It would, from a political point of view, have combined the best elements of two competing objectives: free access to a large market for Canada's resource or "natural" products, and continued protection for its manufactures. It also would have maintained the tariff as a serious source of revenue: too much protection was as inimical to the tariff's revenue purposes as too little. But reciprocity was not to be, and the Conservatives, after fifteen years out of office, had to prove that they could do better.

This challenge, however, could not be met. For the next twenty years, Canada's trade policy lacked direction. The introduction of the income tax in 1917 began to detach the tariff from fiscal policy, adding to the sense of drift. Canada now boasted a continent-wide economy. Most of it was resource-based, but in Ontario and Quebec a respectable domestic manufacturing sector had developed, often producing Canadian versions of British and American products. As Glen Williams has demonstrated, the adoption of a high tariff for manufactures, as well as related laws and policies such as patent and competition laws, had encouraged the development of an import-substitution industrial structure. Industries were geared to the production of goods for domestic consumption, often dependent on imported capital, technology, and management.[1] Coupled with the continued emphasis on infrastructure development for the export of resources and the promotion of food, forest, and mineral exports to Britain, the United States, and elsewhere, the economic development of Canada was cast in a mould from which it proved difficult to escape.

Although the regional tensions created by the two-headed policy of protecting import-substitution industrialization in central Canada and promoting export-oriented resource exploitation elsewhere were evident in the results of the 1911 election, Canadian politicians were learning to create winning political coalitions out of these divergent interests. For the Conservatives, the National Policy had reinforced the growing identification between protection and nationhood. Many Canadians, particularly in Ontario and Quebec, believed that Canada's existence as an independent nation was directly tied to its ability to protect manufacturers from foreign competition. In addition, many Canadians were prepared to support policies that would knit the far-flung population together into a coherent whole within the British imperial family. In later years, the connection between protection and nationalism would become driven more by fear of assimilation into the United States, sentiments which the Liberals would prove more adept at exploiting. In the first thirty years of the new century, however, Canadians' sense of nationhood, at least outside Quebec, was still more a matter of maintaining the imperial connection than of resisting the allure of the American dream.

Conservative trade minister Sir George Foster tries to drum up empire trade in London. Posters in front of the Royal Exchange announce his speech.

Neither brand of nationalism, however, provided a secure basis for sustained economic development. Canada was too dependent on outside markets to support such nationalism. However, it would take two world wars and a depression to prod Canada toward the development of a more broadly based economy and a more outward-looking trade policy. Fundamental to Canada's adjustment to these developments were the revolutionary changes in the trade policies of Britain and the United States that took place between the two world wars.

Canada Looks to Britain

Despite his resounding victory in 1911, Borden had no clear alternative except to continue the pragmatic policy adopted by Laurier and developed by Fielding.[2] It was hard to criticize a policy that seemed to have contributed to the largest and most-sustained economic boom in Canadian history (see table 3.10, p. 77 above). The combination of growing domestic and foreign demand had fuelled a decade of agricultural expansion, railway building, and other public and private investments,

James Fergus Kyle, "Oh What a Change – 1911: Deep Gloom, 1913 – Oh Joy." The Conservatives, who had been deeply depressed by Laurier's coup in negotiating a new reciprocity treaty in 1911, are overjoyed to learn that the new Underwood Tariff in the United States provides Canadian goods with largely the same access, without Canada having to make any concessions of its own.

and had provided Canadians with a rising standard of living. For the first time since Confederation, immigration had outstripped emigration. Industrialization and urbanization were steadily transforming the landscape and providing Canada with the characteristics of a modern economy. The background of a decade and a half of success did not provide much impetus for change. The gradual development of the imperial connection continued as the temporary lurch back to reciprocity was abandoned. Fortunately, the Underwood Tariff, adopted with the return of the low-tariff Democrats to the White House in 1913, gave Canada most of the concessions it had negotiated in 1911.[3] It appeared that Canada, despite James Blaine's strong views to the contrary a generation earlier, could have its cake and eat it too.

The boom years, however, effectively ended within two years of Borden's victory and suggested once again that Conservative government usually coincided with tough times. The period between 1913 and 1922 saw dramatic upheavals in the Canadian economy (see table 4.1). The recession of 1913-14 was followed by the ups and downs of a war economy and the postwar recession of 1920-2. Throughout the period, prices, production, and trade fluctuated erratically. Steel production, railway expansion, and housing construction all slowed, while pulp, newsprint, and automotive production grew steadily. Overall, the percentage of workers employed in manufacturing declined, while the percentage of farm workers increased as Canadians expanded food production for export to the British market.

Table 4.1

Growth in the Canadian economy, 1913-22 (in millions of current dollars)

Item	1913	1918	1920	1922
Merchandise exports	443	1,209	1,267	884
Merchandise imports	655	922	1,429	745
Current account balance	−408	−82	−323	−47
Net long-term capital movement	+542	−136	+143	+237
Domestic investment	405	427	653	362
Capital employed in manufacturing	1,959	2,927	3,372	3,244
Steam railway mileage	29,304	38,484	38,976	39,358
Wheat acreage (000)	11,015	17,354	18,232	22,423
Terms of trade (1913 = 100)	100	117.7	104.3	101.8
Wholesale price index (1900 = 100)	133	266	325	203
Population (000)	7,527	8,243	8,691	8,919

Sources: A.E. Safarian, *The Canadian Economy in the Great Depression* (Toronto: University of Toronto Press, 1959), table 2; O.J. Firestone, *Canada's Economic Development: 1867-1952* (London: Bowes and Bowes, 1958), tables 51 and 83; J.A. Stovel, *Canada in the World Economy* (Cambridge, MA: Harvard University Press, 1959), tables 19 and 27; and F.H. Leacy, ed., *Historical Statistics of Canada,* 2nd ed. (Ottawa: Statistics Canada, 1983).

During the war, exports and imports grew rapidly, but much of this activity was geared to the special needs of war, including Britain's extraordinary food needs and demand for war materiel. By the end of the war, Canada was supplying its share of the shells that were used to reduce the western front to a muddy hell. The temporary basis of much of this trade became apparent in the slump of 1920-2.

Little changed on the trade policy front. Finance Minister Thomas White summed up the lessons learned from the period leading up to the 1911 election in his budget speech of 1914: "The evils of a high protective tariff are too well known to make it necessary that I should discuss them here. The tariff of Canada has not been a high tariff but one affording a moderate degree of protection only."[4] Even though the Canadian Manufacturers' Association continued to press for ever more protection, the Conservatives had learned that enough was enough. They might speak out in favour of protection on the stump, but they were moderate in its application, just as the Liberals electioneered against the tariff but maintained it in office. There was much truth in the jibe that the Tories were against any reduction in the tariff while the Grits insisted it could go no higher.

As illustrated in table 4.2, the trade-weighted incidence of White's tariff was somewhat lower than either of Fielding's tariffs and considerably below that of the last Conservative government. Most of this reduction can be attributed to the impact of rising prices as well as the imperial discount, which for most products was by now one-third off the general rate. The prevalence of specific tariffs meant that during periods of falling prices, the incidence of protection automatically increased, while during periods of rising prices the incidence decreased. The last period of Conservative rule (1878-96) had seen depressed economic conditions and a general

Table 4.2

Trade-weighted average rates of duty, Canada, 1891-1921

Years	Tariff legislation	% of imports duty free	Equivalent *ad valorem* rate (%)	
			Dutiable imports	Total imports
1891-7	Conservative tariffs	37.7	30.5	19.0
1898-1907	Fielding's first tariff	39.7	27.7	16.7
1908-14	Fielding's second tariff	36.7	26.4	16.8
1914-21	White Tariff	35.0	24.1	15.7

Source: Hugh McA. Pinchin, *The Regional Impact of the Canadian Tariff: A Study Prepared for the Economic Council of Canada* (Ottawa: Supply and Services, 1979), table 1-2. Reproduced with the permission of the Minister of Public Works and Government Services Canada, 2001. The findings of this Study are the personal responsibility of the author and, as such, have not been endorsed by Members of the Economic Council of Canada.

decline in price levels; the economic boom of 1895 to 1913 had seen prices rise. In addition, preferences reduced the incidence of protection somewhat during the period 1897 to 1914, although, for most of this period, the trade-weighted incidence of protection on British imports was not markedly different from that on US imports, given the different mix of products involved.[5]

The highest levels of nominal protection were still levied on manufactures and luxury goods, with rates as high as 35 percent for manufactures and even higher for luxuries such as alcoholic beverages and perfume. Holes in the tariff and the use of bounties and remissions, however, ensured that protected Canadian manufacturers could still import necessary industrial inputs that could not be supplied from domestic sources at competitive prices. A third of Canada's imports came in free of duty, including industrial inputs, indicating that the level of effective protection for manufactures was considerably higher than nominal averages would suggest. The result of this carefully calibrated protection was to encourage growth in import-substitution industries. Canadian manufacturers in a range of protected industries generally satisfied three-quarters or more of domestic demand and exported very little of their final product. Prices, given the smaller Canadian market and the high levels of protection, were generally higher than in the larger, more competitive US market. While US tariffs on manufactures were, on average, higher than Canadian tariffs, the benefits of a larger market resulted in more competition and the ability to reap the advantages of scale production.[6]

Once in office, the Conservatives did take some concrete steps toward the further development of a system of imperial preferences. In 1912, Borden visited London and established his credentials as a staunch defender of the imperial connection, while his ministers negotiated the first-ever trade agreement with the West Indies. Even though Britain remained indifferent, Canada now set out to consolidate imperial preferences through trade agreements with its principal imperial trading partners. An innovation in the 1912 West Indies agreement was the concept of bound margins of preference. The Conservatives thus ushered in a contractual commitment to preferences, a commitment the Liberals had studiously avoided, insisting that preferences were freely given and could thus be freely withdrawn if doing so would suit Canadian interests. The new policy eventually complicated efforts to negotiate trade agreements with nonimperial partners, but to the Conservatives that was of little consequence at the time.[7]

War fever and then war, however, soon pushed trade policy into the background. The need for extra revenue was first tackled by adding a tariff surcharge in 1915 of 5 percent on imperial imports and 7.5 percent on all other imports, with a list of exemptions for necessities. Two years later, in 1917, the government introduced a modest income tax as well as various other new taxes, and the following year, additional duties on luxuries like tea, coffee, tobacco, and liquor. The nontrade purpose of these tariffs was confirmed by their removal after the war; the other new taxes, however, remained and were gradually expanded to the point that they provided more than a third of federal government revenue by the end of the 1920s, reducing pressures to increase tariff protection for revenue purposes. Thus the structure of protection at the beginning of the 1920s was largely as it had been in the first decade of the century.[8]

One of the longer-term impacts of the war, although it was not immediately apparent, was the decline in Canada's relationship with the United Kingdom, coupled with a growing attraction to the United States as a trade and economic power. Economic relations during the war had foreshadowed this development, and trade and investment patterns in the years immediately after the war confirmed the subtle change that had taken place. As historian Jack Granatstein has argued: "Although there was a certain reversion towards a more normal trading pattern in the postwar years, Canada had, during the Great War, shifted out of the British economic order and towards, if not yet completely into, the American."[9] The combined effect of business judgment, geography, and consumer preference conspired to erode the influence of imperial history and sentiment.

The Return of the Liberals

As the war years gave way to peace, Borden resigned to be succeeded by Arthur Meighen, a brilliant, arrogant, and uncompromising intellectual and an even more confirmed upholder of the imperial connection. Canada had been transformed by the war. As C.P. Stacey points out, Canada gave much and gained much from the war by providing both new industrial products and food.[10] The immediate effect of the return to a peacetime economy, however, was recession, as wartime demand dried up and the economy adjusted to more normal production patterns. The value of Canada's exports to Great Britain, for example, plunged from $892 million in 1917 to $310 million in 1921, and total exports fell from $1,558 million to $892 million. The US economy failed to take up the slack, as Congress returned to its predilection for isolationism and protectionism.

Against this inauspicious background, Meighen decided to consolidate his hold on power and called a general election for 21 December 1921, confident that the united Tories could defeat the Grits. The Grits had yet to recover from the split in their ranks occasioned by conscription and the migration of some of their members to the wartime Union government. Laurier had died in 1919 and been succeeded by the little-known and untried William Lyon Mackenzie King. On the Western flank, the radical Progressives under Thomas Crerar were likely to undermine Liberal strength. In central Canada, the division over conscription had left bitter feelings between Quebec and Ontario.

Trade policy once again figured prominently in the election. Meighen took a strong stand for protection and the imperial connection, hinting at the evils of Liberal continentalism: "We stand for a tariff based on the principle of protection. Not the kind of protection that will fleece the many for the benefit of the few, but for protection just sufficient to enable Canadian industries to operate in this country, to make Canadian goods for Canadians, to employ Canadian labour, and to build a Canadian market."[11] Crerar took an equally strong stand against the tariff and for reciprocity. King showed his peculiar genius for obfuscation, hinting at positions but never confirming them. His creed was not to offend; the less said, the fewer people would be offended. He promised a tariff for the consumer and producer that would also take care of the needs of all the industries, without defining what any of this would mean in practice.[12]

To Meighen's chagrin, King gained a sufficiently large minority to enable him to govern with the help of a large contingent of Progressives. With Fielding back as finance minister, Canadians were in for another decade of cautious pragmatism.[13] The policy of cultivating a system of imperial preferences continued, with more success as Britain gradually crept toward protectionism, but progress toward more general imperial cooperation cooled. King and Fielding saw imperial preferences as a means to an end rather than as a noble objective. At imperial conferences in the 1920s, King threw cold water on schemes advanced by the Colonial Office and the other dominion prime ministers, particularly the Australian Stanley Bruce, who was cast more in the mould of Borden than King.[14]

To King, further progress in achieving imperial preferences appeared to compromise a more important objective, the achievement of full independence in the conduct of Canadian foreign relations. If there were to be imperial preferences, they would be freely given so that they could also be freely withdrawn or adjusted. He disliked the concept of bound preferences, which would rob the government of the necessary flexibility to react to changing circumstances. Much of the trade promotion and negotiating activity of the period appears to have been aimed as much at demonstrating to the world that Canada was an independent nation as at pursuing trade objectives. The establishment of a Department of External Affairs by Laurier in 1909 had had a similar aim.[15] Efforts by the Colonial Office and by the other dominions appeared to be tilting in another and, from Canada's point of view, undesirable direction. In keeping with King's style, however, much of this activity toward independence was indirect and expressed more in what Canada did not do than in what it did.[16]

Relations with the United States during this period were correct but not as warm as they would become later between King and Roosevelt. With the return of the Republicans and isolationism, US trade policy reverted to the protectionist norm of the second half of the nineteenth century. The Fordney-McCumber Tariff of 1922 (see table 4.11 below) restored high tariff levels, and the Antidumping Act of 1921 took a leaf out of Fielding's own book and provided for the use of antidumping duties as a protectionist trade measure. There was no serious talk of reciprocity on either side of the border. King did, however, take steps to ensure that Canada would have its own eyes, ears, and voice in Washington. Borden's scheme of appointing a Canadian minister who would serve as deputy to the British ambassador was scrapped in favour of a separate mission, and in 1927 Vincent Massey took up residence in a handsome mansion on Massachusetts Avenue built by one of the victims of the Titanic disaster. During a visit by King to Washington in 1927, President Calvin Coolidge and his commerce secretary, Herbert Hoover, tried to interest King in a St. Lawrence Seaway project, but King demurred, concerned that it smacked too much of reciprocity.[17]

The Canadian Economy in the 1920s
Once over the postwar recession, the Canadian economy, particularly the wheat economy of the Prairies, continued to grow and become more dependent on world markets. During the first thirty years of Confederation, Canada had tried in a variety of ways to open up the western territories in order to create a Dominion from coast to coast in fact as well as in name. The effect was negligible. Between 1871 and 1891, the population of the Prairies rose only from about 75,000 to 250,000, concentrated largely in Manitoba. Starting in the mid-1890s, however, Western settlement finally took off. The combination of failed harvests in Europe, cheaper and more efficient transportation methods, and advances in dry-land farming and strains of drought-resistant wheat had made the vast stretches of isolated, dry, but fertile Canadian prairie land economically feasible and attractive to thousands of land-hungry European settlers. By 1911, the population of what had become the three Prairie provinces had mushroomed to 1.3 million, and their gateway, Winnipeg, had become Canada's third-largest city with a population of 150,000. By this time, Prairie wheat had fully supplanted the Ontario crop and become the new export staple, with Quebec and Ontario farmers turning to dairy and fruits.[18]

To sell the new products on world markets, the Dominion government participated actively in developing the necessary commercial and transportation infrastructure, including a trade commissioner service, and negotiated an increasing number of trade agreements that provided access to new markets, often specifically for wheat.[19] By the outbreak of the First World War in 1914, wheat and wheat flour accounted for more than a quarter of Canada's exports to all markets (see table 4.3). With the return to peace, the wheat economy continued to expand. By the end of the 1920s, acreage had increased two and a half times over prewar levels and in the record year of 1928, yields reached 566.7 million bushels of which 407.6 million bushels were exported that year and the next. Wheat represented 28.7 and 31.4 percent of total exports in those two years.

The successful wheat economy had not been preordained. Canada was not alone in learning to reap the wealth of the continental plains and had to compete with US as well as Argentine wheat on European markets. European farmers, in turn, had reacted vigorously to the new competition. In country after country on the European continent, particularly after 1892, European farmers made common cause with manufacturers to petition governments to protect them from the new competition. In the light of high American and Canadian levels of protection on the manufactured exports of Europe, the new combination proved potent and created

Table 4.3

Wheat exports in the Canadian economy, 1871-1939

Crop/ fiscal year	Acreage (millions)	Production (millions of bushels)	Exports (millions of bushels)	Exports ($ millions)	Total exports ($ millions)	Wheat as % of total
1871	1.6	16.7	1.7	2.0	57.6	3.5
1901	4.2	32.3	9.7	6.9	177.4	3.9
1911	8.8	132.1	45.8	45.5	274.3	16.6
1914	11.0	231.7	120.4	117.7	432.0	27.3
1920-1	23.3	263.2	129.2	310.9	1,189.1	26.1
1924-5	20.8	395.4	191.7	251.6	1,069.0	23.5
1927-8	24.1	566.7	352.1	352.1	1,227.4	28.7
1928-9	25.2	304.5	370.4	428.5	1,363.7	31.4
1932-3	26.0	281.8	239.3	130.5	528.0	24.7
1936-7	25.6	180.2	227.9	223.4	1,061.2	21.1
1938-9	26.8	520.6	162.9	109.0	927.0	11.8

Sources: J.A. Stovel, *Canada in the World Economy* (Cambridge, MA: Harvard University Press, 1959), table 4; Mary Hill, *Canada's Salesman to the World: The Department of Trade and Commerce 1892-1939* (Montreal: McGill-Queen's University Press, 1977), tables 11, 14, 16, 24, and 26; and F.H. Leacy, ed., *Historical Statistics of Canada*, 2nd ed. (Ottawa: Statistics Canada, 1983).

significant obstacles for Canadian exports to overcome. By 1913, Canadian wheat faced duties of 35, 38, 36, 37, 40, 43, and 28 percent respectively in Austria-Hungary, France, Germany, Greece, Italy, Spain, and Sweden. Only the United Kingdom, the Netherlands, Belgium, Denmark, Finland, and Russia still provided free entry.[20] After the war, falling prices and burgeoning production continued to make the wheat economy a major focus of international attention. Nevertheless, Canadian producers did well, stimulating the rapid growth of the Prairie provinces. In the first thirty years of the new century, the population of the three Prairie provinces grew almost six-fold to reach 2,353,529, of which two-thirds remained rural.[21]

The burgeoning wheat economy had helped to fuel the investment boom of the 1900-13 period and contributed again in the period 1922-8 (see table 4.4). The first investment boom had been oriented largely toward infrastructure and had benefited industries that supplied, for example, inputs to farm machinery and rails and rolling stock. The second boom was geared more to the expansion of manufacturing and the new resource industries, pulp, newsprint, and mining. In 1929, Canadian factories pumped out 188,721 cars, 4,766,000 tires, 4,021,000 tons of wood pulp, 2,725,000 tons of newsprint, 98 locomotives, and 13,242 railcars. Value added in manufacturing grew 6 percent each year between 1921 and 1929, and employment growth averaged 5 percent per year. Much of this new production was destined for

Table 4.4

Growth in the Canadian economy, 1922-31 (in millions of current dollars)

	1922	1925	1928	1931
Merchandise exports	884	1,241	1,341	601
Merchandise imports	745	872	1,209	580
Current account balance	−47	+273	−32	−174
Net long-term capital movement	+237	−50	−104	+113
Domestic investment	362	708[a]	1,038	622
Capital employed in manufacturing	3,244	3,808	4,780	4,961
Steam railway mileage	39,358	40,350	41,022	42,280
Wheat acreage (000)	22,423	20,790	24,119	26,355
Terms of trade (1913 = 100)	101.8	109.0	111.2	105.6
Wholesale price index (1934-9 = 100)	126.8	133.8	125.6	94.0
Population (000)	8,919	9,294	9,835	10,377

a 1926.

Sources: F.H. Leacy, ed., *Historical Statistics of Canada,* 2nd ed. (Ottawa: Statistics Canada, 1983); *Canada Year Book*, 1932 and 1936 (Ottawa: Dominion Bureau of Statistics, various years); J.A. Stovel, *Canada in the World Economy* (Cambridge, MA: Harvard University University Press, 1959), table 27.

export markets. The value of exports rose 67 percent from their trough in 1921 to their peak in 1928. Exports of agricultural products grew by 17 percent, forest products by 38 percent, iron and steel products by 150 percent, and nonferrous metal products by 238 percent.[22]

The boom at the turn of the century had been in large measure a product of government policy. Efforts to attract immigrants, to build railways and other infrastructure requirements, and to protect domestic manufacturers had all contributed to the growth in population, new investment, added production, and increased trade. The growth in the 1920s, while still benefiting from some of the same policies, was more the result of private initiative, building on the achievements of the earlier period, the demand for Canadian food products in Europe and for newsprint and industrial resource material in the United States, as well as preferred access to the growing markets of the other dominions.

On the trade policy front, the 1920s were characterized by much activity but also by drift and lassitude. As indicated above, the Liberals no longer viewed imperial preferences as an important objective. Canadian imports from Great Britain had steadily declined over the years and in the 1920s, exports also took a major tumble, despite the newly established preferences. The bright spot in the picture was that imperial preferences and related efforts to promote Canadian sales in imperial and other new markets were beginning to pay off. By the end of the decade, a third of Canada's exports went to markets other than the United States and Great Britain, a

Table 4.5

Canada's trade in goods with Great Britain, the United States, and the rest of the world, 1901-39 (proportion of total)

	Great Britain		United States		Rest of world	
Year[a]	Imports	Exports[b]	Imports	Exports[b]	Imports	Exports[b]
1901	24.2	52.5	60.1	38.4	15.7	9.1
1906	24.3	54.0	59.5	35.7	16.2	10.3
1911	24.3	48.2	60.9	38.0	14.8	13.8
1916	15.2	60.9	73.0	27.1	11.8	12.0
1921	17.3	26.3	69.0	45.6	13.7	28.1
1926	16.3	36.6	66.2	36.0	17.5	27.4
1929	15.1	25.3	68.6	42.6	16.3	32.1
1933	24.4	39.9	53.7	31.6	21.9	28.5
1937	18.3	40.4	60.4	36.1	21.3	23.5
1939	15.2	35.6	65.9	41.2	18.9	23.2

a Figures from 1926 are for calendar years; from 1911-21 for fiscal years ending 31 March; and from 1901-6 for fiscal years ending 30 June.
b Domestic product only.
Source: F.H. Leacy, *Historical Statistics of Canada,* 2nd ed. (Ottawa: Statistics Canada, 1983), series G389-400.

Table 4.6

Five leading export and import items, 1910 and 1930 (value in millions of current dollars)

Exports			Imports		
Item	Value	%	Item	Value	%
1910					
Wheat	46	16.8	Cotton and manufactures	33	7.3
Planks and boards	22	8.0	Coal	32	7.1
Cheese	21	7.7	Wool and manufactures	26	5.7
Wheat flour	14	5.1	Rolling mill products	23	5.0
Cattle	9	3.3	Sugar	17	3.8
Total five items	112	40.9	Total five items	131	28.9
1930					
Wheat	189	21.9	Coal	57	5.6
Newsprint paper	133	15.4	Industrial machinery	50	5.0
Wheat flour	43	5.0	Rolling mill products	47	4.6
Wood pulp	39	4.5	Crude petroleum	38	3.8
Planks and boards	37	4.2	Electrical apparatus	30	3.0
Total five items	441	51.0	Total five items	222	22.0

Source: O.J. Firestone, *Canada's Economic Development, 1867-1952* (London: Bowes and Bowes, 1958), table 55, 60.

degree of diversification that has never been reached again (see table 4.5). Some of these exports were manufactures, as Canadian branch plants were given mandates to export to these markets to take advantage of preferences. The growth in Canadian automotive production, for example, was geared to both domestic and other imperial markets. Nevertheless, Canada remained a resource-based economy, and resources continued to be the mainstay of its exports. At the end of the decade, two product groups, wheat and wheat flour and newsprint and pulp, together made up 47 percent of Canadian exports (see table 4.6).

The overall structure of the tariff and its levels of protection were not much altered during this period (see table 4.7). In order to satisfy the rabidly antiprotectionist Progressives, Fielding made a number of cosmetic changes in the tariff (such as reducing the rates on farm machinery), but its basic structure and level remained the same as during his first fifteen years as finance minister. He also continued the policy of allowing drawbacks if imports were used for specific purposes, such as a new 40 percent drawback on machinery for new factories. Similarly, he still showed his fondness for bounties and subsidies instead of tariff reductions. His successors continued in this tradition of minor adjustments as circumstances warranted. In 1927, James Robb finally followed through on an old idea to help depoliticize tariff adjustments: the establishment of an Advisory Board on Tariffs and Taxation. Over the years it would further refine Canadian tariff classification and rates.[23]

Table 4.7

Structure of Canadian protection, 1928 (nominal average rates of duty, selected sectors)

Sector	Preferential[a] (%)	Treaty[b] (%)	General[c] (%)	Impact[d] (%)
All iron and steel products	11	17	19	54
All manufactures	12	17	21	25
All textiles	17	23	28	39
Electrical apparatus and supplies	15	23	27	32
Furniture	18	28	30	–
Glass and its products	13	19	22	72
Leather boots and shoes	16	27	29	6
Petroleum products	9	12	14	33

a Rate for goods imported from Great Britain and the rest of the Empire.
b Rate for goods imported from countries to which Canada owed treaty obligations.
c Rate for goods imported from all other countries, particularly the United States.
d Ratio of imports to gross value of Canadian production.
Source: Royal Commission on Dominion-Provincial Relations, Book 1, Canada: 1867-1939 (Ottawa: King's Printer, 1939), p. 157, table 53.

Arch Dale, "The Milch Cow." The sectional impact of Canadian tariff policy is well captured in this famous cartoon capturing the West's perspective; it takes only a little imagination to add the Maritime point of view.

Liberal tariff policy was popular in Ontario and Quebec, where 80 percent of Canada's manufacturing capacity was located, as was 60 percent of its population and thus the political base of any government. The policy was tolerated in the West as long as the government also paid attention to the need to sell Western resource products and as long as export markets for them were good. When resource markets went sour, the high tariffs on manufactures were resented. Bothwell, Drummond, and English note that "central Canada supplied manufactures to the west at inflated prices, while the west had its wheat and timber on world markets, at unprotected prices. No better recipe for interregional friction could have been devised."[24] By this time, neither Liberal nor Conservative tariff policy was popular in the Maritimes, where bitter opinion held that the tariff protected central Canada at the expense of the rest of the country.

To offset this criticism, Canadian officials busied themselves with the negotiation of general trade agreements as well as specific agreements for the delivery of grain. Over the course of the decade, Canada entered into arrangements with France, Spain, the Netherlands, Italy, Belgium, Czechoslovakia, and Australia, and expanded the agreement with the West Indies. Some agreements exchanged MFN rights, while others exchanged narrower concessions. With the exception of the French agreement, none were of much long-term significance and were the work of officials such as

Dana Wilgress, a trade commissioner who had joined the service in 1914 and seen service in Russia, Germany, and other European centres, who appeared to have a flair for trade negotiations.[25]

Britain Abandons the Good Fight
The Canadian search for wider markets took place against the background of a gradual retreat by the UK government from its historic commitment to free trade. From the late eighteenth until the early twentieth century, Britain had been the world's premier economy, confident, outward-looking, and rich. Since 1846, it had preached and practised free trade and kept its markets open to the products of the world. But, except for the brief interlude ushered in by the Cobden-Chevalier Treaty of 1860, Britain had stood largely alone. With the collapse of the world economy in 1929, British resolve crumbled and the government adopted not only tariffs but the discrimination advocated by its former colonial possessions and long the mainstay of European trade policy.[26]

The Tariff Reform League in the United Kingdom had for three decades pressed political leaders to introduce tariffs in order to foster industrial development, higher employment, and colonial ties. Its views had been firmly rejected by the Liberals and only tentatively accepted by the Conservatives. The pressures of war, however, changed the balance. The staunchly free-trade Liberal government that had ruled in London since 1906 gave way in 1915 to a coalition government that included Lloyd George Liberals, Bonar Law Conservatives, and some members of the newly established Labour Party. Lloyd George's leadership provided an improved basis for prosecuting the war, but his coalition government was also prepared to accommodate the entreaties of the dominions for a greater voice in imperial decisions and a trade policy that would reward their contribution to the cause. The stage had thus been set for a reversal in British trade policies.

In 1915, Britain introduced the McKenna Tariff in order to raise revenue for the war and discourage trade in some commodities, thus leaving more room for war materiel in ships crossing the ocean. At the same time, the old colonial conferences were replaced by imperial conferences, and the dominions were co-opted into a joint war effort and participation in an imperial war cabinet. At the end of the war, additional tariffs were assessed in the 1919 Finance and Key Industries Acts. Lloyd George further fulfilled his commitment to the dominions by introducing, for the first time, an imperial discount of one-third off the tariff. More goods became subject to tariffs in 1921 in the Safeguarding of Industries Act, all subject to the imperial discount.[27] Canadian Tories had finally achieved reciprocal preferences, and with their like-minded colleagues in the other dominions, began to hatch grandiose schemes for a comprehensive system of imperial preferences backed up by other forms of imperial economic and political cooperation.[28]

More important, however, the war had set the stage for even more profound changes in British trade policies and, less directly, Canadian and US policies as well.

Jan Tumlir has written that one of the easily forgotten legacies of the First World War is that it laid the foundation for the intricate involvement of government in society. The war ushered in what he called the planning ideology or the politicization of the economy, involving political authorities in the structure and operation of the economy. The planning, cooperation, and control required by the combatants on both sides of the front not only developed the capacity of governments to take on new responsibilities, but also fostered acceptance of a new government role that would have been unthinkable in the nineteenth century. This change in ideology, when combined with the move toward democracy and universal suffrage, had profound implications for trade policy and for attitudes toward the establishment of a planned international economic order.[29]

Before the war, trade policy in Canada, the United States, Britain, and elsewhere did not have to be "popular"; it needed to appeal only to those elements in society that made a difference – the propertied classes. In the years after the war, however, politicians, in order to retain office, had to devise policies that commanded broader support. These changes were particularly important in Britain, which had entered the war as the unchallenged major world power and which, under successive governments, had pursued a laissez-faire policy that was increasingly seen as unpopular. Protectionism, until the war a decidedly minority opinion, now began to attract sufficient support to require a response, a response that would go beyond the tariff and involve questions of other means to stimulate employment and domestic industry. No longer an unchallenged great power, Britain was saddled with an economy that faced major adjustment burdens, and British politicians began to take more seriously popular calls for protection and government intervention. Britain's conversion to protection, therefore, was driven more by domestic than imperial considerations. Nevertheless, these domestic considerations helped the dominions in pushing for preferences in the UK market.

The introduction of the McKenna Tariff in 1915, imperial preferences in 1919, and more duties in 1921 had opened the door to protection and made proponents of more protection both more vocal and more respectable. Canadian-born newspaper baron Max Aitken, Lord Beaverbrook, used his newspapers to promote not only protection for British industries, but a particular variant thereon, Empire-wide free trade. In his view, and in that of other prominent Conservatives, the economies of other countries were performing better than that of Britain and were doing so on the basis of high levels of protection. While free trade might be intellectually correct, it made little sense when practiced unilaterally. In response, therefore, Britain needed to introduce tariffs to protect its manufactures and promote employment and at the same time to encourage Empire-wide growth by creating a free-trade zone throughout the Empire.

Over the course of the 1920s, political debate raged about the costs and benefits of protection. The misery of a full-scale global depression finally turned the tide. At the end of 1931, unable to fight the depression on the basis of Labour support alone,

Ramsay MacDonald formed a National coalition government made up of Conservative, Liberal, and some Labour members. MacDonald won a resounding victory in the subsequent election, with a strong mandate to introduce protection in line with the policies practised in virtually every other country. In 1932, therefore, Britain finally abandoned free trade. The Import Duties Act of that year imposed an across-the-board rate of 10 percent, exempted Empire goods pending the Imperial Economic Conference later that year, and provided for retaliatory duties of 100 percent on goods from countries that discriminated against British goods. Britain was now fully committed not only to protection but also to discrimination.[30]

Nevertheless, postwar British governments sought to maintain international leadership through both the League of Nations and the Empire. Neither effort led to liberalism and order. Efforts in the League, in the absence of the United States and Germany, proved feeble and became more so over time. Much was discussed, debated, and studied, but little was agreed and implemented. With British hegemony lost and nothing to take its place, international relations lapsed into disarray. As J.B. Condliffe concluded, "Britain lost the will and lacked the power to enforce international cooperation as she had done throughout the nineteenth century."[31] This failure further accentuated the pessimism in Britain about the benefits of free trade and freely convertible currencies. Even John Maynard Keynes, who later played such an influential role in establishing the Bretton Woods system of nondiscriminatory multilateral agreements, despaired about the benefits of open, nondiscriminatory exchanges of goods: "I sympathize, therefore, with those who would minimize, rather than those who would maximize, economic entanglements among nations. Ideas, knowledge, science, hospitality, travel – these are the things which should of their nature be international. But let goods be homespun whenever it is reasonably and conveniently possible, and, above all, let finance be primarily national."[32]

Others agreed with Lord Beaverbrook that the way forward lay through imperial cooperation. Britain would be great again by building a new empire based on economic cooperation and preferences. It was an idea that fitted in well with the growing taste for discrimination in Europe.

The End of the European Treaty System
Between 1860 and 1914, the European countries maintained a system of interlocking MFN agreements built upon the Cobden-Chevalier Treaty of 1860 between Britain and France. Each treaty bound tariffs to agreed levels for periods of up to ten years and fostered a substantial liberalization of trade. The various individual bilateral treaties were linked to each other on the basis of the unconditional MFN clause, i.e., participants agreed to extend MFN status to each other without imposing any conditions. The procedural obligations imposed by the need to gain the approval of trading partners for any upward revisions in tariff levels, coupled with the impact such a change would have on the whole system, provided an adequate

means for maintaining stability. It was a system that "suited unitary nation-states with powerful executives and a tradition of intensive diplomacy."[33]

The Cobden-Chevalier Treaty was renewed in 1871 for a further ten years despite pressure within France and elsewhere to reverse the direction. The system remained intact until 1879 when Bismarck's nation-building tariff in Germany ushered in an era of competitive, destructive tariff increases as well as related steps aimed at protecting home markets and discriminating against particular foreign producers. At the outbreak of war in 1914, only Britain remained aloof from the rush to raise tariffs. In most instances, however, the increases were modest. The period 1879-1914 had seen an erosion in the commitment to freer trade but no marked increase in protection in most of Europe. Tariffs, despite the fact that they served both revenue and protective purposes, only averaged 9.8 percent in France and Germany at the start of the war, substantially lower than rates in the United States and Canada.[34]

The First World War finished what commercial policy had started, completely destroying the treaty system. After the breakup of the Austrian and Turkish empires, customs agents proliferated along the southern and eastern flanks of Europe. By the end of the war, trade barriers were considerably higher all around as various governments moved to protect new industries established by war, safeguard their balance-of-payments positions, and promote employment. Various quantitative restrictions (QRs) and similar nontariff barriers were gradually replaced by more neutral tariffs after the war, which in turn began to march ever higher in the absence of any treaty obligations to impose restraint. Where tariffs proved insufficient, QRs were reintroduced as were exchange controls. Few treaties were concluded aimed at reducing or even stabilizing tariffs, nor was the principle of unconditional MFN rehabilitated. France's decision to abandon an unconditional MFN treaty system doomed any efforts to reintroduce it. The popular appeal of protectionism and its link to nationalism gave the fragile French governments of the interwar years little room to manoeuvre.[35]

Consequently, when recession struck agricultural production in 1928 and gradually spread, hastened by the Wall Street crash of 1929, there were no restraints in place in Europe or elsewhere to prevent countries from adopting policies aimed at exporting their problems. As the recession turned to depression, countries further aggravated the fall in demand by erecting ever-higher barriers to protect their own industries. The US Smoot-Hawley Tariff (see below) was only the most notorious example. Britain's decision to abandon its traditional trade policy, therefore, was but one of a series of steps marking the steady retreat from a system based on liberalism reinforced by interlocking treaty obligations to one that increasingly assumed the efficacy of autonomy and protection. To unsettle matters further, Britain abandoned the gold standard in 1933, followed by many of its trading partners, and the United States devalued its dollar. Currency instability and inconvertibility added another dimension of fragility to international commerce and reinforced the deepening depression.

Throughout the 1920s and into the 1930s, the League of Nations sponsored a series of conferences aimed at addressing the proliferation of protectionist policies.[36] Most were to no avail, because the League lacked the capacity to translate discussions about possibilities into negotiations leading to contractual commitments.[37] Additionally, the refusal of both the United States and France to participate in reconstructing a stable international commercial policy system doomed the League's efforts.[38]

Continental frustration with American isolationism and increasing British fascination with its dwindling Empire led to various plans for European integration, many of them with a decidedly anti-American flavour. The aim of most of these plans, such as the Briand Plan sponsored by France, was to make intra-European liberalization possible and to shut out US goods. Few went beyond the discussion stage, and all collapsed in the face of the recession, the US Smoot-Hawley Tariff, and the subsequent plunge into a prolonged depression.[39]

Intellectual Ferment in the United States

Even before the collapse of the Wall Street stock market in 1929, economic conditions in Europe had been unsettled, with unemployment remaining at high levels, fuelling protectionist sentiment. The United States, however, enjoyed relatively more prosperous conditions behind very high levels of protection. The American economy remained largely isolated from the rest of the world. Influential opinion, however, was beginning to question both the objectives of economic isolationism and the means by which it was maintained.

The first stirrings of this new attitude could be seen in American participation in the Great War. The feeling that the United States had embarked on a great moral crusade continued through President Woodrow Wilson's efforts at asserting a leadership role in settling the peace. While action was short-lived, the ideas evoked by America's brief appearance on the world stage persisted. Wilson's successors and Congress soon drew back into the familiar isolationist shell, but American academics began to take a serious look at the implications of America's new power and influence, including their implications for trade policy. They concluded that a sound, outward-looking American trade policy should rest on two fundamentals: the classic arguments favouring free trade and the more subtle point of nondiscrimination.

Typical of this ferment of ideas was the examination of American trade and commercial diplomacy taking place at the newly established United States Tariff Commission. Chairman Frank Taussig, a professor at Harvard, and his colleagues Jacob Viner and William Culbertson concluded in their 1919 report, *Reciprocity and Commercial Treaties:*

A policy of special arrangements, such as the United States has followed in recent decades, leads to troublesome complications. Whether as regards our reciprocity treaties or as regards our interpretation of the most-favored-nation clause, the separate and individual treatment of each case tends to create misunderstanding and friction with countries, which, though supposed to be not concerned, yet in reality are much concerned ... [The United States should adopt] a clear and simple policy ... of equality of treatment ... Equality of treatment should mean that the United States treat all countries on the same terms, and in return require equal treatment from every country.[40]

The key concept in this report, and in related writings by Taussig, Viner, and other leading American international trade economists, was not so much a classic defence of free trade as an attack on discrimination and its handmaiden in the United States, conditional MFN treatment. The principle of conditional MFN treatment had underpinned the few efforts at treaty making by the United States during the previous century, rather than the unconditional variety that had been the mainstay of the treaty system in Europe. During the nineteenth century, the United States had entered into eleven MFN agreements (as distinct from tariff agreements), but in all of them any additional rights gained by one country had to be bargained for by the other countries, rather than being extended automatically. All that the US MFN clause provided was the right to seek further negotiations and a presumption of success as long as the United States gained equivalent concessions. Since any new concessions granted to the United States would complicate the unconditional MFN agreements these countries enjoyed with other trading partners, US trade negotiations proved singularly unsuccessful. Wrote Viner in 1924, "The most-favored-nation clause in American commercial treaties, as conditionally interpreted and applied by the United States, has probably been the cause in the last century of more diplomatic controversy, more variations in construction, more international ill-feeling, more conflict between international obligations and municipal law and between judicial interpretation and executive practice, more confusion and uncertainty of operation, than have developed under all the unconditional most-favored-nation pledges of all other countries combined."[41]

Equally undesirable to Taussig, Viner, and their colleagues was the increase in tariff preferences and other forms of discrimination. Viner, who had been taught by Stephen Leacock at McGill University at the turn of the century but had subsequently studied and taught at Chicago and Princeton, devoted much of his writing to demonstrating the negative effect of discrimination on international trade, notably in his magisterial *The Customs Union Issue* (1950) and *Dumping: A Problem in International Trade* (1923). Unlike his first mentor, who in 1932 wrote a small treatise in praise of imperial preferences,[42] Viner insisted that such discrimination was inimical to long-term economic growth, telling an audience at the London School of Economics in 1931, "If England adopts protection, a large part of that protection will undoubtedly be protection to colonial and not to English industry ... The threat that if the rest of the world continues to pursue its evil ways England will do as other countries do might perhaps add reinforcement to the growing sentiment for moderation in tariff matters. But the definite and unconditional abandonment of free trade by England would destroy what basis there is for hope in early and wide-spread tariff reform."[43]

Of course, Taussig and his colleagues also advanced the classic arguments for free trade, nowhere more eloquently than in the same much-quoted lecture by Viner:

> The contrast is striking between the almost undisputed sway which the protectionist doctrine has over the minds of statesmen and its almost complete failure to receive credentials of intellectual respectability from the economists. The routine arguments of the protectionist politician differ somewhat in quality from country to country. In my own country they are often magnificent achievements of sustained and impressive oratory, capturing their audiences in spite of – or perhaps by – their absence of any means of intellectual support. In England they are usually not quite so eloquent, nor quite so foolish, nor quite so effective with their audiences ... They are fairly adequately disposed of in any one of a large number of elementary textbooks, and what importance they have is due mainly to the fact that the general public does not read economic textbooks.[44]

Thus, throughout the 1920s and into the 1930s, as the world economic order deteriorated and the relative positions of the United States and the United Kingdom reversed, changes in their respective commercial policies paved the way for a new order. As we have seen, the United Kingdom gradually developed a backward-looking imperial trade policy, while in the United States the ground was being prepared for a forward-looking, internationalist trade policy.[45]

US opinion was preparing for the moment when the United States would forsake a century and a half of isolationism and protectionism and take up the cause of freeing world trade. But whereas Britain had championed unilateral free trade, US free traders anchored their policy in reciprocal reductions in trade barriers. Indeed, the policy's more immediate goal was not free trade but nondiscrimination, and therein lay its genius. Britain had stood largely alone during its period of economic leadership. The United States would successfully pursue a policy that brought most of the trading world into a single system dedicated to the progressive reduction of barriers and the practice of nondiscrimination. It was a system based on American ideas and values that, for the next forty years, ushered in an unprecedented era of growth based on international trade.

For Canada, these developments in the trade policies of its two major trading partners had significant implications. Canadian politicians would look first to one and then to the other for inspiration in response to the misery of depression.

Canada and the "Great Depression"

Canadian economic expansion in the 1920s had been built on precarious foundations and when, following the collapse of the New York stock market in 1929, the world went into depression, dependence on exports of grain, forestry, and mineral products made Canada particularly vulnerable to the protectionist response. Canada's domestic market was small and its economic health critically dependent on international trade. Canada had no security of access to its two major markets. Despite the flood of negotiating activity with European and Commonwealth[46] countries, Canada still did not have a trade agreement with either the United States or Britain and was, therefore, at the mercy of changing policies in these countries.

The notorious (1930) US Smoot-Hawley Tariff Act, for example, not only raised nominal tariff rates to an average of over 50 percent, but it also enacted various other devices to protect American producers from foreign competition, including new antidumping and countervailing duty provisions.[47] Notes US historian Edward Kaplan: "The Tariff antagonized every element of the Canadian population. The tariff on halibut was doubled, offending the eastern provinces; tariff duties on potatoes, milk, cream, and butter were radically increased, angering the populations of Quebec and Ontario; the prairie and western provinces were provoked by increasing duties on cattle and fresh meats; British Columbia and Alberta criticized the high duties on apples, logs, and lumber."[48] Canada had sold more than $21 million in live cattle and almost $102 million in wheat on US markets in 1920-1, when both entered free of duty. Comparable figures in 1930-1 were $764,000 and $6.5 million following imposition of the Smoot-Hawley Tariff.[49] This same depressing pattern was evident in other sectors, but since Canada had no agreement rights, there was little the government could do. More for symbolic than substantive reasons, Canada for the first time decided to retaliate, and Liberal finance minister Charles Dunning brought in a budget in 1930 that contained countervailing duties on US products and a broad extension of preferences for Commonwealth and MFN trading partners. General rates were increased on 54 items and decreased on 46; 35 intermediate rates were increased and 98 decreased; and only 11 British preferential rates were increased compared to 270 decreases. Dunning, rather than adopting the American principle of high tariffs, counterattacked with increased discrimination. Some 589 out of a total of 1,188 tariff items now entered free under the British Preference column.[50]

It was a moderate response. Canadians, however, were no longer prepared to listen to moderation; desperate times called for desperate measures. In the election of that year, the new Conservative leader, R.B. Bennett, insisted that Canada should not only discriminate by strengthening imperial ties but, even more importantly, should structure and administer its tariff so as to ensure that imports would be limited to goods that could not be produced in Canada. Canada should then use its own high tariffs as a bargaining lever to "blast open" world markets. Building on the industrial policy of the National Policy, he would pursue import-substitution even further. Canadians liked his approach and in the election of 1930 gave him a strong mandate.

Once in office, Bennett set to work to increase rates, including those that applied to British goods, although these continued to enjoy a preference. The Tories had always maintained that Grit preferences gave the United Kingdom something for nothing. As he raised rates, Bennett indicated he was prepared to lower British preferential rates in return for preferential concessions in the British market. In the face of falling prices, *ad valorem* rates were converted to specific rates. In addition, much artful use was to be made of administrative devices such as valuation and antidumping duties to increase the protective effect of the tariff.[51]

Nominal levels of protection had declined somewhat during the 1920s, but they had increased elsewhere to such an extent that Canada had the appearance of one of the more liberal countries. The background documents prepared for the World Economic Conference of 1927, for example, calculated the level of the Canadian tariff in 1925 at 23 percent, compared to 37, 29, and 27 percent respectively for the United States, Argentina, and Australia, the other principal resource-based new economies. Protection was calculated to be somewhat higher in Spain and Central Europe, somewhat lower in France, Italy, and Germany, and much lower in Sweden, Holland, Belgium, Switzerland, and Britain. Bennett could thus make a convincing case that there was room for more protection in Canada.[52]

Canada's nominal tariff levels understated the effective levels of protection already in place in Canada (see table 4.8). The combined impact of tariff escalation, holes in the tariff, the use of drawbacks, bounties, and antidumping duties, and such clever administrative devices as valuation, made-in-Canada, and end-use provisions, seasonal rates, content requirements, value brackets, temporary reductions,

Table 4.8

Structure of Canadian protection, 1933 and 1936 (nominal average rates of duty, selected sectors)

Sector	Preferential[a]		Treaty[b]		General[c]		Impact[d]	
	1933	1936	1933	1936	1933	1936	1933	1936
All iron and steel products	10	6	23	21	25	25	33	34
All manufactures	14	10	25	24	30	30	13	14
All textiles	21	20	39	41	45	49	17	16
Electrical apparatus	16	12	30	29	34	33	17	18
Furniture	22	18	32	31	49	49	–	–
Glass and its products	12	7	23	20	26	25	56	67
Leather boots and shoes	24	20	37	37	43	43	2	3
Petroleum products	10	7	15	16	21	18	13	12

a Rate for goods imported from Great Britain and the rest of the Empire.
b The United States was entitled to this rate only after 1935.
c Rate for goods imported from all other countries, including the United States until 1935.
d Ratio of imports to gross value of Canadian production.
Source: Royal Commission on Dominion-Provincial Relations, Book 1, *Canada: 1867-1939* (Ottawa: King's Printer, 1939), p. 157, table 53.

and classification provided Canadian manufacturers with much more protection than appeared to be the case on the surface. Canada had gone further than almost any other country in developing the administration of the tariff as a protective device. Canada was not a liberal trading country, and Liberal policies had offered much more than the claimed incidental protection. Bennett, however, greatly added to this protection.[53]

Clever as this protection might have been from a political standpoint, it did little for a country that needed foreign markets to sell its surplus production and underpin its economic development. During the 1920s, Canadian exports had grown more quickly than those of any other country and Canadians had become critically dependent on these export receipts. The Canadian market could never absorb all this production. The real answer to Canada's economic woes during the depression, therefore, did not lie in increased protection at home but in decreased protection abroad. Canada needed access to markets. For that, Bennett turned to Britain and the Empire.

The Consolidation of British Preferences
As we have seen, the Import Duties Act of 1932 committed Britain not only to protection but to discrimination. The stage was now set for the full-scale development of imperial preferences at the 1932 Imperial Economic Conference in Ottawa. At the 1930 Imperial Conference in London, Bennett had convinced his colleagues of the need for a conference to discuss trade and other economic issues. Here the dominions could establish a true system of imperial preferences as one of the principal tools for rebuilding their shattered economies.[54] The British government reluctantly agreed without making any commitment to Bennett's scheme. But fate intervened. The conference, originally scheduled for 1931, was delayed. As a result, the British delegation came from the newly installed National coalition government, which brought a wholly different perspective to the gathering.

Hosting the Imperial Economic Conference was to be the crowning achievement of the Bennett government, and every precaution was taken to ensure its success. Bennett appointed O.D. Skelton, a former professor of political economy at Queen's University brought in by Mackenzie King to be his principal foreign policy advisor, to take charge of the substantive preparations. Bennett had at first been suspicious of Skelton's political leanings but had learned to rely on him at the 1930 conference. To prepare the trade policy dimension, Skelton established an interdepartmental committee of officials from Trade and Commerce, Finance, National Revenue, and External Affairs, which included Norman Robertson, Dana Wilgress, and Hector McKinnon, soon to be Canada's premier trade negotiating team. They prepared some twenty detailed position papers and showed for the first time that the public service was coming of age and was capable of contributing to the development of policy. To provide advice on monetary matters, Skelton hired a Queen's protégé,

Clifford Clark, who would stay on for the next twenty years as deputy minister of the Department of Finance.[55]

But Bennett was not altogether confident of the advice being prepared for him by these members of the permanent service. He relied on the commissioner of customs, R.W. Breadner, a former official of the Canadian Manufacturers' Association, as well as Bennett's brother-in-law, W.E. Herridge, to advise him on trade matters. Both were inclined to bolster Bennett's natural protectionist inclinations. Breadner had already proven his value to Bennett in the advice he had given on the 1930 and 1931 budgets. Their increased tariff rates were very much in line with CMA thinking. If nothing else, these high rates gave Canada something to bargain with in trying to reduce the high American rates and to interest Britain in an expanded system of imperial preferences.

The conference was a major event not only in the life of the capital but in the evolution of the Commonwealth as successor to the Empire. It coincided with the Statute of Westminster, which gave statutory recognition to the increasingly independent foreign policy role being assumed by the dominions. From now on there would be no legal impediments to the dominions entering into their own treaties. At the conference, Britain's delegation was headed by the president of the privy council, Stanley Baldwin, accompanied by six ministers and more than eighty officials. Canada's delegation was headed by Bennett and included thirteen cabinet ministers and sixty-four advisors. The other dominions were represented by smaller delegations but were equally determined to make the conference the event of the decade.[56]

The work of the conference proceeded on two fronts. Bennett presided over plenary sessions aimed at general debate and the adoption of nonbinding resolutions, while his ministers, as well as the senior members of other delegations, negotiated a series of bilateral accords. Canada had already initiated discussions the previous year with the other dominions and by the end of the conference had concluded or revised trade agreements with Australia, New Zealand, South Africa, the Irish Free State, and Rhodesia. The other dominions concurrently negotiated with each other and with the United Kingdom. In each of these agreements, the members of the emerging Commonwealth had bound preferences to each other and adjusted preferential, MFN (treaty), and general rates up and down to meet each other's requests. Bound concessions were thus further cemented into place on a Commonwealth-wide basis, including with Britain. They would in future become a source of conflict in both bilateral and multilateral negotiations.

The Ottawa conference, despite its failure to construct a comprehensive Commonwealth-wide trade and economic policy, suggested a way to negotiate trade agreements on a bilateral basis within a multilateral and commonly agreed framework. Indirectly, they prepared the United Kingdom, Canada, and the other dominions for the multilateral negotiations to come. As such, the Commonwealth negotiations proved more important and fruitful than efforts in the 1920s and 1930s to negotiate agreements under the auspices of the League of Nations.

For Canada, the most important of the bilateral negotiations involved the conclusion of its first-ever trade agreement with the United Kingdom, a negotiation for which Bennett took personal responsibility. Bennett's objective at the conference, as devised by Breadner, was to gain as much preference as possible without sacrificing the high level of protection now afforded existing as well as potential Canadian manufacturers. Canada was more interested, for example, in convincing Britain to increase its general rates than in lowering its own. More specifically, Canada sought better access for its natural products to the British market in return for concessions on items that were not made or likely to be made in Canada. Bennett was interested in inducing more import-substitution and not at all interested in any export-oriented manufacturing.

The British team, however, were taken neither by Bennett's conduct in the plenary sessions nor by his excessively self-serving approach to the bilateral negotiations. They saw little to be gained from opening the British market to Canadian goods as long as Canada continued to levy high duties on British goods, nor were they interested in increasing discrimination against Britain's European trading partners in return for preferential access to the markets of the dominions. Bennett got nowhere and finally had to concede that Breadner was perhaps not well placed to give disinterested advice. In the end, he turned to Skelton's team of officials and instructed them to patch together a more realistic position and try to convince the United Kingdom that Canada was prepared to make a defensible offer. The conference ended, however, with an agreement that satisfied neither delegation and with the recognition that negotiations would have to be continued later. Skelton's officials were unable to satisfy Britain's offer of free entry for food and industrial raw materials in exchange for duty-free access for Britain's manufactures. The best they could do was widen margins of preference by agreeing to increase the MFN tariff. The Canadian schedule to the agreement contained 215 concessions, of which 83 involved raising rates on imports from non-Commonwealth countries.

Britain and the dominions were not alone in pursuing preferences. The French, Belgian, and Dutch governments also extended preferences to trade with their colonial dependencies, and even the United States gave preferences to imports from Cuba and the Philippines. What differentiated the British system of preferences was both the size of the trade involved and its extension to the autonomous dominions. The result was unquestioned trade diversion at a time when trade was already disturbed. Table 4.9 illustrates the diversion that took place in the United Kingdom's trade with the Empire before and after the consolidation of preferences. In 1928, 35 percent of Canada's exports went to British markets; by 1938, the level had risen to 46 percent. In 1929-30, only 2 to 3 percent of Britain's imports and 5 percent of her exports involved preferential arrangements; by 1937, this had risen to 10 to 11 percent of both imports and exports.[57]

Table 4.9

Imperial preferences and trade diversion in the United Kingdom, 1931 and 1938

Country	% of UK exports		% of UK imports	
	1931	1938	1931	1938
Australia	3.7	8.1	5.3	7.8
Canada	5.3	4.8	3.8	8.6
India	8.3	7.7	4.3	6.1
Irish Free State	7.8	4.3	4.2	2.5
New Zealand	2.9	4.1	4.4	5.1
South Africa	5.6	8.4	1.5	1.6
Rest of Empire	10.1	12.5	5.2	8.7
Total Empire	43.7	49.9	28.7	40.4

Source: Richard Pomfret, *Unequal Trade: The Economics of Discriminatory Trade Policies* (Oxford: Basil Blackwell, 1988), table 3.3.

While the conference did advance the cause of imperial preferences and a policy aimed at encouraging intra-Commonwealth trade, it had a more interesting influence unrelated to these objectives. The conference demonstrated the inadequacy of ministers and prime ministers as lead negotiators. The issues had become too detailed and intricate to be dealt with at the political level. They now needed sophisticated staff work and quiet negotiations at the level of officials to prepare the ground for final ministerial and prime ministerial sessions. The bilateral negotiations with the United Kingdom had shown the shortcomings of the old era as well as the promise of the new. Realization of these changes set Canada on the road toward establishing a modern trade policy developed and delivered by a team of professional administrators and negotiators. Preparation for the conference had encouraged the habit of interdepartmental consultation. It had also limited the advice of outside business consultants in favour of specialists with a strong academic background. Bennett was a big enough man to recognize that he had been well served by Skelton and his colleagues, and he now gave them the room to put Canadian trade policy and negotiations on a more sustainable footing.

The conference also came at a time when the government's main trade policy objectives had become less relevant for Canada, as a result of shifting attitudes and changing trade patterns. The advent of mass transportation and entertainment brought Canadians into increasingly close contact with their neighbours to the south. The war, while it had strengthened government relations between Britain and the dominions, had introduced more balance into popular attitudes toward Britain and the United States. Britain could now do wrong and the United States could occasionally do right. By 1930 the fond attachment to the Empire had become more tenuous, and suspicion of the United States less resolute.

Between 1910 and 1930, Canadian trade had also diversified. Britain's importance had declined as the importance of the United States had increased, and third countries now took a respectable share of Canada's exports (see table 4.5 above). The United States had also replaced Britain as Canada's principal source of investment capital, with the added difference that most of this came in the form of direct rather than portfolio investment.[58] Close economic relations between Canada and the United States were a fact even if government policy did not yet recognize it. The bilateral agreement with the United Kingdom and the arrangements with the other dominions were a positive achievement, as was the network of interlocking preferences these agreements established, but what Canada needed even more was a trade agreement with the United States that would roll back some of the excesses of its protectionist trade policy and remove the need for countervailing tariffs.

An immediate challenge faced the new team of professionals: Canada still did not have adequate trade arrangements with its two main trading partners. In reaching mutually beneficial agreements with the United Kingdom and the United States, however, the negotiators had to take into account the legacy of the Ottawa conference: high rates and contractually bound preferences, the two elements that the Liberal opposition attacked when the results of the conference were announced but that proved most popular with the business community.

The difficulties Canada faced and the role played by Canadian and other trade policies were by now more widely appreciated. The effect on Canada of the 1928 collapse of the world grain market and the precipitous decline of trade as a whole

Table 4.10

Growth in the Canadian economy, 1931-9 (in millions of current dollars)

	1931	1934	1937	1939
GNP	4,693	3,969	5,241	5,621
Merchandise exports	601	648	1,041	906
Merchandise imports	580	484	776	713
Current account balance	−174	+68	+180	+126
Net long-term capital movement	+113	−91	−158	−136
Domestic investment	622	298	633	592
Steam railway mileage	42,280	42,270	42,727	42,637
Wheat acreage (000)	26,355	25,991	25,605	26,757
Terms of trade (1948 = 100)	96.1	91.8	105.1	95.6
Wholesale price index (1934-9 = 100)	94.0	93.4	108.4	99.0
Population (000)	10,377	10,741	11,045	11,267

Sources: F.H. Leacy, ed., *Historical Statistics of Canada,* 2nd ed. (Ottawa: Statistics Canada, 1983); *Canada Year Book,* 1945 (Ottawa: Dominion Bureau of Statistics, various years); J.A. Stovel, *Canada in the World Economy* (Cambridge, MA: Harvard University Press, 1959), table 27.

had been disastrous (see table 4.10). By 1933, exports had fallen to 45 percent of their 1929 levels, while imports had fallen to 31 percent. The volume of Canadian trade recovered by the end of the decade, but because prices remained low, many export industries remained vulnerable. The output of Canadian industry as a whole fell by 30 percent on the basis of constant prices between 1929 and 1933, and had not yet fully recovered by 1938. Unemployment rose from 5 to more than 27 percent and stayed high, exacerbated by the natural disaster of the failed harvests on the Prairies in the middle years of the decade. Most historians have concluded that Canada probably suffered a greater reversal in fortunes during the depression than any other country. The importance of trade to Canada's well-being in the past underlined the need for Canada to find access for its products, particularly in its closest market. The prospect of gaining that kind of access was dim at the beginning of the 1930s but looked increasingly promising as the decade wore on.[59]

The Reversal of US Trade Policy

Just as Bennett concluded that it was time for a change in the way Canadian trade policy was made and executed, a farsighted American came to the same conclusion for his country. The United States Constitution gives Congress the authority to make trade policy, and this it had done for the previous century and a half. Presidents had made suggestions and administered the results, but Congress had set the policy. The main policy-making instrument was the tariff bill, adopted every few years by the two houses, sometimes on the advice of the president and sometimes not. Given the log-rolling that takes place in the American legislative process, the result had historically appealed more to narrow than to broad interests. Said one senator after the passage of the Smoot-Hawley Tariff, "The existing minuteness with respect to rates is partly an absurdity and partly a partisan fraud to cover what the tariff really is – namely a mass of private legislation."[60]

Originally the American tariff, like the colonial tariff in Canada, had been largely geared to raising revenue but increasingly, as America industrialized, it had become equipped to provide protection.[61] After the Civil War, extensive use was made of the free list, that is, goods that entered free of duty, to offset increases in the rates applied to manufactured goods.[62] As a result, the aggregate incidence of the tariff on a duty-collected basis might have declined, but the aggregate incidence of the tariff on dutiable imports continued to increase, providing analysts with statistics to satisfy whatever point they wanted to make. Every three or four years rates were adjusted. With the brief exception of the periods from 1846 to 1860 (the prelude to the Civil War) and 1913 to 1922 (from the Underwood Tariff to the Fordney-McCumber Tariff), the direction was generally to increase protection, taking account of changing producer and user interests.[63] Where it counted, the US tariff was high and wide, successfully shielding the US economy from foreign competition (see table 4.11).

One of the by-products of congressional trade policy making was that the United States had enjoyed very little success in negotiating trade agreements. What was

Table 4.11

Trade-weighted average rates of duty, United States, 1910-61

		% of imports duty free	Equivalent *ad valorem* rate (%)	
			Dutiable	Total
Years	Tariff legislation		imports	imports
1910-13	Payne-Aldrich Tariff	52	41	19
1914-22	Underwood Tariff	66	27	9
1923-30	Fordney-McCumber Tariff	64	39	14
1930-3	Smoot-Hawley Tariff	66	53	18
1934	Reciprocal Trade Agreements Act	61	47	18
1935-9	Reciprocal Trade Agreements Act	59	39	16
1940-8	Reciprocal Trade Agreements Act	63	25	9
1949-61	Reciprocal Trade Agreements Act	51	12	6

Source: Hugh McA. Pinchin, *The Regional Impact of the Canadian Tariff: A Study Prepared for the Economic Council of Canada* (Ottawa: Supply and Services, 1979), table 1-2. Reproduced with the permission of the Minister of Public Works and Government Services Canada, 2001. The findings of this Study are the personal responsibility of the author and, as such, have not been endorsed by Members of the Economic Council of Canada.

negotiated rarely gained Senate approval; what did gain approval was usually not worthwhile. The United States had followed "an independent, autonomous, non-bargaining tariff policy"[64] and had not, for example, participated in the Cobden-Chevalier system of bilateral MFN treaties. As late as 1929, President Hoover could still insist that "there is no practical force in the contention that we cannot have a protective tariff and a growing trade."[65]

The US tariff was thus unaffected by any international obligations. Between 1776 and 1934, presidents had made attempts to negotiate tariff agreements using their treaty-making authority. Only three of these were ever ratified by the Senate and brought into force: the 1854 Elgin-Marcy Treaty with Canada, an 1875 agreement with Hawaii, and an 1898 agreement with Cuba. Only the Cuban agreement was in force by the 1930s. Starting with the McKinley Tariff of 1890, presidents had been given some authority to negotiate reciprocal agreements aimed at opening up foreign markets, but most of the negotiations failed miserably since the authority was based on threat rather than promise. Congress had not given the president authority either to reduce US tariffs or to bind them against further increase; rather, it had authorized him to forego retaliation if the foreign country agreed to extend its MFN tariff to the United States.[66]

US governments had been prepared to live with this situation when US exports were largely confined to the raw materials that were not generally available from other suppliers and that consequently enjoyed easy access. Once the United States

began to export manufactures, however, and found its resource producers competing with, for example, Canadian and Argentine producers, efforts were made to
open foreign markets. These efforts met with little success, as American negotiators
could promise neither lower tariffs, nor unconditional MFN treatment, nor Senate
ratification.[67] Viewed in this light, the aborted reciprocity agreement with Canada
in 1911, proposed by the president and passed by both the House and the Senate,
was even more of an aberration in the United States than it was in Canada. This fact
alone had been enough to earn the distrust with which it was viewed by its Canadian opponents.

Against this background, the Smoot-Hawley Tariff Act of 1930 does not seem all
that noteworthy. In response to the agricultural crisis of 1928, Republican presidential candidate Herbert Hoover had proposed a special session of Congress to raise
the tariff on agricultural goods. Congress obliged, but in response to aggressive
lobbying, quickly turned to the tariff as a whole. The tone of the discussion led to a
wave of domestic and international anxiety. Some thirty-four governments protested what was being proposed, and 1,028 professional economists signed a petition urging President Hoover to veto the act. While some of the criticism was directed
at specific tariff changes, critics noted more generally that the United States was a
creditor nation and as such ought to increase rather than decrease export opportunities for debtor nations, ensuring greater balance in international payments.[68]

The final act pushed tariffs to a height seen only once before in the 1828 Tariff of
Abominations. Given the increasing importance of the United States in the world
economy, Smoot-Hawley contributed to converting a sizeable recession into a severe depression, not only in the United States, but around the world.[69] The product
of hundreds of individual proposals and amendments by representatives and senators responding to special interests, the Tariff Act of 1930 became from the moment
it was proposed a worldwide symbol of the excesses of protectionism. As a result of
falling prices and the large number of specific tariffs, the average rate of protection
on dutiable products reached almost 60 percent in 1931, and, through the continued process of splitting tariff classifications, it provided tremendous scope for arbitrary administration.[70] Even today the names of Smoot and Hawley are synonymous
with protectionism. Both went down to defeat in the 1932 election.

The election of Franklin Delano Roosevelt in 1932 offered an overpowering mandate to roll back the tariff and, more generally, to reform the unsatisfactory system
that had given rise to it. As in Canada, US trade levels had fallen precipitously, and
trade policy came in for its share of criticism and blame, adding fuel to calls for
substantial change. The person assigned to the task was Cordell Hull, a man much
influenced by the work of Taussig and Viner and now appointed as secretary of
state. Hull had been the ranking Democrat on the House Ways and Means Committee when it studied and debated the Smoot-Hawley Tariff Act. He submitted a
minority report that still stands as a compelling defence of the principles of free
trade. Smoot-Hawley offended not only his Southern free-trade convictions but

also his internationalist views that open, nondiscriminatory commerce between nations was a critical ingredient for world peace.

As a Wilsonian Democrat, Hull had long believed that the United States needed to take a more activist and constructive role on the world stage, particularly in economic matters. In 1916, commenting on the role commercial rivalry had played in driving the combatants to war, he told the House of Representatives: "Apart from its essential injustice to the people, [high tariffs] have become a positive menace to the peace of all trade countries. It is naturally utilized for purposes of rank discrimination, practical boycotting, undue preferences, and other irritating practices ... It is a matter of common knowledge that the operation of the many unfair, injurious, and trouble-making trade practices and the strenuous trade conquests pursued under these systems chiefly contributed to the outbreak of the present European war." And then followed his vision of what the United States should do to rectify this menace. He recommended that the president "propose to the governments of all commercial nations that at the close of the present European war an international trade conference be held ... for the purpose of establishing a permanent international trade congress ... [to consider] all international trade methods, practices, and policies which in their effect are calculated to create destructive commercial controversies or bitter economic wars, and to formulate agreements with respect thereto, designed to eliminate and avoid the injurious results and dangerous possibilities of economic warfare, and to promote fair and friendly trade relations among all nations of the world."[71] Experience since the First World War had demonstrated even further the destructive impact of protectionism and isolationism.[72] In 1932 Hull, then a senator, had been a sponsor of the Collier Bill, which had tried to roll back some of the excesses of the Smoot-Hawley Tariff Act. Passed by Congress, it had been vetoed by President Hoover because it provided for tariff reductions through international negotiations, which Hoover saw as a potential intrusion of foreign policy into what he considered to be a matter of domestic policy.[73]

Hull and his State Department advisors diagnosed the beggar-thy-neighbour policies adopted on both sides of the Atlantic as the main culprits fuelling the worldwide depression and damaging American trading interests. The Smoot-Hawley Tariff might be the most conspicuous example, but other nations had adopted equally protectionist tariff policies and had added currency manipulation, discriminatory quantitative restrictions, and other administrative devices to their bags of tricks.

Hull's own preference was to negotiate multilaterally and mount a wholesale attack on trade barriers, but given the legacy of protectionism, congressional jealousy of its tariff-making authority, suspicion of international entanglements, and the discredited multilateral efforts of the League of Nations, Hull proposed a more modest program of bilateral reciprocal trade agreements. In order to negotiate successfully, Hull needed a more satisfactory policy than had existed heretofore. His views, however, were somewhat at odds with the reigning ideology of the New Deal, which saw the main problem as unemployment and took the unorthodox economic viewpoint that the way forward lay through massive government intervention and planning. The economics of John Kenneth Galbraith were more typical of the New Deal than those of Taussig, Viner, and Gottfried Haberler. Indeed, Galbraith's characterization of Haberler was typical of the young New Dealer's attitude to neoclassical economics: "Gottfried Haberler [and other Austrian émigré economists] believed in the competitive and laissez-faire economy that, through its failures, had been lost in Austria and Germany. In the decades following World War II, Austrian economic policy had been a model of successful, undogmatic pragmatism. None can doubt that it benefited greatly from the emigration of these distinguished scholars to the United States ... Like many others, Haberler associated unthinking commitment to the market and automatic resistance to government intervention with scientific competence."[74]

To counter these views, Hull and his advisors developed an innovative new approach. In 1934, over the objection of more typical New Dealers, they first ensured President Roosevelt's backing for a policy of nondiscrimination and freer trade, and then secured passage of the Reciprocal Trade Agreements Act (RTAA), aimed at giving the United States a realistic trade bargaining policy likely to attract the interest of the world. Under the act, Congress for the first time delegated broad trade policy-making authority to the president. The act set broad goals and objectives that the president could achieve through reciprocal trade agreements that would extend unconditional MFN rights, lower US tariffs up to 50 percent, and bind rates for up to three years – all without the need of Senate ratification.[75]

John Letiche has noted that "the objective of the program was not the adoption of 'free' trade at home, or the insistence upon the removal of all governmental controls abroad; rather, it was the more moderate aim of gradually moving, on a democratic basis, toward freer trade at home and freer and less discriminatory practices abroad."[76] Additionally, the act established the machinery and resources to carry out the necessary analysis, consultations, and negotiations. While the RTAA marked a revolution in US trade policy, it did not emerge out of thin air. The ideas on which it was based had been debated and introduced piecemeal for over a generation.[77] What distinguishes the RTAA is that all the ideas tried out in previous acts had now been rolled into one fully articulated program with a clear vision and a means to implement it. The RTA program, while it might have been a cumbersome and slow instrument for reducing tariffs, had the merit of bypassing Congress on the detail of negotiations, making it possible for US officials to conduct serious negotiations.

Over the next six years, until war slowed the program, Hull's team negotiated twenty-two agreements with Canada and Latin American and European nations. By 1947, on the eve of the new postwar multilateral negotiations that would spawn the General Agreement on Tariffs and Trade (GATT), twenty-nine countries had taken advantage of the program to gain improved and secure access to what was by then the largest and most dynamic economy in the world. The average level of US tariffs at the beginning of the program approached 60 percent; by 1947, it had been reduced to under 30 percent for participants in the program. By mutual agreement, the United States and twenty-nine of its trading partners had reduced tariffs, enlarged or eliminated quotas, liberalized exchange controls, bound thousands of tariff levels, and entered into long-term commitments to end discrimination and develop a body of international trade rules.[78]

Economically, the program was also a success. For the period prior to the outbreak of war, trade increased more rapidly between agreement countries than non-agreement countries, and by the end of the 1930s trade was back to its pre-1929 levels. By using the principal-supplier rule as the basic starting point for all negotiations (concessions were generally limited to products for which the agreement country was the principal supplier), the US negotiators had ensured that concessions exchanged would be meaningful and lead to new trading opportunities. Adherence to the unconditional MFN principle ensured that all participants in the program would benefit from all negotiations without necessarily needing to make new concessions.

Adoption of the reciprocal trade agreements program marked a revolution in US trade policy. It radically altered not only the basic orientation of US trade policy (from a built-in bias favouring protection to one favouring liberalization), but also the process by which it was formulated and delivered. Congress now blessed the adoption of a "bargaining" tariff and, through delegation of its power over the detail of tariff making, married the making of trade and foreign policy. The detail of both would now be the responsibility of administration officials, pursuing their work within guidelines established in consultation with the president and the Congress.

As part of that delegation, Congress wrote detailed rules covering other terms of access for imports and assigned their administration to the courts and to quasi-judicial tribunals. Whereas, in the evolution of Canadian trade policy, governments relied on creative and flexible use of the broad instruments available to them, particularly the tariff, Congress and the US administration relied heavily on detailed rule making and legalistic but transparent administration of these rules. By confining its activity to broad rule making and goal setting and leaving the details to the administration, courts, and tribunals, Congress solved for the next few generations the problem of how to deal with the hundreds of special interests clamouring for protection. As a result, the details of trade policy making became a professional, non-partisan activity pursued within broad guidelines that had wide political support.[79]

It is fashionable today to criticize the achievements of the Hull program and note that the United States could have afforded an even more open trade policy in the 1930s. As the only country with a large economy and a chronic trade surplus, it was practising the same policies that in later days it would find so offensive in Japan. All this may be true, but set in the context of contemporary US politics, Hull's achievement was considerable. It committed the United States to a policy of nondiscrimination and gradual trade liberalization and provided a legal and institutional basis for making that policy realizable. This revolution made it possible for Hull to change the direction of US trade policy, a change in direction that had global repercussions.[80]

At the beginning of the 1930s, the United States had adopted a trade policy that contributed to making the depression deeper, longer, and more miserable than might otherwise have been the case. By the end of the decade, the United States had adopted a policy that was pointed in the opposite direction, capable of providing the world with the means to stimulate growth and to prevent recurrence of the excesses of the 1930s. Notes Richard Pomfret: "The 1930 Hawley-Smoot tariff and its aftermath illustrated the dangers of a world trading system based on autonomous tariff policies."[81] The adoption of the reciprocal trade agreements program and the agreements it spawned showed the potential of a return to a world trading system based on interlocking tariff and other trade commitments.

There was one major flaw in the generally positive results that flowed from the Hull program: they did not extend to agriculture. Much of the focus of tariff changes in first the Fordney-McCumber Tariff and then in the Smoot-Hawley Tariff had been in response to the difficulties experienced by the agricultural sector. These problems did not disappear. The response of the Roosevelt administration was to introduce radical changes in the Agricultural Adjustment Act of 1933, which effectively isolated American agriculture from the world market. These changes became the bedrock of American farm policy for the next fifty years, and proved impervious to any proposals for change. As Judith Goldstein concludes:

> In sum, as the United States embarked on the creation of a new liberal international trade regime, its own domestic policy was mired with inconsistencies. Although the State Department was unequivocal on the benefits of multilateral trade liberalization for the American economy, the Department of Agriculture declared simultaneously that under no conditions could the United States delegate control over import protection for farm products. It was not that the intrinsic interests of the agricultural sector were orthogonal to trade liberalization. By the late 1940s, the prosperity of American agriculture was clearly associated with exports: the United States was supplying 39 percent of the world's wheat, 41 percent of the tobacco, and 49 percent of the cotton. Few could ignore the importance of agriculture to America's export economy. Yet both farm groups and elected officials were politically wedded to government controls on price and supply. It would take twenty years for producers and political leaders to realize the costs of this strategy.[82]

For Canada, the effective absence of farm products from the reciprocal trade agreements program was a major disappointment, particularly in later years as the UK and other markets closed to some of Canada's traditional, nongrain farm exports. The result was a resort to protectionist actions that preserved at least the Canadian market to suppliers of some of these commodities.

THE WANDERING BOY

Arch Dale, "The Wandering Boy," 3 May 1933. Canadian manufacturers were not pleased when R.B. Bennett began to court US president Roosevelt following passage of the US Reciprocal Trade Agreements Act.

Canada Responds

Given Canada's long-standing interest in more open and more secure access to the US market, the revolution in Washington called for a response in Ottawa. Already in 1933, Bennett had cautiously shown an interest in opening negotiations, but it soon became apparent that the existing trade policy framework in Washington and the Canadian attachment to imperial preferences made any significant break-throughs unlikely.

Adoption of the reciprocal trade agreements program changed the balance, and it was not long before overtures were again made to Washington. US experience in the first few years of the program showed the benefits of a fully thought out and consistent trade policy, carried out by professional staff with the necessary resources and flexibility to get the job done. It was a lesson also learned in Canada, although on a more modest scale. No minister or prime minister would ever again lead a major trade negotiation. Instead, Bennett turned to the professionals. Norman Robertson, trade and economic specialist at External Affairs, Hector McKinnon, commissioner of tariffs in the Department of Finance, and Dana Wilgress, head of the Trade Intelligence Service at Trade and Commerce, took on the task and for the next twenty years dominated the negotiation of trade agreements for Canada. Wilgress took charge of Canada's export interests, McKinnon looked after Canada's import concerns, and Robertson provided integration and leadership.

Canada-US negotiations were finally joined in the summer of 1935, by which time it was clear that the two countries were prepared to pursue more compatible objectives than had been the case a few years earlier. Both wanted to exchange MFN status, that is, make US goods eligible for the intermediate tariff in Canada while Canadian goods continued to enjoy the MFN tariff in the United States. In addition, Canada wanted to reduce the US MFN tariff on a list of primary products and gain contractual guarantees that certain products would stay on the free list, while the United States wanted to improve access for US manufactures to the Canadian market. US flexibility was somewhat reduced by adherence to the principal-supplier rule; Canadian ability to respond to US requests was hampered by some of its bound margins of imperial preferences. Progress was slower than anticipated, and by the end of August negotiations were suspended to await the results of the Canadian election.[83]

If anything, the return of Mackenzie King proved a positive omen for the Canada-US negotiations. He campaigned on the theme that the absence of trade equalled depression and that renewed trade would spell the end of depression. Increasing protection in Canada had not proved helpful. Canada needed to export. It needed an agreement with the United States that would open markets and set the tone for more such agreements with other countries. Briefed before the election on the progress that had been made, King immediately instructed Robertson and his team to go back to Washington to conclude negotiations in time for signature during his first visit to Washington under the new administration. The officials complied and King and Hull, without much public fanfare, signed the agreement on 15 November.[84]

Implementing the agreement ran into the kind of US strong-arming that often leaves an unpleasant aftertaste in Canada-US trade relations. US treasury secretary Henry Morgenthau believed that Canada's interest in the agreement provided him with leverage to get even with Canadian distillers for their wanton disregard of Prohibition in the 1920s. Even though Prohibition had been lifted three years earlier, he thought they should pay a fine of $100 million if they were to get the benefit of a 50 percent reduction in the US tariff on whisky. Only the strong intervention of President Roosevelt and Canadian agreement to a token fine of $3 million removed Morgenthau's opportunistic opposition.[85]

There had been little public discussion, nor was there much parliamentary debate, but the 1935 agreement marked the end of an era. Ever since the United States had abrogated the 1854 Elgin-Marcy Treaty, Canada had continually sought a return to reciprocity. It had almost achieved success in 1911, only to have the Laurier government defeated at the polls. King had been a young member of that government,

A smiling President Roosevelt and a bevy of Canadian and US officials witness the signing of the 1935 Canada-US Reciprocal Trade Agreement by US secretary of state Cordell Hull and Prime Minister Mackenzie King.

and the election had sent him into the political wilderness for the next ten years. This time, he took no chances. The agreement quietly went into effect in 1936, with no more than a pro forma parliamentary debate.[86]

Strictly speaking, the agreement was not a reciprocity agreement. Nevertheless, it was a fitting heir to that tradition and in many ways contained broader obligations. The 1854 agreement had been a three-line affair to which were appended twenty-eight items that both sides agreed to place on their free list. The 1911 arrangement had been described in a three-page exchange of letters, largely devoted to the approval procedure, and included four schedules of specific tariff concessions. The 1935 agreement was set out in fifteen articles plus two schedules setting out the specific tariff concessions. This time the text was more important than the schedules, since it set out reciprocal obligations to grant most-favoured-nation and national treatment, to extend fair and equitable treatment in state-trading practices and exchange controls, and not to impose quotas except in specified circumstances. As a result of the unconditional MFN commitment, Canada and the United States benefited not only from the specific commitments in the agreement, but also from tariff reductions negotiated with other MFN countries, thus increasing Canada's potential gains.[87]

Despite the fact that the agreement was more extensive than anything that had been contemplated in the past, the two sides rejoined discussions within two years of its signature in order to improve its provisions. By this time Robertson and his team had visited the United Kingdom and renegotiated the 1932 agreement, and the United States had entered into negotiations with Britain to extend the provisions of their 1815 treaty on Friendship, Commerce, and Navigation (FCN). The Canadian team now had four years of experience as trade negotiators, as well as four years of results, and had been able to conclude a more balanced agreement with the United Kingdom in 1936 than was possible in 1932. Canada agreed to improve access for British goods, and both countries agreed to retreat somewhat from the restrictions on their bargaining leverage imposed by preferences. The King government used both the US and British negotiations, and its first few budgets, to roll back some of the higher tariffs imposed by the Bennett government (see table 4.8 above). As well, it continued a policy begun by Bennett of bringing more order into imperial preferences by establishing uniform British preferential (BP) rates applied to all British and Commonwealth products, whether or not there were contractual obligations to do so.

The 1937-8 bilateral negotiations with the United States had a double purpose. They built on the 1935 agreement, and they addressed the serious problem raised for Canada and the United Kingdom by imperial preferences. The 1932 agreement with the United Kingdom, for example, had improved access for UK goods worth $14 million that year but had disadvantaged $36 million in imports from the United States. Similarly, in its 1937 negotiations with the United States, the United Kingdom could not meet a number of requests because of its preferential obligations to the dominions, principally Canada. In order to satisfy the United States, the United Kingdom had to be released from these obligations. Canada insisted that if it was to release the United Kingdom, it wanted a voice in the negotiations. The United States and the United Kingdom reluctantly agreed and a tripartite negotiating process was devised. By the end of the negotiations, the United Kingdom additionally needed to take account of the views of Australia and New Zealand, thus anticipating the multilateral negotiating process in Geneva a decade later.

Within a framework of unconditional MFN negotiations, any bilateral concession is of benefit to all other participants in the system, but when some of the participants are parties to a preferential system, a concession to a nonpreference partner may undermine an existing concession to a preference partner. These were the complications that US, British, and Canadian negotiators faced in 1937-8.[88] Progress was made, however, and at the end of 1938, Canada and the United States signed a much more ambitious agreement than had been possible in 1935. The twenty-four pages of text agreed in 1935 had been expanded to sixty-four. In addition to more tariff concessions, the text had been extensively revised to remove any ambiguities and to take account of the experience of both sides in the intervening two years. Additionally, a number of specific irritants had been resolved in side letters, including a US complaint about high levels of Canadian softwood lumber exports. Again, despite the broad implications of the agreement, public attention focused on specific concessions rather than on the fact that Canada and the United States had entered into a reciprocal trade agreement more extensive than one that had caused a government to be defeated a generation earlier.[89]

Although Bennett in retirement denounced the agreement and the Canadian Manufacturers' Association bemoaned the loss of protection, general opinion was highly favourable. Canadian trade policy had matured, in part because of its professionalization. The removal of ministers from the detail of the policy began also to remove trade policy issues from the high agenda of politicians to the low agenda of the bureaucrats.

More important, the period of drift had come to an end. Canada had adopted a clear-sighted trade policy in tune with its domestic interests as well as with its desire to play a larger role on the world stage. Its economic interests in wider markets would need to be addressed if trade was to continue to stimulate growth in the Canadian economy, but a successful foundation had been laid to accommodate larger ambitions and more beneficial results.

5 MULTILATERAL DREAMS

The successful outcome of the triangular negotiations of 1938 served to stabilize trade relations with the two chief outlets for Canadian products. A goal had been achieved towards which Canadians had been striving ever since the days of Canada's immaturity as a nation. In reaching this goal Canada had won the respect and high regard of her trading partners. The basis was laid for that partnership, which would take the lead towards the promotion of world trade through multilateralism.

–Dana Wilgress, Canada's Approach to Trade Negotiations

By the end of the 1930s, Canadian trade had returned to its pre-depression levels, and investment in both resource extraction and secondary manufacturing had largely recovered. The federal government had appointed a royal commission to examine the state of the economy and federal-provincial fiscal arrangements.[1] The commission's hearings and research constituted the first detailed examination of the Canadian economy and of the forces that would lead to growth or to decline. Its report also heralded the end of the drift and confusion in Canada's domestic affairs, an end to a period of frustration and lost opportunities. Historians John Thompson and Allen Seager conclude, "The decades [of the 1920s and 1930s] have an essential unity ... Both were decades of failure, tragedies of missed opportunities. The previous quarter-century had seen the 'nation transformed' by industrialization, urbanization, immigration and westward expansion. These social and economic changes created regional, ethnic, and class divisions that political structures were unable to bridge ... Canada, wrote Arthur Lower after a lifetime of reflection, 'is a country whose major problems are never solved.' During the decades between the two world wars, however, Canada's political leaders did their best to see that those problems were never addressed."[2] Perhaps not, but Prime Minister Mackenzie King and his advisors had solved one of Canada's oldest problems: how to devise a trade policy that would nurture the domestic economy and give Canada's export industries a secure outlet to their two principal markets. They had established a policy that contained sufficient flexibility to allow Canadians to play a large and constructive role in devising an international economic order sensitive to Canada's needs. The coming war would fortify this policy of national self-determination through international cooperation, and the requirements of war would help to strengthen and diversify the economy.

Until the 1930s, Canada had veered back and forth between the United Kingdom and the United States in its approach to trade issues. Critically dependent on both economies, from the late 1870s it had pursued policies that would give it the maximum possible access without compromising the protection required by Canadian industry, or forgoing the needs of the Canadian treasury. Additionally, trade negotiations had proven a useful demonstration of Canada's status as an independent and self-governing Dominion. In response to the disaster of the 1930s, Canada had first turned to the United Kingdom and the Commonwealth, negotiating the Ottawa preferential agreements. It had then turned to the United States and participated in the new reciprocal trade agreements program.

By the end of the 1930s, the policy was clear: Canada wanted and could have good trade relations with both of its major trading partners and should avoid isolating itself in an alliance with one or the other. It was a policy that enjoyed broad support. The bitter partisan debates of the past seemed to have been buried and the opposition of the Canadian Manufacturers' Association (CMA) and other special interests placed into perspective. Canada was now negotiating and entering into agreements clearly in its own right and pursuing Canadian economic objectives without much reference to the emotional overtones of the British connection or the threat of American dominance. From the point of view of the professionals in Ottawa, however, the American connection seemed to hold more promise for the future. Wrote External Affairs' Norman Robertson to his colleague Lester Pearson: "Triangular trade negotiations – with Australia, South Africa & the Colonial Empire each off at its own peculiar tangent are dreadfully difficult & rather discouraging. I was the last Imperialist in the Dept. of External Affairs – and now I've gone too. You may never have had the 'language difficulty' but I can get on with the Americans a damn sight more easily than with the English & the Australians ... Our direct negotiations with the U.S. are the least of our worries right now. We can cope with them but not with God's Englishmen and the inescapable moral ascendancy over us lesser breeds."[3]

Canada's new-found self-confidence and ability to make agreements with both its trading partners would soon be put to the test. By the end of the 1930s, the United Kingdom and the United States were on a roughly equal footing as Canada's predominant trade and investment partners. War would alter that and, at the same time, greatly improve the prospects for long-term economic prosperity. From 1939 until into the 1970s, the Canadian economy grew prodigiously, underpinning an unprecedented increase in the standard of living. This period of growth saw major changes in the structure of the Canadian economy, completing the transition from farm to factory and ushering in the tremendous growth of the services sector. At the same time, Canadians also discovered that inexorable ties had developed between their continuing prosperity and close relations with the United States.

War and Economic Recovery

War solved the main economic problems of the depression for Canada – unemployment and demand. Canada emerged from the Second World War economically stronger than it had entered it, with a much more diversified industrial structure. While the level of economic activity had by the end of the 1930s almost returned to pre-depression levels, this activity was built on fragile foundations. Neither domestic nor international demand had yet reached the stage at which Canadians could express much confidence about their future, as was well illustrated by the fatalistic tones of the Rowell-Sirois report in 1940. Describing Canada's precarious trading position, the commissioners wrote, "Canada's position in both her trade and financial relations with the outside world is largely that of her position in relation to the United States and the United Kingdom. This position is similar to that of a small man sitting in a big poker game. He must play for the big stakes, but with only a fraction of the capital resources of his two substantial opponents; if he wins, his profits in relation to his capital are very large, and if he loses, he may be cleaned out."[4]

War changed all that, immediately and for many years thereafter. Between 1939 and 1941, in addition to the thousands of men and women taken into the armed forces, domestic employment grew by 50 percent. Unemployment, the main scourge of the depression, had by 1941 become but a bad memory, one that continued, however, to have a profound influence on policy makers. Trade patterns also shifted dramatically. Britain ceased to export and became a major importer of war materiel as well as of food. Canadian exports to Britain increased by 50 percent from 1939 to 1940 and by 300 percent by 1944 (see table 5.1).[5]

One overwhelming factor, however, cast a shadow of continuing doubt over the long-term strength of the Canadian economy. This was not a recovery driven by private demand and supply, but a recovery flowing from the heavy hand of government-controlled mobilization for war. It was the work of many committees and government boards under the direction of C.D. Howe, the government's supreme organizer and friend of business.[6]

Many Canadians feared that this wartime prowess would not translate into peacetime prosperity. They were wrong. The foundations built during the war, when converted to peacetime use, provided Canada with an industrial base that fuelled a strong and sustained period of growth, fundamentally altering the character of the Canadian economy. By the end of the war, Canada was the third most important trade and industrial power in the world, a position that it could not sustain as others recovered, but a position that did change the long-term prospects for Canadian prosperity. Canadian GNP doubled from $5.6 billion in 1939 to $11.9 billion in 1945; by 1957 it had almost tripled again to reach $33.5 billion.

Trade was crucial to this long-term spurt in Canadian economic growth, and trade policy decisions during and after the war played a determining role in shaping the structure and performance of the Canadian economy. But most of the trade

Table 5.1

Canada's trade in goods, 1939-45 (value in millions of dollars)

Year	UK Value	UK %	United States Value	United States %	Rest of world Value	Rest of world %	Total value
Exports							
1939	328	35.6	380	41.2	214	23.2	922
1940	503	43.0	442	37.7	226	19.3	1,171
1941	623	39.7	599	38.2	348	22.1	1,570
1942	696	30.4	881	38.4	715	31.2	2,292
1943	988	34.1	1,147	39.6	763	26.3	2,897
1944	1,194	35.6	1,296	38.6	867	25.8	3,358
1945	948	30.0	1,193	37.7	1,025	32.3	3,167
Imports							
1939	112	15.2	485	65.9	139	18.9	736
1940	137	13.4	711	69.5	175	17.1	1,023
1941	138	10.8	912	71.2	224	18.0	1,274
1942	118	7.8	1,209	80.3	178	11.9	1,505
1943	101	6.0	1,410	83.6	175	10.4	1,686
1944	94	5.4	1,435	82.9	200	11.7	1,730
1945	100	6.6	1,183	78.1	231	15.3	1,514

Note: Totals may not add due to rounding.
Source: F.H. Leacy, ed., *Historical Statistics of Canada,* 2nd ed. (Ottawa: Statistics Canada, 1983), series G389-400.

and economic policy decisions taken during the war, although they would endure well beyond it, were taken primarily for military and related reasons. As Finance Minister J.L. Ilsley explained in his 1944 budget statement, "For the present, the customs tariff is without any great influence on the scope and direction of external trade. Scarcity of supplies, bulk purchasing, import and export permits, and import subsidies – these are the instruments which determine, for the time being, the extent and pattern of world trade."[7] Two decisions were particularly critical to the future of Canadian trade and economic development: the decision to stay outside of the British currency area, or sterling bloc, and the decision to help Britain financially and to meet its requirements for both food and war materiel.

Canada's decision to stay outside the sterling bloc during and after the war had significant long-term implications for its commercial relations with Britain and the Commonwealth as well as with the United States. In the face of the severe drain on its external resources, Britain decided soon after the outbreak of war to end sterling's convertibility. This required a high degree of government regulation of both trade and investment, regulations that would influence UK trade and investment patterns for many years after the war. Invited to join the sterling group, Canada declined. It was prepared to help the United Kingdom, but not to the extent of tying itself into a high-cost, inflexible, closed trade and payments regime. Participating in the sterling group would have weakened Canada's own economic recovery and undermined its capacity to help the Allied cause. It would also have complicated growing trade with a neutral United States. Finally, it would have signalled a return to the imperialism from which the King government had worked hard to distance Canada in the 1920s and 1930s.[8] The result, however, was that Canada's own payments position was made more difficult: pounds earned on exports to the United Kingdom were not convertible to dollars. Increasing trade with the United States during and immediately after the war thus aggravated Canada's own delicate balance-of-payments position.[9]

If Canada could not help on the monetary front, it did what it could to further the cause economically. It retooled and expanded its productive machinery in order to provide Britain and the Allies with the trucks, tanks, artillery, rifles, planes, ammunition, and ships needed to win the war. Steel, chemical, and other basic industries were converted to war production, and secondary manufacturing was expanded to meet the needs of the forces in Europe, North Africa, and Asia. Within two years of the outbreak of war and before the United States entered, Canada was providing the Allies with more than its share of the sinews of war. Two-thirds of Canadian war production was for use by others – half for Britain, the rest for other allies.

Unfortunately, Britain could not pay for all this materiel. In the early stages of the war, Britain liquidated its reserves and its assets held in Canada, but these soon proved inadequate. By early 1941, bolder steps were required, and they needed to be taken by Canada. As a result, Canada agreed to make Britain a billion-dollar gift and to convert outstanding sterling balances into a $700-million interest-free loan. The pattern was repeated several more times. By the end of the war, the British Treasury calculated that Canada had contributed more than $3 billion to the UK war effort. In reality, it was probably substantially more, given the extent of Canadian aid in kind, in grants, and in loans.[10] While enormous in the context of Canadian tax revenues and gross national product, Canada's contribution was not beyond its means. By 1945, Canada was immeasurably wealthier than in 1939. Investment in war industries and the concomitant expansion in employment, savings, and demand had made Canada's economic prospects very different than they had been during the depression.[11]

Canada's generosity to Britain was a calculated gamble combining altruism and shrewd self-interest. Canadian officials wanted the Axis powers defeated and the war brought to a speedy and successful conclusion. They also wanted the United Kingdom to survive and be a good economic partner after the war. As Mackenzie King reflected following a cabinet discussion: "From our point of view, the whole business relates back to making sure of our holding a place in the British market."[12]

King and his colleagues believed that a commercially strong Britain was essential to Canada's future prosperity. Canada's generosity, however, created an increasingly impossible short-term situation: Canadians were shipping war materiel and food to Britain for which the latter could not pay, while importing military components and other goods from the United States that demanded payment. This was an unsustainable balance-of-payments situation. Canada could afford to help Britain in the long run, but it could not finance the dollar drain in the short run. Canada's generosity, while well thought out, did not leave much room for manoeuvre.

The solution to Canada's short-term financial predicament lay in Washington. Although the United States did not enter the war until the end of 1941 and congressional isolationist sentiment required strict official neutrality, President Roosevelt's sympathies – and those of most Americans – were clear. The United States was already putting its economy on a war footing and, within the confines of US political reality, Roosevelt was taking steps aimed at providing aid to Britain and its allies, including Canada. As with Canada, these steps involved both altruism and self-interest. The United States also knew how to drive a hard bargain. The main tool used by the United States was to lend Britain and the Allies the money needed to buy or lease war materiel from the United States in return for a number of considerations, including commitment to the establishment of a nondiscriminatory trade and payments system after the war.[13] Referred to as "the consideration" in contemporary records, this commitment proved a bitter bone of contention between the United States and some of the Allies, particularly the United Kingdom, which felt that the United States was taking advantage of wartime desperation to gain future, unrelated concessions.[14]

Canada did not participate directly in the US lend-lease program, nor did Canada enter into any long-term loan agreement.[15] Lend-lease, however, had important implications for Canada. Initially, it spelled trouble. Canada worried that its financial situation could become even more precarious because lend-lease might divert UK and other orders to the United States. Eventually, however, this was avoided in a manner that also solved Canada's balance-of-payments problem. The United States agreed that Canada could charge the UK lend-lease account for purchases of components needed in the manufacture of war materiel destined for the United Kingdom. Additionally, the United States agreed to procure some of its own defence needs in Canada. The solution was formalized in the Hyde Park Declaration, which provided a basis for Canada-US defence cooperation for the next two years. Although the details may not have worked out exactly as envisaged, over the course of the war the United States bought Cdn$1.187 billion in defence products in Canada under the terms of the Hyde Park agreement, thus considerably easing Canada's balance-of-payments problems.[16]

The decisions to stay out of the sterling bloc and to look to the United States for help in solving the balance-of-payments problem of 1941 were pragmatic and reflected the realities of the moment based on three-way cooperation between Canada, the United States, and Britain, but they also had profound implications for the future. They reflected the decline in the United Kingdom's economic position and the rise in the economic strength of the United States. This pattern became increasingly apparent in the years to come and disposed ministers and officials in Ottawa to take actions and policy decisions ensuring that Canada would not have to choose between the two countries unless it was absolutely necessary, but reserving the option to have solid ties to the stronger of the two if it was advantageous.

Planning for Peace

By 1943, the job of arming the Allies was well in hand and the tide of war was turning, so that governments could turn to the job of planning for a peacetime economy. Given the experience after the First World War, the conventional view was one of foreboding. The worry, in government, business, academia, and throughout society, was that the end of the war would bring a return to the depression. Much postwar planning was predicated on this assumption, an assumption that turned out to be mistaken as Canada converted rapidly and successfully from a strong wartime to a booming peacetime economy. But that was the future; in the middle of the war, with the memories of the depression still fresh, Canadians remained very uneasy about their economic prospects.[17]

Planning took place largely in Finance under the leadership of its deputy, Clifford Clark, bolstered by a special committee set up to look at postwar requirements. The views with which officials had to grapple ranged from those of C.D. Howe and his business advisors, who were confident that industry would rise to the challenge of meeting Canada's economic needs once converted to peacetime requirements, to the more advanced social planning views gaining favour on university campuses, modelled on earlier British and German experiments. Neither extreme appealed to the civil servants and their political master, Mackenzie King. Instead, the government opted for a number of welfare-enhancing programs such as the baby bonus, and established a Department of Reconstruction under C.D. Howe, to ease the transition to peacetime production.[18]

Although considerably less than what academic and other progressive opinion considered necessary to ensure that Canada would not again be ravaged by depression, the various programs still represented a quantum leap forward in government participation in the economy. Financing came from new taxes – largely corporate and personal income taxes. At the outbreak of war, indirect taxes – customs and excise duties and sales taxes – accounted for 58 percent of the federal government's income, with total income accounting for only 8.2 percent of GNP. By 1947, the federal government had doubled its tax bite to 17.6 percent of GNP, but indirect taxes now accounted for only 34 percent. Trade policy, with customs duties down to 8 percent of the total, had clearly become less central to fiscal policy.[19]

Planning during the war was more than a matter of ensuring domestic prosperity. It also involved cooperative efforts to establish a world order that would severely curtail the capacity of governments to export their problems. As in Canada, the common international concern was whether the return to peace would mean the return to depression and, as widely believed, to its progenitor, protectionism. In North America, the challenge was to absorb returning soldiers and convert to peacetime production. In Europe, the immediate challenge was to provide basic needs by reconstructing and rebuilding farms and factories destroyed by six years of war; longer term, the need was for institutions and values that would promote prosperity and obviate the rivalries that had led to war. In both Europe and North America, the array of restrictions inherited from the 1930s posed a serious obstacle to the achievement of prosperity.

Canada's transition to peace turned out to be much smoother than anticipated. Employment and production dipped only slightly and soon recovered. The end of wartime controls was met by a surge of pent-up demand from savings. Most of the growth experienced in the first decade after the war was thus stimulated by domestic demand, both delayed consumer demand and producer capital investment in new productive capacity to meet consumer and export requirements.

Despite the domestic boom, the Canadian economy was still heavily dependent on exports, and there it faced some serious problems. Canada's two traditional markets, the United Kingdom and the United States, were not as open as they could be or needed to be for Canada to take full advantage of its new productive capacity. If Canadian prosperity were to last, it would require a trade and payments regime that would reward Canada for maintaining an open economy and deter others from adopting policies that discriminated against Canadian goods and services. Achieving such a regime would prove to be a quest of many years' duration.

The preference was for a multilateral, nondiscriminatory trade and payments regime that would allow for currency convertibility, multilateral clearing of accounts, and nondiscriminatory access to markets. Canada wanted it multilateral not only to avoid having to choose between the two traditional markets of the United States and the United Kingdom, but also to ensure that the trading partners of Canada's principal export markets could maintain equilibrium in their trade and payments. Bilateral balancing was impossible for a country that supplied most of its needs from the United States but still sold more than half of its exports to other markets. As W.A. Mackintosh told Prime Minister Mackenzie King: "Only by promoting and participating in a collaboration between the United States and the United Kingdom, with the three-fold object of developing coordinated policies for maintaining employment, ensuring relative freedom of trade, and contributing to productive international investment, [could] Canada ... find after the war the larger world economy necessary to her tolerable existence."[20]

Canada was not alone in seeking such a liberal, nondiscriminatory trade and payments regime after the war, at least at the level of ideology if not always in practice. So did the United States, at the same level of abstraction, and the two countries were active partners in their efforts to realize this dream. Canadian officials recognized that such an approach was the most viable means for realizing Canada's objective of prosperity through trade. The United Kingdom and Europe could not and did not share this objective, making increasing integration with the United States inevitable. The alternative for Canada was economic stagnation.[21]

The multilateralist urge was ubiquitous. It went well beyond the establishment of a trade and payments regime and extended to every aspect of Canadian foreign policy. The economic dimension, however, was never far from the surface. It was Canada, for example, which insisted that NATO should go beyond mere military security and include a commitment on economic and social collaboration in article 2 (the so-called Canadian article).[22] While the article never amounted to anything, largely because no other member of NATO shared Canada's vision of a vibrant North Atlantic economic community, its inclusion aptly illustrates the depth of Canada's commitment to the multilateral ideal.[23]

Although Canada preferred an open multilateral system involving both the United Kingdom and the United States, Canadian officials were not shy about flying other kites if opportunity beckoned. The overwhelming sentiment was pragmatism. Economic security was the priority, wherever it could be found. Multilateralism might be the most effective means of achieving Canada's objective of stable trade and economic relations with the United States and the United Kingdom, but not at the expense of other solutions if circumstances dictated. Multilateralism made it possible not to have to choose between the United Kingdom and the United States. If Canadians had to choose, however, they were more likely to favour the United States, where prospects were brighter.[24]

Establishment of the GATT

The successful negotiation of trade agreements with Britain and the United States in the 1930s convinced both King and his advisors of the value of a multidimensional trade policy. Together with the Americans, Canadian officials were convinced that the bilateralism and unilateralism expressed in the beggar-thy-neighbour policies of the 1930s had contributed directly to war. They believed that in a world of strong multilateral institutions the risks of protectionism and isolationism could be significantly reduced. Canadian leaders additionally believed that multilateralism provided opportunities for Canada to influence directly the policies of the major powers in directions favourable to Canada's further development as a nation. Together with UK officials, they also believed that multilateral cooperation based on American leadership would deter postwar US isolationism and prevent the adjustment problems of the 1920s and 1930s.[25]

Even before the United States formally entered the war, cooperative steps had been taken to pursue policies that would plan for a more stable peace than had been the case after the First World War. In the 1941 Atlantic Charter, US president Franklin Roosevelt and British prime minister Winston Churchill had pledged themselves to the establishment of a postwar multilateral trade and payments system.

Canadian officials were brought into the discussions at an early stage.[26] From the perspective of the two major powers, Canada seemed to have a shrewd appreciation of the issues and was prepared to make useful suggestions. From Canada's perspective, participation was essential to avoid a situation in which the United States and Britain made decisions that were inimical to Canadian interests but were hard to change once they had been taken. The triangular negotiations of 1937 to 1938 had suggested that Canada could play a constructive role, and throughout the planning and negotiating stages, Canadian officials sought every possible opportunity to exercise their influence.[27]

Starting with the UK-US lend-lease agreements of 1941, the Allies began planning for a postwar world of strong institutions within a United Nations system. These would include not only the UN itself, but also a group of specialized agencies to tackle problems of aviation (the International Civil Aviation Organization – ICAO), agriculture (the Food and Agriculture Organization – FAO), health (the World Health Organization – WHO), education, science, and culture (the United Nations Educational, Scientific, and Cultural Organization – UNESCO), monetary affairs (the International Monetary Fund – IMF), reconstruction and development (the International Bank for Reconstruction and Development – IBRD), and trade (International Trade Organization – ITO). Older technical organizations such as the International Labor Organization (ILO), the Universal Postal Union (UPU), and the International Telecommunications Union (ITU) were also brought under the aegis of the United Nations.[28]

Already in 1944, the United States had successfully hosted a conference at the Mount Washington Hotel in Bretton Woods, New Hampshire, at which the Allies concluded the articles of agreement for both the IMF and the IBRD. These required careful preparation and major efforts to bridge the gap between US and British assessments of what was required to restore monetary and financial stability to the postwar world. Canada played an important role in finding the compromises necessary to establish a system built on fixed exchange rates, agreed procedures for adjusting them, a modest level of capital reserves to defend agreed rates, and jointly subscribed funds to provide financing for reconstruction and development.

By 1946, all the agencies but the ITO had been established. In that year preparations began in London for a World Trade and Employment Conference to establish an International Trade Organization based on a draft charter already worked out between US, UK, and Canadian officials over the previous three years. At the London conference, the preparatory committee further refined the charter for an ITO. Their work was continued by a drafting committee at Lake Success, New York, early in 1947 and by a second meeting in Geneva during the summer of 1947. For the Geneva meeting, the United States had also proposed that the members of the preparatory meeting and a few others enter into tariff negotiations, building on the tariff-cutting agreements many had already negotiated between themselves in the 1930s. Twenty-three countries ultimately responded.[29]

By arranging a huge jamboree of bilateral, item-by-item negotiations, including between countries that had already exchanged concessions and that were thus looking for deeper, more sensitive cuts, the United States successfully organized what had been considered impossible in 1934 – a multilateral tariff negotiation.[30] By harnessing the power of the unconditional MFN rule as well as the principal and substantial supplier rules, it proved possible to negotiate 123 such agreements containing reductions and/or bindings affecting some 45,000 items in the tariff schedules of the twenty-three participating countries. The result for the United States was a further 35 percent reduction in its tariff protection. To provide rough balance, particularly for smaller and low-tariff countries, negotiators accepted that a binding could be as valuable as a reduction. It thus proved possible to meet the US congressional requirement for reciprocity.[31] In effect, the United States successfully mobilized the mercantilist attitude of most governments to trade (maximize export opportunities and minimize import exposure) in a multilateral tariff-cutting procedure that provided for the gradual reduction of tariffs on a politically acceptable basis.

Any immediate impact on trade patterns, however, would be slight. In order to make progress, the participating countries decided that quantitative restrictions (QRs) would be illegal except in tightly defined circumstances. However, they turned a blind eye to the many existing QRs, which they assumed would disappear as the European economies recovered. The negotiators concentrated on tariff concessions with the only significant country in a position to open its market – the United States, which incidentally made little use of QRs to protect its manufacturing sector. These early concessions worked principally to open up the US and, to some extent, the Canadian markets.[32] Most of the other tariff concessions were prospective; they would not have much impact until the underbrush of QRs was cleared away. As we shall see, the QR problem endured much longer than Canadian negotiators anticipated and for reasons that bore little relationship to the tolerance exhibited in 1947.[33]

In order to tie the various individual bilateral agreements together into a single set of rights and obligations, the delegates had agreed in London in 1946 to take most of the provisions of chapter 4 of the draft charter, the commercial policy chapter, add a few articles to hold them together, provide final provisions, and call it the General Agreement on Tariffs and Trade (GATT). The text of this GATT had been fleshed out at Lake Success and was further refined at Geneva to reflect the continued evolution of the draft charter. The amalgamated results of the 123 tariff agreements were then added as schedules to article 2, the article providing for the tariff concessions traded among the participating countries.

The agreement thus put together was never intended to function as an organization; the participating countries agreed that it would be an interim agreement that would shortly be subsumed into the ITO. The ITO would then supply the institutional muscle to guide international commercial policy and provide the framework within which further tariff negotiations could be organized. Since the US delegation did not have congressional authority to accede to a trade organization but did have authority to negotiate a trade agreement, members of the preparatory committee were consciously seeking to conclude what could be achieved immediately while also laying the groundwork for a more ambitious approach in the longer term. In fact, in the face of congressional criticism that the draft GATT as it stood at the end of the Lake Success meeting contained too many organization-like provisions, US negotiators had successfully insisted on some cosmetic changes at Geneva necessary to make the final text more acceptable.[34]

In order to provide a basis for bringing the new agreement into force before the expiry of the 1945 renewal of the US Reciprocal Trade Agreements Act (RTAA) and before news of the significant tariff cuts that had been agreed began to leak, the negotiators crafted the Protocol of Provisional Application (PPA). Parts I and III of the GATT were judged to be fully consistent with the RTAA and could be brought into force definitively. Part II, which contained many of the trade rules and which amended many of the clauses of earlier bilateral agreements, would be brought into force only insofar as it was not inconsistent with existing legislation. Once the ITO charter was concluded, it would provide the vehicle for bringing part II of the GATT into force definitively. The PPA would allow the interim GATT to fit the mould and time-frame prescribed by the RTAA and allow the US administration to implement it without seeking further legislative authority. In effect, rather than tailoring its suit to fit available cloth, the US administration decided to tailor two suits – one out of available cloth and another if more cloth should become available. Seven other participants joined the United States – including the United Kingdom and Canada – and agreed to bring the new accord into force by 1 January 1948 on the basis of the PPA. Other participants agreed to take the necessary steps to bring it into force on the same basis as soon thereafter as possible.[35]

At Geneva, Canada made concessions affecting about half of the items in its tariff schedule, including some 600 reductions in its MFN rates and 500 bindings of existing rates. The designated items covered about two-thirds of Canada's imports. In return, Canada benefited from concessions by others improving the terms of access for about three-quarters of Canada's traditional exports. Of the various bilateral agreements concluded, the deal between Canada and the United States, building on the 1935 and 1938 agreements, was by far the most extensive. The success of this bilateral agreement, as well as others, confirmed for Canadian trade officials that the multilateral framework was a potent vehicle for promoting Canadian trade objectives.[36]

Canada had also succeeded, together with Britain and the other dominions, in retaining the system of imperial preferences established at the 1932 Ottawa conference. Despite a strong and sustained attack on the system by the United States, imperial preferences were formally recognized as part of the multilateral bargain. The only serious concession was that the system could not be expanded or the margins of preference increased. For Canada, that concession was not difficult to accept. The Liberals under King had never liked the binding nature of the preferences forged under Borden and Bennett, and officials now found that British insistence on those preferences cramped their ability to negotiate concessions of interest to Canada with others, particularly the United States. Nevertheless, the capping of the preference system proved the only issue on which His Majesty's loyal opposition attacked. Conservative leader John Bracken complained that Canada had lost the ability to set its own trade policy and to extend preferences where it saw fit. King, on the other hand, insisted that these negotiations had been the most comprehensive, significant, and far-reaching ever undertaken in the history of world trade and that he took great pride in the constructive role played by Canadians.[37]

Not only with the hindsight of its eventual failure did the 1948 Havana conference to establish an International Trade Organization appear anticlimactic. For the negotiating conference itself, Canada sent its second team. In the telegram traffic back and forth and in King's diary jottings, there no longer appeared to be any sense of urgency. When the IBRD and IMF were established at Bretton Woods in 1944, enthusiasm for postwar cooperation was at its height; by the time the ITO negotiations were seriously under way, postwar complications had already dulled the enthusiasm and raised obstacles to the establishment of a liberal trade regime.

For some of the delegations at both the preparatory meetings and the conference at Havana, there was irony in the positions advanced by the United States and the United Kingdom. With US adoption of the reciprocal trade agreements program and British abandonment of free trade, the two main players appeared to have changed sides. The United States had broken with a protectionist, nationalist, and isolationist past while Britain had forsaken an outward-looking past dominated by adherence to free trade. These diametrically opposed positions meant that much effort was required to reach compromises with which both sides could live. Canadian officials were instrumental in this bridge-building, as they already had been in the planning stages. Canadian goals were less categorical, built on policies nurtured for many years, and were now continued on the basis of a more professional and sophisticated approach. British and American negotiators, on the other hand, were working from trade policies adopted only a little more than a decade earlier and pursued their objectives with the fervour of the newly converted. Canada had learned the virtues of compromise and patience, and its role as a mediator between US and British views of the postwar world came easily.

The biggest issue in the negotiations was when, and under what circumstances, parties to the agreement could discriminate. The United States was generally opposed to any discrimination – except when it came to trade in agriculture; the United Kingdom, however, was determined to provide room both for discriminatory domestic measures to promote full employment and for the defence of its balance-of-payments position. Both positions reflected very different approaches to the problems of postwar reconstruction, based on different economic circumstances.

The most visible symbol of discrimination became the system of Commonwealth tariff preferences adopted at Ottawa in 1932. For the United States, preferences were an evil that needed to be eradicated. For Britain, those same preferences were politically important, symbolic of its glorious past. British, as well as Canadian, negotiators had made it clear throughout both the preparatory discussions and the subsequent negotiations that the preferences could be eliminated in return for a substantial reduction in the still-high US tariff to a level more in keeping with the dominant economic position enjoyed by the United States. US negotiators, on the other hand, while authorized to make substantial cuts, could not meet the aspirations of their British and Canadian counterparts without raising the ire of Congress and bringing the whole project into jeopardy. The solution lay in compromises that left all feeling somewhat cheated but that provided a basis for continuing the attack on high tariffs and discrimination over time.

As a result of the differences between British and American views of trade barriers and discrimination, plus the participation of a large number of developing countries with their own views, the Havana Charter turned out to be a further compromise between principle and practice. Like many compromises, it attracted more detractors than defenders. In the United States, it was criticized by both protectionists and perfectionists, and only a small group of officials and internationalists rose to its defence. In Canada, the government declared it an important step in the right direction but took few steps to ensure its passage, either in Canada or the in United States. Similar lukewarm support in the United Kingdom and elsewhere ensured its eventual demise. Friction between the administration and Congress, and the increasing isolationism of the US Senate, are often cited as the principal reasons for the failure of the ITO to come into being, but the truth is that it did not have strong support anywhere and that few governments lobbied the US administration to seek ratification by the Senate.[38]

Part of the failure to bring the ITO into force can be attributed to official attitudes in Canada and elsewhere to trade barriers and international trade negotiations. For Canadian negotiators, with more than a decade of practical experience under their belts, the challenge at Geneva, Havana, and the various other conferences was to meet a set of conflicting objectives. Their task was to juggle the changing priorities attached to these objectives and to come up with a package that in general met Canadian political and economic needs. These needs included the following:

- promoting order and stability in international trade and monetary affairs
- improving access to world markets by lowering barriers not only to Canada's exports but also to the exports of Canada's customers
- promoting the free conversion of currency
- protecting the freedom to extend imperial preferences
- protecting domestic industry
- advancing Canadian independence and stature.

Achieving these goals required adroit negotiation and management. Protecting imperial preferences, for example, ran directly counter to American zeal for non-discrimination and to the basic principles embodied in the draft ITO charter. Similarly, the desire to maintain protection for domestic manufacturers complicated efforts to induce others to lower their tariffs. Fortunately for the Canadian negotiators, other participants came with a similar mix of conflicting objectives. The Americans were keen to end discrimination and lower barriers, but were limited by the extent of the negotiating authority delegated by Congress. The fact that the renewal of the Reciprocal Trade Agreements Act had been controversial in 1945 and had nearly failed made the American negotiators less sure of their ground than three years earlier. Despite this uncertainty, the US delegation was determined not to let the levels of protection for American farmers erode.[39] The British delegation did not share the American enthusiasm for nondiscrimination and was determined, for its part, to protect the system of preferences that the United Kingdom had reluctantly adopted only a generation earlier. Additionally, for Clement Attlee and his ministers, domestic issues such as full employment were more important than an end to discrimination. As a result, the British delegation sought to build in derogations from the main thrust of the agreement to allow scope for interventionist policies aimed at postwar reconstruction. They were not, for example, as convinced as the Americans of the evils of QRs and subsidies, and they thought there was much to be said for discriminatory government procurement policies.[40]

With these conflicting views to complicate negotiations, the end result was unquestionably complex and subtle, and the benefits of the various compromises were not readily apparent. Dana Wilgress, the head of Canada's delegation, described the problem as follows:

> The Canadian Delegation consistently opposed efforts to weaken the rules designed to reduce trade barriers and to permit the restoration of international trade upon a multilateral basis as soon as possible. The successive stages in the elaboration of a Charter for the International Trade Organization did bring about a weakening of these rules. This arose through the progressive introduction of exceptional provisions or "escape clauses," necessary in order to secure the adherence to the Charter of as many different countries as possible. The Canadian Delegation, when finding that the inclusion of an exceptional provision was inevitable, directed its efforts to restricting the scope of the provision as much as possible. The result of all this has been that the Charter which finally emerged at Havana represents a bold compromise, flexible enough to take care of varying needs of different economic philosophies and of different stages of economic development, yet sufficiently true to the principles of multilateral trade to give rise to the hope that the Organization, when it is set up, will prove to be one of the most successful and most enduring of all the intergovernmental organizations established during the last few years.[41]

A.G. Racey, "The Indigent Opportunist on the Hunt for Initiative and Election Issues." The Liberals, always ready to find their policies in opportune places, toy with Canada-US free trade in 1948.

This optimistic assessment was not widely shared. To the principal trading countries, the interim GATT arrangement, with its more limited objectives and relatively weak institutional structure, began to appear more attractive than the more comprehensive but compromised ITO charter. Several years of experience with GATT confirmed the impression that perhaps the interim arrangement was politically more acceptable than the more permanent ITO.

Trade policy, trade relations, and trade negotiations have less to do with ideology than with resolving practical problems in a manner compatible with both current political and economic environments, and past decisions and experiences. Only later, as patterns emerge, are grand ideas hatched to provide *ex post facto* coherence to new behaviours. The 1947-8 GATT/ITO negotiations provide a good example. Later myth making about the values of multilateralism has obscured the fact that in 1947 multilateralism was new and unproven. Canada faced some real problems and struck out in a variety of directions, as circumstances dictated. As explained below, that course of action included exploring the prospect of a bilateral free-trade agreement with the United States as well as a number of bilateral deals with the United Kingdom. Nevertheless, Canadian determination to establish a multilateral order and make it work became an enduring theme in the pursuit of Canadian trade interests over the next forty years.

In the 1920s and 1930s, Liberal governments had worked hard to loosen the strings tying Canada to a British-dominated imperial destiny. Mackenzie King and his officials became increasingly leery of the dangers that British imperial pretensions posed for Canada's ability to steer its own course. Stronger ties to the United States were in part intended to offset the strong pull of the United Kingdom, a pull that Conservative critics of Liberal policies preferred. Liberal preference for Washington was less a matter of continentalism than of anti-imperialism. In the immediate postwar years, when the roles of Britain and the United States had reversed, King demonstrated that he could be equally suspicious of Washington-inspired continentalism.[42] The goal was neither continentalism nor imperialism but maximum room for Canadian independence of action. Canada's active and consistent pursuit of multilateralism provides visible proof of this desire, but the economic realities had changed, as had the policy attitudes of Canada's two principal trading partners. Nothing illustrates these new circumstances more clearly than the bizarre secret negotiations with the United States launched by Canada in November 1947.

The Aborted Free-Trade Negotiations of 1947-8
At the conclusion of the Geneva negotiations, with discussion continuing on the ITO charter in Havana, Canada sought to improve on the bilateral deal with the United States in separate and secret negotiations in Washington. In Geneva, the Canadian and US heads of delegation had exchanged letters agreeing that the 1938 agreement would remain suspended as long as the two countries were participants in the GATT. Now Canada sought to conclude a more comprehensive replacement for the 1938 agreement.[43]

The direct stimulus for these negotiations was the severe balance-of-payments problem encountered by Canada in the immediate postwar period (discussed in more detail in chapter 6). Canada's large trade surplus with the United Kingdom was more than offset by its deficit with the United States, but Canada could not use its sterling to pay for American goods. To forestall Canadian import restrictions that would inevitably become necessary to protect dwindling American dollar reserves, Prime Minister Mackenzie King concurred with his principal advisors that John Deutsch and Hector McKinnon should proceed with negotiations with the United States in order to find a bilateral solution analogous to the one achieved in similar circumstances in 1941. Canada needed better access to the US market to increase exports sufficiently to offset the dollar drain; Britain needed US dollars with which to purchase Canadian goods. Deutsch and McKinnon, together with Dana Wilgress, had been Canada's principal negotiators in Geneva. Wilgress was now told to proceed to Havana and continue with the ITO negotiations with the help of a group of more junior officials, while his two main collaborators travelled to Washington to seek a solution to the trade dimension of Canada's balance-of-payments problem.

In order to correct the imbalance in Canada-US trade, Canadian officials sought to build on the 1947 GATT agreement by adding products of Canadian export interest to the US free list. US officials, however, had to come to grips with the fact that they had neither the authority from Congress for such a negotiation nor a pressing interest in gaining better access to the Canadian market. Nevertheless, they agreed with the Canadian request to consider a new agreement. Canada's interest was clearly economic, but that of the United States appeared to be largely political. Canada had been and remained a good ally. Canada shared US views of the threat posed by Soviet expansionism in Europe and supported US efforts at containment. Together with the United States, Canada represented the economic strength of the emerging Western alliance. Maintaining a viable Canadian economy, therefore, was politically important to the State Department.

To meet that political objective, however, US officials needed something sufficiently dramatic to capture the imagination of Congress and business, whose interest in the State Department's geopolitical considerations was much less apparent. US officials' initial suggestion that the two countries negotiate a customs union was firmly rejected by the Canadian side. In the end, the Americans suggested a modified customs union that they called a free-trade area. The two sides would enter into an agreement whereby they would, over a period of five years, eliminate all customs barriers, but maintain their full freedom to regulate trade separately with the rest of the world. Canada would be free, for example, to maintain its British preferences. This was an idea that appealed to Deutsch and McKinnon as well as to Mackenzie King and finance minister Douglas Abbott. On this basis, discussions soon made headway. To accommodate an eventual bilateral agreement, Canadian and American officials collaborated in adding, somewhat indirectly through the good offices of other delegations, the concept of free-trade areas to the drafting of the Havana Charter (and thus to article 24 of the GATT).

As described by Deutsch, the proposal had evolved by April 1948 into a plan to negotiate two free-trade agreements, one between Canada and the United States and the other between Canada and the United Kingdom. Both would eliminate tariffs and QRs but retain a few special provisions in politically sensitive areas such as trade in wheat and woollens. The Canada-US agreement would entail immediate removal of barriers by the United States and the phased removal of barriers by Canada over a five-year period. The Canada-UK agreement, which had to date not been discussed with any British officials, would similarly comprise asymmetrical provisions, this time in favour of the United Kingdom in order to give it time to bring its balance of payments into greater equilibrium. Deutsch explained that such arrangements would solve problems created for all three countries by the collapse of the UK and Continental economies as reliable contributors to the triangular trading patterns among countries on both sides of the North Atlantic.[44]

With preliminary negotiations on this plan almost concluded, Prime Minister Mackenzie King took fright at the political consequences, remembering the fate of Laurier in 1911 and fearing that Canadian nationalists would once again confuse patriotism with the maintenance of customs duties and other trade barriers with the United States. Inadvertent or planted articles in *Time* and *Life* extolling the virtues of a customs union had resulted in a series of negative editorials in Canadian newspapers and polite inquiries as to the government's policy. King had seen enough. Fortunately, the exchange crisis that had provided the occasion for the negotiations had abated, in large part because Congress, in providing legislative authority for Marshall Plan aid, agreed that the United Kingdom and Europe could make purchases outside the United States with Marshall Plan dollars.[45] Additionally, King believed that article 2 of NATO would provide a more politically acceptable basis for closer Canada-US economic cooperation, because it would also involve the United Kingdom and Europe. As secretly as the negotiations had begun, they were then abandoned. To make sure that there were no misunderstandings, King went to unusual lengths both to distance himself from the plan and to make clear to ministers and officials that he now opposed the idea.[46]

On both sides of the border, those officials who had participated in the planning were bitterly disappointed at King's about-face and made various efforts to change his mind.[47] C.D. Howe went so far as to assure US officials that once King had retired and his likely successor, Louis St. Laurent, had secured a further Liberal victory in the next election, negotiations could continue. But Howe was wrong. With the exchange crisis in the past, interest in a bilateral deal evaporated. Five years later, when President Eisenhower raised the possibility of a free-trade agreement with St. Laurent, Canadian officials scrambled to ensure that no one took the idea seriously. Canada-US bilateralism appeared to be firmly buried, despite its brief if secret revival.[48]

While a pragmatic response to the exchange crisis of 1947, the free-trade negotiations were at odds with a fundamental tenet of Liberal foreign policy since King's assumption of the leadership in 1919. King had worked hard to provide Canada with its own place in the sun, independent of either the imperial or the American connection. Achieving that goal had required that Canada have close commercial ties with both Britain and the United States. It also required that Canada pursue with vigour improved ties with the less dominant of the two in order to offset the pull of the more powerful and potentially more threatening partner. In the years after the war, the UK connection failed to live up to its requirement of offsetting US power, opening the way to a much higher degree of Canada-US interdependence than King found acceptable. Strengthening ties to the United States through a free-trade agreement would have further compromised King's policy. It is little wonder, therefore, that he turned against it as soon as Canada's financial problems permitted and turned again to finding ways to bolster UK ties. That proved a task beyond Canada's power.

Canada had decided to stick with the dream of a multilateral world ruled by multilateral institutions and procedures. It was a noble decision, but one that would be severely tested over GATT's first decade. That decade would also establish once and for all that the pull of geography made anything other than a continental reality difficult to achieve.

6 CONTINENTAL REALITIES

I learned then and had the lesson confirmed many times later, that while the power of the United States was always in the background in these differences, we were quite able to stand up for our own rights, to work out fair agreements, and to do so without destroying the specially close relationship advantageous to both countries.

– LESTER PEARSON, MIKE: THE MEMOIRS OF THE
RIGHT HONOURABLE LESTER B. PEARSON

To the officials charged with designing Canada's postwar trade policies and to the ministers responsible for deciding what direction to follow, three priorities stood out. In the first place, it was clear that Canadians would not long tolerate a government that could not deliver prosperity; Canadians had had enough of unemployment and deprivation and wanted to realize the promise that generations of political leaders had said was theirs. Second, ministers and officials believed that an important key to prosperity lay in foreign markets and foreign investors; they accepted that the Canadian market was still too small to generate the demand that would sustain long-term growth and that Canadian savings were still insufficient to finance the further development of the Canadian economy. Third, ministers and officials recognized that they had to work within the reality of what other, more powerful nations would decide, both domestically and internationally. During the first dozen years after the war, it was the final point that would repeatedly determine the nature of Canada's own policies. Canadian officials might prefer one policy over another, but ultimately their choices were limited by the decisions taken by UK, US, and European political leaders working with the cards circumstances had dealt them. Canada's dependence on the policy choices of others for its further economic development might irritate some Canadian nationalist critics, but it was a reality that policy makers in Ottawa could not escape.[1]

The reality that stared Canadians in the face in the years immediately after the war was stark: Britain, although it still ruled an empire on which the sun never set, could neither afford that empire nor keep it intact in face of the various challenges to its suzerainty. Its industry and citizens alike were in a parlous state, exhausted by war and broke. By contrast, in the United States, the economic might that had been the key to the Allied victory was everywhere on display. Industry and consumption were both running flat out. In 1947, the United States produced half of the world's manufactures, pumped 61 percent of its oil, and produced 43 percent of its electricity. Canada had little choice. Its destiny lay with the rising power next door rather than with the waning power across the ocean. Sentiments might waver, and efforts to maintain the UK connection might continue, but the facts were clear.[2]

It was not a development welcomed by King or his advisors. Throughout his career, King had pursued one overriding foreign policy objective: the development of an independent Canada capable of seeking its own interests. He was as suspicious of US as of UK designs that might in any way undermine Canada's ability to direct its own course. He thus resisted British efforts to strengthen the Commonwealth as a third force in world affairs but was also wary of what he considered US efforts to absorb Canada.[3] If there had been viable alternatives, King and his advisors would have pursued them. The fact of the matter was that there were few such alternatives.[4]

The damage done by war and the difficulty of reconstruction meant that the British market would for many years disappoint Canadians. The source of Britain's problems was financial, but the effects were felt in trade: its financial problems not only coloured Anglo-Canadian trade relations, but had also influenced the negotiation of the General Agreement on Tariffs and Trade (GATT). Throughout those negotiations, British efforts to maintain room for discriminatory trade measures had been as much driven by balance-of-payments considerations as by trade and employment concerns.

From the perspective of the 2000s, when most major currencies float relatively freely and exchange rate adjustments and balance-of-payments measures are no longer political headaches for the major industrialized economies, it is difficult to appreciate the problems raised by this set of issues. Only developing countries now routinely face the lash of adjusting to currency misalignments and balance-of-payments crises. But in the late 1940s and early 1950s, this was the crunch issue, made more urgent by the fact that the United Kingdom and Europe faced chronic balance-of-payments problems that, while evident even before the war, had been exacerbated by the heavy costs of the war and the erosion of British overseas investments. The obstacles were apparent in the GATT/ITO negotiations, in continuing discussions about emergency financial assistance, and in difficulties in making the International Monetary Fund (IMF) regime operational.[5]

Canada had sought to address this predicament through multilateralism and a series of bilateral trade deals and financial aid packages, to little avail. The UK economy was weak and stayed that way well into the 1950s as a result of the depth of the problem and the policy choices exercised by successive UK governments. The result was a precipitous fall in access for traditional Canadian exports such as wheat, cheese, eggs, bacon, apples, and newsprint. On the other side of the ledger, the United Kingdom proved incapable of supplying Canada with consumer and producer goods that Canadians could use at prices they were prepared to pay. In addition, because of its chronic deficit position, Britain was exercising stringent currency controls, curbing any possibility of private-sector investment. A steady decline in commercial ties to the United Kingdom was inevitable.

UK efforts to maintain and defend a discriminatory sterling bloc also kept other Commonwealth markets less open to Canadian goods than they might otherwise have been. Australia, New Zealand, South Africa, and the rest of the Commonwealth, unlike Canada, had opted at the outbreak of war to cast their lot exclusively with the British market and the sterling bloc. As a result, largely due to the inconvertibility of sterling, they found themselves increasingly tied to the British market, selling their raw materials there and buying British manufactured goods, often at higher prices than they could have found elsewhere, including Canada.

On the other side of the Channel, Canada did not fare any better. European recovery was impressive, but Canada did not gain much from it. Recovery got off to a solid start in 1945-6, suffered a setback in 1947, but was back on course in 1948 and did not stall in any serious way until the 1970s. Critically important factors were Canadian and US financial aid and cooperative efforts under the auspices of the Organization for European Economic Cooperation (OEEC). Steps toward European integration also made a critical contribution. The European Payments Union established in 1950 facilitated capital movements, while the European Coal and Steel Community of 1951, the European Common Market of 1958, and the European Free Trade Association of 1960 eased trade restrictions, complementing efforts in the GATT.[6] But continental European markets had never been well developed by Canadian exporters and, in the late 1940s, were suffering from difficulties similar to those of the United Kingdom: weak demand and access problems flowing from discriminatory balance-of-payments measures. For most of the first decade and a half after the end of the war, Europe developed along lines that emphasized Europe first. These steps toward economic and political integration were welcomed by the United States, and to some extent by Canada, for broad geopolitical reasons, but they had the unfortunate side effect of limiting opportunities for new transatlantic trade and investment.

Non-US markets in the Americas were still a poor prospect. Like Canada, they were rich in resources and poor in capital and manufactures, and thus offered little to a Canadian economy still in the early stages of industrialization. What little opportunity they did offer gradually diminished in the decades immediately following the war. The Caribbean islands were part of the closed sterling bloc, and country after country in Latin America adopted the import-substitution strategy advocated by the UN Economic Commission for Latin America. Efforts to rekindle rudimentary prewar steps to build trade relations with such countries as Brazil and Mexico, therefore, paid few dividends.

Demand across the Pacific was similarly inconsequential. In addition to the problems of postwar reconstruction in Japan and elsewhere, the Chinese market closed

Table 6.1

Canada's trade in goods, 1947-57 (value in millions of dollars)

Year	UK Value	%	United States Value	%	Rest of world Value	%	Total value
Exports							
1947	749	27.5	1,061	39.0	913	33.5	2,723
1949	701	23.5	1,521	50.9	767	25.6	2,989
1951	636	16.1	2,326	58.9	988	25.0	3,950
1953	656	15.8	2,458	59.2	1,038	25.0	4,152
1955	772	17.8	2,598	59.9	962	22.3	4,332
1957	734	15.0	2,931	59.9	1,229	25.1	4,894
Imports							
1947	182	7.2	1,951	77.0	402	15.8	2,535
1949	300	11.1	1,899	70.4	497	18.5	2,696
1951	417	10.2	2,846	69.4	838	20.4	4,101
1953	463	11.0	3,048	72.4	701	16.6	4,212
1955	406	8.9	3,283	72.3	854	18.8	4,453
1957	520	9.5	3,878	70.7	1,090	19.9	5,488

Note: Totals may not add due to rounding.
Source: F.H. Leacy, ed., *Historical Statistics of Canada*, 2nd ed. (Ottawa: Statistics Canada, 1983), series G57 and G70.

in 1949, while the markets of smaller countries were either part of the sterling bloc, disrupted by civil wars, or of so little consequence as to make little difference. Like Latin America, they might become important markets in later years, but offered little potential in the 1940s and 1950s. Efforts to develop these markets, while not unsuccessful, did not begin to lead to significant trading opportunities until well into the 1960s. (See table 6.1.)

As a practical matter, therefore, Canadian producers were left with only two markets that had any immediate growth potential, their own and that of the United States.[7] For most manufacturers, the Canadian market was more than sufficient to meet their capacity to supply. Many were branch plants that had limited mandates; others were content to take advantage of the protection offered by high tariffs and geared their production to a growing domestic market. With the United States, the only realistic alternative market, already well and often more cheaply supplied by its own manufacturers, many of which were related firms, there was little incentive to orient production to anything but the domestic market. For most farmers, the US market was basically available only during periods when US harvests were insufficient. The rest of the time, the US market was closed, even to more efficient Canadian producers, as a result of a variety of nontariff barriers flowing from the

1933 Agricultural Adjustment Act.[8] Only a few specialized products made it through those barriers. For resource and resource-based producers, the US market became the mainstay of existence and US investment the basis for expansion. The boom of 1900 to 1913 had been sustained by UK demand for Canadian foodstuffs and had accentuated Canada's east-west orientation; the boom of 1950 to 1957 was fuelled by a combination of domestic demand and US demand for Canadian raw materials, some of which could be attributed to the military spending for the Korean War.[9]

It was in these sobering circumstances that Canadian ministers and officials tried to devise policies that would increase export opportunities for competitive Canadian producers. They expended considerable effort to find the most realistic and workable trade regime, one that opened markets for Canadian agriculture and resource producers but that protected the vulnerable Canadian manufacturing sector. In order to understand the tangled web of Canadian trade policy that led ultimately to a continentalist result, we turn now to unravelling the four main strands of Canadian trade policy during this period: Canada's inability to maintain meaningful commercial ties with Britain and the Commonwealth; its disappointment in trying to expand access to the European market; its frustration in managing the burgeoning US connection; and its limited success in promoting Canadian interests in the fragile GATT during its early formative years.

The Waning of the British Connection

The end of war found an economically weak and financially troubled Britain and a strong and triumphant United States. Try as it might to help strengthen Britain and avoid the allure of the United States, Canada found itself drawn ever deeper into the US economic orbit and more and more dependent on US economic policy, markets, and capital. Not only did the United Kingdom's weakness force Canada into the arms of the United States, as Jack Granatstein has colourfully argued, but British ineptness in managing relations with Canada and the United States, and in pursuing trade and other negotiations, helped to drive Canada into the US orbit more quickly and with a sense of some satisfaction.[10]

The end of the war did not end the United Kingdom's continuing financial problems, which continued to crowd the trade agenda, making trade negotiations appear marginal at best. By 1946, Canada stood ready once again to extend a loan, this time to the tune of $1.25 billion at 2 percent interest beginning in 1951. At the same time, Ottawa cancelled the $425 million owing under the Commonwealth Air Training Plan, and agreed that the $1-billion loan of 1942 would continue interest-free until 1951. While again motivated by the desire to continue to sell Canadian goods – particularly food – to the United Kingdom, Canada was much more generous than the United States, which in the same year only managed a loan of $3.75 billion on much stiffer terms, in part because Canada's stake in continued trade with Britain and the Continent was much greater.[11]

The year 1946 also saw Canada negotiate a wheat deal that committed Britain to buy guaranteed quantities of Canadian wheat at a fixed price for four years (160 million bushels for two years, declining to 140 million bushels for the next two years, at $1.55 per bushel the first two years declining to $1.00 per bushel the final year). It turned out to be a great deal for the United Kingdom when the international price for wheat rose well above these levels. The deal had been insisted on by Agriculture Minister Jimmy Gardiner and his officials, who saw it as a way to provide a guaranteed market for Canadian wheat farmers, but it was disliked by trade officials, particularly because of the complications it created in relations with the United States.[12]

The following year a new round of Canada-UK trade and financial discussions took place against the backdrop of grim conditions in Europe. An unusually severe winter had followed a wet summer, both leading to great strains on UK and European coal and food supplies. Britain again needed help and again sought it across the Atlantic. This time the cupboard was practically bare in Ottawa. During a Canada-UK food mission that year, Canada tried to shore up trade relations with Britain, while Britain tried for its part to get out of some of its long-term food contracts or sweeten them in order to preserve dwindling dollar credits. The hard line taken by UK officials proved very difficult for Canadian officials to swallow, given the extent of Canadian aid over the preceding seven years and the United Kingdom's continued inability to provide Canada with any hope of tangible returns.[13] Discussions were painful and distasteful not only because of the United Kingdom's continuing weakness, but also because it was becoming abundantly clear that the United Kingdom was turning more and more to the Continent and to sterling members of the Commonwealth and leaving Canada to its own devices, next door to the United States.[14] Currency controls and related QRs made access to the UK market virtually a matter of state trading; there was little room for market-based private transactions.[15]

By 1947, Canada had extended an inordinate amount of credit to the United Kingdom, much of which seemed to be going down a sinkhole. At the same time, Canadians were spending more and more on imports from the United States, again creating an impossible balance-of-payments position for Canada, a situation that was aggravated by a premature decision to relax wartime currency restrictions and let the dollar trade at par (see table 6.2). UK requests for more help and entreaties for more understanding were beginning to lose their appeal.

By this time it was clear that long-term help could only come from the United States – either in the form of private investment or official assistance.[16] By late spring, US officials indicated a willingness to increase credit but only in return for European efforts at self-help. In a commencement address at Harvard on 5 June, Secretary of State George Marshall indicated that the United States would be prepared to help the countries of Europe in their reconstruction in order to avoid their falling into the orbit of the Soviet Union and world communism. Thus the Marshall Plan

Table 6.2

Canada's current account balances, 1946-57 (millions of dollars)

Year	UK	Other sterling	United States	Overall
1946	+500	+164	−607	+363
1947	+633	+242	−1,134	+49
1949	+446	+135	−601	+177
1951	+223	−24	−945	−512
1953	+132	+83	−907	−448
1955	+332	+60	−1,029	−687
1957	+120	+4	−1,579	−1,451

Source: F.H. Leacy, ed., Historical Statistics of Canada, 2nd ed. (Ottawa: Statistics Canada, 1983), series G83.

was born.[17] It would eventually resolve not only the UK exchange crisis but contribute to the full recovery of Europe. All that, however, was in the future. Between the idea and its execution lay a good many false starts. As late as the end of July one State Department official suggested that "the 'Marshall Plan' has been compared to a flying saucer – nobody knows what it looks like, how big it is, in what direction it is moving, or whether it really exists."[18]

Canadian officials were acutely aware of this uncertainty as their own financial situation deteriorated. As a result, on 17 November, Canada adopted severe trade and financial restrictions, concurrent with the announcement of the successful agreement of the GATT, and began exploratory discussions with US officials on various monetary and trade measures that could help ease the crisis. The Canadian situation was not alleviated until the following April when the US Congress finally passed the legislation mandating the Marshall Plan, including the provision that UK and other European purchases of Canadian goods could be made with Marshall Plan funds.[19] In response, the United Kingdom finally took steps to try to smooth some of the ruffled feathers in Ottawa, leading to the establishment of a Canada-UK Continuing Committee to discuss and try to anticipate and resolve problems.[20]

While 1947 was a bad year in Canada-UK relations, it was not atypical. From the early 1940s on, Canada-UK trade and economic relations had become increasingly strained, with Canadian officials feeling none too pleased with British imperial hauteur. The United Kingdom had been prolific in its requests but less so in its appreciation of Canadian help.[21] Canada soldiered on, however, because it was extremely worried about British intentions to pull a cordon sanitaire around the sterling area at the expense of the rest of the world. Under no circumstances did Canada want to see the establishment of two opposing trade blocks, with Canada isolated in a block with the United States and cut off from UK and Commonwealth markets. British attitudes, on the other hand, were coloured by its much bigger problems with the United States and its demands of multilateralism and nondiscrimination in return for financial and other aid. As a result, the North Atlantic triangle was awash with suspicion and mutual recriminations.[22]

Britain, of course, faced real problems, some flowing from the devastation and sacrifice of war, others from lack of confidence about the future and consequent policy choices. Fighting two world wars and weathering a global depression had exhausted Britain. Trying to maintain its role as a great, imperial power proved a burden rather than an asset in this ongoing travail. In addition, British industry was not adjusting; it lacked the capital to rebuild and modernize, and poor labour relations further undermined efforts to set things right. The Atlee government severely complicated Britain's problems with its determination to nationalize the commanding heights of the British economy, often with disastrous results. As a result, Britain produced goods that had little appeal beyond the captive domestic and Commonwealth markets. The artificial conditions created by nationalization and the tight currency controls within the sterling area made it more profitable for British firms to export to sterling customers than to customers in the more competitive dollar markets.[23]

The result was two decades of floundering and inept British foreign and economic policy with major implications for Canada. Although more obvious in the years after the war, the contours of British postwar economic policy had already been apparent during its wartime planning. British scepticism about the benefits of multilateralism and nondiscrimination, a faith imposed on her and other members of the Commonwealth by the United States through article 7 of the wartime lend-lease agreements, is well illustrated by Keynes, the leading economic advisor to the UK government. Britain, he had indicated, would be unable, after the losses of the war, to take the risks of an international economy organized on liberal lines until and unless adequate arrangements were made to solve Britain's international financial problems.[24] His assessment turned out to be a self-fulfilling prophecy. The almost constant application of currency restrictions, concomitant balance-of-payments measures, and other discriminatory restrictions steadily drove Canadian goods out of the UK market. For the same reason, Britain persisted in looking to other, sterling sources of imports, even where these were more costly. It continued to block private investment in Canada. Britain's weakness thus continued to bleed the Canadian connection, making it increasingly difficult for Canada to help prop up the UK relationship with financial aid. As long as Britain continued to seek bilateral deals within the high-cost sterling area, Canadian efforts to reverse the pattern were to little avail.[25]

Marshall Plan assistance did not fundamentally alter the United Kingdom's policy stance. Canada-UK-US discussions in the summer of 1949, for example, considered yet another precarious UK financial situation. Canada and the United States worked hard to dissuade the United Kingdom from isolating itself even further in closed Commonwealth arrangements, with only limited success. Britain agreed to devalue the pound, but at the same time tried to convince Canada to join the sterling area, a policy direction that would have been disastrous for Canada. The United Kingdom's financial situation had become increasingly untenable.

Britain's stringent trade actions to protect the sterling area had the perverse effect of draining Marshall Plan aid from the United Kingdom to the rest of the sterling area, perpetuating the structural problems that were keeping the United Kingdom from recovering and the whole area weak.[26] Britain believed that its future lay in its past and it was, therefore, determined to maintain trade links with the other dominions. While the Empire might no longer be the basis of British strength, UK officials believed that a properly constituted Commonwealth could play such a role, and British effort was consistently geared to that end. For Canada, this meant an irreversible deterioration in its trade with Britain, dictated by UK policies but slowed by Canada's Herculean efforts to keep the British connection afloat. These efforts were consistently unsuccessful because they foundered on British inability to pay, provide quality exports, or simply be reliable as either a customer or a supplier. The policy issue was the shortage of dollars and the efforts to preserve the few Britain gained from US purchases or aid; the problem, however, was much deeper and lay in the United Kingdom's difficulty in adjusting to changing realities.

In 1952, Norman Robertson concluded that "the impression left here by the documents sent here from London is that the British government is looking for a cure to sterling's recurrent crisis in external rather than domestic measures."[27] The unreliability of the United Kingdom as a customer and a supplier had led to the natural conclusion of both sellers and buyers that they were better off concentrating their efforts elsewhere. Noted the *Financial Times* of London: "Once custom has been transferred elsewhere, it is extremely difficult, if not impossible, to regain."[28] In the years that followed, there developed a growing suspicion in Ottawa that London's reluctance to move to convertibility and relax its balance-of-payments controls was at least in part a desire to shield British industry from North American competition.[29]

By this time, however, the damage had been done. Canadian concerns were as much driven by nostalgia as by any realistic expectation that the deterioration in the UK commercial connection could be reversed. Unfortunately for Canada, things were not much better on the Continent.

The Disappointment of Europe

The UK market was not the only market that proved a constant source of frustration to Canadians. Indeed, the decade after the successful establishment of the GATT put the hopes and expectations of Canadian negotiators to the test. They had played a constructive and influential role in the planning and negotiations, and had concluded a settlement at Geneva that, while not perfect, represented a compromise good enough to get rave reviews from the prime minister and from the media. They anticipated that the new policy would deliver and confidently looked forward to the day when European markets would be open to Canadian exporters of agriculture and resource products. Unfortunately, reality proved otherwise. Europe turned inward and shut out all but the goods that could not be produced at home. The fragility of reconstruction is usually cited to justify the continued application of discriminatory restrictions, but it was Europe's determination to pursue full employment policies within closed economies that was the real reason Canadian exporters faced continued disappointment. The move toward integration in the 1950s had the perverse effect of turning the more outward-looking European governments into members of an inward-looking block.

The popular image of Europe at the end of the war is one of chaos and despair, with cities flattened and populations on the move. There is truth to this, but Europe was not in as bad a state of repair as this image of chaos suggests: labour, industry, and capital equipment were in much more plentiful supply and Europe's ability to provide the wherewithal of economic recovery was much more robust than is generally supposed. Workers, factories, machines, and machine tools were ready to hand in 1945 to convert to peacetime production, as were the necessary management and organizational skills and the demand by consumers starved for the goods and services they had done without for fifteen years. There were bottlenecks, to be sure, such as in transportation, but these were quickly overcome. By the first quarter of 1946, for example, European railway traffic had already returned to prewar levels. The harsh winter of 1946-7 brought only temporary setbacks. Fuel and food shortages created problems and slowed recovery, but did not prevent it.[30] Canada's expectations of European markets were not unrealistic.

France, Belgium, Luxembourg, the Netherlands, and Norway were among the countries that had participated in the negotiation of the GATT and were among its original signatories. Led by France, they had also been among the most vocal in insisting on room to maintain discriminatory restrictions for balance-of-payments reasons as well as to allow time for reconstruction. All had participated in the negotiation of tariff concessions and most had made concessions of some value to each other as well as to Canada and the United States. The fruits of these negotiations, however, were more anticipatory than real, because the agreement, as well as its Protocol of Provisional Application, allowed the existing wide range of discriminatory restrictions to stay in place. Due to the continuing problem of currency inconvertibility leading to currency restrictions and discrimination against dollar imports for balance-of-payments reasons, the tariff concessions traded with most European countries remained meaningless.

At Geneva in 1947, the United States, Canada, and other participants in the negotiations were confident that the ITO would provide a sufficiently robust setting to tackle Europe's restrictions and restore multilateral trade within a reasonable time frame. With the failure of the ITO to come into being, that hope was transferred to the General Agreement. At early meetings in Geneva, Annecy, and Torquay, the issue was fervently pressed. As it turned out, however, GATT was not the instrument that would underwrite Europe's recovery and gradually remove the wide array of restrictions. As Alan Milward points out in his study of European recovery, there was a much more complex story that had its origins in the failure to address fundamental economic and political issues during the interwar years, which allowed nationalist and particularist forces to triumph.[31] In the immediate postwar years, European recovery was, if anything, too fast, because of the pent-up demand and the opportunity taken to rebuild and restructure on the basis of what was still a remarkable level of industrial capacity. What made recovery possible was the gradual development of intra-European interdependence through a series of institutions and experiments that gradually allowed foreign trade and investment to work their magic, complemented by help through the Marshall Plan and transatlantic trade. It was not the IMF but the European Payments Union (EPU) that proved critical. It was not the GATT but the European Coal and Steel Community, the European Common Market, and the European Free Trade Association that made the difference. It was not the Americans but the Europeans who reconstructed Europe and created the necessary institutions and procedures that made interdependence into a positive force.

American support for and European determination in the building of these intra-European institutions and arrangements were motivated by political factors, with commercial factors repeatedly pushed to the second rank. Canada did not disagree with the political motives that were central to the story of European integration, but it was acutely uncomfortable with the fact that transatlantic economic and commercial considerations were invariably given short shrift. The United States might be able to afford such an attitude, given the fact that less than 5 percent of its GNP depended on exports; Canada, with a much higher stake in foreign markets, could not. Canada's voice, however, although frequently raised, did not carry sufficient weight to make a difference. Canada stood by helplessly as the potential for greater transatlantic trade underwritten by adherence to the multilateral rules of GATT was repeatedly sacrificed on the altar of European reconstruction and integration.

The political factors behind European integration were relatively straightforward. For the Europeans, particularly the French, integration proved the means to keep the Germans involved in institutions and commitments that would discourage a revival of militarism. It also gave France access to the Ruhr and Saar coal and iron fields, essential to French industrial revival. For the Americans, the Marshall Plan and related efforts to promote European integration were an attempt to create a bulwark against the particularism that had led to the destructive prewar policies, to aid in reconstruction, and to prevent western Europe from falling into the Soviet orbit. The southern flank of Europe had threatened to do so in the late 1940s and early 1950s; it was already too late for the eastern flank.[32]

For both the United States and Britain, European integration and cooperation would work best if they comprised all the countries of Europe and involved commitments to the reduction and removal of tariff and nontariff barriers to intra-European trade. To this end, the United States sponsored the establishment of the Organization for European Economic Cooperation (OEEC), which channelled Marshall Plan aid and encouraged cooperative efforts under its auspices. These steps did not prove sufficient for France and the Benelux countries, which wanted to go further toward integration but maintain restrictions against outsiders. The tortured history of European integration is less important, however, than the consequences for Europe itself and for Canada. As Milward notes, "In the place of a liberal, unified Europe came a closely regulated Little European common market whose twin purposes were to provide for French national security by containing West Germany and to permit its members to continue to pursue a very limited range of common economic policies in a few specific sectors of the economy, which would otherwise have proven impossible."[33] From Canada's perspective, there was a clear lesson here: even the United States with its vast resources could not orchestrate matters in Europe to meet its own goals and objectives; Canada, with far fewer resources, stood even less of a chance.

By the end of the 1950s, Europe had divided into two commercial camps. On the Continent, the Common Market of France, Germany, Italy, and the Benelux countries – the Inner Six – had, through the 1957 Treaty of Rome, set up a tightly controlled customs union with relatively high barriers to outsiders as a result of the Common External Tariff (CET) and the Common Agricultural Policy (CAP). Around them were arrayed the Outer Seven of the United Kingdom, Sweden, Denmark, Norway, Austria, Switzerland, and Portugal in a more loosely organized freetrade area set up by the 1960 Treaty of Stockholm, which provided for free trade in industrial products but allowed members to maintain independent trade regimes against the rest of the world. By this time, currencies had become convertible, and both groups were committed to relaxing the wide range of restrictions that had sheltered them in previous years. For Canada, however, the period of restrictions had been decisive. It had effectively shut Canadian exporters out of important markets.

Canada, however, did try. As soon as the Marshall Plan was set up, Canada's trade commissioners in Europe were instructed to fan out and get to work to convince buyers and governments to use their Marshall Plan dollars to buy from Canada if price and other conditions of supply were comparable. In the first few months, Canada was remarkably successful, garnering almost a quarter of Marshall Plan dollars for purchases from Canada.[34] This success was not to last. European officials, fearful that Marshall Plan dollars would dry up, preferred to channel their overseas purchases to the United States. The bureaucratic, centralized allocation method set up to administer Marshall Plan funds facilitated such decisions.[35] European preferences were a natural response to congressional anxieties about who was extending grants and credits and who should benefit. The administration and Marshall Plan officials might take a broader view, but Congress in the end controlled the purse strings. The extension of Canadian credits, both to the United Kingdom and to France and the Benelux countries, sought to offset European preferences, but the total available could not match the generosity of Marshall Plan dollars.

As early as 1949 Canada watched in frustration as Europe drew deeper into its shell, avoiding its new GATT obligations on the basis of GATT-sanctioned balance-of-payments restrictions. In addition, Britain, facing yet another exchange crisis, prepared to increase discrimination against Canada in favour of the soft-currency Europeans. The lesson learned during this period should have endured: Canadians should have appreciated the full force of Lord Palmerston's maxim that nations do not have friends, they have interests. Many countries in Europe were prepared to have Canada as a friend; few were prepared to accept that better economic relations with Canada represented any compelling interest. However, this was a hard lesson that Canadians did not want to learn. Repeatedly they looked to the United Kingdom and Europe, convinced that ties of blood, sentiment, history, and friendship would translate into trade and investment. They never did.[36]

European discrimination meant that Canada was at the bottom of the list of potential suppliers, even in situations in which Canada had the right product at the best price. The first option was to do without, followed by producing it domestically, buying from another European supplier, buying from the sterling area, buying from the United States, or finally buying from Canada. Even eastern Europe was often the preferred supplier. Canada worked hard to overcome this attitude and promote European prosperity in the vain hope that it would ultimately lead to sales.[37] It did not. Europe took 8 percent of Canada's exports in 1947; 4 percent in 1950; and 6 percent in 1955. Again, circumstances and attitudes beyond the control of Canadian ministers and officials conspired to make the American market the most viable option.

The New Hegemon and the Special Relationship

Circumstances dictated that Canada would become increasingly dependent on the United States as an outlet for its competitive producers and as a source of capital, manufactures, consumer goods, out-of-season fruits and vegetables, services, and much more. In 1946, the United States had taken 38 percent and the United Kingdom and western Europe 47 percent of Canada's exports. By 1948, the pattern had reversed to 50 and 33 percent respectively, and by 1950 the United States was taking 65 percent with the United Kingdom and continental Europe down to a mere 21 percent of the total. (See also table 6.1 above.) The following years saw a great boom in Canadian resource development, stimulated by American demand, financed by American capital, and including oil, gas, uranium, nickel, and iron ore, and related infrastructure developments such as pipelines and the St. Lawrence Seaway. In addition, the cold war and the Korean War further stimulated US investment in Canadian resources as a stable and secure source of supply, and cooperation on defence production drew Canada deeper into the US military supply system.[38]

On the whole, Canada prospered from the relationship, but Canadians were to find that close relations with a hegemon could be trying, particularly once the outwardly oriented Truman presidency was replaced by the more inwardly focused Eisenhower administration. Both administrations, however, were guilty, at least from the perspective of some Canadians, of not being sufficiently solicitous of Canadian interests. Coming to grips with this reality, made enormously more important as a result of the steep growth in economic interdependence, was one of the central challenges faced by Canadian policy makers in the 1950s.

This state of affairs, of course, had already been apparent in the 1940s, but the cooperative spirit that had reigned in the successful pursuit of wartime teamwork and in the postwar establishment of the multilateral trade and payments system had muted the sting of US arrogance and frequent indifference to Canadian problems. By the late 1940s, however, these American mindsets were becoming increasingly annoying. The real test came with the election of General Eisenhower in 1952, bringing twenty years of Democrat administrations to an end. Canadian Liberal ministers and their officials had developed a congenial relationship with the Democrats, often referring to it as a "special relationship." They saw eye to eye on many issues. To both, Congress was the source of problems on the trade front; ministers and cabinet secretaries knew what had to be done in the national interest of both countries.

It was Congress, after all, that had failed to embrace the International Trade Organization and that had gradually begun to curtail the freedom with which the administration pursued its delegated authority to negotiate trade agreements. The reciprocal trade agreements (RTA) program had been renewed without substantial change in 1937, 1940, and 1943. It had been extended with much more difficulty in 1945, providing the basis for the GATT negotiations. It was extended again in 1948, 1949, and 1951, but each time was hemmed in by safeguards such as the escape clause, the national security exception, and peril-point considerations.[39] In the face of Republican majorities in both the House and the Senate, the Truman administration had fought hard to preserve its room to negotiate and had accepted a number of the changes only in an effort to forestall even more limiting modifications. Fortunately, the bark turned out to be much worse than the bite. Between 1947 and 1951, some twenty-one escape clause applications led to only two actions. As a result, the United States had been able to play an effective role in the Geneva negotiations, and Canada had been able to negotiate tariff deals that promised to provide its exporters with new opportunities.[40]

In 1953, however, the Republicans not only retained control of both houses of Congress but also gained control of the White House. This shift provided a real test of the US commitment to the liberal trade program introduced by Cordell Hull and carried on by his successors. Conservatives in Congress immediately set out to test the new administration and called for a return to the Smoot-Hawley Tariff Act of 1930. Eisenhower, however, was not prepared to turn the clock back to that extent and in 1953 successfully secured a one-year extension of the RTA program on the promise that the administration would not engage in any new, substantive negotiations during this period.[41]

In an effort to build a new consensus, Eisenhower appointed the Randall Commission on Foreign Economic Policy to chart a course for the future. Despite intense internal division, the commission forged a report that advocated a general continuation of liberal internationalism.[42] Administration-sponsored legislation to that effect could not gain a congressional hearing, however, and Eisenhower had to be content with another one-year extension of the old act in 1954. Not until 1955, when Congress returned to the Democratic fold, could Eisenhower secure the necessary new legislation, albeit with both the escape clause and peril-point provisions intact. Eisenhower now had new authority to negotiate cuts up to 15 percent over three years from their 1955 levels. Given the US dominance of the global economy in the 1950s, this was not much of an authority, but it represented as much as Congress was prepared to delegate.[43] The act was extended in 1958 with new authority for cuts up to 20 percent from their 1958 levels, but with tighter discipline on presidential discretion in accepting the advice of the Tariff Commission.[44]

Although not prepared to turn back the clock, Eisenhower was not interested in any bold new steps into the future. Eisenhower might personally have been internationalist in his outlook, but other members of his administration were markedly more protectionist in their views.[45] For Canadian trade interests, this was not a happy development. In the words of historians Bothwell, Drummond, and English, "Sure of itself and conscious of its rectitude, the Eisenhower administration treated Canada with friendly unconcern ... On economic matters Eisenhower did not bring back old-fashioned high-tariff Republicanism, but he did enforce a blind devotion to domestic economic interests to the exclusion of America's allies."[46]

The new administration was not ignorant of Canada. Treasury Secretary George Humphrey, as the president of Hanna Mining of Cleveland, had been one of the principals in the establishment of the Iron Ore Company of Canada. Defense Secretary Charles Wilson had been a senior executive of General Motors, and Secretary of State John Foster Dulles owned property in Canada. Like all good Republicans, however, they saw US interests in terms of the narrow concerns of US business or the broader preoccupation with security in all its ramifications. Good relations with Canada played a distinct second fiddle to such considerations. Specific irritants included wheat sales to traditional Canadian markets under the PL-480 program (concessional sales to poor countries)[47] and the use of section 22 of the Agricultural Adjustment Act of 1933 to place import quotas on dairy products (in 1953, adversely affecting Canadian sales of cheese and skim milk powder) and grains (in 1954, adversely affecting Canadian sales of oats, barley, and rye). In 1955, the United States successfully sought a GATT waiver for this kind of section 22 action over the strenuous objections of Canada. Other traditional agricultural exporters, such as Australia, were more muted in their criticism, convinced that without a waiver for US agricultural programs, the GATT as a whole could collapse.[48]

Between 1947 and 1962, US industry initiated 134 safeguard investigations of which fifteen– a modest one per year – resulted in a safeguard measure. Canada, however, often found itself at the wrong end of actions on products such as red-cedar shingles, clover seed, groundfish fillets, and lead and zinc. Canada also found its oil exports restricted on national security grounds, though subsequently excluded as a result of heavy lobbying. Growing Canadian trade with the United States was inevitably increasing the number of irritants as the US complaints system provided scope for US producers to worry about increased competition. In defence of these actions in meetings with Canadians, American officials regularly used the argument that small doses of protectionism acted as an inoculation to prevent the growth of much more virulent strains. This sounded good, but provided little comfort to Prairie wheat farmers, Quebec lead and zinc miners, BC forestry workers, or Ontario dairy farmers.[49]

Among the more galling aggravations was US policy on wheat. Wheat sales had long been one of the mainstays of Canada's export trade, but by the early 1950s, Canada's wheat was in trouble as European markets began to dry up. The revival of the European economies meant not only that Canada was exporting less, but also that it was facing more competition. To this already depressing mix, the United States now added the insult of artificially high agricultural production stimulated by various US income support measures. The United States not only used import quotas to keep Canadian exports out of its market, but also relied on concessional sales to compete unfairly with Canadian exports to third markets.[50] The Eisenhower administration, however, ignored Canadian pleas not to undercut Canadian sales in its traditional markets.[51]

Canadians also learned to appreciate that opening the US market was more than a matter of reducing the high tariffs set in the seventy-five years between the Civil War and the depression. The Byzantine nature of US customs administration and the many detailed rules and procedures in the Tariff Act of 1930 added considerably to the hurdles that needed to be jumped to do business in the world's largest and richest market. While American politicians became fond of describing the United States as the most open economy in the world during this period, their claim was not based on any objective standard of openness.[52]

Despite these handicaps, trade and investment between Canada and the United States grew steadily. In response, the two governments set up various mechanisms to manage relations better, including a Canada-US ministerial committee that allowed issues to be discussed and resolved as early as possible. The Canadian embassy in Washington, upgraded from legation to embassy status during the war, saw its resources increased to ensure that Canadian ministers had early and accurate information on US policy developments as well as the staff to deal effectively with the State Department in pressing Canadian interests. The main hope, however, continued to rest with the General Agreement in Geneva and its broad multilateral rules. There Canada pushed hard to curb the US appetite for the fixes that would appease Congress and to convince the United States to exercise the kind of leadership that while critical to GATT's establishment had been notably absent in its formative years.

The Fragility of Multilateralism

The decade after the establishment of the GATT was a period of both hope and frustration for Canadian trade officials. Rising prosperity at home was tempered by the disappointment of the decline in commercial ties to the United Kingdom, the failure of the European continent to deliver on its potential as a new market and economic partner, and the constant irritation of dealing with the arrogance and self-absorption of the United States. No wonder, therefore, that Canadian policy makers placed such hope in the ability of the new trade arrangement in Geneva to provide them with a means to address their problems. The GATT's early years, however, severely tested the fledgling multilateral trading order.[53] Having expected much, Canadian officials were among the most let down. By the end of the 1950s, they had become pessimistic about the GATT's continuing capacity to meet Canadian objectives. The strong faith in multilateralism exhibited by Canadian negotiators at its birth was not confirmed by results before well into the 1960s. Until then, multilateralism was a fragile reed on which to lean.[54]

The trade policy problems that Canada faced in the period from 1948 to 1958 – from the negotiation and implementation of the GATT to the reintroduction of currency convertibility in the United Kingdom and Europe – were in their immediate sense problems of access. The more fundamental difficulty, however, was the failure of the monetary system, and that failure flowed directly from the profound weakness of the Bretton Woods monetary institutions. The concessions traded between Europe and North America, for example, were meaningless as long as Europe bristled with discriminatory balance-of-payments restrictions. In these circumstances, GATT negotiations, discussions, and dispute settlement could address symptoms but had no capacity to deal with the underlying causes. Without the underpinning of stable, convertible currencies, the GATT's liberal rules could not be made to work.[55]

There were also trade policy reasons why the GATT's early years proved disappointing. The continuing weakness of the European economies – whether perceived or real – disposed the European members to be cautious in their approach to trade issues and in their willingness to make more concessions to the stronger economies across the Atlantic. For example, when Japan acceded in 1955, many European countries invoked the nonapplication provisions of article XXXV to avoid having to open their markets to Japan.[56] At the same time, deeply ingrained congressional protectionism, particularly on agriculture, made the US more circumspect in its leadership than its economic conditions warranted.

For Canada, the most glaring deficiency was the continued application of quantitative restrictions.[57] GATT members had agreed in 1947 to eliminate all QRs (article XI) in accordance with US practice and ideology, at least as far as industrial products were concerned. The logic of the US position was impeccable if the world were to embrace nondiscrimination and rely on tariff negotiations to make trade freer, but the position was not widely shared. As a result, European members maintained their QRs as long as possible, justifying them either as temporarily necessary (for balance-of-payments reasons under article XII, or for economic reconstruction and development reasons pursuant to article XVIII) or permanent (for agriculture – a position strengthened when the United States obtained a waiver in 1955 to maintain its own QRs on agricultural imports).

From the outset, therefore, the GATT at the same time deplored and tolerated the QRs that were a prominent feature of the commercial policies of most of its members, but not of Canada and the United States. Canada hoped that this was a temporary phenomenon of postwar reconstruction, after which the normal rules would kick in and the escape clauses be more strictly applied. It took time before the European members realized that QRs were a double-edged sword. It was not until 1955, for example, that the UK government began to appreciate the extent to which QRs not only safeguarded the United Kingdom's balance-of-payments position but also prevented an expansion of its exports. In short, QRs were a holdover of the beggar-thy-neighbour policies of the 1930s and frustrated a broad expansion of trade on a multilateral basis.

Lack of firm US leadership on trade policy matters also contributed to initial disappointment with the GATT. Liberal US trade policy had been a creature of Secretary of State Cordell Hull, and his leadership had been critical in the realization of, first, the reciprocal trade agreements program, and then the design of a multilateral postwar trade order. Hull's resignation in 1944 left a gap that was not filled until President Kennedy took up the cause of trade liberalization in 1961. Although during the intervening period the United States followed the trail blazed by Hull, it did so without the vision, determination, and leadership Hull and his close circle of advisors had brought to the issue. As a result, the pace, creativity, and depth of commitment necessary to the task were at times lacking, particularly in the State Department.[58]

As a former congressman and senator, Hull had been particularly good at working with Congress and overcoming its prejudices. His successors were not so adept at convincing Congress that the postwar iteration of the reciprocal trade agreements program, as expressed in the GATT, was in the US interest. Congress had become more jealous of its delegation and more leery of the extent to which US producers were being exposed to competition, and made classic mercantilist demands for more export opportunities without exposing the US economy to too many new imports. Of course, the extent of US exposure to foreign competition during this period was minimal, never rising above 4 percent of US GNP during the decade of the 1950s. Many members of Congress, however, insisted on the narrowest view of reciprocity and were suspicious of any efforts to place US trade interests on a broader plane.

Congressional suspicion of the GATT reflected lack of enthusiasm for any arrangement that could put congressional decision making in the straitjacket of an international agreement. Perfectionists additionally argued that the United States would be held to the tight general rules while other countries would be able to make frequent use of the many escape clauses that marred both the ITO and the GATT. Difficulties in making the GATT work further eroded congressional support, in turn undermining efforts to make the GATT work.[59]

Contemporary pessimism about the GATT, however, should not obscure the fact that barriers did decline during the 1950s and that trade did increase (see table 6.3). The 1945 renewal of the RTA Act might have marked the high point of liberalism in the United States, but there continued to be broad support for the RTA program. Congress might not have been a fan of free trade, but it did support freer trade, an objective widely shared among business, academic, and government elites from the late 1940s on. The depression had discredited protectionism, and the success of the RTA program had confirmed the value of a pragmatic liberalism. This was an elitist opinion, not necessarily favoured by the general public, for whom trade and trade policy were not important issues, but it was strongly held among those who designed and implemented US trade policy and those who advised them in the think tanks and in industry. In the 1950s, the liberalism of US trade policy was further reinforced by the new strategic and geopolitical considerations of the cold war, which could usefully be deployed to overcome the misgivings of conservative Republicans. But

Table 6.3

Value and volume of world trade and output, 1948-57

	Value (US$ billions)		Volume (1938 = 100)	
Year	World exports	US exports	World exports	World output
1948	55.01	12.65	93	128
1950	56.78	9.65	112	146
1951	76.02	13.46	123	151
1952	72.43	12.81	121	155
1953	71.43	11.86	125	163
1954	75.69	12.43	134	164
1955	83.95	13.82	148	178
1956	93.27	16.90	162	185
1957	100.56	18.87	170	187

Source: GATT, *International Trade*, 1957-8 (Geneva: GATT, 1959).

liberalism was no longer pursued with the missionary fervour and conviction of Cordell Hull, and there was a greater willingness to accommodate special interests.[60]

A direct corollary of less enthusiastic US leadership was GATT's weak constitutional structure. The ITO had contained a strong institutional component. Efforts to introduce a watered-down version into the GATT failed, largely because the US Congress was unprepared to see the establishment of a strong institution with authority to second-guess its decisions. As a result, "GATT spent the better part of its first ten years of existence waiting and hoping for the creation of a permanent organizational structure. While it waited, it dealt with the pressing commercial policy business of the day by whatever ad hoc arrangements could be fashioned on the spot."[61] In the absence of formal institutional machinery, business was conducted by an informal extension of the preparatory committee; the chairman of the commercial policy committee, Canada's Dana Wilgress, functioned as chairman with the help of the preparatory staff headed by Eric Wyndham White.

The first few sessions of the Contracting Parties concentrated on expanding membership and consolidating tariff concessions. In the process, a number of issues

Canada's Dana Wilgress chairs an early session of the GATT at Geneva, c. 1950.

needed to be addressed, including the problem faced by low-tariff European countries in negotiating with high-tariff countries like France and the United States, both in terms of increasing opportunities for export industries and of moving toward a single European market. Various plans were put forward by Dutch, Belgian, French, and other representatives, who tried to make the GATT the forum for resolving their problems. All foundered on the inability of the United States to move Congress toward the delegation of a new authority that would give it the scope to respond to European offers as well as to UK intransigence in dealing with both preferences and its by now relatively high tariffs. As a result, only modest progress was made in lowering tariffs beyond the initial cuts agreed in 1947 and expanded to new members in subsequent sessions. Additionally, the Europeans looked more and more to intra-European arrangements to cope with conflicts.[62]

Canada participated actively in these discussions. Not only did Wilgress chair the first five sessions, but officials from Ottawa came regularly with a mandate to try to make GATT work and to contribute to resolving the problems Canada was experiencing in gaining access to Europe and in managing relations with the United States. The decade and a half after the Second World War was the golden age of Canadian postwar foreign policy. Canadian officials could be found everywhere trying, often successfully, to combine enlightened internationalism with pursuit of Canada's own interests. A new round of talks was held in Annecy, France, in 1949 to negotiate the accession of Italy, Denmark, Sweden, Finland, Liberia, Greece, and Uruguay. Canada and the United States did not negotiate with each other at Annecy because it was considered too soon after 1947, but both did participate actively in the accession negotiations and benefited from concessions that expanded their MFN advantages. Indeed, Canada pressed its interests with such dogged determination that it gained a reputation for sanctimony; most other GATT members appeared more ready to accept the imperfections of the GATT and its members.[63]

In 1950-1 at Torquay in the south of England, the main issue was the accession of Germany, but Canada and the United States did negotiate with each other to take advantage of what was left of President Truman's negotiating authority. Canada succeeded in negotiating a reasonable deal with the United States involving US concessions on some 400 items affecting $120 million in recent exports. In general, however, the second (Annecy) and third (Torquay) rounds were disappointing to Canadian officials, a disappointment shared by trade officials elsewhere looking for proof that the new technique of multilateral negotiations could bring immediate and tangible results. At Geneva in 1947, it had been possible to negotiate some 123 bilateral agreements, many containing solid concessions. At Annecy and Torquay, some 147 bilateral negotiations were completed, despite a larger potential given the expanded membership, but most involved only limited concessions. Worse, deteriorating conditions in Europe disposed countries to withdraw or modify concessions, as provided for in article XXVIII. Some 300 concessions were modified or withdrawn at Torquay. Nevertheless, at the end of the Torquay conference, plans were made for a fourth round in Toronto in September 1953. Nothing, unfortunately, came of the plans and Canada would have to wait until 1988 before a GATT session was held on its territory (the midterm review in Montreal of the eighth or Uruguay Round).[64]

By the end of the Torquay meeting, when the delegations bravely called for ratification of the ITO, GATT could boast a total membership of thirty-six countries. Despite disappointment at the US decision to withdraw the ITO proposal from congressional consideration, the GATT soldiered on. Plans began to give the GATT a more permanent character. At the sixth session in Geneva at the end of 1951, members devoted considerable attention to the issue but were unable to make much headway in the face of continuing congressional hostility to the GATT as an institution. Dana Wilgress stepped down as chairman, and the session agreed to set up an intersessional ad hoc committee. At the seventh session held in late 1952, again at Geneva, plans were set afoot for a review session to examine the whole future of the agreement. This review session (the ninth regular session) met in Geneva in late 1954. By that time Geneva was confirmed as the permanent site for GATT's deliberations, and the GATT had adopted a workmanlike approach to the conduct of its business.[65]

The review session set about putting the GATT on a more permanent and institutionally satisfactory footing, but proposals to set up an Organization for Trade Cooperation (OTC) failed, as did efforts to strengthen virtually every article of the agreement. In the end, members again showed their caution by amending only those provisions that clearly required change, such as articles XVI (subsidies) and XVIII (reconstruction and development). GATT's new institutional machinery amounted to little more than formalizing practice as it had already developed. The OTC was initially accepted by members but then rejected by the US Congress, and the GATT was revised again to reflect this disappointment. More successfully, a concerted effort was made to eliminate existing QRs and to tighten the exceptions that allowed new ones by introducing more searching consultations. As a result, there was a major retreat from QRs in the second half of the 1950s; by the early 1960s, only a hard core of such restrictions remained in place in Europe. Discussions in the OEEC were critical in moving this issue along. For industrial products, the issue was largely resolved by the early 1960s, but QRs remained in place on agriculture, in some cases not to be removed until the beginning of 1995, pursuant to the Uruguay Round agreement to convert all agricultural nontariff barriers to ordinary customs tariffs.[66]

Following the conclusion of the review session, members stayed on in Geneva for a fourth round of tariff negotiations. These opened in January 1956 with an air of pessimism. Over the previous five years, members had failed to find a generally satisfactory formula for a further wholesale reduction in tariffs capable of reducing average tariff levels to those in place in the low-tariff countries. All that the members were able to achieve was a further round of incremental cuts arrived at through bilateral, item-by-item negotiation based on the offer-request, principal-supplier technique. An across-the-board approach remained too rich for the principal players. The United States had insufficient authority, and the United Kingdom was, once again, unprepared to run the risk of further opening its economy. The failure to meet the aspirations of the European countries contributed to the determination of the Six (France, Germany, Italy, and the Benelux countries) to move toward a customs union that would solve the problem of intra-European tariff disparity, taking the issue outside the GATT and resolving it through a common customs territory. Unfortunately, the Treaty of Rome, which flowed from this development, established a common external tariff at levels closer to those prevailing in France than to those in the Netherlands and other low-tariff countries. The experience of these opening years, however, had not all been negative; much had been learned, including the limits and contours of what was politically possible within the framework provided by the GATT.[67]

The complexity of the first three post-1947 rounds of GATT negotiations can be appreciated by considering the incompatible objectives being pursued by the main participants. The United States administration sought to balance its broad geopolitical aims (the cold war and European unity) with the more prosaic and narrowly conceived trade policy aims required by the reality of its congressionally delegated authority. At Annecy and Torquay, it tried to realize the benefits of a wider GATT membership, including the rest of Europe, as a bulwark against the menace of communism, at the same time negotiating specific tariff concessions as mandated by Congress. The United States wanted to eliminate the evil of imperial preferences but not at the price of substantially lowering its own barriers. It wanted to strengthen multilateralism but was prepared to see Europe take detours for geopolitical reasons.

Similarly, the United Kingdom wanted to strengthen and maintain the Empire and sterling bloc, solve the balance-of-payments problems consequent from this policy, promote a relatively shallow European integration, discourage the deeper integration sought by its Continental rivals, and improve access to the US market for British manufactures. France wanted a European integration scheme that would keep Britain at bay, maintain protection around the continent at French levels, and safeguard access to the Ruhr and Saar coal and iron mines. Canada wanted to restore multilateral trade, enhance access to the US market, keep its traditional markets, and protect fragile manufacturing industries.

These varying and incompatible objectives created complex negotiating circumstances that could only lead to significant results if at least one of the major players was able to exercise strong leadership based on long-term considerations rather than short-term complications. No such leadership emerged in the 1950s. US negotiators found their wings clipped by Congress, and the Eisenhower administration was reluctant to take on Congress and US business. The United Kingdom was equally disinclined to take the long view. Not surprisingly, Canada found both the UK and US positions increasingly frustrating.

American historiography and Canadian romanticism have perpetuated the myth that the American dream of a multilateral trade and payments system anchored in the Bretton Woods monetary institutions and the GATT paved the way for the era of economic expansion and prosperity of the 1950s and 1960s. The reality was somewhat different. The multilateral rules and institutions established in the 1940s led a precarious existence throughout the 1950s and into the 1960s. The IMF multilateral payments system never worked as intended and was finally abandoned in the 1970s for a more flexible approach. The multilateral trade system gradually expanded in the 1950s, because the overly ambitious ITO was allowed to die and the demands placed on the GATT were small and sustainable. It was not until well into the 1960s that the GATT achieved the kind of success that became the basis for the fond memories of the 1980s and 1990s.[68]

The basis for the prosperity of the 1950s and 1960s was instead national economic interdependence, championed in later years as the hallmark of the multilateral trade and payments system of the IMF and the GATT, but originally built on a much more complex set of institutions and relationships. Within Europe, the various schemes for economic integration, involving both trade and payments, were critical. In North America, it was the increasing interdependence of the United States and Canada, and for the United States additionally, the growth of transatlantic and eventually transpacific interdependence.

The poor relations in this system of interlocking national interdependencies were the Antipodes and the developing countries. The GATT system never addressed their needs and aspirations. Indeed, it agreed that they should be allowed to practice autarchy or national self-sufficiency. Australia and the developing countries successfully argued at Geneva in 1947 that their relative poverty should translate into less-onerous obligations. As a result, the GATT's rules played only a minimal role in the growth of the economies of Australia and New Zealand as well as those of the developing countries. It was not until the 1960s and 1970s, when newly independent but unsuccessful national economies in Africa and Asia joined the still unsuccessful national economies of Latin America, that a new consciousness developed about how to bring these countries into a system from which they did not seem to benefit. By then the reputation of the GATT was finally established.[69]

The GATT survived these early trials and built the necessary foundation for its more successful future. Despite contemporary pessimism, its achievements were not insignificant. At Geneva in 1947, 45,000 concessions were traded; at Annecy in 1948, 5,000; and at Torquay in 1951, 8,700. These were consolidated at the Geneva review session in 1955 into a total of 58,700 concessions among the thirty-seven participating countries.[70] Additionally, the GATT had succeeded in stabilizing tariff schedules through bindings and more uniform classifications. It had also, albeit somewhat later than Canadians had hoped, begun to tackle the problem of quantitative restrictions and adopted a schedule for their elimination. Finally, the GATT had developed a pragmatic but effective way of overcoming its constitutional weak-

Canada at the GATT at Geneva, c. 1958.

ness through a series of ad hoc arrangements that had taken on an air of permanence by the end of the 1950s. The most important of these involved procedures to resolve disputes and thus strengthen members' capacity to abide by the rules with the confidence that they could be enforced.

During the first few sessions, disputes were largely resolved by the call of the chair or, if the issue was complex, with the help of a working party made up of interested members. The prestige of Dana Wilgress in the chair added to the willingness of members to abide by his rulings. Three or four issues were resolved at each of the first few sessions, gradually strengthening respect for the rule of law. By the seventh session in 1952, a new approach was introduced involving a panel of experts serving in their personal capacity. Canada's Claude Isbister chaired this first panel, and Jean Royer, the GATT's deputy executive secretary, widely regarded as a master of the GATT's rules, assisted the panel. It addressed some twelve complaints raised by members, which suggested that this could be a more satisfactory long-term approach. Over the next six years, some forty complaints were assigned to panels, and many were successfully resolved as a result of the capacity of the panellists and the secretariat to help the disputants understand the issues involved and the GATT provisions affected. By the end of the review session in 1955, members began to refer to these procedures as customary, and the secretariat referred to them in its written reports.[71]

The approach to rule enforcement and dispute resolution that evolved over this first decade was grounded in the understanding that the GATT was a contractual arrangement that involved a mutually satisfactory balance of concessions among its participants. Any action – or inaction – by a member that upset this balance gave other members – or contracting parties – a right to seek redress. The concept of a multilateral code of conduct that would condition members' economic policies was still novel in the 1950s, and GATT members approached the issue of enforcement and dispute resolution cautiously. Nevertheless, by the end of the decade they had succeeded through a process of trial and error in developing a unique set of procedures that, while still largely grounded in diplomatic concepts of conciliation and negotiation, laid a firm foundation for the prospect of moving toward adjudication.

By the end of the 1950s, the postwar problems that had preoccupied the first generation of officials who had negotiated the GATT and managed its fragile existence had thus been resolved, and a new range of problems needed to be addressed. Despite the prevailing pessimism about what the GATT had accomplished, the GATT was by now both resilient and robust enough to adapt further and prove capable of addressing such new issues as regional integration and new members. In effect, GATT had succeeded in consolidating the trade regimes of its member countries into the beginnings of a relatively uniform, stable, and predictable international regime.

Nevertheless, Canada's geographic proximity to the United States, coupled with the disappointments of the UK, Commonwealth, and continental European markets, had deepened Canada's reliance on the United States as both its principal export market and its main source of imported goods, services, capital, and technology. Canada had found the multilateral option attractive because it allowed the country to chart an independent course and maintain good trade relations with its two most important trade and investment partners. Circumstances beyond Canada's control had made this dream impossible to achieve. Even more critically, the structure of protection in Canada and the United States had created an interdependence in the two countries' industrial and economic structures that would have a profound influence on Canada's further economic development. As we shall see, not everyone was pleased with this turn of events, and some were prepared to blame the federal government and its advisors for selling out to the United States.

7 THE STRUCTURE OF PROTECTION AND ITS IMPACT

A policy of trade restrictions is a treacherous instrument even for the attainment of its ostensible object, since private interest, administrative incompetence and the intrinsic difficulty of the task may divert it into producing results directly opposite to those intended.

– JOHN MAYNARD KEYNES, THE GENERAL THEORY
OF EMPLOYMENT, INTEREST AND MONEY

The tilt of Canada's economy toward continentalism during the 1950s had been less a matter of design than of circumstance. The markets of Europe, Latin America, and Asia had all been virtually closed to Canadian exporters in the decade after the Second World War. The American market, on the other hand, while still shielded by relatively high levels of protection for agricultural and manufactured goods, at least welcomed Canadian resources and industrial inputs. Even more importantly, American capital was available to make up for the shortage of Canadian capital and to help develop Canada's resource and manufacturing sectors. The political and economic circumstances of the first decade and a half after the war further reinforced the natural links between the American and Canadian economies flowing from geographic proximity. All other links, while perhaps desirable, proved anaemic at best. Canada's dream of a multilateral world had been tempered by a continental reality.

Growth in the Canadian economy postwar, however, was dictated more by domestic demand than by exports. During earlier periods of strong economic expansion in Canada – the middle of the nineteenth century, the opening years of the twentieth century, and the decade after the First World War – growth had been fuelled in large part by foreign demand. By contrast, in the late 1940s and throughout the 1950s, it was the combination of pent-up demand denied during fifteen years of depression and war, the baby boom, and high levels of immigration that drove growth in the Canadian economy. Indeed, in 1959 merchandise exports at 14.0 percent of GNP reached one of their lowest levels in Canadian history. Over the next decade, they began to increase steadily to reach 19.7 percent of GNP in 1970, a level still well below what had been achieved in the 1920s (see table 7.1).

Table 7.1

Merchandise trade and the Canadian economy, 1950-70

Year	Domestic merchandise exports (current $ millions)	GNP at market prices (current $ millions)	Exports/ GNP (%)	Canadian share of world trade (%)
1950	3,139	18,491	17.0	5.3
1951	3,950	21,640	18.2	5.1
1952	4,339	24,588	17.6	5.9
1953	4,152	25,833	16.1	6.2
1954	3,934	25,918	15.2	5.8
1955	4,332	28,528	15.2	5.7
1956	4,837	32,058	15.1	5.7
1957	4,894	33,513	14.6	5.4
1958	4,890	34,777	14.1	5.7
1959	5,151	36,846	14.0	5.7
1960	5,392	38,359	14.1	5.1
1961	5,889	39,646	14.8	5.1
1962	6,387	42,927	14.9	4.9
1963	7,082	45,978	15.4	4.8
1964	8,238	50,280	16.4	5.0
1965	8,745	55,364	15.8	5.0
1966	10,326	61,828	16.7	5.4
1967	11,338	66,409	17.1	5.6
1968	13,720	72,586	18.9	5.8
1969	15,035	79,815	18.8	5.6
1970	16,921	85,685	19.7	5.4

Sources: F.H. Leacy, ed., *Historical Statistics of Canada,* 2nd ed. (Ottawa: Statistics Canada, 1983), series G57 and F75; IMF, *International Financial Statistics,* various years.

Reliance on domestic demand rather than on exports also reflected the structure of protection in Canada and the rest of the world. There was a large gap between the promise of the new Genevan faith and its reality. Although there had been some progress in lowering tariff and other barriers, Canadian industry still relied on relatively high levels of protection in 1957, ensuring that domestic firms enjoyed a substantial price advantage over their foreign competitors. That protection not only penalized Canadians by denying them access to a wider range of goods at competitive prices but also explained much of the inflow of foreign investment in the manufacturing sector. US investment in Canada's resource sector – investment that grew dramatically in the 1950s, fuelling exports of resource products to the United States – reflected the abundance of economically viable resources in Canada and low levels of protection on exports of those resources to the United States. Similarly, US – and Canadian – investment in Canadian manufacturing was driven not only by high levels of protection in Canada, but also by high levels of protection in the United States. The expansion of Canada's manufacturing capacity continued in the import-substitution pattern that had been established even before Canada had become a nation, dictated by both Canadian and foreign patterns of protection.

That protection involved more than what nominal tariff rates would suggest. Various studies in the late 1950s through the 1960s – from John Young's pioneering study for the Gordon Commission through various studies for the Private Planning Association and the newly established Economic Council of Canada – suggested the extent and depth of protection in both Canada and the United States.[1] Concluded one such study: "Canadian producers of highly processed industrial materials and manufactured goods are generally oriented to the relatively small domestic market and do not obtain the maximum economies of specialization and scale. The cost disadvantages resulting from the latter situation are increased in comparison with the United States at least by two related factors: there tend to be more Canadian producers in relation to the size of the market than in the United States and not infrequently Canadian plants produce a wider variety of products in relation to total output than American plants."[2]

In a survey of the composition and structure of exports and imports of industrial countries in 1963, Canada's exports of manufactured products (19 percent) ranked lowest, with Norway next at 31 percent. Canada was second in terms of exports of industrial materials at 39 percent, with Norway number one at 41 percent. Canada was second to Denmark in exports of primary products at 42 percent. In terms of the extent of processing taking place before export, Canada ranked a distant last and had shown little improvement in the decade since 1954, increasing the share of manufactured exports only from 17 to 19 percent. Conversely, Canada ranked highest in the percentage of its imports that were fully manufactured: 63 percent, tied with Norway. Clearly, Canada's revealed comparative advantage lay in primary resources but, unlike other resource-rich countries, Canada did relatively less with its resources before export, a situation partially explained by the structure of protection at home and abroad.[3] The authors of one of the studies prepared for the Gordon Commission concluded: "Given access to the United States market Canadian industry would prove competitive in some sectors of advanced manufacturing which do not depend so directly on natural resource availabilities ... Inadequate size of markets is at the heart of Canada's relative disadvantage over a broad range of secondary manufacturing industries. In the broadest terms, Canada's inability to develop more effectively along these lines can be attributed in substantial measure to the restraints imposed by United States commercial policy. There can be few other general propositions about the Canadian economy which have

Ed Franklin, "I've Got Skins, Pelts, You Know," 9 April 1981.
Canadian efforts to increase trade with the United States
continue to be frustrated by US indifference.

stronger roots in economic analysis and logic."[4] Determining where scope for improvement in Canada's trade and economic performance could be found requires consideration of the various elements in the trade policies and customs administrations of Canada and its principal trading partners as they existed at the end of the 1950s.

The Tariff
Since Canada's earliest days as a nation, the tariff had been the principal instrument of protection available to the government. As in the United States, it had also been an important source of revenue. After 1917, however, when both countries began to rely increasingly on taxes on personal and corporate incomes, the share of the tariff in total government revenue had steadily declined. In 1957, tariff revenues of $554 million made up 6.5 percent of the total revenue of the Canadian federal government.[5] The continued existence of the tariff by this time was almost exclusively a matter of industrial policy, although since responsibility continued to reside

in the Department of Finance, its officials were prone to protest piously that it continued to play an important fiscal role.

Analysis of the tariff is often cast in terms of the average rate on dutiable and total imports. In 1957, the average incidence of the Canadian tariff was 10.1 percent on all imports and 17.2 percent on dutiable imports. A total of 39 percent of imports entered duty-free. On total and dutiable imports from the United States, the average incidence was 10.5 and 16.6 percent respectively; on total and dutiable imports from the United Kingdom it was 7.2 and 16.6 percent respectively, suggesting that the preferences enjoyed by the United Kingdom were more helpful on duty-free than dutiable products.[6] In the other direction, the overall incidence of the US tariff on all imports from Canada was 2.4 percent in 1957, and 6.1 percent on dutiable imports.[7] Some 60 percent of imports from Canada entered duty-free. Given the preponderance of resources and industrial materials in Canada's export profile, these figures are considerably lower than the averages for US imports from all sources: 5.8 percent on all imports and 10.8 percent on dutiable imports.[8] Such analyses, however, can be misleading. Trade takes place through "holes" in the tariff; very little trade takes place in highly protected product categories. Trade-weighted averages suggest a lower level of protection than may in fact be the case, while simple averages do not reveal the extent of dispersion among high and low rates.

The nature and competitiveness of a country's industrial structure also may have an impact on trade-weighted averages. In the late 1950s, many US products were able to jump over Canadian tariff rates of 10, 15, and even 20 percent, whereas rates of 5 percent or less were sufficient to keep Canadian products out of the US market. Additionally, the effective rate of protection afforded by nominal rates is conditioned by the structure of protection for related upstream and downstream products. This cascading protective effect results from the fact that if the raw material enters free of duty, but products at the next stage of processing attract a tariff of 5 percent, that 5 percent tariff is charged on the full value of the import, representing a much higher effective rate on the actual value added by the next stage of processing. It is necessary to look beyond nominal and average rates to gain a more accurate picture of the structure and effect of protection in the late 1950s.[9]

Canada had a three-column tariff in 1957: a general tariff applicable to those very few countries to whom Canada did not extend most-favoured-nation (MFN) status, either by treaty or unilaterally, such as some of the oil-producing countries in the Middle East and some communist countries; the MFN tariff applicable to all GATT countries as well as others to whom Canada extended MFN status; and the British preferential (BP) tariff applicable to imports from all Commonwealth countries. Some 1,450 of the 2,038 items and subitems in the Canadian tariff provided for a BP margin of preference. The margin varied from product to product. On automobiles, for example, it was substantial (BP free; MFN rate of 17.5 percent); on other products, such as manufactures of wood, it could be small (BP rate of 17.5 percent; MFN of 20 percent).[10]

The MFN rates on manufactured products were generally in the 15 to 25 percent range, on semi-manufactures in the 5 to 10 percent range, while rates on raw materials tended to be free or very low. The effective rates on manufactures, therefore, were considerable, often as high as 40 percent. Some of the highest rates, including many on agricultural products, were expressed in specific terms, such as so many cents per pound or unit. When translated into *ad valorem* equivalents, these could range as high as 50 percent or more, depending on the value of the import. Powdered and sheet glue, for example, protected by a rate of 22.5 percent plus five cents per pound, could translate into 54 percent *ad valorem*, as it did in 1954 on imports from the United States. Rugs not otherwise provided for (nop) attracted a rate of 25 percent plus five cents per square foot, which brought the average *ad valorem* rate on imports from the United States to 40.5 percent in 1954.[11]

The structure of the Canadian tariff was the product of its historical development. The structure in effect in 1957 had been adopted initially in 1907.[12] Individual items had been added and various categories divided and subdivided in response to producer interests. Additionally, Canada had introduced various tariff programs, discussed below, adding to the complexity. Noted the chairman of the Tariff Board in 1948: "The Canadian tariff as it stands today is easily one of the most complicated in the world ... Where the United States will have one rate ... we may have ... as many as five different rates on one and the same commodity."[13] The result was a complex tariff structure and classification scheme that was unique to Canada and that added to the protective effect of the tariff.[14] Canada did not adopt a modern, systematic tariff classification scheme until 1987 when it converted to the Harmonized Commodity Coding and Description System (HS) developed by the Customs Cooperation Council and based on the Brussels system long used in Europe.

In the United States, the tariff had similarly developed in response to producer interests. Although the high levels of tariffs enshrined in the Smoot-Hawley Tariff Act of 1930 had been gradually reduced as a result of the reciprocal trade agreements program, the United States still boasted some of the highest tariffs among industrialized countries. By the 1960s, the United States basically applied a two-column tariff: the general rate and the MFN or GATT rate. There remained a few preferences in favour of Cuba and the Philippines, but these were of marginal economic importance. Communist countries in particular were singled out for treatment under the general rate, that is, the rates established by the Smoot-Hawley Tariff Act.

The classification of the more than 8,000 tariff rates set out in the act has been called "tedious, archaic, ambiguous, hopelessly complex and virtually impossible to administer."[15] An item could be classified in one category if its material of chief value was wood, quite another if made chiefly of plastic or steel. Some items depended for classification on their use in the United States. Over 125 different classifications of leather gloves appeared in the schedule. Value brackets specified different rates depending on the assessed value of the imports for duty purposes. For some products, the schedule specified minimum and maximum *ad valorem* equivalents for specific duties.[16] Customs agents were, of course, interested in classifying goods at the higher rates, whereas importers sought to have goods classified at lower rates. It is not difficult to understand, therefore, why before the United States adopted the HS system in 1988, customs classification was one of the more lucrative areas of practice for US trade lawyers. At the end of 1959, 130,610 classification appeals and 88,381 reappraisement appeals were pending before the US Customs Court.[17]

The dispersion of rates in the US schedule was more complex than in most other countries, owing in part to the historical development of the tariff. Until 1934, the tariff had been the product of thousands of amendments by individual members of Congress responding to constituency pressures. As a result, the classic structure of low rates for raw materials, intermediate rates for semi-manufactures, and high rates for end-products did not always hold true. Thirty years of negotiations based on the principal-supplier rule had further complicated the rate structure.

Although the overall incidence of the US tariff had reached reasonable levels by the end of the 1950s, there continued to be items that attracted astronomical duties. On manufactured goods, only 14.5 percent of rates were 10 percent or lower and 41 percent were over 20 percent, with 3.3 percent over 40 percent.[18] Table 7.2 provides examples of typical *ad valorem* equivalent rates on products that Canadian-based firms were supplying to the Canadian market, often using Canadian industrial materials, products that could potentially have been exported to the US market under more open market conditions.

In a 1952 study of the US tariff, the US Tariff Commission calculated that 373 items, largely manufactured products, paid duties over 45 percent, with rates as high as 335 percent. The list did not include products with tariff rates so high as to prevent imports altogether.[19] The addition of new products to the list was based on a "rule of similitude," that is, they were classified on the basis of products they most resembled. The small rolling balls used in ballpoint pens, for example, were classified as parts for fountain pens dutiable at 72 cents per dozen plus 40 percent *ad valorem*, which worked out to about 2,400 percent *ad valorem*. "Ornamented" items attracted higher duties than others. A plain tablecloth was dutiable at 12.5 percent but one with a fringe at 42 percent.[20]

Items on the US free list enjoyed more than duty-free status. They were exempt from a number of other protective devices, including liability for antidumping and countervailing duties. Thus, for Canadian negotiators, adding products of export interest to Canadian producers to the free list was always an important, but not easily achieved, goal. Due to price increases, some specific rates set in 1930 had been reduced to no more than nuisance levels by the late 1950s, but remained in effect because the Smoot-Hawley Tariff Act prohibited the automatic transfer of goods to the free list. In 1957, Canada exported $350 million in goods to the United States that paid duties under 2 percent *ad valorem*.[21]

Table 7.2

US duties on manufactured goods of export interest to Canada, 1957

Product	Ad valorem equivalent rate (%)	Product	Ad valorem equivalent rate (%)
Aircraft	12.5	Furniture	24
Articles made of textiles, except		Glass	23
clothing	30	Glassware	35
Articles of pulp, paper, paperboard	16	Ingots, blooms, billets, bars	12
Other paper, paperboard	12	Leather manufactures	17
Automobiles	8.5	Metal manufactures	23
Building materials, not glass, clay	14	Organic chemicals	33
Buses, trucks	10.5	Pig iron, sponge iron, ferro-alloys	9
Coal-tar, dyestuffs	81	Pipes, fittings, cast	10
Common packing, wrapping paper	14	Plumbing, heating, lighting fixtures,	
Explosives	17	fittings	22
Finished forms of iron, steel	11	Tires and tubes	19
Other iron, steel	21	Travel goods	30
Floor coverings, tapestries	21	Wood manufactures	19
Fur clothing	33	Woollen, worsted fabrics	46
Furs, dressed or undressed, dyed	31	Yarn, thread, synthetic or artificial	32

Source: Randall Hinshaw, *The European Community and American Trade: A Study in Atlantic Economics and Trade* (New York: Council on Foreign Relations, 1964), 90.

As far as Canada's other trading partners were concerned, the UK tariff was relatively lower than those of Canada and the United States, but contained rates on processed goods that effectively encouraged imports of raw materials and discouraged imports of more highly processed products. Canada enjoyed a margin of preference in the UK market. Most importantly, along with other Commonwealth countries, Canadian producers could sell many food and industrial raw materials to their UK customers free of duty, favourable terms of access that were threatened by the on-and-off discussion during the 1960s regarding Britain's entry into the Common Market.

The EEC's Common External Tariff (CET) had been calculated on the basis of the arithmetic average tariff applied by its members before the Treaty of Rome, and favoured the higher rates of the larger members like France and Italy rather than the lower rates of the smaller Benelux members. Once the CET was fully deployed at the end of the 1960s, Canadian producers had to face a relatively high tariff that rigorously applied the principle of tariff escalation. The overall incidence of the CET in 1958 was calculated to be 7.4 percent, but rates ranged from an average of

0.3 percent on raw materials to 5.9 percent on semi-manufactures, and 14.8, 13.6, and 17.2 respectively on foodstuffs, capital goods, and other industrial goods.[22] Additionally, the Six were in the process of developing their Common Agricultural Policy (CAP) on the basis of a set of measures that involved minimum prices for local production defended by a system of flexible tariffs (dubbed variable levies) at the border that effectively precluded imports of a wide range of food and other agricultural products that competed with EEC production.

In Japan, the tariff was not an important factor in trade decisions. A combination of import quotas and currency restrictions made exporting to Japan a major challenge; few Canadian manufacturers tried and even fewer succeeded. In 1962, Japan began a process of liberalization that involved, initially, upward revisions in the tariff as quotas were relaxed and eliminated. Nominal tariff rates for most raw materials were set at free or very low rates; rates for imports of intermediate industrial inputs were set in the 5 to 15 percent range; the rates on most finished goods, including machinery, were set above 20 percent, sometimes well above. Additionally, however, habits learned during the period of heavy government direction continued on a more informal basis with a system of administrative guidance. As well, the absence of competition laws and other regulatory structures allowed a high level of cooperation between firms as well as between the corporate and government sectors. From a Canadian perspective, the Japanese governing structure made exporting anything other than desired raw materials difficult, but it also facilitated efforts to restrain Japanese exports of low-cost goods when those became a problem for Canadian competitors.[23]

Protection in Commonwealth markets, though mitigated by the availability of preferences dating back to the 1930s, remained high. Most had thrown in their lot with the British sterling bloc and had added currency restrictions to the other array of barriers that needed to be breached. By 1957, most of these restrictions had been relaxed, but high tariffs, even after taking account of the Commonwealth discount, meant that trade could recover in only a few narrow segments where protection was low and market complementarity was high.

The structure of protection in most developing countries was such as to make trade extremely difficult. Most did not have convertible currencies and were able to use currency restriction as an effective means of regulating international trade. In addition, high tariffs and discretionary import quotas made sales to these countries troublesome on anything but a government-to-government basis for essential goods and services. Discretionary sales to private buyers were virtually impossible to organize without elaborate campaigns that were beyond the resources and interests of most Canadian firms.

Tariff Programs

Simply stated, the tariff is a discriminatory tax that is paid on imports but not on domestic products, providing the government with revenue and domestic producers with protection. Over the years the revenue dimension of the tariff had declined, but the artful way in which the tariff could be administered as a tool of industrial policy had not. If anything, officials had learned to apply a wider array of administrative devices in order to enhance the tariff's protective effect in specific circumstances.

The first area for enhancing protection was the matter of determining the classification of the product for customs purposes. The definitions in Canada's Customs Tariff were sufficiently opaque to provide scope for different interpretations, with customs officials prone to classify products into higher duty categories and importers seeking to classify them into lower categories. Differences of view were ultimately resolved by the Tariff Board on the basis of public hearings and expert testimony. The net effect, however, was often to discourage and harass first-time exporters or importers of new product lines.[24]

Establishing value for duty offered a further opportunity to increase protection, an area of customs administration in which Canadian officials had developed a world-class reputation.[25] During the 1930s, various provisions of the Customs Act, such as minimum values for duty and advances for dumping margins, allowed Dominion customs appraisers, for example, to raise a nominal tariff of 40 percent on taffeta to 250 percent.[26] Most abuses of this kind had been eliminated in reforms when Canada implemented the GATT, but not all. Further changes were implemented in 1958, many of which reintroduced modified versions of some of the more arbitrary provisions used in the 1930s.

By the late 1950s, some three-quarters of the goods entering Canada were valued for duty purposes on the basis of their "fair market value," or the price at which the same goods were offered for sale in the home market. For the vast majority of transactions, customs officials accepted the invoice price as the fair market value. Only if they had reason to believe that this was not the case, such as pursuant to a complaint from a Canadian producer, did they investigate and look behind the invoice price. Establishing fair market value in such instances, however, provided a wide area of administrative discretion, particularly when insufficient home sales required customs officials to "construct" a fair market value. Where fair market value could not be established, customs officials could use ministerial prescriptions establishing often arbitrary values for duty. Ministerial prescriptions were mandatory for various classes of imports, including used or obsolete goods, job lots, remnants, close-outs, discontinued lines, and surplus goods. Canadian valuation provisions, therefore, continued to allow a high level of administrative discretion aimed at protecting Canadian producers.[27]

One of the more ingenious customs devices adopted in Canada was the made/not-made rule. The Customs Tariff specified that imported goods competing with goods "of a class or kind" made in Canada should be taxed at a higher rate than goods not made in Canada. From one perspective, this provision ensured that Canadian firms could concentrate on a few products and import the remainder of their line. It also assured consumers and industrial users that they did not pay duties unnecessarily. At the same time, it provided a built-in guarantee of tariff protection, without the need for legislative action, to any manufacturer prepared to begin operations in Canada. Normally a product was deemed "not made" if less than 10 percent of consumption was satisfied by domestic producers. The regulations, however, created fine distinctions and conditions that again provided substantial scope for administrative discretion and manipulation. Determinations could be appealed to the Tariff Board. Producers or importers not satisfied with Tariff Board rulings could appeal to the minister of finance and seek changes in the offending regulations.[28]

A further wrinkle in tariff classification, often used in combination with the made/not-made regulations, was the wide use of end-use provisions. Products were classified under one tariff item if used for one purpose and under a second item if used for another. Industrial inputs, for example, were often taxed at a lower level than the same product destined for final consumption. Again, this provision ensured officials the scope to achieve various industrial policy objectives.[29]

Finally, Canadian officials had learned to make artful use of duty remissions, drawbacks, and waivers. Manufacturers could recoup, or draw back, the cost of the tariff, for example, on imported materials incorporated into products for export. Duties could be remitted if the manufacturer satisfied various industrial policy objectives favoured by the government. The Customs Act provided the government with considerable discretion to lower or eliminate duties on almost any basis it saw fit, a power that it could use to good effect to meet economic objectives, but that could also lead to administrative abuse. Increasing use of the quasi-judicial Tariff Board, however, had made use of this discretion less a matter of political fiat and more a matter of policy inscribed in regulations.

The United States had its own ingenious ways of enhancing the protective effect of its tariff, particularly through valuation and classification rulings. As already noted, the complexity of the US tariff provided a rich vein of classification rulings for US officials to tap to increase the effective levels of protection. Valuation could be equally complex. In 1956, Congress amended the valuation provisions of the Tariff Act by introducing a simplified system that established four bases for determining value for duty, in the order in which they would be applied: export value, US value, constructed value, and the American selling price. In addition, however, Congress decreed that as a result of these amendments, no level of existing protection could be reduced by more than 5 percent. As a result, the Treasury Department maintained a "final list" comprising 15 percent of all imports, to which the old, much more complex and arbitrary valuation system applied. In effect, in 1957, the United States maintained nine different ways in which value for duty could be assessed on dutiable imports.[30]

Consequently, although the average US tariff on dutiable Canadian imports had decreased from 30.2 to 6.1 percent between 1937 and 1957, and that of Canada on US imports from 22.9 to 16.6,[31] it would take more than the reduction of average tariff levels to allow Canadian-based firms to reap the benefits of specialization and econo-mies of scale. Before manufacturers would be prepared to invest to supply more than the Canadian market, they needed to be convinced that a wider array of pro-tective measures had been eliminated: in Canada to provide the goad of competi-tion; in the United States to provide the reward of a larger market.

In the United Kingdom, Europe, Japan, and elsewhere, similar aspects of cus-toms administration added to the protective effect of the tariff. If nothing else, the wide variety in administrative practices, the ingenuity of trade officials in invent-ing new rules and procedures, and the determination of customs officials to do their best in collecting revenue and protecting domestic producers, ensured that success in exporting to a new market did not come easily.

Other Protective Measures

The basic tariff and its administration do not tell the whole story of protection in Canada, the United States, or elsewhere. As one 1960 study concluded after com-paring Canadian and US protection: "One of the most striking features of the analysis is the variety and complexity of the methods used by each country to keep out the other's goods. Tariffs are probably the principal barrier, but few people in either country appreciate the extent to which the tariffs of each country have been sup-plemented by other forms of protection."[32]

One of the more ingenious ways Canadian officials had learned to protect Cana-dian producers from low-cost foreign, particularly US, competition was the appli-cation of antidumping duties. First introduced by Finance Minister W.S. Fielding in 1904, the antidumping system had developed over the years into one of the most cherished forms of protection available to Canadian producers. Fielding had main-tained in 1904 that the use of antidumping duties to deal with unusually low-priced imports was preferable to a general increase in tariff protection covering all im-ports. It was an argument that continued to appeal to Canadian authorities, despite the fact that Canadian producers were already protected by tariffs and related pro-grams that were far from insignificant.[33]

What distinguished the Canadian system from similar regimes was its automa-ticity. Canada's valuation system, which determined value for duty on the basis of the fair market value in the home market, automatically provided the customs authorities with a dumping margin if the export price was lower than the fair market value. The Customs Tariff prescribed that antidumping duties equivalent to the difference between the sale price and the fair market value, up to a maxi-mum of 50 percent, be assessed if the import was of a class or kind made in Canada or if it competed directly with goods made in Canada. Of course, in the vast major-ity of cases, customs accepted the invoice price as the fair market value and no dumping duty was assessed. The Canadian Manufacturers' Association was of the view that customs officers should be much more vigilant but, given staff resources, there was a limit to what could reasonably be expected. The amount of dumping duties actually assessed, therefore, was much smaller than the word "automatic" would suggest.

Because this administrative system exempted goods of a class or kind not made in Canada, some Canadian officials were prepared to defend the absence of an injury test, as required by GATT article VI. Since antidumping duties could be imposed on goods of a class or kind not made in Canada if they competed with similar goods produced in Canada, critics in the United States, United Kingdom, and elsewhere were not easily convinced by this line of reasoning and made the Canadian system one of their principal targets in the Kennedy Round of GATT negotiations (1963-7).

The United States introduced its own Antidumping Law in 1916 as an extension of its domestic antitrust legislation but replaced it in 1921 with one more closely modelled on the Canadian law and aimed at protecting domestic producers rather than ensuring fair competition. It was amended in the Smoot-Hawley Tariff Act of 1930 and became the basis of the provisions in the GATT. The US law involved a bifurcated process: the Treasury Department determined dumping and the Tariff Commission determined material injury.[34] Given continued high levels of tariff protection and the opportunities to increase protection through various valuation provisions, the law was not often applied. In 1960, no Canadian goods had been subjected to a US antidumping duty since the early 1930s, although a few products had been investigated, including hardboard in 1957.[35]

Another mainstay of the protective system in effect at the end of the 1950s, particularly for agricultural products, was the use of quantitative restrictions (QRs). GATT article XI prohibited QRs except in the agricultural and fisheries sectors. As we shall see below in the discussion of trade in agricultural products, Canada made less use of QRs than the United States at this time. The United States used quotas or tariff-rate quotas to respond to escape-clause petitions. While resort to escape-clause measures had occurred much less often than the number of petitions would suggest, Canadian exporters had been affected by actions on lead and zinc ores.

Finally, a range of other nontariff barriers could and did exert a significant influence on trading patterns. By 1960, purchases of goods for government use were beginning to become significant, and preferences in favour of domestic suppliers were being introduced on both sides of the Canada-US border. US Buy America legislation became a growing source of frustration for competitive Canadian suppliers. Excise taxes and various processing fees, some of which applied only to imports, further complicated cross-border trade. Similarly, technical specifications and product standards, health and sanitary requirements, labelling and marking requirements, patent and copyright laws, and other regulations could also be administered to give domestic suppliers an added advantage.[36] As one study of these barriers at the end of the 1950s concluded, "Canadian administrative or indirect trade barriers undoubtedly impose a burden on many U.S. firms exporting to Canada, just as similar U.S. barriers impose a burden on many Canadian firms exporting to the United States ... these 'invisible' barriers are multitudinous, and make their effect felt in a variety of ways ... The most restrictive effects, however, appear to be on ... companies entering the ... market for the first time, or on firms marketing new products ... For it is in these areas of trade that the problem of uncertainty is most keenly felt."[37]

For Canadian producers, the various devices in place in Canada and the United States were of greatest interest in influencing investment and production plans. A much more limited experience in Europe and Japan in the 1950s had exposed Canadian producers to only some of the various administrative and other procedures used in those countries. Efforts to broaden their market base in the 1960s and 1970s, however, provided them with no shortage of lessons in the ingenuity of trade and customs officials. Japanese authorities proved particularly adept at implementing regulations and procedures that were difficult for foreign suppliers to satisfy, thus providing domestic producers with a level of protection far more potent than nominal tariff protection and normal customs procedures would suggest.

Role of GATT Negotiations

The GATT had made an important beginning in trying to open the markets of industrialized countries. The negotiators had correctly identified the tariff and currency instability as the two most important and most visible barriers to international trade in goods. They tackled the problems of monetary policy in the International Monetary Fund and those of the tariff and other barriers in the GATT. Over time, their goal in the GATT was to see tariffs reduced and even eliminated where possible. At the same time, they had decreed that the tariff would be the only acceptable form of standing protection. All other forms of protection, particularly QRs, had either been outlawed or their use stringently constrained by the rules of the agreement.

These broad goals, however, had been severely circumscribed by the number of exceptions built into virtually every article of the agreement as well as by the overarching exception of the Protocol of Provisional Application. With some limited exceptions, many of the protective devices used by Canada, the United States, and others predated the GATT and did not need to conform to GATT's requirements. Both the Canadian and US valuation systems, for example, were inconsistent to some extent with GATT article VII but were not brought fully into conformity until 1984 and 1980 respectively as a result of the Tokyo Round negotiations. Similarly, Canada did not apply an injury test before assessing antidumping duties, a practice inconsistent with article VI and not amended until after the Kennedy Round.

The GATT was also limited to trade in goods. Trade in services, such as transportation, insurance, and other "invisible" transactions, was either governed by other regimes, such as the network of bilateral agreements that controlled air transport, or relied on comity. Those aspects of international commerce covered by the ITO charter but "lost" when it was not ratified, such as restrictive business practices, investment, and commodity trade, were the subject of periodic discussions in the GATT and in various UN bodies over the course of the 1950s. Governments remained, however, ambivalent about the need to negotiate binding multilateral accords to address these secondary aspects of international trade.

As a practical matter, therefore, the first four rounds of GATT negotiations had only scratched the surface of what was required to create a more uniform set of commercial policy regimes among its members. Tariffs had been reduced and the outline of a uniform code of commercial practice had been delineated, but it would take four more rounds of negotiations, each more ambitious than the last, to achieve in practice what had been outlined in theory in 1947. Not until the conclusion and implementation of the Uruguay Round of GATT negotiations in 1995 did members of GATT's successor, the World Trade Organization, come close to achieving the objective set in 1947: a uniform code of practice governing members' trade policies.

Impact on Structure of Trade and of the Economy
Given the structure of protection in place at the end of the 1950s and into the 1960s, it is not surprising that Canada's exports continued to be crowded within a narrow range of products. Agricultural products (principally wheat and other grains), metals and minerals, lumber, pulp, and newsprint made up fully three-quarters of Canada's exports to the United States (see tables 7.3 and 7.4). On these products tariffs were low or free, often also eliminating the possibility of other forms of administrative protection. On the Canadian import side, a much wider range of products entered, despite nominally higher tariffs than in the United States and Europe. Three-quarters were manufactured goods, some benefiting from duty-free entry as a result of end-use or not-made-in-Canada provisions, but many more successfully jumping over tariffs between 10 and 25 percent and competing with domestic manufacturers. As a result, while average Canadian tariffs tended to be higher, they were no more restrictive than those in vogue elsewhere.

Both Canadian and US manufacturing firms had developed primarily to serve their domestic markets and continued to do so in the 1950s and 1960s. The difference was that the US market, more than fifteen times larger than the Canadian market, allowed manufacturers to reap the benefits of specialization and scale; the smaller size of the Canadian market had led to a pattern of industrial fragmentation, with most plants pumping out small runs of too wide a variety of goods to achieve economies of scale. As a result, Canadians, although enjoying comparable choices to their American neighbours, paid considerably more and earned considerably less. An increasing number of contemporary analyses confirmed that Canadians were productive and hard-working, but the structure of the economy, much of it conditioned by Canadian and foreign levels of protection, made it almost impossible to close the Canada-US productivity gap – estimated to be as high as 35 to 40 percent – without allowing freer trade between the two countries.[38] One 1967 study suggested that bilateral free trade would provide Canada with a 10 percent

Table 7.3

Composition of Canada-United States trade, 1957: Top twenty Canadian exports and imports

Canadian exports to the United States	% of total	Canadian imports from the United States	% of total
Newsprint	21	Nonfarm machinery and parts	14
Wood pulp	8	Autos, trucks, parts	8
Planks and boards	7	Rolling mill products	7
Nickel[a]	5	Electrical equipment	5
Petroleum	5	Coal	3
Aluminum[a]	4	Engines and parts	3
Iron ore[a]	4	Tractors and parts	3
Uranium ores and concentrates	4	Aircraft and parts	2
Copper[a]	2	Books and printed matter	2
Farm machinery and parts (except tractors)	2	Cotton, raw and fabrics	2
Fish, fresh and frozen	2	Farm implements and parts (except tractors)	2
Whisky	2	Fresh fruit and vegetables	2
Abrasives	1	Petroleum and products	2
Barley	1	Tourist purchases	2
Cattle, chiefly beef	1	Cooking and heating equipment	1
Fertilizers	1	Iron ore	1
Fur skins	1	Medical, optical, dental equipment	1
Nonfarm machinery and parts	1	Refrigerators	1
Pulpwood	1	Synthetic plastics	1
Zinc[a]	1	Tools	1
Total	76	Total	61

a   Primary and semimanufactured

Source: Grant L. Reuber, *The Growth and Changing Composition of Trade between Canada and the United States* (Montreal: Private Planning Association for the Canadian-American Committee, 1960), 38.

boost in its GNP, largely by wiping out the productivity gap.[39] Multilateral free trade, of course, would have an even larger impact.

A further determinant of the patterns of production in trade in Canada was the extent of foreign ownership. In the 1920s and 1930s, American firms had invested in Canada to serve the Canadian market and sometimes other Commonwealth markets as well. In the 1940s and 1950s, currency and other restrictions had made those markets marginal at best. Most US investment in Canada in the 1950s sought to exploit Canadian resources for US industrial users or to serve Canadian consumers

Table 7.4

Composition of Canadian exports, 1961 (%)

Commodity	All countries	US	UK	Others
Live animals	1.2	2.0	negligible	0.3
Food, beverages, tobacco	20.8	9.6	26.2	38.0
Crude materials	20.8	22.4	22.5	17.0
Fabricated materials	48.3	56.6	48.4	33.2
End products (inedible)	8.8	9.1	2.9	11.3
Special trade transactions	0.2	0.3	negligible	0.2
Total	100.0	100.0	100.0	100.0

Note: Totals may not add due to rounding.
Source: F.H. Leacy, ed., *Historical Statistics of Canada,* 2nd ed. (Ottawa: Statistics Canada, 1983), series G415-28.

with familiar US household and other products. Various studies in the 1950s and continuing into the 1960s attempted to understand the extent to which the boardroom prejudices of US branch-plant operations in Canada influenced the pattern of Canadian imports and exports. Did US branch plants tend to buy their inputs from familiar US suppliers or from the lowest-cost supplier, whether US or Canadian? Were US branch plants prevented from competing with parent or other affiliates outside Canada? One of the studies prepared for the Gordon Commission concluded, "No simple generalization will explain adequately the whole range of purchasing behaviour. What is clear, however, particularly with respect to manufacturing enterprises, is the observable fact that imports from the parent, and from the parent's suppliers, remain high."[40] Others in the years to come would be less even-handed, determined to prove that the high level of US investment in Canadian manufacturing had had a devastating effect on Canadian trading patterns.

Any efforts by the government to change the patterns of Canadian trade and investment required major adjustments in the structure of protection both in Canada and in its existing or potential trading partners. In Canada, any such changes needed to deal head-on with those industries – foreign or Canadian-owned – that depended on the existing structure of protection. Abroad, such changes had to be negotiated and paid for, and prove politically acceptable to economic interests in those countries. Officials were steeped in these realities; their political and academic critics were not. As a result, there was more talk about change than actual change in the direction and contours of Canadian trade and economic policy. Public debate over the next few decades might at times reach a fever pitch, but it did not produce concrete results.

It would be wrong to suggest that Canadian manufacturers had a monolithic view of the benefits of protection. Resource-based firms, of course, such as those in the forest products and metals and minerals sectors, were often very outward-oriented and found protection in Canada's major markets the principal source of their trade policy worries. Some manufacturing firms, such as makers of agricultural machinery, were active in world markets and had adjusted well to full competition in Canada as a result of the elimination of the tariff on their products. The transportation equipment and other sectors knew that without some restructuring, their future looked bleak (see chapter 9). Smaller, Canadian-owned manufacturing firms tended to be more wedded to protection than the branch plants of American or other multinational firms; many of them relied on the Canadian Manufacturers' Association to represent their views, which, until the late 1970s, tended to be at the most conservative or protectionist end of the spectrum. Some industry-based groups, however, such as the Canadian Trade Committee (CTC) sponsored by the Private Planning Association (PPA), or the Canadian-American Committee (CAC) sponsored by the PPA in Canada and its sister organization, the National Planning Association, in the United States, initiated studies and made statements espousing a much broader range of views than is often appreciated.[41] What distinguished their views from those of academic critics was their healthy respect for the limits of Canadian independent action and their deep scepticism about the willingness of Canada's trading partners to move to freer trade.

Throughout the 1960s, business groups considered a variety of plans that sought to improve the trade policy basis of Canada's economy, including Canada-US free trade and Atlantic free trade. Some were efforts to deal with the impact on Canada of British entry into the EEC; others addressed the issues raised by deepening Canada-US trade and investment ties. Nothing came of these plans, but they did provide ministers, officials, and business leaders with a more informed basis for discussion of the narrow range of real options available to Canada. Largely excluded from these discussions was Canada's academy. With the exception of economists commissioned by think tanks such as the Economic Council or the Private Planning Association (later the C.D. Howe Institute), the dominant themes being explored in Canada's universities, particularly in political science departments, were those of economic nationalism or autarchy. Little came of these themes in the 1960s, but by the 1970s they began to exert a clear influence on both debate and policy.

The Trials and Tribulations of Canadian Agriculture
Unlike the earlier booms of the twentieth century (1900 to 1913 and 1922 to 1928), agricultural trade did not play a significant role in the postwar boom of the 1950s. The Prairie wheat economy, if anything, lagged behind, and agricultural exports in general failed to make up for lost markets with new export outlets. Mineral and forest resources remained the mainstay of Canada's export trade, with manufacturing developing further to meet domestic demand.

The rapid growth of the wheat economy in the first three decades of the twentieth century had come to a crashing halt in the 1930s with the onslaught first of the global depression, itself pushed over the edge by the collapse of the international grains market in 1928, and then of a severe drought. By the middle of the decade, Prairie grain farmers were in desperate straits, dependent on government not only for relief but also for the marketing of their grain and for various policies aimed at stabilizing farm incomes. The establishment of the Canadian Wheat Board in 1935, complemented by continuing efforts to negotiate bilateral and multilateral wheat agreements, aimed at returning the Prairie farm economy to a more sustainable state of affairs.[42]

The extraordinary circumstances of war did not provide as much help to the wheat farmer as to the rest of the economy. Prices remained low, and when they began to rise in 1943, the government stepped in to use its emergency powers to suspend trade in wheat and add to the powers of the Wheat Board, making it the exclusive marketing agent for the wheat farmer. The Wheat Board announced the prices it would pay, bought the grain, stored it, and marketed it abroad. Once established, these powers remained the core of government policy through the 1990s.

In the years immediately after the war, as the grain trade returned to more normal circumstances, the government sought to provide a stable market in the United Kingdom for Canadian wheat through a four-year agreement. As we saw earlier, it turned out to be a bad bargain. The farmers and their champion in Ottawa, Jimmy Gardiner, had bet on deflationary conditions. In reality the price of wheat rose, but the price paid to Canadian farmers declined. Farmers lost an estimated $300 million during the first two years of the agreement alone. Chastened, Canada joined in successfully negotiating a multilateral wheat agreement in 1949, but its price provisions also proved too pessimistic. Not until its renewal in 1953 did agreement prices match market prices.[43]

To make matters worse, weather conditions in the first half of the decade produced bumper crops not only in Canada, but also in the United States. Try as it might, the Wheat Board could not market the growing glut, particularly in the face of aggressive US competition and giveaways under its PL-480 food aid program. By 1955, the United States had a carryover of more than a billion bushels of unsold wheat. Two years later, Canada also passed the billion-bushel mark in stored wheat. The combined impact of soaring production and declining sales brought new disaster to the Prairie wheat economy. The Prairie farmers' cash income reached a high of $1.46 billion in 1952; by 1955, it had fallen to prewar levels of $420 million. Without new outlets, the prospects for the Western farm economy again looked grim.[44]

Farmers in the eastern half of the country did not fare much better. Their export markets in the United Kingdom and Europe had collapsed in the 1940s and 1950s without compensating new markets in the United States, Latin America, or Asia. This situation made farmers increasingly dependent on the home market and more inclined to look to government to protect their home market than to find new markets abroad. Cheese, eggs, ham, bacon, apples, and similar farm commodities gradually disappeared as mainstays of Canada's export trade.[45] Instead, farmers expected marketing boards, tariffs, and even quotas to protect them from foreign competition. Although the establishment of supply management still lay in the future, a growing reliance on marketing boards suggested the change of direction that had taken place.

Even at the best of times, farmers face circumstances that make their incomes prone to instability. Income support and stabilization, however, did not become the focus of serious government attention until the 1930s, when the economic dislocations of that period gradually convinced governments that they should intervene. In many ways, these rural programs have their urban/industrial equivalents in unemployment and welfare schemes for individuals as well as in various investment and other incentives at the firm level. What distinguishes rural income support from urban unemployment schemes is the much more direct impact such programs can have on production and their much greater capacity for distorting market allocation of resources.

Marketing boards, with or without control over production, became one of the instruments of choice in Canada to strengthen farmers' ability to reap profitable returns on their investment. Based on successful experiments in Australia, marketing boards were introduced in Canada in the 1920s. Fruit and vegetable growers in British Columbia and Ontario, caught between the monopsonistic powers of food processors and distribution agencies and the perishability of their product, sought to enhance their bargaining power by establishing voluntary cooperatives through which they would bargain with their customers. In effect, farmers were organizing to increase their market power in ways analogous to unions in the industrial sector, substituting collective for individual bargaining. Their efforts met with limited success, however, because of the difficulty of ensuring the total cooperation of all farmers engaged in producing a particular commodity.

To ensure compliance, marketing boards sought and gained provincial legislation to compel participation when the majority of farmers agreed, again analogous to the legislation that gave unions their authority. These ran into constitutional difficulties that the federal government sought to remedy, with limited success. The courts ruled that provincial boards could not take production, pricing, or marketing decisions that would affect interprovincial trade, a federal jurisdiction, and that the federal government could not regulate production, a provincial matter.[46]

Through a combination of federal-provincial agreements, federal and provincial legislative initiatives, and carefully developed board mandates, these constitutional constraints were gradually ironed out through such legislation as the federal Agricultural Stabilization Act of 1958 and equivalent provincial legislation. By the 1960s, the existence of more than a hundred marketing boards across the country bore testimony to the extent to which they had become an integral part of Canadian agriculture. None of these boards, however, exercised sufficient authority or market power to affect international trade. They had very limited authority to regulate interprovincial trade and none to regulate international trade. Most marketing boards, therefore, operated in a market-based environment. Nevertheless, they were symptomatic of an increasing orientation to the home market and away from export markets.

Canadian farmers were not alone in looking more and more to the home market. Farm programs in the United States, Europe, and elsewhere had gradually developed a mindset that farm economics differed from that of the rest of the economy, and government policies had responded with programs likely to consolidate the conviction that open international markets were a problem rather than a solution. Governments routinely guaranteed farmers specific, often high, prices and then dumped the resulting surplus on world markets at fire-sale prices. As crop prices were driven up by artificial price and other supports, they led to overproduction, often depressing world prices and decreasing export opportunities at anything but highly subsidized prices.[47]

In the United States, imports of farm products were covered by a wide array of restrictive regulations, ranging from prohibitive tariffs to absolute prohibitions. Quotas or prohibitions were in effect on a whole range of dairy products as well as on wheat and wheat flour, oats, rye, and barley. GATT panels and other bodies had been highly critical of US quotas on a variety of agricultural products pursuant to section 22 of the Agricultural Adjustment Act of 1933. The United States succeeded in gaining a GATT waiver for such quotas in 1955, however, making further protest moot.[48]

By the late 1950s, developments in US trade policy were beginning to have a strong influence on the further evolution of Canadian agriculture. As already discussed, the system of price supports and public disposal of surplus grains had had a devastating impact on the Canadian grain industry. High levels of protection in the dairy sector added to the forces that disposed Canada to adopt its own protectionist schemes.

In the second half of the 1950s, Canada began to place quotas and prohibitions of its own on dairy and poultry imports. In 1956, turkeys were placed on the Import Control List and imports were held to annual quotas far below domestic demand. Cheddar cheese was also placed on the Import Control List in 1956, joining butter, butter fat, and dried skim milk powder. By the second half of the 1950s, the Wheat Board exercised not only control over trade in wheat, oats, and barley, but also over any product containing more than 25 percent of these grains by weight. In 1957 and 1958, importers needed licences and Board permission to import a wide range of products including pasta, cake mixes, and animal feeds.[49]

Efforts by the federal government to use trade negotiations, either at the GATT or in bilateral and multilateral commodity agreements, to address problems in agricultural trade proved of limited value. As long as the United States pursued policies aimed more at protecting the American farmer than at promoting more liberal and stable agricultural trade conditions, Canadian efforts were doomed to failure. When

American negotiators tried to reverse the pattern of intervention and protection in the 1960s, they found that the Europeans had learned their lessons too well. It would take a further thirty years before agricultural issues could be successfully tackled in multilateral negotiations, and, by that time, Canadian negotiators found that Canadian interest in open markets had considerably cooled.[50] For Canadian agricultural trade officials, the decade of the 1950s is remembered as one of opportunities lost because of American narrow-mindedness.

The Making of Trade Policy in Canada

In Canada, trade policy was essentially developed and implemented by a small group of professionals in the Departments of Finance, Trade and Commerce, and External Affairs. At first supervised by an interdepartmental committee chaired by Norman Robertson, its work was soon delegated to a subcommittee chaired by the director of the economic division in External Affairs. Wrote Undersecretary Lester Pearson to the Canadian ambassador to the United States, Hume Wrong, in 1948: "I have been aware for some time of the need in Ottawa of a central body which should give full consideration on a co-ordinated basis to any action which various Government Departments might be contemplating and which might conceivably affect Canada's External Trade Policy. Recent developments, such as the signing at Geneva of the General Agreement on Tariffs and Trade, ... and our position at the World Trade Conference in Havana, have made it more essential than ever that officials of the various interested Departments of Government maintain close liaison before finalizing any new procedures which they propose adopting."[51] The original group led by Robertson, McKinnon, and Wilgress, which in later years included John Deutsch, Mitchell Sharp, C.M. Drury, and Louis Rasminsky, gave way to veterans recruited in the years immediately after the war. Louis Couillard, a veteran of the ITO negotiations, was the first officer appointed to manage GATT affairs on a full-time basis. In 1956, Canada assigned a Trade and Commerce officer, Mel Clark, to the permanent mission in Geneva to liaise with the growing secretariat. He was succeeded by an officer from External Affairs, Frank Stone, in 1959. Other members of this group included a long list of officials who went on to more senior positions throughout government in the years to come, including future deputy ministers such as Ed Ritchie, Gordon Robertson, Gerry Stoner, Simon Reisman, Jim Grandy, and Jake Warren. They were highly talented men dealing with an issue considered crucial to Canada's further development as an independent and economically strong nation.

At any one time, however, the membership of the group was small, rarely more than a dozen or two. In Washington, London, and elsewhere, similar small groups of officials staffed other central trade policy units. US interests might have been much more extensive and far-flung, but its trade policy community was no larger than that of Canada. In London, the group was somewhat smaller. The usual bureaucratic penchant for ever-increasing specialization and staffing was not present.

In all three capitals, there was an appreciation of the delicate balance between mastery of detail and an overview of the whole field.

In all three capitals, these small groups of officials learned the details so essential to the formulation of trade policy, developed the broad lines of that policy, and attended the meetings and negotiating sessions where this policy was put into effect. As required, two or three members of the Canadian group travelled to Geneva to participate in sessions of GATT's contracting parties and to compare notes with their colleagues from London, Washington, and elsewhere. More of them travelled to Annecy, Torquay, and Geneva to participate in the next three rounds of multilateral trade negotiations. Before their departure, Canadian officials discussed their negotiating agenda in their interdepartmental subcommittees, had their deliberations approved by interdepartmental committees of deputy ministers, and finally gained cabinet endorsement. In Geneva and elsewhere, undisturbed by politicians, provincial officials, and journalists, they pursued the instructions they had previously prepared, returning after a period of weeks or months to write a report for their deputies and ministers explaining how they had carried out these instructions. The result was usually implemented by Order-in-Council or in a budget and rarely occasioned either parliamentary or public notice.[52]

Throughout this period, Canadians gained a reputation for being solid and professional participants, carefully balancing their government's short-term political interests with their deeply held conviction that multilateralism in general and the GATT in particular were critical to Canada's future economic prospects. This conviction translated into Canadians playing a large role in the GATT's development, chairing various committees and working groups, injecting ideas and proposals into discussions, finding formulas that could overcome stalemates among the major players, and otherwise making themselves an indispensable part of the GATT's fabric. Most prominently, Dana Wilgress served as chairman of the first five annual sessions of GATT; others, however, were equally visible in subsequent years.[53] Their persistence paid rich dividends in later years, giving Canada a voice and influence that belied its weight in international trade and proved critical as Canadian policy adjusted to changing realities.

Canadians also gained a reputation for being chisellers. They shrewdly gained concessions while making few. Hector McKinnon, one of Canada's lead negotiators in the 1930s, 1940s, and 1950s stated at the end of the Torquay negotiations in 1951 that "our purpose in every agreement is to get all we can and give as little as possible."[54] In the 1960s and 1970s, European negotiators delighted in characterizing Canadians as free riders. At home they used their administrative tools, such as valuation and dumping, to keep business interests happy. They invented techniques such as voluntary export restraints with Japan[55] and performance-based duty remission orders to deal with particular problems in ways that did not contravene the letter of the GATT. Their inventiveness was like that of their colleagues in other governments: quick to complain when others broke the rules but convinced that their own techniques were within the pale. Canadians contributed not only to the management and elaboration of the international trading system, but also to cynicism about it.

Much energy was spent at home, in Washington, and in Geneva on ensuring that the Americans played their leadership role. Reluctant to make many major concessions of its own, Canada was quick to tell the Americans of the importance of maintaining a liberal trading order and of showing the way. In 1953, for example, extensive diplomatic effort was expended on convincing the US administration to move expeditiously on a new round of multilateral negotiations and to forestall a protectionist threat in Congress, some of it related to Canadian trade interests such as threatened restrictions on imports of lead and zinc. After a visit to Ottawa by President Eisenhower, US embassy chargé Woodbury Willoughby reported to the State Department, "Canadians no less convinced vital importance leadership by US in reducing world trade barriers and apprehensive delays will result in action by Congress prejudging general policy or leading to unfavorable reactions abroad."[56]

The most important sources of information and inspiration for their work were generated within their own circle. Analysis by junior staff, discussion among themselves, testing ideas and advice on ministers, and negotiating and consulting with colleagues in other capitals provided them with most of the pertinent information and ideas that they needed. In addition, however, many of them consulted with business and academic contacts, particularly those whose advice was congenial to their own. Formal, mandatory consultations with business groups were still far into the future. Participation in occasional meetings of the Canadian Trade Committee, the Canadian-American Committee, or the British-North American Committee, all sponsored in Canada by the Private Planning Association, provided opportunities to take the pulse of informed business, labour, and academic opinions. Stints advising Royal commissions, such as the Gordon Commission, further broadened contacts and outlooks. But first and foremost, Canada had by the end of the 1950s developed a highly competent group of professional trade negotiators and policy advisors, confident that they knew what was best.

The Triumph of Professionalism

Both the bilateral and multilateral negotiations of the 1940s and 1950s demonstrated how far the professionalization of trade policy had come. Robert Spencer has written, "There is much to suggest that the government, both led and assisted by a gifted company of expert advisers, had moved ahead of Canadian public opinion ... The role of officials in contemporary Canadian government looms very large; and not least in international affairs where the complexity of problems to be faced made expert knowledge essential ... The traditional role of the civil service is to plan and to recommend. But the special nature of foreign policy made it natural and inevitable that to these should be added the function of persuasion."[57] In subsequent years that role would expand even beyond persuasion. Donald Creighton, in an acerbic treatment of Canada during the period of Liberal hegemony, sought to capture what the professionalization of the public service in Canada had meant for the political process.

> In traditional British and Canadian practice, civil servants had been unpolitical and impartial advisors, equally separated from both parties and ready to serve either. Twenty years of Liberal rule had shattered this convention for ever. The Canadian civil service, like Canadian business, had become identified with the Liberal Party in one huge and omnipotent establishment. Civil servants were intimate friends of Liberal ministers; they were committed to Liberal policies which they had largely framed themselves; they rejoiced at the success of Liberal stratagems, which were not infrequently of their own invention. In Canada civil servants and Liberal politicians were simply two divisions of the same armed forces – different members of a large, rapidly growing, and extremely happy family. Government by party had virtually ceased to exist. Instead, the Liberals had become the party of government.[58]

Creighton was both right and wrong. There may indeed have developed a congeniality between ministers and officials during the long Liberal hegemony from 1935 to 1957 that made them see eye to eye on many issues. But this congeniality was unrelated to any partisan spirit. While there were a few celebrated instances of public servants becoming Liberal ministers (starting with Mackenzie King himself in 1908 and continuing with Lester Pearson, J.W. Pickersgill, Mitchell Sharp, Guy Favreau, and C.M. Drury), most of the senior mandarins of the period had no particular party loyalty. Indeed, Arnold Heeney was offended when Mackenzie King suggested that Heeney could serve him better as a partisan secretary to the cabinet than as a career secretary.[59] Rather, the senior mandarins had their own view of policy, and it was this view that they recommended and in many cases implemented.

The bureaucratic view of matters often prevailed, resulting in remarkable continuity in the basic policy orientation of Canadian government. The mandarins had the expert knowledge of the issues, of the technical and administrative problems, and of the decision-making process. Ministers advanced their views on the major issues that were politically important in the life of a particular government and thus influenced this policy development. But even for these major issues, the details of policy were developed by civil servants and kept in tune with the general policy orientation of the senior mandarins. The senior civil service – deputy ministers and assistant deputy ministers and, particularly, the top officials in the principal agencies such as Finance, the Privy Council Office, and External Affairs – dominated the day-to-day business of government, unencumbered by the problems of elections.

This is not to suggest that ministers, the cabinet, and Parliament made no difference; they did, but in technically demanding areas, the expertise of the permanent bureaucracy often proved as decisive as political instincts. Obviously the ministry of the day set the tone and signalled its priorities. The bureaucracy, in turn, in developing advice, weighed what the government of the day was likely to consider acceptable, often inserting its political judgment for that of ministers. It took a very determined and creative minister to insist on a policy at odds with established bureaucratic priorities in areas of bureaucratic technical expertise. Only on issues that mattered politically to ministers might it be necessary to oppose the policy preferences of the bureaucracy, and then only on those occasions when the political antennae of senior officials had failed to provide a suitable compromise.

This ordering of the political process was not, however, a coup d'état orchestrated by power-hungry mandarins indifferent to the democratic process, but a natural result of the complexity of modern government and the consequent burdens placed on ministers by the parliamentary system. A similar development took place in Britain but not in the United States. In the United States, the separation of powers between Congress and the administration, as well as the tradition of staffing all senior positions in the administration with political appointees, ensured much firmer political control over the direction of government. The price paid was lack of continuity; every four years, the new appointees had to learn the limits and process of government. In Canada and Britain, on the other hand, it was a rare minister that regularly bested the mandarins, as demonstrated so convincingly in the brilliant BBC comedy series, *Yes Minister*. If anything, the situation was even more one-sided in Canada. Constituency affairs and other demands regularly took ministers out of Ottawa for days at a time.

The practical effect of this professionalization of the public service and of government in Canada was a smooth continuum in policy. The nonpartisan tradition in trade policy ushered in under King meant that by the 1950s Canada boasted an uncontroversial, cautious, civil service trade policy. Officials analyzed the information, drew up the options, recommended the preferred course of action, and implemented the inevitable decision.[60] But while outwardly bland, the process did not lack internal conflict. The machinery of interdepartmental consultation and decision making ensured that all the options were indeed seriously examined. Within the closed confines of bureaucratic meetings, there were sharp differences of view based on departmental mandates and priorities. The object of interdepartmental consultation, however, was to resolve these differences early in the process and, preferably, before they reached the level of deputies. Should the issue require ministerial direction, it was usually a matter of the minister or cabinet concurring in the recommended course of action.[61]

As matters turned out and despite strongly held views to the contrary among senior mandarins in Ottawa, it was the United States that maintained a neutral public service. The development of policy remained clearly under the control of political appointees, with the mandate of the civil service confined to technical advice. In Canada, on the other hand, the civil service remained nonpartisan only in the sense that the mandarins were not aligned with any political party. Policy development, however, was far from neutral. Canada had, in fact, a powerful civil service that largely controlled its own destiny and that of government. Notes Jack Granatstein in his study of the origins of this mandarin form of government:

> The Ottawa Men had to face the challenge of creating a governmental structure, a foreign policy, and an international monetary policy for a country that had never had them. There were also the difficulties of working within what amounted to a one-party system, for the Liberals were in power from 1935 to 1957 ... the mandarins created the mechanisms – notably in the Privy Council Office and Prime Minister's Office – through which the Prime Minister and Cabinet could shape, direct, and control the course of events in Canada to the extent they chose or were able. In the process they also created a central government structure and system in which great power and influence flowed to them as well – a necessary, and probably not entirely unwelcome or unplanned concomitant.[62]

Creighton's criticism was therefore not completely wrong, but it did go too far. The public service had not become a branch of the Liberal Party of Canada. Rather, ministers, in the face of complexity and growing pressure, had delegated much of the responsibility for policy making to the public service, and the public service had stamped public policy with its own values and priorities. Trade policy offers one of the best examples of the benefits that flowed from this development. From the early 1930s until well into the 1970s, there developed a remarkable continuity in Canada's approach to international trade issues. It was an approach that fostered prosperity, but it reached its limits in the 1980s. By then, ministers began to encounter problems in their efforts to chart a course at odds with perceived bureaucratic values.

Prosperity, Continentalism, and Its Critics
Creighton's dissatisfaction with the Liberal hegemony from 1935 to 1957 was, of course, predicated on more than the process of government and the relationship that had developed between politicians and senior public servants. He did not like the policies that had been devised and pursued nor the results of those policies in terms of Canada's economic development and foreign relations. His was the criticism of the Tory nationalist who disliked the individualism of classical liberalism and the continentalism that flowed from Canada's geography. Like George Grant in his *Lament for a Nation*, Creighton preferred the ties of history, Empire, and sentiment to those of geography, technology, and economic interests.

By the mid-1950s, Creighton's and Grant's Tory nationalism was matched by a newer breed of economic nationalist who deplored the US connection because it tied Canada into the preeminent capitalist economy and undermined Canada's ability to act independently. Ironically, Grant's high Tory nationalism had its most profound and lasting effect on those ultimately attracted to statist, left-wing anti-Americanism. For these economic nationalists, the benefit of the end of the imperial British connection had been completely eroded by a neocolonial economic connection to the United States. What they wanted was a Canada that could pursue its own destiny, often defined as anything but that of the United States. Creighton's and Grant's Tory nationalism was rooted in fantasies of the past; the new economic nationalism tended to be rooted in dreams of the future as a statist, classless society. Both brands of nationalism eschewed classic liberal individualism, the basis for much of the policy thinking in Ottawa during this period. Tory nationalists preferred communitarianism; nationalists of the left preferred collectivism. Both were suspicious of the market; both preferred a larger role for government; and both saw the United States and its technological wizardry as the embodiment of all that was wrong with modern society.[63]

Neither of these ideologically based criticisms of Canadian postwar trade and economic policy recognized the limitations placed upon Canadian decision makers by the realities of Canada's economic position in the period immediately after the war, nor did their proponents accept the limitations placed upon decision makers by the realities of contemporary ideas and values.

There had always been a persistent strain of anti-Americanism among Canada's intellectual elite, particularly at the University of Toronto where scholars like Creighton, Harold Innis, and Frank Underhill plied their trade, but they had spoken for few but themselves. This was as true in the mid-1950s as it had been in earlier periods.[64] By the middle of the decade, most Canadians had many good reasons to be satisfied. The depression and the war were by now but bad memories. Canadians had begun to enjoy a high and rising standard of living and an increasing range of government services. For the first time in Canadian history, the growth in the economy – output rose 64 percent between 1944 and 1957 – had come largely from domestic demand. New investment had risen 249 percent while government capital spending during this period had risen by 776 percent. Domestic demand outpaced foreign demand to the point that exports steadily declined as a percentage of GNP.[65] The economy had become more diversified and capable of providing Canadians with a growing cornucopia of goods and services and with high-paying jobs. Canada had become more urbanized and the quality of life, at least materially, had improved with it. Canadians could look with satisfaction at a government that had delivered the prosperity it had promised. General optimism was also reflected in the rapid growth of the population, from an estimated 12,823,000 in 1948 to about 16,610,000 in 1957. A quarter of the increase had come from immigration with the rest supplied by the baby boom. Unlike during earlier periods, few Canadians left.[66]

And yet elite opinion makers in university common rooms and Ottawa living rooms were able to mine a growing unease with the fact that this prosperity had come on the basis of a much closer economic integration with the United States. A small but influential number of Canadians were becoming uncomfortable with the fact that the east-west orientation of the country, so painfully staked out in earlier decades, had been seriously eroded by this development.

The integration was also much more than a matter of investment and trade figures. The influence of the United States on all aspects of Canadian life had markedly increased. With it had come changing attitudes toward the United States with significant implications for the future conduct of what had by now become not only Canada's most important trade and economic relationship, but the only relationship that really mattered. Most Canadians were generally happy with the close ties that existed between the two countries, taking a keen interest in American politics, television, movies, books, and magazines and enjoying visiting back and forth on holidays and business, but a growing minority found these ties distasteful, both because of their dislike of things American and because of the feared impact they would have on Canada's ability to control its own destiny and define its own values.

By the middle of the 1950s, this broad strain of unease could be found reflected in the pages of the final report of the Royal Commission on Canada's Economic Prospects and its supporting research. Set up in the summer of 1955 and chaired by Toronto business scion Walter Gordon, the Gordon Commission, in its hearings and deliberations, became a lightning rod for anxiety about the close relationship that had developed between Canada and the United States.[67] The commission's final report celebrated the positive dimensions of the relationship but also warned about its perils. It noted that "Canada and the United States live in a kind of symbiosis – two organisms separate and distinct, each with its own ends and laws; but highly interdependent, indissolubly sharing the same continental environment and, in spite of a great disproportion in wealth and economic power, each necessary to the other."[68]

In its interim report of December 1956 the commission had provided a well-thought-out, carefully reasoned assessment of the benefits and perils of foreign direct investment, particularly by US investors (see table 7.5 for the extent of such investment). Its final report constituted a splendid picture of Canada at mid-century, with lots of useful statistics, and a detailed assessment of the structure of the economy and the role of savings and investment. The latter served as the basis for much of the commission's speculation about the future, including its warning about the dangers of an over-reliance on foreign investment, and its moderate recommendations on how to encourage more domestic investment and less reliance on foreign sources of capital. Its thirty-three volumes of research supplied a wealth of statistical and analytical material to back up the final report, including a detailed study of Canada-US economic relations, a study of Canadian commercial policy, and separate volumes on recent and anticipated import and export patterns.[69]

Others, however, were less prepared to be as sober in their analysis or as moderate in their assessment and recommendations. In the years that followed, a whole

Table 7.5

US and other foreign direct investment in Canada, 1948-57 (billions of dollars)

Year	Total capital	Total FDI	US FDI	Total resident-owned capital
1948	16.0	5.1	3.7	10.9
1951	20.8	6.5	4.9	14.3
1952	23.0	7.4	5.6	15.6
1953	25.7	8.3	6.4	17.4
1954	28.2	9.1	7.0	19.0
1955	30.4	9.9	7.6	20.5
1956	34.0	11.5	8.7	22.6
1957	37.6	12.9	9.9	24.8

Note: Totals may not add due to rounding.
Source: F.H. Leacy, ed., *Historical Statistics of Canada,* 2nd ed. (Ottawa: Statistics Canada, 1983), series G255, G262, G269, and G276.

industry would develop dedicated to examining the evils of foreign, particularly American, investment and the problems created for Canadians by the uncritical march toward continentalism under the leadership of Mackenzie King and Louis St. Laurent, and directed by their US-born minister of everything, C.D. Howe. Walter Gordon became the inspiration for a growing army of Canadian political scientists providing the grist for this more virulent strain of economic nationalism. Several generations of students would be nurtured on the myths and theories developed by this brand of scholarship to the point that it would become difficult to separate fact from fiction in academic discourse.

As these myths and theories took hold among a growing number of opinion moulders, policy makers felt more and more compelled to respond. As a result, Canadian trade and economic policy over the succeeding thirty years became more and more shaped by considerations that flowed from or responded to nationalist economic analysis. But because such policy was grafted onto the policy base laid during the first postwar decade and the deeply ingrained business reality of close ties between the Canadian and US economies, a growing tension developed between continentalist economic reality and nationalist political ideals.[70]

The basic line of argument that had developed by the end of the 1950s ran as follows:

> Canada's contemporary situation is that, while dependence on the outside world as a whole is decreasing, dependence on the United States is increasing. Of fundamental importance is the relative decline of Great Britain as a source of capital and as a market, depriving Canada of its historic counterpoise to the weight of the United States. Current

concern over the relations of Canada and the United States reflects the absence of this traditional balance ... In broad outlines the [resulting] situation is a simple one: United States capital flows into Canada principally to accelerate development in sectors that will serve the United States market. Since the United States is already a highly industrialized economy with a very productive agricultural sector, the market demand that it exerts on Canada is predominantly a demand for industrial raw materials.[71]

In short, Canada's dependence on the United States for investment capital and as a market was perpetuating Canada's role as a supplier of staple products to its metropolitan market and stunting the development of a more diversified, independent economy.

The point that Canada had become more integrated into a continental economy was, of course, well taken. The statistics were clear. Less compelling was the assumption among many of the critics of postwar trade and economic policy that trade and investment were not critical to Canada's economic development. For many nationalists, a mild socialism or statism translated into the belief that Canada would be a better place if there were less foreign influence through trade and investment. For the policy makers in Ottawa, however, to have chosen the nationalist or noncontinentalist route would have been deliberately to have chosen a poorer Canada. There was not enough capital in Canada – or in Britain for that matter – to finance Canada's further economic development, nor was there enough demand for Canadian goods in Europe and elsewhere to maintain Canadian exports at acceptable levels.[72] Policy makers thus opted for prosperity and the only available means to prosperity, more trade and investment with the United States. The specifics of this option involved a combination of multilateral negotiations and relatively unfettered investment from the only possible source, US corporations. That there was a price to be paid was appreciated.[73] Both ministers and officials would have much preferred more diversified trade and investment patterns, and they worked hard to encourage them, but to little avail.

First and foremost, Canadian policy makers were pragmatists. Among their nationalist critics, however, pragmatism and nationalism did not mix. To them, C.D. Howe came to epitomize all that was wrong with Canada by the end of the 1950s. He had been content to help create the conditions that made it possible for private investors to develop the nation, without regard to the nationality of those investors. Given Canada's trading heritage and the impact on Canada of the collapse of world trade in the 1930s, it is hard to imagine what other options were available.

Ironically, the course chosen by Howe and his colleagues contributed to Canada's more rapid economic development, ultimately making Canada less dependent on foreign markets and foreign capital. The rapid rise in US capital inflows in the 1950s reflected not only the interest of US investors in Canadian resources, but also the fact that Canada was running a chronic current account deficit. That deficit was in turn the result of the rapid development of the economy, as manufacturers imported capital machinery in order to expand their productive capacity and consumers spent their new prosperity on imported consumer goods and tourism in the United States. That deficit was offset by the inflow of capital, making it possible for Canadians to enjoy the benefits of the new prosperity and a growing economy. The total inflow of investment capital, however, was less than during earlier periods, including the periods before and after the First World War. In 1946, Canada's gross liabilities to foreigners stood at $7.8 billion while foreigners' gross liabilities to Canadians stood at $4.0 billion. Canada's net position was thus minus $3.8 billion, or 32 percent of GNP. In 1969, Canada owed foreigners $48.8 billion, but was owed $28.1 billion by foreigners for a net of minus $20.7 billion or 35 percent of GNP, hardly a major change and not enough to warrant either the charge of a Liberal sellout or the hand-wringing about the imminent demise of Canada.[74]

As Canada began to reap the benefits of the more diversified economy that resulted from the rapid growth of the first two decades after the war, the role of foreign investment steadily declined. Canadians were by then able to generate enough savings to provide much of the needed capital for further expansion, and enjoyed a much richer and more comprehensive array of social programs. Indeed, it would be Canada's addiction to the latter that would create a new requirement for foreign capital in the 1980s, but this time a foreign capital to underwrite consumption rather than investment.

The acid political test, of course, was that the pragmatic policies pursued by governments during this period led to steady growth and spreading prosperity. Few Canadians were prepared to place that prosperity at risk in order to see whether the utopian idealism of the nationalists would create even more prosperity – either in absolute or distributional terms. While there was always the hope that taking from the rich and giving to the poor would result in more people being better off, there was also the nagging fear that everyone might be worse off. The nationalists did not promise more prosperity, only more control and other political values of dubious merit to most Canadians. Some nationalists were even prepared to hint that there would be a cost in prosperity for these values, making the message one that only the comfortable middle-class intellectual could embrace with any enthusiasm. Entrepreneurs and business managers were not about to self-immolate, and the working class and poor wanted more, not less, prosperity. Thus the nationalist refrain appealed to selected members of the public service, secure in their permanent jobs, and to university intellectuals, with equally secure tenured positions.

Nevertheless, by the mid-1950s there seemed sufficient discontent to bring into question the continued ability of the Grits to deliver. The cumulative impact of various political and economic factors swept the Grits from office in 1957 and installed a minority Tory government under their new leader, John Diefenbaker, bringing to an end a government that had served Canada well but had become somewhat tired and arrogant in the process. In twenty-two years, the Liberals had at one time or another offended a lot of groups, including the Prairie wheat farmers, who were convinced the government was not doing enough to sell their wheat on glutted world markets or compensating them enough for losses, as their American competitors were being compensated. Could Diefenbaker and his ministers respond to these and other complaints and do better? Did the bureaucracy have ideas that had not been offered to or accepted by the Liberals?

8 PROFESSIONALISM AND NATIONALISM
The Diefenbaker Years

> The gulf between orthodox economic thinking and the intuitive notions of do-it-yourself economics is widest in the sphere of international economic relations in general and trade policies in particular. The professionals, and those who think like them, are very much in a minority. Perhaps the sharpest difference between minority and majority lies in their respective conceptions of where national interests lie in international trade.
>
> – David Henderson, Innocence and Design

The election of John Diefenbaker and the Tories in 1957 not only marked the end of twenty-two years of uninterrupted Liberal rule, but also led to the first political test of the professionalism of Canada's public service. The early development of a professional public service had predated the Liberal hegemony, but it had reached its maturity under Mackenzie King, responding to the crises of depression and war. By most accounts, the professionals had served Canada well. They had provided good advice and good administration in dealing with the challenges of the previous three decades. The resulting policies had underpinned a remarkable growth in Canada's prosperity, successfully defeating the twin scourges of depression and war.

But not everyone agreed, including John Diefenbaker and some of his closest advisors. To them, the relationship between the senior ranks of the public service and the Liberal party had been too close for comfort. They were determined to put their own stamp on public policy and ensure that the role of the public service was limited to implementing the will of Parliament and pursuing priorities established by cabinet. The senior public service, for its part, was equally determined to demonstrate that its leaders were not Liberal partisans but professional administrators and policy advisors.

Trade policy figured prominently among the issues that came under close scrutiny. Diefenbaker shared the view that the Liberal hegemony had tied Canada too closely to the American economy. Even worse, it had often disposed Canadian officials to opt for American policy preferences. This tilt toward continentalism had been at the expense of Canada's historic ties to Britain and the Commonwealth and was pregnant with implications that reached far beyond mere trade and economic interests.

The Tories, as the party with the strongest ties to traditional Canadian business, were also not convinced that the Liberal zeal for a more open economy, as pursued in the GATT and elsewhere, was necessarily the best option. It not only smacked of what Donald Creighton called the new, US-dictated Genevan faith, but it was also beginning to expose Canadian manufacturers to a level of competition that they were not convinced was in their best interests.

Of course, had the professionals been able to deliver on the promise of stable, better access to the markets of the United States, Europe, and Japan in the 1950s, it would have been easier to demonstrate that their preferred course made sense. As we have seen, they could not. The European market remained essentially closed until currencies finally became convertible and balance-of-payments restrictions were removed, developments which did not take place until the closing years of the 1950s. The US Congress continued to insist on its stingy approach to tariff reductions, and the Eisenhower administration showed little inclination to challenge this attitude. Japanese and other overseas markets remained largely closed to anything but essential imports. Thus, for Canadian-based manufacturers, restructuring their production to take advantage of foreign markets made little sense. The necessity of protecting their home market from more competitive US, Japanese, and other imports was more than a matter of traditional mercantilism; their natural inclination had been reinforced by the realities they faced elsewhere.

By the end of the 1950s, GATT had become the bedrock of the professionals' trade policy. Nevertheless, within a few years two important bilateral deals were concluded with the United States: the Defence Production Sharing Arrangements (DPSA) and the Canada-US Automotive Products Agreement (the Auto Pact). In both instances, important Canadian industries dominated by US-based multinationals gained special status in the US market. In both cases, the issue was not a matter of free trade but of complementing other policies (defence) or avoiding a nasty dispute (the threat of a US countervailing duty case involving a duty remission project for automatic transmissions). These developments took place against the background of diminishing reliance on Commonwealth preferences and on exports to the United Kingdom.

It is tempting to speculate whether more success in GATT's early years in opening foreign markets to Canadian manufactures would have created more outwardly oriented manufacturing firms in Canada by the 1960s. Certainly the initial confidence created by their wartime success in helping to supply the Allies with the sinews of war suggests that such a development would have been possible. Nevertheless, a decade and a half of experience had demonstrated that only a narrow range of resource-based products could rely on export markets, confirming for many Canadian-based manufacturers that this natural state of affairs ought not to be disturbed without better evidence than had been offered to date. Studies by various academic and think-tank economists that showed the potential of foreign markets flowing from GATT negotiations in the 1960s were, not surprisingly, met with deep scepticism by Canadian manufacturers. Instead, they found it relatively easy to exploit Tory protectionist and anti-American sentiments.

W.A. Mackintosh, writing in 1922, in an essay that sought to provide an economic explanation of the main developments in Canadian history, noted, "To Canadians of the present generation political writings of fifty years ago read strangely. Annexation, commercial union, Zollverein, Canada First, Imperial Federation, these have no place in contemporary politics. We are less sensitive on these points. It is difficult to realize that Canadians ever believed in them. The difference is not in Canadians. It is in the economic background. When frustration of Canadian progress was overcome, and a period of expansion resulted, Canadian nationality was assured, and policies which cast doubt upon that nationality fell away."[1]

Fifty years later, sentiments had turned a further 180 degrees and assimilation, economic integration, and cultural identity were once again at the forefront of Canadian anxieties. These anxieties, however, were more a matter of concern among university and other elites than among ordinary Canadians, and it was ordinary Canadians who had elected John Diefenbaker. He was prepared to adopt the rhetoric of nationalism but proved incapable of translating that rhetoric into concrete action. It would take another decade before nationalist sentiments actually led to policy initiatives. In the meantime, Canadians were first treated to the indecision and bumbling of the Tories and then to the bungling and vacillation of the Grits.[2]

Neither Diefenbaker's successful 1956 leadership campaign nor his winning electoral campaign in 1957 offered much insight into either his domestic or foreign economic policy. Diefenbaker, though clearly a man of deep convictions, was not much given to introspection about policy issues. His five years in office confirmed that he merely reacted to events and was not prone to long-term planning or the pursuit of clear objectives. Many of his decisions were coloured by personality clashes and reflected his strong sense of paranoia. For those charged with preparing policy advice for his government and implementing its decisions, Diefenbaker's leadership turned out to be a trying experience.[3]

Some of his ministers, on the other hand, left a strong and positive legacy, despite the increasing problems within the cabinet. Donald Fleming and George Hees, for example, ably executed their mandates. Indeed, Hees is fondly remembered by the Trade Commissioner Service as one of its most enthusiastic and supportive ministers. Ultimately, however, Diefenbaker himself left a strong mark on issues of central policy and it is his legacy that must be considered. From a trade policy perspective, that legacy was largely a matter of bluster and indecision.

Diefenbaker and the British Connection
Within a few weeks of assuming office, the new prime minister announced that Canada would switch 15 percent of its trade from the United States to Great Britain. He appears to have developed the policy impromptu after playing a significant role (in his mind) at the Commonwealth heads of government meeting in London.

Les Callan, "Pretty Bubbles in the Air," 1 October 1957. Prime
Minister Diefenbaker's unrehearsed proposal of a 15 percent
increase in Canada-UK trade leads to some unexpected scheming
by the UK at the Commonwealth finance ministers' meeting in
Mont Tremblant, Quebec.

Pressed on his return on 7 July by reporters about how serious he was about strengthening Commonwealth trade ties – a promise that had featured prominently in his
election campaign, as well as in efforts to get Commonwealth agreement to hold a
finance ministers' meeting in Canada – he indicated that he was prepared to see a 15
percent shift. Subsequent analysis by the civil service as to what this would involve
did not deter his enthusiasm, but it did show the limits of what could be done.[4] At
the time, it would have required a doubling of UK exports to Canada, a willingness
by Canadians to forgo the purchase of goods they wanted in order to buy goods of
inferior quality designed for British circumstances (such as small refrigerators and
cars that did not start on cold winter mornings), and a capacity by UK customers
to absorb twice the value of Canadian shipments they were purchasing.

It would also have required Canada to take discriminatory steps inconsistent
with the GATT unless the two countries first negotiated either a free-trade agreement or a customs union. To that end, the UK government proposed that Canada
enter into a Canada-UK or broader Commonwealth free-trade area (an idea that

had been briefly broached by the United Kingdom during the 1946-8 GATT/ITO discussions in response to the dogged efforts by the United States to undo British preferential tariffs). In September 1957 at the Commonwealth finance ministers meeting at Mont Tremblant and later in Ottawa, the United Kingdom formally made this proposal, catching Finance Minister Donald Fleming and his officials off-guard. There was no response and the issue was gradually allowed to die.

Nevertheless, there was a small grain of sense in Diefenbaker's impulse. Throughout the postwar years Canadian exports to the United Kingdom and the Continent had been handicapped by the myriad balance-of-payments, currency, and other restrictions maintained by most governments. By 1957, the prospect of these restrictions finally being lifted appeared real and could have led to a surge in Canadian prospects. It is only with the benefit of hindsight that we can appreciate the extent to which commercial ties with UK customers and suppliers had been severed and new ones with the United States put in place. It is questionable, however, that Diefenbaker had any appreciation of this aspect of his policy preference.

Rather, Diefenbaker's impulse smacked of naïveté and nostalgia. He seemed to have little appreciation that trade policy, like all branches of foreign policy, is not solely within the control of a single government. Rather, it requires the active cooperation of at least one other government, either in the negotiation of new agreements extending improved access or other commitments, or in the implementation of various other concessions. Additionally, he seemed not to appreciate that the size, composition, and direction of trade flows result from the decisions of thousands of private producers and consumers. These decisions may be influenced by government policy, but a shift of such proportions would have taken some pretty heroic or draconian policy measures. At the time, Canadians would have been unlikely to shun the many desirable products they were buying from the United States and substitute less desirable products from the United Kingdom, nor would Canadian producers have been willing to forgo receipts from good US customers and turn to less certain UK customers. If Diefenbaker had indicated a desire to increase sales to the United Kingdom and to improve UK sales opportunities in Canada, a variety of measures could have been pursued with these goals in mind. But any policy geared to a massive switch in buying and selling patterns suggested a politician who spoke before he had given much thought to what was involved or before he had sought the advice of his officials. Events proved that the policy denoted no more than a nostalgic preference, with no conception of how to pursue it and no follow-through.[5]

Further Frustrations from across the Atlantic

The sharp mandarin reaction to Diefenbaker's unrehearsed proposal was in part a reflection of the fact that over the previous five years officials had thoroughly considered a range of options to diversify (rather than divert) Canadian exports and imports. Unfortunately, none proved workable or even negotiable. They too had been frustrated by persistent US protectionism and worried about its impact on a Canada becoming ever more dependent on the US market. They had learned, however, that there were limits to pious hopes. The problem and its solution lay less in Canadian policy and more in the realities of markets and in the policy choices exercised by others.

In response to the lessons learned over the previous decade, the assumptions underpinning Canadian trade policy in 1957 were: 1) that Europe would not be able to get its act together, and 2) that the US Congress would refuse to provide the president with a mandate sufficiently bold to cut tariffs significantly. Within a few years the Treaty of Rome (1957), the Treaty of Stockholm (1960), and the US Trade Expansion Act (1962) undercut this prevailing wisdom. The two basic assumptions of Canadian trade policy had been challenged, and Diefenbaker and his ministers were incapable of any creative adjustments. Their lukewarm support of the US Trade Expansion Act and their hostility to the reality (rather than to the ideal) of European integration undermined Canada's ability to take advantage of changing opportunities. Instead of riding the international trend toward freer trade, Diefenbaker preferred the comfort of traditional, modified Tory protectionism.

To add insult to injury, in 1961 the UK government began to take deliberate steps to enter the new European Common Market, steps that would eventually require it to turn its back not only on Canada but also on the rest of the Commonwealth. The inability of officials to provide Diefenbaker with policy proposals that would prevent this disaster for Canada added to his convictions that the public service was hopelessly compromised by Liberal sympathizers.[6]

Britain's decision to tie its future to Europe rather than to the Commonwealth was taken for reasons perfectly consistent with other aspects of Canadian policy, namely the desirability of intra-European cooperation both as a bulwark to the immediate menace of communist expansionism and as an answer to the longer-term problem of intra-European aggression. Diefenbaker and his cabinet saw merit in these broader foreign policy considerations, but they could not come to grips with the extent to which a strengthening of Commonwealth ties and a deepening of European integration were mutually exclusive. British politicians found this reality equally wrenching but nevertheless compelling. At times Diefenbaker and his ministers suggested that they understood but then slipped back into nostalgic whining about the cost of these developments to Canadian trade and other interests. What really hurt, of course, was that the loosening of Commonwealth trade ties added to the forces driving Canada into the American orbit. US support for European integration did not help Canadians to accept these changes in power alignments.

Throughout the 1950s, Europeans, with US and sometimes Canadian encouragement, had been discussing various projects aimed at creating a more unified Europe. The first successful step had been the creation of the European Coal and Steel Community in 1951 among France, Germany, Italy, and the Benelux countries. Failure to achieve a major breakthrough in multilateral negotiations at the GATT in

Geneva in 1955-6 had spurred a second wave of discussions leading to the establishment of the European Economic Community (EEC) through the Treaty of Rome in 1958. The United Kingdom had participated in many of these discussions, and British leaders had been among the earliest proponents of intra-European cooperation.[7]

By the mid-1950s, however, the United Kingdom had become sceptical about the direction of European integration and worried about the impact its participation would have on the Commonwealth.[8] Britain wanted something both more and less: it wanted wider participation, and it preferred to pursue economic integration through an industrial free-trade area rather than through a comprehensive common market. It preferred intergovernmental cooperation to supranational integration. Such an approach would be less threatening to British sovereignty and would allow Britain to maintain its links with the Commonwealth. These sentiments had a basis in the reality of the United Kingdom's trading patterns. As late as 1960, only 15 percent of its trade was with members of the EEC, 43 percent was with Commonwealth countries, and 42 percent was with the rest of the world, principally the United States and other European countries.[9]

Soon after the formation of the Common Market, Britain accepted Sweden's invitation to participate in the negotiation of a free-trade area among the nonparticipants to the EEC and in 1960 signed the Treaty of Stockholm establishing the European Free Trade Association (EFTA) among the United Kingdom, Norway, Sweden, Denmark, Switzerland, Austria, and Portugal. The details of the circumstances that had led to two competing approaches to regional integration in Europe – the UK-led EFTA and the French-led EEC – are less important than its results, which were undesirable. The United States and Canada, for broad geopolitical reasons, had supported European political and economic cooperation, but they did not welcome the establishment of two rival camps. Some of the potentially discriminatory effects of both the EEC and the EFTA were tackled in the 1960-1 Dillon Round of GATT negotiations (see below), but to little avail. US efforts were hemmed in by congressional protectionism, and EEC efforts were frustrated by lack of cohesion and common purpose.

The United Kingdom's response to Diefenbaker's impulsive announcement to shift 15 percent of Canada's trade to the Commonwealth must be considered in the light of these ongoing developments. If Canada had been serious about negotiating a free-trade area, and extending it to the Commonwealth, there were British officials prepared to explore that avenue. Indeed, the participation of the United States, Canada, and Britain in an Atlantic free-trade area also held some attraction and continued to reverberate through the halls of universities, business groups, and think tanks in all three countries for the next decade or more.[10] Despite the failure of Diefenbaker's first trade policy initiative, his disposition to find some way to strengthen commercial ties with the mother country, unrealistic as that preference might have been, continued to animate his thinking in subsequent years.

To be sure, UK accession to the Common Market did spell clear and immediate problems. In 1960, Canadian exports to the Six were valued at roughly $440 million or 8 percent of total exports; exports to the United Kingdom amounted to $915 million or 17 percent of the total. In both cases wheat, other food products, and industrial raw materials made up the bulk of these exports. About three-quarters of Canada's exports to the Common Market entered free of duty because they constituted largely raw materials at the earliest stages of processing. Some 97 percent of Canada's exports to the United Kingdom entered free of duty. More importantly, $376 million of those exports enjoyed a Commonwealth preference. UK entry into the Common Market would not only wipe out those preferences but would in some instances result in reverse preferences. Canadian exports of wrapping paper, which entered the United Kingdom free of duty and thus enjoyed a 14 percent preferential margin, would face an EEC tariff of 18 percent should the United Kingdom enter the Common Market. Wheat, barley, newsprint, aluminum, lead and zinc, industrial chemicals, and other exports to Britain would face similar, if perhaps less dramatic, reversals in fortune. As a result of EFTA tariff cuts, Norway was already threatening Canada's place as the principal supplier of aluminum to Britain. With such examples clearly in mind, Canadian officials could not view UK entry into the Common Market with equanimity; Canada stood to lose some real commercial benefits that could take years to replace.[11]

Curiously, Canadian business leaders were less concerned than Canadian officials. In their view, Britain had become an increasingly less attractive market and the European market offered little immediate prospect, whereas the United States was a proven and growing trading partner. If Britain decided for its own reasons to cast its future with Europe, business could and would adjust and evaluate new opportunities as they developed. Such a bloodless assessment was not for Diefenbaker and his ministers. As Jack Granatstein concludes, the British connection was more than a matter of trade. The Conservatives "had been fighting for ... the idea of the Commonwealth as it existed in John Diefenbaker's mind, a British-led community of nations that fought the good fight and co-operated on all things."[12]

In the end Canada was spared having to come to terms with British accession to the Common Market for at least a decade. French president Charles de Gaulle vetoed the project in 1963 and again in 1967. A Common Market that France could dominate politically and that would ensure German involvement in European affairs was one thing, but a Common Market that included Britain and some of the Nordics could dilute French preeminence more than the French president considered tolerable. Although supportive of European political cooperation, de Gaulle had been sceptical of the supranationalist approach of the Treaty of Rome, preferring instead an intergovernmental approach. More fundamentally, de Gaulle was not convinced that Britain's interest in Europe rested on positive or constructive foundations. Britain was turning to Europe because it saw no alternatives and would, in his view, continue to be a negative force in the Common Market's further

Peter Kuch, "Tying up the ECM," 1962. Canada's John Diefenbaker and Australia's Robert Menzies tie British prime minister Harold Macmillan into knots over Britain's efforts to negotiate accession to the European Common Market.

evolution. Last but not least, de Gaulle saw British entry as providing too much opportunity for American influence.[13]

Not until the end of 1969, after de Gaulle's departure, did France lift its veto. Even then it took nearly three years of arduous negotiations to find the basis for British entry. Politically it was a hollow victory, which meant the end of the Commonwealth as anything more than a symbol but did not make the British into Europeans. EEC membership was more a matter of resignation than of embrace.[14] Accompanied by Denmark and Ireland, the United Kingdom entered the Common Market on 1 January 1973. The Norwegian electorate narrowly defeated the referendum on accession, preferring to remain with the less demanding EFTA and denying continental Europe access to its fishery and offshore energy resources.

The long delay in British accession to the Common Market postponed the day of reckoning for Canada. Canadian exporters continued to enjoy their preferences to the UK market for at least another decade. The uncertainty created by de Gaulle's veto for most of the 1960s also cast a long shadow over Canada's approach to GATT multilateral negotiations and further strengthened its ties to the American economy. Rather than looking to an EEC that might soon include the United Kingdom, Canada continued to treat Britain and the EEC as separate interests.

Despite his anglophilia, Diefenbaker had very little appreciation of Britain's continuing difficult economic straits and its limited room for manoeuvre. Both his cavalier proposal of the 15 percent shift as well as his hostility to British membership in the EEC were based on self-serving and erroneous perceptions. He was convinced that the United Kingdom was plotting to break up the Commonwealth and the British preferential system, and indicated that Canada would retaliate for any loss of preference. In the event, Canada did nothing to enhance UK access to the Canadian market. In fact, it took a number of measures that reduced it. Increased tariffs on woollens and rubber footwear, a ministerial prescription to increase the value for duty on cars, and continued resort to automatic dumping duties all sent confusing signals across the Atlantic.

Diefenbaker and the American Connection

If Diefenbaker's anglophilia did not translate into any constructive policies, neither did his anti-Americanism. He had never been shy about his dislike of the Americans as a nation. In September 1957 he asked an audience at Dartmouth College in New Hampshire whether a country can "have a meaningful independent existence in a situation where nonresidents own an important part of that country's basic resources and industry?"[15] At the end of the first year of Tory rule, US ambassador Livingston Merchant reported to President Eisenhower that "the last year has seen the development of a strident, almost truculent nationalism" in Canada, and an increasing sensitivity to the problem of living next door to the United States.[16]

Despite the continued rhetoric, there was little serious effort to reduce Canadian dependence on the US market or to reduce US investment in Canada. Diefenbaker's ministers used the occasion of the first meeting of the Joint Canada-US Ministerial Committee to express their desire to try to diversify Canadian trade. In return they received little more than a sarcastic rejoinder from US secretary of state John Foster Dulles that that was Canada's business. Dulles also reminded them that the United States was a cash customer that provided Canadians with the goods they wanted.[17] It was not the best way to start a meeting aimed at resolving Canada-US trade irritants. But as Dulles and his colleagues soon learned, the Diefenbaker government's bark was worse than its bite. Indeed, it rarely bit and when it did, it was likely to hurt itself as much as its intended victim.

The real problem was that the United States was critical to Canada but that Canada, at least insofar as trade and investment were concerned, was of little more than marginal importance to the United States. In 1957, Canadian merchandise exports to the United States represented 11.6 percent of Canadian production, but amounted to no more than a trickle of 0.8 percent of consumption in the vast US market. In the other direction, imports from the United States represented 16.7 percent of Canadian consumption, but less than 1 percent of US production.[18] Dulles could afford to be sarcastic. If Canada were to disappear from the face of the earth, only a few American firms, workers, and consumers would notice.

Even though Diefenbaker and his ministers expressed a strong preference for doing relatively less business with the United States and more with the rest of the world, they had to confront the fact that a lot of Canadian exports did go to the United States and that not all US citizens welcomed those exports. As Ronald Anderson told readers of the *Globe and Mail,* "If any Canadian manufacturer succeeds in winning any substantial market in the United States, a way will be found to keep him out."[19] Various irritants over the years, and their seeming insolubility, added to the sense of frustration experienced by Diefenbaker and his ministers in dealing with the Americans. Continuing quotas on lead and zinc, new quotas on oil, PL-480 concessional sales of wheat, undercutting of Canadian wheat sales to Japan, the nonrenewal of contracts for Canadian uranium, regulatory interruptions of natural gas sales, efforts to try to reduce sales of softwood lumber, US sales to reduce its strategic stockpiles, and other problems seemed never to go away.

Canada, of course, contributed its own share of irritants to Canada-US relations. Various tax measures initiated by Donald Fleming, for example, including a 15 percent withholding tax on the patriation of profits, sought to make a statement about the desirability of US investment, to little practical avail but some annoyance. Efforts to encourage the development of Canadian periodicals through discriminatory restrictions on Canadian editions of *Time* and *Reader's Digest* did not sit well with their owners and congressional friends. Sales by Canadian subsidiaries to China and Cuba were seen as provocative acts undermining US policy.

On a personal level, Diefenbaker was prepared to get on with President Eisenhower and his administration. His discomfort with the American connection did not come into full flower until the Kennedy administration, and he was at his most hostile on defence and security matters. But it was precisely on defence-related issues that Diefenbaker demonstrated early in his government the extent to which he was unprepared to follow through on his emotional instincts. Indeed, his actions deepened Canadian trade and investment ties to the United States. The occasion for this unexpected turn of events was the difficult decision to scrap the Avro Arrow. The result was the series of understandings and administrative arrangements collectively known as the Defence Production Sharing Arrangements (DPSA).

The Defence Production Sharing Arrangements

The problem of the Avro Arrow had been inherited from the Liberals, as had the elements that came together into a solution. Canada had developed a respectable defence industry during the war and had maintained it afterward, supplying both Canadian and some US and British military requirements. It did not take long, however, for Canadians to learn how readily military procurement lends itself to the exercise of industrial policy. The military everywhere tend to be averse to buying their products off the shelf. They prefer that their weaponry, logistics, communication, transportation, and other requirements be met on the basis of rigorous and unique specifications. No army, navy, or air force has the same needs as those of any other nation. Terrain, borders, resources, and missions all vary and, therefore, need distinctive equipment. The Canadian military is no different but, unlike the US and British military, does have to face the harsh reality that Canada's forces are much smaller and the country's financial resources more limited. Nevertheless, by the 1950s, "Canadian industry was producing a wider range of more sophisticated military equipment than it ever had ... It had developed an advanced electronic industry. It was selling to the U.S. at least six kinds of aircraft."[20]

The military also tends to be patriotic and prefers to buy its equipment from local suppliers. In 1951, to encourage and organize local procurement, Canada had established a Department of Defence Production. It worked closely with the Department of Defence and with Canadian suppliers to ensure a Canadian presence in the industry and to provide Canadian-based firms with the help needed to maintain a profitable level of production. Various incentive programs and preferences ensured that, where possible, Canadians would supply their own military. One of the arguments deployed, then and now, was that a domestic defence industry creates a wide range of industrial spin-offs that more than offset the extra expense of relying on domestic suppliers. In short, military procurement is an important component of any modern industrial policy.

In the early 1950s the government determined that Canada needed an all-weather interceptor fighter aircraft and that A.V. Roe (or Avro) in Malton – a British subsidiary – would be the lead company in developing the aircraft. By the mid-1950s much progress had been made in designing the Arrow, including an engine to be developed in Canada by Orenda Engines. Experts considered it a superb design. The problem was that the whole project had become ruinously expensive. Its continued economic viability was further undermined when it became clear that the fighter would be too sophisticated for reserve pilots and could only be flown by the air force itself.[21] This realization had reduced the potential Canadian order from 500 to 100 aircraft and had sent the cost of each individual aircraft through the roof. Some estimates suggested that the cost of one Arrow would be equal to fifteen times the cost of its predecessor, the CF-100. More bad news arrived when it was learned that the US air force was not interested. It found the Arrow unsuited to its requirements and not competitive with designs being developed by American firms. No other air force expressed any inclination to buy the Arrow; each had its own favourites.

The Liberal government had been aware of these sobering facts but had agreed to keep the project alive for a little longer to see if future developments might make matters a little less grim. In 1957, when the Conservatives were asked to pour more millions down this sinkhole, the government balked. By this time the Canadian military had lost its initial enthusiasm, particularly when it became evident that the Arrow would suck up all available money for military procurement and leave the generals and the admirals without any funds to meet their own forces' needs. The government delayed a final decision when officials informed it of the economic and industrial consequences of terminating the project: thousands of sophisticated jobs would be lost and cancellation charges could add $170 million to an already large sum spent without anything tangible in return.[22] By this time, the Canadian defence industry employed some 45,000 people and supported another 100,000 jobs in related industries.[23]

By 1958, however, it was clear that the Arrow was a liability of enormous proportions, and early in 1959 Diefenbaker and his cabinet agreed to close down the project. To make sure there could not be a later resurrection, Diefenbaker ordered that the five existing prototypes be cut up and sold for scrap. All that remains today is the nose of one of the prototypes housed in the Aviation Museum in Ottawa. A.V. Roe responded by immediately laying off 14,000 workers,[24] many of whom would eventually migrate to the United States and help NASA put a man on the moon. There was no question that A.V. Roe had put together a first-class team; their talents, however, were more in tune with the financial resources of the US space agency than of the Canadian military.

To address the disaster that the termination of the Arrow project spelled for the Canadian defence industry, the government turned to the United States. As far back as the 1941 Hyde Park Declaration issued by President Roosevelt and Prime Minister King, the US military had been prepared to purchase some of its requirements from Canadian suppliers to offset to some extent the flow of military equipment northward. Canada had always needed to procure some of its military requirements offshore, and increasingly, it preferred US to British or other equipment. Arrangements between Canada and the United States in the early 1950s built on the Hyde Park experience and allowed Canadian suppliers to contribute to the US military effort in Korea.[25] Two-way trade in military equipment, however, remained in the US's favour. Between 1951 and 1958, Canada sold $586 million in military equipment to the United States, but bought $690 million.[26]

The government now proposed and the US government accepted that these arrangements be expanded with a view to ensuring that Canadian suppliers would continue to participate in US military supply contracts. Canada agreed that it would replace its aging CF-100 fighters with CF-105 Voodoos purchased in the United States and would add to its antiaircraft defence by equipping the Canadian air force with Bomarc missiles. More generally, Canada agreed that it would build on established agreements on military cooperation, such as the 1957 establishment of an integrated North American air defence system (NORAD), and rely on the United States as its principal supplier of sophisticated weaponry and other military requirements. In return, the United States agreed to remove various barriers to Canadian firms' ability to sell equipment to the US military, including the tariff on a range of goods provided to US military contractors and some Buy America procurement preferences. Access to US defence research projects was increased and was gradually expanded over the next decade.[27] In 1963, the Liberals agreed that the arrangements should be managed so as to ensure a rough balance in two-way trade in defence materiel. In 1966, Canada agreed to eliminate many of its own tariffs on military products.[28] Various administrative and other arrangements further consolidated a robust two-way trade, which would become a major political liability during the Vietnam War, but which also ensured the continued viability of a Canadian defence industry. In the first seven years of the program (1959-65), the US military procured $1,174.2 million in high-value end-products and research contracts in Canada.[29]

The asymmetrical terms of the DPSA reflected the differing objectives of the two countries. For the United States, the DPSA was largely a matter of security, complementing NORAD, NATO, and other cooperative defence arrangements. The US delegation to the DPSA discussions was exclusively made up of officials with defence-related responsibilities. For Canada, security factors were important, but so were trade, industrial, and broader economic considerations. The Canadian delegation reflected these preoccupations in both the negotiation and administration of the DPSA. Responsibility for the DPSA was housed in the Department of Defence Production. With the demise of that department in 1963, it moved to the new Department of Industry, and in 1968 to the amalgamated Department of Industry, Trade, and Commerce. The DPSA may have addressed military procurement, but it was also an instrument of industrial policy, and some of its most important elements involved trade policy instruments.

Already in 1958, the Canadian defence industry was dominated by branch plants of American defence contractors, but it also included some British and Canadian enterprises. Under the DPSA, the American presence increased, as US firms bought out British and some Canadian firms, and the Canadian operations of McDonnell Douglas, General Dynamics, Pratt and Whitney, Boeing, Rockwell, and others became an integral part of the US defence procurement system. Additionally, however, the Canadian operations contributed components to civilian projects, including various aviation and space projects. Pratt and Whitney, for example, designed and built a range of engines for small turboprop aircraft in Montreal, including the short take-off and landing aircraft developed and built in Toronto by de Havilland. CAE became the world's premier builder of simulators for civil aircraft. By killing the Arrow project, the Diefenbaker government brought an end to the dream that Canada could develop and fund large defence projects on its own. By negotiating the DPSA, it strengthened the foundation for a viable aviation, avionics, and electronics industry in Canada. Ironically, however, the DPSA further consolidated the continental orientation of the Canadian economy, despite Diefenbaker's stated desire to move in the opposite direction.

Trade and National Security: The Problem of US Extraterritoriality

During the remaining years of the Diefenbaker government, there were not many more triumphs on the trade and economic front with the United States. Indeed, in the final year and a half of Diefenbaker's watch, the antipathy between him and President Kennedy, occasioned by both clashes of personality and matters of policy, reached such a height that Canadian officials could not use their own personal relationships to overcome it. The urbane Charles Ritchie, upon his appointment at the beginning of 1962 to replace Arnold Heeney as ambassador to the United States, found the atmosphere so chilly that he wondered what good he could do.[30] The most difficult issues between Canada and the United States involved matters of defence, but these spilled over into matters of trade and investment.[31]

One of the more pressing issues was the American penchant for thinking that what was good for Washington was good for the rest of the world. As far back as 1917 the United States had had a Trading with the Enemy Act on its books. This had since been extended with the Foreign Assets Control Regulations administered by the Treasury Department. These laws prohibited US citizens from engaging in commerce with countries with which the United States was at war. During the 1950s, they were aimed primarily at isolating communist countries, particularly the People's Republic of China and North Korea.

Such laws were clearly the business of the US government. More troubling was that they also prohibited foreign subsidiaries of US firms from doing business with the enemies of the United States. This had already caused conflict between Canada and the United States in the 1950s when a number of Canadian subsidiaries had been told by the State Department to forget about sales to China. The most notorious instance had been a 1957 order to Ford to block the sale of a thousand trucks from its Canadian subsidiary. The Canadian government indicated to Ford that the only law that applied was Canadian. Ford decided to cut its losses; the sale did not proceed.[32]

As a first step in trying to resolve the issue, Diefenbaker and President Eisenhower, in the context of a broader discussion about defence-related issues, had issued a Joint Statement on Export Policies in July 1958 promising annual consultations and case-by-case exemptions from the US law where warranted.[33] Although not wholly satisfactory, this approach was in keeping with the general tenor of exemptionalism, an important aspect of the special relationship between the two countries that had developed over the previous twenty years.

In 1961, however, extraterritoriality reached new heights of US intrusiveness. The successful overthrow of the corrupt Batista dictatorship in Cuba had installed a communist regime under Fidel Castro almost on Miami's doorstep. Not only did Castro make clear that US gamblers and gangsters were no longer welcome, but he nationalized the properties of US mining, sugar, hotel, and other firms and refused to provide them with compensation on any basis other than their book value. US interests were severely burned. US-Cuba relations were made even more complex first by the aborted effort to overthrow the Castro regime at the Bay of Pigs in 1961, and then by the Cuban missile crisis a year later. Both events had rankled with Diefenbaker, who thought that President Kennedy had behaved recklessly, particularly when he failed to consult him over the missile crisis.

Canadian trade and investment interests in Cuba had also been harmed by the Castro revolution, but most Canadian businesses had settled their losses or adapted. As a result, Canada continued to enjoy relatively normal trade relations with Cuba, and Canadian firms were prepared to do business there. The value and volume of Canada-Cuba trade remained modest, but US authorities were not amused. In October 1960, they imposed a limited trade embargo and on 4 September 1961,

Congress authorized a complete ban on trade and investment with Cuba. Most Americans felt that Canada should join in the embargo and help bring the embarrassment of a communist regime in the western hemisphere to a hasty end. Canadians did not see it that way, and their government saw no reason to disagree.[34]

Through ad hoc consultations, the Canadian government negotiated exemptions in various instances from the Cuban embargo, but this was obviously an unsatisfactory basis on which to resolve the issue of principle. It was an aspect of US foreign direct investment that few could defend, marking a clear affront to Canadian sovereignty and reinforcing opposition to the growth of the US investment presence in Canada. Over the years the issue periodically resurfaced as US heavy-handedness placed the executives of Canadian subsidiaries and their US parents in no-win situations. Passing Canadian blocking legislation made the government feel better, but it did little to resolve the issue.

Muddling Through: Trade and the Canadian Economy

One of the problems in the Canada-US trade relationship was that Canadians bought a lot more from the United States than Americans bought from Canada (see table

Table 8.1

The direction of Canadian merchandise trade, 1958-63 (millions of dollars)

Year	US	UK	Japan	EEC	Other America	Central planning[a]	Rest of world	Total
Exports								
1958	2,808	772	105	420	241	30	415	4,791
1959	3,083	786	140	314	238	40	421	5,022
1960	2,932	915	179	439	255	47	488	5,256
1961	3,107	909	232	466	308	247	487	5,755
1962	3,608	909	215	455	302	197	492	6,179
1963	3,766	1,007	296	475	357	316	582	6,799
Imports								
1958	3,460	519	70	237	457	16	292	5,050
1959	3,709	589	103	292	461	17	339	5,509
1960	3,687	589	110	293	420	19	364	5,483
1961	3,864	618	117	318	447	21	384	5,769
1962	4,300	563	125	335	474	23	437	6,258
1963	4,445	527	130	342	536	27	552	6,558

Note: Totals may not add due to rounding.

a PRC, Cuba, and the USSR and its COMECON satellites.

Source: F.H. Leacy, ed., *Historical Statistics of Canada*, 2nd ed. (Ottawa: Statistics Canada, 1983), series G381, G384, and G401-14.

8.1). In a period of fixed exchange rates, this meant that Canada and the United States had to pay careful attention to the balance of payments, as the Diefenbaker government learned in 1962 (see below). A bilateral trade imbalance, however, was nothing new. Canada's trade with the United States had been in deficit for more than a century, but it was usually offset by Canada's surplus with the rest of the world. This triangular pattern had gradually eroded in the 1950s, but the chronic trade imbalance with the United States had not. By 1961, Canada was threatening to hit the billion-dollar mark on its current account deficit for the sixth year in a row. At a macroeconomic level, the books were balanced by the massive influx of US investment. In the long run, however, Canada would need to bolster its export performance to the United States.

Trade with the United States, of course, had increased by leaps and bounds over the previous decade. US resource investments in Canada, for example, were predicated on selling metal, mineral, forest, energy, and other resource products to US customers. The problem was that Canadians bought a lot more in the United States, from consumer products to machinery and equipment. To balance the current account Canada had to sell more manufactures in the United States. As the prime minister told US state governors in Montana in June 1960: "Canada does not ask for favours, but the reduction of the imbalance requires a greater increase of imports of Canadian manufactures into the United States."[35] To meet this challenge, adjustments had to be made not only in Canadian trade policy, but also in that of the United States: US barriers to Canadian exports needed to come down. The DPSA made a contribution, but more was needed. As officials repeatedly told the prime minister, the negotiation of better terms of access to the US market had to be pursued at the GATT in Geneva. Unfortunately, GATT negotiations did not produce positive results during Diefenbaker's tenure (see below).

The challenge for the Tories was heightened by the fact that they had come into office at the end of one of the longest and most sustained periods of economic expansion in Canadian history. There had been a number of recessions during the twelve years between 1945 and 1957, but the secular trend had been one of steadily rising incomes and employment. This expansion had come to an end in 1957 and did not resume until 1961. The economy continued to grow, but it suffered more fits and starts than in the previous decade, leading to high levels of seasonal unemployment. More importantly, it failed to meet rising expectations. By the late 1950s governments had convinced themselves and the electorate that they could manage the economy and solve its problems. Failure to do so was now a clear political liability.[36]

The Tory approach to trade and related problems was very much coloured by these difficulties, including its approach to GATT negotiations. Canada was frustrated as well by the chronic deficit in merchandise trade with the United States and by the likelihood of a further deterioration in trade with the United Kingdom. Each undermined the balance of payments, and each added to the need for foreign capital, largely in the form of foreign direct investment.[37]

To some Canadians, the solution to slow economic growth was to boost Canadian exports through more aggressive marketing efforts, a view strongly held by George Hees. To give him the opportunity to prove his point, in 1960 Diefenbaker moved him to Trade and Commerce, where he worked tirelessly at promoting Canadian exports and at encouraging the Trade Commissioner Service to help Canadian businesses to expand their overseas markets. One of his first steps was to call all the trade commissioners home to an Export Trade Promotion Conference. They were then sent across the country to impress upon Canadian business the need for more vigorous salesmanship. He revitalized the use of trade missions and trade fairs as critical components of Canada's export promotion efforts. For years to come, incoming trade commissioners were handed tie clips with the minister's logo, YCDBSOYA – You Can't Do Business Sitting on Your Ass.[38]

Some export-reliant companies felt they could perform better if the government provided them with more advantageous export credit terms than they could get from the banks. In 1959, the government responded by establishing the Export Finance Corporation and expanding the mandate of the Export Credits Insurance Corporation.[39] The Export Finance Corporation never got off the ground, as Canadian banks failed to come through with their share of the necessary credit, but some of its mandate was transferred to the Export Credits Insurance Corporation, providing it with a somewhat improved basis for the funding of exports to risky markets. While these initiatives could not match the power of the US Export-Import Bank, they did become an important factor in Canada's modest but growing success in nontraditional developing country and communist markets.[40]

Others felt that Canada's dollar was overvalued, pushed up by a combination of tight money and high inflows of US investment capital. Bank of Canada governor James Coyne objected strenuously to any suggestions that he was making money expensive, though he did suggest that Canada's reliance on foreign investment was not only creating short-term strains on the economy but also jeopardizing Canada's future prospects. He urged Canadians to live within their means and to rely more on their own savings for capital investment. The government might not have disagreed with his second point but found his speeches an extraordinary departure from form. Civil servants provided advice to the government; they did not criticize government policy in public. His days as governor were numbered.[41]

Easing the money supply and lowering the value of the dollar, however, did hold some attractions. Since 1950 Canada had technically been in violation of the IMF by maintaining a floating rather than a fixed exchange rate. Canada's excuse was its proximity to the United States and its heavy dependence on the US market. A floating rate, however, enables a government to use monetary policy to affect the exchange rate, and when the Conservatives began actively to try to lower the Canadian exchange rate in 1961, markets did not react favourably. Reducing the value of the dollar might have helped to boost export sales, but it also had more deleterious effects, including a flight of capital and a precipitous reduction in Canada's reserve position. In response, the government decided on 2 May 1962 to peg the dollar at 92.5 US cents. Pressure on the dollar mounted, however, and on 24 June, the government announced a series of balance-of-payments measures, including a temporary surcharge on selected imports. The fact that an election was fought during May and June added to the air of crisis and charges of economic mismanagement. The government insisted that its course had been right, but events brought home to many Canadians that playing with the dollar was perhaps not the best way to boost export sales.[42]

Despite the deep freeze into which Canada-US relations had descended by 1962, the Canadian government was not shy about asking the US Export-Import Bank to provide it with some necessary foreign exchange to help the country weather the balance-of-payments problem created by its rash monetary policies.[43] US authorities also tolerated the temporary surcharge and the devaluation of the Canadian dollar. The first harmed US export interests; the second boosted Canadian exports. The *Winnipeg Free Press* observed tartly that Canada had needed to seek help "almost as if it were an underdeveloped Asian state in need of charity. And that aid, let us never forget, came from two countries most damaged by Canada's tariff increases and most viciously attacked by the Canadian government."[44] The measures did the trick, however, and stabilized the Canadian economy, an objective US officials were more prepared to take seriously under Kennedy than had been the case under Eisenhower, even if they found Diefenbaker an increasingly irritating and unreliable member of the Western alliance.

As usual, there were those who insisted that Canada's balance-of-payments problems were caused by too many imports. Canada had been too quick to open its market and Canadian officials were not zealous enough in administering the customs rules. Complained one disenchanted contributor to *Saturday Night:* "Imports continue to flow through Canada's leaky tariff walls, but our biggest customer has, in effect, told Canadian manufacturers to keep out."[45] In his view, the rapid rise in imports in the 1950s had been at the expense of Canadian production and Canadian jobs; it was time the government did something about imports and protected Canadian jobs by raising tariffs, tightening the antidumping provisions, and otherwise slowing down the increase in imports. Import-competing sectors, such as the textile and clothing industry, were among the most vocal critics of the previous decade of trade liberalization, but the automotive industry also complained about the surge in imports from Britain, and the electronics industry worried about rising imports from Japan. The Canadian Manufacturers' Association embarked on a Buy Canadian campaign, and some of its more embattled members called on the government to negotiate more voluntary export restraints with Japan, Hong Kong, and other low-cost suppliers.[46]

The government did take some steps to respond to the concerns of the more protectionist elements of Canadian business. Voluntary export restraint agreements were negotiated with low-cost suppliers of textile products, beginning a trend that would not be arrested until the 1990s, of extralegal provisions to deal with politically inconvenient imports from developing countries. In 1958, the government revised the Customs Act, partly in order to revamp valuation and related provisions, and restore some of the scope for administrative discretion. In 1960, Finance Minister Donald Fleming announced that new legislation would empower the minister of national revenue to redefine goods so that more would qualify for higher made-in-Canada duties. Vigorously opposed by the opposition, the amendments died in the Senate before they could lead to problems with Canada's trading partners. The reality, however, was that as a result of GATT obligations, the scope for unilateral tinkering had been severely circumscribed. The *Kingston Whig-Standard* could complain about the ghost of R.B. Bennett stalking the House of Commons, but there was little the Conservatives could do to return to those days.[47] Those options had been effectively buried at Geneva in 1947. Governments could still deal with the political inconvenience of rising imports, but they had to find more ingenious ways than in the past.

During the exchange crisis of 1962, the government felt the lash of its international obligations. Not only did Canada have to go hat in hand to the IMF to gain permission to draw down $300 million in foreign reserves, but it also had to justify its tariff surcharge to GATT's balance-of-payments committee, the first and only time Canada has found its policies examined by that committee. While such examinations are not onerous, it was a comedown for Canadian officials, who had spent more than a decade, in the colourful phrase used by an Australian minister, polishing Canada's halo. Now they had to explain the use of a surcharge rather than quotas – as required by GATT's provisions – to deal with the government's mismanagement of its monetary policy. It did not add to their credibility that they were urging deeper tariff cuts and other trade liberalizing efforts by others. The fact that the restrictions were already being eased by the end of 1962, however, helped Canada's case considerably.[48]

Diefenbaker and the GATT: The Dillon Round

By 1958, the GATT was Canada's principal trade agreement with thirty-seven countries. It guaranteed Canadian firms reliable terms of access to their major markets. In return, Canada agreed to be an equally dependable market. The level of reliability was still more a matter of potential than reality, but the direction of GATT's further development was clear. Tinkering with tariff levels and valuation provisions could now only take place in the light of Canada's obligations under the GATT. Major changes required negotiations with the other members.

At the 1957 meeting of the contracting parties, the GATT had set up a panel of experts to examine trends in international trade in light of the end of postwar reconstruction and the return to convertible currencies. Chaired by Professor Gottfried Haberler of Harvard, the panel was asked to consider what initiatives GATT might pursue to address three major challenges: 1) the organization of a new round of tariff negotiations with a mandate to tackle tariffs seriously on a horizontal rather than an item-by-item basis; 2) the mounting problem of barriers to trade in agriculture; and 3) the emerging problems of developing countries.

The Haberler panel reported in October 1958 and provided GATT members with what they had sought: a strong intellectual basis for doing what was implicit in the mandate of the panel.[49] Tariff negotiations needed to be reorganized to provide scope for much deeper and more meaningful cuts; barriers to agricultural trade were more than a matter of tariffs; and the problems of developing countries needed to be addressed on a continuing basis and involve special and differential treatment. At the November meeting of trade ministers, GATT decided to establish three committees to examine each of these issues in greater detail. In addition, Douglas Dillon, undersecretary of state for economic affairs in the Eisenhower administration, proposed that members launch a new round of negotiations to take advantage of what remained of US negotiating authority.[50] The fifth round of multilateral negotiations of the GATT in Geneva in September 1960 were known as the Dillon Round in honour of this proposal.

The principal US objective for these new negotiations was to try to reduce the impact of the discrimination flowing from the formation of the European Economic Community. The Common External Tariff (CET) adopted by the Six involved rates generally representing an arithmetic average between those of high-tariff France and Italy and those of low-tariff Germany and the Benelux countries. The result was that US exporters faced some new hurdles in Europe, particularly in Germany and the Benelux countries, which were not wholly offset by lower entry barriers to France and Italy. US officials wanted to reduce these tariffs to the greatest extent possible. Canada shared this objective, but also saw the Dillon Round as an opportunity to tackle some of the more pressing high tariffs in the US schedule on products of export interest to Canada.[51]

The round was organized to address two issues: 1) the EEC's obligations under GATT article XXIV:6 to offer compensation to any GATT member affected by the increases in bound rates flowing from the establishment of the CET; and 2) a general effort to reduce further the industrial tariffs of all members. It proved a disappointment. In anticipation of the second half of the exercise, the EEC was reluctant in the first half to provide satisfactory compensation. EEC officials preferred to deal with the issue of compensation on the basis of the arithmetic average of the individual tariffs of the Six. Other GATT members did not find this an attractive solution and insisted on trade-weighted averages. In the end, the issue of principle was abandoned. Instead, during nine months of arduous negotiations, each delegation sought to ensure that those of its particular export interests harmed by increases in the CET from individual pre-CET bound rates were compensated by equivalent reductions on other items of export interest to them. The final result was a series of compromises that left a sour taste for many of the participating delegations. Canada was able to gain adjustments on EEC tariffs affecting $250 million in Canadian exports.[52] Failure to shape the Common Market along liberal lines, however, had further consolidated the EEC as an inward-looking block.[53]

In the general round, the EEC opened with an across-the-board cut of 20 percent as a gesture of goodwill following the difficult compensation discussion. As well, it was prepared to make substantial further cuts in its tariffs if the United States and others were prepared to reciprocate. Only the United Kingdom was amenable to matching EEC cuts. The US ability to do so was severely hemmed in by the limits of its authority. Not only could it not go beyond the 20 percent cut authorized by the 1958 extension of the RTA, but many products of export interest to the EEC and others could not be cut the full 20 percent because of the legislation's peril-point provision, among others. Congress had reintroduced the peril-point provision, which required the US Tariff Commission to establish the level below which any further cut in each tariff might result in injury to US producers, that is, be economically meaningful. The president was required to report to Congress whenever he had breached the peril point, a requirement that effectively throttled any room for negotiating manoeuvre. Additionally, no tariff could be cut more than 2 percentage points, which meant that many tariffs could not be cut the full 20 percent.[54]

The result was much less than the participants had hoped. World exports in 1962 totalled US$139 billion (see table 8.2); the Dillon Round cuts affected only 3.5 percent of that trade. The EEC tariff, which was the main target of the negotiations, was reduced from an arithmetic average of 10.2 percent, to 9.1 percent as a result of the compensation negotiations, and to 8.6 percent as a result of the general negotiations.[55] The trade-weighted average for dutiable products, of course, stood at much higher levels.[56] The US and UK tariffs had been reduced by similar small margins. From a Canadian perspective, minor US tariff concessions covering less

Table 8.2

Value and volume of world trade and output, 1958-64

Year	Value world exports (US$ billions)	Unit value world exports (1953 = 100)	Volume (1953 = 100)	
			World exports	World output
1953	78.3	100	100	100
1958	105.7	100	135	124
1959	113.6	99	146	134
1960	126.1	100	161	144
1961	131.9	99	170	149
1962	139.0	99	179	159
1963	151.7	100	194	168
1964	170.1	102	213	179

Source: GATT, *International Trade,* 1966 (Geneva: GATT, 1967).

than $65 million in Canadian exports – or 2 percent of the total – were a major disappointment.[57] For its part, Canada had not been prepared to make many concessions of its own following the decision to exclude agricultural products.[58] Canada made minor concessions on a total of fifty-nine tariff positions covering $63 million in imports.[59] Canada did, however, benefit from the MFN rule; without making many concessions of its own, it gained tariff reductions on the $4.9 billion in trade covered by the Dillon Round agreements, including on $85 million in exports to the United States and $114 million in exports to the EEC.[60]

The Dillon Round demonstrated the extent to which item-by-item negotiations based upon the principal-supplier rule had been exhausted. The approach pioneered in the 1934 US Reciprocal Trade Agreements Act had served well the need to develop a consensus in the United States favouring tariff negotiations and liberalization. It had succeeded in reducing some of the more egregious excesses of the US tariff. But negotiators were now beginning to tackle tariff cutting that would be economically meaningful. The item-by-item rule provided opponents with an easy target. A new approach would be required to reduce the influence of special interests and promote more satisfactory results. At a ministerial session of the GATT convened at the end of October 1962, contracting parties agreed to begin work on finding a better formula, establishing a working party chaired by Canadian official Rodney Grey to prepare for new negotiations, which would start with a ministerial meeting scheduled for May 1963.[61] At the same meeting, Trade and Commerce Minister George Hees intervened with a speech that would become a regular part of Canada's litany: "Canada is prepared to examine seriously any methods which would facilitate further progress in reducing tariff barriers. We would, of course, expect that they would take into account the special position of countries like our own, which depend on a more limited number of exports than the larger industrial countries or groups."[62] More important, however, was the need for the US government to find a more acceptable basis upon which to pursue negotiations. Congress would need to be persuaded to delegate a more flexible negotiating authority to the president.

The US Trade Expansion Act of 1962

President Kennedy had inherited the Dillon Round from the Eisenhower administration. Bound by the terms of the 1958 Trade Agreements Extension Act, there was little that he could do to make the negotiations more successful. Instead, he and his advisors chose to cut their losses and prepare for a major new assault the following year. They succeeded with the passage in 1962 of the Trade Expansion Act (TEA), the first major overhaul of US trade negotiating authority since 1934. For the first time since Cordell Hull, an American political leader was prepared to put the full weight of his office behind an effort to liberalize trade. Like Hull before him, Kennedy saw increased trade not only as a stimulant to the domestic economy, but also as a means of strengthening ties between nations. He thus wanted legislation that would allow him to develop a stronger basis for transatlantic cooperation among the United States, the EEC, the United Kingdom, and Canada. As he told Congress in his 1962 State of the Union address: "We need a new law – a wholly new approach – a bold new instrument of American trade policy." The TEA became the centrepiece of his 1962 legislative program and was signed into law on 11 October 1962.[63]

The TEA established a new beginning. It provided the president with a five-year authority to 30 June 1967, enough time to mount a major attack on foreign trade barriers as well as respond to the requests of others. The act provided the president with authority to cut tariffs by 50 percent from 1962 base levels, and to go to free for tariffs below 5 percent. Additionally, the negotiators could go to free for those sectors in which the United States and EEC together accounted for 80 percent of world trade. In practical terms, this provision, which could be used only if the United Kingdom were to become a member of the EEC, created a strong incentive for the EEC and Britain to complete their negotiations. Rather than a peril-point provision, the act introduced an adjustment assistance section clearly heralding a new attitude. Congress now accepted the revolutionary idea that US industries might have to adjust to import competition. In effect, the TEA acknowledged that cutting tariffs should lead to both increased exports and imports.[64]

The act also reformed the machinery for the conduct of negotiations. Congress had become increasingly disillusioned with the State Department as the lead agency for managing trade negotiations. It found State's trade negotiating priorities to be too easily influenced by foreign policy considerations. Instead, the TEA established a new, cabinet-level official, the Special Representative for Trade Negotiations (STR), to be housed in the executive branch but with reporting requirements to the House Ways and Means Committee and the Senate Finance Committee. The addition of various procedural and consultation requirements sought to give Congress and business interests more influence and oversight over negotiations. State was now reduced to the role of one of the agencies, along with Treasury, Commerce, Agriculture, and the Tariff Commission, working with the STR in developing and implementing policy within the framework set by the TEA. This change, little noticed in Canada in 1962, had grave consequences for a country that had made a career out of working with the State Department to solve bilateral problems on the basis of a special relationship.[65]

Passage of the TEA provided a lesson in what it took for a president to get the kind of legislation that he wanted to pursue broad national interests and overcome narrow local or sectoral interests. Kennedy and his advisors worked tirelessly for the better part of a year building support in Congress and among affected interests. They succeeded in isolating the most powerful opposing interests and successfully appealing to the imagination and vision of others. The most vocal opponents to trade liberalization were legislators from New England and the South worried about rising imports of low-cost textiles and clothing. Kennedy satisfied their political needs by promising to take action to restrict those imports. The result was a 298-125 vote in favour in the House and a 78-8 vote in the Senate.[66]

Imports of textiles and clothing represented only 7 percent of US production in 1960, but the trend was such as to alarm enough industrialists and legislators to imperil the whole trade expansion program. In 1961, the United States sponsored adoption by the GATT of a Short-term Arrangement on Trade in Cotton Textiles, followed in 1962 by a Long-term Arrangement. Both agreements provided for agreed departures from GATT's disciplines by allowing the negotiation of discriminatory quotas on low-cost products. Failure to negotiate such arrangements would lead to the imposition of unilateral quotas. While a pragmatic response to the political imperative of securing passage of the TEA, these textile arrangements cast a long and troubling shadow across GATT's claim to being a liberalizing and nondiscriminatory trade arrangement.[67]

To implement the TEA and prepare for negotiations, Kennedy appointed Christian Herter, former governor of Massachusetts and secretary of state in the final year of the Eisenhower administration, as his Special Representative for Trade Negotiations. Herter had long experience in Washington politics and, though not versed in the detail of trade negotiations, knew what it took to work with Congress and business and labour interests. The detail of policy formulation and negotiations could be left to specialists. By the end of 1962, Herter had a team in place and was ready to implement the act and launch negotiations.[68]

To ensure that his call for new negotiations would not be in vain, Kennedy had waged two campaigns in the fall of 1961 and throughout most of 1962: one to gain congressional approval for a sweeping new negotiating authority and the other to develop international support for a new round of multilateral negotiations. The latter had not always run smoothly. Not all major trading nations were ready for another assault on tariffs so soon after completing the Dillon Round. The EEC, for example, expressed some reservations, and French officials were, not unexpectedly, opposed. Gradually, however, US diplomatic efforts overcame these reservations so that by the fall of 1962 a broad consensus had emerged favouring an early launch.

John Diefenbaker was among those initially unimpressed. He was suspicious of Kennedy's motives and fearful that a new round would lead to a further assault on Commonwealth preferences and to heightened pressure on the United Kingdom to join the Common Market. As a result, he and his ministers could mount little more than the faintest praise for the initiative, further contributing "to the image of Canada during this period as a frightened and irritating advocate of the status quo."[69] In Geneva, however, Canadian officials were already fully engaged in preparing for negotiations.

Once Congress passed the TEA, Diefenbaker's suspicions had receded, but by this time the damage had been done. His efforts to take credit for calling for a ministerial conference to launch the new round caused more heads to shake in

Washington and elsewhere. By this time, Diefenbaker was a spent political force. His antics still garnered some support among those who found his anti-Americanism bracing, but to a growing number of Canadians his achievements became more and more difficult to discern and the liabilities continued to mount. Among these achievements, however, was a reversal in the fortunes of the Prairie wheat farmer.

Diefenbaker and the Prairie Wheat Farmer

When John Diefenbaker, the Prairie populist, won the 1957 election, Prairie wheat farmers had reason to believe that someone in Ottawa would pay attention to their problems. Their plight was real. Silos were bulging with unsold wheat; the Americans were undercutting Canadians everywhere with concessional or dumped sales; and the world glut was driving prices to levels that severely reduced Prairie incomes. C.D. Howe's gibe during the election campaign to one complaining Manitoba farmer that he looked well fed to Howe had been mercilessly exploited by Diefenbaker and his colleagues. The Liberals had lost all but six seats on the Prairies. Now Diefenbaker had to deliver.[70]

The 1957-8 crop year began with over a billion bushels of unsold grain. The Canadian Wheat Board had worked hard to try to sell wheat, barley, oats, and other grains, but for over a decade its officials had repeatedly butted their heads against aggressive US salesmanship and, since 1954, against the provocation of US giveaways under PL 480. Diefenbaker assigned political responsibility for the Wheat Board to his first minister of trade and commerce, Gordon Churchill. There was little Churchill could do about the weather, which continued to be favourable, ensuring that bumper crops would continue to add to the challenge faced by the Wheat Board. Churchill tried hard to sell wheat, but there was no breakthrough. The pattern of US competition in traditional Canadian markets continued, but Canada was actively seeking new markets.

As early as 1952, Canadian officials had made tentative forays behind the Iron Curtain and had achieved modest success in selling wheat and barley to Poland, Czechoslovakia, Yugoslavia, and Hungary, often on credit terms. In 1955, then secretary of state for external affairs Lester Pearson had led a mission to Russia to explore, among other things, the potential for wheat sales there. The result was the successful conclusion a year later of the first Canada-Russia trade agreement, involving an exchange of most-favoured-nation treatment and a Soviet commitment to buy 1.2 million to 1.5 million bushels of wheat over the next three years. The amount was still modest, but the agreement laid the foundation for more to come. Similarly, Canada had made modest sales to the People's Republic of China despite the fact that it had not extended diplomatic recognition to China. Canada had shown that, despite the cold war, it was prepared to do business with the Russians and the Chinese.[71]

The breakthrough came in 1960, when responsibility for the Wheat Board had passed to the newly appointed minister of agriculture, Alvin Hamilton. Discussions with

Duncan Macpherson, 12 May 1962. Prime Minister Diefenbaker feeds wheat to the Chinese tiger.

the Chinese indicated that they were prepared to enter into long-term purchase commitments if the terms were right. The result was a major agreement signed on 22 April 1961 under which China agreed to buy up to 5 million metric tonnes of wheat and one million metric tonnes of barley between 1 June 1961 and 31 December 1963. Other agreements followed as Canada built a relationship that became critical to the Canadian wheat economy.[72] Two years later, in September 1963, with the Liberals now in office, the Wheat Board concluded a similar deal with the Russians, this time for the delivery of 5.3 million metric tonnes of wheat and 500,000 tonnes of flour before the end of the 1963-4 crop year. Some Canadians expressed reservations about trading with these communist countries, but the general consensus was that the Canadian wheat farmer deserved no less.[73]

A series of new, multilateral International Wheat Agreements, negotiated in 1956, 1959, and 1962, continued what had become familiar commitments: exporters contracted to supply wheat at an agreed maximum price if prices reached that level, and importers contracted to buy at an agreed minimum price if prices fell to that level. Wheat did not always trade within the band of minimum and maximum prices nor did all important exporters and importers always participate. The United Kingdom, for example, had declined to participate in the 1953 IWA. On balance, however, these agreements added to the stability of trade in wheat, if only because of the amount of information that needed to be gathered and shared among participating countries and the resulting discussion of possible solutions to problems in the grains trade.[74]

By 1962 the world's grain trade had clearly fallen into a pattern of commercial, concessional, and communist sales. The IWA covered commercial sales; US PL 480 dominated concessional sales; and the Canadian Wheat Board had become the main player in sales to communist markets. US discontent with Canadian sales to communist markets began to gradually undermine its willingness to cooperate through the IWA. It was extended by one-year protocols until 1967, when it was necessary to do some serious reconsideration of the international governance of the grains trade.[75]

The Tories were clearly committed to helping Prairie wheat farmers. Selling their wheat was critical. In addition, however, the government was prepared to provide other assistance. Through the Agricultural Stabilization Act of 1958, the government provided new price supports to some twenty-four products on the basis of federal-provincial-producer cost sharing and helped to solve the problem of setting up provincially organized marketing boards. The 1961 Agricultural Rehabilitation and Development Act expanded the services available from the Department of Agriculture and provided assistance to farmers to leave the land or take unproductive land out of production, to modernize their farms and equipment, and otherwise to strengthen the rural economy. A decade later the program would be rolled into the Department of Regional Economic Expansion and become part of the largest government subsidy program in Canadian history. In 1961, Canada was rich enough to start subsidizing farmers. By the early 1970s, the government believed the country could afford to subsidize whole regions of the country.

There were not many positive achievements on the trade policy front during the Diefenbaker years, but sales of wheat marked a conspicuous exception. Like the export promotion crusade spearheaded by George Hees, those sales owed a lot to the willingness of Alvin Hamilton to be unconventional and to give officials in the Wheat Board the room to try new approaches. Wheat sales also maintained strong support for the Tories on the Prairies. The Tories survived the 1962 election with a minority government, but by April 1963 Canadians were prepared to give Lester Pearson and the Grits a chance. Prairie votes and Diefenbaker's campaigning skills, however, denied them a majority in both the 1963 and 1965 elections. Although Prairie farmers have long memories, their support is not enough to form a government. Ironically, more wheat was sold under the Grits in the years that followed, but the Tories continued to take credit for the breakthrough.

During his nearly six years in office, Diefenbaker never overcame his suspicion of the senior bureaucracy. He remained convinced that External Affairs was full of "Pearsonalities" and that other senior officials were all friends of the leader of the opposition. Nevertheless, he learned to trust Bob Bryce, the secretary to the cabinet, could not get along without Basil Robinson, had respect for Norman Robertson at External Affairs, and generally learned to work with a range of officials, albeit never easily. Professionalism involves constancy, smoothing out the hills and valleys and creating predictable, stable circumstances. It is uncomfortable with mercurial moods and off-the-wall impulses. Nor is it well suited to feeding ill-conceived prejudices and nostalgic preferences.

Ironically, by 1963 there were Liberal partisans who shared some of Diefenbaker's suspicions that senior officials could not be trusted to carry out the new government's program. Tom Kent, Pearson's principal policy advisor, expressed strong reservations about officials, particularly after meeting with some of them and being told that many of the ideas high on the Liberal agenda were impractical and likely to create more problems than they would solve.[76] Walter Gordon decided that he could not do justice to his first budget solely on the basis of the advice of officials in the Department of Finance, and brought in outside advisors to help him.[77] Like Diefenbaker before them, the newly elected Grits failed to appreciate the extent to which good policy must respond to the realities within which Canada operates, including the necessity of adapting to the policy preferences of other countries. Officials could be as nationalistic as Diefenbaker or Gordon, but it was a nationalism tempered by a clear appreciation of the limits of idealism. The next five years would continue the roller-coaster ride of trying to find the balance between the professionals' preference for pragmatic solutions to specific problems and their critics' zeal for more idealistic and nationalistic approaches.

9 NATIONALISM AND PRAGMATISM
THE PEARSON YEARS

More integration, in my mind, means a richer and more prosperous Canada; and nobody is as independent as the man who can afford to pick up his own cheques.

– HARRY JOHNSON, THE CANADIAN QUANDARY

The Liberal electoral triumph on 8 April 1963 was somewhat marred by the lack of a majority. At the beginning of the campaign, the Liberals had enjoyed a commanding lead in the polls and were looking forward to forming a strong government. But they had too easily dismissed the Chief. Diefenbaker might have lacked something as a prime minister, but as a campaigner he had no equal. Jowls shaking and eyebrows arching, he warned Canadians of the perils of a party that had made a career of grovelling to the Americans. His dire warnings gained few votes for the Tories, but they raised enough doubts about Lester Pearson and his colleagues to cause a quarter of Canadians to vote NDP and Créditiste. The result for Pearson was a mandate that was less than commanding, a clear signal that he had to tread the line on Canada-US relations with particular care.

For Pearson, the American connection was not a matter for debate. Geography and economics made it imperative to get along with the Americans, even if this did not mean always acquiescing in US priorities and preferences. He could agree with Peter Newman that it was "quite impractical for our politicians to adopt poses of exaggerated independence. The fact is that we are not independent in the vital areas of defense and trade. The future prosperity and even the existence of Canada depend directly on the goodwill of the USA. This doesn't mean that we should toady to Washington. But it does mean that we can hardly expect our point of view to carry much weight, if our chief emissary in future bargaining with the US president is a politician elected on the basis of blatant anti-Americanism."[1]

Nevertheless, the Liberals' appreciation of US relations had undergone a subtle metamorphosis. Once in the wilderness of opposition, they had also begun to question the policies of the previous twenty years, finding inspiration in the nationalist ideas espoused by Walter Gordon, placed in charge of the finance portfolio, and his admirers. But whereas Tory criticism of those policies had been grounded in nostalgia for the British connection and the comfortable protectionism of earlier years, Liberal critics were more worried about Canada's ability to control its own destiny, ranging from ownership and control of the Canadian economy to the capacity to foster Canadian culture and identity.

The trade policies of the previous twenty years, so carefully crafted by the professionals in Finance, Trade and Commerce, and External Affairs, thus continued to be denounced. First, Diefenbaker's small-town, Prairie populism had found those policies wanting; now Walter Gordon's urban economic nationalism wanted to make adjustments. Both points of view questioned the foundation of Canada's postwar prosperity, drew on traditional anti-Americanism, and butted their heads against reality. The policies of the previous twenty years were deeply embedded in Canada's treaty obligations, in Canadian law and practice, in Canada's economic structure, and in Canadians' expectations about prosperity. They could not be easily undone or turned around.

Circumstances beyond Canada's control remained a constant element conditioning Canadian policy. If there was to be change, it had to flow from cooperative action involving more than just Canada. John Diefenbaker had wanted to change the fundamental character of Canada's trade dependence on the United States by looking to Britain and the Commonwealth. Walter Gordon was determined to make the Canadian economy less reliant on American investment capital and international trade in general. As nationalistic as Diefenbaker, Gordon drew on the ideas of the interventionist left rather than the imperialist past. The professionals in the bureaucracy found this brand of nationalism as difficult as Diefenbaker's to translate into practical policy choices. They had deemed Diefenbaker's quixotic desire to shift 15 percent of Canada's trade from the United States to the United Kingdom to be impractical. They found Walter Gordon's desire to make Canada less reliant on US capital and markets just as ill-conceived.

Of course, the public service was not without political allies. Gordon's nationalism may have appealed to some of the more outspoken members of the Liberal party, but the party also housed pragmatists who could appreciate the benefits of what had been achieved and who were not eager to weather the costs and uncertainties that could flow from any major changes in direction. In the end, their caution ruled the day, ensuring continuity for the policy direction adopted in the 1930s and cemented into place as a result of negotiations in Washington and Geneva over the succeeding years.

Pearson and the American Connection

Diefenbaker's tortured relations with President Kennedy and his advisors played more than an incidental role in the 1963 election. Indeed, presidential advisor McGeorge Bundy claimed that he "once approved a White House communiqué that led to the downfall of ... John Diefenbaker."[2] Could Pearson do better at responding to Canadians' heightened sensitivity to American influence? It was clear that he enjoyed good personal relations with the young president. He was intimate with other power brokers in Washington and was not shy about using those connections to advance his interests. But the Canada of the mid-1960s was not the Canada of the 1940s and 1950s, and Pearson knew it. Bringing Walter Gordon into the cabinet was more than a matter of rewarding friendship; it also recognized the need to respond to the demands of budding economic nationalism. Similarly, relying on Tom Kent as Pearson's principal policy advisor ensured that his government would pursue more interventionist policies than had been espoused by Louis St. Laurent and C.D. Howe, including some that would bring conflict with the Americans.[3]

Pearson's pragmatic assessment of the reality of close economic ties to the United States was clearly set out in one of his earliest speeches as leader of the opposition, in 1958. In discussing the three trade policy options available to Canada, he dismissed "a trade policy of maximum self-sufficiency [as] simply one of economic isolationism with particular reference to the U.S.A. Such a policy might well be disastrous for Canada; do irreparable damage to us, especially to those continental economic relationships which, after all, and whether we like it or not, are essential to our prosperity and our stability."[4] By 1963, his personal views might not have changed, but he was prepared to let Gordon, Kent, and other members of his government pursue policies aimed at strengthening Canada's self-sufficiency and reducing its ties to the United States.[5]

Diefenbaker had demonstrated that getting under the skin of the Americans on virtually every file was a sure way of frustrating the attainment of Canadian objectives. Pearson was more selective, reflecting the outlook of most Canadians. In 1963, Canadians were generally still well disposed to the United States and particularly to its energetic young president. The Vietnam War would change that and make anti-Americanism a creed with which more and more Canadians could identify.[6] The war did for Canadian attitudes to the United States what the Suez crisis had done for attitudes to Britain in 1956. It introduced a cynicism about the exercise of power that corroded attitudes along a much wider range of issues than those related to defence and security, and gave economic nationalism a respectability that it might not have attained otherwise. In 1963, support for economic nationalist experiments remained fragile, as Walter Gordon discovered in his first budget. By the time he returned to cabinet in 1966 he could count on much wider support.

Pearson's initial reaction to growing concern about US economic dominance was the classic response of the diplomat. This was an issue that needed to be talked about, particularly with US investors, urging them to be good corporate citizens by increasing the number of Canadians in senior positions and on boards of directors.[7] Ministers like Mitchell Sharp and Robert Winters agreed, and each responded to specific incidents in Canada-US relations by establishing guidelines for corporate behaviour.

Walter Gordon did not share this view. As he had already shown in his 1957 commission report and in his book, *Troubled Canada,* he was deeply disturbed by growing US dominance of Canadian economic life. That attitude hardened as a result of US invocation of the Trading with the Enemy Act to interfere with Canadian trade with Cuba and China.[8] Here was a good example of how the confidence grounded in US notions of manifest destiny could take a mild Canadian concern raised by US economic hegemony and turn it into a legitimate grievance. At the same time, he and other Liberal nationalists naïvely believed that US officials would calmly accept Canadian efforts to demonstrate their sovereignty in ways that could harm US interests. Gordon's first budget as Pearson's finance minister set out to test those convictions.[9]

In his first budget address, Walter Gordon protested that salvation from Canada's problems "did not lie in isolationism ... in withdrawing unto ourselves and ignoring the currents of progress and change around us ... We are a great trading nation dependent on our relationships with our friends throughout the world ... The way of the future, the way of prosperity, the way of national pride, involves the fullest participation in the world around us in an economic sense as in every sense."[10] Perhaps, but this wider world apparently did not include the Americans or their capital. He had already indicated that Canada would take as niggardly a position as possible in the Kennedy Round of GATT negotiations (see below). Now he announced confiscatory tax measures aimed at driving foreign – or, more accurately, American – direct investment out of the Canadian market. He pronounced that Canada would increase the withholding tax on the patriation of profits by foreign-controlled firms from 15 to 20 percent, and reduce it from 15 to 10 percent for those with 25 percent Canadian equity participation. He further provided that companies that met the 25 percent Canadian ownership criterion would enjoy, for tax purposes, a faster write-off of investments in machinery and equipment. As a final touch, he announced a 30 percent tax on nonresident takeovers of, or substantial foreign investments in, Canadian-controlled firms.[11]

Gordon had been warned by his officials that a 30 percent takeover tax would have dire consequences.[12] He was determined to proceed, however, and paid the price. A howl of protest, more from Canadians than Americans, about the budget's confiscatory and discriminatory elements forced him to back down, earning the Pearson government the eternal reproach of the left. Within a month little was left of the minister's proposals and what might otherwise have proven a reasonable budget had gone down in history as a singular failure.

Gordon's baptism by fire into the reality of Canada-US economic relations was not yet finished. A month after tabling a budget aimed at curbing US capital flows into Canada, he had to send his officials to Washington to seek an exemption for Canada from US measures that sought to slow the exodus of US capital from the United States. By the mid-1960s, the United States was beginning to face a serious balance-of-payments problem. As the reference currency in an interlocking system of fixed currencies, US authorities had felt that they did not need to adjust monetary policy to address inflationary and other pressures. As a result, the US dollar was becoming overvalued, leading to a decline in the traditional huge merchandise trade surplus but not in the outflow of US capital, and a deteriorating balance-of-payments situation. On 18 July 1963, the US administration announced an interest equalization tax on foreign borrowings in the United States in an effort to equalize the cost of borrowing long-term capital in the United States and Europe.

Canada viewed this new tax with alarm. Within hours of the US announcement, Canadian stock prices took a precipitous dive, and Canada's loss of foreign exchange exceeded anything that had been experienced during the 1962 payments crisis. To stem the tide, Gordon had little choice but to send a team to Washington to negotiate an exemption. Led by Louis Rasminsky, the governor of the Bank of Canada, officials sought to convince US authorities that Canada was not the source of their problem. Indeed, it was absolutely critical to the stability of Canada's financial markets and its balance-of-payments position that US capital inflows not be impeded. They were needed to compensate for the continuing huge US merchandise trade surplus with Canada, amounting to over a billion dollars in 1962. US authorities were sympathetic but wanted assurances that Canada would manage its monetary reserves prudently and not add to US woes. This the government was ready to do, and by 22 July the two sides had reached an understanding that exempted Canada from the US measure.[13]

The deal amounted to a full retreat for Walter Gordon. The special relationship was intact, if somewhat besmirched.[14] By this time, in the words of historians Bothwell, Drummond, and English, the Americans were convinced that "Canada's finance minister possessed limited competence but abundant paranoia."[15] However, though Gordon and his nationalist supporters had been wounded by their early losses, they were not yet dead. Two more attempts at reducing the American presence in Canada would further test the mettle of the nationalists, the patience of the Americans, and the steadfastness of the pragmatists. The first was a victory for the pragmatists; the second a draw.

The Pearson government had inherited the unresolved issue of the status of Canadian editions of US magazines. The 1961 O'Leary Commission had recommended that advertising in such magazines should lose its tax-exempt status, thus encouraging advertising in Canadian media and the growth of new media expressing Canadian points of view. Diefenbaker had, as usual, dithered and nothing had come of the proposals. Gordon, Kent, and others were determined to act, but others in the government had no appetite for a further fight with the Americans, particularly in the face of a strong campaign by *Time* to ensure that its Canadian edition would not lose tax-exempt status. Not until his April 1965 budget did Gordon finally act on the O'Leary recommendations. Exemptions, however, were granted to *Time* and *Reader's Digest* on the basis of their long-standing presence in Canada. Gordon argued that the special deal for *Time* and *Reader's Digest* was the price of getting

American approval for the Auto Pact (see below). Perhaps. More generally, however, it suggests that the pragmatists in cabinet were unprepared to adopt another symbol of Gordon's campaign. The issue, of course, did not go away. It would resurface in 1975, with more satisfactory results for the nationalist cause, and would ultimately become the basis of a dispute under the rules of the World Trade Organization in 1996.[16]

The Mercantile Bank affair proved a messier matter before it was settled. The Mercantile Bank was a small, Dutch-owned merchant bank, which had the distinction of being the only foreign-controlled banking institution in Canada. When National City Bank of New York, owned by a branch of the Rockefeller family, proposed to purchase the bank and use it as a base for expanding in Canada, it was told in no uncertain terms by Gordon and his officials that this would not be welcomed. National City was taken aback. After all, Canadian banks had been operating quite profitably in the United States for more than a century. Surely Canada would behave sensibly. National City Bank went ahead with the deal and Gordon responded with amendments to the Bank Act that would have required National City to sell three-quarters of its stake to Canadian investors. US officials took some exception to the draconian terms of the legislation and regarded them as a forced divestiture of an American investment.

Gordon's revisions to the Bank Act, however, died on the order paper when the government called an election in 1965 in a vain effort to gain a majority. The amendments were not revived until Mitchell Sharp was in charge of the Finance portfolio. Sharp was not opposed to the general amendments of the Bank Act, but he was prepared to make some small changes to give National City the time to develop its operations in Canada and find Canadian partners. The US government took the view that US willingness to exempt Canada on issues that mattered to Canada, as it had on automobiles, the interest equalization tax, and similar matters, should be matched by a willingness to try to accommodate specific American concerns, such as the National City Bank. Sharp could see the sense in such a stance. Gordon could not. He took the view that the Mercantile Bank affair was a matter of principle that could not be compromised.

Cabinet, bilateral, and public discussion of the issue generated much heat in the first half of 1967. Eventually, the revisions in the Bank Act were approved, placing severe limits on any bank with more than 25 percent foreign ownership and more than a 10 percent stake by any individual investor. The following year, Edgar Benson, Sharp's successor, negotiated an accommodation providing Mercantile with time to acquire Canadian partners. In the end, Mercantile Bank found enough Canadian investors, but it was not a success and was eventually absorbed by the National Bank of Canada.[17]

Despite the inauspicious beginning created by Gordon's first budget and the strains generated by issues such as the *Time* and *Reader's Digest* and Mercantile Bank affairs, ministers tried hard to put Canada-US economic relations on a more constructive footing, a goal shared by their US colleagues. At the first two meetings of the Joint Committee on Trade and Economic Affairs, cabinet-level officers wrestled with how to effect a more harmonious relationship. At the September 1963 session, they agreed "that early consideration be given by the two governments to the best means of elaborating and strengthening the basic principles of economic cooperation between Canada and the United States."[18] George Ball, the US undersecretary of state, came armed with a list of suggestions for consideration, including establishing working parties on joint energy problems, on the balance of payments, and on the extraterritorial application of economic laws. At the April 1964 meeting of the Joint Committee, they reviewed the usual range of irritants and problems, including energy trade and trade in automotive products, as well as a preliminary report prepared by special envoys Arnold Heeney and Livingston Merchant.[19]

Heeney and Merchant had been appointed by Pearson and US president Lyndon Johnson in January 1964 to inquire into what could be done to reduce the level of noise in Canada-US relations and to consider more fruitful ways to resolve disputes. Both had been ambassadors of their respective countries to the other for two terms, and both had long experience in each other's affairs. They diligently set about their work and in eighteen months produced a thoroughly professional report, *Principles of Partnership,* containing many thoughtful recommendations.[20] Unfortunately the mood in Canada, fuelled by growing distaste for US conduct in Vietnam and resurgent nationalism and anti-Americanism, left little room for the kind of sober reflection found in the report. Critics in particular zeroed in on the report's recommendation that "it is in the abiding interest of both countries that, wherever possible, divergent views between the two governments should be expressed and if possible resolved in private, through diplomatic channels."[21]

While many in the media dismissed these sensible recommendations as further proof of the foul designs of the United States on Canada, Heeney and Merchant had done little more than encapsulate what had in fact been the basis of managing good relations between the two countries for two generations. This arrangement had been severely tested during the Diefenbaker years and further undermined by Gordon's budget and his bellicose response to the Mercantile Bank affair, but it continued to be the way the professionals would approach problems between the two countries. Nothing illustrated this better than the negotiations already in train to resolve a potentially nasty dispute involving automotive trade. These negotiations demonstrated that there remained much goodwill between officials and a mutual desire to resolve problems. That would remain the case for a further five years until President Nixon brought them to a rude end. Throughout this period, while the usual range of trade irritants continued, the most difficult issues revolved around the problems generated by the worsening US balance-of-payments position, adding to protectionist sentiments in Congress and increasing anxiety in the US administration. US balance-of-payments problems would finally be resolved by Nixon in August 1971.[22]

The Canada-United States Auto Pact

Policy efforts to improve Canada's competitive position in the auto industry provided a further test of the Pearson government's efforts to build better relations with President Kennedy. By the end of 1963, however, Kennedy had been swept away by the tragedy of Dallas. The automotive negotiations took place with the Johnson administration and plumbed whether the Kennedy glow would last. The negotiations also provided a further reminder of the limits of economic nationalism, with Walter Gordon brooding over the negotiation of an agreement that would further consolidate the continental integration of one of the largest industrial sectors in Canada. The circumstances leading to the Auto Pact provide a textbook example of the impact of both US and Canadian trade and industrial policy on investment and production patterns in Canada.

The Auto Pact's origin lay in attempts to address the weak competitive position of the Canadian automotive industry, which flowed from a variety of factors including technological developments, the revival of the European industries, the weakening benefits of traditional links to British and Commonwealth markets, and the structure of the Canadian industry. Investment in Canadian automotive production had followed classic import-substitution patterns. Canadian entrepreneurs, such as the McLaughlin family in Oshawa, had started by building cars under licence from American firms. The consolidation of a number of smaller firms in the United States into General Motors in the 1920s had swept the Canadian operations into the larger firm, and the new parent company had continued to invest in Canadian production. Ford had made similar inroads in Canada, as had Chrysler and some of the smaller and more specialized producers of trucks. Given the high tariff walls of the 1920s and 1930s, it had made sense to assemble cars and trucks for the Canadian market in Canada. The preferences available on Canadian-assembled cars and trucks in the United Kingdom, Australia, and other Commonwealth countries had provided the basis for a respectable export trade. In the years 1931-4, for example, Canada had exported 27.6 percent of its domestic automotive production.[23]

The war had brought that trade to an end as automotive production facilities were converted to meet wartime needs. When these plants returned to normal peacetime production after 1945, they enjoyed boom times keeping up with burgeoning domestic demand. Little attention needed to be paid to exports in the postwar economy. There was at best a limited market in Europe for the large, gas-guzzling family saloons favoured in both Canada and the United States. More importantly, the major auto assemblers now preferred to meet demand in Europe, South Africa, and Australia with branch-plant operations producing vehicles designed for those markets. As a result, the Canadian production facilities concentrated on producing a narrow range of vehicles for the Canadian market, satisfying the rest of demand with US imports.[24]

The pattern of trade and production established by the major vehicle producers was also conditioned by the structure of the tariff. The basic Canadian tariff on cars and a specified range of parts had been bound in GATT negotiations in the 1950s at 17.5 percent, but producers could import parts not made in Canada duty-free if they maintained a specified level of production in Canada. This level was 50 percent of the factory cost for most producers of commercial vehicles and 60 percent for most producers of passenger vehicles; somewhat lower levels applied to firms producing fewer than 20,000 vehicles and even lower levels for firms producing fewer than 10,000. Some parts, including engines and brake linings, were protected with a tariff of 25 percent. This pattern of protection increased the level of effective protection for vehicles to well beyond 17.5 percent and encouraged the use of domestically sourced parts. At the same time, the US tariff of 6.5 percent on passenger cars and 8.5 percent on trucks discouraged production in Canada for sale to the United States.[25]

By the 1960s, the North American automobile industry, in the words of Paul Wonnacott, "was a comfortable oligopoly."[26] It was an oligopoly, however, that brought more comfort to Americans than Canadians. As a result of the established pattern of protection, Canadians paid considerably more for cars than did Americans and had to choose from among a narrower range of vehicles. In addition, Canadian workers earned about 30 percent less than their US counterparts. When the costs of the excise tax, the manufacturers' sales tax, and the extra costs of Canada's less efficient distribution system were added, Canadians often paid as much as 50 percent more than Americans did for the same car. It is little wonder, therefore, that Canadian consumption of vehicles was a third less on a per capita basis than that of Americans. It is also not surprising that by the end of the 1950s Canadians were turning to cheaper imports, principally from the United Kingdom, Germany, and Japan. In 1960, 28.1 percent of the sales of new vehicles in Canada represented imports, compared to 7.6 percent in the United States. Prospects for the Canadian industry did not look promising: unemployment in the automotive industry was rising, as were costs.[27]

To address the competitiveness gap, the Diefenbaker government in 1960 appointed economist Vincent Bladen, dean of the Faculty of Arts and Sciences at the University of Toronto, to investigate the Canadian automotive industry and compare its structure and competitiveness to those of other countries. Following an exhaustive inquiry, Bladen found that only GM was making a modest profit in Canada. He concluded that short, fragmented production runs were the principal reason for the inefficiency of the Canadian industry. He recommended, among other things, that the government adjust protection in Canada to reward firms prepared to export by letting them count their export sales as part of their domestic production base, thus allowing them to import more parts on a duty-free basis. Bladen suggested, in addition, that cars imported by Canadian producers qualify for duty-free entry as long as the minimum Canadian production levels were maintained. With these conclusions, Bladen indicated that the future of the industry lay in narrowing its lines of production and increasing its exports. The means for achieving this objective lay in the more efficient deployment of the Canadian tariff.[28]

By specializing and increasing production for export, Canadian-based firms would be able to come closer to achieving economies of scale. Contemporary studies of scale in the industry indicated that firms producing at levels below 300,000 units per year were operating under a severe handicap and that the benefits of economies of scale would continue to rise up to a level of 600,000 units per year. In 1960, General Motors, the largest producer in Canada, manufactured a total of 175,086 passenger cars in Canada. Total Canadian production that year by the Big Three only reached 379,083 vehicles, barely enough even if production were consolidated into a single plant to reap some benefits of economies of scale.[29] The answer to the competitiveness problem of the Canadian industry obviously lay in producing more cars and trucks for export.

The Conservatives did not adopt the specifics of the Bladen plan, but instead decided to take the thrust of his recommendations and use the instruments at the government's disposal to encourage increased production in Canada for export. On 31 October 1962, the government reimposed the suspended 25 percent duty on automatic transmissions but provided that manufacturers could recoup the costs of this tariff, as well as the tariff on imports of engine blocks, by increasing exports of parts above base levels established in the year ending 31 October. A year later, the Liberals broadened the program to provide for the full remission of duties on imports of vehicles and parts based on increased levels of production in Canada. For every dollar of production added in Canada beyond the base levels achieved the previous year, producers could import a dollar of parts and vehicles free of duty.[30] Canada had gone about as far as it could go within the parameters of existing trade and production patterns and the structure of Canadian and US protection. If producers responded to these incentives and increased production in Canada through exports, the cost structure in Canada might come down to more competitive levels, benefiting both producers and consumers.

Discussion of Canada's various policy approaches had already figured prominently on the agenda of the September 1963 and April 1964 meetings of the Joint Canada-US Committee on Trade and Economic Affairs, with US officials expressing alarm about Canada's approach.[31] The plan, however, was never given an opportunity to prove itself. In May, acting on a complaint from the Modine Manufacturing Company of Racine, Wisconsin, US authorities began an investigation into whether or not the Canadian scheme constituted a bounty or grant within the meaning of section 303 of the Smoot-Hawley Tariff Act of 1930. Should the Modine complaint be upheld, and the odds favoured that it would, Canadian producers exporting to the United States would face not only the US tariff, but also a countervailing duty fully offsetting the benefits of the Canadian duty remission scheme. As a result, no industrial restructuring was likely to take place and Canadians would continue to pay a high premium for production in Canada.

Walter Gordon was furious, as were his officials, if not for the same reason. Gordon's shouts down the telephone line to Treasury Secretary Douglas Dillon,

Prime Minister Lester Pearson and US President Lyndon Johnson sign the agreement establishing the Canada-US Auto Pact at the LBJ Ranch, 15 January 1965.

however, proved to little avail. Nevertheless, to head off such a provocative development, President Johnson and Prime Minister Pearson agreed that officials should try to work out a mutually acceptable solution. Exemptionalism would be given a further test. Favouring the successful negotiation of an alternative plan was the fact that virtually all vehicle production and a significant share of parts production in Canada took place in wholly owned US subsidiaries. Over the years these US firms had made large investments in Canada and were well disposed to any plan that would allow them to make better use of these facilities, reducing their costs and raising the prospect of increased sales in Canada.

Throughout the summer and fall of 1964, teams of US and Canadian officials worked furiously at out-of-the-way places like the Seigniory Club in Montebello, Quebec, to find the basis for a mutually satisfactory solution.[32] Anxious cabinet discussions weighed the pros and cons of various approaches, with Walter Gordon agonizing over yet a further increase in US control of the commanding heights of the Canadian economy. By the end of the year, they had succeeded, and in January 1965, Prime Minister Pearson, accompanied by Secretary of State for External Affairs Paul Martin, flew to the Johnson ranch in Texas to sign the Canada-US Automotive Products Agreement.[33] Finance Minister Walter Gordon, whose officials had been key to the success of the negotiations, regarded the agreement with mixed emotions. Although he recognized the need for a solution to the problem Canada faced in trying to increase the productivity and long-term viability of its automotive industry, he regretted that the solution lay in an agreement that would further consolidate the position of the major US firms in Canada.[34]

The solution enshrined in the agreement proved deceptively simple. Canada and the United States entered into a unique sectoral arrangement so structured as to meet the competing objectives of the two countries. On the US side, the objective was to clear the way for the Big Three to rationalize their production in North America. For Canada, the goal was to ensure continued Canadian participation in that rationalization. In the words of the agreement, it would enable "the industries of both countries to participate on a fair and equitable basis in the expanding total market of the two countries."[35] The result was an agreement with asymmetrical obligations. Canada agreed to make its protection more efficient, and the United States agreed to exempt Canadian-origin parts and vehicles from its protection. On the US side, original equipment parts and vehicles produced in Canada were granted duty-free entry provided they met a minimum level of Canadian and/or US value-added. On the Canadian side, qualified firms could import original equipment parts and vehicles from anywhere in the world provided they maintained at least a 75 percent ratio of Canadian production of vehicles to their Canadian sales of vehicles and ensured that vehicles produced in Canada maintained a level of Canadian content, measured in dollar terms, equivalent to the level attained during the 1964 model year.[36]

In typical Canadian fashion, however, Canada was not confident that the agreement alone would be sufficient to ensure restructuring of the industry on a basis favourable to Canada. As a result, the government sought letters from the Big Three producers in which they agreed to increase the level of Canadian value added on a continuous basis. In addition to a minimum growth commitment, the firms agreed they would continuously augment the value of Canadian production by at least 60 percent of the value in the growth in Canadian sales. US officials considered the safeguards, both those in the agreement and those contained in the industry letters, to be temporary transitional measures but failed to write this stipulation into the agreement. A three-year review provision might have provided a basis for their elimination, but Canada successfully maintained that they continued to be necessary.[37] As a result, the safeguards stayed in place.[38] This was managed free trade. As Tom Kent saw it: "Far from abandoning the role of government intervention in the market, the Auto Pact used it to induce the industry to structure its production in a way more beneficial to Canada both than it had under the old tariff regime and than it would have done in an integrated 'free' market."[39]

The agreement successfully passed the hurdle of US Senate consent in 1965, although not without some concern being expressed about its impact on US employment. The United States also succeeded in gaining a waiver in the GATT allowing it to introduce preferential treatment in favour of Canada. The structure of the industry and of international trade in 1965 was still such that producers in Japan and Europe did not raise alarms at this clear contravention of GATT's principle of nondiscrimination. Canada claimed that its obligations were being implemented on a nondiscriminatory basis, a claim that other GATT members did not challenge.[40]

From a Canadian perspective, the Auto Pact marked a huge achievement and seemed a clear vindication of the policy of exemptionalism. Canadian negotiators had successfully appealed to US geopolitical instincts and negotiated an agreement that clearly favoured Canadian objectives. President Johnson was not far off the mark when he told Canadian ambassador Charles Ritchie, "You screwed us on the auto pact."[41] It guaranteed for Canada a clear share of the production of one of North America's most important industries. Its backward and forward linkages were of such critical importance that they soon became the mainstay of the Ontario economy. By 1980, the Auto Pact was directly responsible for more than 100,000 jobs and at least as many more in upstream and downstream industries.[42] The traditional Canadian deficit in automotive trade was gradually wiped out and replaced by a consistent surplus. By 1970, Canada enjoyed a merchandise trade surplus with the United States. In 1966, Canada enjoyed a global merchandise trade surplus; by 1970 this had reached $2 billion (see table 9.1). The gap between the cost of North American cars to Canadian and American consumers disappeared and, in some years, exchange rate fluctuations could lead to Canadians paying less for an identical car. The available choice was identical.

Not all Canadians were prepared to congratulate the government on its sagacity in negotiating the Auto Pact. Indeed, Canadian members of the United Auto Workers Union (UAW) were not at all clear that they would benefit and, in the usual bleat of organized labour, preferred the devil they knew to the one they didn't. Walter Reuther, the US head of the UAW, however, was satisfied and in 1965 that was what counted.[43] Canadian managers of the Big Three were similarly ambivalent, fearing that integration would eliminate what little autonomy they had. Only Ford Canada president Karl Scott expressed unreserved support.[44] But for once, in the words of historian Robert Bothwell, "The law of unintended consequences operated strongly in Canada's favor."[45] The agreement was a huge success and even the Canadian Auto Workers, nationalist successor to the Canadian arm of the UAW, convinced itself that it had always favoured the agreement. On the agreement's twentieth anniversary, General Motors CEO Roger Smith could tell the American Parts Manufacturers' Association that the agreement "is assuredly the most successful trade policy in the history of our industry. And despite some shortcomings, it remains – in my mind at least – an excellent example of a rational and responsible way to resolve thorny trade issues between nations."[46]

The success of the Auto Pact as industrial policy led the Canadian government to use its duty remission technique as the basis for granting Auto Pact status to a growing number of specialty vehicle producers. The technique became popular in other industrial sectors and was used repeatedly in the 1980s to lure Japanese automotive investment to Canada. These so-called transplant firms did not gain Auto Pact status, but Canada did grant them a variety of incentives, including duty remission programs, to convince them to locate some of their North American production facilities in Canada. From a trade policy point of view, the Auto Pact was

Table 9.1

The direction of Canadian merchandise trade, 1964-71

Year	US	UK	Japan	EEC	Other America	Central planning[a]	Rest of world	Total
Exports								
1964	4,271	1,200	330	555	436	619	683	8,094
1965	4,840	1,174	316	626	433	418	717	8,525
1966	6,046	1,123	394	662	496	583	785	10,089
1967	7,088	1,169	572	709	482	275	825	11,121
1968	8,997	1,210	607	774	544	307	887	13,325
1969	10,211	1,096	625	873	589	160	890	14,443
1970	10,563	1,481	810	1,226	750	311	1,261	16,401
1971	11,683	1,380	829	1,129	734	397	1,244	17,397
Imports								
1964	5,164	574	174	406	581	39	549	7,488
1965	6,045	619	230	514	548	59	618	8,633
1966	7,204	672	270	613	523	88	701	10,072
1967	7,952	649	294	635	551	100	693	10,873
1968	9,051	696	360	698	682	105	769	12,360
1969	10,243	791	496	831	714	109	947	14,130
1970	9,917	738	582	849	691	94	1,081	13,952
1971	10,951	837	803	984	755	111	1,177	15,618

Note: Totals may not add due to rounding.
a   PRC, Cuba, and the USSR and its COMECON satellites.
Source: F.H. Leacy, ed., *Historical Statistics of Canada,* 2nd ed. (Ottawa: Statistics Canada, 1983), series G381,
G384, and G401-14.

the crowning achievement of the 1960s, far outstripping any Canadian gains from simultaneous GATT negotiations.

The principal architect of the Auto Pact, Simon Reisman, had been part of the Canadian team in Geneva and Havana negotiating the GATT and ITO. He had continued to play an influential role in Canadian trade policy developments as director of Finance's International Economic Relations Division. He had been seconded to the Gordon Commission in 1956 as one of its directors of research and had co-authored or directed the commission's trade policy studies. By 1964, Reisman was the deputy minister of the Department of Industry and from that perch concluded that multilateralism was good but concrete results were better. Among the influences leading him toward the negotiation of a bilateral Canada-US sectoral trade agreement were the difficulties Canada had faced in GATT negotiations, first during the Dillon Round and again during the Kennedy Round. In both negotiations

Canada had learned that its most immediate needs, better and more secure access to the large market to the south, could not be easily reconciled with the multilateral framework. US willingness to make concessions to Canada was hemmed in by the MFN rule requiring that any such concessions had to be shared with the Europeans and the Japanese. Congress was not ready to make such concessions. The Auto Pact, on the other hand, although it occasioned some grumbling in the US Senate, garnered sufficient support to provide Canada with the kind of access it needed to encourage a more efficient and rewarding use of North American resources. There was a lesson here that would continue to percolate with Reisman and among similarly minded officials. In the meantime, Canada continued to do its best in multilateral negotiations, playing the game of maximizing new export opportunities but minimizing exposure to new import competition.

Canada at the GATT: The Kennedy Round Negotiations

As we saw in chapter 8, President Kennedy had proposed a new, ambitious attack on global trade barriers, including those maintained by the United States. He wanted to revitalize the momentum initiated more than a decade earlier by the GATT, the Marshall Plan, the OEEC, and European integration with a bold new plan to lower barriers on a global basis. By the beginning of 1963, he had succeeded in gaining both international support and a robust negotiating authority from Congress for a new round of multilateral negotiations to pursue his vision. John Diefenbaker had been a reluctant participant in this consensus. Lester Pearson had let it be known that the new government was prepared to be more enthusiastic.

To confirm this new attitude, Kennedy dispatched his Special Trade Representative, Christian Herter, to meet with newly installed Minister of Trade and Commerce Mitchell Sharp on 26 April 1963. They would go over preparations for the ministerial meeting in a few weeks in Geneva, which would officially confirm GATT members' commitment to the negotiations. Canada had an important role to play. One of Sharp's assistant deputy ministers, Jake Warren, was chair of the contracting parties that year, and Rodney Grey from Finance was chairing the working party preparing for the negotiations. Sharp assured Herter that Canada would be an active and willing participant in the negotiations. He was confident that preparations were well in train for a good beginning. Herter came away from the meeting satisfied that the bad old Diefenbaker days were over.[47]

Much of the preparatory work for the May conference had long been under way, and officials had concluded that Canada's economic structure made the US linear approach problematic. The United States had proposed that governments come prepared to negotiate across-the-board cuts based on a to-be-negotiated formula. Canada needed to improve access for its resource-based and agricultural exports. Cutting tariffs on a formula basis, however, would not zero in on those of greatest interest to Canada; indeed, a formula cut in Canada's own tariffs could create a problem for Canada's fragile manufacturing sector. Despite the acknowledged difficulties of the item-by-item, offer-request technique, officials had concluded that Canada would do better by sticking with it.

Canada had pursued its trade objectives in successive rounds of GATT negotiations by seeking more open and secure access to larger markets for Canadian exports of industrial raw materials, foodstuffs, and selected manufactured goods. As payment for concessions by the United States and others, Canada had agreed to modest reductions in selected tariffs protecting Canadian secondary industry. Canadian negotiators had skilfully exploited GATT's bargaining technique by emphasizing Canadian export over import interests. It was a policy that had proved popular with Canadian business. Canadian officials in 1963 were not convinced that they needed to depart from this approach. In Walter Gordon, they found a ready ally; Mitchell Sharp went along, but with less conviction.[48]

Sharp was not alone in his reservations. Dana Wilgress, the retired dean of Canadian trade negotiators, had already counselled Canadians to engage in more constructive negotiations, noting that "Canada has a great deal to gain and, if normal precautions are taken, little to lose from following a positive policy of active participation in the tariff negotiations to be held under the auspices of the GATT."[49] His views were echoed in a variety of other studies from academic and think-tank analysts. Officials, however, took a more cautious view, reflecting the anxiety of the Canadian manufacturing sector as articulated by the perennially protectionist Canadian Manufacturers' Association.[50]

By inclination a free trader, Sharp, like Wilgress, was convinced that Canada had much to gain from the negotiations. As he told a Toronto audience on 6 May 1963, "We shall be tough, but not reluctant bargainers." He did not believe that "the answer to Canada's problems of unemployment, under-utilization of resources or the balance-of-payments difficulty" lay in protection.[51] As a former senior trade official, he had the background and experience to fit quickly into his portfolio, but as a member of the government, he had to pursue a consensus position developed in concert with his cabinet colleagues. Not surprisingly, Walter Gordon's inclinations were toward caution in opening Canada's doors to more trade and exposing the Canadian economy to more competition. He worried not only about Canada's further integration into the US economy, but also about the impact of more imports on Canada's balance of payments. Admittedly, Canada was in a difficult position, given the extent of its trade deficit with the United States ($1.116 billion in 1962) and the resource-based structure of its economy. Cutting tariffs on manufactures on a reciprocal basis could pose short-term adjustment challenges.

In preparation for the Geneva ministerial meeting, the UK government had invited Commonwealth trade ministers to meet first in London and discuss their general approach to the negotiations "within the family." Sharp took the occasion to make clear to his Commonwealth colleagues that the new government in Ottawa did not view the decline of the Commonwealth in Canada's trade position with alarm, nor was it going to lecture Britain about its obligations to keep the family together. The new government would take a pragmatic rather than nostalgic approach. The breakdown in the talks between the United Kingdom and the EEC in January had changed the equation somewhat. In the upcoming GATT negotiations, Britain would continue to be an important player in its own right, and Canada would bargain vigorously to protect its access to the UK market. At the same time, Canada was not prepared to make the preservation of preferences an important part of its bargaining strategy, as some Commonwealth countries preferred and as the Diefenbaker government had intimated. As negotiations proceeded in Geneva, Canada chose to play its cards cautiously, whereas the other dominions decided not to play at all, maintaining even higher levels of protection, with serious long-term consequences.

In Geneva, Sharp outlined Canadian reservations about the linear approach. At the same time, he insisted that Canada was prepared to play, but on a different basis.[52] If others would reciprocate, they would find Canada a ready and willing partner. On his return, Sharp told the House of Commons that he had told Canada's trading partners that the proposed tariff-cutting formula "would not yield the necessary mutuality of trade and economic benefit for Canada." But he had assured them that "Canada would play its part and make concessions in Canadian tariffs commensurate with the benefits" it received. Others, he believed, were prepared to recognize Canada's special situation and work toward a mutually acceptable solution.[53]

The United States and the EEC, however, were determined to proceed on the basis of the linear approach. Their experience in the Dillon Round had clearly demonstrated the limits, for them, of the offer-request, item-by-item approach. They were not of one view on the best formula, but they were agreed that the old way was no longer appropriate. At the same time, they saw some reason in Canada's position and reluctantly agreed to let Canada participate on the basis of the older approach.[54] The EEC was more unhappy than the United States. EEC officials were concerned that Canada would get a free ride, gaining access to the EEC market on the basis of the MFN rule, without offering equivalent improved access for EEC products to the Canadian market. US negotiators were more sympathetic, but worried about the "recrudescence of Canadian nationalism" and the "narrow and short-run self-interest that characterized the Canadian position."[55]

The government appointed Norman Robertson in February 1964 to head the Canadian negotiating team and to chair the newly established Canadian Tariffs and Trade Committee. Robertson had enjoyed a distinguished career in the Department of External Affairs, twice its undersecretary, twice high commissioner to the United Kingdom, and ambassador to the United States. By 1964, he was ill and needed a rest. In recognition of his past fondness for trade negotiations, his old friend Lester Pearson thought this position would be more rewarding and less taxing. Hector McKinnon, the retired former head of the Canadian Tariff Board and Robertson's colleague in the negotiations with the United Kingdom and the United States in the 1930s, was appointed vice-chair.[56] The government gave the two veterans a mandate to consult with industry and gather its views before commencing negotiations in Geneva. Throughout 1964, the committee held hearings and received briefs, some 450 in total, fleshing out ministers' and officials' sense of Canadian industry's priorities and sensitivities. As is often the case, more briefs set out negative concerns than positive targets. Overall, however, Canadian industry projected a more positive image than had been the case a few years earlier during the Dillon Round.[57]

By the fall of 1964, Robertson had taken up residence in Geneva to pursue the negotiations, together with a team of seasoned officials under the leadership of his deputy, Maurice Schwarzmann, from the Department of Trade and Commerce.[58] With advances in transatlantic air transportation, officials like Bobby Latimer from Trade and Commerce and Rodney Grey from the Department of Finance regularly supplemented the team from their Ottawa base. Canada thus gradually prepared its offer and request list. The government's minority position made it skittish about being too far out front. In November 1964, for example, the government instructed the delegation to pull the Canadian package on offer just before it was tabled, and it took all of Robertson's contacts and powers of persuasion to turn things around.[59]

Along with fifteen other countries, Canada tabled its offer on 16 November 1964. It involved a general ceiling that would significantly reduce high tariffs, with some exceptions for sensitive items. For items below the ceiling, various cuts were proposed including reductions of up to 50 percent on a range of semi-manufactures, plus reductions to free for industrial raw materials and tropical products. In return, Canada sought full 50 percent cuts on all items of potential and actual export interest to Canada, the inclusion of agricultural products in the formula, equivalent tropical products offers by others, and agreement on the reductions of margins of preference.[60] It was a handsome offer and, if it held, would provide a basis for significant new trade opportunities. There were many conditional elements, however, which could gradually lead to its erosion. The offers of the other fifteen full participants involved lists of exceptions from the linear formula agreed earlier. The stage had been set for the detailed negotiations to begin. Time would tell how much of the initial offers would survive to become part of the final package.

Delegations now proceeded to intensive bilateral discussions. Canada, for example, held a total of eighty-eight meetings with the Americans. Robertson found the discussions tedious and his instructions from Ottawa confining and insufficiently forthcoming to give him the room to make any interesting counteroffers and deals. He was unable to capitalize on the receptive mood of the US and other delegations, thus missing a significant opportunity to broaden markets and adjust to greater competition. He soon tired of the shadow-boxing and became more and more frustrated by the extent to which Canada had been marginalized by both circumstances and its own lack of imagination. He was relieved of his boredom before the summer of 1965 and succeeded by another veteran, Sidney Pierce, Canada's ambassador to Brussels, as ill health forced his retirement.[61]

Once negotiations are launched, it is easy for negotiators to become captive to the process. Momentum pushes participants in the direction taken and it is very difficult to change one's bearings. Having chosen not to participate in the linear approach, Canada had to fit its offer-request strategy into a negotiation revolving around a formula approach. It was not always an easy fit. The logic of the negotiations involved reciprocity. The obligation to extend all tariff concessions on a most-favoured-nation basis meant that delegations carefully measured the extent to which concessions proposed were matched or, even better, surpassed by concessions offered. Such calculations may make little economic sense, but they are critical to ensuring political support for the final results.

The political arithmetic of trade negotiations entails trading politically popular gains in access to foreign markets for politically risky reductions in access to one's own market. Export interests can thus be harnessed to offset complaints from import-competing interests. As both ministers and officials knew all too well, however, it is much easier to raise the ire of import-competing interests than to earn the praise of export-oriented ones. A natural inclination to be cautious is hence a necessary prerequisite for a tariff negotiator. In Canada, the Department of Finance carried the burden of defending Canadian import interests, while the Department of Trade and Commerce took the lead in pursuing Canadian export interests. This kind of tension between the champions of the two competing interests is a normal part of any negotiation.[62]

The linear approach did not solve the problem of balancing competing interests, but it did shift the burden of proof somewhat in favour of export interests. The US proposal was that all delegations should start with an offer to cut industrial tariffs by 50 percent across the board and then negotiate exceptions to this formula. The US delegation was right in arguing that this approach changed the onus from deciding which items to include in a country's offer to deciding which items to exclude. But the formula also favoured a country that had many high tariffs and a wide dispersion in its tariff rates, such as the United States, and was less attractive to a participant with somewhat lower and more uniform tariff rates, such as the EEC. Not surprisingly, the EEC had been a reluctant convert to the US formula, and the proof of the round would still need to be found in tedious negotiations examining the quality and value of each and every participant's offer and weighing those offers against one's own offer.

As a rule of thumb, negotiators relied on the quantity of imports covered by each concession to measure the value of offers, but needed to take account also of the depth of cuts as well as the capacity of any cuts to lead to new export opportunities. The principal and substantial supplier rules ensured that delegations would only trade concessions with countries that had a significant economic interest in the trade of the item being considered. Market size was a further important consideration in determining what to trade with whom.

To facilitate the task of bargaining about these kinds of details and of calculating the political concessions involved, delegations had a strong disposition to deal with the issues on a sector-by-sector basis and, to the extent possible, to try to balance export gains and import concessions within a sector. From the beginning it had been agreed that agriculture would not be included in the general linear approach but would be handled on an offer-request basis. The EEC's disposition was to defend its Common Agriculture Policy and concede as little as possible. Given its goal of self-sufficiency in agriculture, the EEC had little reason to seek a balanced agreement in the agriculture sector, a frustrating position for traditional temperate-zone agricultural exporters like Canada, the United States, and Australia. Without the weight of agriculture gains, however, these delegations would be hard put to satisfy the EEC's goals in the industrial areas. Sectoral balance was important, but so was overall balance.

It had also been agreed at the outset that the Kennedy Round would tackle a number of nontariff issues that had gained in prominence, and ministers had confirmed that progress should be made where possible. Two such issues were addressed during the negotiations: antidumping and valuation procedures. In both cases, delegations were looking for agreement to bring the practices of members more in line with the requirements set out in the General Agreement and, where the GATT's rules were not clear, to clarify them. The United Kingdom, United States, and EEC, for example, were determined to bring Canada's antidumping regime into line with the requirement in article VI for an injury test, and the United Kingdom and EEC wanted to reform some of the procedures used in the United States. Canada and the United States, on the other hand, were interested in making the EEC system more transparent. On valuation, the EEC and others wanted the United States to abandon its American Selling Price provision, particularly in the chemicals sector.

A complicating factor in the nontariff area was that the US Congress had not authorized the administration to make concessions requiring changes in US law. It had authorized reductions in US tariffs but not in other forms of protection. The Trade Expansion Act of 1962 had not changed the continuing official disdain with which Congress viewed the GATT. It remained an executive agreement that did not enjoy the formal approval of Congress. US negotiators believed that a good deal would help them to convince Congress to make any necessary changes in US law flowing from negotiations on nontariff issues. Time would tell.

Finally, it had been agreed that special efforts should be directed to improving the basis for the participation of developing countries in the trading system. When the GATT had been negotiated, only a few developing countries had participated and even fewer had decided to accede to the new agreement. By the early 1960s, however, the decolonization of Africa, the Caribbean, and the Pacific regions was creating newly independent countries at a fast and furious pace. By 1963, GATT boasted a membership of sixty-two countries, with a further six countries having acceded provisionally and five applying the agreement on a de facto basis. The number of countries participating in multilateral trade negotiations had more than doubled to fifty, and more were waiting in the wings to determine whether this was a process that met their needs.

The 1958 Haberler Report had identified a number of areas where GATT could respond more positively to the aspirations of developing countries. Since then a working party had been studiously engaged in fleshing out a consensus on steps GATT members could take to strengthen the agreement in directions favourable to developing country interests. At a special session of the contracting parties in November 1964, members had agreed to adopt three new articles dealing with the special problems of developing countries. Further steps were now part of the negotiating agenda.[63]

It is not necessary to record the detail and drama of the Kennedy Round negotiations here as they have been well captured in separate accounts by two American participants.[64] In brief, difficulties emerged between the United States and the European Common Market, between Brussels and the EEC member states, and between the US administration and Congress. Each of these struggles prolonged the negotiations and made it more difficult to maintain the momentum first established by President Kennedy in 1962-3.

The round was complicated and prolonged, for example, by French president Charles de Gaulle's attack on the EEC in an effort to change it from a supranational into an intergovernmental arrangement. His attack put the EEC negotiators on a very short leash and threatened to derail the whole project. The Luxembourg compromise in January 1966 setting out a new consensus on the decision-making structure of the EEC brought the French back into the fold and broke the stalemate.

Similarly, US efforts during the round to address agriculture and the EEC's Common Agriculture Policy (CAP) were marred by the hollow resonance of the US agriculture waiver of 1955. This waiver had established that US law and priorities took precedence over US international obligations – a precedent that was not unnoticed by the other players. US agricultural export objectives in Europe were frustrated by the successful implementation of the CAP and led to the chicken war: US exports of frozen chickens to Germany and the Netherlands, which had quadrupled in the late 1950s, fell off precipitously once the CAP's provisions were fully implemented in the early 1960s. Not satisfied with the compensation the EEC was prepared to offer, the United States retaliated by raising its own tariff on various sensitive products, including alcoholic beverages and motor vehicles.

The chicken war suggested that the United States was not used to a challenge to its hegemony and had difficulty adjusting to a player prepared to adopt its own brand of hardball. US efforts also had an unrealistic air about them, given both the sociopolitical difficulties that success would have engendered for the EEC's agricultural regime, the glue that held the Common Market together, and the relative unimportance of trade in agricultural products to the US economy. Andrew

Shonfield observes that "what the United States was doing in this instance was to try to impose a new set of rules of behaviour which were designed to maximize its own competitive advantage in one segment of international trade."[65]

For Canada, the negotiation of the Auto Pact throughout much of 1964 meant that the delays occasioned by the tiffs between Brussels and Washington and Brussels and Paris were of less significance than they might otherwise have been. Successful conclusion of an agreement in the auto sector was potentially of greater weight than the Geneva negotiations. More to the point, the consequences of failure in the auto negotiations would have been immediate and painful, whereas failure in the Kennedy Round, although disappointing, would have been a matter of benefits not achieved rather than pain avoided.

In the end the negotiations concluded, as all negotiations must, and with more success than much of the hand-wringing during them would have suggested possible. The imminent demise of US negotiating authority at the end of June 1967 concentrated the minds of the negotiators wonderfully. The increasingly ugly mood in Congress about the possible erosion in protection and the rise in imports, further exacerbating an already difficult balance-of-payments position, made it clear that either seeking an extension or looking to a new mandate would be imprudent. Too much had been committed to these negotiations not to cobble together a package that all but the most zealous could find acceptable.

During the first half of 1967, delegations achieved their goal, and on 30 June, GATT's secretary general, Eric Wyndham White, gavelled the round to a conclusion. Forty-six of the fifty participating countries signed the Final Act.[66] The results were wide and deep: industrial tariffs were cut on average by 35 percent, based on formula cuts with exceptions, bringing the overall incidence of the tariffs of the United States, EEC, and Japan to below the 10 percent range. For the first time, the United States made cuts into protection that were serious enough to have a real impact and increase import competition. EEC tariffs were reduced to the levels of the low-tariff members before the Treaty of Rome, in effect restoring US access to Europe for industrial products and preventing the trade diversion that had been feared. The round succeeded in unleashing once again the trade potential of the United States, Germany, Japan, and the United Kingdom, which, together, accounted for 60 percent of world trade.

The results on industrial tariffs were not matched on agriculture. The EEC and other importers such as Japan and the EFTA countries were unprepared to make major concessions. One of the principal US negotiating objectives, shared by Canada and other exporters of temperate-zone agricultural products, therefore had to be shelved for a further effort in future rounds.[67] As a result, in US trade policy folklore, the Kennedy Round came to be considered a failure. Additionally, US manufacturers could not take full advantage of the cuts in industrial tariffs because of monetary factors. The overvalued dollar continued to make US exports expensive but imports competitive. The mood in the US Congress as a result of these circumstances was becoming ominous.

A new grains agreement, however, did compensate somewhat for the failure on agriculture. Negotiations conducted in the grains group were incorporated at the end of the round into a new International Grains Arrangement (IGA), replacing the expired International Wheat Agreement (IWA). The IGA entered into force 1 July 1968 for an initial three years and entailed commitments on both price and food aid. Unlike the single-price IWA, the IGA established price ranges for fourteen types of wheat. To end the ruinous competition in concessional sales, members entered into a food aid convention that committed them to providing a minimum volume of wheat as aid to poor countries. Additionally, the institutional arrangements provided an improved forum for adjusting the commitments to changing circumstances.[68]

For developing countries, the results were also disappointing.[69] The tropical products offers they had sought gradually thinned as negotiations proceeded. The reductions in tariffs were concentrated in areas for which they were not major suppliers; in their areas of comparative advantage – agricultural products, raw materials, and consumer products – they benefited little or not at all. Indeed, the arrangement on cotton textiles and clothing, adopted as a temporary expedient in 1961, was extended for a further three years in 1967. The industrial countries were not yet ready to make a serious run at the issues that preoccupied the developing countries, particularly in the absence of any tangible offers from these countries. Industrial countries were prepared to pay lip service to the principle of nonreciprocity in their negotiations with the developing countries, but this was a difficult concept to put into practice. Part IV of the GATT, adopted at the special session in 1964, similarly exhibited more political rhetoric than contractual commitment and never gained the status its authors had hoped. The issue of developing country participation in the trading system would remain a challenge, not to be seriously addressed until the Uruguay Round of negotiations at the end of the 1980s.

From Canada's perspective, concessions had been gained covering $3 billion in exports, including the reduction or elimination of duties on lumber, paper, fish, agricultural, and other products of export interest to Canada. The United States had agreed to implement the full 50 percent cut on more than half the items of interest to Canada and to eliminate tariffs of 5 percent or less on $560 million in Canadian exports. In return, Canada had provided concessions on Canadian imports worth $2.5 billion, $1.9 billion coming from the United States. Canada agreed to eliminate the 7.5 percent tariff on machinery not made in Canada and to reduce the tariff on made-in-Canada machinery from 22.5 to 15 percent with a commitment that the overall impact of the machinery tariff would be reduced to 9 percent.[70] Canada was disappointed in the outcome on agriculture but pleased with the acceptance of commitments providing the basis for the new grains arrangement.

Trade and Commerce Minister Robert Winters told Canadians, "It may be that the Kennedy round will be regarded in the future as a crucial turning point in the transformation of Canada from a resource-based economy to one of the most advanced industrial trading nations of the world."[71] Finance Minister Mitchell Sharp added that "no country has more to gain from the Kennedy round than Canada."[72]

Once again Canada had been able to strike a better deal with the Americans than with anyone else. Coupled with the breakthrough of the Auto Pact two and a half years earlier, Canada and the United States had taken a giant step toward reducing barriers between them. Little was gained from either the EEC or the Japanese other than what would come from MFN reductions negotiated with others. Integration between the Canadian and US economies would continue. The much vaunted desire to diversify Canada's trading patterns had been throttled again by the reality that only the Americans had sufficient interest in the Canadian market to make concessions that were helpful to Canadian exporters. Nevertheless, the *Globe and Mail* thought the overall package offered sufficient opportunities to Canadian business that "it may well provide us with our best hope of maintaining an independent Canada."[73]

Other Commonwealth dominions solved their problem by making virtually no contribution to the negotiations. Dissatisfied with the gains available on agricultural products, they decided to keep their high tariffs on manufactures. Australia did not conclude a single bilateral agreement, and New Zealand and South Africa made small concessions covering less than 3 percent of their trade. Of course, they gained improved access as a result of the MFN rule, but the high level of protection for their small manufacturing sectors continued, with long-term consequences that would require painful adjustments in later years.[74]

More generally, the linear countries had agreed to cut tariffs on two-thirds of their dutiable imports. Canada had limited its own reductions to about half of its dutiable imports, earning the opprobrium of the EEC for many years to come. Its concern that Canada would get a free ride had been realized. Canada, for its part, found its bilateral negotiations with the EEC less than satisfactory, maintaining that the EEC had not been prepared to make a single concession to Canada for which it had not already been paid in bilateral settlements with other delegations. Efforts in the closing days of the negotiations to find a basis for a more amicable settlement failed. Mutual recriminations would continue across the ocean for some time, extending well into the next round of negotiations. Some US negotiators harboured similar misgivings about Canada's participation, but conceded that in their bilateral settlement Canada had been forthcoming and had made many concessions of interest to the United States.

For Canada, one of the more difficult issues was the negotiation of a new antidumping code. As Rodney Grey, the negotiator, has noted, Canada was responding first of all to the desire of the United Kingdom, United States, and EEC to bring Canada's system of automatic antidumping duties into line with the provisions of

GATT article VI, particularly by subjecting the imposition of antidumping duties to a material injury test. At the same time, there were many problems with the Canadian system that needed to be corrected. Negotiating a code provided an opportunity to address these issues and get paid for them. Negotiators always find it attractive to get paid for doing something sensible. Additionally, there was growing fear that US manufacturers would make increasing use of US antidumping procedures. Better international rules would help to keep this trend honest. Nevertheless, Canadian manufacturers, particularly those in import-sensitive areas, liked the Canadian system and were reluctant to give it up for a system involving more transparent procedures and tougher standards. For Canada, therefore, the successful negotiation of the Antidumping Code required careful political management as its requirements were implemented into Canadian law.[75]

Canadian participation in the final phase of the negotiations had been directed by a somewhat more pragmatic team of ministers. Walter Gordon had resigned from cabinet after the 1965 election when he failed to deliver the majority he had predicted. Mitchell Sharp then moved to Finance, and Robert Winters replaced him at Trade and Commerce. By this time, Gordon had succeeded in alienating virtually every segment of the Canadian business community. With Diefenbaker still leading the Tories, some businesspeople felt they had been effectively disenfranchised. To rectify the situation, Pearson convinced Winters to rejoin his government. Back in the cabinet after an eight-year stint on Bay Street, Winters, together with Sharp and C.M. "Bud" Drury, provided the voice of pragmatism and business good sense. The change may not have materially altered Canada's approach to the negotiations, but it did facilitate its participation in the final months.

The Kennedy Round results were well received in Canada. As Canadians celebrated the Dominion's centennial, 1967 was a year of exceptional self-confidence. Montreal's Expo 67 added to the air of optimism. The announcement, competing with the Queen's centennial tour for editorial space, garnered big headlines across the country on 29 and 30 June. The tone was positive and built on the government's press releases emphasizing how much Canada had gained and how relatively little it had paid. The *Winnipeg Free Press,* while noting in its coverage that "Canada remains one of the more highly protectionist countries in the world,"[76] was unstinting in its praise: "The riches opened up to Canadian industry by the Kennedy Round of tariff reductions are almost impossible to exaggerate. In return for incredibly minor concessions to the products of other countries, this already prosperous and favored land has been offered opportunities which are limited only by the willingness of its people to exploit them and by the vigor and competitiveness of its business community."[77]

The results got a much rougher reception in Washington. A resurgence of protectionism in the US Congress, stimulated by problems related to monetary policy and the Vietnam War, was leading to a decrease in US sales abroad and an increase in imports, shrinking the traditionally large surplus in US merchandise trade. That shrinking surplus, coupled with the continuing outflow of US investment capital, had resulted in a serious balance-of-payments situation. Since Congress could do little about monetary policy, it was turning its attention to dealing with the symptoms through trade policy. The tariff package automatically became law by virtue of the provisions of the Trade Expansion Act. The nontariff elements, however, particularly the Antidumping Code and US commitment to adjust the American-selling-price valuation method on selected chemicals needed congressional approval. This was vigorously denied. To make sure the point was not missed, Congress began considering various bills to impose unilateral quotas on textile and other low-cost products and increases in tariffs. Sabre rattling about the GATT being nothing more than an executive agreement added to the ugly mood. For Canada, these developments were ominous and put a strain on the relationship.[78]

By the end of the Kennedy Round, it was clear that GATT's mandatory requirements – the end of discrimination and the implementation of the code of good trade policy practice embedded in its various articles – had been much less successful than its nonobligatory aspects – the negotiated reduction in tariff barriers.[79] For most of the decade, the focus of attention had been on the negotiation of new commitments leading to further reductions in tariffs. The day-to-day activities of the GATT as a forum for the discussion of members' obligations and the resolution of disputes had taken a decided back seat to these negotiating efforts. As a result a large backlog of issues relating to members' implementation of their obligations would gradually begin to crowd GATT's agenda. By the end of the 1960s, the special circumstances that had given the United States such a commanding competitive edge over its main trading partners had also come to an end. The economies of Europe and Japan had fully recovered and in many areas, European and Japanese

Table 9.2

Value and volume of world trade and output, 1965-71

Year	Value world exports (US$ billions)	Unit value world exports (1960 = 100)	Volume (1960 = 100) World exports	World output
1960	128.0	100	100	100
1965	186.5	103	141	130
1966	204.0	105	151	139
1967	214.5	105	159	145
1968	239.5	104	180	155
1969	273.0	108	197	164
1970	312.0	114	213	170
1971	348.0	120	226	176

Source: GATT, *International Trade,* 1972 (Geneva: GATT, 1973).

firms were now fully capable of competing with US suppliers. The Kennedy Round further unleashed these competitive forces. As illustrated by table 9.2, world trade expanded rapidly in the 1960s, more than doubling in volume terms and far outpacing world output. As competition increased, the GATT was called on to solve a growing list of problems. Gradually, the institution was being transformed from a venue for negotiating more liberal trade conditions into a forum for governing the conduct of world trade. The next round, the Tokyo Round, would play a critical role in accelerating this transformation.

The Emergence of More Diversified Trade Relations

During the Diefenbaker-Pearson decade, Canadian trade grew prodigiously. In Canada's centennial year, the country's share of world merchandise trade peaked at 6.3 percent, and exports as a share of Canada's GNP reached 18.4 percent the following year. The United States' dominant position in Canada's trade was by now well established, with the US market consistently taking more than half of Canada's exports and US exporters supplying roughly two-thirds of Canada's imports. The rapid growth in trade, however, also meant increases in Canadian exports to other markets, with the surplus earned in these markets making up for Canada's deficit in trade with the United States.

At the beginning of the period, the Commonwealth countries (principally Britain, the dominions, and the West Indies) comfortably commanded second place among Canada's trading partners. During the course of the decade, however, rapid growth in trade with Japan and Germany, and more modest growth in trade with France and other European markets, as well as with Latin America and communist countries, created a more diversified pattern of trade relations. A surge in the number of independent countries during the 1960s added to the number of countries with which Canada traded. In 1966, signature of an agreement exchanging MFN treatment with Korea brought the number of countries with which Canada enjoyed formal trade relations to a total of 104.[80]

The multilateral provisions of the GATT remained the principal basis for governing the conduct of trade with most of these countries, but an increasing array of other instruments were being developed to advance Canadian economic interests. For the more important of these countries, Canada exchanged ministerial visits and set up permanent committees of ministers or senior officials to provide a focus for a periodic review of relations, problems, and opportunities. Annual meetings of the Joint Canada-US Committee on Trade and Economic Affairs were a regular feature of the management of relations with the United States. The Canada-UK Continuing Committee established in 1949 was elevated into a Canada-UK Ministerial Committee on Trade and Economic Affairs in 1967. A Canada-Japan Ministerial Committee was established in 1961 and tried to meet at least once a year. A Canada-Caribbean Trade and Economic Committee first met in 1967. High-level visits were exchanged with France, Germany, and various other countries, and the ministers of trade and commerce complemented the work of their officials by leading trade missions to some of the more promising new markets.

By the beginning of the 1960s, exports to Japan had reached interesting levels, with two-way trade approaching $300 million a year, ranking Japan as Canada's third-most important trading destination. Most of Canada's exports were concentrated in a narrow range of industrial raw materials and wheat; Japan's exports consisted largely of low-cost consumer products. The low cost of Japanese products occasioned much anxiety among Canadian competitors and prompted the government to follow the US lead and negotiate export restraint agreements with Japan on such items as flatware and cotton clothing. Unlike the European countries, Canada and the United States did not invoke article XXXV (GATT's nonapplication clause) when Japan acceded to the GATT in 1955. As a result, the two felt entitled to ask Japan to restrain its exports to acceptable levels. Most meetings of the Canada-Japan Ministerial Committee during the 1960s were, therefore, dominated by complaints from Japan about the imbalance of trade in Canada's favour and insistence by Canadian ministers on Japan's continuing need to exercise restraint.

Various other multilateral institutions provided further opportunities for contacts among ministers and senior officials. The Organization for European Economic Cooperation was transformed at the end of 1960 into the Organization for Economic Cooperation and Development (OECD), providing a forum for discussion and analytical work among member governments and for ministerial discussions at least once a year. The Commonwealth Economic Consultative Council continued to meet annually, involving either the trade or the finance minister and sometimes both in discussions with their Commonwealth colleagues. By the end of the decade, a permanent Commonwealth Secretariat had been established, headed by Canadian diplomat Arnold Smith, and meetings began to focus on the special problems faced by the newly independent members of the Commonwealth.

The extension of export credits and export credits insurance by the government facilitated the expansion of trade with some of the newly emerging markets. Other complementary efforts to enhance trading links included expanding or strengthening the range of auxiliary economic agreements. A new air agreement with the United States in 1966 greatly promoted business travel to Canada's number-one market. Similar, if less ambitious, agreements with other countries opened up new opportunities. New agreements were also negotiated to avoid the problem of double taxation.

Canada had always been a strong supporter of commodity agreements negotiated between producers and consumers that aimed at stabilizing world prices. A succession of international wheat agreements had been a critical component of Canadian agricultural trade policy. The rapid increase in the number of exporters of primary commodities made international discussion of these issues a matter of growing urgency in the 1960s. The ill-fated International Trade Organization had contained extensive provisions relating to commodity agreements. With the ITO's failure to come into force, responsibility for general discussion of international problems relating to trade in primary commodities had been assumed by a UN Committee on Commodities. Additionally, however, a number of commodity-specific organizations had been established, including some that administered commodity agreements with economic provisions involving price, production, and purchasing commitments.

By the middle of the 1960s, international commodity discussions extended to a number of commodities of critical importance to Canada. In addition to the International Wheat Agreement, Canada participated in the work of the Lead and Zinc Study Group, the Rubber Study Group, the Cotton Study Group, the International Tin Agreement, the International Sugar Agreement, the International Coffee Agreement, and the International Cocoa Agreement, as well as in a variety of ad hoc discussions involving other primary commodities such as oils and oilseeds, tungsten, and pulp and paper.

In 1963, in preparation for the first meeting of the United Nations Conference on Trade and Development (UNCTAD) to be held in Geneva in 1964, responsibility for commodity issues was assigned to this new arm of the United Nations. Canada took a keen interest in the work of UNCTAD, not only because of its effort to address international commodity policy issues, but more generally because of its potential for shaping responses to the trade and economic problems of developing countries. By 1968, however, when UNCTAD held its second session in New Delhi, Canadian trade officials were beginning to express alarm about the highly interventionist and discriminatory nature of the policy prescriptions favoured in UNCTAD discussions. In the years to come, trade officials would tread warily as aid and foreign policy officials waxed enthusiastic about Canada's opportunity to do good through UNCTAD and similar organizations.

Canadian Business in the 1960s

The period 1948-73 marked one of the longest and most sustained booms in Canadian history. With the exception of the years 1957-61, when growth faltered and unemployment reached politically uncomfortable levels, this period was marked by high levels of expansion and only brief, intermittent recessions. It was the Tories' bad luck to be in office during the only period when there was a marked slowdown. Some of this was due to their mismanagement of the economy; some was pure bad luck. For many Canadians, however, it confirmed that Tory times were bad times. Between 1957 and 1961 the economy averaged only 2.9 percent growth. In 1962 it hit 7.1 percent and continued at that pace or close to it for the next decade.[81]

For Canadian business, the quarter-century following the Second World War was one of rapidly expanding opportunities. In the first part of this period, those opportunities involved a rapid expansion of the resource sector to serve the American market. Forest, energy, and mining companies, some Canadian, some American,

Table 9.3

Composition of Canadian exports, 1968

Commodity	Total ($ millions)	US ($ millions)	Total (%)	US (%)
Live animals	59	51	0.4	0.6
Food, beverages, tobacco	1,554	489	11.7	5.4
Crude materials	2,468	1,373	18.5	15.3
Fabricated materials	4,855	3,351	36.4	37.2
End products (inedible)	4,351	3,703	32.7	41.2
Special trade transactions	38	31	0.3	0.3
Total	13,325	8,998	100.0	100.0

Source: F.H. Leacy, ed., *Historical Statistics of Canada*, 2nd ed. (Ottawa: Statistics Canada, 1983), series G415-28.

tapped Canada's huge storehouse of resources, particularly in BC and the more remote parts of Ontario and Quebec. Even Saskatchewan benefited as Canada became the world's largest supplier of potash to help fertilize the green revolution. In the second half of the period, the expansion involved more investment in manufacturing, particularly once the Auto Pact created the basis for rapid growth in the auto sector and its suppliers, from steel to textiles and plastics. Once the Kennedy Round tariff cuts and the Auto Pact began to take hold, the share of processed and finished goods in Canada's export profile also began to rise, particularly in exports to the United States (see tables 7.4, p. 187, and 9.3).

American investment made a critical contribution to the first part of this expansion, but by the time Canadians began to worry about it, the US share of the economy was already declining as Canadian savings and wealth generated by the boom became the basis for further growth and investment. Canada had its own share of capitalists and of multinational companies, as well as a growing number of small and medium-sized enterprises. The chartered banks and other financial institutions were wholly Canadian-owned and were active not only in Canada but also in the Caribbean and elsewhere. Noranda, Alcan, Macmillan Bloedel, and others were major players in the resource sector. Canadian Pacific was by this time a Canadian company. The Irving family dominated the New Brunswick economy, rapidly outpacing the Beaverbrook legacy. Ken Thompson was building a global media giant and the Southam family strengthened its own place in the newspaper game. The Argus Corporation used its brewing profits to build a major holding company. Retailing remained almost exclusively in Canadian hands. The list goes on. To be sure, in the resource and manufacturing sector, the dominant players were American multinationals, but even here, more and more Canadian entrepreneurs were finding niches to supply, distribute, or even manufacture their own products. Licensing and franchising allowed Canadian businesspeople to benefit from widely recognized brand names but to retain control over production and distribution.

The problem of over-reliance on foreign investment had already disappeared at the time that worries began in earnest and was of little consequence when action finally began to be taken. As Michael Bliss points out in his history of Canadian business: "High levels of foreign ownership had been a fact of Canadian economic life since French and English traders first arrived to take over from the aboriginal peoples ... The economic nationalism of the 1960s reflected a revolution of rising expectations rather than a rational response to a worsening problem. The alarm about foreign ownership was not a function of its seriousness as a national problem. That seriousness was decreasing ... Fear of foreign ownership was a perverse expression of Canadians' sense of power in the 1960s."[82]

For the Canadian business community by the end of the 1960s, the issue was not foreign ownership but whether the business sector could continue to grow and expand on the basis of the Canadian market alone. The resource sector had long ago determined that its prosperity was critically tied to access to foreign markets. For most resource firms, only a small proportion of production was destined for final consumption in Canada. More critical for them was the extent to which they processed their products in Canada before export. In the first half of the century, much of their production had been exported at very low stages of production. In the 1950s and 1960s, they wanted to turn pulpwood into more than newsprint and to manufacture kraft paper, paper board, and even fine papers. They were prepared to smelt copper and iron ore in Canada and turn it into wire, cable, bars, and pipes. To do that, Canada would have to make more progress in reducing the carefully calibrated protection of Europe, the United States, and Japan. Much progress had been made in the Kennedy Round. More was required before Canadian-based firms dared to make investments in world-scale facilities to upgrade Canadian resources.

The manufacturing sector similarly was becoming more conscious of the limits imposed by the small Canadian market. Technological improvements in production methods were pointing to the growing need to achieve economies of scale. The productivity gap between Canada and the United States, despite the growth in the Canadian economy, continued to hover around 25 to 30 percent. Only access to a larger market could provide the basis for reducing this gap. Improvements in transportation and other distribution technologies were making the limits imposed by geography less and less critical. Willingness to invest in plants to serve larger markets, however, was critically dependent on the terms of access to larger markets. Again, the Kennedy Round had made a start, but there was still a long way to go.

With the establishment of the Department of Industry in 1963, the government signalled a new willingness to guide and influence investment in Canada. Before 1963, the main focus of industrial expertise, and thus of industrial policy, had resided in the Department of Finance through the deployment of the tariff and related programs. Additionally, the Department of Trade and Commerce, through its marketing efforts, had developed its own knowledge of the supply capabilities of the Canadian economy. Finally, the Department of Defence Production worked closely with the defence sector and administered the various defence procurement programs, including the DPSA.

The new Department of Industry set out to find ways and means to strengthen the manufacturing sector in Canada. It worked closely with industry and with other government departments to determine what programs were required to encourage investment in manufacturing and further processing in Canada. Through its regional development programs, it was also mandated to spread the benefits of industrialization to the peripheral regions of Canada. A new era of government involvement in economic development was thus ushered in. Canada had done well in the postwar years, but the government now suggested it could do better, and the key to doing better lay in more government involvement.

Pearson appointed Bud Drury as his first minister of industry and Dave Golden, formerly with the Department of Defence Production, as his deputy, soon to be succeeded on his early retirement by Simon Reisman. Under Reisman, the new department grew rapidly and became a significant player in bureaucratic policy making. Tom Kent, who during his career in Ottawa had a number of run-ins with Reisman, notes that Pearson considered Reisman "the most dedicated and aggressive empire-builder of all the bureaucrats of the time."[83]

Developments on the Agricultural Front

Canadian agriculture fared less well in the quarter-century after the end of the Second World War. The Prairie wheat economy enjoyed record crops for much of the period, but these record crops did not translate into higher incomes. The glut in world grain markets continued to depress prices. Not until the huge sales to China and Russia in the 1960s did Prairie wheat farmers finally reap rewards. The pressure to sell their wheat, however, continued to be one to which the government had to respond. Having taken over the marketing of wheat with the establishment of the Wheat Board and its conversion into a monopoly, the government had set up an expectation that it could not always meet.

The rest of the agricultural sector had its own problems. The Ontario and Quebec dairy and the BC, Nova Scotia, and Ontario horticulture sectors had grown on the basis of exports to Britain. As the British market gradually waned, they found it increasingly difficult to find new markets and looked to government to preserve at least the domestic market. The Agricultural Stabilization Act of 1958 set an important new precedent about the role governments were prepared to play. From then on, both the federal and provincial governments became involved in guaranteeing farm income by supporting prices equivalent to average prices in previous years. While not as distortive as the more politically determined price support systems that had been introduced in Europe and the United States, the guarantees did reduce the role of markets in determining what a farmer would plant and what price

Merle Tingley, "OK Dammit, but Let's not Rush It," 15 May 1964. Secretary of State for External Affairs Paul Martin appears in no hurry to recognize China, despite the continuing allure of a hungry population and the prospect of further wheat sales.

he would realize. Rising expectations throughout the 1960s increased pressure on governments to find new and better ways to ensure that the farm sector would share in Canada's new prosperity.

The Clash of Ideals

Canada's new prosperity was not universally hailed. On university campuses and in other conclaves of the elites, there was much hand wringing about the basis of Canada's wealth and the policies the government had pursued. Critics had looked to Walter Gordon to turn things around, but little had happened. Gordon had worked hard to effect a revolution in Canada's approach to economic policy in general and to relations with the United States in particular. He had had some success, but his more senior colleagues in cabinet did not support him on the main thrust of his policy preferences and found him an increasingly irksome associate. Not only was he unwilling to work with his cabinet colleagues and with officials in trying to find the best way to pursue his priorities and preferences, but too often he went over their heads to the prime minister or went public in an effort to drum up support.

His cabinet critics were prepared to acknowledge that Gordon had played a large and constructive role in the revival of Liberal fortunes, but he was also a pain in the neck. Many were not sorry to see him go after the debacle of the 1965 election. His second stint in cabinet in 1967, first as a minister without portfolio and then as president of the Privy Council, proved even more troublesome. During his absence, he had written another book, *A Choice for Canada: Independence or Colonial Status,* and had extensively promoted its ideas during a cross-country speaking tour.[84] His return to cabinet naturally raised questions – in his mind, in those of his colleagues, and in those of the public – as to whether the government was now ready to embrace his program. It turned out that the answer would be as imprecise as it had been earlier, leaving everyone frustrated. Without a portfolio to keep him busy, he exercised a licence to meddle in the affairs of other ministers, not always with happy results in terms of either policy or politics.[85]

The prime minister did follow through on one of his promises to Gordon and allowed the establishment of a task force under his direction charged with providing an analytical basis for Gordon's intuitive assessment that foreign investment, particularly American foreign direct investment, was bad for the Canadian economy. Gordon asked University of Toronto economist Mel Watkins to head up this inquiry, and together with a group of colleagues Watkins set out to gather the necessary information and prepare the required analysis. Drawing on a vein of analysis that was not unique to Canada – similar anxieties were being expressed by European and even American scholars who were consumed by a "storm over the multinationals"[86] – Watkins and his colleagues produced a report that "proved" all of Gordon's concerns and became the inspiration of a whole new literature in Canada.[87] Little came of the report's recommendations. It would take a further half dozen years before political pressure mounted sufficiently to require a mild policy response, one that would not satisfy Gordon and his supporters but that would alienate many members of Canada's business establishment and roil the waters of Canada-US relations for a decade thereafter.

With his second departure from cabinet on 10 March 1968, Gordon became an angry old man. By 1967, he had succeeded in building a sizable following, particularly on university campuses. Ironically, some of his most vocal supporters were disaffected American social scientists like Cy Gonick, editor of *Canadian Dimension,* one of the many earnest organs that popped up in the late 1960s and early 1970s to argue the case for an independent, socialist Canada. They kept the flame alive. Gordon was also willing to put his personal fortune at the disposal of the cause and helped to found the Committee for an Independent Canada (1970), the Canada Studies Foundation (1970), and the Canadian Institute for Economic Policy (1979), a think tank dedicated to providing an analytical basis for Gordon's policy intuitions. Thus over the next fifteen years Gordon was able to exert more influence on government policy than he had been able to do as a member of the government.

Richard Cooper, more than thirty years ago, noted the challenge to modern governments of sustaining a high level of prosperity based on international trade. International agreements, he wrote, "both enlarge and confine the freedom of countries to act according to their own lights ... The central problem of international economic co-operation ... is *how to keep the manifold benefits of extensive international economic intercourse free of crippling restrictions while at the same time preserving a maximum degree of freedom for each nation to pursue its legitimate economic objectives.*"[88]

That was the challenge to which Gordon had put his considerable energies and talents from the mid-1950s through the mid-1970s. In the end he did not succeed in convincing sufficient numbers in either the cabinet or the Liberal caucus to adopt the radical policies he thought necessary. His more cautious and pragmatic cabinet colleagues, particularly Mitchell Sharp, believed the problems Gordon had identified were not as severe nor the solutions as necessary as he claimed. They preferred a more incremental approach, one that included working with the government of the United States through a combination of international rule making and specific exemptions from some of the more difficult US policy choices. In this approach, they had the full support of the professionals in the public service. Gordon never learned the critical role the public service plays both in developing and implementing policy. Sharp, the former mandarin, did know and used this knowledge to his advantage.

On the trade policy front, the years from 1963 to 1968 had proven reasonably successful. Certainly they were more fruitful than the previous half decade. The Auto Pact provided the basis for the development of a large, productive secondary manufacturing sector in Ontario, demonstrating once again the critical role of foreign direct investment in Canada's economic prosperity. The Kennedy Round further consolidated and strengthened the world-class position of the resource sector in supplying forest and mining products to markets in the United States and, increasingly, Europe and Japan. Other manufacturing industries had seen some erosion in their protection, but not enough to induce those industries to look beyond the domestic market. With the exception of the grains sector, agriculture had not fared as well, and had become more and more dependent on the Canadian market. Trade relations with the United States had improved from the early 1960s, but there were storm clouds on the horizon. New opportunities in more distant markets were beginning to be realized even as the interdependence of the Canadian and US economies deepened.

On its trade policy record, the Pearson government should certainly get a passing grade. There were other areas of achievement, including the flag, social legislation, and more. But there had also been much bumbling. Pearson's style of government looked increasingly old-fashioned. In Canada's centennial year, he turned seventy. Canadians wanted someone younger and more energetic. They wanted to put the

Diefenbaker-Pearson decade behind them. Pearson agreed and resigned to make room for a new leader. Diefenbaker did not and had to be removed kicking and screaming. If nothing else, he would not be soon forgotten.

The leadership campaign to succeed Pearson cast the prime minister in a new light. Some thought he possessed special powers to have kept a cast of such disparate individuals together with at least a semblance of order. Only later would the memoirs begin to reveal the extent of the turmoil within his cabinet. Others found it hard to distinguish between the disintegration of the Diefenbaker cabinet during its final days and the disintegration evident in the Pearson cabinet at the end of its tenure.

Pearson's successor took the lesson well. Not for him the hurly-burly and broken field running of his predecessors at 24 Sussex Drive. What was needed was a firm hand at the tiller and a system to provide direction. Individualism would be replaced by logic, analysis, and collective decision making. Both senior officials and ministers would be tutored in concepts of accountability and responsibility. Equally, there would be little room for passion and nationalism. Ironically, however, Trudeau would preside over more nationalist experiments than were tried under either of his predecessors. Similarly, the professionals would find his systems approach even more trying than Diefenbaker's impulses and Pearson's bumbling. One thing remained constant and just as frustrating: other governments still controlled much of Canada's destiny, as Trudeau would find out soon and often. And like Diefenbaker and Pearson, there was little he could do about it, much as he might try.

10 REVIEWS AND OPTIONS
THE TRUDEAU YEARS

Freedom is the most important value of a just society, and the exercise of freedom its principal characteristic. Without these, a human being could not hope for true fulfillment – an individual in society could not realize his or her full potential. And deprived of its freedom, a people could not pursue its own destiny – the destiny that best suits its collective will to live.

– PIERRE ELLIOTT TRUDEAU, PRIME MINISTER, 1968–79, 1980–4

When Canadians went to the polls on 25 June 1968, they were still full of the self-confidence generated by Canada's centennial celebrations. The economy was equally buoyant. Since the 1961-2 recession, it had grown by 68 percent, fuelled by domestic demand, new investments, and export growth. Unemployment was down to 4 percent and inflation was equally low. Many also felt a smug sense of moral superiority, scornful of the sorry record of US political turmoil punctuated by political assassinations, race riots, campus upheavals and, most of all, the quagmire of the war in Vietnam. There had been spillovers of the US rebellion against the old order, but at a less menacing level. Canadians were equally prepared to bury the past and take a gamble on a more exciting future. The man who symbolized Canada's new cheekiness was Pierre Elliott Trudeau, and Canadians gave him an overwhelming mandate, handily defeating the Conservatives and their new leader, Robert Stanfield.

Little was known about Trudeau. First elected to office less than three years earlier, he had captured media attention in a gutsy performance at a federal-provincial gathering on the constitution as Pearson's newly appointed minister of justice. At the Liberal leadership conference in April 1968, he had successfully challenged a bevy of much better known and more experienced cabinet warhorses, skilfully alternating charm and contempt to put distance between himself and his colleagues. Once in office, he moved quickly to consolidate his power by proroguing Parliament and calling an election, not even allowing time for the traditional parliamentary tributes to his predecessor.

His pizzazz promised an end to the bumbling politics of the previous decade. Where Trudeau would take the country was less clear, but many felt it would involve a change for the better. In previous incarnations as a journalist and law professor, he had shown a capacity for rational analysis and biting criticism of the policies of both the Quebec and federal governments, but had provided few hints as to his own preferences and priorities. Neither the run for the Liberal leadership nor the subsequent electoral campaign clarified matters. Canadians liked his style and that was enough.

In the first few months after the campaign, Trudeau's approach to governance became clearer, at least to his cabinet colleagues and to the bureaucracy.[1] He was obviously of the view that Canada needed policies based less on political instincts and experience and more on systematic analysis and deliberation. He wanted ministers to decide jointly, to accept responsibility collectively, and to know and understand the policies they were choosing and why. He insisted that officials provide the ministry with carefully reasoned decision documents setting out the options and their pros and cons. His would be a government of first principles, rational policies, and collegial responsibility.[2]

In the first year, a range of policy issues were subjected to detailed examination, of which the reviews of defence and foreign policy garnered the most attention. Both went through countless drafts before finally hitting the desired note. Neither proved of lasting value. The foreign policy review in particular, issued in six trendy booklets, was quickly dismissed as a banal collection of platitudes that took needless pains to offend and offered little guidance for the future.[3] Trudeau's desire to increase Canada's policy autonomy and ground foreign policy more firmly in domestic interests denied thirty years of Canadian statecraft geared to finding ways to increase Canada's capacity to influence the policies of others.[4] Canadian officials had worked assiduously to develop international agreements and institutions to manage interdependence and give Canada a voice in shaping a world where it would otherwise be no more than a minor player. This very Canadian stance had had deep roots in Canadian interests but was more subtle than the new prime minister appeared to appreciate. Over time, he would gain a better understanding of the nuances of Canada's role in the world, but not before subjecting ministers, officials, and the country to a long and not always fruitful learning process.

Missing from the foreign policy review was any discussion of relations with the United States and consideration of the trade and economic dimension of Canada's foreign relations. The first lacuna was explained away as too important and pervasive a relationship to be encompassed within a single review; the second reflected a curiously narrow appreciation of Canadian interests in the world beyond its borders.[5] In the end, it did not matter. Like so much of the Trudeau era, the delivery never lived up to the promise. The next sixteen years would see many more brilliant initiatives. Few would ever translate into sustainable laws and policies, some due to lack of follow-through, many more due to the realities imposed upon a relatively small economy heavily dependent on relations with larger economies.[6]

There were good reasons why so much Canadian trade and economic policy had been improvisational rather than based on rational principles. Canadian policy makers of necessity had to find the narrow path between the constraints imposed by domestic politics and the limited opportunities offered in a world of larger powers responding to their own domestic constraints and imperatives. There were forces at work that suggested that nimble footwork would be even more essential in the 1970s than it had been in the 1950s and 1960s, including:

- serious problems in the IMF world of monetary rules, involving misaligned exchange rates and a burgeoning US balance-of-payments problem
- a rise in US protectionism, spurred by the Vietnam War, monetary problems, and related macroeconomic factors
- growth in regional trade agreements, particularly, but not exclusively, in western Europe
- the rise of Japan as a potent new economic force and competitor
- the emergence of developing countries as an insistent new voice in world economic affairs
- the concomitant emergence of the oil-exporting countries and their successful use of the Organization of Petroleum Exporting Countries (OPEC) to foment an energy crisis
- declining productivity growth within the industrialized economies, accompanied by rising unemployment and accelerating inflation
- growth in trade and monetary disputes that could not be resolved purely on diplomatic terms
- rising nationalist sentiments at home demanding greater Canadian control over the economy.

It took time before Trudeau and his ministers appreciated the challenges for Canada posed by these developments and the narrow scope for action available to Canadian governments. Even then, ministers periodically rebelled and struck out in directions that cost more than they gained or promised more than they could deliver. It would make the next sixteen years exciting, but would leave a legacy of even tougher times requiring tough policies.

Two events symbolized the foreign economic challenges with which Canadians had to come to grips in the early 1970s: one was the series of trade and monetary measures adopted by US president Richard Nixon in 1971 to address US balance-of-payments problems, the other was Britain's entry into the European Common Market in 1973. Both contributed to the development of a series of trade and foreign policy initiatives that would preoccupy Canadians for more than a decade, few of which proved of lasting worth. By the early 1980s, it was clear that the two constants that had emerged in the decade following the Second World War would continue to dominate Canadian trade policy choices: the relationship with the United States and the importance of the GATT-based trade relations system. Much energy would be expended on exploring alternatives to both but to little avail.

The search for counterweights to the United States also had an echo in a number of domestic policy initiatives. Witheringly dismissive of nationalism when it reared its head in the guise of Quebec separatism, Trudeau proved much more ambivalent about its economic manifestation. More interested in constitutional and legal issues, Trudeau was bored by the nuances of economic policy and was generally content to rely on his ministers and advisors to set the direction.[7] The result was a fecklessness in his government's approach to economic issues, including a willingness to entertain such nationalist experiments as the Foreign Investment Review Agency (FIRA), the National Energy Program (NEP), and the Canada Development Corporation (CDC). Each was conceived largely in response to domestic policy pressures, but each stirred up serious trade and foreign policy entanglements.

A Decade of Economic Turmoil

When Pierre Trudeau assumed office in April 1968, he inherited an economy at the top of the business cycle. The buoyant times evident during the Pearson years continued for nearly five more years, and then came to a crashing halt, ending a quarter-century of sustained expansion and ushering in a decade of uncertainty. Canada was not alone in experiencing economic turmoil (see table 10.1), suggesting that international forces played a large role. Domestic factors, however, were also important, including the impact of policy choices that tried to shield Canadians from international pressures and avoid desirable adjustments.

The unsettled global conditions had a significant impact on Canada's trade performance (see table 10.2), although rising inflation hid the full impact of the slowdown in the growth in Canada's merchandise exports and imports. The real value of exports declined in the period 1973-5, while imports stagnated. Over the next six years, recovery in both exports and imports remained at disappointing levels. Many Canadians fretted about Canada's declining share of world trade. More important, however, were growing signs that Canadian firms were not meeting

Table 10.1

Economic indicators, G7, average percentage change, 1973-80

	Canada	US	UK	FRG	France	Italy	Japan
Real GDP/GNE	3.3	2.8	1.7	2.7	3.2	3.3	4.4
Employment	3.1	2.2	0.2	−0.4	0.4	1.1	0.9
Unemployment rate	7.0	6.4	5.0	2.9	4.5	6.6	1.9
Productivity	0.2	0.6	1.5	3.1	2.7	2.2	3.4
Consumer prices	9.1	8.8	15.1	5.0	10.6	16.0	9.9
Capital formation	2.6	1.4	−0.5	1.3	0.7	−0.7	2.4

Source: Canada, Department of Finance, *The Current Economic Situation and Prospects for the Canadian Economy in the Short and Medium Term,* Budget Statement, November 1981.

Table 10.2

Growth rate in the value of Canadian merchandise trade, 1968-81
(average annual percentage changes in current and constant [1971] dollars)

	1968-73		1973-5		1975-81	
	Current	Constant	Current	Constant	Current	Constant
Exports						
Agricultural commodities	14.2	6.1	16.1	−6.0	14.6	7.5
Crude petroleum	27.1	20.1	43.5	−20.9	−3.2	−21.8
Other crude materials	10.6	8.9	2.4	−11.4	18.1	0.2
Fabricated materials	11.1	5.4	9.6	−10.5	20.7	7.8
End products	14.0	11.2	11.7	1.1	15.9	6.3
Motor vehicles and parts	14.5	13.7	9.0	2.4	12.6	3.6
Total	13.2	8.2	14.5	−5.6	16.6	5.8
Imports						
Agricultural commodities	15.4	6.6	18.9	3.3	11.6	2.9
Crude petroleum	20.4	12.5	87.1	−7.4	15.6	−6.7
Other crude materials	10.4	4.2	11.7	−14.9	22.6	12.8
Fabricated materials	12.0	9.2	17.8	−2.7	16.1	3.4
End products	14.2	11.7	18.2	4.2	14.4	3.1
Motor vehicles and parts	15.2	13.7	16.4	8.9	11.7	1.7
Total	13.5	10.0	22.0	2.0	14.7	3.2

Source: External Affairs Canada, *A Review of Canadian Trade Policy* (Ottawa: Supply and Services, 1983), tables 13 and 14.

global competition. Canada's macroeconomic policy stance for much of the period exacerbated rather than facilitated the adjustment challenge.[8]

From the late 1940s until the early 1970s, Canadian governments had pursued macroeconomic economic policy largely on the basis of countercyclical budgeting in an effort to stimulate economic growth and full employment while maintaining budgetary discipline. By the 1960s, however, governments began to believe that they could do more, and proponents of what became known as the Keynesian consensus decided that governments could also repair the economy's failings and redistribute income to create a more just society, regionally and individually.[9] To these ends, the Pearson government had pursued an activist social agenda, convinced that in a richer Canada, governments could do more to help poorer Canadians. The Trudeau government decided to go even further, trying to shape Canada's economic development along politically more acceptable lines.[10]

Trudeau's vision of a Just Society originally involved equal opportunity for every Canadian to succeed and excel, regardless of race, sex, ethnic origin, or similar factors.

Over the course of his four mandates, however, the goal increasingly became equal results, a much more expensive and intrusive proposition. Trudeau thus presided over a government often eager to expand the role of the state consistent with the expanding Keynesian vision. Some seven departments, fourteen ministries of state, and 114 new agencies, boards, and commissions were created during the Trudeau years to advance regional development, science and technology, urban affairs, the environment, international development, and more.[11] Throughout government, officials learned the rewards of policy and program activism.

The core of Keynesian demand management, countercyclical budgeting, involved a fairly straightforward, even mechanistic, application of fiscal policies on both the revenue and spending side. The second dimension, redistribution, could be expensive but if managed prudently held more attraction. The third, tackling market failures, opened a potential Pandora's box of social and economic experimentation that could easily bankrupt a government, particularly when coupled with the notorious difficulty of convincing politicians that they should retrench during boom years in order to allow room for expansion during bad years. Instead, the combined impact of all three dimensions, at both the federal and provincial levels, was steady growth in the size of the government sector, and rising inflation.[12]

Canada was not alone in heading down the primrose path of Keynesian optimism; virtually every OECD government thought it had found the magic formula for solving society's most basic social and economic ills, and continued to promise more and more government-centred solutions. Rising expectations added to governments' convictions that they should and could do more. Between 1948 and 1973, Canadians had enjoyed a quarter-century of unprecedented growth in their prospects, leading many of them to think that rising prosperity was their birthright. Ministers and some of their political and bureaucratic advisors agreed and were eager to oblige, leading to an unsustainable spiral of demands and promises.

Key players in the Trudeau government, such as economic advisor Joel Bell and staffers at the newly established Science Council,[13] worked assiduously to implement an industrial strategy. In their view, trade policy as an instrument of industrial policy had been eroded by the liberalization of tariff and other border measures. By the 1970s, in their view, traditional trade policy was failing to meet any useful goals. Instead, now that Canada was a richer country, Bell and others wanted to "mobilize large sums of money to influence the structure and performance of an industrial economy" and institute various interventionist programs to create more Canadian-owned champions.[14] Business columnist Andrew Coyne notes acerbically that "if the welfare state was largely the work of its predecessors, the Trudeau government gave us the pervasive state."[15]

As early as the late 1960s, some senior officials were beginning to worry about growing signs of runaway inflation and counselled the need to let the economy adjust. They saw the economic slowdown of 1969-70 as a healthy sign that should be allowed to follow its course. Pierre Trudeau and his ministers, however, insisted that the anticipated increase in unemployment would be unacceptable. They would not allow market signals to deter their dream of creating a Just Society, matching US president Lyndon Johnson's equally inflationary Great Society.

The federal government's efforts to apply Keynesian demand management was complicated by the federal structure of the government and large regional disparities. The smaller provinces did not command the same resources as the larger ones, which added to the conviction that the federal government should – and could – tackle both personal and regional disadvantage. Additionally, more than any other member of the OECD, Canada faced the fastest-growing labour force, spurred not only by the baby-boom bulge, but also by rising participation by women in the labour force and continuing high levels of immigration. Accommodating these additions added to inflationary pressures. Finally, there developed a high level of resistance on the part of both government and industry to the need to adapt and adjust to new economic forces, particularly in the weaker manufacturing sectors, adding to the attraction of the crank solutions offered by nationalists and interventionists.

In the United States, the 1971 Nixon trade and economic measures were among the first steps taken to address the complications created by rising inflation, an overvalued dollar, and a growing balance-of-payments problem (see below). The federal government, however, decided not to take any fiscal or monetary measures to address this first of a number of international shocks that would buffet the Canadian economy in the 1970s and further increase inflationary pressures. Instead, it preferred to rely on moral suasion and set up a Prices and Incomes Commission to convince Canadians to moderate their wage and price demands.

In 1972, not satisfied with the government's economic record, Canadians hesitated in their support for the Liberals and reduced them to a minority government. The Pearson experience had suggested that minority mandates tended to produce more attentive and democratically accountable governments. The Trudeau minority of 1972-4 taught Canadians that such governments could also be expensive. Dependent for support on the interventionist and nationalistic New Democratic Party, the government became even more inclined to spend and regulate to achieve its objectives and solve problems.

The OPEC-induced oil shock was next, as the Middle East oil producers succeeded in quadrupling the price of crude oil, adding further supply-side international inflationary pressures to go along with the already sharply rising prices of grains, fertilizers, and other basic commodities. Fears of scarcity – encouraged by groups like the Club of Rome and the emerging environmental movement – added to and prolonged this global spike in commodity prices. Canada, blessed with its own supply of Western oil, decided to shield Canadians from the direct impact of the oil shock by imposing a one-price policy, averaging out the controlled price of domestic oil with the high cost of imported oil required in Quebec and the Atlantic provinces. It also wound up the Prices and Incomes Commission and replaced it with a Food Prices Review Board with a mandate to monitor food prices, but without any greater impact than its predecessor.

Unfortunately, the commodity boom of the first half of the 1970s was followed by the commodity bust of the second half, sending the terms of trade of Canada's resource-based economy up and down like a yo-yo. Canada's customers, squeezed by the high prices of the first half of the cycle, had begun to find alternative sources and not all came back to Canadian suppliers, adding to Canada's trade woes. Throughout the decade, as Canada was continually buffeted by external forces, the question of whether to adjust was more ducked than faced, the government preferring made-in-Canada policies to adapting to external pressures.

Faced with the evils of both inflation and unemployment, the 1972-4 minority Liberal government targeted only unemployment in its stimulative budget of 1973-4, indexing tax brackets and lowering rates. As a result, Canada averted much of the impact of the global recession of 1974-5, opting instead for a larger dose of inflation and future problems. A nagging new problem also emerged: growing signs that productivity growth was slowing, a development shrouded by the large nominal increases in the economic numbers generated by galloping inflation.

In 1974, Canadians agreed to give Trudeau a new majority mandate, agreeing with him that the mandatory wage and price controls advocated by the Conservatives were undesirable. In the fall of 1975, however, Trudeau finally decided the time had come to fight inflation with his own version of wage and price controls. The program, administered by an Anti-Inflation Board, met with a moderate level of success, but also suggested that the real solution lay in macroeconomic discipline. The following year saw the government looking for middle ground, exercising some fiscal and monetary restraint and moderating its penchant for interventionism. In response, economic performance improved somewhat. In 1978, apparently having learned about the benefits of fiscal restraint from German chancellor Helmut Schmidt at the annual G7 Economic Summit, the prime minister came home to announce a cut of $2 billion in spending, even before discussing it with his minister of finance. In order to help bring the spiralling demands of spending portfolios under control, Trudeau and Privy Council clerk Michael Pitfield also hit upon the establishment of a Board – later Ministry – of Economic Development to help set government-wide priorities and trim the appetite of activist ministers and their officials.

Over the course of the 1970s, proponents of Keynesianism discovered more and more market failures requiring government action. Rather than being deterred by clear market signals of looming economic problems, Keynesians maintained that the boom of the postwar years was the direct product of demand management and that, with patience, their efforts would be rewarded. Those who held that the boom years had been grounded in the fiscal caution of the King and St. Laurent governments were dismissed, not always logically, as heartless, or were accused of trying to turn Canada into a miniature replica of the United States.

The results of this exuberant application of Keynesianism, however, were not encouraging. GDP growth fell from 7.7 percent in 1973, to 4.4 percent the following year, to 2.6 percent in 1975 and stayed in that range for the rest of the decade, only marginally above population growth. Unemployment steadily climbed from 5.3 percent in 1974 to 6.9 percent in 1975 and reached 11 percent in 1982, while inflation averaged over 10 percent from 1974 through 1982. Some of the inflation was the result of international forces; more was due to purely domestic factors, although other countries were experiencing similar problems as a result of similar policy choices. The value of exports declined in real terms, further depressing investment.

The profligacy of the 1970s also sent budgetary deficits spiralling out of control. Between 1968 and 1985, the federal government doubled its spending, in real dollars, on each citizen, reaching some $4,750 in current dollars in 1985. Concurrently, per capita tax revenues steadily declined, ensuring a growing deficit crunch. Andrew Coyne calculates that "net federal debt in fiscal 1968 ... was about $18 billion, or 26 percent of gross domestic product; by [Trudeau's] final year in office, it had ballooned to $206 billion – at 46 percent of GDP, nearly twice as large relative to the economy ... In 1984-85, total spending exceeded revenues by more than 50 percent. The deficit that year, at $38.5 billion, was nearly equal to 9 percent of GDP ... Every dollar of the $300 billion added to the debt during the Tory years was interest on the debt the Liberals had left behind."[16]

By the end of the 1970s, inflation appeared to be abating, only to be heated up again by the second oil shock in 1979; this led to more experiments with tax cuts, but without any clear indication of a government with a sure sense of direction or priorities. Canadians by this time had lost confidence in the Liberals, although they were not wholly prepared to put their full trust in the Conservatives and their new leader, Joe Clark. The result was the fifth minority government in twenty-two years, this time led by the Tories. It did not last long. By February 1980, Canadians opted once again for the Grits, handing Trudeau his fourth mandate.

Initially attracted to a full dose of activism, which included a National Energy Program (NEP), an effort to craft an industrial strategy, and two stimulative budgets, Trudeau and his ministers finally accepted defeat in the face of overwhelming international forces pointing in the opposite direction. The economic turmoil of the 1970s had fully discredited demand-side Keynesianism and stimulated a reaction from supply-side monetarists. In the United States, Paul Volcker, chairman of the Federal Reserve, confronted by President Ronald Reagan's stimulative combination of tax cuts and new military spending, decided the time had come to wring inflation out of the US economy, a view shared by most central bankers, including Canada's Gerald Bouey. US and other interest rates reached unprecedented levels, leading to a global recession. Canadians found themselves renewing mortgages at rates in the high teens, while short-term treasury bills peaked at 22.75 percent. Canada did not escape the recession this time. The Trudeau government abandoned wage and price controls, opting once again for moral suasion, urging large employers and provincial governments to adopt its "6 and 5" program of voluntary wage and price restraints, aimed at keeping wage and price increases to a maximum of 6 and 5 percent respectively.

Trade policy was not immune from the policy activism of the 1970s and early 1980s. A plethora of initiatives were pursued in an effort to change the direction and content of Canadian trade and investment flows. Alliances, agreements, and common cause were sought with a variety of nontraditional partners, all in an effort to diversify Canadian trade and industrial patterns, increase the range of the Canadian economy, and reduce dependence on US markets and capital. Few of them made much long-term policy sense and most tilted against the natural forces of geography, consumer preference, and business judgment. As we shall see in chapter 12, the structure of the Canadian economy was by this time experiencing fundamental changes, suggesting the need for wrenching adjustments. The scope for change, however, was again conditioned by the policy choices exercised by the Trudeau government in response to external forces, and nowhere more so than the forces emanating from south of the border.

No More Uncle Sugar

Throughout the Pearson years, ministers and officials had skilfully deployed their personal ties to senior officials in the Kennedy and Johnson administrations to solve problems in the Canada-US relationship. Although not always successful, they had succeeded often enough to give some support to the perception that Canada and the United States enjoyed a special relationship. By the end of the 1960s, however, the credibility of this claim was showing considerable strain. The culprit was the US Congress. Never as convinced of the importance of good foreign relations as administration officials, members of both the Senate and the House had shown increasing frustration with the course of US foreign trade and economic policy and had begun to lash out at the most visible targets.[17]

By the end of the 1960s, the US economy was beginning to face a serious balance-of-payments problem. The roots of that problem lay in macroeconomic issues and the role of the US dollar as the reserve currency in a system of interlocking fixed exchange rates.[18] As in Canada, a panoply of social and economic programs were placing increasing strains on the treasury. When coupled with the military expenses generated by the war in Vietnam, the result was an unsustainable level of inflationary pressures, increasingly evident in the US balance-of-payments position. Congress was not well placed to deal with these fundamental problems, but it could address symptoms.[19]

The clearest symptom was the erosion in the traditional US merchandise trade surplus due to an increase in imports of standard-technology products such as textiles, clothing, footwear, and household products, and eventually of more sophisticated products such as steel, machine tools, and automobiles. US firms, used to their competitive supremacy and comfortable in their still well-protected market, were not prepared to address increased international competition, and many decided that the solution lay in political activity rather than adjustment. The result was a further increase in protectionist pressures on government and a variety of political responses, including expansion of the textile restraint program and the first steel program involving voluntary export restraints (VERs) with Japan.[20]

Until the mid-1960s, merchandise trade constituted only a small fragment of US economic activity, with exports rarely exceeding 5 percent of US GDP and imports usually an even smaller fraction. Thereafter, with the impact of the Kennedy Round tariff cuts, European and Japanese economic recovery, and the increase in the number of developing countries, US imports began to rise, reaching about 8 percent of GDP by 1980 and 12 percent by 1990. An overvalued dollar ensured that US exports did not grow as rapidly. By the early 1970s, the historical US merchandise trade surplus had been replaced by what would become a chronic deficit. In response, Congress began to balk at administration initiatives and to show a keen preference for more "results-oriented" trade policies.

The Johnson administration had succeeded in bringing the GATT's Kennedy Round to a successful conclusion, in part because many in the administration were working to preserve President Kennedy's legacy and believed that they could overcome congressional opposition at the conclusion of the round. They were wrong. The tariff cuts negotiated during the round were implemented automatically, but Congress refused to amend US legislation to accord with the new Antidumping Code, to adopt the reductions in the chemicals tariff schedule, or to change the American-selling-price valuation provisions.[21] In 1968, President Johnson sought a new Trade Expansion Act involving approval of the nontariff provisions of the Kennedy Round negotiations and extending his negotiating authority to 1970. Congress not only rejected the president's initiative, but passed various sector-specific pieces of legislation at odds with US GATT obligations, including quotas on imports of low-cost textile products.[22]

The US congressional attitude was difficult for non-Americans to grasp. The US system of divided authority virtually guarantees that there will be tensions between Congress and the administration. Support for freer trade and for the GATT remained strong among American elites in the administration, the media, the universities, the think tanks, and even within some business and labour groups, but there was also evidence of equally strong interest in protectionist policies, attitudes that were often echoed in the Congress. For many American political and business leaders, free trade in theory might be regarded as part and parcel of the "American way," but free trade in practice often proved inconvenient and unpopular and needed to be addressed in ways that did not undermine US ideological commitment to it. Any increase in imports from the rest of the world, for example, had to be characterized as unfair and as taking advantage of US generosity.[23]

To add to the confusion, throughout this period Congress and the administration were engaged in an elaborate ritual setting out the limits of each other's roles in the making and implementation of US trade policy, a ritual largely for domestic consumption, but in which foreign interests were regularly called to account. The delicate balance between the president's delegated authority and Congress's continuing desire to maintain sufficient control to address its own political priorities made the shaping of Washington trade policy an exceedingly complex process. It was not always easy to divine the difference between genuine concerns and posturing, between long-term strategic objectives and short-term tactical manoeuvring, either in Congress or in the administration. The complex congressional system of committees and the exercise of congressional seniority added to the Byzantine nature of these gyrations and made it difficult for Canadian and other foreign governments to sense when and where to make representations in the US capital.[24]

The pressures generated by the war in Vietnam convinced Johnson not to stand for a second term. Vice-president Hubert Humphrey failed in his bid for the White House, and a Republican administration under Richard Nixon inherited the task of managing the legacy of Johnson's determination to fight both a war on poverty at home and a military campaign in Southeast Asia. With the Special Trade Representative (STR) now responsible for trade negotiations, secretaries of state William Rogers and Henry Kissinger needed to pay little attention to trade policy.[25] They could concentrate on peace, security, and other major geopolitical issues, including détente, the war in Vietnam, disarmament, the recognition of China, and peace in the Middle East. Trade was now out of the State Department's hands. This relative neglect of trade issues further encouraged protectionist sentiments, particularly since Nixon was disinclined to take the office of the STR seriously and staffed it with nonentities.[26]

In 1969, Nixon sought a modest trade negotiating authority and approval of the valuation and antidumping provisions of the Kennedy Round. The administration's draft bill also included a new program to stimulate exports and reverse the decline in the merchandise trade surplus: the Domestic International Sales Corporation (DISC). Congress had its own ideas. Many members, and their business supplicants, found quotas much more attractive, with Ways and Means Chairman Wilbur Mills himself introducing a bill for footwear quotas. State and STR officials vigorously opposed the quotas and other protectionist bills and supported Nixon's proposals, but senior officials from the Department of Commerce testified in favour of some of the quota provisions, reflecting their closer ties to US business interests.

The House Ways and Means Committee drafted a protectionist bill in 1970 – known as the Mills Bill – which wended its way through the House and the Senate Finance Committee but died, having largely served its purpose, in the Senate at the end of 1970. While it failed, it still sent a powerful message to the administration and to the rest of the world about the state of congressional thinking. The administration hemmed and hawed about the Mills Bill, but finally gave up trying to shape it into a useful policy instrument. Instead, Nixon appointed a blue-ribbon presidential commission chaired by industrialist Albert Williams (the Williams Commission), to provide a new political and intellectual basis for trade initiatives in the 1970s. Its 1971 report did make a major, if indirect, contribution to US policy.[27]

The year 1971 proved to be a watershed. The Bretton Woods monetary system collapsed when on 15 August President Nixon announced the end of the gold standard, imposed a 10 percent surcharge on all imports, introduced measures to tax overseas investment capital, and imposed wage and price controls.[28] As Nixon told his staff, "We have too long acted as Uncle Sugar and now we've got to be Uncle Sam."[29] The tough approach of Treasury Secretary John Connally and his officials added to US friction with its major trading partners, not to be resolved until Connally's departure and his replacement by the more diplomatic and cerebral George Shultz. Even Shultz, however, let it be known that the era of the United States as the world's Santa Claus was over. US officials used the Nixon measures skilfully over the next few years to effect the changes the United States wanted in international trade and monetary policy.[30]

The breakdown of the Bretton Woods monetary system illustrated the problem of finding an acceptable basis for coordinating monetary and macroeconomic policies among the increasingly interdependent major market economies. The Nixon measures helped to concentrate the minds of the European governments and eventually led to new monetary and macroeconomic management techniques. One of them was the convening of annual economic summits among the major economies, following the initial summit held in 1975 at the invitation of President Giscard d'Estaing of France. Summits promoted the conditions and discussions which ultimately paved the way for a new round of multilateral trade negotiations and a reduction in trade and monetary tensions.[31]

The era of clear US hegemony seemed to have come to an end. The United States remained the largest, most powerful, and most important economy, but US leadership was less easily accepted by its trading partners. It would have to work harder to earn it. Bullying others, however, remained an important characteristic of US policy making and made trade relations and trade negotiations much more difficult in the 1970s than they had been in the 1950s and 1960s. For Canada, it added an ominous dimension to a relationship that had become increasingly important, and to which there seemed few viable alternatives. Nevertheless, the search for counterforces would become a major dimension of Canadian policy, made more compelling as trade and economic relations with the United Kingdom became more and more marginal.[32]

The Canadian Reaction

For Canadian officials, the Nixon measures of August 1971 came as a blow, while the uncompromising stance of the president and Secretary Connally added to their anxieties. To them, the Nixon administration had effectively ended the special

Table 10.3

The direction of Canadian merchandise trade, 1971-81 (millions of dollars)

Year	US	Japan	UK	Other EEC	Rest of world
Exports					
1971	11,683	829	1,380	1,129	2,375
1973	16,671	1,807	1,588	1,552	3,203
1975	21,074	2,130	1,795	1,583	5,203
1977	30,319	2,513	1,929	2,727	6,018
1979	43,519	4,083	2,589	4,661	9,465
1981	53,667	4,487	3,321	5,379	14,040
Imports					
1971	10,951	803	837	984	2,043
1973	16,502	1,011	1,005	1,477	3,330
1975	23,641	1,205	1,222	2,074	6,573
1977	29,630	1,803	1,281	2,358	7,083
1979	45,571	2,159	1,928	3,691	9,521
1981	54,131	4,040	2,234	4,065	14,195

Source: F.H. Leacy, ed., *Historical Statistics of Canada,* 2nd ed. (Ottawa: Statistics Canada, 1983), series G57, G401-14, and G441; Statistics Canada, *Summary of Canadian International Trade* (Catalogue 65-001) for the period 1977-81.

relationship, a relationship based on a mutual understanding that broad geopolitical interests should, when necessary, overrule narrow commercial policy concerns. In response, Canada doggedly asserted its right to control its own destiny. Canadians had become increasingly alarmed about the extent of the US role in the Canadian economy, and the combined impact of the 1971 Nixon measures and the more strident defence of US commercial interests released the restraints on Canadian statecraft. The Canadian government now found the economy newly vulnerable to external forces and was unsure which course to take. Trade was becoming steadily more important to the Canadian economy, dominated by trade with the United States (see tables 10.3 and 10.4). Canada needed secure access to world markets to ensure that its economic development would continue. The means for accomplishing Canada's goals, however, were less certain at the beginning of the 1970s than they had been for a generation.[33]

In the opening years of Trudeau's first mandate, Canada-US relations had not drawn much attention. Indeed, officials on both sides agreed at the conclusion of the 1970 meeting of the Joint Ministerial Committee that there was no further need for these annual rituals.[34] Officials would deal with the usual myriad of issues and ministers would get involved if needed. Neither Trudeau nor Nixon – nor his national security advisor, Henry Kissinger – saw any need for them to get involved in

Table 10.4

Merchandise trade and the Canadian economy, 1971-80

Year	Domestic merchandise exports (current $ millions)	GNP at market prices (current $ millions)	Exports/ GNP (%)	Canadian share of world trade (%)	Volume index
1971	17,877	94,450	18.9	5.4	100.0
1972	20,129	105,234	19.1	5.4	109.4
1973	25,461	123,560	20.6	4.8	121.1
1974	32,591	147,528	22.1	4.4	116.5
1975	33,347	165,343	20.2	4.4	108.1
1976	37,576	191,031	19.7	4.4	121.0
1977	43,506	213,308	20.4	4.1	131.9
1978	51,681	235,654	21.9	3.9	145.0
1979	64,317	268,941	23.9	3.7	147.6
1980	74,259	302,064	24.6	3.4	145.7

Sources: F.H. Leacy, ed., *Historical Statistics of Canada,* 2nd ed. (Ottawa: Statistics Canada, 1983), series G57, and F75; IMF, *International Financial Statistics,* various years; Statistics Canada, *Summary of Canadian International Trade* (Catalogue 65-001); *National Income and Expenditure Accounts: Annual Estimates* (Catalogue 13-201-XPD); *Bank of Canada Review* (February 1984).

the micromanagement of the relationship. That is not to say that Trudeau was indifferent. During his first trip to Washington, he gave the national press a new but abiding cliché: "Living next to you is in some ways like sleeping with an elephant. No matter how friendly and even-tempered is the beast, one is affected by every twitch and grunt."[35] Cartoonists would add the mouse to complete one of the most enduring images of the bilateral relationship.

There were issues on the agenda, and not all of them provided a foretaste of things to come. In the innocent days before the OPEC-induced energy crisis, for example, it was Canadians who were interested in a continental energy pact as they looked for secure access for Canada's surplus oil, gas, electricity, and uranium. The Americans, on the other hand, were worried about national security and preferred to develop domestic supplies, even if they cost more, and found various ways to frustrate Canadian ambitions. There was also the usual range of problems on the agriculture and fisheries fronts. On the Canadian side of the ledger, rising nationalist sentiment, particularly regarding the high levels of American foreign direct investment and the dominance of US magazines, film, television, and other cultural products, was already causing concern in the US embassy in Ottawa. But these were the kinds of issues that Kissinger had characterized as "small problems" that could be left to the technicians.[36]

The Nixon measures, however, could hardly be dismissed as small. Even Kissinger learned from their aftermath "that the key economic policy decisions are not technical, but political."[37] In Canada, the potential for harm was perceived to be huge, and would have been even larger if officials had known that Secretary Connally had been prepared to sacrifice the Auto Pact. Only a last-minute intervention from the State Department had removed its cancellation from the list of measures to be taken to restore the US balance of payments.

Within days, Canadian officials had trooped to Washington to explain that Canada was not part of the problem and should be exempted from the measures. The United States had taken balance-of-payments measures in 1968 and had been prepared to exempt Canada. Connally rudely disabused them of any idea that history would be repeated. He considered Canada very much part of the problem. Imports from Canada represented a quarter of the US total, and new US investments in Canada, while perhaps less than those in Europe, also represented a sizable outflow. Over the next four months, tense discussions underlined that indeed there had been a major departure from previous bilateral relations. Early in December, the prime minister met with the president and sought assurances that "it is neither the intention or the desire of the United States that the economy of Canada become so dependent on the United States in terms of a deficit trading pattern that Canadians will inevitably lose independence of economic decision."[38] He received those assurances and when, two weeks later, having achieved its objectives on the monetary front, the United States lifted the surcharge, Trudeau looked like a hero.

A divide, however, had been crossed. Neither Canada nor the United States was prepared to return to the *status quo ante*. Indeed, President Nixon underlined this point in an address to Parliament the following April:

> It is time for us to recognize that we have very separate identities; that we have significant differences; and that nobody's interests are furthered when these realities are obscured ... Mature partners must have autonomous independent policies; each nation must define the nature of its own interests; each nation must decide the requirements of its own security; each nation must determine the path of its own progress ... No self-respecting nation can or should accept the proposition that it should always be economically dependent on any other nation. Let us recognize once and for all that the only basis for a sound and healthy relationship between our two proud peoples is to find a pattern of economic interaction which is beneficial to both our countries and which respects Canada's right to chart its own economic course.[39]

Canadian nationalists could not have put it more clearly. This was a path they were eager to trot and they now found a government more willing to oblige. Based on ideas formed during the August crisis, Secretary of State for External Affairs Mitchell Sharp had been working with his officials to craft a policy that would clearly set out Canada's own priorities and "determine the path of its own progress." In the fall of

Duncan Macpherson, "But Of Course – Trade Relations in America are Most Amicable," 1975. Prime Minister Trudeau assures Japan's prime minister that North American trade relations are "most amicable" as he pursues the Third Option.

1972, in a special issue of his department's house organ, *International Perspectives,* Sharp set out three options for the future conduct of Canada-US relations:

- Canada can seek to maintain more or less its present relationship with the United States with a minimum of policy adjustments;
- Canada can move deliberately toward closer integration with the United States; or
- Canada can pursue a comprehensive long-term strategy to develop and strengthen the Canadian economy and other aspects of its national life and in the process to reduce the present Canadian vulnerability.[40]

It did not take a genius to figure out Sharp's preferred course. For the next decade, Canada would pursue the third option. The clear purpose lacking in the 1968 foreign policy review had been found, as had the missing discussion on Canada-US relations.

The new strategy was pursued on two fronts: internationally, Canada took deliberate steps to strengthen ties and enhance trade and investment opportunities with other trading partners; domestically, Canada pursued policies of self-reliance, aimed at making Canada less dependent on foreign capital, more capable of supplying its own needs, and giving it a stronger sense of self. As luck would have it for those committed to the establishment of a more "independent" Canada, such as the Committee for an Independent Canada formed by three icons of Canadian economic nationalism, Walter Gordon, Peter Newman, and Abraham Rotstein, the 1972 election forced Trudeau to tilt even further in their direction.[41] Devastated by his electoral losses, Trudeau learned that in politics it is often better to be popular than wise. Beholden to the NDP, which now held the balance of power and itself was being pulled leftward by the Waffle faction, Trudeau and his ministers proved quick studies in one of the most ancient and sacred of Liberal rituals: co-opting the views and policies of their most threatening rivals.[42] By 1974, the NDP cupboard had been stripped bare of anything that could be converted into Liberal strategies. In the June election, Trudeau regained the majority he craved.

As a technique for managing trade relations with the United States, the Third Option proved less than helpful. Indeed, some officials blithely ignored it. Finance Deputy Simon Reisman dismissed it as "theatrical, mystical, idealistic ... You know, we're a North American country."[43] But then, as Robert Bothwell observes, "Trudeau was never very much at home with Americans, and never entirely came to grips with the significance of the United States in Canadian life."[44] Because trade with the United States continued to expand, issues and irritants in the relationship also increased. US officials could appreciate Canadian anxieties about overdependence on the US market, but they did not appreciate some of the consequent policy measures, whether in the realm of investment (the Foreign Investment Review Agency), energy (differential pricing and export controls), or culture (various measures to increase Canadian content in publishing and broadcasting). All were considered confiscatory and discriminatory. The net result was a deterioration in Canada-US relations. The Trudeau years not only saw an end to the special relationship of the 1950s and 1960s, but also witnessed the growing perception in Washington that Canada was becoming a "problem" country. Sharp came to have his own regrets, remembering that "the Third Option came to be invoked enthusiastically by the government and by others to support policies that were far more nationalistic than my paper had proposed, a consequence that I deplored."[45]

In the embattled climate of the mid-1970s, the US government rediscovered its trade remedy legislation. US antidumping and countervailing duty regulations, as well as section 337 procedures to address unfair methods of competition (usually limited to patent infringement cases), had been around for many years, but the number of cases per year was small and the number of positive findings even smaller. In the early 1970s, however, as import pressure mounted, US firms pressed their claims more insistently, and US agencies became more willing to make positive findings, including against Canadian products.[46]

US antidumping and countervailing duty procedures, however, were not wholly consistent with US GATT obligations, and section 337 was considered at odds with the GATT's national treatment requirements. With the failure of the Congress to adopt the amendments mandated by the Kennedy Round Antidumping Code, US antidumping procedures were also somewhat out of line with practice in Canada, the European Community, and Australia, the other major users of antidumping procedures. Quarterly meetings of the GATT's Committee on Antidumping Practices, which at this time was still able to consider individual cases, provided regular opportunities to remind US officials of their failure to conform.

US countervailing duty (CVD) procedures were even more controversial. The United States was the only country that made use of countervailing duties. Canada, for example, did not arm itself with this weapon until 1977 and did not adopt the necessary regulations to implement the provision until 1981. Up until 1972, the United States had used CVDs sparingly and limited them to cases of export subsidies on imports subject to duty upon entry into the United States. In that year, however, the Treasury Department accepted a complaint about regional development incentives enticing the Michelin Tire Corporation to locate a plant near Halifax, Nova Scotia, and found the assistance to be countervailable. With this case, the United States opened a new chapter in trade relations, declaring that it was prepared to offset unilaterally the effects of a potentially wide range of foreign government programs by subjecting products exported to the United States that benefited from such programs to CVD procedures. Even more provocatively, the United States had yet to introduce an injury test into its CVD proceedings, as required by GATT article VI, claiming the protection of GATT's 1947 Protocol of Provisional Application. To prove that the Michelin case was not an isolated example, the next few years saw industry after industry bring cases that tested the ambit of the now much more interesting CVD statute, including cases involving Canadian exports of groundfish, glass beads, and optic liquid level sensors.[47]

The era of the special relationship was clearly over. As an alternative for managing relations with the United States, however, the GATT did not seem to appeal to Canadian officials. They had always seen the GATT as an instrument for negotiating improved access to the US market, not as a tool for pursuing Canadian rights and enforcing US obligations. To many officials, such an approach risked more than it would gain. During the GATT's first twenty-five years, Canada had not once used its consultation and dispute settlement provisions to address an issue with the United States. Exemptionalism had proved a much more effective tool of Canadian tradecraft. Even as the temperature rose in the early 1970s and the United States began to flex its muscles through the use of CVD and section 301 procedures, Canadian officials continued to counsel caution to their political masters. Congress was in an ugly mood; the administration was not much better disposed; this was no time to try out an instrument that the one disdained and the other regarded with some suspicion.

On a more positive note, President Ford and his secretary of state, Henry Kissinger, while unable to stem the tide of congressionally mandated actions, could inject a more civil tone into relations. More importantly, they recognized in the prime minister and his senior ministers experienced officials who could be helpful in difficult multilateral discussions with the Europeans, Japanese, and other players. French president Giscard d'Estaing had deliberately excluded Canada from the 1975 Economic Summit at Rambouillet, concerned that the presence of a second-tier nation like Canada would diminish France's great power pretensions. Ford and Kissinger had no such worries and welcomed Canada to the next meeting in San Juan, Puerto Rico. The Summit Five became the Summit Seven with the balancing addition of Italy, and thus it remained through 1999, after which the addition of Russia made it eight.[48]

In President Jimmy Carter, elected in 1976, Trudeau found for the first time a US statesman who was both bright and personable, a man as much a master of his own brief as was Trudeau. Even more gratifying, Carter exhibited humanitarian instincts similar to those of the prime minister, as did some of his leading cabinet officers. Relations between the two governments, therefore, reached a more cordial level. Multilaterally, Canadians found US officials closer to them on a range of issues than they had been for more than a decade. Bilaterally, there were efforts to resolve various issues from fishing and boundary waters to uranium sales and gas pipelines. Unfortunately, for all Carter's intellect, his mastery of Washington politics was disappointing. Some of his cabinet colleagues, such as Special Trade Representative Bob Strauss, proved to be among the best, while others like Secretary of State Cyrus Vance were more urbane than effective. Vice-president Walter Mondale from Minnesota turned out to be Canada's strongest asset in Washington, determined to keep relations with Canada on an even keel. Trudeau and his ministers, for their part, while not backing away from the nationalist experiments of 1972-4, did not add to them, thus assuring a relatively tranquil period in Canada-US relations. From a trade perspective, the main focus during this period was the conclusion of the Tokyo Round of GATT negotiations in Geneva, discussed in chapter 11.

Contractual Links and Other Counterweights

The Canadian government's reaction to the provocation posed by the 1971 Nixon measures was in part conditioned by the conclusion to the long-running drama of Britain's entry into the European Community (EC).[49] For the members of the EC, the Kennedy Round had demonstrated that they could act together and pursue a common commercial policy. The end of the Kennedy Round had coincided with the final implementation of the Treaty of Rome and the full establishment of the Common External Tariff and the Common Agricultural Policy. The Kennedy Round had also confirmed for the United Kingdom that its future lay with the EC. For the next six years, UK governments concentrated on achieving EC membership and, once French president Charles de Gaulle had left office, EC negotiators were able to respond positively. For the EC, therefore, the years immediately after the Kennedy Round were consumed with efforts to enlarge the Community and to reach accommodation with the members of the European Free Trade Association (EFTA).[50]

Britain, accompanied by Ireland and Denmark, finally joined the Community on 1 January 1973, and the EC and the remaining EFTA members – Norway, Sweden, Finland, Austria, Switzerland, Portugal, and Iceland – concluded bilateral industrial free-trade agreements (FTAs) with the EC.[51] The United Kingdom's problem of commercial relations with its former colonies was solved in 1975 through revisions in the EC's aid and trade pact – renamed the Lomé Convention – involving most of the newly independent countries of Africa, the Caribbean, and the Pacific. These further steps consolidating regional integration in Europe posed new challenges to Canada and the United States. Liberal opinion in the two countries had envisioned a transatlantic agreement as part of an ongoing program of liberalization following the Kennedy Round. There were many enthusiasts in the universities and think tanks who had begun to contemplate an Atlantic Free Trade Area involving Canada, the United States, and the United Kingdom. Such an agreement within the English-speaking world would create a counterweight to the EC and provide a forum for eventual, deeper commitments. British entry into the EC brought this romantic notion to a conclusive end.[52]

European recovery and renewed self-confidence created new tensions in relations with the United States. The misalignment of exchange rates that had become increasingly evident in the 1960s also made it possible for US-based firms to make major investment inroads in Europe, using the high value of the dollar to buy European assets at bargain prices.[53] At the same time that the high dollar made European exports to the United States competitive, it made US exports to Europe expensive, adding to the looming monetary crisis. US efforts in the late 1960s and early 1970s to solve the monetary problem through protective actions to slow down imports met a hostile reception and increased tension around the Atlantic. Proposals for a new round of negotiations to improve access to European markets and thus increase US exports fell on equally deaf ears.[54]

For Canada, the 1960s had seen a further deterioration in its trade with the United Kingdom, while trade with the members of the EEC had become more interesting. Two-way trade with Britain and the six members of the EEC stood at $1,291 million and $657 million respectively in 1958, the year the EEC entered into force. By 1973, UK trade had only grown to $2,593 million while trade with the Six had reached $3,029 million in current dollars, with Canada enjoying a healthy surplus, always an attractive feature for mercantilist-minded ministers and their senior officials. Over the same period, Canadian merchandise trade as a whole had grown five-fold from $9.8 billion to $48.8 billion. The expanded EC thus commanded about 12 percent of Canadian two-way trade. Obviously, while the loss of preferences in the UK market would have an impact, the more important lesson to be drawn was that there was more potential on the Continent, a potential that might be advanced more effectively with the United Kingdom as an EC member.

Even more interesting had been the growth in trade with Japan. By the early 1970s, Japan had emerged as a major competitor for European and US firms, but also as an attractive market for Canadian resources. For US and European firms, competing head-on with Japanese firms at home and abroad proved a major challenge, particularly since Japan appeared to be successful at limiting imports to those products it wanted – raw materials and foodstuffs – while keeping foreign manufactured goods off its shelves through the use of nontransparent administrative guidance and similar measures.[55] Canada's leading firms, on the other hand, focused on the industrial raw materials and foodstuffs Japan lacked, found a much more hospitable climate, while large Japanese trading corporations, such as Mitsubishi and Mitsui, actively courted Canadian firms in an effort to cement relations with reliable sources of the most important industrial raw materials.

Between 1958 and 1973, two-way trade mushroomed from $75 million to $2,818 million, with Canada enjoying an almost two-to-one advantage. The major inroads by Japanese automotive, machinery, and electronic firms into Canadian markets were still in the future, while Japan's disruptive exports of low-cost textiles and clothing appeared to be moderating. On balance, therefore, Japan seemed to offer great potential as a trading partner.

A number of other East Asian economies, particularly Taiwan, Hong Kong, Korea, and Singapore, were successfully emulating the Japanese model of export-led growth, adding to import pressures in vulnerable, labour-intensive, standard-technology sectors.[56] Both the United States and the EC countered by adopting a range of measures that did not fit well into the GATT system of nondiscrimination. Tariffs were ineffective against the rising tide of low-cost products; only quantitative restrictions were a reliable stopgap, whether legal or not, which injected a corrosive new dimension into attitudes toward the GATT rules.[57] Again, as an exporter of food and raw materials, Canada enjoyed more balanced trade relations with these countries. The disruption caused by low-cost imports was also less of a problem in Canada, in part because Canadian tariffs were higher than equivalent US and EC tariffs, and Canada's valuation system – still not brought into conformity with GATT requirements – provided Canadian manufacturers with an extra measure of protection. It would not be long, however, before Canada would find many imports from these countries a mixed blessing.

Thus, as the temperature in Canada-US relations remained on the boil after the Nixon shock, the government looked to establish new external counterweights. The first step was to use its old ties with the United Kingdom as a springboard to a "contractual link" with Europe. From Canada's perspective, a Canada-EC agreement could provide a basis for influencing policies in Europe and improving access for Canadian goods. It would also remind Europeans that Canadian interests were distinct and separate from American interests. Finally, Canada hoped to attract European investment partners, diversify Canadian trade and investment patterns, and reduce Canada's vulnerability to US unilateralism. As the prime minister told a London audience, "I am in Europe to meet with heads of government of member states of the European Economic Community. I have conveyed to each of them, as

I did to the European Commission in Brussels, the desire of Canada to enter into a contractual relationship with the Community – one that would ensure that both the Community and Canada would keep the other informed, would engage regularly and effectively in consultations, would not consciously act to injure the other, would seek to cooperate in trading and any other initiatives in which the Community might engage."[58]

The Europeans were initially puzzled by the Canadian request. Under the terms of the GATT, Canada already enjoyed most-favoured-nation relations with all the EC member states. Early in the discussions, both sides also established that neither was interested in a preferential trade agreement. Dispatches from the front suggested that most Canadian journalists were equally puzzled.[59] It took Canada nearly four years of lengthy discussion and frequent visits by ministers and even by the prime minister to gradually explain its objective. In the end, the Europeans accepted that what Canada wanted was more symbolic than real and agreed in the summer of 1976 to an anodyne Framework Agreement on Commercial and Economic Cooperation. It set out in very general terms commitments to consult and establish a range of working groups to examine the scope for investment, industrial, and other cooperative ventures.[60]

European puzzlement was in part conditioned by the prime minister's earlier indifference. After all, one of his first impulses had been to pull Canadian troops out of NATO and otherwise downplay the need for close political and security relations on the Continent. During his first two governments, the Continent was not sufficiently important to warrant an official prime ministerial visit. On the trade front, EC officials had still not fully recovered from their view that they had been euchred by Canada during the Kennedy Round, and that Canada had been excessively demanding in settling its compensation claims arising from British entry into the EC. Even after the conclusion of the contractual link, Europeans remained sceptical, particularly when they could not convince the Canadian government to source some of its defence needs from European suppliers or to pressure Air Canada into buying Airbus jets.

On the Canadian side, officials in the Department of External Affairs waxed eloquent about a new era in Canada-Europe relations and the opportunities the contractual link would create. They could justifiably take pride in the fact that their tenacity and skill had brought Canada a link no other country shared. In that, they had the support of some officials in Industry, Trade and Commerce and elsewhere who considered the agreement a useful technique for managing economic relations with the EC, giving them an opportunity to review – and perhaps resolve – a growing list of irritants on a regular basis. But by the 1980s, trade officials had become more reserved in their assessment. They found the agreement at best a sideshow, rarely capable of resolving issues and confirming their view that the diplomats in the Pearson Building were more concerned with form than substance.

Canadian and European business leaders were even more reserved. A spokesman for the Canadian Manufacturers' Association called it "a bland bucket of fog."[61] But without active business support and participation, many of the goals of the agreement stood little chance of success. Missions were mounted and discussions joined, but both sides quickly learned that the policies and programs on both sides of the Atlantic that stood in the way of greater economic interaction were in no way affected by the Framework Agreement. The Common Agriculture Policy, tariff escalation, product standards, and similar barriers hampered Canadian export interests, while FIRA, interprovincial barriers, government procurement preferences, and similar policies continued to bother the Europeans. Not surprisingly, concrete results were minimal.[62]

In an effort to provide geographic balance, the government initiated a similar exercise with Japan. The 1976 Canada-Japan Framework for Economic Cooperation sought to broaden and deepen commercial relations. Concurrently, the two business communities set up the Canada-Japan Business Committee (CJBC).[63] Like the Europeans, the Japanese agreed to annual consultations and more business missions to raise the profile of each other's business sectors, but again to little long-term avail. Both governments operated on the assumption that trade between the two countries should be complementary rather than competitive, and neither took any steps to encourage the development of intra-industry trade. Japan continued to buy Canadian resources and to invest in further resource development, but stubbornly maintained tariff and other measures that ensured that Canada would sell its resources at low stages of processing. Canadian suppliers of intermediate and finished goods continued to find the Japanese market tough to penetrate. Canada, for its part, relaxed restraints on imports of Japanese consumer goods, but these were already being replaced by more competitive products from lower-cost suppliers.[64]

While a small coterie of officials continued to keep these expressions of the Third Option alive at External Affairs, both proved illusory instruments for diversifying Canada's trade relations. Historian Robert Bothwell predicted in 1976 that "the third option, so sensible, so necessary, so obvious, is an attempt to secure the triumph of politics over geography ... The contractual link with Europe, when concluded, will turn out to be a modest achievement."[65] It did not take long for events to prove him right. Trade with Europe and Japan as a share of total Canadian trade had already reached its peak in the early 1970s. In 1973, the EC and Japan took 12.3 and 7.1 percent respectively of Canada's merchandise exports; in 1981, their shares were down to 10.8 and 5.5 percent. The United States' place in Canadian trade continued to expand and Sharp's first option remained the basis for Canada-US relations. More ominously, from the perspective of Sharp and others, by the early 1980s there was even serious talk of pursuing the second option as the process of silent integration continued to draw the Canadian and US economies closer together (see chapter 12).

The Conundrum of Developing Countries

The arrival of the East Asian economies as forces to be reckoned with in international commerce drew further attention to the problem of the role of developing countries in the trading system. GATT's 1958 Haberler Report had noted the necessity of paying attention to their needs, but little had been done other than the adoption of the largely hortatory provisions of Part IV of the GATT in 1964. During the Kennedy Round, promises that their demands would be accommodated had featured prominently at the beginning, but had been largely ignored in the closing stages. By the early 1970s, developing country members clearly outnumbered industrialized countries in the GATT, but the GATT remained focused on the issues of greatest concern to its leading members.[66]

The developing country case received a major and unexpected boost in 1973 when a group of developing countries in the Middle East, most of whom had never been active in international affairs, were not parties to the GATT, and had not even been major players in UNCTAD and UN affairs, seized the moment of the Yom Kippur War to insist on greater rents from their only economic asset, crude oil. Through concerted action by the Organization of Petroleum Exporting Countries (OPEC), they succeeded in quadrupling the export price of crude oil.[67] The following year, general turmoil in world commodity markets convinced developing countries that they finally had a chip to play in demanding changes in the way the world economy worked. They wanted greater say and more direct benefits. For the next decade they pushed their agenda in every possible international economic forum. While ultimately unsuccessful, their campaign added to the unsettled global trade and economic conditions that dominated the 1970s.

Canadian ministers and officials were not always sure how best to address the issues raised by developing countries. Humanitarian considerations inclined them to take a sympathetic stance and pursue a generous aid strategy. Long-established Commonwealth ties disposed Canada to be particularly keen on discussions in that forum and to respond to the hopes and aspirations of the newly independent countries in Africa and the Caribbean. Canadian experience as an exporter of resource products facing barriers to exports of further processed products to the markets of the United States, Europe, and Japan further tilted Canadian sympathies.[68] More sober trade and economic considerations, however, led to sceptical assessments of some of the dubious claims advanced by the more militant members of the newly formed Group of 77.[69]

In these conflicting circumstances the government – or, more accurately, the prime minister – sought to become a player in North-South discussions. Trudeau and some of his closest advisors, particularly Ivan Head, his foreign policy guru, were convinced that Canada had a lot in common with developing countries and could make common cause with them on a range of economic issues.[70] It took a while for all members of the government to become attuned to this new direction in Canadian foreign policy. In 1966, for example, Mitchell Sharp as finance minister was "inclined to doubt that new preferential tariff systems would be of much assistance to developing countries ... The real difficulty facing most of the developing countries is that their industries, by and large, are simply not efficient enough."[71] Six years later, however, Canada followed the lead of others and introduced its own scheme of tariff preferences for developing countries, albeit one carefully calibrated to avoid encouraging a flood of inconvenient low-cost imports of textiles, clothing, and footwear.

On the pure aid front, Canada had initially been a major instigator of the Commonwealth's Colombo Plan aid and had continued to focus its effort on Commonwealth countries. Gradually, however, Canadian aid lagged behind others. In 1960, Canada contributed only 0.19 percent of its GDP to aid, one of the lowest among the OECD donor countries. In 1968, Trudeau determined that his government would do better and also make the aid more effective. To that end, he converted the External Aid Office into the Canadian International Development Agency (CIDA) with a broad mandate to raise Canada's profile in developing countries through a more aggressive Canadian presence. His motives were a combination of both altruism and enlightened self-interest. As he told an Edmonton audience that year, "We must recognize that, in the long run, the overwhelming threat to Canada ... will come from the two-thirds of the peoples of the world who are steadily falling farther and farther behind in their search for a decent standard of living."[72] By 1975, Canadian aid had reached 0.54 percent of GDP and Canada was in the forefront of those espousing the UN standard of 0.7 percent. More difficult was the challenge of dealing with the deep-seated structural problems faced by developing countries and the role of international rules and institutions in addressing these problems, particularly in light of the radically different perceptions of these problems and solutions in the North and in the South.

The developing countries had since 1964 focused on the UN Conference on Trade and Development (UNCTAD) as the primary institutional vehicle for advancing their program. At ministerial meetings in Geneva (1964), New Delhi (1968), Santiago (1972), Nairobi (1976), and Manila (1979), and at lower-level preparatory meetings in Geneva, they pressed for implementation of an increasingly ambitious program of reforms in the way the international economy functioned. In addition to calls for increased aid flows, debt relief, changes in the monetary system, and preferential trade arrangements, debate raged over the behaviour of multinational corporations, international maritime shipping arrangements, the protection of intellectual property, and more. UNCTAD's most important function, however, lay in addressing the special problems of trade in resources and here Canada had both an expertise and clear interests to defend.

For countries dependent on the exports of one or a few resource products, international price fluctuations can play havoc with the stability of export earnings and, consequently, orderly economic development. This sensitivity to the impact of price fluctuations on the stability of export earnings is not unique to developing countries, and Canada had been a proponent of efforts to stabilize trade in grains since the 1920s. Not surprisingly, the prime minister and his advisors believed Canada could be helpful in addressing the problems faced by developing countries. At the same time, Canadian resource firms, as well as buyers of developing country resources, were wary of any schemes that would do more than share information and make markets work better. From their perspective, such private-sector institutions as the London Metal Exchange and the Chicago Commodity Exchange were effective instruments for smoothing out market imperfections. Anything more, in their view, was likely to do more harm than good.[73]

With these competing views to guide them, Canadian officials learned to play a complex role over the course of the 1970s and into the 1980s. They needed to satisfy prime ministerial and other dispositions to be helpful and constructive participants in increasingly acrimonious North-South discussions, and at the same time ensure that Canada made no commitments that would undermine fundamental and immediate Canadian trade interests. At meetings of GATT, the United Nations and its various organs, and the Commonwealth, and at ad hoc venues such as the Conference on International Economic Co-operation in Paris (co-chaired by Secretary of State for External Affairs Allan MacEachen), Canadian officials danced their delicate minuet with great skill, satisfying short-term political imperatives without compromising long-term economic interests.

Concurrently, ministers and officials tried to broaden the base of Canadian experience in developing countries through trade missions, various new institutional linkages such as industrial cooperation agreements and ministerial consultative committees, the deployment of more trade commissioners, more generous export credit arrangements, and other techniques. No one could accuse Canadians of not trying to expand and strengthen trade and economic ties with the countries of the Third World. Again, however, the payoff for these efforts turned out to be meagre at best. These were classic foreign policy measures, providing more sustenance in the short than the long run. Trade with developing countries at the end of the 1970s stood almost exactly where it had stood a decade earlier.

For a resource-based economy with a weak manufacturing sector, the scope for expanded trade with most developing countries was minimal. Export of Canadian grains was one staple, although a significant proportion was distributed on a concessional basis as food aid. The markets for Canadian forestry and mineral products were also limited. Canada did have some interesting prospects to sell subway systems, nuclear reactors, engineering services, and similar high-end items, but these were one-time sales that took a long time to come to fruition. In the other direction, while Canada was a good customer for tropical products such as coffee, tea, cocoa, orange juice, and similar items, and dependent on imports of crude petroleum for the eastern part of the country, it was more difficult to welcome textiles, clothing, footwear, and other standard-technology products that the more advanced

Anthony Jenkins, "*Eh Juan, Wake Up, The North-South
Dialogue Appears to be Headed Our Way,*" *13 April 1982.
Trudeau becomes a player in the North-South dialogue,
including as chair of a conference in Mexico.*

developing countries were producing in abundance but that politically astute Canadian competitors were eager to keep to a minimum.

Over the 1970s, trade with a few countries in East Asia and Latin America showed some early promise, but as with the promising EC and Japanese markets, the kind of patient nurturing and investment required was in short supply among Canadian businesses. Many were prepared to admit that in the long run these markets might mature into interesting second-tier partners, but in the short term they had payrolls to meet and stockholders to satisfy. Their resources to pursue potential rather than immediate sales were limited. Various government export development programs were helpful but in the end could not erase the severe handicaps that had to be overcome in developing small, distant, and unstable markets. As illustrated in table 10.5, the shares of Canadian exports and imports held by developing countries remained modest.

The prime minister's political desire to be a constructive participant in advancing the cause of developing countries may have been well meaning, but it suffered

Table 10.5

Canadian merchandise trade with leading developing countries, 1981:
Top twelve export markets and import suppliers

Country	Value ($ millions)	Share (%)	Major products
Exports			
China	1,007	1.20	Wheat, wood pulp, fertilizers
Venezuela	829	0.99	Motor vehicle parts, newsprint
Mexico	734	0.88	Skim milk powder, newsprint
Brazil	690	0.82	Wheat, sulphur, newsprint
Saudi Arabia	461	0.55	Cars, trucks, lumber
Cuba	453	0.54	Wheat, wheat flour, other cereals
South Korea	447	0.53	Coal, wood pulp, fertilizers
Algeria	380	0.45	Wheat, prefab buildings, lumber
India	348	0.42	Newsprint, sulphur, edible oils
Iraq	321	0.38	Cars, wheat
South Africa	262	0.31	Sulphur, cars, wood pulp
Taiwan	237	0.28	Sulphur, copper ores, coal
Imports			
Venezuela	2,385	3.01	Crude petroleum
Saudi Arabia	2,273	2.87	Crude petroleum
Mexico	996	1.26	Crude petroleum, tomatoes
Taiwan	729	0.92	Outerwear, footwear, consumer electronics
Hong Kong	675	0.85	Outerwear, games, toys, watches
South Korea	608	0.77	Outerwear, footwear, consumer electronics
Brazil	431	0.55	Coffee, orange juice, aluminum
Algeria	424	0.54	Crude petroleum
South Africa	403	0.51	Raw sugar, metals and ores
China	220	0.28	Outerwear, edible oils, furnishings
Cuba	196	0.25	Raw sugar, fish and marine animals
Singapore	175	0.22	Rubber, consumer electronics

Source: External Affairs Canada, *A Review of Canadian Trade Policy* (Ottawa: Supply and Services, 1983), tables 28 and 29.

from some fundamental limitations. In the closing years of the 1970s, as Canadian fiscal problems began to erode Canada's aid disbursements and the ever more strident demands of developing country militants soured discussions in the UN and other forums, Canada gradually became more nuanced in its approach to developing countries.

Throughout this period, the GATT loomed as important as ever to the professional trade policy community, while some of these other foreign initiatives seemed peripheral to Canada's central trade interests. To the prime minister and his cabinet, however, the GATT was an instrument valued by the civil service, but one that was not well suited to addressing more immediate political problems or opportunities. Revealingly, the chroniclers of Trudeau's foreign policy never once mention the GATT or multilateral trade negotiations. Neither their interviews nor their perusal of the record placed the GATT high on the Trudeau government's radar screen.[74] Nevertheless, as we shall see in chapter 11, Canada had major, long-term interests at stake in GATT negotiations, and that is where the trade policy professionals deployed their best resources, consciously working to advance Canadian interests far away from the political limelight. Active public and political attention was more likely to undermine their work than advance it. Fortunately, some also remained in Ottawa to participate in working out some of the government's domestic economic policy priorities, many of which seemed equally peripheral, but potentially more troublesome.

The Search for an Industrial Strategy

For many Canadians, including some of the government's brightest political advisors and like-minded colleagues in universities and think tanks, the holy grail of Canadian economic development was a Canadian-owned, world-class manufacturing sector. For them, the thrust of Canadian trade and industrial policy in the 1950s and 1960s had pushed Canada in the exact opposite direction, fostering a foreign-controlled, branch-plant economy. They saw evidence of Canada's "arrested" economic development on every front.[75] US multinational firms owned the commanding heights of the Canadian economy, pursuing utilitarian activities to satisfy Canadian domestic demand, but reserving more valuable research and development, management, and other functions for US and other locations. Canada's large deficit in trade in end products proved that US investors were exploiting Canada's storehouse of raw materials and retarding Canada's development of its own world-class manufacturing facilities. For economic nationalists in and out of government, here was a situation that needed desperately to be reversed with a heavy dose of strategically deployed industrial policy.

Industrial policy, of course, was not unknown in Canada.[76] Indeed, federal governments had deployed trade, transportation, and other tools of industrial development from Canada's earliest days, and provincial governments had tinkered with various other programs to promote their own economic development. More the product of circumstance and opportunity than grand strategy, much of Canada's industrial structure was the result of earlier efforts to foster the development of a Canadian manufacturing sector. In the absence of a large continental market of their own, however, Canadians required export markets to develop world-class manufacturing firms. Similarly, in the absence of large pools of domestic capital, little would have been accomplished without infusions of foreign capital. The path between what was desirable and what was possible had been narrow and not always straight.

Also often ignored in the industrial policy debates of the 1960s and 1970s was the relative decline of the manufacturing sector as an employer. By 1975, only 22.1 per-cent of the labour force was employed in manufacturing, representing 26.5 percent of Canadian economic output. As in other OECD countries, Canadian manufac-turing had become steadily more efficient and capital-intensive, requiring fewer workers for the same level of output.[77] Over the postwar years, employment growth had been concentrated in services, particularly in business and personal services, demand for which was a direct outgrowth of increasing prosperity. By 1975, 61.6 percent of Canadians were employed in the services sector, double the proportion of thirty years earlier. Ironically, these trends also reflected the relatively higher productivity growth in the goods producing sectors of the economy. Over the dec-ade 1961-71, productivity had grown at an average rate of 2.63 percent annually in real terms, all of it contributed by the goods producing sectors of the economy.[78]

Within manufacturing, the auto industry was steadily becoming the mainstay of the Ontario economy, both directly and indirectly, as a customer of a wide range of other industries, including steel, plastics, rubber, textiles, and glass. The Auto Pact had cleared the way for a major rationalization of the assembly facilities of the major North American car makers as well as of a growing number of both captive and independent parts suppliers. The structure of the Auto Pact and its safeguards favoured assembly in Canada, but by the late 1970s Canadian parts suppliers were also beginning to make significant contributions to employment and output. In 1987, the Canada-US Free Trade Agreement listed 194 firms in Canada as eligible for Auto Pact status, that is, eligible to import parts from all over the world without paying duty, and another dozen with near-Auto Pact status.

In protecting and promoting a domestic manufacturing sector, Canada had re-lied more on tariff and related measures than most other countries. By the 1960s, however, the extent to which the tariff could be used was beginning to be curtailed by international trade agreements that both reduced the level of the tariff and cir-cumscribed the discriminatory use of various tariff-related and other industrial programs. In response, governments began to look to other types of policies to promote industrial development. In 1963, the federal government had established a Department of Industry to devise and administer programs to advance Canada's industrial development, including the various programs that had formed part of the postwar Department of Defence Production. The new department set out to gain a clearer understanding of Canada's wider industrial structure and the types of programs and policies that could advance Canada's industrial development.

In 1969, the Trudeau government integrated the industry portfolio within the Department of Industry, Trade and Commerce (ITC) and established a separate Department of Regional Economic Expansion. Both departments were mandated to explore what government could do to enhance Canada's industrial and regional development. Their establishment was spurred by growing concern with a number of characteristics of the Canadian economy:

- The persistent productivity gap between Canadian and US manufacturing
- The domestic orientation and lack of international competitiveness of Canada's secondary industrial sector
- The high level of foreign – particularly American – control of Canadian manufacturing
- The concentration of manufacturing in the Quebec to Windsor corridor, and the concomitant regional economic disparities
- The large deficit in Canadian trade in "end" products, i.e., finished goods, and the related large trade surplus in resource products exported at low stages of processing
- The relatively low levels of spending on research and development by Canadian industry

Over the years, industry officials developed an increasingly detailed appreciation of the strengths and weaknesses of various sectors of the economy and devised new tariff programs, taxes, subsidies, procurement preferences and offsets, and other programs to promote industrial development or shield industrial decline. Increasingly, the conviction grew among these officials and their political masters, with the active encouragement of a growing legion of academic and think-tank commentators, that Canadian industrial firms and their managers were incapable of addressing the known deficiencies in Canada's industrial structure without a helping, and even guiding, hand from government.[79] Proliferating Crown corporations, a favourite technique of Canadian governments to address market failures, further reflected the conviction that governments were often better placed than industry to respond to emerging opportunities and technologies. The absence of much evidence of success was often attributed to failure to pursue the recommended strategy with sufficient enthusiasm and follow-through.

Activists throughout Ottawa saw government programs and policies as critical to the development of Canadian champions. Without positive government programs, they feared Canada would have a much smaller industrial base and a less certain future. In the words of Eric Kierans, who served in Trudeau's first cabinet, "The missing element in Canadian development has always been a lack of entrepreneurship."[80] In his view, government was essential in providing a substitute for this critical element. As a result, subsidies and capital assistance to business increased five-fold during the Trudeau years, while a range of tax incentives or expenditures added further to the cost of pursuing the dream of the preferred industrial structure.[81]

Trudeau may personally not have been deeply committed to these policies and programs, but those who were learned to work with his ministers to pursue the programs dear to their hearts.[82] After 1971 and the Nixon shock, Trudeau and his ministers were even more receptive to new ideas. While one group of officials worked to diversify Canada's trade relations, others sought to find ways to diversify the Canadian economy and make it less vulnerable to the vagaries of US policy and economic performance.

Despite their best efforts, the industrial strategists never achieved their goal and complained in later years that the senior civil service and business had frustrated their ambitions and reduced their efforts to a series of ad hoc policies rather than a coherent strategy. In the words of Joel Bell, he and like-minded colleagues had sought "a sensible framework within which [the government] could respond to requests for support and restructuring; a notion of where and how it might usefully concentrate or apply its muscle; a forward-looking alternative to backing into crisis responses, where money was being spent and government was getting involved or intervening in any event, but less constructively, it seemed."[83] Such a "sensible program" was never put in place, and as the government's fiscal position deteriorated in the later 1970s and early 1980s, such a program became more and more of a chimera.

Industry welcomed some of the programs that were implemented and learned to lobby effectively for certain types of assistance, such as subsidies, procurement preferences, selected protection, and tax incentives. At the same time, industry leaders were not above criticizing the government for failing to meet their needs in other areas of government policy, including fiscal, monetary, and competition policy. Industry was also critical of another aspect of activist government: regulations touching virtually every aspect of Canadians' lives. With the establishment of such new departments and agencies as Consumer and Corporate Affairs (1967), Communications (1969), Environment (1971), Science and Technology (1971), the Canada Development Corporation (1971), the Foreign Investment Review Agency (1974), and the Industrial Renewal Board (1976), the scope for government interference and hectoring grew rapidly, souring government-business relations. Indeed, in 1976 the minister of industry, trade and commerce, Jean Chrétien, asked businessman Roy MacLaren to head a task force on business-government "interface." Its September report recommended that the government and business spend more time talking to each other.[84] It did not address the real problem: business was losing confidence in the government's economic judgment. Business leaders did not like many of the activist programs and policies the government was pursuing. To make that point more effectively, they founded a new organization to represent the views of Canada's leading 150 firms: the Business Council on National Issues.

The most controversial of the various activist initiatives was the creation of FIRA. The issue of foreign ownership had first come to public attention as a result of the

1957 Gordon Commission. Since then, it had become a staple of activist complaints and the subject of a growing pile of academic and official studies, each more strident than the last. The 1968 Watkins Report had been followed in 1970 by a parliamentary committee inquiry known as the Wahn Report, after its chair, Toronto MP Ian Wahn. In 1972, the government itself published a massive study prepared under the direction of the minister of national revenue, Herb Gray.[85] The burden of each of these studies was that foreign direct investment (FDI) was, on balance, beneficial, but that the extent of foreign – read American – control was undesirable and a threat to Canadian sovereignty. The studies all intimated that foreign control brought with it undesirable side effects that needed to be addressed.

Not everyone agreed with this analysis. Indeed, most economists thought the problem was exaggerated and the benefits of FDI undervalued.[86] In any event, the extent of foreign control was declining as a more prosperous Canada was generating sufficient savings to create a larger domestic capital pool. Nevertheless, the Trudeau minority government of 1972-4 decided it would be prudent to act and established an agency that would "review" takeovers and greenfield foreign direct investments to determine whether the result would be of "net benefit" to Canada. The agency would make these determinations by examining, for example, the effect of the investment on employment, economic activity, productivity, technological development, product variety, and Canadian participation in management. The criteria were sufficiently vague and nontransparent to allow FIRA's administrative practices to evolve on a basis consistent with prevailing political winds and economic climates.

Over the next ten years, FIRA would receive 7,947 applications, reviewing 7,132 of them. Of those, it allowed 5,981 and disallowed 435, while 637 were withdrawn by the investor before certification.[87] Its real impact, however, is difficult to judge.[88] The bases of most approvals were set out in confidential undertakings negotiated by the agency. The extent to which foreign investors changed their plans, adapted them to meet the agency's requirements, or gave Canada a miss will never be determined with any precision. Anecdotal evidence indicates a high level of flexibility in the application of the rules. The fact that approvals were reviewed by cabinet – clogging cabinet decision making for the whole ten-year period – suggests a high level of potential political interference. During the period when the agency reported to Herb Gray as industry minister (1980-2), industry complaints about political involvement were particularly frequent.

FIRA's work also provoked strong representations from officials in the United States, the United Kingdom, Germany, Japan, and other major sources of foreign capital. Investors from these countries, however, were often reluctant to involve their home-country authorities. They were not eager to share the confidential undertakings they had accepted or to sour relations with the Canadian authorities. Instead, foreign officials tended to hear from disgruntled investors who had failed to satisfy FIRA in one way or another, adding to the negative image Canada gained

*Roy Peterson, "You Have Nothing to Fear but FIRA Itself," 26
March 1982. US concern with FIRA finally led to a GATT panel,
which found some of its practices inconsistent with Canadian
trade obligations.*

as a potential location for investment. In addition, a decision by a 1984 GATT panel
that some of the undertakings enforced by FIRA were inconsistent with Canada's
international trade obligations added to the agency's troubled status.[89] The counterproductive impact this image created for Canadian growth, trade, and industrial
development convinced the Conservatives under Brian Mulroney to turn the mandate of the agency on its head. After 1985 its primary task became the promotion of
foreign investment in Canada, with screening limited to a few sensitive sectors,
such as energy and culture.

The activism of the 1970s, however, did not lead to much change in the basic
structure and performance of Canadian industry. If anything, there was depressing
evidence of just how difficult it is for governments to pick winners and how easy it
is for losers to find governments.[90] Government support for declining industries
such as textiles, clothing, footwear, and furniture underlined the extent to which
political and market judgments differ. Additionally, the economic turmoil of the
decade undermined investor confidence and added to the woes of the weaker parts
of the manufacturing sector.

Efforts by the Economic Council and like-minded university economists to convince the government that the time had come to let international competition become the main instrument of industrial development were not well received. Instead,
the government became increasingly attracted to the nostrums promoted by economic nationalists, although generally within the limited confines prescribed by

the GATT. To industrial policy advocates, the structure of the economy – what goods and services are produced, by whom, and where – was a matter of public policy and concern. To critics, the structure of the economy was largely a matter of market forces, with public policy limited to addressing market failures. The Trudeau government, not always sure where it stood in this debate, often tried to satisfy both sides with the not unpredictable result of satisfying neither.

Other initiatives aimed at making the government a more activist player in re-making the Canadian economy suffered similar fates. The dream of a Canadian Agricultural Export Corporation (Canagrex), for example, a particular favourite of Eugene Whelan, the minister of agriculture, was never realized, nor were his plans for more supply management schemes. Previously, however, Whelan had enjoyed much more success in getting his agricultural versions of activist industrial policy through cabinet.

Throwing in the Towel on the Agricultural Front

As already noted in earlier chapters, the Canadian farm sector had lagged increasingly behind the rest of the economy in sharing in the new prosperity. Technological developments added to the woes of all but a small number of successful, capital-intensive farmers. In 1951, one in five Canadians still lived on the farm; by 1979, that proportion had fallen to one in twenty-two. By that time, the number of farms in Canada had fallen to 300,000, employing fewer than half a million people. Additionally, about half of those working farms counted on nonfarm income to make ends meet.[91]

Consistent with the general trend toward greater involvement of government in the economy, Canadian federal and provincial governments substantially increased their roles in the farm sector. As the authors of one report concluded, "Government intervention in the food system is pervasive. Beyond the farm gate, governments are involved in regulation in such areas as food safety, plant and animal health, and grading, packaging, and labelling standards ... Governments also promote the development of the farm and food system through their activities in the provision of research and extension services, factor supplies, infrastructure, and public goods, and through commercial policy and foreign market development. A third major component of government activity in agriculture is ensuring adequate farm incomes."[92]

Historically, Canadian governments had used transportation policies and related infrastructure investments to help stimulate the development of export-oriented agricultural production, a policy that had met with some success. Canadian farm products had gained a large place in world, but particularly UK, markets. In the immediate postwar period, efforts to expand markets for Canadian grains had also met with success. Concurrently, however, the persistent deterioration in Canada's overseas agricultural markets for dairy, poultry, horticultural, and some red meat products had led eastern Canadian agricultural interests to turn inward.

By the 1970s the combined impact of rising urban incomes, stagnant farm incomes, and uncertain overseas markets convinced the federal and provincial governments to take further steps to stabilize and even enhance farm income through a combination of direct and indirect subsidies, stabilization programs, marketing boards, and supply management. In 1965, 8.5 percent of aggregate net farm income flowed from government support programs. By 1977 it reached a new high of 36 percent, and averaged 24 percent for the decade as a whole.[93]

In the 1950s and 1960s, Canadians could legitimately complain that the farm programs pursued by the United States and Europe were distorting world trade in agricultural products. By the end of the 1970s, however, Canadian farmers had themselves fully converted to what has been called "farm fundamentalism."[94] They increasingly implored the government to practise its own brand of protectionism and give Canada's marketing boards authority to manage trade and production levels.

As discussed in chapter 7, a series of federal-provincial agreements, federal and provincial legislative initiatives, and carefully developed board mandates had gradually ironed out constitutional and political obstacles to deploying the full potential of marketing boards. By the 1960s, there were more than a hundred such boards across the country, most of which operated in a market-based environment.[95] Matters changed in the late 1960s, in reaction to both interprovincial and international problems. For example, new production, management, and shipping techniques greatly enhanced the supply of eggs and poultry available for sale on an interprovincial basis.[96] Surplus production was leading to falling prices, falling incomes, and intense interprovincial rivalry as excess production in one province was offered for sale in others to maintain the production quotas of provincially based marketing boards. Provincial governments sought help from the federal government to bring this chicken and egg war to an end.

In 1970, after intense federal-provincial discussions, the federal government finally proposed legislation that would permit the organization of marketing boards with authority to implement supply management schemes consistent with GATT article XI:2(c)(i), the provision that spells out the conditions under which governments can use border restrictions to defend supply management. The original proposal was couched in generic terms and was bitterly opposed by other commodity groups, particularly the cattle producers. They feared that once governments gained control of the market, the independence of producers would be at risk. It took more than a year of intense debate to overcome this opposition by limiting authority for national supply management to the most seriously affected sectors: poultry and eggs. The first board, the Canadian Egg Marketing Agency, began operation in 1973, and was followed by a national turkey marketing agency in 1974 and a chicken marketing agency in 1978. Supply management for fertilized eggs and chicks was introduced in 1989.

Concurrently, problems in the management of the mandates of a number of provincial marketing boards for fluid and industrial milk led to the creation of the Canadian Dairy Commission in 1966 with authority to act as a national dairy marketing board. Supply management authority for industrial milk, however, was not implemented until 1974. The supply management of fluid milk, markets for which are largely local, remains limited to individual provinces and is not underwritten by any import restrictions. Nevertheless, supply management has succeeded in steadily reducing the number of farms engaged in milk production, from some 455,000 farms in 1951 to fewer than 30,000 farms with commercially viable quota levels by the end of the 1990s.

The operation of supply management is relatively simple and straightforward. As Barry Wilson explains, "Domestic demand is predicted, the anticipated market is divided among farmers with quota ... prices are set at levels high enough to cover production costs plus profit, and imports are controlled to ensure that the administered domestic prices are not undercut by cheaper foreign produce ... the board that issues quota and controls the system operates an effective domestic monopoly under the authority of federal and provincial legislation."[97] Understandably, farmers like it, but consumers face prices that are higher than they would be under open market competition. Additionally, the longer the system stays in place, the greater the rigidity that it engenders, for example, in creating barriers to entry into the industry, and retarding adjustment to changing technology, consumer preference, and other competitive conditions.

In the years to follow, governments tried to address these problems with limited success. Solutions often proved or appeared worse than the problem. At the same time, criticism of supply management's shortcomings by consumers, economists, and other governments deterred any appetite for extending supply management to other commodities.

Unlike their counterparts in the United States and elsewhere, however, Canadian governments had chosen a policy measure – supply management – that was wholly consistent with Canada's international obligations and was least likely to distort international markets. The combined effect of stringent import, price, and production controls isolated the Canadian market and limited the costs of the scheme to Canadian consumers. Surplus production proved a temporary, introductory phenomenon, and disrupted world markets only in the first few years of supply management. The potential loss of the Canadian market counted for little, given the minuscule performance of others in that market during the period when it was one of the most open markets in the world.

US schemes with similar objectives had not only proved a heavy burden for US consumers and taxpayers, but had also become one of the principal contributors to the instability of world agricultural markets. The US Congress, in an effort to woo and reward the farm vote, consistently set price and loan guarantees well above world price levels, encouraging overproduction, leading to the dumping of surplus supply, and further depressing world prices. US intervention in the US agricultural markets might have succeeded in raising prices and incomes, but at a very high cost that went well beyond US borders.

Nevertheless, supply management would increasingly bedevil efforts by Canada to bring greater sanity to world trade in agriculture and did for agriculture what the National Policy had done for the industrial sector, creating competing import-sensitive and export-oriented sectors. The grains and red-meat sectors, concentrated in the West and highly dependent on world markets, now found their trade policy goals increasingly frustrated by the determination of the dairy, poultry, and horticultural sectors, concentrated in the East, to maintain supply management and other forms of protection. In the next two rounds of GATT negotiations, Canadian capacity to influence the outcome of world agricultural trade policy would be frustrated by the tension between these two goals.

The later years of the 1970s had not been kind to Canada. Buffeted by international forces ranging from the OPEC-induced oil crisis to the collapse of the Bretton Woods monetary system, the federal government had struck out both at home and abroad in attempts to find counterweights to the traditional pillars of Canadian economic development: the US economy and the resource sector. Much effort was expended on contractual links, North-South initiatives, and industrial and agricultural policy programs, but by the end of the decade there was little evidence that much had changed. Throughout this period, however, Canadian trade officials had laboured in obscurity pursuing Canadian trade interests at the GATT in Geneva. Perhaps these negotiations offered better prospects for long-term Canadian prosperity in the more demanding circumstances of the late twentieth century.

11 THE GATT SHALL PROVIDE
CANADA AT THE TOKYO ROUND

On the international plane, there is only one system which provides in legal form a framework of rules and procedures governing international trade and trade relations and which embodies the legal rights and obligations between its member countries. This system is the General Agreement on Tariffs and Trade.

– OLIVIER LONG, GATT DIRECTOR GENERAL, 1968–79

For much of Canada's history, trade policy shaped the contours of the country's industrial development. Tariffs and related instruments encouraged the growth of a domestic manufacturing sector, while trade negotiations encouraged the growth of export markets for resource producers. These policies led to a bifurcated industrial structure, a heavy reliance on foreign capital, and an increasing dependence on trade with the United States. In the 1970s, criticism of Canada's economic situation and the policies behind it sparked a search for alternative courses of action. However, the status quo was not to be easily overcome, and various alternatives proved largely ineffectual.

Given Canada's dependence on foreign trade, it is not difficult to appreciate the extent to which trade policy continued to take priority over industrial policy. As Atkinson and Coleman explain, in these circumstances, "The critical question is which type of policy, trade or industrial, takes pride of place. If governments stress industrial policy as the primary means to economic growth and stability, then an anticipatory approach is ordinarily employed, with trade measures applied on a case-by-case basis at the sector level. If, however, a liberal trade policy is emphasized, then industrial policy becomes a supplementary tool, normally reactive in character and often applied primarily at the level of the firm."[1] From the 1930s on, Canada had pursued liberal trade policies, supplemented by reactive firm- and sector-specific industrial policies as required.

Those most committed to changing Canada's trade and industrial patterns in the 1970s complained in later years that senior officials and business leaders had frustrated their efforts to give industrial policy precedence. Joel Bell and his colleagues insisted, for example, that their efforts to implement an industrial strategy had been frustrated by senior officials, while Tom Axworthy complained that Canadian business was unwilling or unable to make the investments and efforts necessary to diversify exports beyond established patterns.[2] Similar complaints were echoed by officials in the departments and agencies responsible for assisting Canadian manufacturers and exporters in addressing the competitive challenges they faced. Trade commissioners, for example, frequently voiced the view that Canada needed an export strategy and an export trading corporation to give it effect.[3] Similarly, officials in the industry branches of government often complained about the lack of entrepreneurship in Canada and the need for greater government assistance and direction.

There is some truth to these charges. Nevertheless, to senior public servants such as Simon Reisman, Jim Grandy, and Ed Ritchie, respectively the deputies at Finance, Industry, Trade and Commerce, and External Affairs in the early 1970s, the pattern and approaches of the past had achieved results that they were reluctant to reverse. In their view, the incremental, pragmatic, and economically cautious approach of the previous thirty years had produced a track record consistent with Canadian capabilities, priorities, and circumstances. More could certainly be done, but new programs and policies were most likely to work if they continued the same basic pattern. Radical departures were, in their view, neither warranted nor likely to succeed. They recognized the basic realities within which Canadian government policies operated, including the capability and interest of Canadian firms. In Canada, trade and investment are primarily private-sector activities. Governments can facilitate or frustrate these activities, but ultimately they do not trade or invest. Those cases in which governments had engaged directly in economic activity – such as Crown corporations – did not provide much evidence that government could do better than the private sector.

The relatively small Canadian market imposed a second limitation. Without access to foreign markets, Canadian industrial production was unlikely to attain the competitive scale needed to finance innovation and other desirable features. Additionally, both business leaders and experienced trade officials had a clear understanding of the real – as opposed to potential – size of the opportunities offered by foreign markets. In the case of Japan, for example, Canadian exporters faced some formidable barriers involving not only market access, but also costs, consumer interests and preferences, and institutional barriers. Even large, well-financed US and EC firms, backed up by the muscle of their much bigger governments, were finding the Japanese markets tough sledding in areas for which there were Japanese suppliers. European and developing country markets offered their own difficulties. Over time, Canadian firms might find niches in these markets, but only if they earned enough from Canadian and US markets to finance the effort.

Given these realities, Canadian officials had used the policy instruments at their disposal to nurture trade and industrial patterns that would provide Canada with growing prosperity. The pace of the desired adjustment, however, was dependent on both external and domestic factors. Externally, it required Canada's major trading partners, particularly the United States, to open up their markets to Canadian suppliers and accept the discipline of international rules to underwrite this market access. Domestically, it required governments, firms, and workers to accept increasing levels of foreign competition and to make constant efforts to upgrade and adjust domestic production. The mutually reinforcing impact of these external and domestic dimensions was key to the incremental nature of this strategy.

The machinery program offers a good example of how trade negotiations can be used to achieve industrial policy objectives. Canada for many years maintained a provision that allowed Canadian industrial firms to import sophisticated machinery from abroad at a lower tariff rate if they could demonstrate that the machinery was not available from domestic sources. During the Kennedy Round, Canada agreed to eliminate the 7.5 percent tariff on machinery not made in Canada and to reduce the tariff on imports that competed directly with made-in-Canada machinery from 22.5 to 15 percent, with a commitment that the overall impact of the machinery tariff would be reduced to 9 percent. The revised program satisfied two competing objectives: access by Canadian industry to the best machinery available and the development of a competitive Canadian machinery industry. The Kennedy Round commitments succeeded in providing a basis upon which both could be pursued, but not without some grumbling from Canadian machinery providers, who thought their Canadian customers too often bought from abroad when a reasonable substitute was available from domestic sources. Nevertheless, over the course of the 1970s, the industry rationalized as it reduced product lines and became steadily more export-oriented.[4] In the Tokyo Round, the machinery and similar programs would be squeezed further in an effort to ensure that Canadian industry would become more competitive and less dependent on the domestic market alone. The values of the National Policy were gradually being adjusted to the more demanding circumstances of a country increasingly dependent on more than trade in resources.

To the trade professionals, this strategy was centred in the rules and negotiations of the General Agreement on Tariffs and Trade (GATT), and in this they had the general support of Canadian business. Getting the most out of GATT negotiations, however, was not automatic. There were many benefits to multilateral negotiations, but there were also some drawbacks. First, Canada was one of many and had to accept the reality that the United States and the EC set much of the agenda. Second, in multilateral negotiations, the final result is the common denominator with which all the major players can live. Third, the payoff from multilateral GATT negotiations is long term, while political needs are often much shorter term. Finally, making the GATT work and endure required that governments pay due attention to systemic concerns, concerns that were more likely to preoccupy permanent officials than ministers and business leaders. The latter looked for more immediate goals and results and often found GATT's procedures slow and cumbersome.

On the domestic side, there were also complications that needed to be taken into account. Canadian industry, for example, did not speak with a single voice. Some industries regarded GATT liberalization as a problem, exposing them to more competition than they thought they could handle, while others saw it as providing opportunities to adjust and compete more effectively in larger markets. These perspectives were not new, but as the Canadian economy had grown more diversified, the arguments had become more sophisticated. The efforts of those promoting various industrial policies tended to complicate trade-negotiating mandates. For example, at the same time that one set of Canadian officials was negotiating rules to discipline the use of government procurement preferences and subsidies as industrial policy tools, others were actively trying to make greater use of them.

Within the context of the demanding international economic circumstances and deteriorating economic conditions at home discussed in the previous chapter, trade officials recognized that they would need to deliver convincing evidence that their preferred approach worked. From the conclusion of the Kennedy Round in 1967 through the conclusion of the Tokyo Round in 1979, therefore, they worked tirelessly to ensure that both the existing GATT disciplines and new negotiations responded to Canadian needs and priorities. In this, they cooperated closely with Canadian industry and with their colleagues in other departments and the provinces.

Trade officials clearly had the support of the ministry as they pursued their mandates, but it was a different kind of support than that available on higher-profile initiatives. The decision to set up a special cabinet committee chaired by the deputy prime minister and secretary of state for external affairs, Allan MacEachen, to direct the Tokyo Round negotiations, for example, recognized the need for sustained political support. MacEachen had a sound appreciation both of what made long-term economic sense – he held an advanced degree in economics, which he had taught before entering politics – but he also possessed very sensitive political antennae and commanded the respect of his colleagues. From 1968 to 1979, Trudeau rotated five ministers through the trade portfolio, four through Finance, and three through External Affairs, each with different political sensitivities. Each contributed to Canada's participation in the GATT and the Tokyo Round negotiations, but neither constituted a major political priority for any of the ministers.

Nevertheless, while the GATT may not have been central to the government's immediate political consideration of the various issues that roiled international economic relations in the late 1960s and early 1970s, the GATT was also not idle. Steadily but unspectacularly, it responded to those Canadian interests and priorities identified by senior officials and adopted by ministers.

GATT in the Early 1970s

At the close of the Kennedy Round negotiations, the consensus among governments was that it would be a long time before there would be a further negotiation of similar scope and duration focused on tariffs. Nontariff barriers, however, were another matter. By the end of 1967, officials were already establishing the groundwork for an even more ambitious undertaking. Their discussions soon took on an air similar to the preparations for the original GATT negotiations. The next round would not be just another tariff-cutting conference but involve a major effort to reform the GATT and to recognize the changes in its membership, in the trade policies of its principal adherents, and in the nature of the international economy.

There were those who were prepared to launch far-reaching negotiations within a year of the conclusion of the Kennedy Round, but as we have seen, none of the governments of the major players was politically prepared for such a significant initiative. In the United States in particular, Congress made it abundantly clear that it was in no mood to grant the administration authority for another major negotiation in the immediate future. The EC, for its part, was preoccupied with enlargement. Finally, it would take time to create the necessary information and analytical base to make any new round a success.

To this end, governments at the 1967 annual session of the contracting parties gave the Secretariat a mandate to begin elaborating a firmer information base for an aggressive attack on both tariff and nontariff barriers. On the tariff side, the Secretariat was charged with developing a more uniform basis for measuring tariff concessions, while on the nontariff side, members needed to determine precisely what was involved. By this time it was clear that trade was being affected by a much wider range of government policies, practices, and participation in the economy than had been considered within the pale at the time the GATT was negotiated. The result was an unforeseen variety of restrictions and distorting influences. The evidence was perhaps most acute in the agriculture sector, but it was not absent in other areas. What was lacking was any systematic investigation and analysis of the nature of nontariff measures and their susceptibility to negotiation.[5]

As a result of a concerted effort of cross-notification, the GATT was able to develop an inventory of some eight hundred nontariff barriers (NTBs). The Secretariat then catalogued these into about thirty distinct types organized into six broad categories (see table 11.1). Both the inventory and the typology then became the subject of intense discussions among interested governments in working groups, as they attempted to flesh out what future negotiations would entail.[6] The senior trade official in the Canadian permanent mission in Geneva, Percy Eastham, played a leading role in this endeavour, chairing the subgroup on technical barriers to trade; this subgroup distinguished itself by preparing a draft agreement. Another member of the mission, Peter Clark, chaired the GATT's Budget Committee and was the first Canadian member of the newly established Textiles Surveillance Body. Both were carrying on the tradition of ensuring that Canada assumed an active role, using their offices to deploy the hard work, solid information, and good ideas being generated by their colleagues in Ottawa and around the world.

Canadian officials had from the start been among the most enthusiastic supporters of the NTB inventory. Already early in 1968, Pearson's last minister of trade and

Table 11.1

GATT illustrative list of nontariff measures

Group 1: Government participation in trade
Countervailing duties
Export subsidies
Government procurement
State trading in market economy countries
Trade diverting aids
Other restrictive practices

Group 2: Customs and administrative entry procedures
Antidumping duties
Consular and customs formalities and documentation
Certificates of origin
Consular formalities and fees
Customs clearance documentation
Samples requirements
Valuation

Group 3: Standards
Packaging and marking regulations
Standards

Group 4: Specific limitations on trade
Discriminatory bilateral agreements
Export restraints
Licensing
Minimum price regulations
Motion picture restrictions
Quantitative restrictions

Group 5: Charges on imports
Credit restrictions for importers
Discriminatory taxes on automobiles
Fiscal adjustments at the border or otherwise
Prior deposits
Restrictions on foreign wines and spirits
Special duties on imports
Statistical and administrative duties
Variable levies

Source: Adapted from Sydney Golt, *The GATT Negotiations, 1973-75: A Guide to the Issues* (Montreal: C.D. Howe Institute – British North American Committee, 1974), 31.

commerce, Robert Winters, had sent out 5,000 letters to Canadian business interests seeking their views on the kinds of impediments they had experienced trying to sell their products in foreign markets.[7] Canadian trade officers at embassies abroad had similarly fed information to their colleagues in Ottawa on their own experience with NTBs. Eastham, Clark, and the other Canadian participants thus came well armed to add a Canadian perspective to this effort to build an information base for future negotiations. In the government procurement group, for example, instances of the frustration experienced by Canadian firms trying to sell goods to US federal, state, and local government agencies offered a rich source of specific cases. This was not work that attracted much political or public attention. Rather, it was the critically important task of chopping away at the mine-face of trade policy, steadily preparing the basis for future breakthroughs. In the long run such efforts paid handsome dividends in opening markets and providing business and governments alike with transparent and nondiscriminatory rules, larger dividends than flowed from the politically more appealing negotiation of contractual links and other "framework" agreements.

Concurrently, members of the Organization for Economic Cooperation and Development (OECD) pursued related work in its Trade Committee and in other bodies that similarly aimed at developing a firmer information and analytical base for future negotiations. OECD discussions on government procurement were particularly important. Indeed, the OECD launched negotiations on government procurement restrictions that proceeded in tandem with the Tokyo Round negotiations until they were folded into the GATT negotiations in 1976.[8]

In 1971, in a further effort to provide analytical and political ammunition for future negotiations, OECD ministers established a high level group of former officials and academics under the chairmanship of Jean Rey, former president of the EC Commission, to examine the state of the multilateral trading system and provide advice on the "opportunities for further progress towards the general objective of a greater liberalization of international trade." Canada's Wynne Plumptre, a former senior official in the Department of Finance and by this time a professor at the University of Toronto, was among the dozen eminent members of this group. The group reported at the end of the following summer in a document that more than met expectations. It recommended a new round of multilateral negotiations and provided a detailed rationale for their launch. More importantly, the report provided a detailed assessment of and plan of action for the areas the group considered critical. Not all of its recommendations were ultimately taken up by governments during the Tokyo Round. Consideration of services and investment, for example, was not pursued until the Uruguay Round (1986-94). On the whole, however, the Rey Group provided governments with a solid assessment of the negotiations in prospect.[9]

Meanwhile, the GATT's regular activities also kept officials in Geneva and national capitals busy as they sought to solidify the GATT's position as the principal

Table 11.2

Value and volume of world trade and output, 1969-80

	Value (US$ billions)		Volume (1970 = 100)	
Year	World exports	US exports	World exports	World output
1969	273	–	92	95
1970	312	–	100	100
1971	350	–	107	105
1972	415	47.8	116	110
1973	575	68.6	130	119
1974	836	95.0	137	122
1975	875	103.1	127	120
1976	991	110.7	142	128
1977	1,125	114.7	148	133
1978	1,303	135.5	155	139
1979	1,635	170.6	163	144
1980	1,989	209.6	163	145

Source: GATT, *International Trade 1984-85* (Geneva: GATT, 1985), table A1 and various other years for value of US exports.

arbiter of world trade. At the conclusion of the Kennedy Round, Eric Wyndham White retired after twenty years at the helm, to be replaced by a Swiss official, Olivier Long. Among his early initiatives, Long made creative use of the Consultative Group of Eighteen (CG-18), set up on ad hoc basis by his predecessor, as a forum for the discussion of broad trends and issues in world trade. The CG-18 was made up of representatives from the capitals of the GATT's leading members, developed and developing alike. It became an important sounding board, rather than a negotiating forum, for addressing some of the problems the GATT's contracting parties faced during the difficult period following the Kennedy Round.[10]

The first issue facing members was the steady deterioration in world economic conditions and the consequent rise in protectionist pressures. While world trade continued to grow throughout the 1970s, it did so less robustly than during the previous decade. As illustrated in table 11.2, the volume of world trade grew by only 63 percent over the course of the decade, barely keeping ahead of the volume of world output. Already in 1970, the director general warned member governments that in his view "protectionist influences ... are today making themselves felt more strongly than at any time since the 1930s."[11] For some of the smaller members, including Canada, Sweden, and Switzerland, rising protectionist sentiments in Washington and Brussels also appeared to threaten the continued health of the multilateral trading system. The representatives in Geneva of these smaller countries consequently banded together in a Ginger Group dedicated to promoting the welfare of the system and the launch of a new round of negotiations.[12] In their view, a new round would dampen protectionist pressures by providing governments with an important outlet for addressing issues on a collective basis.

Two other issues had assumed increasing importance: how to integrate the developing countries more fully into the GATT system and how to address the conundrum of state-trading practices and thus welcome countries with centrally planned economies into the GATT's fold. On the first issue, the action had clearly shifted to various UN forums. Nevertheless, the GATT did take steps to accommodate one of the problems faced by developing countries. (The phrase "developing countries" replaced the phrase "less developed countries" around this time, an early example of political correctness. The old abbreviation, LDCs, however, continued to be applied.) Based on preparatory discussions in UNCTAD and the OECD, the GATT adopted a waiver in 1971 allowing members to introduce preferential tariff rates in favour of LDCs. Between 1971 and 1976, some twenty developed GATT members implemented general systems of preferences (GSP) in favour of developing countries. Canada introduced its system in 1974, generally providing to all developing country products either free entry or the lower of either the British preferential tariff or one-third off the MFN tariff. The EC had already brought its system into force in 1971. The United States followed suit in 1975.[13]

The problem of state trading was equally challenging. With the exception of Czechoslovakia, which was an original member, none of the centrally planned economies in Europe was a GATT member. Poland and Yugoslavia had applied for accession in the 1950s, but their applications had languished for years. Given the central role of the state in their production and purchase decisions, nonmarket economies do not fit easily into a system which assumes that such decisions are determined by market forces. Yugoslavia's case was easier because its economy left some room for market-based enterprises. Yugoslavia was granted observer status in 1950, became a provisional member in 1962, and finally gained full membership in 1966. The following year, terms of accession were agreed with Poland. Romania acceded in 1971 and Hungary in 1973. In all three cases, the protocols of accession specified that these countries would make their trade regimes more transparent, commit to increasing imports from GATT members, and enter into periodic consultations regarding their progress in meeting import targets. In effect, however, East-West political considerations disposed the GATT's leading members to bring these countries into the GATT on terms that were fundamentally at odds with its basic principles and objectives. Canada was at the forefront in welcoming these countries into the GATT. Canadian experience in selling wheat and other agricultural commodities to these countries disposed officials to take a forward-looking approach.[14]

The pragmatism that allowed the GATT to accommodate the demands of both developing and state-trading countries also had its less attractive side. Since 1961, when the United States had successfully initiated negotiations for a special arrangement to address the problem of trade in low-cost cotton textiles, GATT members had periodically extended this temporary solution in order to allow more time for orderly adjustment. Arguing that low-cost imports caused "market disruption," GATT members had been allowed to negotiate or impose discriminatory restrictions on such imports to give their markets time to stabilize. By the early 1970s, it was clear that the problem of market disruption had spread to the full range of textile and clothing products. GATT members responded by negotiating a new, more comprehensive arrangement popularly known as the Multifibre Agreement (MFA). Like its predecessors, it provided for an organized derogation from the GATT's nondiscrimination requirements, somewhat undermining the claim that the developing countries' desire for reverse discrimination could not be accommodated within the confines of the GATT. The claim was particularly hollow because the problem of market disruption seemed to be largely a matter of developing countries exploiting their comparative advantage of low labour costs.[15]

For Canada, the problem of imports of low-cost textiles and clothing had been a relatively minor issue, easily contained within the provisions of, first, the cotton textile arrangements and, then, the MFA. In 1976, however, tighter US and EC quotas led to a rapid surge in exports to Canada and triggered the decision by the Trudeau government to impose global quotas on all imports of clothing pursuant to GATT article XIX (emergency action). The United States and the EC found the Canadian response highly offensive, since it included quotas on their exports, as well as those of developing countries. Insistent claims for compensation, as allowed under article XIX, convinced the Canadian government to replace the global quotas with comprehensive bilateral restraint agreements with most of the suppliers of low-cost textiles and clothing, a network of agreements that ultimately extended to more than thirty countries. The episode proved a watershed in Canadian relations with developing countries. On balance, Canada was regarded as more favourably disposed toward their interests than the United States or the EC, but the purity of its voice had become somewhat sullied.

A further focus of GATT activity became the settlement of disputes. The US government rediscovered dispute settlement in the 1970s, and brought it to a new level through the deployment of section 301 of the Trade Act of 1974. Section 301 had been added to US trade legislation by the Trade Act of 1974. It provided procedures for US private interests to launch complaints about foreign trade and industrial practices that "burdened" US commerce, and for formal US government action to address such practices, including through GATT dispute settlement procedures. By the end of the decade, the EC and Canada had also begun to make greater and more strategic use of dispute settlement. All three governments were exploring both the usefulness and the limits of the GATT's dispute settlement provisions.[16]

The proliferation of dispute settlement cases demonstrated clearly that the GATT's existing procedures could be used to discipline trade, that they could be used to create negotiating leverage, and that there were limits to what the United States and the EC would tolerate from each other or from others. The fact that other contracting

Table 11.3

Canada, the GATT, and trade disputes, 1962-79

1962	US complaint concerning the application of values for duty on potatoes imported from the United States
1974	Canadian complaint regarding EC obligations to compensate Canada under Article XXIV:6
1975	US complaint regarding the imposition of import quotas on eggs under article XI:2(c)(i) as part of the implementation of supply management
1975	Canada joins the EC in a complaint involving US DISC program
1976	EC complaint regarding the withdrawal by Canada of tariff concessions on lead and zinc pursuant to article XXVIII:3
1979	Canadian complaint regarding quantitative restrictions imposed by Japan on imports of leather

parties participated in a number of these cases and supplied the panels with briefs further underlined the importance of these proceedings both in their own right and as fodder for future negotiations. While many of the cases created political discomfort for those countries in which practices were found wanting, on balance the settlements generated a positive momentum supporting rule making as important and beneficial. They also suggested that it was important to resolve negotiating issues on the basis of clear and detailed texts. Ambiguity only fuelled more disputes and allowed issues to be settled on a basis beyond the control of national governments. The disputes also illustrated the continuing ambivalence among politicians about the value of a rules-based system: to the extent that GATT findings confirmed their views or political needs, such a system was beneficial; to the extent they did not, it was inconvenient and even irrelevant.[17] (See table 11.3 for Canada's involvement in GATT disputes.)

Canada became fully embroiled in GATT's dispute settlement provisions in 1974 in a dispute with the EC arising out of the negotiations to settle compensation claims, pursuant to article XXIV:6, following the entry of the United Kingdom, Ireland, and Denmark into the Community. Canada was not satisfied with the results and finally took unilateral action by withdrawing tariff concessions on lead and zinc. This move in turn led to an EC complaint that Canada's retaliatory measures were more valuable than the estimate of its original claims. The second panel's findings led to a satisfactory settlement.[18] Canada was at the receiving end of a complaint by the United States in 1975 that the quotas set by Canada on eggs as part of the introduction of supply management were too low. This issue was settled with the help of an examination of the issues by a working party, one of the last instances in which a working party rather than a panel was used in a dispute settlement case.[19]

The most interesting and difficult case involved a US export promotion tax scheme implemented in 1971 as part of the Nixon measures, the Domestic International Sales Corporation. The EC complained that the DISC program amounted to a prohibited export subsidy, and Canada later joined in that complaint. The United States countered by charging that the territorial tax systems of Belgium, the Netherlands, and France had a similar effect and were thus also prohibited. The case continued a long-standing controversy over the impact of direct and indirect taxes on exports. The United States took the view that rebates of indirect taxes on exported products, such as value-added taxes, provided an advantage to European firms. US state and federal governments relied more on direct taxes, such as income taxes, which the GATT provisions indicated could not be rebated on exports. This so-called border tax adjustment issue had never been resolved to the satisfaction of either side. The US introduction of the DISC program, however, constituted a unilateral declaration to resolve the issue in its favour as well as a direct challenge to the GATT rules.[20]

A single panel of tax experts was appointed to examine the case and reported in 1976 with a complex set of findings which indicated that the DISC indeed amounted to a prohibited export subsidy and that the European tax schemes contained elements that could be considered GATT-inconsistent and in need of some adjustments. The EC and Canada were eager to adopt the panel's report, but the United States blocked adoption for the next five years, waiting until after the conclusion of the Tokyo Round to accept a heavily compromised decision. Even then the United States waited a further three years to implement the report by making some cosmetic changes that transformed the DISC program into the FSC program (Foreign Sales Corporation).[21]

The DISC case showed the limits of dispute settlement. Important cases involving the major players could lead to stalemates. The lesson was that dispute settlement, if it was to work to the benefit of all, needed some fundamental reforms. For one thing, it was important that the parties to a dispute should not be involved in the decision-making process. Equally, however, it was evident that issues concerning highly complex matters such as tax schemes might be beyond the GATT's competence. Nevertheless, the successful conclusion of a number of other difficult but less complex matters over the ensuing years – including a number of cases involving Canada, for example, the US complaint about Canada's investment screening procedures – indicated that dispute settlement procedures, properly used, could add an important dimension to making the GATT – and the trade regime more generally – work more effectively.[22]

In the years following the Kennedy Round, therefore, activity in the GATT reached a new level. Although the GATT continued to enjoy a relatively obscure place on the political radar screens of member governments, it occupied a growing amount of attention from trade specialists in capitals and required a beefed-up permanent presence in Geneva. Canada's representation to the GATT by this time included the deputy permanent representative of the Geneva mission – Frank Petrie from 1967

GATT finally gains headquarters in 1977 appropriate to its growing importance.

to 1970, Percy Eastham from 1970 to 1973, Frank Stone from 1973 to 1977, and Bob Martin from 1977 to 1981 – as well as two other members of the mission on a regular basis. In addition, the ambassador was available for heavy lifting as required. In 1980, the government appointed as its ambassador to Geneva an official – Don McPhail – with extensive trade policy experience, in recognition of the growing role trade and economic issues played in the activities of the Geneva mission to the European seat of the United Nations and the various specialized agencies headquartered there.

By this time, the GATT's regular activities included annual sessions of the contracting parties, usually held at the end of November, monthly meetings of the Council of Representatives, and periodic meetings of a range of committees and subsidiary bodies, including the Antidumping Practices Committee, the Dairy Management Committee, the Textiles Committee and the Textiles Surveillance Body, the Balance-of-Payments Committee, the Trade and Development Committee, the Budget Committee, working parties to examine regional trade agreements, accession negotiations, and other policy issues, and dispute settlement panels. In 1973, with the commencement of the Tokyo Round negotiations, activity at the GATT had reached a new level.

The Secretariat had grown commensurably to keep up with these increasing demands, although it remained small by UN standards. It had clearly outgrown the temporary buildings scattered throughout the park surrounding the Palais, the European seat of the UN. While the GATT remained an interim agreement, it clearly was there for the long term, and its lack of a permanent seat had become a handicap. The Swiss government agreed, and in 1977 it provided the GATT with a permanent home of its own. The Centre William Rappard, on the shores of Lake Geneva, originally the home of the International Labour Organization, had been refitted for the GATT and the UN High Commission for Refugees (UNHCR). Over the next decade, as GATT work expanded further, so did its need for space; by the early

1990s, UNHCR had moved to its own building, and the GATT could finally claim a permanent seat of its very own. It was in this splendid building that the drama of the final stages of the Tokyo Round would be played out.

Launching the Tokyo Round Negotiations

By August 1972, there was a broad consensus favouring the launch of a new round of multilateral negotiations, with the conspicuous exception of the US Congress. Officials in both the Johnson and Nixon administrations had seen the utility of a new round, but had not succeeded in convincing a sceptical Congress. The fallout from the August 1971 measures to address the US monetary crisis had, however, changed the mood sufficiently to get the ball rolling. The EC, Canada, and Japan were all in a receptive mood, and the output of the OECD Rey Group, the US Williams Commission, and the GATT work program had created a solid intellectual foundation for negotiations reaching well beyond the traditional issue of lowering tariff barriers. It took a further two years, however, before the necessary US legislation was passed with the Trade Act of 1974.[23]

By this time the EC had expanded to include the United Kingdom, Ireland, and Denmark, and had established preferential arrangements with the rest of western Europe, with members' former colonial possessions, and with some of their near neighbours around the Mediterranean. Developing countries had become the most numerous members of the GATT, and the Japanese assault on Western markets had begun in earnest. The cozy postwar club of like-minded countries, all of roughly similar economic clout except for their leader, the United States, had disappeared. Up until the Tokyo Round, there had continued to be broad acceptance that one of the fundamental purposes of the GATT was to provide a forum for the gradual liberalization of trade, even if in their individual policies member countries sometimes honoured this principle only in the breach. Now the emphasis changed to rule making and to the management of trade relations and disputes. The challenge was whether the negotiations would lead to substantive and liberalizing results or focus on procedural and management-oriented issues.

Preparations for the round had established that it would be dominated by the United States and the EC, with Japan still not ready to become an equal partner. No clear coalition of smaller players seemed capable of providing a counterforce sufficient to change the fact that the Tokyo Round would be a bilateral negotiation masquerading as a multilateral negotiation. Its impact, however, would be multilateral; all the other players would have to participate, even though in the end they would not determine the final outcome. For Canada, the challenge would increasingly be finding the best means of influencing the major players in order to shape the outcome in ways beneficial to Canadian interests.

Each of the two principal protagonists operated within constraints that enormously complicated their ability to cut a satisfactory deal. For the United States, the continuing tensions between the administration and Congress, exacerbated after 1974 by the Watergate scandal and the concomitant collapse of the congressional seniority system, coloured every aspect of the negotiations. Congress still considered the GATT to be an executive agreement, implemented on a provisional basis. Any new agreement thus required congressional authority to negotiate and congressional approval to implement. Getting either required extensive effort on the part of the president and his advisors to engage the support of members of Congress and the interests most adept at influencing them.[24]

The EC operated under similar constraints. The Commission was empowered by the Treaty of Rome to negotiate on behalf of the member states, but on the basis of a mandate established by them. Getting a mandate required careful and sometimes difficult internal negotiations among the nine member states and the Commission. As in the United States, this complex environment encouraged skilled private interests to find opportunities to advance their views, further complicating the process. Once these internal negotiations were completed, the Commission had very little flexibility in exercising its mandate in Geneva.[25]

Despite the US lack of negotiating authority, the negotiations were formally launched in September 1973 at a ministerial meeting in Tokyo with 102 countries participating. By this time the GATT could boast eighty-three members, but the contracting parties had decided that the negotiations should be open to any country contemplating membership. The political focus of the ministerial meeting was the role and interests of the developing countries, and this emphasis was clearly articulated in the ministerial declaration. The rest of the declaration, however, had been carefully negotiated prior to the meeting and reflected the positions and priorities of the major players.[26] Inauspiciously, once the ministerial meeting concluded, there was little more that could be done until the US delegation was in a position to negotiate.

The United States Gains Authority

President Nixon's request for new trade authority continued to experience heavy weather and delays in Congress, many of them unrelated to trade issues. War in the Middle East and congressional anxiety about East-West détente also intervened. A further delay resulted from the combined impact of President Nixon's resignation following the Watergate scandal and a major difference of view between Congress and the administration on granting MFN status to the Soviet Union. The Trade Act finally passed at the end of 1974, nearly two years after the US administration had committed the United States to a new round of negotiations. The act's provisions, however, were more than enough to arm negotiators with a sweeping new mandate. The provisions included:

- a five-year negotiating authority to 4 January 1980 and expedited or fast-track approval procedures, including a requirement for extensive business, labour, and congressional consultations throughout the negotiations and the approval process
- a linear tariff-cutting authority and power to address a range of non tariff barriers

- fine-tuning of the trade remedy laws, relaxing procedural and substantive criteria, and giving import-competing interests greater assurance of the availability of relief, as well as the inclusion of an expanded "fair trade" provision, section 301, to address fairness in US export trade and the enforcement of US trade agreement rights
- authority to extend a general system of preferences (GSP) in favour of developing countries
- renaming of the Tariff Commission as the US International Trade Commission and expansion of its authority
- expanded adjustment assistance programs
- the Jackson-Vanik amendment to address the thorny issue of MFN treatment for the Soviet Union and its satellites; the administration was authorized to extend MFN treatment to the USSR in return for assurances that the USSR would permit its citizens freedom to emigrate.

On balance, the Trade Act of 1974 was an internationalist piece of legislation for which congressional approval would have seemed impossible only a few years earlier. By the end of 1974, however, Nixon had resigned, Gerald Ford had succeeded him in the White House, and the Trade Act had easily passed Congress. The act clearly set out a US negotiating position that reflected a consensus among the administration, Congress, and leading trade and labour interests, and it provided procedures allowing the US delegation to exercise leadership and conclude a big agreement.[27]

To keep the United States from dominating the establishment of the agenda and the modalities of the negotiations, the EC adopted and published its own decision – the Overall Approach – similarly setting out its objectives and negotiating limits. The document asserted the EC's equal status with the United States and reiterated that US bullying tactics, such as the 1971 Nixon measures, would be counterproductive. To underline the point, the EC insisted that progress in the trade talks be directly related to satisfactory discussions on monetary stability and other broader trade and economic issues.[28]

Canada Defines Its Interests
By this time Canada had developed a more diversified industrial base and was exporting a wider variety of products. While the United States remained Canada's principal market, officials concluded that any hope of seriously diversifying Canadian trade required full participation in the round. Canada's objectives, therefore, reflected its more sophisticated industrial structure and determination to be a player. Canada was seeking to:

- reduce foreign tariffs facing current and potential Canadian exports, particularly low "nuisance" tariffs

- enlarge the number of markets into which Canadian products could enter duty-free, including the United States
- eliminate or reduce nontariff barriers inhibiting Canadian exports, particularly technical barriers and government procurement preferences
- encourage investment in the production of more highly processed raw materials and foodstuffs, as well as fully manufactured goods
- lower Canadian tariffs consistent with a more competitive international environment, but limit tariff concessions in areas of particular employment and import sensitivity, such as textiles and footwear
- ensure that agreed-upon reductions in Canadian protection would be phased in over a period of time sufficiently long to permit orderly adjustment to the new trading environment
- reach desirable changes in international trading rules with respect to countervailing and antidumping duties and emergency safeguard actions, while limiting the capacity of foreign governments to act arbitrarily against Canadian exports
- strengthen the rules and procedures for the settlement of disputes.[29]

In a departure from its approach during the Dillon and Kennedy Rounds, Canada made it clear from the outset that it would participate fully. Nevertheless, officials sought to find a formula that would meet important industrial and export policy objectives on a basis that would be politically palatable. Canada entered the round with the highest tariffs in the industrialized world. As a way out of the difficulties posed by the structure of its economy and its high dependence on resource exports, officials had developed the "sector" approach: Canada would propose that the main resource importers substantially reduce their tariffs on raw materials and semiprocessed resources, in return for which Canada would reduce its tariffs on finished goods in the same sector.[30] Officials hoped that the sector approach would allow Canada to make a major contribution in liberalizing world trade based on maximizing the benefits of its strong resources base.

Leaders of all the parties in Parliament welcomed the launch of negotiations and urged the government to participate vigorously. The minister for industry, trade and commerce, Alistair Gillespie, in a speech in Toronto on his return from Tokyo, enthused that the negotiations "hold tremendous potential for Canada, especially with our abundance of resources and the government's policy that, where competitive, these resources be processed in Canada prior to export."[31]

To ensure the effectiveness of its participation, Canada took steps even before the official launch in Tokyo to gauge the views of industry and other interests. As the negotiations approached, the government appointed a Canadian Trade and Tariffs Committee chaired by retired trade official Louis Couillard to meet with interested parties. In the first year of its operation, the committee received some four hundred briefs setting out the hopes and anxieties of the Canadian private sector.[32] As during the Kennedy Round, there were many anxious voices, but also many that looked for new opportunities in the US, EC, Japanese, and other markets.

By the end of 1974, Canada had selected a team of seasoned officials to lead the Canadian effort in Geneva, supported by officials in Ottawa as required. Rodney Grey, a veteran of both the Dillon and Kennedy Rounds and by this time the assistant deputy minister responsible for trade and tariffs in the Department of Finance, was appointed to head the delegation. He was backed up by Mel Clark, former director general of the Department of Industry, Trade and Commerce's Office of General Relations, and a team of specialists drawn from ITC, Finance, Agriculture, and External Affairs. They had engaged Eric Wyndham White, GATT's first director general, to provide strategic advice. The team set up quarters in Geneva by the beginning of 1975, separate from Canada's regular permanent mission, emphasizing that it was dedicated to a single task, the conclusion of a multilateral agreement favourable to Canadian interests.

The Issues

Other delegations were similarly in residence by the beginning of 1975, ready to begin the arduous task of building the basis of a big agreement. The Tokyo Declaration called for negotiations based on the principles of mutual advantage, mutual commitment, overall reciprocity, and MFN. The goal was to achieve "an overall balance of advantage at the highest possible level."[33] These principles and objectives, however, provided substantial room for posturing and significant scope for negotiation. In pursuing their task, the negotiators were able to build on the extensive preparatory work that had already been in progress for some seven years. The negotiations revolved around five principal sets of issues: tariffs, agriculture, nontariff barriers, safeguards, and the participation of developing countries.[34]

Tariffs

As with the Kennedy Round, the major players were agreed that the tariff negotiations would be organized around a formula approach. The basis for the formula, however, varied from player to player. Both the Rey Group and the Williams Commission had favoured a broad linear reduction and had even indicated that in many sectors it should be possible for the industrialized countries to aim for tariff-free trade linked to a ten-year transition period. While some delegations could identify with such an ambitious objective, no delegation came armed with sufficient authority to put it into play. The United States had sufficient authority to make a further 50 percent cut feasible but was keen to reduce the level of effective protection in the European Community. The EC sought greater convergence in tariff levels, reducing the wide dispersion and eliminating the peaks in the US tariff. Canada proposed sectoral negotiations to address the problems posed by its industrial structure. Japan was interested in as liberal a formula as possible, secure in the knowledge that access to its market was determined by more subtle measures than the tariff.

Tariff negotiations can involve a highly complex ritual of calculating off-setting concessions to satisfy the myriad interests that want to know what a government "gained" in return for "sacrificing" its protection. The astute negotiator learns how to create elaborate constructions to measure such gains and concessions, which may have a basis in fact, but which often involve "might-have's" and "could-be's." At the end what counts is confidence that there is political balance, with more happy than sad faces among interested parties. Many months were devoted to finding a formula that would satisfy the disparate interests of the major players.

Agriculture

The Tokyo Declaration recognized that there were sectors with special characteristics that might need to be handled separately. The Williams Commission had given agriculture high priority, and US negotiators had expressed a strong resolve that this time agriculture would not be swept under the rug. The EC, on the other hand, was determined to prevent any erosion in the Common Agricultural Policy (CAP) and sought to build on its Kennedy Round proposal of establishing commodity-specific "margins of support" that would consolidate rather than eliminate protection. As noted by Gilbert Winham: "The EC was simply unwilling to allow trade to exact a social cost it had already declined to pay."[35] In the EC view, managing international trade in agriculture through commodity agreements would help to stabilize world markets. Smaller agricultural exporters like Canada and Australia had girded their loins for yet another attempt at prying open the markets of the United States and Europe and at waging a frontal assault on the many foreign distorting programs that undermined the export basis of their farm economies. Given the wide disparity in views, the basis for a large agreement appeared elusive as discussions began.[36]

Nontariff Barriers (NTBs)

Work since the Kennedy Round had developed an agreed typology for considering NTBs. Many of the issues they raised, of course, were not new. Indeed, much of the GATT was devoted to establishing rules that would limit the capacity of governments to use NTBs to undermine their tariff commitments. Nevertheless, the extent and impact of NTBs had grown, partly in response to the pressures generated by tariff reductions, partly because tariff reductions had made traders more aware of nontariff measures affecting their access to markets. Existing GATT rules thus needed to be clarified, tightened, amplified, or expanded to address the numerous problems that had been identified. Negotiating about such a diverse range of issues, however, would require much ingenuity.[37]

The Williams Commission had considered negotiations aimed at reducing the distorting impact of NTBs to be both necessary and feasible, a judgment in which others concurred. US negotiators had placed the issue high on their agenda. They had gained the necessary authority from Congress to address NTBs and the commitment that Congress would consider the resulting agreements on their merit and without amendment. The US goal was to develop precise, binding rules to curtail the abuse of the wide range of nontariff measures. The EC was equally prepared to address NTBs, but preferred a more nuanced approach that would allow it to retain more flexibility to respond to emerging issues.

Canada shared much of the US perspective, but Canadian officials were nervous that some of the issues on the agenda, such as valuation, could cut deeply into traditional Canadian ways to address the concerns of import-competing sectors. On the other hand, access to the US government market could open up many new opportunities for competitive Canadian firms, while stronger rules governing the application of countervailing duties or the use of technical barriers to trade would create a much more stable and predictable world for Canadian traders.[38] Other smaller participants harboured similar hopes and worries. Developing countries, many of which used a wide variety of these measures as the basis for their economic development policies, cast a wary eye on this aspect of the negotiations. The goal was to negotiate new codes of conduct to address these matters, modelled on the Antidumping Code negotiated during the Kennedy Round.

Safeguards
The rapid growth in exports from Japan and from some of the more competitive developing economies in East Asia, such as South Korea and Hong Kong, had led to a rash of voluntary export restraint and similar grey-area measures. The Tokyo Declaration had indicated that these needed to be addressed. The Williams Commission had devoted considerable space to the issue, emphasizing the importance of adequate adjustment assistance to allow for an orderly transition to changing comparative advantage. The EC, on the other hand, preferred a more flexible approach to the requirements of GATT article XIX, allowing for the application of discriminatory measures when specified criteria were satisfied, such as market disruption, and subjecting these measures to multilateral control and surveillance. Market disruption was the euphemism adopted to refer to the impact of low-cost, competitive exports from East Asia. The developing countries considered the EC position to be a threat to the integrity of the principle of nondiscrimination and, even more, to be a direct challenge to the kind of preferential treatment they were seeking. Canada shared this first concern and had some sympathy for the second.[39]

Participation of Developing Countries (LDCs)
The Tokyo Declaration had zeroed in on this issue as central to the new round, recognizing that by 1973 the majority of GATT members were developing countries. The adoption of Part IV had done little to alleviate LDC concerns, and discussion in UNCTAD had further fanned the flames of dissatisfaction. The Williams Commission had expressed pious hopes about greater efforts to address the problem, but its language indicated the extent to which LDC aspirations for reverse

preferences and room for greater government intervention in the economy did not square with US ideology and values. Given the prime minister's disposition to play a constructive role, Canadian officials carried a complex brief to be as helpful and accommodating as possible without compromising other, fundamental interests.

The gap between rhetoric and reality made this a difficult issue to bring to a successful conclusion. Nevertheless, there were issues on which it seemed possible to make some progress. LDCs wanted to gain better access to OECD markets for their tropical products. They wanted to see the discriminatory regime for textiles and clothing made less restrictive. They wanted to hold the line on safeguards. They shared some of the concerns of traditional food exporters, although many depended on food aid and thus were content to see production surpluses disposed of in this way.[40] The OPEC-induced oil crisis at the onset of the negotiations convinced the LDCs that if they maintained solidarity, they had negotiating power. US and EC interest in enhancing security of supply and, after 1976, the Carter administration's less doctrinaire position on markets and commodity agreements suggested that the Tokyo Round might lead to a breakthrough.

Course of the Negotiations
Between the launch of negotiations in September 1973 and the summer of 1977, little of consequence happened. A major international negotiation involves a significant investment of political commitment, and between 1973 and 1977, none of the leading governments were prepared to make that commitment. There were too many pressing problems on the agenda. The outbreak of war in the Middle East in October 1973 unleashed a series of political and economic events that more than occupied the available attention of political leaders.

The deep division between the United States and the EC on the approach to agriculture was another reason for delay.[41] Senior members of the Nixon administration, as well as of the US negotiating team, were convinced that a deal that did not include major progress on agriculture could not be sold to Congress. They insisted that agricultural issues had to be folded into the rest of the negotiations and should not be treated separately. The EC, on the other hand, could not bend on agriculture. Having concluded a laborious internal negotiation to establish the Common Agricultural Policy (CAP) and then having adapted it to the entry of Britain, Ireland, and Denmark, the EC was in no position to make any major changes in either the goals or the operation of the CAP. For the EC, no deal was better than a deal that eviscerated the CAP. US insistence that the CAP had to be on the table was seen at best as an effort to put the EC on the defensive on the whole range of issues, and at worst as obtuse myopia on the part of US officials. Until this issue was settled, however, it was difficult to make much progress at all except at the most technical level.

Between the first meeting of the Trade Negotiations Committee (TNC) in late 1973 and the beginning of serious negotiations early in 1977, the outward appearance was that the negotiations were marking time. In one sense, this was true. Until the United States became fully engaged politically, little could be decided. The United States did not gain negotiating authority until early in 1975 when President Ford finally signed the long-delayed Trade Act of 1974. Presidential politics further delayed full US engagement until after the 1976 election. The appointment of Bob Strauss as newly elected president Jimmy Carter's special trade representative gave the negotiations a new air of reality, and a whirlwind of activity in the first half of 1977 culminating in the Downing Street Declaration by the Summit Seven gave the impression that the negotiations were finally on track.[42] On the sensitive issue of agriculture, Strauss was prepared to be wholly pragmatic. What mattered was a good result, not the technique employed. If the EC preferred a separate discussion on agriculture, the new administration was prepared to bend. In return, the EC enthusiastically endorsed Strauss' plan for an expedited timetable.[43]

The negotiators, however, had not wholly wasted the intervening three years. Work had proceeded in six groups: tariffs, nontariff measures, agriculture, sector negotiations, tropical products, and safeguards. A seventh group on "framework" issues was added in 1976, devoted largely to the question of special and differential treatment for developing countries. In these groups, and in a range of bilateral, plurilateral, and other meetings, underbrush was being cleared away, ideas were being put forward and rejected or shaped to appeal to broader interests. Limits were being established and the strength of commitments tested. Clearer political engagement might have given these discussions more urgency and a greater sense of reality, but good negotiators know how to adapt to shifting constraints. Given the range and complexity of the agenda and the number of players involved, there was much to be said for allowing time to sharpen and ripen arguments and positions before the negotiations were lifted to a new, more urgent level.

The GATT's first six rounds had focused on reducing tariffs, and governments had gained considerable experience in finding the necessary political support for their results. During the Tokyo Round, the tariff negotiations formed only part of a much larger negotiation. Governments were much less experienced in the political economy of bringing such a complex undertaking to a successful conclusion. It had been more than a generation since they had negotiated the original agreement, and only a part of that negotiation had succeeded. The Treaties of Rome and Stockholm had involved considerable rule writing, but among much smaller and more homogeneous groups of countries. Negotiating a series of codes on a diverse range of nontariff issues, therefore, constituted a major challenge.

Given the dominance of the EC and the United States in the negotiations, the results needed to satisfy the conflicting objectives and values of both. In a manner reminiscent of the original GATT negotiations in the 1940s, the United States continued to push for an outcome rich in clearly articulated and enforceable rules, while the EC, like the United Kingdom a generation earlier, preferred a more flexible outcome that would provide greater room for the rules to be developed through practice and subsequent negotiation. Nevertheless, the commitment in the early stages of the negotiations to the elaboration of codes to address nontariff issues clearly suggested that the balance between these competing American and European values had shifted permanently toward those of the United States. The growing penchant of both the EC and the United States to resort to formal dispute settlement in the 1970s further underlined this change in emphasis. Both the EC and the United States had determined that even in a bipolar world, agreed rules and procedures for the resolution of disputes were preferable to continued resort to power and negotiation.

By the end of 1977, it was clear that the missing level of political commitment had been found, and ministers and officials began to speak confidently of concluding the negotiations by the fall of 1978. The US negotiating deadline of 4 January 1980 seemed far off, but given the complex requirements of the Trade Act, it would take US officials the better part of a year to satisfy them following the conclusion of negotiations. The end of 1978 was, therefore, a prudent target date.

By the end of February 1978, a working hypothesis had been accepted for the tariff negotiations based on a Swiss formula, and the United States, EC, Japan, and many others had tabled their tariff offers and requests listing the products they would be prepared to subject to the formula, and those they would except from it to varying degrees. Canada was conspicuous by the absence of its offer. Canada had placed much faith in the sector discussions, hoping that they would yield results that would provide Canada with better access for its resource-based products at higher stages of processing. The United States, EC, and Japan, however, had not expressed much interest, and, with adoption of the Swiss formula, the sector discussions collapsed.[44] Ministers and officials now scrambled to develop a political basis for a settlement based on the Swiss formula. As Frank Stone explains, Canada announced that its "acceptance of the Swiss formula would depend, among other things, on the substantial elimination or reduction of many of the relatively low tariffs facing Canada's industrial exports; the elimination, reduction, or bringing under effective control of certain non-tariff measures; and a greater liberalization of tariff and non-tariff barriers in the key resource-based sectors – of Canada's trade."[45] Time would tell whether this critically important requirement could now be met.

The negotiations on nontariff measures had settled down to the elaboration of a series of codes on customs valuation, industrial standards, government procurement, and subsidies and countervailing duties. Each presented challenges, but the nature of what would be required was beginning to take shape. The group on safeguards was similarly working on a supplementary agreement. The sticking point was whether it would provide for the application of discriminatory measures and on what terms. The negotiations on agriculture were not going well. The United States had tabled an ambitious set of requests aimed at *liberalizing* world trade in agriculture. The EC, more interested in *managing* world trade in agriculture, had eyed the US request with some trepidation but had not made much headway on its own agenda. Negotiations focusing on dairy and meat in Geneva, and on grains at the International Wheat Council in London, were leading to the prospect of agreements providing for more transparency and consultations.[46]

The aspirations of the developing countries were not gaining the attention promised by the Tokyo Declaration. Indeed, throughout the negotiations, developing countries invested much more energy in broader political discussions in the United Nations and UNCTAD than in pursuing their interests in the multilateral trade negotiations. The eagerness of some of the more insistent LDCs to transform the GATT from a passive into an active instrument of change did not appeal to most of the core members, but the rhetoric of the North-South dialogue required that the issue not be confronted directly. Canada was among those most dedicated to finding a way to appeal to broader LDC participation, but it did not make much progress.

Multilateral trade negotiations can be extremely labour-intensive. The range of subjects discussed and the complexity of the issues involved require a deep level of expertise. For large players like the United States and the EC, it is not unusual for dozens of specialists to be engaged. Each code required a lead negotiator as well as various specialists from interested agencies and directorates around Washington, Brussels, and other capitals. Generally, the Tokyo Round engaged a much larger number of players from capitals, with the resident team in Geneva often playing a support role or providing continuity and strategic advice. To conclude its tariff negotiation with the EC, for example, the United States sent twenty-one people to Geneva for the final year of the negotiations.[47]

For smaller players, such complex negotiations can constitute a major challenge. Canada, for example, found its resources severely taxed and in the summer of 1977 made significant changes. To back up Ambassador Grey and his team of senior trade specialists in Geneva, the government appointed J.H. (Jake) Warren to take command of the Ottawa end of the negotiations as Canadian Coordinator for Trade Negotiations (CCTN). He was provided with a small team of trade officials whose main function was to ensure coordination among the many specialists in various departments around Ottawa working on individual aspects of the Tokyo Round file, as well as to promote effective communication with provincial officials and private-sector interests. In the final year of the negotiations, Warren met almost daily with a core group of senior officials from Industry, Trade and Commerce, Finance, External Affairs, and Agriculture, supplemented as required by working-level officials and specialists from every agency with programs, policies, or laws that might be affected. He also met almost weekly with a special cabinet committee chaired by Deputy Prime Minister Allan MacEachen, established to maintain political oversight and direction.[48]

The keen interest of provincial governments in trade negotiations was a new development, raised by provincial responsibility for some of the issues under negotiation, including government procurement preferences, liquor board sales and distribution practices, and product standards. In addition, the provinces insisted that the negotiations as a whole affected the full range of their economic development policies and demanded a voice in the formulation of the government's negotiating positions. Both Warren in Ottawa and Grey in Geneva expended considerable energy in ensuring that provincial ministers and officials were comfortable with the issues and ready to lend public support at the conclusion of the negotiations, without in any way compromising the federal government's ultimate responsibility.[49]

For even smaller participants such as New Zealand, the Nordics, and most of the developing countries, the resource requirements often went beyond their capacity, mandating that their representatives in Geneva learn to participate strategically. Because much of the real negotiation was taking place in bilateral and plurilateral meetings among the major delegations, a large part of the task of Geneva-based representatives of smaller players was to glean intelligence from the major delegations and the Secretariat in order to advise their governments on developments critical to their interests. Embassies in major capitals supplemented this information by cultivating their own contacts within each capital's trade policy community.

The greater use of computers made it somewhat easier to gather, store, and analyze information, particularly in the tariff negotiations. Juggling information about the tariff schedules, offers, and requests of several dozen players can be extremely demanding, and the Tokyo Round negotiators found that the technical work done by the Secretariat in the years immediately after the Kennedy Round in providing a more uniform basis for reporting and analyzing trade and tariff data was tremendously helpful. The use of computers, however, did not fully come into its own until the Uruguay Round, when the almost universal adoption of the Harmonized System of Tariff Nomenclature had further standardized information and eased the task of analyzing and comparing the quality and value of tariff offers and requests.

Like Canada, all the major players had organized more formal procedures for integrating the views of domestic interests into the negotiating process. In the case of the United States, the Trade Act of 1974 had mandated the establishment of a dense network of private-sector advisory bodies, as well as more formal consultation requirements to ensure congressional oversight.

Conclusion and Results
All negotiations must eventually come to a conclusion. The negotiators can successfully spin the technical dimensions of the negotiations out as long as necessary; in the end, however, the conclusion is not determined by them but by their political masters, who must decide whether the balance needed to address the claims of competing interests has been achieved. In Bob Strauss, the United States had found a political operator with a superb sense of how and when to drive a negotiation to a conclusion. From his entry on the scene at the beginning of 1977 through the spring of 1979, it was his dominating personality that propelled the negotiations. Making full use of G7 summits and bilateral and plurilateral meetings with the

other principal players, he orchestrated the negotiations to a successful conclusion, gaining for the United States the essential core of its objectives, but fully prepared to let smaller issues slide for the sake of the overall package.[50]

For Canada, the final year of negotiations involved extensive engagement at political and official levels. In Geneva, Ambassador Grey and his team were now engaged in a heavy round of bilateral and plurilateral discussions, feeding the results back to the team in Ottawa and depending on Ottawa for fresh input and instructions. As a member of the Summit Seven, Canada was involved in discussions at the highest level steering the negotiations to a conclusion. Finally, both Geneva- and Ottawa-based officials met frequently with their counterparts in Brussels and Washington to craft the complex set of codes that would form the heart of the result on nontariff barriers. Canada was particularly keen, for example, to ensure that the United States adopted an injury test in its countervailing duty proceedings and relaxed its Buy America provisions in government procurement. Thus Canada found itself as involved as it had been during the original GATT negotiations, and the quality of its participation ensured it a significant influence.

Despite Strauss's superb leadership, the Tokyo Round concluded with more of a whimper than a bang on 12 April 1979. Various issues remained unresolved, including the bilateral settlement of the US-Japan tariff negotiations and the safeguards negotiations. Efforts would continue on both fronts beyond the deadline, successfully in the case of the first, unsuccessfully in the case of the second. The strong sense of accomplishment that had characterized the concluding session of the Kennedy Round was not evident at the final formal meeting of the Tokyo Round. Many of the developing country delegations were particularly dissatisfied. They had harboured high hopes in the early stages of the negotiations, only to see their most important objectives gradually relegated to the sidelines. For the major delegations also, satisfaction had to wait. The principal part of the negotiations involved texts that had to be ratified and implemented into domestic law. Until that had been accomplished, the job of the negotiators was not really finished. Indeed, much of the next nine months was devoted to an intense round of domestic negotiations about the details of implementation, as well as careful monitoring of what the other major players were doing. The extent to which the results would be implemented faithfully into US law was particularly important.[51] Nevertheless, despite disappointments and shortcomings, the negotiators had succeeded in bringing together a large package of rules, concessions, improvements, and commitments on tariffs, NTBs, agriculture, safeguards, and framework issues.[52]

Tariffs

The tariff deal covered US$155 billion in trade in 1979, or approximately 10 percent of world trade in goods. It involved both a high degree of tariff harmonization and a reduction in protection. The formula required that the higher the tariff, the deeper the cut. As a result, the cuts expanded and opened up more certain export opportunities. In the case of industrial products, tariffs on most manufactured goods in the EC and Japan were reduced to the 5 to 7 percent range at the end of the eight-year phase-in period, while raw materials were, with some exceptions, to enter these markets free of duty or at low rates. For the United States, average tariffs on manufactured goods were in the area of 4 percent, although some products such as certain chemicals, textiles, and footwear would continue to enter at much higher rates; most industrial materials would enter free or at very low levels. Canada agreed to reduce its industrial tariff to an average of between 9 and 10 percent. Most industrial raw material imports continued to be free of duty so that the overall incidence of the tariff was reduced to the 4 to 5 percent range. Like other participants, Canada made no reductions – or comparatively small reductions – in the level of Canadian tariffs on certain items such as textiles, clothing, footwear, toys, flatware, other consumer products, and ships.

The overall tariff package amounted to a further reduction in the tariffs of the industrialized countries of 33 percent on a trade-weighted basis, or 38 percent as a simple arithmetic average, in line with the levels achieved during the original 1947 negotiations and during the Kennedy Round. For the industrialized countries, virtually all tariffs on industrial products were now bound against further increase. Only a small percentage of the tariffs on industrial products traded among the industrialized countries were not reduced. Fully a third of that trade would no longer be subject to any duties. Developing countries made few concessions and received few in return, but they would benefit from the broader concessions by virtue of the MFN rule, while the GSP schemes in force in all the industrialized countries were calibrated to deliver automatic reductions as a result of MFN cuts.

Nontariff Barriers
The negotiations on nontariff issues resulted in the conclusion of new agreements or codes governing subsidies and countervailing measures, government procurement, licensing, technical barriers to trade (or product standards), and valuation. There were also revisions to the Kennedy Round agreement on antidumping. These codes represented a major change in the GATT, from broad statements of principle to detailed constructions of rules that clarified and amplified the original rules. In addition, Canada, the United States, the EC, Japan, and Sweden concluded a sectoral agreement governing trade in civil aircraft that provided, inter alia, for the elimination of tariffs on virtually all trade in civil aircraft and parts.

Agriculture
In the end, there was no major breakthrough on agriculture; the EC successfully held the line. Nevertheless, participants did agree to reductions in tariffs on a range of fish and agriculture products. A large portion of that trade, of course, was already duty-free, but cuts on tariffs affecting a further $15 billion in trade were agreed. In addition, two commodity agreements were concluded on bovine meat and dairy

products providing for consultation and other transparency provisions. Separate from the GATT but in a related negotiation in London, members of the International Wheat Council had concluded a new wheat agreement as well as a food aid convention. Nevertheless, agriculture would continue to be handled largely outside the GATT's normal framework of rules.[53]

Safeguards
It did not prove possible to conclude the safeguards negotiations. The gap between the EC and the developing countries was too wide, particularly after both the United States and Canada expressed strong reservations about the desirability of a code embracing discriminatory measures. As a face-saving gesture, it was agreed that negotiations continue with a view to their conclusion as soon as possible.

Framework Issues
A series of understandings and decisions were reached in the Framework Group, which clarified or amended existing obligations and practices. These included: agreement on an "Enabling Clause" allowing industrialized countries to extend differential and more favourable treatment to developing countries, such as their respective GSP schemes; a text setting out obligations relating to safeguards taken for development purposes; a declaration clarifying obligations relating to balance-of-payments measures; an understanding codifying practice regarding notification, consultation, dispute settlement, and surveillance; and an understanding regarding export restrictions and charges. The overall impact of these agreements was to create a firmer basis for the GATT's role in the management of trade relations.

Implications for Canada
For Canada, the package represented both major achievements and disappointments. The failure of the sector approach meant that low tariffs on slightly processed industrial materials, particularly in the EC and Japan, would continue to inhibit further processing in Canada. On the other hand, improved access across a wide range of products of export interest to Canadian firms would create new opportunities in the US, EC, Japanese, and other markets. On balance, the new codes had achieved Canadian objectives. Canada was pleased with the government procurement code but disappointed in its rather small coverage. US withdrawal of its offer to include small business set-asides was particularly disappointing. (US Buy American laws set certain areas of government procurement "aside" for small businesses, even should a foreign firm be able to overcome preferences and other obstacles. For Canada, the small-business set-aside was particularly galling because what might be a "small" business in the United States would be a good-sized firm in Canada.) Canada hoped that the US obligation to implement an injury test as a result of the subsidies/countervailing duty code would bring balance into this difficult area of international trade. Acceptance of the valuation code was a major Canadian

Duncan Macpherson, "Well What's on the Agenda Today?" 27 June 1979.
Prime Minister Joe Clark and Finance Minister John Crosbie make a brief
appearance on the world stage and brush up on the Tokyo Round.

concession, requiring significant changes in Canadian practice and some erosion
in protection; Canada successfully entered a reservation that allowed it to delay
implementation until 1984. Failure on safeguards, the small package on agriculture,
and limited US reductions in tariffs on petrochemicals and transportation equipment were also major letdowns. Canada had been among those most prepared to
meet the aspirations of the developing countries and shared their dissatisfaction.[54]

On the import side, Canada agreed to substantial reductions in its tariffs, many
of which required major adjustments, although industrial users and consumers
would benefit from lower-priced imports. Adjustments in the machinery program
were among the most important concessions Canada made to the United States,
binding a number of special items, including machinery supplied by US firms, at
free. The Tokyo Round's chronicler and analyst, Gilbert Winham, suggests that this
was the price Canada paid for changes in the US Wine Gallon Assessment tax system, a concession that was critically important to Canada's large, export-oriented
distilling industry.[55]

Prime Minister Trudeau and the Liberals were in power in Ottawa throughout
the negotiations. In April 1979, however, as the director general gavelled the negotiations to a conclusion, Canada was in the middle of an electoral campaign. On 22
May, Canadians gave Joe Clark and the Conservatives a slim mandate to form a
government. Nothing could have better demonstrated the nonpartisan nature of
trade policy in Canada than the smooth transition. The results of the negotiations

were first announced by Deputy Prime Minister Allan MacEachen on 12 April, and then again by new Tory trade minister Robert de Cotret in July, both on the basis of briefing and press material prepared by the public service. While there was some initial anxiety among officials, it was quickly dissipated in the face of the great mass of detail that ministers would have to digest if they wanted to make a policy change. Not unexpectedly, the Tory ministers chose the safe course and proceeded to implement their predecessors' trade deal.

In terms of bureaucratic objectives and management, the Tokyo Round was a huge success. The provinces, whose growing interest in international affairs included trade policy, had been fully engaged and supportive. Business, more than ever before, had been consulted extensively and brought into the process. The central place of the GATT in the grand scheme of things had been confirmed to an extent few would have imagined at the beginning of the decade. Canadian officials were ready to greet the 1980s with the same enthusiasm about the benefits and possibilities of multilateral trade cooperation with which they had greeted the original GATT in the 1950s.

The Tokyo Round results were well received in Canada. The government had worked hard to discuss the issues with the provinces and the private sector, both of which were satisfied that Canada had done as well as could be expected in a multi-lateral negotiation dominated by the United States and the EC. The media were similarly prepared to judge the negotiations a qualified success. The *Globe and Mail* was typical in its assessment. It noted that Canada had gotten off comparatively lightly in earlier rounds, but that this time Canada had not escaped. It concluded, however, that with good effort by Canadian business, Canada would be a better country: "Canadian pessimists can look upon the changes in GATT as a blow to our trading hopes. Canadian optimists can look upon them as a challenge to our competitiveness."[56]

Wally Dennison, writing in the *Winnipeg Free Press,* reported widespread satisfaction in the business community, quoting Bill Fréchette of the Canadian Manufacturers' Association, who characterized the results as "a constructive outcome; the systematic effort to eliminate nontariff barriers augurs well for future trade."[57]

Richard Gwynn, writing in the *Montreal Star,* was less confident. He concluded that because Canada had gained more from the Americans than from the EC and Japan, the pull of continental geography would increase, making the noble objectives of the Third Option pursued by the Liberals less and less realistic. "Our trans-Atlantic ties of sentiment, of culture, of history, of shared values and of common political systems, are indissoluble. Our trade with Europe, West Germany excepted, has ceased to grow ... There isn't any third option."[58] Gwynn was right. The Third Option was dead or, more accurately, stillborn. One of the perverse results of the Tokyo Round, as with earlier rounds, was that it would provide far more opportunities for Canadian exports in the United States than anywhere else, and as Canadian exporters responded, they pointed to further issues with the United States that needed to be resolved. Multilateral negotiations, far from providing a basis for diversifying Canadian trade patterns, reinforced the patterns determined by geography, business judgment, and consumer preference.

The impact of eroding protection afforded to Canadian manufacturers, already evident during the 1970s and part of the fuel for industrial policy enthusiasts, would accelerate in the 1980s. Canada's bifurcated industrial structure was becoming increasingly untenable and would require both industry and government to face some critical choices. The Tokyo Round had confirmed Canada's deep commitment to a degree of liberalization hitherto unfamiliar to many Canadians, as well as strongly affirming the continuing importance of rules and the means to enforce them and settle disputes. The first accepted what had long been advocated by economists; the second reflected bureaucratic experience and preference. Both had long been resisted but would ultimately effect a revolution in the structure and performance of the Canadian economy, and require Canada to confront the full implications of deepening but silent continental integration.

More broadly, the Tokyo Round helped to unleash forces that initially led to a deep protectionist reaction but ultimately fostered, first, unprecedented levels of intra-industry trade and investment among the OECD countries, and then recognition by developing countries that they needed to find their place in a rapidly globalizing economy.

THE TWILIGHT
OF THE NATIONAL POLICY

For almost three decades after the conclusion of World War II, Canadians earned high incomes by exploiting a large resource base and exporting to a large and fast-growing US economy. Beginning in the middle of the 1970s, the structure of the world economy began to shift in a number of ways, increasing the relative supply of goods produced with unskilled labor and reducing the relative importance of natural resources in production. Canada faced prospects of generating income through the export of manufactured goods and services or enduring a declining relative standard of living.

– Richard G. Harris, Trade, Money,
and Wealth in the Canadian Economy

Pearsonian postwar diplomacy had suggested to Canadians that they could play a special and important role on the world stage, especially in matters of war and peace and trade and economic affairs. Canadians had been instrumental in the founding of the United Nations and, during its first decade, had been able to exercise strong moral leadership. The world had recognized this role by honouring Lester Pearson with the Nobel Peace Prize. Similarly, Canadians had played a large role in the establishment of the postwar multilateral trade and payments system and in providing early leadership for it. It came as something of a shock in 1975, therefore, to learn that President Giscard d'Estaing of France had invited the leading industrialized countries to a conference at Rambouillet just outside Paris to discuss trade and financial matters and had failed to invite Canada's prime minister. Some Canadians, however, delighted in this snub. Senator Grattan O'Leary, for example, wrote, "A great deal of Canada's inflated posture in foreign affairs can be attributed to Mike Pearson, who rose to prominence in the postwar years as our Minister in charge of External Affairs, and as Prime Minister very often acted as though he continued to occupy his old position. Recently the Rambouillet incident ... provided a more realistic measure of our status ... I find little excuse for the world-wide vagabondage of minor government officials on self-assigned missions to the far corners of the globe."[1]

It was a snub, however, that seriously preoccupied Canadian officials and much effort was devoted to ensuring that Canada would participate in the 1976 summit in San Juan, Puerto Rico, hosted by US president Gerald Ford. This effort proved successful, but the French slight reflected a reality that Canadian officials were finding difficult to accept. The world had changed, as had Canada, and not everyone believed that Canada was a major player or should consider its destiny to be inextricably linked to the health of multilateral institutions dominated by other players and their concerns.

Throughout the postwar years, the multilateral exchange of rights and obligations had been central to Canadian trade policy. The GATT had proved an efficient means of achieving the fundamental Canadian trade objectives of open and secure access to world markets within a stable international trading order. But as the 1980s dawned, it appeared to some that the means had become the end. Canadian trade policy seemed less concerned with Canada's further economic development and its dependence on secure and open access to foreign markets, and more with maintaining a specific trade and payments system. The central focus of Canadian trade policy appeared to be systemic and bureaucratic rather than economic and political.

It is not surprising, therefore, to find that not everyone agreed that the Tokyo Round had been a triumph of Canadian tradecraft. It was surprising, however, that the main critic should be Canada's chief negotiator. Rodney Grey had retired soon after the conclusion of the negotiations and within weeks suggested that there were disturbing dimensions to the results that he believed to be inimical to the interests of smaller countries like Canada. He pointed out that the negotiation of codes setting out rules on the application of antidumping and countervailing duties had further cemented into place a system of "contingency protection," based on remedies that could be applied when certain conditions were present. In his view, this system was suited to the politics and administrative capacities of large economies such as the United States and the European Community, but was difficult for smaller countries like Canada to apply. It reflected power-based rather than rules-based multilateralism and could create sufficient anxiety and uncertainty for traders and investors to more than offset the gains flowing from the reductions in tariffs and the introduction of new rules governing technical standards, government procurement, and other nontariff barriers.[2] Although Grey was first dismissed as an alarmist, Canadians soon learned that his assessment was both shrewd and unsettling. The implementation of the Tokyo Round into US law made private-sector access to US trade remedies easier and the chances of success more certain. Within a year, the number of cases began to mount, including against Canada.

Grey's deputy, Mel Clark, disagreed. Emphasizing the positive aspects of the round's results, he noted that Canada and the other main players had made important concessions to each other and created valuable new export opportunities.[3] It was not difficult to list them, as the government did in its press package and in ministerial statements.[4] Nevertheless, by embedding the antidumping and countervailing duty systems more firmly into the trade policies of the United States and the EC, by failing to conclude a safeguards agreement that would have arrested the growth in grey-area measures, by managing only a very small package on agriculture, and by allowing continued departures from the letter and spirit of the GATT, the character of the GATT seemed to have subtly changed from an agreement dedicated to the *liberalization* of trade to one that paid a high premium for *managing* trade.

Stability and predictability are, of course, important values in interstate relations and had always been significant goals of GATT negotiations. But a system that pays more attention to managing trade relations and less to liberalizing trade is endorsing different values. The shift in emphasis from liberalization to management during the Tokyo Round had important implications. The balance of advantage in the trading system seemed to have shifted to the two major players, the United States and the EC, at the expense of many of the smaller countries. This may not have been the objective of the negotiators, but it soon seemed to be the result.

In a similar note of caution, US GATT scholar John Jackson indicated that the implementation of the codes on a smorgasbord basis had exacerbated the GATT's constitutional weaknesses. GATT members could now choose whether to implement all, some, or none of the Tokyo Round codes.[5] Most developing countries decided that they would not implement the codes, and the result was the further evolution of a multitier GATT, with some members applying all the rules, and others accepting only some.

Combined with the impact of the major global recession in 1981-2 and the resultant rise in protectionist sentiment in the United States, Europe, Canada, and elsewhere, these disturbing analyses tended to tarnish the glow from the successful conclusion of the round. Within a brief few months, officials found that they had more on their plates than they had bargained for. Further discomfort was created by new efforts to pursue a series of nationalist experiments that ran diametrically opposite to the policy confirmed by the results of the Tokyo Round. Thus trade officials found that they were under siege from two directions: critics within their own ranks questioned the benefits of GATT negotiations, while critics inside and outside of government pursued initiatives fundamentally at odds with the foundations of Canadian tradecraft.

Nationalism and Economic Turmoil Revisited

The Conservative government of Prime Minister Joe Clark, which approved and implemented the results of the Tokyo Round negotiations, proved short-lived. Eight months after assuming office, it lost a vote of confidence in the House of Commons and the confidence of the people in the resulting election. On 18 February 1980, Pierre Elliott Trudeau and his colleagues were once again returned to office. Already during the campaign, Trudeau had signalled a willingness to listen to the more nationalist and interventionist members of his party. Back in power, the nationalists were given the opportunity to advance policies to address the challenges they believed Canada faced in the more competitive global markets of the 1980s (see table 12.1). At the top of their agenda was a renewed effort to give Canada an industrial policy that would provide the government in Ottawa with the power and

Table 12.1

Trade and the Canadian economy, 1980			
Population	24,089,000	Labour force	11,522,000
GNP ($000)	289,859	GNP per capita ($)	12,107
Merchandise exports ($000)	76,170	Merchandise imports ($000)	68,360
Total exports (goods and services)		Total imports (goods and services)	
as share of GNP (%)	27.4	as share of GNP (%)	29.4
Main exports (%)		Main imports (%)	
Wheat	5.1	Industrial materials	22.5
Newsprint	4.8	Motor vehicles and parts	20.3
Woodpulp	5.2	Producers' equipment	22.4
Nonferrous metals and alloys	6.1	Consumer goods	16.2
Motor vehicles and parts	14.7		
Other manufactured goods	19.0		
Main customers (%)		Main suppliers (%)	
United States	63.3	United States	70.1
United Kingdom	4.3	United Kingdom	2.9
Other EC	8.3	Other EC	5.2

Source: Organization for Economic Cooperation and Development, *Economic Surveys: Canada* (Paris: OECD, June 1982).

resources necessary to steer the economy into directions they considered necessary and desirable.

Already in the closing years of the 1970s, officials had set out to explore what a fully articulated industrial strategy might entail.[6] A massive exercise in consultation and analysis led by officials at Industry, Trade and Commerce (ITC) produced a pile of papers documenting the structure, strengths, and weaknesses of the Canadian economy, at sectoral, regional, and functional levels. Before the results of the "tier one" and "tier two" studies could be fully translated into the "tier three" policy program, however, the election of 1979 intervened and dulled enthusiasm for the anticipated high level of spending and intervention required. Indeed, the establishment of the Ministry of State for Economic Development (MSED) in 1978 as a superministry dedicated to coordinating the spending and program appetites of economic ministries had already slowed matters significantly. Gordon Osbaldeston, who as deputy at ITC had overseen the first stages of the industrial policy consultations, exhibited remarkably less enthusiasm for them as the first deputy at MSED.

The return of the Liberals, however, provided a renewed opportunity to test the industrial strategy waters, and the prime minister appeared willing to try. His appointment of Herb Gray to the ITC portfolio was certainly interpreted as a signal of a greater willingness to move in this direction, as was the throne speech promising more stringent application of the FIRA investment review process, establishment of a National Trading Corporation, more strategic use of government procurement contracts, and greater effort to encourage Canadianization of the economy. Despite the widespread use and long-standing existence of various industrial development programs,[7] industrial policy advocates now insisted that Canada lacked an industrial strategy.[8] In many cases, of course, this charge amounted to little more than a complaint that the favoured programs were lacking or underfunded.

More fundamentally, however, industrial policy advocates insisted that the mere existence of a range of policies and programs did not constitute a strategy. A strategy required an integrative plan that brought the various programs and policies together into a coherent national strategy, allowing business, labour, and government to work together toward a common purpose. Such programs and policies needed to be "anticipatory" rather than "reactive."[9] Advocates often asserted that Japan, Germany, Sweden and other countries had such an integrated, coherent approach.[10] Canada, they inferred, was a captive of the American model, a criticism that, by definition, required no further elaboration.

The government's first and most celebrated foray into micromanaging the economy was the National Energy Program (NEP). Developed as part of the government's October 1980 budget – and thus worked out largely in secret, with little consultation inside or outside government – the NEP set out to remake the energy sector in Canada on a basis that would make the federal government a major player as participant, regulator, and tax beneficiary. Based on five years of tinkering in response to the fallout from the 1973 OPEC crisis, the NEP was spurred on by the second energy crisis of 1979. Unfortunately, it was based on assumptions about oil prices and economic growth that turned out to be wildly unrealistic. It also created major rifts between the federal government and the producing provincial governments, between the federal government and the oil industry, and between Canada and the United States. In the end, while the program succeeded in rearranging federal-provincial financial interests in the industry, and increasing Canadian participation, the Trudeau government had already backpedalled on some of its major components before the Mulroney government finished the job of dismantling the NEP in 1984-5.[11]

While finance and energy officials were busy concocting the NEP, officials in ITC and other ministries were busy cooking up an industrial strategy, another part of what Stephen Clarkson and Christina McCall have called the "heroic delusion" of the final government of Pierre Elliott Trudeau.[12] Industry officials, armed with boxes of material generated over a decade of consultations, reviews, and analysis, finally had in Herb Gray a minister ready to implement a full-blown strategy. The first version was placed before cabinet in the fall and drew negative reviews. While the strategy contained some bold ideas, it also contained a lot of warmed-over ones, as well as requests for major funding and potential problems with Canada's trading partners. As one official noted, "It might perhaps best be treated as a piece of campaign literature for next fiscal year's appropriations, were it not for the fact that ... many of the measures will have adverse effects on relations with our trading partners, and with the United States in particular."[13]

Others agreed and even Gray's deputy, Robert Johnstone, had difficulty mustering any enthusiasm. In preliminary cabinet discussions, many of Gray's colleagues found his ideas more interventionist and expensive than they were prepared to contemplate. Business shared this view and made no secret of its concerns.[14] Without many allies in cabinet and few outside, Gray's plan stood little chance. He was determined, however, to try. Over the winter in interdepartmental discussions, officials steadily whittled away at the analysis and the proposals, only to be hauled back by the minister, determined to pursue his core ideas. As an alternative, officials turned to Osbaldeston and his minister, Bud Olson, at the Ministry of State for Economic Development, to bring forward a version based on more traditional analysis and focusing on Canada's resource strengths. The result was a deep rift in cabinet requiring the prime minister, atypically, to provide guidance on an economic issue.

Trudeau tasked Allan MacEachen, now serving the government as both deputy prime minister and finance minister, to chair an ad hoc cabinet committee, supported by Osbaldeston and his officials, to bring forward a new document. In his instructions, however, the prime minister clearly stated his preferences: "I remain convinced that the primary engine of economic development must be a dynamic private sector and that the marketplace is in most circumstances the best allocator of scarce resources. The role of government must be to complement these functions ... and where necessary supplement private initiative."[15] The infighting between ministers and their officials continued, but with MacEachen and Osbaldeston clearly in the political and bureaucratic drivers' seats, the result was a foregone conclusion. Attached to MacEachen's ill-fated 1981 budget, *Economic Development for Canada* provided a relatively anodyne industrial strategy focused on the spinoffs that would accrue to both Canada's regions and industrial sectors from government-backed major projects.[16]

The global recession of 1981-2 made even this modest program a nonstarter. Induced in part by the determined efforts of central bankers in the United States, Canada, and elsewhere to bring inflation under control, the recession severely retarded Canadian economic growth (see table 12.2) and, as we saw in chapter 9, put the finishing touches to Canada's unsustainable fiscal position. By the time Canada had absorbed this further body blow, the appetite for expensive industrial and other strategies had been completely exorcised. To signal the change in direction, Trudeau assigned Gray to guard the government's purse strings at the Treasury Board and put the much more business-oriented Ed Lumley in charge of a reorganized Department of Regional Industrial Expansion (DRIE). In early 1982, despairing of any

Table 12.2

Merchandise trade and the Canadian economy, 1981-6

Year	Domestic merchandise exports (current $ millions)	GNP at market prices (current $ millions)	Exports/ GNP (%)	Canadian share of world trade (%)
1981	80,985	344,657	23.5	3.8
1982	81,825	361,772	22.6	3.7
1983	88,506	394,114	22.5	4.2
1984	109,543	431,249	25.4	4.7
1985	116,145	463,858	25.1	4.6
1986	116,588	489,264	23.8	4.3

Sources: IMF, International Financial Statistics, various years; Statistics Canada, Summary of Canadian International Trade (Catalogue 65-001); and National Income and Expenditure Accounts: Annual Estimates (Catalogue 13-201-XPD).

useful program initiatives, Trudeau had integrated the industry and regional development portfolios and hived trade off to a renamed Department of External Affairs and International Trade. He had also asked officials to bring forward a thorough review of Canada's trade policies. Not happy with the direction of Canada's economic development, Trudeau was reverting to his urge of more than a dozen years ago. He wanted officials to present ministers with thoroughly analyzed and discussed policy options. If industrial policy was a bust, could trade policy do better?

Trudeau appeared to have been motivated in part by the virulent reaction of Canadian firms to his interventionist economic initiatives as they found themselves caught in the crossfire between Canadian nationalism and US protectionism. US president Ronald Reagan may have professed a deep attachment to market disciplines, but many members of the US Congress were still firmly committed to fair trade, an elastic concept that provided justification for a range of protectionist measures. As a result, the leading proponent of an open, multilateral trading regime appeared to be adopting a new, more aggressive mien. Justified as protecting US rights, many of the specific measures adopted also appeared to have strong nationalist and protectionist aspects to them. US trading partners were not sure they liked this version of market economics.[17] For Canadian exporters, increasingly dependent on the US market, this was an ominous development.

Canadian government efforts in the 1970s to diversify trade away from the United States had not proved successful. By the early 1980s, neither the EC nor Japanese arrangements had made much difference. Business had not taken them seriously. Reflecting perhaps useful expressions of essentially political relationships, the inescapable conclusion was that framework agreements, unaccompanied by the exchange

Table 12.3

Direction of Canadian merchandise exports, 1960-84 (percentage)

	1960	1970	1980	1983	1984
United States	55.8	64.4	63.2	72.9	75.6
United Kingdom	17.4	9.0	4.3	2.8	2.2
Other western Europe	11.3	9.8	10.6	5.8	5.0
Japan	3.4	4.9	5.9	5.3	5.1
Other Asia	2.2	2.9	4.0	4.4	3.8
Other	9.9	9.0	12.0	8.8	8.3
Total	100.0	100.0	100.0	100.0	100.0

Source: Richard G. Lipsey and Murray G. Smith, *Taking the Initiative: Canada's Trade Options in a Turbulent World* (Toronto: C.D. Howe Institute, 1985), 47.

of new rights and obligations beyond those in the GATT, could not be effective in gaining improved and more secure access to larger markets. They were certainly insufficient to induce restructuring of the Canadian economy to the more competitive footing required in a rapidly changing world. The Trudeau government's 1971-2 assessment of a growing and irreversible dependence upon the United States had been sound; its prescription to diversify away from the United States had ignored economic reality. If the government was going to put greater emphasis on trade policy as the basis for its economic development policies, Trudeau wanted a thorough assessment of what had worked and what had not.

As Canada slid into recession, the deep and seemingly permanent dependence of Canada's economic well-being on the US market could no longer be denied. The Canadian market alone was not large enough to ensure continued growth. Geography, corporate links, and consumer preferences overwhelmed all choices but that of the United States. The European and Japanese economies remained attractive and valuable secondary markets but would never attain the status of the US market. Indeed, between 1960 and 1984, the share of Canadian exports commanded by European and Japanese markets slipped from 32 to 12 percent, while the US share grew from 56 to 76 percent (see table 12.3). Developing countries would continue to grow but offered limited opportunities for resource-based Canadian firms. More to the point, developing countries had become formidable competitors for many of Canada's resource exporters.

Canadian trade policy interests had also been undermined by various protectionist compromises. The government's commitment in 1975 to introduce supply management for the dairy and poultry sectors, its decision in 1976 to impose global quotas on imports of textiles and clothing, and its resolve in 1979 to do the same for footwear were but three indications of hardening attitudes in Canada toward adjustment. There was clearly a growing gulf between Canadian export interests and efforts to shield the domestic market from new competition.[18] An earlier generation of trade policy practitioners had proven very successful at sailing close to the wind, finding the narrow space for manoeuvre between international obligations and domestic political imperatives. The new generation seemed less adept at finding that space, in part, perhaps, because the available space had shrunk. Ministers were less willing to heed the advice of their officials. They were looking for alternatives and did not like what they were hearing.

Everyone agreed that the future lay in developing stronger secondary and tertiary manufacturing sectors and service industries. To industry officials, industrial policy was the key that would open the door to their development. Trade officials insisted that it would require open and secure access to larger markets, particularly the large markets of the US Northeast and Midwest, many of them situated within a day's truck drive of Canada's industrial heartland. The challenge lay in gaining that access on a basis that would induce Canadian industry to restructure. The mood in the United States, however, seemed less than receptive to any Canadian overtures. The Tokyo Round had demonstrated that gaining better access was possible, but securing that access was much more difficult. Contingency protection had, if anything, made access *less* secure.

The US Search for Level Playing Fields

US implementation of the results of the Tokyo Round had successfully demonstrated that the new, fast-track procedures set out in the Trade Act of 1974 worked. The administration had collaborated closely with Congress in preparing the necessary legislation and, by the end of the year, Congress had passed the Trade Agreements Act of 1979. It carefully balanced the obligations the administration had accepted in signing the Final Act of the Tokyo Round and the continuing concern of both private and congressional interests that US firms be able to deal with competitive pressures at home and abroad. Responsibility for administering the trade remedy laws was shifted from the Treasury to the Commerce Department in a move legislators felt would send a signal to industry that the laws would be interpreted and applied in a manner that would be more likely to provide relief.[19]

US trading partners had monitored the progress of the US implementation process with some care and on occasion had pointed to interpretations of the new codes that would quickly lead to disputes. Wherever possible, US legislation had found room for creative and usually restrictive interpretations. The definition of material injury enshrined in the new law, for example, was a standard that would be easier to meet than that envisioned by the negotiators. US officials had accepted some but not all of the concerns voiced by their EC, Japanese, and Canadian colleagues. If nothing else, the legislative process in the United States had provided early proof of the fears expressed by Rodney Grey.[20] The full proof, however, would come in the application of the laws. It did not take long before the evidence began to roll in.

Macroeconomic policies pursued throughout the Reagan years exacerbated the impact on US trade policy of structural changes in the US economy. These policies generated enormous budgetary imbalances, reflected in an overvalued dollar and the burgeoning US trade deficit. The overvalued US dollar effectively imposed a heavy burden on exports and a subsidy on imports. The consequence for the United States was a loss of market share in both domestic and export markets and a further weakening of the steadily diminishing constituency for a liberal trade policy.[21]

In response, Congress aggressively reasserted its constitutional responsibilities for the conduct of trade policy. Until 1985, the Reagan administration generally ignored growing congressional frustration and concern. Congress filled the vacuum by wielding the threat of legislation and acquiring a taste and capacity for bringing political pressure to bear on the administration for protectionist actions to serve constituency interests. In the face of criticism, US officials and legislators retorted that they were only searching for means to "level the playing field." To most foreign observers it seemed more like an effort to move the goal posts.[22]

The greater economic importance of a strong trade performance to the United States and the seeming permanence of the US trade deficit also eroded the legitimacy of deploying trade policy to serve broader US political and economic objectives. In the 1950s, for example, the United States had lent strong support to the formation of the European Common Market, absorbing the costs of discrimination against US trade as the price of fostering a stable and more prosperous Europe and shoring up a bulwark against communist expansionism. Thirty years later, US political leaders were no longer willing to accept discrimination against US exports to sustain important bilateral relationships or, indeed, to maintain the multilateral trading system.

With US tariff levels greatly reduced, the basic obstacle to unimpeded Canadian access to the US market had become US trade remedy laws. The 1974 Trade Act had signalled the new mood. The 1979 Trade Agreements Act confirmed it. A new Trade and Tariff Act passed in 1984 further illustrated the new congressional attitude. It included not only new authority for the president to negotiate bilateral and multilateral trade agreements, but also a wide range of amendments to the trade remedy system, adding to the capacity of US producers to gain import relief and giving the administration the ability to pursue export issues. The act also had a strong flavour of unilateralism, particularly in the enhanced section 301 procedures to enforce US "rights" in export markets. It marked the first time since 1930 that Congress had foisted a piece of trade legislation on a reluctant administration. Between 1930 and 1984, all significant trade legislation had been sponsored by the administration and then adjusted by Congress. The 1984 act was sponsored by Congress and adjusted in negotiations with the administration.[23]

Throughout the 1970s and into the 1980s there had developed a proliferating and aggressive use of trade remedy legislation by US industry. Prior to 1970, import-affected industries generally failed to obtain relief under US domestic procedures.

Between 1955 and 1968, 371 antidumping cases were investigated, but duties were imposed in only twelve cases. The success rate for escape clause or emergency safeguard (section 201) action was similarly low. In the 1970s, a more accommodating attitude reflecting, and in part fuelling, the rise of protectionism, made the launch of cases more advantageous for domestic industry. By the 1980s, the Commerce Department found itself at the centre of a flood of new petitions. Ten separate countervailing duty investigations were launched in 1980; 27 in 1981; 146 in 1982; 30 in 1983; 55 in 1984; and 43 in 1985. This increase was paralleled on the antidumping side. Canadians, who in earlier years had enjoyed a special relationship, found themselves in the thick of the controversies. Between 1980 and 1987, forty antidumping, countervailing duty, and escape clause actions were launched against imports from Canada, and eighteen of these led to import restrictions. Resort to section 337 exclusion orders was similarly on the rise. Of course, Canadian industry was not unfamiliar with the utility of antidumping investigations and was beginning to experiment with the countervailing duty procedures available since 1977.[24]

For Canada, the increasing resort to trade remedies in the first half of the 1980s was but one part of a deteriorating bilateral trade relationship. The Reagan administration also took sharp exception to various Canadian policy initiatives in the opening years of the decade, particularly the more aggressive application of the Foreign Investment Review Act under the direction of Herb Gray and the implementation of the National Energy Program. More broadly, President Reagan's priorities seemed to point in an entirely different direction than those of the restored Liberals in Ottawa. Tiffs on the cultural front, on acid rain and other environmental issues, on the fisheries front following the collapse of the East Coast Fisheries Treaty, and on energy files all added to an increasingly embattled relationship. The absence of any personal rapport between the prime minister and the president further complicated efforts to manage the growing range of irritants.[25]

In agriculture, the growing subsidy war between the European Community and the United States fuelled further deterioration in agricultural trade conditions and undermined the health of Canada's outward-oriented grains and red meat sectors. Canada had already decided to shield most Eastern farmers from international competition through supply management. Dealing with the problems of Western farmers required progress in tackling the distorting impact of domestic and export subsidy programs.

The GATT Will Still Provide

The instinctive reaction of trade officials in Ottawa was to turn to the GATT to help them address some of the problems raised by the growth in protectionism, in Canada-US disputes, and in deteriorating agricultural trade conditions. The results were disappointing. The Tokyo Round had sanctioned the use of trade remedies and had further consolidated agriculture's status as beyond the normal rules. Discussion in Geneva confirmed that others shared Canadian concern with the rise in US trade remedy cases, but all agreed that only a major new negotiating round might create the circumstances for finding a more satisfactory balance between multilateral discipline on, for example, subsidies, and unilateral discipline through countervailing duties. The fact that others – including Canada and the EC – were making wide and more frequent use of trade remedies dulled the moral force of complaints about US abuses of these procedures,[26] but the situation confirmed Rodney Grey's grim analysis of the future of the trading system. In speeches and articles he stressed the extent to which GATT members had strayed further and further from their original objectives, determined to manage rather than liberalize trade.[27] The focus of activity in Geneva in the first few years of the 1980s did nothing to refute this assessment.

Other analysts shared Grey's pessimism. Books and articles from university and think-tank analysts bemoaned the new passion for industrial policy, the increasing resort to grey-area measures, the abusive use of trade remedies, the growing fascination with bilateral reciprocity, and the willingness to use unilateral measures to bully smaller countries. At a conference sponsored by the newly established Institute for International Economics in Washington, paper after paper prepared by now retired leading officials of the 1970s recited a litany of the risks to the multilateral trading regime.[28] In some ways it was gratifying to see a growing number of scholars and commentators take an interest in the GATT and the trading system. At the same time, it was disheartening that their interest had been piqued by the system's shortcomings rather than its strengths.

Discounting the usual emotional letdown at the conclusion of a major negotiating round, the focus in Geneva did seem to be on the management of trade. Nevertheless, national delegations and Secretariat officials alike felt under pressure to prove that the GATT could address the woes of the trading system. The challenge fell first of all on the desk of the new director general. Olivier Long, who had directed every stage of the Tokyo Round, retired and was succeeded at the end of 1980 by Arthur Dunkel, a fellow Swiss with long experience as a national participant in GATT affairs.

Dunkel's first major challenge as director general came in managing the renewal of the GATT Multifibre Agreement (MFA). This temporary expedient, which chose the lesser of two evils – an organized and agreed derogation rather than a spate of GATT-illegal measures – had by 1981 been in place in various manifestations for twenty years. The challenge that faced Dunkel was how to extend it in a manner that satisfied both industrialized and developing countries. In these negotiations, he indicated the extent to which he was prepared to play an active and personal role. As chairman of the Textiles Committee, he pioneered the use of the "green room" informal process – discussions in the small conference room next to his office – to coax the members of the committee to find the means to extend the MFA for a further period.[29] By the end of 1981, it was clear that the Long era was over and the Dunkel era had begun.

Ed Franklin, "Geneva Welcomes the Ministers of Trade," 26 November 1982. Secretary of State for External Affairs Allan MacEachen plays GATT's 88 broken keys as chair of the 1982 ministerial meeting.

Renewal of the MFA was played out against the background of the deteriorating economic conditions of the 1981-2 global recession. The period of the Tokyo Round had seen a constant rise in so-called grey-area measures, and an attempt to negotiate a code of conduct aimed at bringing these under control. That effort had failed, and the end of the round as well as the economic problems of 1981-2 had unleashed a renewed spate of questionable measures, including efforts by the United States and Canada to control imports of Japanese cars and US-EC disputes about trade in steel. In response, in various capitals and at meetings of the GATT's Consultative Group of Eighteen and the OECD Trade Committee, the idea developed that management of these pressures would be easier if there were renewed political commitment both to GATT's principles and to a work program to further elaborate them. While discussion was not couched in terms of launching a new round, there was broad consensus that the absence of a round made it more difficult to keep protectionist pressures in check. Consequently, at the November 1981 meeting of the contracting parties, members decided that the 1982 meeting would be held at the ministerial level. Its purpose would be "to examine the functioning of the multilateral trading system, and to reinforce the common efforts of the contracting parties to support and improve the system for the benefit of all nations."[30]

Canada had been among the earliest and most enthusiastic proponents of a ministerial meeting. Its ambassador in Geneva, Don Mcphail, as chair of the Council in 1981 and of the contracting parties in 1982, actively worked to advance a more forward-looking and constructive agenda for the GATT. But the 1982 ministerial meeting proved generally disappointing. Chaired by Canada's secretary of state for external affairs, Allan MacEachen, it achieved little of substance. Cynics in Geneva began to refer to it as a McPhailure.

At one level, the ministerial meeting *was* a disappointment. Once again, it proved impossible to reach agreement on safeguards. Rather than adopting a clear statement about future priorities, including such difficult new issues as trade in services, investment, and the protection of intellectual property, ministers adopted a convoluted text setting out areas for study and further discussion.[31] The difficulties in reaching agreement on the outstanding issues and on a work program clearly fell well short of expectations. Ministers, particularly United States Trade Representative (USTR) Bill Brock, had raised prospects that the meeting would grapple with the fundamental issues and provide the multilateral trading system with new vitality and direction. There had been insufficient time to prepare for the level of consensus such a result would have required.[32]

At the same time, however, the meeting did confront some difficult issues and indicated the extent to which more homework was required. While ministers did not authorize the work program Brock and others had sought, they did begin to lay the basis for future work on services and related issues by mandating examination of a number of national studies. Ministers indicated where work was required to solve problems rather than how to actually solve them.

The response in various capitals, but particularly in Washington, was that the GATT was no longer at the forefront in addressing real problems. The administration had hoped that an aggressive and forward-looking GATT work program would provide a constructive signal to help contain protectionist pressures, but as long as its purpose and agenda remained unclear, GATT considerations would not be central to US policy. US policy makers – congressional and administration alike – felt no qualms about aggressively pursuing trade remedies, bilateral grey-area measures, and unilateral section 301 actions, all geared to satisfying immediate political needs. Members of Congress added to the air of unease among US trading partners by tabling a growing pile of proposed amendments to US trade legislation, few of which fit easily into the existing GATT provisions.

The United States also turned to bilateral negotiations, openly welcoming a Canadian overture in 1983 to explore bilateral sectoral arrangements, negotiating its first free-trade agreement (FTA) with Israel in 1984, and entering into preliminary discussions with Canada the following year toward the negotiation of a full-fledged FTA.[33] In September 1985, the day after the G5 finance ministers – from the five leading centres of global finance: the United States, Britain, France, Germany, and Japan – succeeded in establishing a coordinated approach to monetary matters (the Plaza Accord) that would help the embattled US dollar by sharply raising the value of the yen and the Deutschmark, US president Reagan announced an even more far-reaching willingness to consider bilateral arrangements. In future the United States would get tough with its trading partners and explore bilateral solutions. Although committed to a new round of GATT negotiations, the United States was not going to sit around waiting for others to come around to its views.

The same kind of scepticism and cynicism was apparent elsewhere, including in the EC. It soon began to imitate the United States, aggressively pursuing its rights and using both GATT-legal and GATT-illegal measures to force solutions to its short-term trade policy problems. Taking a page out of the US book, it adopted a "new commercial policy instrument" – similar to the US section 301 process – to pursue EC trading interests. Trade relations soured among the United States, the EC, Japan, and Canada. Attitudes toward the need for developing countries to participate more fully and pull their weight in the trading system similarly hardened.

Throughout the early 1980s, economic troubles in Europe led to discussion of Eurosclerosis. The early vitality of the European integration movement seemed to have evaporated and given way to a defensiveness about maintaining the European market for Europeans. The EC had expanded from the original six to nine in 1973. Greece joined in 1980 and Spain and Portugal in 1986, doubling the original membership. By this time, pressure was mounting to rekindle and strengthen the internal integration process in order to address the competitive challenges coming from the United States, Japan, and newly industrializing countries like South Korea and Brazil. The GATT seemed remote from these troubles, and energy focused on what could be done within the institutions of the Community.[34]

There was one aspect of the GATT to which members did increasingly resort: dispute settlement. Issues that in the past would have been left to bilateral discussion and eventual resolution through negotiations were now being litigated (see table 12.4). Canada launched complaints against the EC (access for high-quality beef), and the United States (a prohibition on imports of tuna and the use of exclusion orders in patent infringement cases). The EC and United States complained about Canadian measures, including practices under the Foreign Investment Review Act and the import, distribution, and pricing of alcoholic beverages. The United States complained about EC practices and the EC hauled the United States before panels. Both mounted major challenges of Japanese practices. Even developing countries joined in, complaining, for example, about EC sugar policies.[35]

This new level of dispute settlement activism was much more legalistic than what had developed in the 1950s and had been revived in the 1970s. Pleadings before panels became more complex and sophisticated, and panel reports became longer and longer in an effort to reflect the creative range of arguments being advanced in the pleadings. The increasing resort to trade remedies like antidumping and countervailing duty procedures signalled what some commentators began to call the judicialization of trade relations.[36] In earlier years, the GATT had provided a

Table 12.4

Canada, the GATT, and trade disputes, 1980-4

1980	Canadian complaint concerning access to the EC for high-quality beef from Canada
1980	Canadian complaint regarding the prohibition by the United States of imports of tuna from Canada
1981	Canadian complaint regarding a US section 337 exclusion order on imports of certain automotive spring assemblies from Canada
1982	US complaint regarding administration by Canada of its Foreign Investment Review Act
1984	EC complaint regarding the import, distribution, and sale of alcoholic drinks by Canadian provincial marketing agencies
1984	Canadian complaint regarding EC administration of quotas on imports of newsprint
1984	Canadian complaint regarding US restrictions on certain sugar-containing products pursuant to its 1955 waiver
1984	South African complaint about Canadian (Ontario) restrictions on the sale of gold coins

Sources: GATT, BISDs, various years.

framework of rules and a forum within which governments could negotiate the resolution of conflicts. By the 1980s, GATT-sanctioned domestic procedures and dispute settlement provisions encouraged firms and governments to solve their problems through litigation. Before 1980, both GATT and national trade officials had strenuously, and proudly, resisted inroads by officials with legal training onto their turf. In the 1980s, the GATT established a legal division, and national officials learned to rely on their legal colleagues for advice in leading them through the new minefield of GATT-based litigation.

The GATT as an institution and forum for managing trade liberalization and sponsoring multilateral negotiations was evolving. It was no longer a select club of twenty-three, but rather a complex organization struggling to overcome its institutional inadequacies. Since the first round of GATT negotiations in 1947, the GATT had grown to over ninety contracting parties, with a further twenty or more countries applying the GATT on a de facto basis. Consensus, accordingly, had become much more difficult to achieve. Most of the new entrants were developing countries that benefited from GATT rights until they became too competitive in traditional products such as textiles, clothing, and steel and were then subjected to import quotas or "voluntary" export restraints. These countries accepted – perhaps understandably – few of the GATT obligations and consequently pursued mercantilist trade policies based on import substitution. They were, moreover, wary of efforts led by the United States to reform the GATT and extend its principles into new areas such as services, intellectual property, and investment. The result by the early 1980s was the breakdown of the contracting parties into regional groupings with consensus on action resulting from arduous discussions of texts rather than policies. While industrialized countries, of course, retained the capacity to negotiate within the framework of the GATT, the task of determining negotiating agendas and timetables had become enormously more difficult than in earlier years.

The reduction in the number of developed countries capable of playing an independent role further undermined Canadian confidence in the GATT. During the Kennedy Round, the EFTA countries – the seven members of the European Free Trade Association, including Britain – had been full and independent participants. Together with Canada, Australia, and New Zealand, they had formed a group of smaller countries among which alliances could be forged in pursuit of common interests on particular issues. These independent participants had then been able to wield increased bargaining power and leverage against the larger countries. By the time of the Tokyo Round, most of these former allies had become part of the EC either through accession, as in the case of the United Kingdom, Denmark, and Ireland, or through free-trade agreements for industrial products, as in the case of Sweden, Norway, and other members of the EFTA. Not only were such countries no longer independent participants, but they identified their principal trade policy interest as the preservation of their preferences in the enlarged European market. Multilateral trade liberalization no longer held the same attraction for them. By the early 1980s, western Europe had become one large free-trade area governed by arrangements loosely blessed by the GATT but essentially outside it.

Canadian ministerial dissatisfaction with the GATT and with the safe but dull trade policy of the past had already surfaced in the late 1970s. Jean Chrétien, for example, as minister of industry, trade and commerce, had clearly been frustrated with the advice he was receiving from officials on textile and clothing policy. During the difficult days of 1975-6, when import pressure from low-cost countries surged and officials continually warned ministers of Canada's obligations under the GATT and other agreements, Chrétien publicly called them "boy scouts" and persisted in a policy that involved not only stepping outside of accepted international practice but also abrogating two bilateral textile restraint agreements the government had already initialled. His outburst marked the end of an era. The easy consensus between ministers and officials on trade policy appeared to be over.

Ministerial cynicism about the GATT mounted in the opening years of the 1980s, particularly after the 1982 ministerial meeting, as it became clear that Canadian officials were unable to defend FIRA and other Canadian policies against adverse findings by dispute settlement panels. Political frustration, however, was not uniquely Canadian. Canadian ministers' sentiments were echoed in a more general plea from the irrepressible Hubert Humphrey in the United States, who implored that "we need a new, fresh, buoyant, forward-looking economics to replace the tired old economics telling us we can't do the things we want to do – the things we have to do." Canadian politicians shared this frustration. The answer, however lay not in a new economics but in a comprehensive reassessment of the policies and assumptions of the past century. They had worked well, if perhaps more from a political than economic perspective. But they had also wrought changes which made these policies and assumptions less and less responsive to Canada's domestic and international circumstances.

Changes in the Global Economy

When governments negotiated the basic framework of postwar international trade and economic rules, trade in goods was the main vehicle of economic integration.[37] In 1950, for example, the total volume of world trade in goods and services represented less than 10 percent of world production. The bulk of this trade consisted of raw materials; most of the rest was made up of finished products; very little trade involved parts and components. Most trade flowed from transactions between unrelated firms with clear national identities. The main barriers to trade were government measures imposed at the border (tariffs and quotas) or differential treatment in taxation and regulatory requirements (e.g., commodity taxes and mixing requirements). Relatively high tariffs helped to maintain nationally segmented markets for most manufactured products. Most exchange rates were fixed, and maintaining a positive current account balance was an important goal of government policy.

In the 1950s, most economic activity was undertaken by nationally organized firms that designed, engineered, manufactured, marketed, and serviced a range of related products largely within the confines of the firm. Firms were hierarchically organized and many employees stayed with a firm for their full working lives. Employees felt themselves to be part of their company, and companies felt themselves to be part of a national economy. Most firms – and their products – had clearly identifiable national origins and foreign investment generally involved the establishment of miniature replicas of such firms. Foreign direct investment and trade, however, represented only a small proportion of global economic activity.

Government policy – domestic and international – reflected these facts of economic life. The GATT assumed that trade among national economies was pursued by private entrepreneurs working largely within the confines of national borders. The GATT regarded conflicts between firms in one country and firms in another as involving national interests that could be resolved through intergovernmental consultation. As negotiated in 1947, GATT conceded the regulation of domestic economic life – competition policy, for example, or farm income stability – to be largely within the purview of national governments. It was indifferent to such regulations as long as they did not involve overt discrimination between domestic and foreign products except as provided by the GATT-sanctioned border regime.

Business and government attitudes to international trade also reflected the prevailing economic theory that international trade flowed from comparative advantage, a relatively static condition based on national endowments of the principal factors of production: resources, capital, and labour. The trade regime was based on the principle that government policies that distorted the most efficient allocation of these factors were likely to lower national and global welfare while the removal of such barriers was likely to raise welfare.[38] Similarly, trade and investment were considered to be alternative ways of pursuing comparative advantage; the establishment of a foreign branch-plant was thought to replace production in the home country that would otherwise have been exported to the foreign market.

Few of these assumptions and characteristics remained valid by the 1980s. The liberalization of trade, for example, did not lead to greater sectoral specialization at the national level. Rather, it had led to tremendous growth in intrasectoral trade as countries exchanged cars for cars and steel for steel, leading to much higher levels of international competition in domestic markets than anyone would have anticipated in the 1940s and 1950s. Trade in goods, while it grew twice as fast as production and by the early 1980s constituted more than 20 percent of world production, was by then less important than international investment, capital flows, and exchanges of knowledge and technology as instruments of international economic integration. The value of world trade in goods had become but a fraction of the annual value of capital movements while fully a fifth of the value of world trade consisted of services. After 1973, most major currencies floated freely, their values adjusting constantly and instantaneously on world markets. The IMF had been transformed from an instrument for regulating currency values and payment balances to a banker and economic advisor to developing countries.

The fundamental shift from the predominantly industrial, nationally organized international economy of the past to the information-based, globally organized economy of the future took place during the 1970s. This transformation to a new, more globally integrated economy saw the traditional engines of economic growth – basic industries such as steel, cars, railways, and construction – give way to new industries. Although resources and manufacturing did not disappear as generators of wealth, more important contributions were coming from services, technology, and other knowledge-intensive activities. In an effort to remain competitive, traditional manufacturing firms gradually relocated some or all of their activities to low-wage economies, fundamentally altering the skills profile demanded in high-wage OECD countries. Relatively fewer low-skill manufacturing jobs were required, and those that remained needed to be able to compete with low-skill workers around the globe. Demand for the vast army of middle managers that had kept the large manufacturing facilities of the past running smoothly also declined. In their place, industry recruited people with broader, multipurpose skills rather than highly specialized, narrow skills.

Manufacturing increasingly became science-based rather than resource/energy-based, while economies of scope were creating ever more differentiated product markets. Production also became more disaggregated. Rather than concentrating the whole manufacturing process – from conception to sales – within one mega-firm, many of the steps in the production process began to be outsourced to more skilled and efficient outside suppliers able to sell their expertise or components to various assemblers. General Electric, for example, continued to market a wide range of household products, but ceased to manufacture many of them.

Global corporations and networks involving local and regional firms began to rely on a more fragmented and decentralized approach to design, engineering, production, marketing, and service. They organized themselves more horizontally than their counterparts from an earlier era and made much greater use of expertise and resources outside the firm. Even manufacturing, the heart of the industrial firm of the past, became an activity that could be assigned to outside specialists, more skilled and cost-efficient than the firm interested in marketing the final product. Branch-plants and transnational companies were evolving into global firms and networks experimenting with strategic alliances such as joint production, cooperative R&D ventures, licensing arrangements, contracting out and brokering among local, regional, and global corporations and networks, as basic techniques in organizing their activities. The result was a tremendous growth in intracorporate and intrasectoral trade in parts and components as well as an increasing reliance on activities taking place far from corporate headquarters or ultimate markets.

New forms of specialization also resulted in the development of strategic links between global corporations and local suppliers and distributors worldwide. The stability in corporate organizations and relationships that was an integral part of economic life in the 1950s and 1960s was replaced by a new premium on fluidity and flexibility. Prevailing theories about economic growth and international exchange also became much more intricate and varied, robbing governments of the moral and intellectual certitude that had underpinned the trade regime of the 1950s and 1960s. New ideas about economic growth, dynamic comparative advantage, the international division of labour, the complementarity of international trade and investment, the role of technology, the importance of trade in services, and the management and organization of production, as well as the role of government policies, all challenged the conventional foundations of trade policy and made governments less certain about the direction of future domestic and international policies and arrangements.[39]

Developments in the way business was being organized and pursued had profound implications for government policy issues and for the functioning of the international trade and payments system. The policies, institutions, and structures of the past – domestic and international – needed to catch up to these new realities. Just like firms, governments had to face the challenge of a world going global.

GATT and the Global Economy

The GATT-based trade relations system had been built on the basis of goals and principles that had generally stood the test of time:

- From an *economic* perspective, it had raised national and global welfare by taking advantage of the international division of labour through the reduction of barriers to international trade, thus promoting efficiency, productivity, and competitiveness.
- From a *legal* standpoint, it had provided rules and procedures for the equitable and expeditious settlement of disputes on the basis of transparency, nondiscrimination, and due process.
- Insofar as *business* was concerned, it had fostered an international business climate based on predictability, stability, and fairness.
- *Politically,* it had established a set of rules to manage stable interstate trade relations while protecting national sovereignty; domestically, it had fostered the equitable distribution of the benefits of international trade while permitting orderly adjustment to greater international competition.

To achieve these goals, the GATT system had pioneered a specific set of tools, rules, and techniques. Some were present from the outset, such as the techniques for negotiating tariff concessions. Others were introduced and developed over time, such as codes governing antidumping and countervailing duties or the procedures for settling disputes.

Closely linked to the GATT were a series of regional agreements – prominently the European arrangements, but also agreements in Latin America and elsewhere – based on the same principles and techniques and broadly consistent with its requirements. Collectively, this global trade relations system had proved a positive force in the international economy and could lay claim to many achievements. Trade had been liberalized; tariffs had been cut; old-fashioned discriminatory quantitative restrictions had been virtually eliminated; and many potentially harmful practices had been restrained. It had created the conditions necessary for the extensive economic integration among the OECD economies. Its rules had provided private investors with the necessary confidence to expand their horizons. Its periodic negotiating rounds had maintained momentum toward increasing trade liberalization.

The postwar trade regime had been dominated by the United States. US economic strength as well as geopolitical interests had given it both the power and the inclination to lead. By the 1980s, US leadership had become less confident, but a new equilibrium that recognized the importance of the EC and Japan, as well as the stake held by smaller countries, remained to be established. There was no longer a clear leader setting the tone and direction of international economic discussions nor a sufficient unanimity of views among the major players to provide a basis for bold progress. Thus, at the same time that there was a clear need for a major renovation of the global trade regime, the techniques, attitudes, and structures of the past were maintaining an inertia that hampered creative responses to the challenges of deepening interdependence and global integration.

Implications for Canada

The changes that were taking place in the global economy and in the roles of its major players involved important consequences for Canada. Canada had prospered as a result of its resource wealth and its location next door to the United States. The former had encouraged Canada to develop a strong, resource-based economy geared to reaping rich rewards in the era when coal, steel, lumber, wheat, and fish were the basis for prosperity; the latter had secured for Canadians the many advantages of living near the premier economy of the industrial era.

For much of its history, Canadian trade and economic policy, as embodied in the National Policy, had aimed at exploiting these twin advantages. Resource exploitation was encouraged through tax, transportation, and trade policies. Agricultural policy sought to exploit Canada's vast resource base and apply technology to get products to world markets. Manufacturing was advanced through import-substitution and branch-plant investment policies. Social policy smoothed out the rough edges while cultural policy sought to develop a distinctive Canadian identity. On the whole, these policies had worked to the satisfaction of most Canadians. The economic inefficiencies that flowed from maintaining a federal state could be tolerated because of the wealth generated by the export of resources and the high wages generated by the manufacturing sector. Regional development policies, for example, that reflected political rather than economic priorities, were seen as a relatively small price to pay for maintaining east-west cohesion.

The structure of the economy by the end of the 1970s exhibited the impact of these policies. Canada could boast the second-highest standard of living in the world which, married to a set of social and other programs, made Canada one of the most pleasant places in the world to live. But there were also some disturbing realities that made it difficult for Canada to adjust to a more globally organized, information-based economy.

As a commodity producer, Canada found itself squeezed between global excess capacity and declining demand (see table 12.5). On the supply side, Canada had become a high-cost producer, mining more remote or deeper sites, harvesting less-than-prime and more remote timber, fishing a declining stock, and farming marginal land. While Canadian producers had become more cost-efficient, they were still experiencing difficulty competing with LDC suppliers whose bottom line was the need for foreign exchange rather than profits. On the demand side, new materials and more efficient manufacturing methods were fuelling a precipitous decline in industry's appetite for Canada's traditional resource products. Between 1970 and 1990, for example, Japan steadily increased its manufacturing output on the basis

Table 12.5

Composition of Canadian exports, 1960-84

	1960 (%)	1970 (%)	1980 (%)	1983 (%)	1984 (%)
Food and beverage	18.8	11.4	11.1	11.6	9.7
Crude materials	21.2	18.8	19.8	15.9	15.8
Fabricated materials	51.9	35.8	39.4	33.3	32.0
Manufactured end-products	7.8	33.8	29.4	38.9	42.1
Special transactions	0.3	0.2	0.3	0.3	0.4
Total	100.0	100.0	100.0	100.0	100.0

Source: Richard G. Lipsey and Murrary G. Smith, *Taking the Initiative: Canada's Trade Options in a Turbulent World* (Toronto: C.D. Howe Institute, 1985), 15.

of steadily decreasing resource inputs. Recycled fibres harvested in the urban forest rather than virgin fibres from northern Ontario and Quebec became the new staples. Fibre optics rather than copper marked the future.

As a manufacturer, Canada produced very few world-class products; most production was for the domestic market. Without fundamental restructuring, manufacturers faced a precarious future. They could no longer count on a protected domestic market as a secure base for their operations. The domestic market had become both too small and too open. In effect, manufacturers had to become more competitive not only to gain international markets but to keep a reasonable share of the domestic market.

Other problems also reflected some of the underlying weaknesses Canadians had to tackle if they were to make the transition toward an economy that could pay its way in the tougher global economy of the future:

- Interprovincial trade barriers and a range of province- and nation-building policies added to the cost of doing business in Canada and deflected investment to other jurisdictions.
- Overcapacity in traditional manufacturing as well as agriculture and food sectors required government intervention to prop up uncompetitive sectors.
- An inefficient and costly distribution system added considerably to consumer costs and reduced consumer choice.
- A range of regulatory and other barriers hampered rather than facilitated international commerce and adjustment to meet more cost-efficient and innovative competitors.
- Regional disparities and linguistic tensions added to making Canada a difficult country to govern and a difficult country in which to do business.

Throughout the 1980s, the World Competitiveness Forum's report card on Canada provided a sobering assessment of the problems the country faced. In terms of the factors critical to success in a resource-based global economy, it did very well; factors that determined success in an industrial economy were not too bad; but the factors critical to the new, global, information-based economy were those on which Canada consistently scored low, particularly outward and forward orientation. While the criteria used by the Forum may have been highly subjective, they reflected the assessment held of Canada by business and opinion moulders around the world. In the tough world of global competition for capital and markets, perception can be more potent than reality.[40]

Reviewing Canadian Trade Policy

These were the circumstances and considerations that faced Canadian officials in 1982 as they responded to cabinet's request for a review of Canadian trade policy. Unfortunately, these global factors did not seem as pressing to officials. Rather, they demonstrated how difficult it is to reverse bureaucratic inertia. As during the industrial policy discussions of two years earlier, officials generated boxes of analysis and consumed hours and days in internal discussions and in consultation with business and other interests. Much of the effort was worthwhile. Indeed, the documents that formed the main product of the review provided a useful, detailed description of the state of the economy, the role of trade in it, the instruments and institutions available to influence the flow of trade and investment, the strengths and weaknesses of the various industrial sectors of the economy, and much more.[41] But it was essentially a static review that celebrated the past rather than anticipating the future. It failed to come to grips with the fundamental changes taking place in the Canadian and global economies.[42]

One senior ambassador consulted as the review wended its way through the bureaucracy, Klaus Goldschlag, captured its essence well. "Some may see it as being basically conservative in its assessment. I am not one of those who believe that the world trading order or Canada's place in it are likely to benefit from the reversal of policies that have been put in place over the years with careful regard for the facts of life."[43] True enough, but given the wrenching difficulties Canada faced and the problems evident in the multilateral trading order, a bolder approach might have yielded better choices. Some cabinet ministers also proved remarkably acute when they complained that officials were trying to use the review to cement further into place an approach to trade policy that relied on multilateral rule making to bind the government's future policy choices.

The review thus offered a solid, professional assessment of the Canadian trade policy of the past, but it failed to look to the challenges of the future. As such, it typified the limits of official documents. Nevertheless, it did add to the growing debate in Canada about how to order Canada's trade relationship with the United States. The chapter devoted to Canada-US relations suggested a modest possibility:

Canada and the United States could negotiate sectoral free-trade agreements to address the growing range of irritants between the two countries. While constituting only a small portion of the review, the sectoral free-trade concept soon became the main focus of public discussion. The choice made in the trade policy review to examine, however cautiously, bilateral arrangements with the United States was based on an assessment of the mood of the country and a pragmatic and deliberate conclusion that there a change in emphasis should be considered.[44]

Emerging Interest in Bilateral Free Trade with the United States

That line of analysis had also begun to emerge in other places. Developments in the domestic economy, the inability of GATT to respond to immediate Canadian economic concerns, and the attitudes of US policy makers to the changing world economy and the US place in it were leading to an insistent reexamination of Canada-US free trade. A modern argument favouring direct negotiations with the United States in order to obtain more open access had been set out in considerable detail by the Senate Standing Committee on Foreign Affairs in three reports issued in 1975, 1978, and 1982.[45] The reports responded to an increasingly popular view among influential members of the Canadian business establishment and were based on extensive public hearings. The reports echoed the views of export-oriented, resource-based industries as well as of most professional economists, although these groups had reached similar conclusions for different reasons. Internationally competitive companies were prepared to welcome any move to reduce artificial barriers to a market of 240 million and limit potential irritants in an economic relationship that was already largely integrated. Economists, on the other hand, consider most trade barriers to be irrational obstacles to efficiency and increased prosperity.

A detailed expression of the economists' view had been set out in the 1975 report of the Economic Council of Canada, *Looking Outward*.[46] It ranked Canada-US free trade fifth among a number of possible strategies. Ahead of it were multilateral free trade; free trade with the United States, the EC, and Japan; free trade with the United States and the EC; and free trade with the United States and Japan. The Council's assessment, however, was that Canada-US free trade was probably the most attainable of these five options. The Council's report built upon the work of such economists as the Wonnacott brothers, John Young, Ted English, Harry Johnson, and others who had long argued that the small Canadian economy could not afford to isolate itself from the world economy by maintaining high barriers to imports.[47] This point of view had been well summarized by Young in his study for the 1957 Royal Commission on Canada's Economic Prospects chaired by Walter Gordon, as follows: "The principal result of this analysis can be summarized in a sentence. In general and over the long run, increases in protection can be expected to lead to economic losses and decreases in protection to economic gains for the country as a whole. This follows not only from the direct effect the Canadian tariff has on the Canadian economy, but also from the effect Canadian commercial policy has on the treatment accorded this country's exports."[48]

Duncan Macpherson, 10 July 1975. The Economic Council recommends withdrawing tariff support from Canadian business in its 1975 study, Looking Outward.

These economists all shared the view that small economies dependent on trade with larger economies needed free, stable, and secure access to at least one large market in order to reap the benefits of specialization and long production runs available to industries in Europe, the United States, and Japan because of large domestic markets. Such benefits could be made available to Canada through open trade agreements. In the 1960s, they had argued for Atlantic free trade; in the 1970s, they turned increasingly to North American free trade. The lingering legacy of the National Policy of high tariffs, however, continued to dominate official views.

By the mid-1980s, three-quarters of Canada's merchandise exports were going to the United States (see table 12.6), and it was on the basis of a North American economy that the private sector was making its growth plans. In the first half of the 1980s, trade with the United States had continued to grow, while that with the rest of the world remained essentially stagnant. Canadian-based manufacturers were convinced that improved access would stimulate further growth. Indeed, most manufacturers naturally concluded that the US market was basic to their export success in third markets. They realized that for many Canadian manufacturing firms, future diversification of trade patterns depended on a sound North American economic base. If these companies could not compete in the United States and find customers south of the border, they would not find them in Europe, Japan, or developing countries.

Table 12.6

The direction of Canadian merchandise trade, 1981-6 (millions of dollars)

Year	US	UK	Japan	Other EEC	Rest of world	Total
Exports						
1981	53,667	3,321	4,487	5,379	14,040	80,895
1982	55,847	2,269	4,568	4,708	14,031	81,825
1983	64,528	2,449	4,728	4,194	12,608	88,506
1984	82,796	2,443	5,629	4,478	14,197	109,543
1985	90,417	2,409	5,707	4,273	13,338	116,145
1986	90,297	2,552	5,915	5,252	12,391	116,588
Imports						
1981	54,131	2,234	4,040	4,065	14,195	78,655
1982	47,866	1,904	3,527	3,805	10,754	65,856
1983	54,103	1,810	4,409	4,150	11,114	75,587
1984	68,450	2,317	5,710	5,930	13,346	95,754
1985	73,817	3,281	6,115	7,067	14,076	104,355
1986	77,337	3,721	7,626	9,090	14,903	112,678

Note: Totals may not add due to rounding.
Source: Statistics Canada, *Summary of Canadian International Trade* (Catalogue 65-001).

During the consultations on the trade policy review, business leaders had stressed the need to build Canada's trade policy on domestic foundations, but within the realities imposed by the international trading system and the international competitive environment. Two basic themes were constantly repeated: because the US market is basic to Canada's economic well-being, it was crucial to get the Canada-US relationship right; and economic nationalist experiments such as FIRA and the NEP were souring relations with the United States and interfering with good business judgment. All those consulted also stressed that while sound export and import policies were significant, more important for Canada's economic development and trade performance were sound domestic policy instruments, that is, fiscal, tax, and monetary policies supported by appropriate industrial policies.[49]

Despite the shortcomings of the government's trade policy review, its suggestion that Canada explore the prospect for sectoral accords with the Americans had unintended consequences. At the press conference releasing the documents in September 1983, the new minister for international trade, Gerald Regan, placed almost all the emphasis on this obscure corner of the review. The media duly reported that Canada would be seeking free trade with the United States.[50] Together with his officials, Regan initiated further work on this dimension and consultations with his American counterpart, Bill Brock. The Americans welcomed the proposal if for no other reason than the prospect it offered of reversing the previous three years of rising acrimony in the relationship.[51]

In the end, the sectoral initiative did not succeed. Some chose to believe that lack of time robbed the Liberals of an opportunity to prove its value. Others, more realistically, accepted that it is virtually impossible to find the necessary momentum and political support to negotiate free trade along sectoral lines. In any event, the initiative had the merit of adding momentum and renewed political legitimacy to a debate that had long been banished from Canadian politics. The next government, whatever its political stripe, would need to address the larger issue spawned by the initiative.

Was Canada ready to contemplate a full-fledged free-trade agreement with its southern neighbour? As it turned out, Canadians were ready for that and much more. Over the next decade, they would successfully negotiate not only a bilateral free-trade agreement with the Americans, but extend it to Mexico, and, together with the Americans, use it as a critical building block in negotiating a wholesale renewal of the multilateral trading system in the establishment of the World Trade Organization. After more than a century of sheltering behind the protective wall of the National Policy, Canadians were ready to test their resolve and transform Canada from a trading nation to a nation of traders.

13 FULL CIRCLE

THE NEW RECIPROCITY

The picture of weak and timid Canadian negotiators being pushed around and browbeaten by American representatives into settlements that were "sell-outs" is a false and distorted one. It is often painted, however, by Canadians who think that a sure way to get applause and support at home is to exploit our anxieties and exaggerate our suspicions over US power and policies.

– LESTER PEARSON, MIKE: THE MEMOIRS OF THE
RIGHT HONOURABLE LESTER B. PEARSON

Over the course of Canada's first century, Canadians had consistently elected leaders who knew the virtues of governing from the centre. The success and political longevity of Mackenzie King could in large part be attributed to his genius for sensing the middle ground of the moment. John Diefenbaker had not fit that mould and Canadians had quickly grown tired of him. In 1968, they had opted for charisma and colour and for the next sixteen years had enjoyed the ups and downs of a government led by a man they could not fathom, always found fascinating, often admired, but other times loathed. By the winter of 1983-4, Pierre Trudeau knew it was time to step aside and, in a bitterly fought contest, the Grits opted for a new leader who had become increasingly alienated from Trudeau, his style, and his politics. John Turner had left the Trudeau cabinet in 1975 and had built a following among media pundits and disaffected Liberals from his perch on Toronto's Bay Street. He had campaigned as a fiscal conservative, in tune with the increasingly conservative temper of the times. Installed as prime minister, however, he faltered and seemed incapable of using the office to consolidate the momentum of the leadership campaign.

The Tories, meanwhile had also changed leaders, rejecting the hapless Joe Clark for the untried Brian Mulroney. The new leader had waged an impressive campaign to bring the always fractious Tories together and forge a coalition of supporters in Quebec and the West. His reputation as a consummate practitioner of the art of compromise shrouded the fact that he also espoused some basic conservative principles. Impressed by the success of Margaret Thatcher in Britain and Ronald Reagan in the United States, he wanted Canada to become a more entrepreneurial and market-oriented society, less reliant on government direction and support. Arguably, as a conservative, he wanted to restore Canadian virtues and methods of an earlier era and roll back the excesses of the postwar welfare state. More fundamentally, however, he represented a harder-nosed assessment of what it would take for Canada to remain a player in the rapidly globalizing economy.

In the September 1984 election Canadians decided that they had had enough of the Grits, at least for the time being. They did not believe that Turner represented anything other than a continuation of a government that had grown tired and arrogant. From Newfoundland to British Columbia, they were ready to give Mulroney and the Tories a chance and provided them with an overwhelming mandate. For the next nine years, Canadians would experience a very different kind of leadership and a fundamental redirection in governmental priorities.

In the end, however, by trying to be both a man of principle and a master of brokerage politics, Mulroney satisfied Canadians on neither front and proved once again that Canada is a difficult country to govern. By the early 1990s, it seemed, they wanted him to compromise when he stood on principle, from free trade to the goods and services tax (GST) and related economic policies, and to stand on principle when he brokered compromises, particularly on the Meech Lake and Charlottetown constitutional accords. Like Trudeau, however, he left a legacy that would alter the nature of the country and could not easily be undone. Trudeau's proudest achievement was the Charter of Rights and Freedoms, Mulroney's the Canada-US Free Trade Agreement. The one constitutionalized personal freedom and equality, the other enshrined economic freedom and nondiscrimination among Canada's international legal obligations. Both committed future governments to their policies and programs, Trudeau by empowering the courts, Mulroney by strengthening the role of international trade tribunals, starting with procedures established in a Canada-US free-trade agreement. Both proved controversial and far-reaching, reflecting fundamentally different conceptions of Canada as a country and Canadians as a people.

Competing Views of Bilateral Free Trade

The pursuit of bilateral free trade with the United States, of course, was as old as the country, but it had been effectively banished from public discussion by the 1911 election. That changed in the 1980s. The combined impact of the Trudeau government's interventionist policies of 1980-1 and the sharp recession of 1981-2 had convinced increasing numbers of Canadian business leaders that something needed to be done about Canada-US relations and about Canada's longer-term economic prospects. They had been joined by economists and other analysts who suggested that the answer lay in bilateral free trade with the United States. These views were sharply opposed by political and other analysts concerned about the impact of such an agreement on Canada's capacity to pursue a wide range of political, social, cultural, and economic objectives.

The focus for much of this debate in 1983-5 was the research and consultations of the Royal Commission on the Economic Union and Development Prospects for Canada, chaired by Donald Macdonald. Macdonald had held various portfolios in Trudeau cabinets and then returned to private life in 1977, but had returned to Ottawa in 1982 to head the commission. Throughout 1984, it was an open secret that the commission was struggling with the issue of Canada-US free trade and leaning toward a positive recommendation. Much of its work responded to the theme of letting markets work, in keeping with the more conservative tenor of society in the 1980s. Nationalists on the commission staff and at commission-sponsored seminars later lamented that the commission had been captured by neoclassical economists.[1] In November 1984, Macdonald went public and declared that Canadians should be prepared to take a "leap of faith."[2] While his choice of words may have been unfortunate, he nevertheless greatly advanced the credibility of those espousing bilateral free trade and brought the debate to the front page.

What was at issue were two competing views of Canada and of Canadian society – a free-enterprise view and an interventionist one. During the postwar years, both Liberal and Conservative governments had steered a course between these two positions without fully endorsing either. In the 1980s, government had to make a choice – Canada could no longer have its cake and eat it too. As political scientist Gilbert Winham wrote: "In economic terms, and even in political terms, Canadians tend to define themselves in relation to the United States. The US economy is viewed at once as both an enormous attraction as well as a serious threat to Canada, and the same could probably be said for American society in general. All this produces a conflict of purpose, which is compounded by the fact that free trade necessarily incites an enormous dose of Canadian nationalism."[3]

The public debate about free trade in the 1980s, of course, was only dimly related to any deep political differences. Such differences are not the basis of Canadian politics, at least not between the mainstream parties. Whatever differences of principle there may have been between these two parties, they were not so profound and strongly held as to prevent rapid adjustments to the changing winds of circumstance and popular fashion. The basis of partisan opposition in Canada is that whatever the government proposes, the other parties must oppose. While there are issues on which it is assumed that no partisan gain can be expected from dissent, most issues marshal opposition. An issue like free trade, which obviously evoked conflicting images for many Canadians, occasioned extremely vigorous political debate.

Although the free-trade debate of the 1980s was essentially without roots in modern partisan political philosophy, the Conservative embrace of free trade in 1985 may have been somewhat facilitated by the fact that since 1935, the Tories had held office for only seven years. They came to the issue, therefore, unencumbered by the complication of defending previous policy choices. For some Liberals, on the other hand, criticism had to be tempered by the reality of almost fifty years of Liberal policy. As the political debate wore on, however, fewer and fewer politicians felt bound by the past.

Similarly, the pleading of special interests should not be confused with real divisions between Canadians. The case for protection, for example, may be cast in terms of patriotism and protecting the Canadian way of life, but it is nevertheless, the privileging of the few at the expense of the many. The Canadian wine industry, for example, presented a heartrending case to the federal and provincial governments that it could not exist without five layers of special protection: forced consumption of locally produced grapes, import duties, provincial monopoly importation and distribution powers, discriminatory listing practices, and differential pricing practices. The overall price effect of these measures was a premium of 100 percent or more on imported wines; to the extent that wine is price-sensitive, Canadian producers needed only to be half as good as foreign producers to compete on the Canadian market. Most of these practices had been declared illegal under GATT rules, and in the free-trade negotiations, the government would finally agree to phase them out. Some sectors of the industry were able to adjust and thrive; others disappeared. The government, in effect, decided that Canadians in general had a more compelling case than did the wine industry. The wine industry provided an extreme example of protection in Canada, but there were other segments of the Canadian economy that also benefited from special protection. Some would see their protection retained, while for others it would disappear. Such changes evoke strong views, but the debate in Canada in the 1980s went well beyond these kinds of concerns.

At heart, the debate was not between Conservatives and Liberals or even between Conservatives and New Democrats, although the latter may have had a better claim to a grounding in political and economic philosophy than the two mainstream parties. It was also not the classic debate between the special interests of protection and general economic welfare. Rather, it was a debate that revolved around two very different conceptions of what a free-trade agreement with the United States would involve.

There were those who saw it as a trade agreement similar to, if somewhat more comprehensive than, previous trade agreements. As such, they saw it as a practical tool that would help the Canadian economy adjust to the competitive challenges of the future. It would incorporate rules that would guide future trade and investment decisions and ensure that such decisions would not be frustrated by capricious action by either the Canadian or US governments. They accepted that the Canadian economy is highly integrated into the world economy and that Canadians needed to recognize both the benefits and challenges that come with that integration. They believed that Canadian identity was secure and unlikely to be much affected by a further evolutionary step in managing trade and economic relations with the United States. This was the point of view of Canadians whose point of departure was largely economic and whose theorists were academic economists. To them, the time had come for the government to pursue a policy that had made sense for many years and was now badly needed to prepare the country for the competitive challenges of the next century.

Others saw a free-trade agreement as symbolic of the end of Canada as an independent country. They decried the degree of integration that had already taken place and argued that close economic, cultural, and political interaction with the world, but particularly with the United States, had already begun to erode a distinctive Canadian identity. A free-trade agreement, by recognizing that closeness in contractual terms, would not only sap the will to turn the tide but even prevent a future government from taking the necessary steps to introduce laws and policies that in their view would nurture a more independent and self-reliant Canada. They had no confidence that the United States government would be bound by a body of rules, but rather, were convinced that Americans would use the agreement as a tool to bind Canada even closer to their economic destiny. To them, a free-trade agreement would accelerate the importation of American values and destroy Canadian values. This was the point of view of economic and other nationalists. Their point of departure was largely political and their theorists were largely academic political scientists. To them, the government was bent on pursuing a policy of economic expediency at the expense of the country's fundamental values.

These were profound differences that had little to do with trade policy and everything to do with opposing views of the nature of the modern world, of Canada's place in it, of the role of government in society, and of the nature of Canada. These were not differences that readily lent themselves to rational debate. The free-trade debate, as a result, acted as a magnet, attracting a host of seemingly peripheral claims about free trade and the United States: concerns about what it would mean for protecting the environment, for advancing the role of women in society, for the fight on poverty, for reducing regional disadvantage, for controlling pornography, for pressing Native land claims, for strengthening social policy, and for promoting an indigenous culture. The debate became symbolic of the hopes and fears of many Canadians for the future of the country and its priorities.

While these many competing claims at times appeared to be not only irrelevant but even silly, they were in reality manifestations of a debate that had solid historical roots. The more extravagant assertions, however, tended to obscure the serious issues at stake. Indeed, concerns essentially unrelated to free trade were used by opponents to raise fears about the potentially negative implications of any bilateral trade agreement with the United States. Wrote David Frum in *Saturday Night,* commenting on a collection of essays by the cultural elite, "The protectionists definitely have the fun side of the great free-trade debate ... Free trade will raise Canada's standard of living and create jobs. Substantiating that claim requires much toilsome research, expressed in measured and even technical prose. The protectionists, on the other hand can sit down at the typewriter and write any old thing that pops into their heads ... What's wrong with [their views] isn't that they are overwrought or vituperative; it's that their authors simply do not consider themselves bound by the customary standards of evidence."[4]

The debate also showed ignorance of Canadian and international trade policy and practice, and of their historical development. Critics who stated their preference for GATT negotiations, for example, seemed to have only the vaguest notion what the GATT involved. With one breath they condemned national treatment (enshrined in GATT article III) and with another counselled that the government should rely exclusively on the new round of GATT negotiations to achieve Canada's trade policy objectives.

Equally bewildering was the wholesale dismissal of all other perspectives, whether found in government documents, remarks from foreign politicians such as Britain's Margaret Thatcher, Germany's Helmut Kohl, or Japan's Noboru Takeshita, or analysis from economists at the OECD or the IMF. For these opponents, the debate was about the nature of Canada and grounded in pre-economic concepts of international trade. The views of foreigners were considered presumptuous and irrelevant.

Hidden behind these criticisms of free trade was the fact that economic, cultural, and other nationalists were as unhappy with the previous fifty years of Canadian trade and economic policy as they would be with any US free-trade initiative. The free-trade debate brought into public consciousness an awareness of where Canada stood in the tough competitive world of the 1980s and some Canadians did not like it. Since trade policy had not been an issue of public controversy for half a century, most Canadians, even those with a sophisticated knowledge of the world around them, were unfamiliar with the requirements of the GATT and of Canada's many other trade agreements. While some professed a preference for multilateral negotiations, many of their criticisms in reality took issue with obligations Canada already had under the GATT and other arrangements or was actively seeking in the GATT context. In effect, the critics wanted Canada to return to a world that never existed. That was not an option the government could pursue. Instead, it needed to consider the merits and pitfalls of a bilateral free-trade agreement that would reach beyond the GATT and provide Canada with a more open and more secure relationship with its overwhelmingly largest trading partner.

Refurbishing Relations with the United States

The process that would lead to the conclusion of a bilateral free-trade agreement with the United States started on 4 September 1984, the day the Tories swept to victory in a wave of public enthusiasm for a change from the perpetual Grits. The new prime minister had made economic renewal and refurbished relations with the United States key elements in his platform. As a symbol of the new approach, he made a whirlwind visit to Washington on 26 September, nine days after being sworn in, to confirm to a smiling Ronald Reagan that the days of confrontation were over and an era of cooperation about to begin. *Globe and Mail* reporter Bill Johnson, in a remarkably prescient article, speculated that the visit also marked the opening shot in the quest for free trade.[5]

Johnson's speculation was not as strange as it might at first seem. Despite Mulroney's curt dismissal of free trade during the election campaign, once in office he had to confront the stalled sectoral trade initiative introduced by the Liberals in 1983. Debate in the country had already moved beyond that initiative and both provincial politicians and business leaders were calling for a serious examination of the full free-trade option. Additionally, refurbished relations with the Americans required a serious look at the management of bilateral trade relations and something more than a reiteration of Liberal policy. Whatever the new cabinet's personal predilections, free trade with the United States was an issue the new ministry had to face from the moment it took office. For the next four years bilateral free trade would dominate not only the government's trade policy agenda but increasingly its economic and finally its political agenda as well.[6]

Unencumbered by the policy baggage of twenty years in office, the new government proved it was ready to take a serious look at the free-trade option. Over the next twelve months, without any strong preconceptions, it consulted widely and listened to every Canadian with an idea and an interest. It studied the issue from every angle and cautiously, step-by-step, began to shape the debate. The first key statement came from Finance Minister Michael Wilson in an 8 November 1984 economic statement. *A New Direction for Canada* set out the new government's leading economic priorities, including consideration "as a matter of priority, and in close consultation with the provinces and the private sector, [of] all avenues to secure and enhance market access. This will include a careful analysis of options for bilateral trade liberalization with the United States in the light of various private sector proposals, as well as preparations for and opportunities provided by multilateral trade negotiations."[7]

Free trade fit in well with the government's other initiatives in the economic area, such as dismantling the Foreign Investment Review Agency (FIRA) and the National Energy Program (NEP), reducing government spending, replacing the manufacturers sales tax with the GST, reducing business subsidies, privatizing Crown corporations, and deregulating many sectors of the economy. During the government's first year in office, Deputy Prime Minister Erik Nielsen led a massive effort to discover the full extent of government programs, subsidies, and regulations, to map out specific proposals to address the government's desire to place Canada on a more businesslike, competitive footing, and to reduce the role of government in the economy.[8] Thus, despite the new prime minister's curt dismissal of bilateral free trade during his successful run for the Conservative leadership in 1983, the issue was squarely on the country's – and the government's – agenda by the end of 1984.

By the following February, Wilson's colleague, Minister for International Trade Jim Kelleher, had issued a discussion paper, *How to Secure and Enhance Canadian*

Access to Export Markets, which set out the government's thinking on the emerging multilateral and bilateral trade agenda. It invited Canadians to tell the government whether they favoured a continuation of the sectoral bilateral initiative, preferred some other form of bilateral cooperation, or were prepared to go further and endorse pursuit of a comprehensive bilateral free-trade agreement. The paper carefully avoided casting multilateral and bilateral negotiations as alternatives, insisting that "the choice for Canada is not between multilateral or bilateral approaches to trade but how both avenues can be pursued in a mutually reinforcing manner"[9] to secure more open and secure access to foreign markets.

After five months of internal debate, the government now joined a public debate that had already attracted considerable attention across Canada in academic seminars, at business conferences, and in newspaper editorial rooms. An April 1984 Environics poll suggested that more than three-quarters of Canadians favoured free trade with the United States. Kelleher, during a cross-Canada tour to gauge reaction to his discussion paper, heard from a broad spectrum of Canadians confirming that view. While there were some Canadians who strongly opposed any bilateral negotiations with the United States or any form of trade liberalization, the majority of the business and professional opinion makers who showed up at his breakfasts, lunches, and open meetings claimed that they were prepared to see the government try to negotiate a comprehensive agreement with the Americans.[10]

While Kelleher toured the country, a task force of officials prepared the ground for a meeting of the prime minister and US president Ronald Reagan in Quebec City. The prime minister had indicated that the meeting afforded a solid opportunity to put improvements in trade relations front and centre on the bilateral agenda. The president agreed, and in their 17 March 1985 Quebec Declaration on Trade in Goods and Services, the two leaders took the next critical step on the road to free trade. Declaring themselves "convinced that an improved and more secure climate for bilateral trade relations will encourage market forces to achieve a more rational and competitive production and distribution of goods and services," they charged their two trade ministers "to establish immediately a mechanism to chart all possible ways to reduce and eliminate existing barriers to trade and to report to us within six months."[11]

Kelleher and newly appointed USTR Clayton Yeutter set to work and on 17 September recommended that the two governments proceed to the negotiation of a comprehensive bilateral trade agreement and set out their respective agendas.[12] By then momentum had carried the issue much further in Canada. Meetings with the provincial premiers and trade ministers had demonstrated a strong federal-provincial consensus favouring negotiations, with only Ontario cautious about the implications. Confidential consultations chaired by former senior trade official Tom Burns had indicated broad support in the business community.[13] The same message had been conveyed to a special parliamentary committee established to hold hearings over the course of the summer. In a 23 August 1985 report it recommended that the government proceed to negotiations.[14] Finally, on 5 September 1985, the long-awaited report of the Macdonald Royal Commission strongly urged the negotiation of a comprehensive bilateral free-trade agreement.[15] Based on three years of hearings and detailed study, the report, endorsed by twelve of the thirteen commissioners, was met by a wave of equally strong endorsements in editorials across the country.

When the prime minister finally rose in the House of Commons on 26 September, his announcement that the government would explore with the Americans the feasibility of a bilateral agreement appeared anticlimactic. The following week, formal letters were exchanged between the prime minister and president setting out their views of the negotiations, and everything appeared ready for the next stage.[16] Two years of debate had thoroughly prepared the country for the decision. While support for the initiative was strong, there had by this time also developed a determined and articulate opposition. Over the next two years the government's commitment to the initiative would be severely tested as one group after another sought to derail it.

Preparing for Negotiations

Once the government had announced its decision to proceed with free-trade negotiations with the United States, the next logical steps were to appoint negotiating teams, establish the necessary consultative and analytical resources, and prepare for formal negotiations. But first US president Ronald Reagan had to obtain authority from Congress to pursue the negotiations under the so-called fast-track authority. US negotiating authority had been extended and refined in the 1979 Trade Agreements Act and the 1984 Trade and Tariffs Act, both of which had included a specific authority to negotiate bilaterally with Canada. This authority ran out on 3 January 1988, placing a time limit on the negotiations, but one considered to be well within reason. Both Mulroney and Reagan were determined to conclude any agreement within their respective electoral mandates.

The complicated fast-track procedures had been devised to manage the trade negotiating difficulties for the United States posed by the separation of powers. As long as US officials did not stray from the authority delegated to the president, followed the procedural steps indicated, and consulted regularly with two principal committees concerned (the Senate Finance Committee and the House Ways and Means Committee), they could negotiate with some confidence and promise that any agreement they concluded stood a good chance of being implemented as negotiated. Preparations were thus set in train for a start to negotiations early in 1986, in the confident expectation that the necessary procedural steps would be completed by then. After all, preliminary soundings by the US administration over the course of the summer had indicated that the members of the two committees were well disposed toward Canada and welcomed the negotiations. Unfortunately, this was not the way the scenario played out.[17]

It took the US administration more than two months of internal wrangling to send the necessary notice to the two committees. In the Senate, strong displeasure with administration management of trade policy led to an unexpected brouhaha and a cliff-hanger tied vote on the negotiations. The Finance Committee appeared initially inclined to disapprove the request by a substantial margin, and the president had to use all of his powers of persuasion to achieve the close vote. Approval to proceed finally came on 23 April, but not before setting alarm bells ringing in Canada about the capacity of US officials to manage the negotiations.

During the intervening months, the two sides had picked chief negotiators and prepared for negotiations. Mulroney had appointed Simon Reisman, a retired deputy minister with a long and distinguished record as a trade negotiator, while the US administration had selected its ambassador to the GATT, Peter Murphy. Reisman had long been on record as strongly favouring a bilateral free-trade agreement, and his crusty, no-nonsense reputation and experience made him an eminently acceptable choice to take on what by then had been dubbed the most important negotiation in Canada's history. By May 1986, Reisman had assembled nearly a hundred advisors, specialists, and support staff and housed them in a penthouse suite in downtown Ottawa. Responsible for both multilateral and bilateral trade negotiations, Reisman had inherited Sylvia Ostry as his deputy for multilateral negotiations and appointed Gordon Ritchie to be his deputy for the bilateral negotiations. A team of assistant negotiators took charge of federal-provincial relations, industry liaison and analysis, legal advice, and the details of the negotiations. Each of them, in turn, was assisted by a bevy of senior and junior advisors.

At the same time, Trade Minister Kelleher had established a forty-member International Trade Advisory Committee (ITAC) and fifteen Sectoral Advisory Groups on International Trade (SAGITs) to provide the government with industry advice. Modelled on the US private-sector advisory system, the Canadian system aimed at providing business with direct access to ministers and the negotiators. As negotiations proceeded, senior members of Reisman's team periodically briefed the SAGITs and sought their advice on particular issues. The minister, accompanied by Reisman or Ritchie, met regularly with the ITAC. Provincial involvement had been addressed by establishing a Continuing Committee on Trade Negotiations (CCTN) made up of senior officials from each of the provinces and the two territories who met monthly with Reisman to be briefed on progress and to share ideas. The prime minister had also agreed to meet regularly with the premiers (over the course of two years, they had twelve meetings to discuss the trade negotiations, each occasion providing the media with a circus of both pertinent and irrelevant comments as Canadian politicians played the perennial federal-provincial relations game). Finally, a special cabinet committee had been struck to oversee the negotiations and provide Reisman with detailed instructions. Originally chaired by Secretary of State for External Affairs Joe Clark, it was taken over by Pat Carney in July 1986 when she replaced Kelleher as trade minister.

By May 1986, Reisman and his team were as ready as they would ever be. The Americans, however, were not at the same stage of preparation. With the exception of the appointment of Murphy in April, little had been done. Housed in the Office of the United States Trade Representative, the US team had opted for a very different negotiating apparatus. Unlike the highly hierarchical and tightly structured Canadian team, Murphy had a personal staff of three, including Bill Merkin, the senior USTR officer who had been responsible for much of the preparatory work, and for the rest of his team would have to rely on the resources of USTR and other agencies interested in trade. Those officials who joined the team would pursue the negotiations in tandem with their other responsibilities. Even Murphy and Merkin were not relieved of their other chores. Merkin continued to be responsible for day-to-day Canada-US trade issues, while Murphy became the senior USTR manager of trade relations with Canada and Mexico. In addition to conducting the negotiations, Murphy was also expected to maintain a regular schedule of congressional briefings and consult with the US private-sector advisory committees. For none of these tasks was he given any extra staff. Any assistance he required would have to come from other USTR staffers already busy with their regular assignments.

Preliminary Sparring

Between the end of May and the end of September 1986, Reisman, Murphy, and their senior advisors met five times, twice in Washington, the other times in the boardroom of the Trade Negotiations Office in Ottawa, at a lodge in Mont Tremblant, Quebec, and at the cabinet retreat in the Gatineau Hills outside Ottawa. These five sessions were billed as a preliminary round needed by the two teams to establish the negotiating agenda and priorities, forge a working method, gain each other's confidence and generally set the ground rules for the more detailed negotiations to follow. Each session lasted two days and was devoted to two or three main negotiating issues. Each side took turns presenting its views of the issues in an effort to set out the parameters within which the negotiations would be pursued.

Each plenary session sought to advance the discussion far enough to establish a working or fact-finding group to pursue more detailed discussions and prepare draft negotiating proposals for consideration. By the end of September, the two sides had set up working groups on intellectual property, customs matters, agricultural trade, services, government procurement, and subsidies as well as fact-finding groups on automotive trade, energy, fisheries, and state and provincial barriers. Each group was jointly chaired by senior members of each negotiating team, assisted by such technical advisors as the issues required. As negotiations proceeded, groups were also established to deal with financial services, investment, dumping, safeguards, dispute settlement, alcoholic beverages and, finally, a legal group to integrate the work of the other groups, consider institutional issues, and prepare the draft text of an agreement. The establishment of some groups came only after much tactical manoeuvring to determine whether sufficient progress had been made on other issues to warrant further consideration on a matter of greater interest to one side or the other. Investment, financial services, and contingency protection (subsidies, dumping, and safeguards), for example, all involved such jockeying.

Two other aspects of the negotiations had also become clear by the end of the summer. Federal-provincial wrangling during the spring over the provincial role in the negotiations had attracted intense media interest, but nothing had prepared either Reisman or Murphy for the media circus that would dog them as negotiations proceeded. Murphy and Reisman became household names in Canada. Strangers stopped them in airports; the daily press reported their every pronouncement. Unfamiliar with the issues under negotiation, the media concentrated on personalities and on the sensational, aided in their quest, often unwittingly, by the mercurial Reisman and the laconic Murphy. If nothing else, reporters could file a story comparing the different styles of the two chief protagonists. Additionally, every public utterance by more junior members of the two teams, as well as of uninvolved officials, was scrutinized for consistency and twisted into major news stories.

Never had a trade negotiation been reported in such breathless detail and never before did a government have to manage its trade agenda under such relentless scrutiny. The detailed media attention soon began to influence the conduct of the negotiations and the approach to the issues. The media debated whether the Auto Pact was on or off the table, whether culture and social programs would be affected by the negotiations, whether supply management would be compromised, whether investment would be included, and whether Canada would gain exemption from US trade remedy law. Endless media speculation and the regular antics of Question Period in the House of Commons fed one another. All the public airings required briefs, spooked the development of negotiating positions, and generally coloured the professional pursuit of negotiations.

A further complicating factor was that the government had simultaneously to conduct negotiations and manage the usual range of trade irritants. At any given time, there are dozens of "cases" requiring the attention of officials responsible for managing the US-Canada relationship. Most of them are never reported in the daily press and involve technical issues in which ministers rarely become involved. Only the most contentious issues are ever elevated to the ministerial level. But the media hype of the negotiations led to a much more detailed scrutiny of these irritants, and ministers were called on to explain complicated technical issues as if the very essence of Canada depended on how the issue was resolved. During the preliminary period, US decisions involving shakes and shingles and softwood lumber, consideration of a highly protectionist US Omnibus Trade Bill, and unguarded comments about the exchange rate all threatened to derail the negotiations before they had even pulled out of the station. As negotiations proceeded, other issues regularly cropped up to provide a fertile field for mischief, particularly culture, the Auto Pact, and agricultural supply management measures.

O.K. EVERYTHING ON THE TABLE.

*Duncan MacPherson, "Everything on the Table," 24 May 1986. The
scope of the negotiating agenda was one of the many phony issues that
delighted cartoonists and editorialists alike during the FTA
negotiations.*

Used to negotiating in the quiet isolation of Geneva, Canadian and US negotiators had never confronted such a carnival atmosphere. GATT negotiations attracted at best two or three visits by reporters per year, many of whom would leave without filing a story, given the numbing complexity and sheer tedium of the issues involved. Only official announcements of the final result had ever attracted any serious media interest and then under circumstances that were easy to control. It was little wonder, then, that the barrage of media attention began to assume a place at the table, often occasioning sharp exchanges between the negotiators as to who had been indiscreet. Both chief negotiators began to use press scrums to stake out positions or to attack or discomfort the other, often inadvertently reducing their own room for manoeuvre and complicating the negotiations.

Review
At the end of the September 1986 session, Reisman and Murphy agreed that they would not meet again until after the US midterm elections in November. They reasoned that they needed to give the working groups time to make some progress before bringing any issues back to plenary for further broad policy consideration. In addition, they wanted to sit back and consider what they had learned from the

preliminary sessions and what they needed to do to ensure that they were in a position to conclude a mutually acceptable agreement a year later.

On the Canadian side, preliminary conclusions were not optimistic. Both the first five plenary sessions as well as opening meetings of the various working groups had revealed a wide gap in approach and philosophy between the two teams. Reisman had come armed with a single vision of a comprehensive agreement that would establish the rules of the game for Canada-US trade relations for the next few generations. He wanted to establish national treatment as the norm for the movement of virtually all goods and services between the two countries. If the United States was prepared to accept his vision, he was authorized to extend this principle of nondiscrimination to the US priorities of investment and intellectual property. Reisman saw an agreement that would proceed from general principles to the details necessary to make it work. This was a vision he had explained to ministers, to provincial ministers and officials, to the business community, and to anyone prepared to listen.

Murphy, on the other hand, had not revealed any vision. Indeed, even after five sessions it was difficult to divine any plan to his approach. He seemed to be driven by the pressures generated by individual irritants, by the views of special interest groups, and by the worry of possibly unhelpful precedents for his government's global trade interests. More than anything else, he seemed risk-averse, determined not to make any early commitments. Unsure of the degree of support he could count on from within the administration, Murphy constantly worried about the views of members of Congress. His team, led by middle-level officials from other agencies, appeared to be equally concerned about congressional opinions and determined not to sacrifice any of the powers and authorities of their home agencies. Rather than acting as the leader of a tightly knit group, Murphy presided as the nominal chair of a collection of individualists, each with his or her own agenda.

The differing importance of the negotiations in the two capitals seemed to have influenced the makeup of the two teams and the approach to the issue. By now the centrepiece of the Mulroney government's economic agenda, the bilateral negotiations seemed to have all the necessary resources and ideas to carry them to a successful conclusion on the Canadian side. On the American side, the negotiations appeared a poorly prepared orphan able to command only meagre resources and virtually bankrupt of ideas and vision. With these differences clearly apparent by the end of the five preliminary sessions, from an Ottawa perspective the way forward appeared decidedly uphill.

Murphy's approach to the negotiations, of course, reflected the Washington decision-making process. Only in very rare instances does a strong and unified approach to an issue survive from conception to final implementation. Decisions emerge out of a highly brokered political market involving not only conflict between the administration and Congress and the pressures of various interest groups, but also conflict among the various agencies that make up the executive branch and even among factions within those agencies.

While there were clear US interests in the bilateral negotiations, these were not so strong as to place the negotiations high on the political agenda or to transcend the constant political infighting that dominates official Washington. Murphy thus faced officials from Treasury, Agriculture, Commerce, and other agencies with objectives entirely different from his own. He did not have the political clout or administrative authority to bring them around to his point of view. Treasury officials denied him any role in negotiating financial services and were reluctant to let him speak on investment; Commerce officials jealously guarded their prerogatives in the area of trade remedy law; and Agriculture officials made clear that there was little room for concessions on the US side, although they insisted Canada had much to give. In the face of these internal difficulties, it is not surprising that Murphy opted for a cautious approach geared more to the resolution of irritants than the negotiation of a comprehensive and visionary agreement.

One positive development was that Reisman and his senior officers had completed the process of obtaining clear and detailed mandates from cabinet and gained the full support for that mandate from provincial officials. By the time the two teams were ready to engage again at the end of the year, every issue had been brought before cabinet for a preliminary consideration and agreement on Reisman's negotiating instructions. Not since the King government had ministers been so intimately involved in the detail of a trade negotiation. Despite the ongoing public wrangling in Canada, the official effort was in good shape.

Serious Negotiations

With the US midterm elections over, negotiations resumed. Between the sixth plenary session in November 1986 and the twentieth plenary on the banks of the St. Lawrence River in Cornwall in mid-August 1987, each major negotiating issue was given at least two or three thorough airings at the level of the chief negotiators. As spring gave way to summer, the pace quickened, and over the course of the summer, plenary meetings were held almost weekly. Some working groups met even more frequently. Even if progress was uneven, there was no shortage of effort as the negotiating deadline of early October loomed ever larger.[18]

While little progress was being made in defining the contours of an agreement, both working group and plenary sessions were developing a hierarchy of issues. Some proved technically demanding but did not raise major political problems, including the elimination of the tariff, rules of origin, technical barriers, and similar traditional issues. More problematic were negotiations involving some of the more sensitive sectors, such as agriculture, culture, energy, and textiles. Some of the newer issues also proved both technically and politically challenging, including services, intellectual property rights, and government procurement preferences. The most difficult issues revolved around trade remedies, dispute settlement, and investment. The first two were crucial to Canada; the third was a deal breaker for the United States. On all three issues, technically useful work was being done but there

Duncan MacPherson, "Mulroney Marries Carney and Reisman,"
4 July 1987. The appointment of Pat Carney as trade minister in
July 1986 provided cartoonists with a new theme to mine.

was little evidence that the two sides were moving toward agreement. Indeed, for even the straightforward issues, the gap between the two remained alarmingly wide.

By late winter 1986, many technical matters had been thoroughly discussed and the main problem areas determined. Missing was any clear consensus on the shape of a final agreement. With the exception of a few relatively uncontentious issues, Canada continued to propose while the Americans lay in the weeds. Even for issues on which the United States was the main demander, such as services, intellectual property, and investment, US proposals proved either poorly thought-through or insensitive to Canadian concerns. On issues critical to Canadian interests, such as contingency protection and dispute resolution, the US team had by midsummer put forward no detailed positions.

In frustration, the Canadian side began to explore alternative ways to get the message across and cut through Murphy's reticence. In December 1986, Trade Minister Carney invited new US Senate Finance Committee chairman Lloyd Bentsen to visit Canada with some of his colleagues so that ministers could explain the issues directly to them and gauge their interest. Bentsen expressed keen support for a very comprehensive agreement and was confident that such an agreement would be welcomed by Congress. In January, the prime minister invited Vice-President George Bush and Treasury Secretary Jim Baker to Ottawa for a tongue-lashing on the inadequacy of the US response. The result was an affirmation in the annual state of the union address that the president attached the highest priority to the conclusion of an agreement. In early April, the prime minister discussed the issue with the president and his senior advisors during the third bilateral summit in Ottawa and received assurances that the US administration understood Canada's concerns and would be responsive to them. The president used the occasion of an address to Parliament to assure Canadians directly of the importance he attached to the negotiations. In June, at the Venice Economic Summit, the prime minister once again appealed to the president to give the issue more priority and received promises that he would. At periodic meetings between Joe Clark and Secretary of State George Shultz, between Pat Carney and USTR Clayton Yeutter, and between Finance Minister Michael Wilson and Treasury Secretary Baker, the message was repeated.

Each time Canada raised the political stakes, it received the necessary assurances as well as heavy media attention, but the message did not penetrate to the level of Peter Murphy and his colleagues. Indeed, Murphy expressed increasing irritation with these high-level sorties, each of which required him to brief more senior officials and keep his fingers crossed that they would not compromise his tactic of playing out the string. That was the only tactic available to him. For most sessions with Reisman, his team was rarely sufficiently prepared and sure enough of its ground to tackle the issues head on. Instead, Murphy counted on Reisman's temper, calculating that a few well-aimed barbs would use up the available time for any given session.

From a Canadian perspective, American responses and ideas remained deficient. By midsummer, the two sides were no closer to an agreement than they had been a year earlier. Both continued to read from different scripts, and neither side seemed ready to adopt the other's approach. Nevertheless, Murphy and Reisman determined that they would exchange complete drafts of an agreement in mid-August, based on the labours of the working groups but also clearly setting out each other's positions. A Canadian team had begun preparing such a text as far back as January and by midsummer had produced a draft that was true to the Reisman vision but also took account of American sensitivities and discussion at plenary sessions and working groups. Intense discussions inside the Canadian team had further honed the document into a single, integrated text for the next stage of the negotiations.

The Americans, in order to avoid having to work from a Canadian text, quickly set to work to produce a similar text. In a matter of two weeks, the US legal team stapled together a draft from various proposals tabled by US team members or prepared by them for eventual tabling. The two documents were exchanged the third week of August. The Canadian draft presented a fully integrated text proceeding from the principle of national treatment and prepared in a single drafting style. The US draft presented a collection of disparate texts that in places contradicted each other and had little in common. For the first time, the difference in approach and attitude between the two sides stood out in sharp relief.

Both teams made a valiant effort in the final weeks of August to bridge the obvious gap but to little avail. The only solid achievement was recognition by the Americans that they had a long way to go. There were no breakthroughs. The two sides remained far apart.

Impasse in September

By the beginning of September, Reisman and Murphy had presided over twenty plenary sessions. Some dozen working groups had held numerous technical meetings. Canada had made dozens of negotiating proposals and finally had tabled a complete text of an agreement. Almost two years of preparations and more than a year of negotiations had resulted in a detailed appreciation of the issues. Public debate and controversy had sharpened public awareness. It was now or never.

Reisman had also met some eighteen times with the Continuing Committee on Trade Negotiations, and the prime minister had met six times with the provincial premiers. Dozens of consultations with the ITAC/SAGIT advisory system had honed Canadian positions. Weekly meetings with ministers had kept them engaged in the detail of the negotiations. By now all these groups were becoming somewhat impatient with the lack of visible progress. While Reisman may have assured them that the negotiations were on schedule, he too had become increasingly disappointed. With only a month to go, it was clear that the negotiations had reached an impasse. Something dramatic was required. If the effort could not be rescued, a plan was necessary to disengage with grace and to repair the damage of failure.

The prime minister and his key ministers and advisors had by now concluded that Reisman and Murphy would probably not wrap up the negotiations successfully. Further political appeals were unlikely to lead to substantial results. What was needed was a second front. To this end, Reisman was encouraged to give it one more try but was instructed that, if by the third week of September he had not achieved a breakthrough, he was to suspend negotiations. Meanwhile, the prime minister's chief of staff, Derek Burney, working together with Finance Minister Wilson and Trade Minister Carney, began to make exploratory soundings on a political settlement. In an exchange of letters with White House Chief of Staff Howard Baker, Burney was told that Treasury Secretary Jim Baker was the president's point man.

Reisman presided over two more negotiating sessions, both in Washington. These came to naught and on 23 September, he staged a dramatic walkout and declared the negotiations over, charging that the United States was not responding on elements fundamental to Canada's position. The Americans at first considered Reisman's walkout a media stunt but soon put their crisis team into full gear. Burney and the two ministers made two pilgrimages to Washington to explore the parameters for reconvening the negotiations with Baker, Yeutter, and their closest advisors. On Thursday 29 September, the Burney team concluded that the negotiations were over; the Americans were not capable of delivering on Canada's basic requirements regarding dispute settlement and contingency protection.

But the next day Burney, Wilson, and Carney, accompanied by the whole of the negotiating apparatus, flew back to Washington and in a dramatic series of events hammered out the elements of an agreement. Baker, following further consultations with Congress, agreed that the US side was now prepared to work on a compromise proposal first advanced by Florida congressman Sam Gibbons that would allow appeals of trade remedy cases to be decided by a bilateral panel. This breakthrough was the bellwether that would allow progress on many other issues.

Breakthrough

The two teams worked at breakneck speed all weekend. Several times it looked as if an agreement would again escape them, but finally, minutes before midnight on 3 October, the final breakthrough came. Many details remained to be worked out, but Canada and the United States had concluded an agreement. Despite the conviction only a few days earlier that it could not be done, the two governments had succeeded. US determination not to fail and Canadian adherence to its bottom line had paid dividends. It was clear that US attitudes had changed dramatically. Driven to avoid failure, US officials were prepared to make compromises in areas where previously they had only reluctantly considered Canadian demands. The focus of hard bargaining over the course of the weekend had been trade remedies and dispute settlement, but many other intransigent issues had also been settled.

Prime Minister Brian Mulroney meets with key members of his free-trade team, Gordon Ritchie, Derek Burney, and Simon Reisman, 1988.

Balancing the US desire not to fail had been Canada's determination to have an agreement that made economic sense and that would stand the test of time. Canada had been prepared to compromise on the short-term issues on which the United States needed to be seen to be making progress but had insisted that the basic agreement be sound. The tariff was to be eliminated over ten years, and most other access issues had been resolved to the mutual benefit of both countries. The security of access issue, so important politically, had been only partly resolved, but a solid basis had been laid for making things better. Canadian sovereignty had been protected by the establishment of a good general dispute settlement mechanism. A start had been made on services trade, access had been eased for Canadian business visitors to the US market, and balanced commitments had been concluded on investment.

Over the next eight weeks the two sides translated the mutually agreed 35-page memorandum of instructions into a 250-page legal text and 2,000 pages of tariff annexes. However, one more session at the political level was necessary to tie up the loose ends. The weekend of 2-3 December, Burney worked with US deputy treasury secretary Peter McPherson to work out the final details that could not be resolved through legal drafting. Finally, on 11 December 1987, the package was released for public scrutiny. On 2 January 1988, the president and the prime minister signed the final text of the agreement.

Results

Canada's purpose in seeking negotiations with the United States in 1985 had been three-fold:

- The most important, if least publicized, goal was to effect *domestic economic reform* by eliminating, at least for trade with the United States, the last vestiges of the National Policy and constraining the more subtle new instruments of protection. By exposing the economy to greater international competition, Canadian firms would need to restructure and modernize, become more efficient and productive, and rely increasingly on foreign markets.
- The most publicized objective was to provide a *bulwark against US protectionism*. By gaining more secure and open access to the large, contiguous US market, Canadian business would be able to plan and grow with greater confidence and gain an incentive to accept the challenge of increased competition from the United States.
- Finally, the agreement was meant to furnish an improved and *more modern basis for managing Canada-US relations*. Since 1948, the GATT had served this function but had increasingly proved insufficient. New and more enforceable rules combined with more sophisticated institutional machinery would put the relationship on a more predictable and less confrontational footing.[19]

These objectives were largely achieved in the 1987 agreement and its implementing legislation. The agreement required Canada and the United States to eliminate the tariff and either remove a wide variety of other import barriers and domestic practices or bring them under codes of conduct based on the principle of national treatment. The trade-liberalizing elements of the agreement were to be phased in over a period of up to ten years, thus providing industry with the time to adjust to more competitive conditions.[20]

The preamble and first chapter of the agreement set out the basic aims and objectives of the two governments and the philosophical framework for the agreement as a whole. Chapters 3 to 13 set out a conventional free-trade agreement, fully consistent with GATT article XXIV, the article specifying the requirements for such agreements. The link to the GATT was critical. Many of the clauses of the agreement were drawn directly out of the GATT or provided agreed interpretations of GATT provisions.[21] For example, the requirement that Canada could not arbitrarily restrict exports of energy to the United States and had to share resources in the event that it did impose restrictions was based on existing GATT requirements.

Chapters 14 to 17 made a cautious start on the new issues of services, business travel, investment, and financial services. Generally, the two governments decided to freeze the status quo but agreed that in any future laws and regulations, they would treat each other's service providers, investors, and business travellers as they treated their own. The two countries had made a similar commitment with regard to trade in goods in 1935 and had then gradually rolled back and eliminated areas where they did discriminate, a job they in effect finished in 1987. They agreed that they would try to do the same for the service industries and investors under the FTA.

Chapters 18 and 19 achieved a more secure basis for managing the trade and economic relationship. Chapter 18 took well-established GATT dispute settlement practices, translated them into agreed rules and procedures, and applied them to the rights and obligations of the agreement as a whole. In chapter 19, the two sides accepted that disputes between the two countries regarding the application of antidumping and countervailing duties should be subject to binational dispute settlement. Both countries could continue to apply their respective trade remedy laws, but they also agreed to replace judicial review of domestic decisions by binational review.

Finally, the agreement provided a framework for the negotiations of the future. Where either side was not prepared to go as far as the other, provisions were made to continue negotiations. At least ten articles throughout the agreement anticipated continued negotiations. The most important of these related to subsidies, anticompetitive pricing practices, and government procurement.

There were also disappointments. It had not been possible to find a mutually acceptable basis for addressing bilateral problems plaguing trade in agriculture.

Both sides hoped that the newly launched Uruguay Round of GATT negotiations would prove more propitious in this regard. The excision of softwood lumber from the agreement left a hole that would continue to haunt Canada-US trade relations. Canada's insistence on exempting culture from the agreement maintained a further area of continued tension. On balance, however, these exceptions covered only a small proportion of total trade, ensuring that for the vast majority of businesses on both sides of the border, important new opportunities had been introduced.

Managing its commercial relations with the United States had always been a challenge for Canada. The explosive mix of Americans' unbridled pursuit of manifest destiny and Canadians' overdeveloped sense of paranoia makes it difficult for a government to maintain the confidence of the electorate. On occasion, Canadian officials had sought to exploit natural US neighbourliness to develop a "special relationship," only to learn time and again, as Allan Gotlieb observed, that in the highly fragmented system of US decision making, legislators have special interests more often than enduring friends.[22]

A foreign government, no matter how friendly, can only rarely rise to the status of a special interest. To reduce the natural disadvantages that a small, trade-dependent country has in dealing with its superpower neighbour and ensure that legitimate Canadian interests would not be not too quickly sacrificed on the altar of political expediency, Canada needed the clout that comes from formal agreements with binding procedures. As Derek Burney, Gotlieb's successor in Washington and one of the principal architects of the FTA, concluded: "Canada's pursuit of trade agreements, of rules and of dispute settlement mechanisms is not a matter of high-mindedness. It is a matter of survival. It is a reality that is brought home to us on a daily basis. As a small country living next door to a global power, we need these rules to reduce the disparity in power and thus allow us to reap the benefits of our proximity."[23] The FTA raised the legal status enjoyed by Canadian interests to unprecedented heights.

Implementation and Electoral Trials

In Canada, the obligations set out in international agreements do not automatically become law but may need to be implemented through legislation. Under the Crown prerogative, the government is fully competent to negotiate and enter into international treaties, but it must seek parliamentary approval to enact their provisions into domestic law if they go beyond existing legislation. To that end, the government tabled Bill C-130, An Act to Implement the Free Trade Agreement between Canada and the United States of America, in the House of Commons in June 1988. The act would implement the terms of the agreement into Canadian law, enact consequential amendments to 27 previous acts of Parliament, and provide authority to amend dozens of regulations and Orders-in-Council as required. The hearings on the bill provided for a further round of protracted debate among opponents and proponents of the agreement, this time with the benefit of both the specifics of the agreement and its implementing legislation.

As described by political scientists Bruce Doern and Brian Tomlin, the debate pitted two distinct brands of nationalism against each other. "One was centred in the anti-free trade forces, founded on the defence of the powers of the Canadian state as the crucial glue for Canada's unity and independence. The other brand was a nationalism based on the market in which the pro-free trade coalition asserted a new entrepreneurial confidence in the ability of Canadians to compete with the best in the world."[24] There was little room in such a debate for compromise and sober reflection. In Parliament, Liberals and New Democrats pulled out all the rhetorical stops and in committee hearings, opponents and proponents did battle with a new level of intensity. The media tried to keep up with the bewildering array of assessments, with pundits and editorialists doing their best to dissect and weigh the validity of the claims and counterclaims. Finally, however, in the face of Liberal determination to use its majority in the Senate to force an election, the prime minister agreed and called an election for 21 November 1988.

The spectre of a repeat of the 1911 election seemed to stare free traders in the face. Canadian electoral campaigns normally coalesce around one or two themes and the differing approaches of the contesting parties to them. In 1988, however, the election became almost exclusively a referendum on the FTA. The prime minister, ministers, leaders, and other senior parliamentarians criss-crossed the country to press their views of the agreement on an unusually alert public. Normally reticent third parties, such as business and other groups, entered the fray with an enthusiasm and concern rarely seen in Canada. Polling organizations reflected an engaged but fickle electorate, as support for the two competing views ebbed and flowed.[25]

By election day, however, the forces favouring the agreement seemed to be in the ascendant. The outcome was decisive. The Conservatives garnered 170 of 295 seats and a clear majority spread across the country. The Liberals won 82 and the NDP 43 seats. Opponents claimed that the election did not give the government authority to proceed with such an important issue because the Tories only commanded 43 percent of the popular vote, while the two main opposition parties commanded 52 percent between them. The remaining 5 percent was largely won by the pro-free-trade Reform Party. In effect, the electorate appeared to be split down the middle. Under Canada's first-past-the-post electoral system, however, the only number that counts is the number of seats in the House of Commons.[26]

When Parliament reconvened, Prime Minister Mulroney moved quickly to reintroduce the legislation that had died on the order paper when Parliament was prorogued for the election. This time, the bill moved rapidly through both houses, with both Liberal leader John Turner and NDP leader Ed Broadbent accepting the judgment of the people. Free trade received royal assent on 30 December 1988.

In the United States, there was little of the public debate and drama seen in Canada. While there was tension, it was of a kind only known and appreciated by

Washington insiders. As required by the fast-track legislative process, the president had notified Congress of his intent to enter into the agreement on 3 October 1987 and had formally signed it, concurrent with Prime Minister Mulroney, on 2 January 1988. Over the next six months, administration officials worked with members of the House Ways and Means and Senate Finance Committees to prepare the implementing legislation and the required "Statement of Administrative Intent." Canadian officials carefully monitored these developments to ensure that US law did not interpret the agreement in ways that undermined Canadian interests. Efforts by some senators to introduce amendments that would have emasculated some of the FTA's provisions were successfully curtailed. The legislative package sent to the Hill in July then went through the steps set out in the fast-track procedures and passed both the House and Senate by handsome majorities in August and September.[27]

On 1 January 1989, the agreement entered into force, finally ending a quest that had been a constant theme of Canadian trade politics for more than 140 years. In the first few years, as anticipated, Canadian firms and individuals went through some painful adjustments, made more severe by the simultaneous effort of the Bank of Canada to wring inflation out of the economy. By the mid-1990s, however, it was clear that the pain was beginning to pay off. Studies by various economists suggested that the FTA was having exactly the impact originally sought by business leaders and the government: a more secure and open border was encouraging more rational investment decisions, leading to both more cross-border trade and investment and a more efficient allocation of resources. A 1998 study prepared by the Royal Bank of Canada, examining the first decade of bilateral free trade, concluded that implementation of the FTA resulted in:

- a substantial increase in bilateral trade and a boost in the productivity of the Canadian manufacturing sector
- a substantial increase in two-way foreign direct investment flows
- a combination of both transitional job losses and export-based job creation
- improvement in settling trade disputes.[28]

The numbers on which these rather cautious conclusions were based are impressive. As indicated in table 13.1, the value of two-way trade between Canada and the United States, which had stagnated during the decade ending in 1989, exploded over the next ten years, with merchandise exports to the United States almost doubling as a share of Canadian GDP (from 15 percent to 28.4 percent) from $101.9 billion in 1989 to $271.5 billion in 1998), led by the manufacturing sector. Import growth was equally impressive, increasing from $88.1 billion to $203.3 billion. Two-way trade in services grew at a similar prodigious rate, almost doubling from $32.4 billion to $58.9 billion.

One econometric analysis of the data concluded that two fundamental factors were responsible for the extraordinary performance of Canadian exports: economic

Table 13.1

Canadian trade with the United States, 1989-98 (millions of dollars)

Year	Merchandise		Service	
	Exports	Imports	Exports	Imports
1989	101,851	88,103	12,820	19,658
1990	111,557	87,875	13,016	22,396
1991	109,694	88,415	13,998	24,407
1992	125,670	96,469	14,473	25,164
1993	150,657	113,987	16,098	26,352
1994	184,179	137,345	18,417	27,380
1995	209,894	150,755	19,742	28,858
1996	223,479	157,494	21,493	30,544
1997	245,090	183,926	24,174	30,228
1998	271,458	203,346	26,687	32,200

Note: Merchandise figures on a customs basis; services figures on a balance-of-payments basis.
Source: Statistics Canada, *Summary of Canadian International Trade* (Catalogue 65-001).

growth in Canada's major trading partner, the United States, and trade liberalization of goods and services.[29] It also pointed to the fact that trade grew in both directions, suggesting that monetary policy and currency fluctuations played a less important part in the story than trade liberalization in the growth of trade and investment in the Canadian economy in the 1990s. This conclusion was strongly supported by other studies that indicated that the greatest growth was recorded in sectors liberalized by the FTA.[30]

Much of the growth in trade was concentrated in intra-industry and intra-corporate transactions, as the manufacturing sector rationalized production in the face of declining barriers and enhanced opportunities. The reward was higher productivity in sectors benefiting from increasing competition and opportunity, despite pressures in the opposite direction from non-trade-related factors.[31] Investment data also suggested deepening integration of the two economies (see table 13.2), as both Canadian and US firms participated in cross-border positioning through mergers and acquisitions to strengthen their competitive positions in a more integrated North American and globalizing world economy. Additionally, Canadian firms became more active players in the global economy through foreign direct investment. In 1997 Canada for the first time became a net exporter of capital, a trend that accelerated in 1998 and continued in 1999.

While the focus of most analyses of the FTA was on its impact on trade and investment, a further important dimension was its impact on the movement of people. Easing restrictions on temporary business travel was not on either the Canadian or US negotiating agenda in 1985. It was added at the behest of Canadian

Table 13.2

Canadian foreign direct investment, 1989-98 (millions of dollars)

Year	Outward Canadian FDI		Inward Canadian FDI	
	US	World	US	World
1989	56,578	89,851	80,427	122,664
1990	60,049	98,402	84,089	130,932
1991	63,379	109,068	86,396	135,234
1992	64,502	111,691	88,161	139,918
1993	67,677	122,427	90,600	141,493
1994	77,987	146,315	102,629	154,594
1995	87,596	164,205	113,206	168,352
1996	95,006	181,358	120,370	179,515
1997	102,815	205,701	131,917	196,713
1998	126,005	239,754	147,345	217,053

Source: Statistics Canada, Catalogue 67-202-XBP.

business advisors, particularly in the financial services sector, who pointed out that the full benefits of reducing trade and investment barriers would not be realized without addressing the excessive regulatory structure that hampered business travel between the two countries. Chapter 16 of the FTA turned out to be a very pleasant surprise, borne out by the growth in the number of Canadian business travellers to the United States.

The raw figures for border crossings over the first decade indicate a peak in 1991, at the height of the cross-border shopping phenomenon stimulated by the high value of the Canadian dollar. This kind of traffic steadily shrank thereafter, in step with the declining value of the Canadian dollar. More detailed analysis reveals some interesting trends. Truck traffic increased from an average of 20,000 vehicles per day in the period 1986 to 1991, to an average of 30,000 vehicles per day by 1996. In response, governments moved to twin bridges by adding a second span, such as for the Bluewater Bridge joining Sarnia and Port Huron, and otherwise to increase border infrastructure. The tonnage of goods moved by rail increased by similar magnitudes, again concentrated in the period after 1990, while air traffic of both passengers and goods increased even more dramatically, particularly after the entry into force of the complementary open skies agreement and the development of cross-border commercial alliances between Canadian and American carriers. Business travel, which takes place largely by air, increased steadily. Finally, the number of Canadians and Americans taking advantage of the ability to reside temporarily in the other country to pursue trade and investment opportunities steadily rose. Until 1989, the number of Canadians residing temporarily in the United States as students or workers held steady at about 17,000 per year. By 1998, that number had risen to 98,000, of whom more than 75,000 were taking advantage of the TN visa program, which allows Canadian professionals to work temporarily in the United States.[32]

Finally, binding dispute settlement procedures, a critically important dimension of managing relations between the two countries, proved their worth. Both countries made extensive use of these procedures, and, despite discomfort on individual issues on both sides of the border, the procedures worked well in enhancing the rule of law in relations between Canada and the United States and reducing the temperature of disputes. International agreements do not eliminate conflicts – in fact, they may increase the number of issues that need to be resolved – but rather provide a better basis for resolving them. Agreements make it possible to bring conflicts to an end and to settle contentious issues. A profound misreading of the FTA led to popular Canadian complaints about the rash of Canada-US trade disputes in the late 1980s and early 1990s. Canadians benefit from this process as the rules become clearer, trade and investment conditions become more stable and predictable, and the capacity of governments to favour local producers is constrained.

The continuing areas of stress in the relationship remain precisely those for which either or both governments had not found the political will to reach agreement, ranging from agriculture to culture, and from trade remedies to softwood lumber. Over time, these flash points may yet be amenable to mutually satisfactory resolution, but they proved too much for both governments in the 1980s and continued to sour relations in the 1990s.

From a Bilateral FTA to a Trilateral NAFTA and Beyond

The most telling vote of confidence in the FTA, however, did not come from Canada, but from Mexico. Within two years of the conclusion of the FTA, Mexican officials began to make cautious soundings in Washington and Ottawa to determine the extent to which the US and Canadian governments were prepared to extend the same rules and obligations to Mexico. By June 1990, US president George Bush was prepared to enter into negotiations to test Mexican resolve, and by the following February the three countries had agreed to try to negotiate a trilateral agreement.[33]

The Mexican request posed a difficult political test for Canada. The Mulroney government had shown considerable courage in pursuing and sticking to its free-trade agenda in the face of relentless opposition. By 1990-1, however, adjustment to the agreement was going through its most difficult phase, as firms adapted their business plans and practices to the new circumstances, gearing up to serve the larger North American market by becoming more specialized, closing down some lines, and increasing production for others. Some firms closed, others expanded, and still others pursued new alliances and marketing strategies. Labour unions, in particular, were pointing to employment losses in some manufacturing sectors as proof of the deleterious effect of free trade. The immediate instinct of ministers, therefore, was that a new round of bruising free-trade discussions held little political appeal.

Adding the Mexican market might ultimately pay dividends, but not before exacting further adjustment pains and political controversy. The fact that Mexico represented a low-cost, developing economy further dulled enthusiasm. While the claim that products from such economies can overwhelm the markets of industrialized countries may rest on dubious economic foundations, it does evoke powerful fears easily exploited by opponents of freer trade. Additionally, there was some concern, in government, business, and other circles, that the United States might use trilateral negotiations to exact new concessions from Canada in such sensitive areas as culture and agriculture.

Nevertheless, after reviewing the issues, ministers agreed that Canadian interests would be better served by participating in a trilateral negotiation than by watching the Americans and Mexicans from the sidelines. Ministers were impressed by the argument that a bilateral Mexico-US agreement might erode some of the advantages Canada had gained in its own agreement. They were particularly concerned by the prospect of Mexico gaining advantages that would attract investments that might otherwise go to Canada. Fears about the United States pursuing a "hub-and-spoke" trade strategy added to the forces favouring participation.[34] After Canada dithered for a few months and discussed matters with US and Mexican officials, the three governments agreed in February 1991 to proceed trilaterally on the basis of two critical understandings: there would be no backsliding by either Canada or the United States from their existing obligations in the FTA, and Canada would step aside if its participation became a stumbling block to a deal between Mexico and the United States.

Over the course of the following eighteen months, while the primary focus of negotiations was the extension of the FTA regime to Mexico, Canada and the United States applied the lessons learned in three years of living with the FTA to make improvements. Like the bilateral Canada-US negotiations, the final deal was forged in a two-week marathon negotiating session at the Watergate Hotel complex in Washington in August 1992 involving the three trade ministers – Michael Wilson for Canada, Jaime Serra for Mexico, and Carla Hills for the United States – and a full panoply of negotiators from all three countries.[35] The result was an agreement that continued the policy regime ushered in by the FTA, but that significantly improved upon it. The rules were made more precise, the coverage more extensive, and the procedures more transparent. The story of the negotiations and the details of the NAFTA are sufficiently complex and interesting to warrant a study of their own.[36] What is important to emphasize is that the successful conclusion of the NAFTA demonstrated the extent to which bilateral free trade had become the basis of a consensus favouring a more open and outward-looking Canadian economy.

The NAFTA did not greatly change access for the United States or Mexico to the Canadian market, but it did fundamentally alter Canadian and US access to the Mexican market. For example, most automotive products – by far the largest Mexican export to the Canadian market – entered Canada duty-free under the terms of the Canada-US Auto Pact. At the same time, the Mexican Auto Decree virtually excluded Canadian firms from the Mexican market. The NAFTA, after a period of transition, opened up the Mexican automotive market to full Canadian and US participation. NAFTA allowed Canada to maintain the Auto Pact safeguards, continue quotas to support supply management for poultry and dairy products, exempt the cultural industries from the NAFTA as they were from the FTA, and maintain the government's freedom to act in the area of social services.

Canada insisted that the NAFTA enhance the FTA and in no way erode the benefits Canada had already realized as a result of either the GATT or the FTA. It succeeded in protecting or improving all of Canada's FTA benefits. The NAFTA either incorporated by reference, replaced with trilaterally agreed improvements, or made generic all the FTA obligations between Canada and the United States. As a result, Canada and the United States agreed to suspend the FTA as long as they are both parties to the NAFTA. Essentially, the rights and obligations set out in the FTA remained in effect, but in an updated and improved agreement.[37]

Based on the model developed during the FTA negotiations, ministers and senior officials again consulted closely with the Canadian private sector, both through formal consultative arrangements established for this purpose and in discussions with a wide range of private-sector groups, labour representatives, environmentalists, and academics. Intensive federal-provincial consultations again mirrored the private-sector collaboration. Meetings of Canadian ministers responsible for trade had by now become a regular part of federal-provincial cooperation. During the NAFTA negotiations, six meetings of ministers were supplemented by discussions by telephone and in person, as well as many meetings and discussions between officials to consider every aspect of the negotiations. As a result, Canadian negotiators could deal confidently with their US and Mexican counterparts not only on the traditional trade policy agenda that falls largely within the federal government's jurisdiction, but also on the increasing number of issues of shared jurisdiction and provincial competence.

In this regard, the NAFTA set important precedents by adding provisions addressing the environment and labour adjustment. In the environmental provisions, all three countries confirmed their commitment to sustainable development and agreed that their trade obligations under specified international agreements (for example, endangered species, ozone-depletion, and hazardous wastes) would take precedence over the NAFTA. They agreed not to establish "pollution havens" by lowering standards to attract investment. Panels dealing with contentious issues that involved environmental issues would have access to scientific expertise. The NAFTA also incorporated the GATT exemption that allows governments to protect their environments even when the necessary measures conflict with the agreement.

Free Trade as the New Norm

In Canada and the United States, the NAFTA was negotiated by Conservative and

Republican administrations. Its full implementation, however, fell to successor Liberal and Democratic administrations. The fact that in both cases political leaders who had, in opposition, expressed considerable scepticism about freer trade, ultimately agreed to implement the agreement, suggests that a fundamental change in attitude had taken place. In neither country were the new governments prepared to turn back the clock. By the end of 1992, freer trade had become the norm while its critics had become marginalized. Fringe movements continued to oppose the agreement, but mainstream politicians on both sides of the border accepted that what had been achieved by their predecessors could not be undone.

In the United States, President Bush notified Congress of his intent to enter into the agreement but accepted that implementing legislation would have to wait until after the November election. He hoped to use the NAFTA as a wedge issue during the campaign. The Democratic candidate, Bill Clinton, however, refused to be drawn into an either/or proposition. Instead, he indicated that the problem was not free trade per se, but the lack of attention to other issues, including the need to address the social impact of freer trade.

His campaign, focused on the economy, won the day, bringing twelve years of Republican rule to an end. Once in office in January, Clinton set out to prove that a Democratic administration could negotiate a more balanced deal. It did not take long for officials to devise an elegant solution: the three governments would negotiate complementary side agreements on the environment and labour standards and consider how best to add an "anti-surge" provision to deal with any unmanageable labour adjustment challenges. During the first half of 1993, the three governments succeeded in this task: agreements established institutions and procedures to help maintain and enforce national environmental and labour standards. They also allowed private parties to complain and seek redress if any of the three governments failed to live up to their own labour and environmental laws and regulations. The adjustment issue was quietly buried with an anodyne statement about consultations.[38]

The US administration then moved on to the delicate task of stickhandling the implementing legislation through Congress on the basis of the fast-track procedures. In Canada, the Conservative government had already introduced a massive omnibus bill, An Act to Implement the North American Free Trade Agreement, into the House of Commons, providing for implementation of NAFTA, consequential amendments to twenty-nine previous acts of Parliament, and authority to make regulations as required. By the end of June, the bill had been passed by both the House and Senate and awaited only royal assent, a step that would follow ratification in the United States and Mexico, and a federal election.[39]

In the 25 October federal election, Liberal Jean Chrétien gained an overwhelming mandate, reducing the Tories under new leader Kim Campbell to two seats in the House of Commons. As a consequence, officials in both countries expressed some anxiety that the hard work of the previous two years might be disowned and never implemented into law. US officials were particularly nervous as implementing legislation had reached the decision stage in Congress. This fear was never realized. While Chrétien made some politically necessary statements calling for the renegotiation of provisions related to energy, subsidies, and dumping, the appointment of Roy MacLaren as Minister of International Trade brought a man of deep free-trade convictions to the task of implementing the agreement. Further discussions also indicated that although the prime minister – and his party – had opposed free trade while in opposition, he was not prepared to turn back the clock and undo the Canada-US Free Trade Agreement. He also soon saw the NAFTA and its accession clause as important steps toward diversifying Canadian trade patterns. Beyond seeking a pledge from the US administration to work toward resolving antidumping and countervailing duty issues on a mutually beneficial basis, by mid-November, Chrétien and his cabinet were content to bring NAFTA into force.

In Mexico, although there was some opposition to the agreement and the peasant uprising in Chiapas gave opponents in both Canada and the United States scope for new charges about Mexico's somewhat dubious democratic credentials, President Carlos Salinas and his party commanded sufficient support in the country and in the legislature to pass the implementing legislation without much difficulty. The only issue for Canadian and US officials was whether the Mexican administration would be up to the task of modernizing its laws, regulations, and procedures sufficiently to live up to the more exacting requirements of the agreement.

In the United States, the Clinton administration had since midsummer waged a protracted campaign in both Washington and around the country to build support for the agreement. Reminiscent of the excesses of the debate in Canada on the merits of the FTA, Americans indulged in an orgy of claims and counterclaims about freer trade and the threat posed by Mexico as a developing country. The side agreements, so arduously negotiated over the course of the summer, appeared to do little to mollify labour and environmental critics. The most colourful and memorable phrase came from Reform party presidential candidate Ross Perot. He claimed that the NAFTA would result in a giant sucking sound of jobs disappearing into Mexico as industry rushed to take advantage of Mexico's cheap labour. In the final weeks, as is often necessary in the US legislative process, President Clinton appeared prepared to make an increasing range of unrelated and even unsavoury concessions to opportunistic but wavering members of Congress. In the end, the agreement passed House scrutiny by a surprisingly comfortable margin of 234-200 on 17 November. Three days later, the Senate also gave its approval.[40]

With ratification by all three countries, the way was now clear for the NAFTA to enter into force on 1 January 1994. Interestingly, the ratification vote in the US Congress also paved the way for the successful conclusion of the other major trade objective of the Bush administration inherited by the Clinton administration: the Uruguay Round of GATT negotiations, which since 1986 had provided some of the background to first the FTA and then the NAFTA negotiations.

14 THE NEW MULTILATERALISM

CANADA AT THE URUGUAY ROUND

> We have an important and historic opportunity to make a comprehensive and lasting contribution to strengthening the world trading system. In an increasingly interdependent world characterized by the globalization of investment, technology, finance and production, this initiative for a new WTO will help the world's traders and investors face the next century with more certainty and confidence.
>
> – JOHN CROSBIE, MINISTER FOR INTERNATIONAL TRADE, 1988–91

The Canada-US Free Trade Agreement effected a fundamental change in Canadian trade policy and the management of Canadian trade relations with the United States. Nevertheless, the multilateral trading system also remained important to Canada. Notwithstanding the central importance of the US market, Canadian producers could also benefit from exploiting new and better opportunities in other markets. The GATT remained Canada's only contractual trade agreement with most other market-economy countries. Canadian multilateral bargaining power, however, had been considerably enhanced as a result of the FTA and then the NAFTA. In all previous rounds, Canadian negotiators had needed to focus most of their energy on the United States. With the conclusion of the FTA, they could concentrate on other potential markets. Careful deployment of this leverage might bring greater gains in non-US markets than those available during previous multilateral negotiations.

Thus, despite Canada's preoccupation with bilateral trade with the United States for much of the 1980s, efforts to revitalize the GATT and make it more responsive to the changing structure of global trade and production also continued. For some critics of bilateral free trade, the multilateral GATT provided a continuing and more attractive alternative. But GATT had its own problems and challenges to meet, and Canada was an active and often creative participant in efforts to address those challenges. If nothing else, Canadian policy demonstrated the extent to which the GATT and bilateral negotiations represented complementary rather than alternative strategies.[1]

By the middle of the 1980s, the GATT had been in existence for almost forty years. During those years, its founding members had amply demonstrated that their judgment in 1948-50 to live with the "interim" GATT was not as foolish as it might have appeared to some at the time. The GATT had gradually developed both a permanence and an institutional structure which, while not as lofty as originally envisaged for the ITO, proved pragmatic and enduring. Six further rounds of successful negotiations had consolidated and extended the original agreement's reach and had ensured that its rules and procedures would contribute to the rapid expansion of world trade. Nevertheless, by the middle of the 1980s, it was equally clear that the gap between the rules enshrined in the GATT and the realities of globalizing business had widened to the point that, without a new round to revitalize and expand the rules and procedures, the GATT was in serious danger of becoming irrelevant. Indeed, some commentators had already come to this conclusion and were convinced that the multilateral trade regime would not be renewed.[2]

Member governments, however, were not as quick to dismiss their confidence in an agreement that had become the keystone of the international trade relations system. To prove their point, ministers gathered in Punta del Este, Uruguay, in September 1986 and found the necessary compromises to launch a new round. The purpose of this new round was to strengthen the GATT's rules and procedures and expand its disciplines to a wider range of international economic activities. The United States was again the prime mover in initiating the round, looking for a revitalized agreement that would have broad appeal but still satisfy the specifics of the US trade agenda. Other players brought varying perspectives, ranging from a strongly supportive Canada to a cynical EC to disapproving developing countries like India and Brazil. Nevertheless, all participants saw some potential benefit in a new round even though they emphasized vastly differing issues as key to satisfying their needs. The wide range of both issues and players promised to make the negotiations the most complex and protracted commercial negotiations ever undertaken.

Canada had from the outset been one of the strongest proponents of a new round. It had been at the forefront in the early 1980s demanding that ministers play a larger role in the GATT's affairs. It had enthusiastically endorsed the US call to expand the mandate of the next round of negotiations beyond the traditional focus on barriers to trade in goods. It had also been an active participant in finding the necessary compromises to build a consensus that would allow the negotiations to begin on as broad a basis as possible. Its officials had been among the most insistent at G7, OECD, IMF, and other forums in calling for the necessary analytical work to prepare for future negotiations.

Some Canadians found the government's pursuit of concurrent bilateral and multilateral strategies puzzling. Such critics, however, failed to grasp the nature of Canada's enthusiasm. For Canada, the GATT had always been first and foremost a means to an end. For more than half a century, the first objective of Canadian trade policy had been harmonious and profitable relations with the United States. The GATT had helped in resolving problems between Canada and the United States, but its failure to do so in the first half of the 1980s had convinced Canadian political and business leaders of the need to explore the prospect of bilateral agreements within the framework of the GATT. Indeed, the successful conclusion of the free-trade agreement with the United States at the end of 1987 provided Canadian officials with a rare opportunity to address multilateral negotiations without being constrained to meet pressing bilateral objectives. In the Uruguay Round, Canada could add to what had already been achieved with the United States bilaterally and concentrate on broader objectives and other partners.

There was one exception to this generally liberal position. Canada's brief on agriculture was complex and politically sensitive. The FTA had not solved Canada-US agricultural trade issues. Canada shared the views of other grain-exporting countries that a way had to be found to place agricultural trade on a more principled and less subsidized footing, but it was unprepared to open the Canadian market to dairy and poultry imports. For more than a decade already, these two sectors had been reserved for Canadian producers on the basis of supply management schemes that Canada considered to be consistent with GATT disciplines and that should not be undermined by new rules to deal with GATT-inconsistent policies. Few other governments agreed, which undermined Canada's capacity to pursue other objectives.

More generally, Canada, like other OECD countries, looked for progress on three fronts: a package on agriculture that addressed the rising cost of subsidies as well as the distortions in domestic and export markets but still left some room for domestic income and price support programs; new rules on the most important barriers to growth for the industries of the future; and scope for continued adjustment by traditional industries at a pace that would not undermine political support for the maintenance of an open multilateral trade regime. While such traditional issues as safeguards, subsidies, antidumping and countervailing duties, textiles, tariffs, and customs procedures obviously needed to be addressed, they required very delicate handling. In some cases, traditional concession swapping would work; in others, rule writing would be required, with some industries interested in liberalizing and others in tightening existing rules.

That was the view from the industrialized end of the telescope. Developing countries (LDCs) had a different perspective. Their economies were also being transformed by the globalizing forces of technology and the reorganization of production. For them, the key to future growth lay in gaining better and more secure access to rich OECD markets for the export-oriented traditional manufacturing facilities now locating in their territories. This goal would require further liberalization along traditional GATT lines. The extent to which the LDCs needed to open their own markets was a matter of some controversy. Some agreed that the discipline that came with an open economy would work as well for them as for OECD countries; others were not yet ready to open their markets fully, certainly not their services sectors. Rules that impinged on their ability to use investment and technology policies as instruments of development also raised serious political difficulties. Many of the LDCs were food importers and were not worried about the availability of cheap surplus agricultural products, but food exporters among them were desperate for a regime that would bring order to the current chaos. Developing countries were thus keen to participate and had something to offer, but their priorities were likely to guarantee difficult and protracted negotiations.

Two topics illustrate the complexity and ambition of the agenda: agriculture and the new issues (services, investment, and intellectual property). In the case of agriculture, negotiators faced a perplexing set of issues that had proven resistant to change in every previous negotiation. The combined impact of waivers, exceptions, derogations, and protocols of accession had effectively removed agriculture from the discipline of many of the GATT's rules. The new issues presented a different challenge: negotiators not only had to devise proposals about what to negotiate, but also had to think through how to negotiate. Preliminary analysis and discussion suggested that the old way might not work in the new circumstances. Each set of issues offered more than enough complexity to challenge any negotiator; combined, the challenge was formidable.

Leaders and Coalitions

As in previous negotiations, the United States was the prime mover both in initiating the round and in setting the pace, but it was less dogged than in the past as it struggled with growing ambivalence at home about the value of multilateral trade rules. Although eager to see the launch of a new round, particularly one that would address the concerns of the new free-trade coalition, US officials were less prepared to make the necessary concessions to stimulate the interests of US trading partners and maintain the momentum of the round, particularly once the end of the cold war decoupled trade and foreign policy considerations. Wary of potential congressional hostility, US officials advanced a negotiating agenda that was a delicate mix of market-opening and market-protecting objectives. The agenda aimed at creating and maintaining US industry support for a trading system that would be more open than closed and a round that contained more pluses than minuses.[3]

The European Community was the second most dominant participant in the round, often playing the role of spoiler. While not averse to a new round and prepared to address many of the same issues as the United States for many of the same reasons, the EC was not willing to go either as fast or as far as the United States and found US pressure tactics increasingly irritating and counterproductive. Perhaps more fundamentally, the EC's energies were focused at least as much on matters related to the deepening and broadening of the Community as on external matters.[4] The EC continued to be preoccupied with consolidating its internal market, expanding the EC to new members, and addressing necessary internal reforms.

Japan played a leading role in the preparatory and early stages of the negotiations, although in the closing stages, as it became clear that a successful round would call for some serious concessions, Japan seemed to be retreating to its more familiar defensive shell. It had found multilateral negotiations to be an effective means for containing the impact of US and EC protectionism. As a consequence, its principal objectives included tightening discipline on antidumping actions, rules of origin, and trade-related investment measures (TRIMs), all favourite EC and US measures to harass Japanese competition. Japan shared an interest in effective intellectual property rules and generally favoured the establishment of a GATT-like regime for services. Defensively, Japan was vigorously opposed to any erosion in its agricultural protection.[5]

The hesitant leadership and limited vision of the big three were to some extent offset by the active and often constructive role played by a growing number of developing countries. By the closing stages of the round, many of the more advanced economies in Asia and Latin America were acting on the fact that they were able to add economic clout to moral and political arguments. They had learned to maximize their limited bargaining leverage through alliances such as the Cairns Group and a shrewd willingness to make trade-offs. In effect, they had learned how to use the bargaining strategies of smaller industrialized countries such as Canada, Australia, and Switzerland.

For the smaller industrialized countries, the arrival of the leading developing countries on the stage of serious trade negotiations proved a godsend. A number of them had found themselves increasingly marginalized as the role of middle powers eroded, first in the face of the sterile East-West and North-South confrontations of the 1950s, 1960s, and 1970s, and then with the development of a tripolar economic world. By the mid-1980s, only Canada, Australia, and New Zealand remained as small, fully independent industrialized countries, with the EFTA countries not sure whether their interests were best protected as independent voices or as EC satellites. Only Canada had found a channel for ensuring its views were heard as a member of the Summit Seven and of its offshoot, the periodic quadrilateral trade ministers' meetings (Quads) among the EC, United States, Canada, and Japan.

The realization that the developing countries were prepared to participate in the negotiations in order to advance specific economic interests rather than on the basis of posture and ideology made it possible for the smaller industrialized countries to dust off their alliance-building skills and find common causes. During the early preparations, they came together in Geneva in various informal groups to plot strategy and tactics. From the beginning, Australia and Switzerland proved they had the sharpest elbows, and Colombia, as a result of its able representation in Geneva, emerged as the consensus spokesman for the more pragmatic developing countries. Canada, trading on its status as a member of the Summit and the Quads, proved an indispensable link between the smaller countries and the big three and learned to play the "honest broker" card with great skill, pursuing its traditional role of enthusiastic cheerleader for any agreement that advanced the cause of international rule making.

The capacity of the group of more than forty smaller countries to build and maintain issue-specific and process-oriented alliances became an important engine that kept the round going in the face of faltering big-three leadership. The coalition builders made it possible to make progress on issues on which the big three could not lead but could acquiesce. They ensured that the necessary intellectual leadership and creativity were present to get the round started and keep it going. However, in the final analysis they did not collectively possess the economic clout to dictate ultimate success or failure, which still depended on the United States and the EC and, to a lesser extent, Japan. A successful conclusion of the negotiations demanded a package that satisfied all four major participants: the big three and the preponderance of the coalition of smaller members. Since the issues that mattered to the smaller countries were not always those that mattered to the big three, the contours and content of the final agreement had to be truly multilateral. That required not only progress on the traditional agenda to satisfy the smaller players, but also a way through the thicket of new issues advanced by the large players.

From the outset, Arthur Dunkel proved he would be a much more activist director general than his predecessor, Olivier Long, who had seen his role strictly as a neutral international public servant. Long had made active use of his office, but he was more inclined to place pressure on delegations to meet informally on their own to resolve issues than to do so under his leadership. Dunkel saw himself as a catalyst. In that role, he became a tireless participant in the negotiations, cajoling delegations, encouraging the development of coalitions, building public support through speeches and a much more active publications program, travelling to capitals, presiding at informal meetings in the "green room" next to his office, hosting

Dale Cummings, "Roll out the GATT Barrel," 18 December 1993. Cummings captured well the mercantilist basis of GATT negotiations, with governments trying to gain on the one hand what they were unwilling to give up on the other.

dinners at his home, and invoking one-on-one meetings with recalcitrant delegations. Long's style had suited the era of a GATT dominated by the United States and
the EC, when the views of the Secretariat were neither sought nor appreciated.
Dunkel's style was more suited to a GATT with a much broader active membership,
prepared to welcome a director general who could help the process of coalition building and move the big three in directions likely to benefit the membership as a whole.

Dunkel was backed up by a Secretariat that had grown considerably during the
1980s and was capable of providing the analysis and advice required by the smaller
members. Small by UN standards but widely recognized as very capable, the GATT's
permanent staff proved during the 1980s that they had the necessary expertise and
analytical skills to move beyond their traditional service function and to contribute
constructively to the negotiations.

Launching a New Round

Preparations for the new round started in earnest in 1983 when Dunkel appointed
a blue-ribbon group, headed by Swiss banker Fritz Leutwiler, to examine the trading system and make suggestions for reform.[6] The Leutwiler Commission reported
in February 1985, recommending, inter alia, a new round to address a range of old
and new issues. Its report confirmed that the idea of a round to refocus trade discussions had gained increasing currency beyond the United States and Canada. In
the EC, Japan, Australia, and elsewhere, business and academic voices were calling
for a new round, and governments were beginning to see some merit in moving
beyond the sterile confrontation and process discussions to a negotiation. By the
middle of 1985, the G7 countries collectively endorsed the idea of a round at their
Bonn Summit, although the French expressed strong reservations. What was less
clear was what a new round would attempt to achieve.[7]

The lack of clear focus on traditional issues fuelled suspicion among some developing countries, particularly Brazil and India, that a new round would concentrate
on new issues but leave older problems unresolved. They feared that this would result in the industrialized countries gaining new rights and disciplines at the expense of the interests of developing countries. To slow down any move toward a
decision, some developing country delegates in Geneva, schooled in the tactical
manoeuvring of UNCTAD, used every procedural trick in the book to frustrate
efforts to launch a new round.[8]

The ability of India and Brazil and a few others to block the will of the majority
demonstrated the changes that had taken place in the GATT. Their voice – made
more powerful by the Geneva habit of maintaining LDC solidarity – was sufficiently important that it could no longer be ignored. Their ability to thwart consensus, of course, was aided and abetted by the still lukewarm support for a new
round in Europe. Although the EC Commission could see advantages in negotiating new rules for services and investment, member states were not prepared to pay
for these new rules with a major reform of agricultural trade.[9]

The combined impact of India-Brazil recalcitrance and EC ambivalence had added to US and Canadian frustration with the GATT process and had stimulated interest in solutions outside the GATT negotiating framework. Ironically, US resort to section 301 procedures aimed at India and Brazil, as well as US pursuit of bilateral solutions and the rise in trade remedy cases, gradually helped to bring some of the more moderate LDCs out of the India-Brazil camp. Opinion also began to shift in the EC as some member states concluded that there was more to gain than to lose from a new round; section 301 could just as easily be directed at them. The nasty trade disputes in the first half of the 1980s had indicated the length to which US interests were prepared to go.

By careful use of both threat and promise, the United States and its allies were able to forge a growing coalition of members prepared to initiate a more formal preparatory process. By the fall of 1985, sufficient support had been garnered for the establishment of a preparatory committee (Prepcom) to plan for a ministerial meeting in September 1986.[10] With the disappointment of the 1982 ministerial meeting still fresh in their minds, the trade policy professionals in Geneva and in national capitals knew that the next ministerial meeting had to be better prepared, with a clear set of objectives and the means to attain them.[11]

These prenegotiations served a number of functions. Not only did they help to forge the necessary consensus to launch a round and determine the major contours of the negotiation, but they also framed the basis for the political management of the round and public perceptions about its potential and importance. Markers were being put down that would be used later to determine success or failure and to establish what would be politically acceptable and what would not. Governments cannot easily make grandiose claims about the significance of something, walk away from those claims later, and still declare success.[12]

Throughout the first half of 1986, Dunkel chaired periodic meetings of the Prepcom, which allowed delegates to continue the process of formally stating their positions and voicing their concerns and misgivings. The real work, however, took place at lunches and dinners and in smaller meetings held in delegation conference rooms throughout Geneva. There the critical alliance building and networking were being pursued, and the real temper of the negotiations was being gauged. At the same time in the major capitals, other officials worked at the critical tasks of fleshing out proposals and building consensus among business and other interest groups on national objectives and priorities.

By midsummer, officials had developed a draft declaration that anticipated a major expansion of the GATT's mandate. Not surprisingly, agriculture proved the most difficult issue. There were three basic approaches: an EC view, supported by the other Europeans, which preferred a go-slow approach; the views of the emerging group of agricultural exporters – who would the following month constitute themselves as the Cairns Group – who wanted a breakthrough on agriculture but accepted that if the EC were pushed too hard, there would be no deal at all; and the

United States, which wanted a big deal or no deal. The major issue was the extent to which new rules would discipline export subsidies; the major problem was France. The deadlock was finally broken by a new text of the declaration to launch negotiations drafted by Colombia and Switzerland, with the help of New Zealand, which reflected the emerging Cairns Group approach.[13]

Little more could be done at the Prepcom level. The professionals had worked hard and carefully and had produced a realistic draft declaration that provided a solid basis for ministerial discussion and decision. While there remained issues to be negotiated, they had been reduced to a manageable number in proportion to the unwieldy setting of a ministerial meeting where the political egos of nearly a hundred countries had to be massaged and satisfied.

At the meeting in Punta del Este, a resort city at the mouth of the Rio Plata in Uruguay, the difficult issues remained agriculture and the new issues (trade in services, investment, and intellectual property protection). The broadly agreed declaration that finally emerged set out an ambitious agenda and time frame that promised to tackle some of the deep-seated problems undermining the GATT's continued viability, extend its discipline to agriculture, textiles, and grey-area measures (such as voluntary export restraints and orderly marketing arrangements), continue the process of liberalization, bring the GATT into line with the changing nature of the global economy by addressing trade-related intellectual property and investment issues, and launch negotiations on services.[14] It identified a range of specific areas for negotiation as follows:

- *Traditional issues*   A broad range of functional and sectoral areas consistent with the GATT's traditional agenda were identified for negotiation: tariffs, nontariff measures (particularly customs practices), subsidies and countervailing duties, the operation of the Tokyo Round codes (including those on antidumping, standards, customs valuation, and government procurement), safeguards, trade in agricultural products, tropical products, natural-resources-based products, and textiles and clothing.
- *New issues*   The deepening integration of the international economy, the changing nature of international business, and shifts in countries' comparative advantages had highlighted a number of areas of international economic activity that were not covered to the same extent by rules and obligations as trade in goods. Increases in the international exchange of services, the proliferation of foreign direct investment, and the growing importance of knowledge-intensive activities all pointed to the desirability of an international code of conduct to cover these activities based on existing GATT concepts. All three issues were included on the agenda, albeit in forms somewhat reduced from those originally envisaged: the trade-related aspects of investment and of intellectual property protection and trade in services.

- *Systemic issues* Four areas were singled out for negotiations to improve the architecture and operation of the GATT-based trade relations system: a standstill and rollback of GATT-illegal measures; a review of the GATT's articles, particularly those addressing balance-of-payments measures and state-trading practices; consideration of ways to streamline and strengthen the GATT's dispute settlement procedures; and a general review of the functioning of the GATT system, including its role in reviewing the trade policies of members and the relationship between the GATT and other international institutions, as well as the constitutional basis for the GATT.[15]

The Punta Declaration set up four bodies to manage the negotiations: a Trade Negotiations Committee (TNC), a Group for Negotiations on Goods (GNG), a Group for Negotiations on Services (GNS), and a surveillance body to monitor the standstill and orchestrate the progressive dismantling of existing illegal trade restrictions. During the remaining months of 1986, delegations in Geneva agreed on how to organize for the negotiations. Dunkel would chair both the TNC and the GNG while Colombian ambassador Felipe Jaramillo would chair the GNS. The GNG was subdivided into a further fourteen negotiating groups to address each of the objectives set out in the declaration. By the end of January 1987, the TNC approved "guidance" documents for each of the negotiating groups as well as for the surveillance body. By the beginning of 1987, the preliminaries were over and substantive negotiations could begin.[16]

The New Geneva Mood

The intense preparatory work that characterized the period from early 1985 to the end of 1986 had created a momentum that proved hard to stop. All the major participants had built up political will, interests, and ideas that now fed the machinery set up to pursue the negotiations. As a result, the round moved ahead with almost unprecedented speed. The first few years of the negotiations also saw a flurry of dispute settlement activity. Various countries, but particularly the United States and the EC, rushed to bring complaints to the GATT either to resolve issues or to create negotiating leverage. Agricultural measures were a favourite target: thirteen of nineteen panels established between the launch of the negotiations and the Brussels ministerial meeting in December 1990 addressed agriculture issues. For example, the United States initiated a series of complaints for which the primary purpose seemed to be to test the limits of the exemption for agriculture provided by article XI. The United States also launched complaints against the EC on oilseeds and against Canada on salmon and herring.[17]

Not to be outdone, the EC demonstrated that it had also learned the utility of the GATT complaints procedures and launched claims against the United States on its Superfund tax, its customs user fee, and its section 337 procedures (on unfair methods

Table 14.1

Value and volume of world trade and output, 1980-95

Year	World exports (US$ millions)	US exports (US$ billions)	Unit value World exports (1980 = 100)	Volume World output (1980 = 100)
1980	1,989	212.9	100	100
1981	1,963	225.8	100	101
1982	1,844	206.0	97	99
1983	1,807	194.6	100	101
1984	1,915	210.2	108	108
1985	1,950	218.8	111	111
1986	2,137	227.2	116	114
1987	2,512	254.1	122	117
1988	2,858	322.4	133	123
1989	3,085	363.8	142	127
1990	3,437	393.6	149	131
1991	3,504	421.7	155	131
1992	3,755	448.2	161	131
1993	3,743	464.8	167	131
1994	4,230	515.5	185	136
1995	5,033	583.8	200	140

Sources: GATT, *International Trade 1984-85* (Geneva: GATT, 1985), tables A1 and A34; GATT, *International Trade 1990-91* (Geneva: GATT, 1991), vol. 2, table A1; World Trade Organization, *Annual Report 1996* (Geneva: WTO, 1997), vol. 2, tables A1 and A3.

of competition, usually involving patent issues). Japan found itself at the receiving end of complaints about the distribution of alcoholic beverages and its agreement with the United States on trade in semiconductors. The United States then turned around and complained about the EC's use of dumping duties to get at so-called screwdriver assembly plants. Other countries followed suit, so that the period 1986 to 1990 proved one of the busiest in the GATT's dispute settlement history.[18]

The heat generated by both disputes and negotiating controversies in 1987 provided a false picture of the health of the trading system. In fact, 1988 marked the sixth year in a row that world trade had increased at a dynamic rate (8.5 percent by volume, 14 percent by value), again outpacing growth in world production (see table 14.1). Global exports of merchandise reached US$2.86 trillion; services exports added another US$625 million. At the annual session of the contracting parties at the beginning of November, chairman Alan Oxley of Australia took a very optimistic view of developments in the round and in the trading system. He concluded that the standing and authority of the GATT had been enhanced by the round and pointed to the effective and frequent use of dispute settlement and the number of new accessions and unilateral reductions in trade restrictions by developing countries and others as illustrative of the GATT's new vitality.[19]

The United States shared in this expanding world market, but this fact was obscured by the continuing budget and current account deficits flowing from Reaganomics. Trade continued to be a negative issue in Washington. Japan was widely regarded as the main culprit, but other countries were also being branded as systemic "unfair" traders, the main evidence for this label being large bilateral trade deficits. As a result, Congress continued to be preoccupied with the trade file. At the end of 1986, the House of Representatives passed a frankly protectionist new trade act, and the Senate continued work on its own version. Administration efforts to dampen this mood fell on deaf ears as Congress continued to work throughout 1987 and into 1988 on a new trade bill. A massive administration-drafted Trade and Competitiveness Act, introduced early in 1988, disappeared as quickly as it had appeared. Congress had its own ideas and was not looking for administration advice. It finally delivered its own Trade and Competitiveness Act in May 1988, minus the worst excesses of the various bills under consideration, but more protectionist and nationalistic than any trade act since 1930.[20]

The Midterm Review

It was within this embattled atmosphere that USTR Clayton Yeutter and his advisors hit upon the idea of a midterm review and "early harvest." Reports from Geneva indicated that progress was being made and that the pace of negotiations was far more positive than the sour preparatory period would have suggested possible. It seemed to make sense to take advantage of these positive developments and use them as concrete evidence that the negotiations were a good idea and would result in tangible benefits for the United States.[21]

Yeutter found support in Canada, Australia, and to some extent Japan, which saw a midterm review as a way of deflecting pressure from the perennial favourite US and EC blood sport of Japan-bashing. The EC, however, believed that a midterm review would detract attention from the tough work ahead. An early harvest would reduce the principle that nothing was agreed until everything was agreed, put additional pressure on the EC on agriculture, and erode EC willingness to address the full range of issues. Various developing countries expressed similar concerns, worrying that progress on new issues would limit headway on old issues.[22]

Despite these misgivings, the United States and its allies continued to push for a midterm review, and by the beginning of 1988, a basis for it began to emerge with indications that agreement on dispute settlement procedures and functioning of the GATT system (FOGS) would be relatively uncontroversial. Additionally, however, the United States and the Cairns Group insisted that there had to be something on agriculture. The EC matched this ambitious demand by insisting that there also had to be something on services, calculating that this rather woolly area could be used effectively as a roadblock to agreement on agriculture.[23] In February, the Trade Negotiating Committee formally agreed that there would be a midterm review and accepted Canada's invitation to hold it in Montreal in December. Ministers would be asked to gauge progress on the full range of issues based on reports from each of the negotiating groups and in addition to take decisions where progress warranted.[24]

The midterm review convened in Montreal on 5 December at the Palais des Congrès with more than ninety ministers and a thousand delegates in attendance, dogged by over 600 journalists. As in Punta two years earlier, ministers were tasked to chair groups and negotiate away square brackets. Almost two years of negotiations and careful preparation at first paid off, with early breakthroughs on tropical products, dispute settlement, and the functioning of the GATT system. As well, far-reaching texts on services and tariffs were quickly agreed. Four issues, however, proved particularly knotty: textiles and clothing, safeguards, intellectual property, and agriculture. On agriculture, the United States wanted a commitment to the objective of complete liberalization, but the EC would commit to no more than a gradual reduction in support levels. No basis existed for bridging this gap, particularly since the EC was not all that interested in an early harvest.

After three days and nights of tough discussions, ministers admitted defeat and went home. To stave off the potential disaster of another failed ministerial meeting, Dunkel suggested that work continue in Geneva at the level of senior officials. Ministers agreed, and over the next four months Dunkel pursued discussions in capitals and in Geneva and gradually prepared the ground for the deadlocks to be broken. Consensus was achieved on agriculture, for example, by agreeing that the long-term objective was to reduce agricultural support substantially, without specifying what was meant by either "long-term" or "substantially." By April 1989, Dunkel felt confident enough to convene a meeting of senior officials who worked out the necessary package of early harvest and negotiating mandates to bring the midterm review to a successful conclusion.[25]

Two decisions had the benefit of providing constructive fuel for future negotiations. The Trade Policy Review Mechanism (TPRM) – which would subject the trade policies of member states to periodic scrutiny in a series of published documents – would create pressures to counter the normal bias in favour of protection, while the streamlined dispute settlement procedures further underlined that GATT law was becoming a more serious and reliable basis for resolving conflict and keeping member states' practices in line.[26]

Back to the Main Event

Once the Montreal interlude was behind them, negotiators could get back to the painstaking, professional task of working out detailed negotiating proposals, rank-ordering the issues, and looking for common ground among positions. From May 1989 through the fall of 1990, these tasks preoccupied most of the negotiators, who made significant technical progress. Texts were tabled, studied, and recast, and gradually worked into composite negotiating texts. The round had now reached the critical stage when posturing had to be translated into concrete proposals and the differences in position reflected in bracketed language had to be reconciled.[27]

Canadian officials played key roles in the discussions, with a core group of permanent officials in Geneva under the leadership of Ambassador John Weekes providing day-to-day coverage, and a much larger group of specialists from various departments in Ottawa flying back and forth. Some of them, like agriculture specialist Mike Gifford and tariff negotiator Kevin Gore, were veterans of the Tokyo Round negotiations. By the end of 1987 they, along with others like Meriel Bradford and John Curtis, could also lay claim to having participated in the successful Canada-US bilateral negotiations. At the beginning of 1990, Weekes and his team were joined by Gerald Shannon, former deputy minister of trade, now assigned to Geneva to take overall charge of the negotiations. Ideas developed in the bilateral Canada-US negotiations were now deployed in efforts to find acceptable bases for multilateral negotiations. Weekes chaired the negotiating group examining the functioning of the GATT system, and the head of the team in Ottawa, Germain Denis, would eventually chair the key market access group. Both had participated in the Tokyo Round negotiations and were well versed in the hard work of building coalitions and brokering deals that brought others together while satisfying Canadian objectives.

Experience with the FOGS group was critical in convincing Canadian officials, with the enthusiastic support of Minister for International Trade John Crosbie, that the time had come to find a better way than had been found during the Tokyo Round to address the complexity of a multitude of interlocking agreements. At first hesitantly but with increasing confidence and the active support of the EC, Canada advanced proposals to establish a multilateral trade organization to implement and administer the many agreements under discussion. With the help of University of Michigan GATT scholar John Jackson, Debra Steger and other members of the Canadian team developed the contours of what would eventually become the Agreement Establishing the World Trade Organization.[28]

While the working groups went about their labours, the TNC continued its task of plotting grand strategy and maintaining momentum. In late July 1989, still flush with the euphoria of having successfully cobbled together a satisfactory midterm review in April, the TNC decided that a final ministerial meeting would take place in Brussels, 3-7 December 1990. The Punta Declaration had committed governments to a four-year negotiation, and the TNC was determined to live up to that commitment.

Deadlines are a necessary evil. Without them, negotiations could go on forever; there is always some reason for at least one major participant to slow things down, such as an inconvenient election. Unrealistic or artificial deadlines, however, can also pose a problem. Crafting a complex, multiparty agreement takes time; forcing the pace is likely to lead either to agreements that cannot stand the test of time or to failure. In multilateral trade negotiations, deadlines are often the product of US trade legislation. The effective deadline was that negotiations had to conclude by the first week in March 1991 so that the president could notify Congress of his intent to enter into the resulting agreements at least ninety days before his authority expired on 31 May. While there was provision for a two-year extension, neither the administration nor US trading partners were eager to learn what price Congress might exact for a request to extend.[29]

Based on the state of the text of the Final Act, however, it was clear that December 1990 was too early. That deadline would mean that the professional negotiators dedicated to the task had had only four years to put together one of the most complex international agreements ever contemplated and to gain the approval of the more than a hundred participating governments. Available time had been reduced by the crucial months and energy devoted to the midterm review in Montreal. Four years might have seemed long enough in September 1986, but as December 1990 approached, the period seemed very short indeed. Large and significant gaps remained, particularly on agriculture and services.

The Brussels Ministerial Meeting

For the fourth time in less than a decade, GATT ministers met to discuss how best to govern world trade. The scene was Brussels, the seat of the European Commission, where on 3 December 1990, ministers and their officials gathered to put the finishing touches to a 400-page draft text that represented the distillation of some 1,300 proposals and working papers and four years of work. The text was full of square brackets indicating where political guidance was needed before technical solutions could be found. As at Punta and Montreal, various ministers were tasked to lead negotiations on selected issues based on the draft Final Act. In some areas, they made rapid progress, such as services, textiles, and nontariff measures; in others, such as agriculture and tariffs, stalemate stared them in the face.[30]

The biggest stumbling block was clearly agriculture. The gap between the United States, the EC, and the Cairns Group could not be bridged. Not only were their approaches to the issues too different, but the baggage of four years of negotiations as well as jockeying for leverage through dispute settlement procedures had loaded the process to the point that no amount of brokering and arm-twisting could create the trust necessary to build consensus. The United States insisted that it had to get the whole loaf, while the EC was equally adamant that it could not go beyond its commitments on CAP reform, which at this time were still in a formative rather than agreed stage. To underline the point, farmers from all over the Community staged demonstrations throughout Brussels which, if they did not impress the US delegation, certainly impressed EC commissioners and the world media.

After four days of trying, the chair – Uruguay's foreign minister Héctor Gros Espiell – announced that although much progress had been made, more time was needed to achieve consensus in certain key areas. Dunkel was again charged with undertaking intensive consultations and reconvening the process when he felt a successful conclusion was within reach. He was instructed to work on the basis of the draft Final Act as moved along at Brussels.[31]

From both the US and EC perspectives, however, the package as it stood was not saleable.[32] The very fact that it was a professional tour de force made it a major political albatross. Its complexity and comprehensiveness made it too easy for the losers – such as EC and eastern Canadian farmers – to zero in on their problems, but very difficult for the winners to explain what they stood to gain and why they cared. In neither the United States nor in the EC were there sufficiently powerful supporters to provide an effective counterweight to the inevitable wailing and gnashing of teeth that would come from the losers. The challenge to Dunkel and his Geneva colleagues, therefore, was only partly to continue negotiating a Final Act in which they could take professional pride. It was also a matter of identifying the elements that would make the product politically salvageable. For ministers and their government colleagues, that was the main challenge. They had to find forces at home to offset the negative voices; without them, further consultations and negotiations could not rescue the round.

The Negotiations Lose Momentum

The disappointment of Brussels took a while to sink in. In the first half of 1991, little substantive progress was made. Only the agriculture group met to try to find the road to success. It soon became clear that this road ran through Brussels and Washington: the United States needed to obtain a two-year extension of its negotiating authority, and the EC needed to make progress on CAP reform and the negotiation of farm prices for 1991-2. At midyear, high-level statements of political commitment emanated from both the OECD annual ministerial meeting in June and the Summit Seven meeting in July in Paris, but without the desired result.

By September, however, Dunkel was confident that behind-the-scenes efforts over the previous months could now be translated into results, and he began an intensive campaign to meet an end-of-the-year deadline. In some areas, the negotiators completed provisionally agreed texts with no square brackets, many substantially improved over the draft texts tabled in Brussels. The structure of an agreement on agriculture was also beginning to emerge. Negotiations on trade-related intellectual property rights (TRIPs) were close to a satisfactory conclusion. Offers on specific commitments on services started to make the services agreement (GATS) economically real. The agreement on textiles was virtually finished. Problems, however, had emerged on subsidies, antidumping, safeguards, and other issues. The extra time afforded by the Brussels failure was not only being used to improve the texts, but was also giving some governments an opportunity to rethink their positions. The United States, in particular, was beginning to backtrack on some issues, encouraging others to revisit their pet peeves.[33]

In order to prevent further unravelling and encourage delegations to look at the negotiations as a seamless web rather than as a series of independent agreements,

Dunkel decided to issue a revised Final Act that took account of the changes and improvements that had been agreed in the previous months and that filled in gaps and solved problems where delegations had been unable to resolve their differences. While he consulted closely with key delegations and worked with the chairs of each of the negotiating groups, a text was prepared on his own authority which did not commit any of the players. Rather, Dunkel and his advisors tried to capture a balanced, hopefully satisfactory outcome.

On 20 December 1991, Dunkel gave each of the 108 participating governments his version of a new and revised draft Final Act.[34] Some 500 pages long, it set out draft agreements on twenty-eight specific items, that is, the whole agenda with the exception of commitments on market access for goods and for services. The text responded admirably to the objectives set at Punta del Este more than five years earlier. Dunkel called on governments to determine whether they could live with it as a whole, rather than to focus on individual details at this stage. In effect, he challenged governments to proceed immediately to a final push involving the negotiation of two protocols on market access and services, and agreement on the Final Act: "This has not been a Round in which initial objectives have been steadily whittled away to produce 'diplomatic,' but impractical solutions to difficult and complex problems. Quite the contrary; ambitions have risen with time, not fallen. The results we have already secured are relevant, precise, balanced and urgently needed answers to some of the biggest economic challenges of the day. They are results from which every trading nation will gain."[35]

The Dunkel text contained a significant number of technical improvements over the Brussels text. Virtually every individual agreement had been clarified and improved. The total product constituted a formidable professional result, but it could not address the fundamental divide. The United States and the EC had by now developed a bunker mentality, particularly on agriculture. Neither was prepared to make meaningful concessions to the other; both had created critical hostages in their bilateral consultations, in their public pronouncements, and in their highly publicized disputes. Rather than becoming easier, finding the basis for agreement had become more difficult. The good work of the other negotiators and of Dunkel was helpful, but further progress had by now become totally dependent on the EC and the United States finding the basis for a bilateral settlement. Frustrating as this may have been for the remaining governments, this was the reality that they all had to accept. Technical work proceeded, particularly among a select group of legal advisors looking at ways to clean up the text and remove any ambiguities, but the negotiations proper were on hold by the beginning of 1992. The momentum that had been there at the end of 1990 and again at the end of 1991 had gradually begun to dissipate.

The real work of the negotiations was now taking place in Brussels, Washington, and various other locations in the United States and Europe, where senior US and EC officials sought to bridge the gap between the two major delegations. Periodic

Quad meetings provided the cover that problems were more than strictly a matter of US-EC negotiation. Other delegations knew that whatever the two giants agreed would largely decide their fate. Whatever influence most of them had been able to exert had by this time been exerted. Insistence by various delegations that they still had problems that needed fixing had in essence become a sideshow for domestic consumption and of little relevance to the fate of the round.[36]

Fresh Blood and New Momentum
Throughout 1992, US and EC officials had worked hard to effect a final settlement and came close on several occasions, only to see one side or the other step back. By the end of January 1993, the US negotiators no longer had the stomach for concluding. The Uruguay Round would not be a legacy of the Reagan-Bush years. Rather, it became a challenge for a new administration. President-elect Bill Clinton had hinted that he was prepared to see the round conclude in the dying days of the Bush administration and had intimated a willingness to live up to its commitments. Once in office, however, the new administration felt no compulsion to conclude an agreement on the basis of its predecessor's approach. It had its own priorities and concerns, such as environmental and labour adjustment issues, which it felt were not being addressed adequately in trade agreements. The more populist elements in the Democratic party were pressing for a "fair" trade agenda, which the rest of the world perceived as protectionist and threatening to the existing trade regime. Nevertheless, new USTR Mickey Kantor pursued furious diplomatic efforts in the opening weeks of the new administration which confirmed that the new team was not hostile to the round, would seek congressional authority for an extension of the fast-track, and was prepared to entertain ideas on how the package could be improved. The round was not dead. Success remained a possibility, although the parameters of what success would entail had become even murkier.

There was also a changing of the guard in Brussels. A new Commission took office in January 1993 and, although many of the faces were the same and Jacques Delors was still president, its priorities were different. Sir Leon Brittan, previously responsible for competition policy, had been put in charge of the trade portfolio. He had his work cut out for him. The delicate agriculture reform package that had been key to putting the EC in position to close would not hold forever, nor were EC industrial leaders any more impressed than their US counterparts with some parts of the package. Sir Leon had no difficulty appreciating the intellectual appeal of the package as it stood, but he was aware that its political appeal was fragile and could begin to unravel at any moment. Other priorities were pressing. With the successful conclusion of the EC-92 Single Market Program, as well as CAP reform, the Commission had to address the challenges to the EC's further political cohesion and expansion. Additionally, the end of the cold war had profoundly altered the EC-US relationship and added a new toughness and confidence to the EC's approach to transatlantic and global issues.

There remained one other important piece of new business. The new blood in Washington and Brussels needed to be matched by new blood in Geneva: Dunkel had to go. He had indicated a desire to retire at the end of a successful round in 1991. That had not happened, and he had agreed to stay one more year. The EC and the United States now decided that the time had come for a new director general to bring the round to a conclusion.

Peter Sutherland was chosen to replace Arthur Dunkel. A former attorney general of Ireland and the EC commissioner for competition, he possessed the credentials, contacts, youthful vigour, and dominant personality sought by the United States and the EC. He radiated a no-nonsense confidence, more interested in results than debating points. He had superb business and political contacts on both sides of the Atlantic and was not shy about using them.[37] By 1 July 1993 he was in place, together with three new deputies, Warren Lavorel of the United States, Anwarul Hoda of India, and Jesús Seade of Mexico, all of them Geneva veterans steeped in the lore of the Uruguay Round and ready to add to the new push.

The new director general wasted no time in establishing his presence. Even before moving into his new office, he had been working the phones to convince the Summit Seven that their meeting in Tokyo at the beginning of July would provide an opportune time to do something more useful than the ritual call for a successful end to the round; he wanted them to agree on a concrete market access package that would provide the momentum he needed for his first meeting as chairman of the Trade Negotiating Committee. The details of what was achieved – very little was in fact agreed beyond broad principles – mattered little. A carefully orchestrated media campaign convinced those who needed to be convinced that the new US president was a fellow to be reckoned with, that his USTR could deliver, and that Sir Leon Brittan was a tough guy prepared to make a good deal. Additionally, Peter Sutherland and his new team were confirmed as the kind of brokers who could make things happen. The round was definitely on again.[38]

The following week, more careful press briefings suggested that the road ahead would be a tough slog, but that both the United States and the EC now had their shoulders to the wheel and the new director general was ready to put the rest of the apparatus to work with a view to concluding within the new time frame. At the July meeting of the TNC, momentum was restored, and the remaining delegates working at the mine face of the negotiations could return with renewed purpose to the painstaking work of crafting market access commitments and honing the texts of the several dozen agreements in play.[39]

The Final Push
With the media and delegates convinced that the round was back on track and the timetable firm, Sutherland turned his attention to one of the most critical deficiencies in its prosecution up to that point: the development of politically powerful

constituencies committed to a big result. While there continued to be room for improvements, the essential contours of a successful outcome for the round had been clear since the end of 1990. What had been missing, however, was the political will to cut through the inevitable difficult issues and reach the necessary compromises. That will would not emerge until US and EC political leaders became convinced that there were sufficient domestic interest groups committed to a successful outcome to outweigh the hue and cry coming from those who felt threatened by more open, rules-based international trade and investment, such as farmers, textile workers, and economic nationalists. Sutherland's political experience told him that no agreement could survive on its professional merit alone; it also needed the committed and sustained support of politically powerful audiences, and national delegations had not done their political homework.

In the absence of adequate national efforts, Sutherland set out to develop the necessary constituencies himself. He and his staff, working in harmony with other international organizations, took the wealth of available material that would make the point and repackaged it for much broader and politically useful consumption. A flurry of press releases and studies developed two mutually reinforcing themes: a successful outcome would add a significant percentage to the world's wealth, while failure would usher in a period of rancour that would subtract an even more significant portion from existing wealth.[40] By the end of September, he had succeeded in creating the necessary atmosphere for putting pressure on the EC and the United States to cut through their differences.[41]

For the new US administration, however, its first real test on the trade front was to get the North American Free Trade Agreement (NAFTA) through Congress. In this it succeeded on 17 November 1993; formidable forces were arrayed against the new president, largely from within his own party; equally formidable forces were marshalled to support him from among Democrats and Republicans, former presidents, and other political icons as well as business and academic leaders. The result was a solid victory for the president.

The message for the Uruguay Round negotiators was crystal clear. The US administration was committed to trade liberalization and international rule making and could deliver the US Congress in the face of formidable and sustained opposition. Any deal that had the full support of the administration was not likely to be frustrated by Congress. Both Clinton and Kantor had achieved stature as serious players in Geneva.

While the United States concentrated on getting the NAFTA through Congress, the EC worked on defining a closing mandate that could accommodate the French and everyone else. A series of summits of trade, foreign, and agriculture ministers plus detailed staff work gradually provided Brittan with a measure of the possible. The French government abandoned its posturing and agreed that a successful round was worth fighting for. Heavy pressure from the United Kingdom and the other more market-oriented member states kept the bottom line honest. Behind the scenes, discussions with the Americans, Japanese, and other leading delegations filled in the details and prepared the ground for the final push.[42]

Conclusion and Results

The way had now been opened to bring the round to a successful conclusion. The underbrush had been largely cleared away by the negotiators in Geneva, Brussels, Washington, and elsewhere. It was time for the two principals, the United States and the Community, to come to some agreement on a basis that they could carry at home and in Geneva. This was the task to which Kantor and Brittan now bent themselves on a virtually full-time basis. Slowly, the package began to come together. The horse trading went on for days and well into the nights, but by 14 December 1993, the deal was done.

All that remained was to hold the line for twenty-four hours while the details were communicated to the other delegations and put together into a final package to be considered by the TNC. Good staff work throughout the final three weeks ensured that other delegations were largely ready to conclude. With some necessary drama to cement the agreement into place and accommodate those delegations that needed to demonstrate their distaste for the way big powers feel they can railroad their wishes through a multilateral conference, the substantive negotiations of the round came to an end. Late in the afternoon of 15 December 1993, well before midnight in Washington, Peter Sutherland brought down the gavel and declared the negotiations over.

There remained work to be done, but the basic deal was now cast in stone. Over the next three months, that is, before the final conference of ministers in Marrakech, officials and lawyers polished the text, filled in some of the missing details, reviewed individual country schedules, removed as many ambiguities as possible, and ensured that the Final Act reflected the agreement reached on 15 December. What had been agreed was monumental by any standard. It involved no less than a complete overhaul of the multilateral trading system, providing a new framework within which to consolidate and strengthen a broad range of new and old obligations that together would put international trade on a much firmer and more open foundation.

The Final Act involved some forty separate agreements collectively amounting to the largest commercial agreement ever negotiated on such a broad basis. In order to provide an integrated set of obligations, and at the same time remove the institutional ambiguity that had hampered the GATT in its first forty-plus years, the centrepiece of the new trade regime would be a World Trade Organization. It would provide the organizational framework within which members could pursue rights and obligations set out in three main agreements: an amended General Agreement on Tariffs and Trade dubbed the GATT 1994, a new General Agreement on Trade in Services (GATS), and a new Agreement on Trade-Related Intellectual Property Rights (TRIPs). Fleshing out the rights and obligations contained in the revised GATT were a series of codes, most of which were revised versions of the Tokyo Round codes (sometimes radically revised, as in the case of subsidies), and decisions and understandings on a range of matters including dispute settlement, the trade policy review mechanism, and the interpretation of various GATT articles.[43]

Appended to the revised GATT and new GATS were 26,000 pages of detailed schedules setting out in very specific terms the market access commitments of individual members. The schedules appended to the GATT 1994 contained not only traditional tariff bindings, but also commitments on other product-specific border measures. On the thorny issue of agriculture, a detailed agreement had been worked out involving the conversion of all border measures into ordinary tariffs (tariffication), minimum access commitments, reductions in export and production subsidies, and clear discipline on domestic support measures. Finally, to overcome the problems created at the end of the Tokyo Round of a hierarchy of obligations resulting from the less-than-universal adherence to the codes, the Final Act was to enter into force on an all-or-nothing basis. With the exception of four so-called plurilateral agreements (on procurement, aircraft, dairy, and bovine meat), signature of the Final Act meant acceptance of all the agreements. The agreements had much to recommend them, including:

- *Breakthroughs*   The conclusion of multilateral agreements on agriculture, subsidies, intellectual property, and services represented a major advance in international rule making. Agreements on textiles and clothing resolved long-standing, festering problems. Other agreements introduced general rules of nondiscrimination to areas of increasing importance in international trade, such as services and intellectual property. The objection of some of the leading developing countries to the expansion of the GATT to these new areas had been neatly overcome by integrating the new and the old into a world trade body with a broad mandate.
- *Strengthening of the GATT system*   The agreements on safeguards and textiles and clothing ensured that the erosion of the GATT's basic principles flowing from the proliferation of grey-area measures and the cynical MFA regime would be reversed. Agreement to establish a World Trade Organization to provide oversight, improvements in the dispute settlement procedures, and the introduction of a permanent Trade Policy Review Mechanism (TPRM) indicated that the Final Act could in fact be implemented and become the basis for a dynamic and more modern trade relations system.
- *Improvements in market access*   The protocols providing for specific commitments on reductions and bindings in tariff schedules and other product-specific border measures, access to most services markets, and enhanced commitments on government procurement all suggested that the momentum of multilateral trade liberalization had been restored. Reductions in overall tariff levels were close to 40 percent, bringing tariffs among the industrialized countries down to little more than a nuisance factor in all but a few sectors. Of particular interest

were the extent to which developing countries had agreed to take on hard obligations for the first time, the extent to which members were prepared not to protect preferences established by the new regionalism, and the number of sectors in
which industrialized countries had opted to move to tariff-free trade.

- *Clarification and modernization of the GATT system*   A range of agreements,
such as those involving rules of origin, preshipment inspections, improvements
to the codes on import licensing, customs valuation, and technical barriers, provided a more secure basis for trade and continued the transition from general to
specific rules and procedures. These agreements also confirmed the further transition to a more law-like and less political approach to dispute settlement.[44]

Looked at from the perspective of the GATT's principles and the values of an
open, nondiscriminatory international trade and investment regime, there were a
number of disappointments that could become issues shaping the trade agenda of
the future. The revisions in the antidumping (AD) and countervailing duties (CVD)
agreements as well as the new code on trade-related investment measures failed to
come to grips with the fundamental problem of fair competition in an open global
economy. While perhaps politically necessary to keep the United States and to some
extent other major traders on side, the AD and CVD agreements maintained rules
that favoured power-based trade relations propped up by flawed economic thinking. The growing conflict between competition and trade policies would need to be
addressed in a future round. Additionally, the TRIMs agreement failed to capture
the importance of foreign direct investment as an agent of international integration and economic development. There was still need for a multilateral investment
code that addressed the full range of issues related to discriminatory regulation of
the conduct of business.

Despite these disappointments, the round had succeeded in reversing the gradual
shift away from multilateral agreements to regional ones and reestablished the
primacy of a universal set of rules and institutions. As such, it provided a stronger
framework for the continued evolution of a trade relations system based on the
principles of nondiscrimination, transparency, due process, consultation, and
cooperation. It laid an impressive foundation for continuing the process of applying these principles to a wider range of international economic transactions, and
it continued the transition from a set of broad principles and general rules aimed
at shallow integration to a much more detailed and complex set of rules capable of
fostering deep integration. The round demonstrated that it was possible to negotiate, on a multilateral basis, rules of general application involving positive norms
that went well beyond the self-denying prescriptions of the original GATT.
Finally, it signalled that it was possible to negotiate international agreements of
some scope and significance in the absence of effective, sustained leadership by
the major players.

Implementation

In a development reminiscent of the conclusion of the Tokyo Round, Canadians went to the polls shortly before the conclusion of the negotiations and opted to change the colour of their government. In 1979, Liberals had negotiated and Conservatives had implemented the results; Conservatives were in office for the duration of the Uruguay Round negotiations, until the Liberals replaced them in the final months of 1993. In Roy MacLaren, the new government appointed its most internationalist minister, a man firmly committed to multilateralism and to freer trade who was able to overcome in short order the misgivings of his more nationalistic colleagues, many of whom had campaigned vigorously against the Canada-US FTA and had expressed deep reservations about the course of the Uruguay Round. The new minister of finance, Paul Martin, fully shared MacLaren's positive assessment of the round, as did other senior members of the cabinet, including Industry Minister John Manley and Secretary of State for External Affairs André Ouellet. The transition, therefore, presented fewer problems than officials had feared. Canadian sensitivities on agriculture, however, had not changed and preoccupied the new government as much as its Tory predecessor. But in the end even this stumbling block was overcome, and the government enthusiastically endorsed the results of the negotiations.

The Canadian media focused on the agriculture dimension, with most commentators regretting that more had not been accomplished to relieve the plight of beleaguered Prairie grain farmers and deploring that too much had been done to continue to shelter dairy and poultry farmers. The deal as a whole was generally well received, with editorialists and pundits making good use of the material developed by the GATT and other international secretariats to demonstrate the impact of the agreement on global economic welfare. The *Montreal Gazette* concluded that "all in all, Canadians have reason to celebrate this deal."[45] The *Globe and Mail* told dairy and poultry farmers to get real in an editorial entitled "The Protection Racket Loses Its Grip." It noted that "the inordinate fuss, here and abroad, over agriculture, obscuring all else and indeed threatening at times to destroy the entire GATT round ... testifies to the ambitious scope of the talks."[46] Many Canadian newspapers ran an alarmist piece from the *Guardian* arguing that the results served only to fatten the purses of industrialists at the expense of poor people throughout the developing world, but had the good sense to balance it with editorials indicating that even the poor stood to benefit from a deal that reduced barriers to trade on a worldwide basis and strengthened the rule of law.[47] David Crane in the *Toronto Star* pointed out that for the first time the GATT had crafted an agreement that would bring direct benefits to developing countries such as India, Brazil, Turkey, Indonesia, Malaysia, and Thailand.[48]

As with the Canada-US Free Trade Agreement and the North American Free Trade Agreement, the government moved expeditiously to implement the results

Brian Gable, "GATT and the Marketing Boards," 15 December 1993. Canada's desire to shield its marketing boards from GATT disciplines proved one of the more difficult issues in the Uruguay Round negotiations.

of the negotiations into Canadian law. Enabling legislation was tabled in the House of Commons in the fall of 1994 and, following extensive hearings and discussion, passed in time for the new agreements to enter into force as envisaged at the beginning of 1995. Echoing the experience of the FTA and NAFTA, the WTO Agreements Implementation Act amended some 26 separate acts, demonstrating once again the extent to which trade negotiations and trade agreements had evolved since the founding of the GATT nearly five decades earlier. The provinces similarly enacted a range of implementing legislation, illustrating the growing importance of trade agreements to their mandates.

On 1 January 1995, the core of GATT members succeeded in bringing the new WTO into force. Within two years, the time frame envisaged in the Final Act, all the GATT contracting parties had succeeded in completing their domestic ratification procedures and had thus become "original" members of the WTO. The original GATT had been negotiated and implemented among twenty-three countries. Its replacement, the WTO, attracted 125 original members with more than thirty further countries signalling their intent to accede. What had been impossible in 1948 finally came to fruition in 1995: an international trade organization with a claim to universal support and membership. Critical to this success had been the nearly fifty years of generally constructive experience under the "interim" GATT. One of the little-noticed by-products of the implementation of the WTO was the end of the GATT's status as an "interim" agreement implemented by its members on a provisional basis. After forty-seven years, the GATT had finally attained the status of a definitive set of obligations forming an integral part of a permanent organization, thanks in part to Canada's ingenious proposal to establish a World Trade Organization to implement the results of the Uruguay Round.

The Canadian Trade Revolution

The bitter political debate in Canada on the merits of the 1989 Canada-US Free Trade Agreement, and its echo in the debate on the North American Free Trade Agreement four years later, was not repeated in the case of the Uruguay Round negotiations. While the content of all three negotiations was remarkably similar, a half-century of positive experience with the GATT and multilateral trade negotiations had made it difficult for all but the most strident critics of trade liberalization and international rule making to make a credible case that the round, and its results as enshrined in the WTO, posed a palpable threat to Canadian interests. Indeed, the Uruguay Round attracted very limited attention in Canada beyond professional and special interests. Like previous GATT negotiations, the round was perceived as esoteric and remote from more pressing Canadian concerns. Once again, however, enlightened Canadian self-interest had prevailed in the emergence of a much-strengthened multilateral system reinforcing liberalism and the rule of law in international trade and economic relations.

The ease with which the results were implemented into Canadian law by a new government, however, suggested that the ghosts of freer trade had been exorcised more generally from Canadians' collective anxieties. The Liberal government under the leadership of Prime Minister Jean Chrétien fully accepted that the trade policy revolution of the previous decade could not be undone. While Chrétien himself had not been in Parliament during the FTA debate, he had fully accepted the critical Liberal position during the NAFTA debate and had given full rein to its most vocal critics in his party, including Lloyd Axworthy, Sheila Copps, and Brian Tobin. Once in office, however, the new government took no steps to undo the agreements. It implemented the NAFTA within months of taking office, insisting only on some minor cosmetic statements about the urgency of addressing contingency protection measures. It similarly implemented the results of the Uruguay Round without any major changes, extolling the new WTO's virtues and dismissing its critics.

If nothing else, Chrétien exemplified the pragmatism of one of his most successful predecessors, Mackenzie King. Like King, Chrétien eschewed an ideological approach, preferring instead to rely on a shrewd capacity to read the politics of the moment. By 1993, he was confident that Canadians had accepted that freer trade, whether pursued bilaterally, regionally, or multilaterally, was here to stay, and that little would be gained by trying to reverse a decade of fundamental change and consequential adjustment in the structure of the economy and the attitudes of Canadians. Indeed, over the next few years, Chrétien and his ministers demonstrated the full extent of their commitment to freer trade by negotiating free-trade agreements with Israel, Chile, and Costa Rica, and entering into discussions to extend free trade more widely, including through a hemisphere-wide Free Trade Area of the Americas and possibly equally broad arrangements among the members of Asia-Pacific Economic Cooperation (APEC). His government even shrugged off criticism from Canadian economic nationalists and participated actively in the negotiation of an ultimately ill-fated and ill-timed Multilateral Agreement on Investment sponsored by the OECD.

As such, Chrétien proved a more adept politician than his immediate predecessors. While Canadians had accepted the free-trade revolution, they continued to harbour deep misgivings about the government that had pursued it. Canadians had returned the Conservatives to office in 1988 less because they had confidence in Prime Minister Mulroney and his team and more because they had little confidence in John Turner and Ed Broadbent. Throughout their second term, the Tories had continued their economic program of deregulation, privatization, tax reform, and freer trade, but the impact of a global recession and efforts by the Bank of Canada to nip new fears of inflation in the bud had made their management of the economy seem less adept. The NAFTA and the Uruguay Round had occupied pride of place on the trade policy front, and met with reasonable success. More generally, however, the government seemed to have lost its sense of purpose and seemed incapable of recapturing Canadians' trust. Despite the convincing mandate provided by the 1988 election, the government steadily lost support and by the third year was enjoying approval ratings in the teens. Prime Minister Mulroney appeared in particular to have become the lightning rod for dissatisfaction.

In February 1993, at the still relatively young age of 53, he decided the time had come to return to corporate life and let someone else suffer the slings and arrows of Canadians' fickle attitudes. His successor, Kim Campbell, who as justice minister had captured the media's attention and favour and who handily defeated Jean Charest in the leadership contest, could not translate the initial euphoria of the leadership change into a winning electoral campaign. The fragile coalition of Quebec and Western conservatives held together by Mulroney disintegrated under her leadership, allowing the return of the Liberals in the October election.

Despite their resounding defeat in the 1993 election, the Tories had served Canada well during their nine years in office, particularly in their trade policy. Their successful pursuit of freer trade on three fronts had succeeded in burying the legacy of the National Policy and had prepared the ground for a much more outward-oriented and competitive Canadian economy. The full acceptance and further development of this policy thrust by the Liberals after 1993 bore eloquent testimony to the wisdom of that choice. At the same time, however, the success of that policy and its continued rejection by a small but vocal segment of the Canadian electorate would create new challenges for Canadian policy makers.

15 CANADA IN A GLOBALLY
   INTEGRATED ECONOMY

You see things; and you say, "Why?" But I dream things that never were; and I say, "Why not?"

– GEORGE BERNARD SHAW

In many ways, 1995 marked an important divide in the historical development of Canadian trade policy. A few years earlier, 1987 seemed to have a similar claim. The conclusion of the Canada-US Free Trade Agreement that year witnessed the end of a quest that had started with Britain's repeal of the Corn Laws in 1846: free and secure access to the giant market to the south. It also symbolized the end of the National Policy and successive governments' determination to deny the forces of economics and geography in favour of politics and sentiment. And yet, the year 1995 provides a more attractive, more Canadian claim. It closed ten years of revolutionary churning that included not only the negotiation of an historic free-trade agreement with the United States, but also its extension to a poor, developing country, Mexico, and the establishment of a new, more robust, more comprehensive multilateral trade regime. Within one decade, Canada had satisfied its yearning for open, secure access to the United States, for reaching out to the developing world, and for confirmation of its fifty-year commitment to multilateralism. With their economy now firmly rooted in the reality of a North American economy, Canadians could pursue their vocation for global involvement, with a special nod to the challenge of integrating developing countries more firmly into the world trade relations system.

From a wider, global perspective, 1995 also marked a critically important divide in the history of international economic cooperation, as important a year as 1948 when twenty-three countries implemented the General Agreement on Tariffs and Trade and ushered in one of the most remarkable periods of economic growth in human history. The GATT was critically important in underwriting that growth. The successful implementation of a rules-based trade relations system fostered the

John S. Pritchett, "The Global Economy, the Deep, Dark Woods."

development of an international economy in which the barriers to trade between nations were sufficiently low, and the rules and procedures governing interstate economic relations were sufficiently stable, to allow firms and individuals in one nation to sell their goods routinely and confidently in the market of another.

The conclusion of the Uruguay Round of multilateral trade negotiations at the end of 1993 and the successful implementation of the World Trade Organization (WTO) on 1 January 1995 may prove to have been similarly pregnant with opportunity. Both events underlined a commitment to ensure that the preponderance of world trade will continue to take place under a nondiscriminatory system of rules. They fortified the rule of law rather than might. They reinforced the commitment of governments to economic growth based on competition rather than intervention. They may even point to the end of the road for those sectors of national economies that rely on walls and government support, like textiles, clothing, and agriculture, and the triumph of more consumer-oriented policies. Together with the successful pursuit of regional integration agreements like the North American Free Trade Agreement (NAFTA) and the European Union (EU), these events also signalled the beginning of a new era of rule making for a global economy.

The Reality of Deeper Integration

Canada's experience over the past century and a half generally tracked broader, global trends, from its early colonial experience to the current challenge of dealing with the impact of globalization. By the 1990s, the reality of deeper integration – or globalization – had been well documented. Annual reports by the GATT and WTO provided clear evidence of the contribution of trade policy and institutions in establishing an enabling environment for this deeper integration. The period 1950 to 1999 witnessed steady integration through trade and investment. For the whole of this period, the volume of world trade grew at a rate 1.6 times faster than that of world production. The volume of world output increased by a factor of six while the volume of world trade in goods multiplied by a factor of nineteen. By the end of 1999, the value of world trade in goods and commercial services had reached nearly US$6.9 trillion. The ratio of world trade in goods and services to output had almost quadrupled since 1950 (see table 15.1). More remarkably, the pace of integration had steadily accelerated. Integration grew rapidly in the first two decades after 1950, slowed perceptibly in the period 1974 to 1984, recovered between 1984 and 1989, and continued to grow rapidly in the 1990s.[1]

Table 15.1

World merchandise exports, production, and gross domestic product, 1950-99 (Index, 1990 = 100)

	Value				Volume							
	Exports				Exports				Production			World
	Total[a]	Ag	Mi	Mf	Total[a]	Ag	Mi	Mf	Total	Ag	Mi	Mf	GDP
1950	2	7	2	1	9	26	18	5	18	37	29	13	19
1955	3	8	3	2	13	30	27	7	24	42	37	19	25
1960	4	10	4	3	18	41	39	11	30	49	45	24	30
1965	6	12	6	4	26	50	49	17	41	55	60	35	39
1970	9	15	10	8	41	61	77	29	54	63	76	49	50
1975	26	36	42	21	52	65	79	42	65	72	82	60	61
1980	59	71	115	45	68	86	91	58	78	78	99	75	73
1985	56	63	88	49	75	90	79	72	86	90	86	84	84
1990	100	100	100	100	100	100	100	100	100	100	100	100	100
1995	145	139	108	152	136	126	126	137	107	109	109	106	108
1999	160	131	115	175	174	143	147	182	120	118	115	122	120

Notes: World merchandise production differs from world GDP in that it excludes services and construction.
Ag = agriculture products; Mi = mining products; Mf = manufactures
a   Includes unspecified products.
Source: World Trade Organization, *International Trade Statistics 2000* (Geneva: WTO, 2001), table II.1.

During the first few postwar decades, integration was most pronounced among the OECD economies, but since the early 1980s Asia and, more recently, Latin America have begun to participate more actively in this integration process. Open economies have shown markedly faster progress in economic development, with a number of them converging on OECD income levels by the 1990s. Among OECD economies, only Japan has not increased its participation in the global economy, remaining stagnant at a level of around 10-11 percent of GDP being exported. Among non-OECD economies, those in central and eastern Europe were only just beginning to show improvement by the end of the 1990s, while those in Africa and the Middle East remained mired in earlier economic patterns.

Although continuing growth in world trade levels is the most obvious indicator of expanding integration, increases in flows of foreign direct investment (FDI) reveal the same thing. World FDI inflows exceeded US$865 billion in 1999, with developing and transitional economies accounting for nearly a quarter of the inflow of world investment. The impact of these investment flows is illustrated by three developments: the rising proportion of trade represented by intra-industry trade, the increasing importance of trade in intermediate inputs, and the growing share of transactions occurring on an intrafirm, intranetwork, or other interrelated corporate basis. The value of production by the foreign affiliates of global firms now routinely outstrips the value of world trade in goods and services.

The most important but most difficult indicator of integration to measure is the flow of information and technology. The last quarter of the twentieth century saw not only an explosion in the absolute amount of knowledge and technology but also, more significantly, a rapid increase in its availability and usefulness to a growing share of the world's population. An unknown but large quantity of information and technology is being traded within private and proprietary networks, adding to the ability of firms to do business globally. Only a proportion of this trade is captured within official trade statistics, which thus underestimate the true value of world trade and the full richness of new patterns of economic integration.

By the 1990s, many countries had reached the stage at which an increasing share of national economic activity was conditioned by extranational transactions and influences. Few goods, services, capital, and technology were still produced wholly within a single national economy. At the same time, the border regimes in place in most countries acted as little more than nuisances to extranational transactions. Having escaped the limitations of time, space, and resources, firms were also finding ways of escaping the reach of national regulation or finding that national regulation in one jurisdiction conflicted with that in another. The national regulatory structures so painfully built up over the previous century and a half were beginning to serve as impediments to further economic development rather than as adjuncts or facilitators. They were more likely to lead to conflict than to harmony.

In the competition for investment in employment-generating facilities, for example, governments increasingly found global firms claiming that various regulatory requirements stood in the way of favourable investment decisions. The choice was either to join a race to the bottom by easing regulatory requirements or to lose new investments. In response, governments have begun to consider ways to recapture democratic control over the market, but in a manner geared to the new reality of a global economy rather than of a group of interlinked national economies. There are, of course, those who argue that one of the happy by-products of globalization is that some of the less sensible regulations and policies adopted by governments in the past may need to be reconsidered. Examples of past regulatory excesses have not been difficult to find, but few argue that government regulation has no place or deny the clear benefits to governments' determining standards of competition, consumer protection, or labour practices. What is being questioned is the detail and extent of regulatory activity, not its existence.

The challenge for governments is to determine the extent to which globalization has undercut their ability to regulate market behaviour and develop a regime that will allow them to maintain governance through cooperative action. An international regime might well recapture the political authority that has been lost as a result of the silent integration flowing from deepening globalization. Even more to the point, cooperative, jointly agreed international rules may provide an effective antidote to the tyranny of unilateralism by the powerful. The most potent threat to the sovereignty of most nation-states in the twenty-first century may not come from the fruits of cooperative action but from the extraterritorial application of unilateral definitions of appropriate standards by the United States and other powerful actors.

Lessons from the Recent Past about the New Rule Making

Trade agreements have traditionally dealt with the policies and programs that governments use to influence the quality and quantity of goods, services, capital, and technology that flow across national frontiers. That was still what trade agreements were largely about by the beginning of the 1990s, but, slowly and steadily, governments have begun to consider how, in a more globalized economy, decisions about where to invest and to what purpose are influenced by a much broader range of policies and measures than in earlier periods. The primary goal of trade liberalization agreements has always been to reduce barriers to international transactions and thus to contribute to economic growth and prosperity. Meeting this goal has political and social as well as economic impacts which, as the global economy becomes more open and integrated, are becoming sharper and more important.

As previously noted, the decade 1985-94 witnessed a variety of initiatives aimed at upgrading the old trade and payments regime and making it more responsive to the demands of a more integrated global economy. In Europe, the EC-92 program and a number of related initiatives sought both to deepen and to broaden the impact of the European integration program first launched in the 1950s. New directives and new agreements transformed the European Community of ten nations in

1980 into a European Union of fifteen nations by the turn of the century, each committed to an extensive range of integrating rules and institutions. A further dozen or more countries were actively preparing themselves for eventual membership. In North America, first the FTA and then the NAFTA provided a different blueprint for cooperation. Institutionally less integrative than the EU, the NAFTA may eventually require steps to make it more responsive to the forces of silent integration. Additionally, talks among the thirty-four democratically elected heads of government in the Americas suggest the potential for an integration agreement among all the nations of the western hemisphere. In Asia, various subregional arrangements may prove precursors and confidence-builders for as-yet-undefined regional integration schemes. Multilaterally, the Uruguay Round substantially upgraded the GATT-based trade relations system into a more comprehensive and more modern set of rules, institutions, and procedures. A new round of negotiations, launched in November 2001 at a ministerial meeting in Doha, Qatar, is likely to deepen and extend these rules.

The decade 1985-94 also saw a fundamental reversal in the attitudes of developing countries toward a global economy and toward rule making. The GATT/IMF trade and payments regime may have served the interests of OECD members, but it failed to prepare developing countries for the realities of an international, let alone a global, economy. By acquiescing in their quest for special treatment, the old regime had relegated the LDCs to second-class citizenship. OECD members had reaped the benefits of internalizing a set of liberalizing and converging external obligations, but developing countries continued to run isolating import-substitution policies, with the full blessing of a trade regime fundamentally at odds with those very policies.

Most developing countries had turned their backs on this strategy by the opening years of the 1990s. Many adopted unilateral reforms that opened their economies and welcomed trade and investment. During the Uruguay Round, developing countries accepted a range of new obligations and agreed that, in many instances, special and differential treatment should be limited to the least developed. Mexico accepted the full range of obligations in the NAFTA and successfully sued for membership in the OECD. The sterile intra-LDC agreements of the 1960s were replaced by more outward-looking and more realistic agreements. Latin American countries appeared ready to take on new responsibilities within the formal confines of regional agreements, while Asian countries, because of different values, experiences, and priorities, seemed to prefer less formal approaches. All, however, were actively engaged in experimenting with new obligations.

These developments are both a response to the changing nature of commerce in the global economy and a basis for further expansion of global rules. If nothing else, regional and multilateral discussions are providing governments with critically important negotiating and administrative experience. The intellectual property provisions in the NAFTA and WTO, for example, marked an important new departure in rule making. Governments agreed to extend a specified level of protection to the owners of intellectual property and to use trade sanctions to enforce them. Protection is extended to all owners of intellectual property rights, regardless of their residence or place of business. Governments agreed that in a global economy, the terms of trade that apply include a guarantee of the property rights of owners of intellectual property. It is not difficult to conceive how a similar pattern of rule making can be applied to other kinds of private rights and conditions.

Similarly, the investment provisions in the NAFTA reflect a much broader appreciation of investment rules than was evident in earlier agreements. They are geared to the whole range of factors involved in international business, including trade in goods and services, the transfer of technology, and strategic alliances, and they cover the conduct of business rather than just investment. They involve an integrated and extensive set of generic rules as well as important new provisions for investor-state dispute resolution. Efforts to negotiate a similar agreement among all the members of the OECD failed in 1998, largely because the problems experienced by OECD members in their investment relations were minimal and the resultant commercial payoffs would, as a result, have been minor relative to the political problems perceived or anticipated.[2] Negotiating about such issues on a broader scale, however, may lead to more positive results.

The NAFTA side agreements set out an interesting experiment in rule making as it relates to environmental protection and labour market regulations. Rather than negotiating substantive rules about these issues, the three participating governments put in place dispute settlement mechanisms that allow interested parties to ensure full compliance with existing domestic laws and procedures in all three jurisdictions. These mechanisms recognize the interface between trade and social issues and acknowledge that differing regulatory regimes can have trade and investment effects, but also accept that trade agreements may not be the best place to establish detailed rules to govern international environmental cooperation.

Not all the new experiments in rule making, however, have been constructive. The governments of economically powerful states have sought to implement solutions that export their political problems by penalizing divergent policies practised in other jurisdictions. In many cases, preferred solutions could lead to new barriers to trade, with countervailing duties and similar restrictive measures being the weapons of choice. Calls for new rules to address environmental protection and fair labour standards, for example, include worrisome protectionist elements that could result in the segmentation of markets rather than their further integration.

The old debate about fair trade may be entering a new and more difficult phase. A whole range of policy differences among states is being cited as creating unfair competition. Those worried about unfair trade seek the adoption of measures that safeguard a country's own policy preferences while penalizing the choices of other nations by excluding their products from the marketplace. An idea that has been around for some time is being retooled for new circumstances, with consequences that may not always be intended.

To forestall these unintended consequences, trade policy analysts have begun to consider whether international rules – globally or regionally – could be negotiated to constrain the ability of powerful states to act unilaterally. In return, smaller states might need to bring their policies more into line with those of the powerful. In short, in order to avoid the tyranny of the powerful, it might be in the interest of smaller countries to behave cooperatively and thus constrain the coercive capacity of larger countries. The challenge is to find the balance between coercion and co-operation that would appeal to the political needs of both the small and the large.

The New Political Economy of Trade Negotiations

In the 1950s and 1960s, as governments negotiated the trade agreements that established and nurtured a more open and stable multilateral trading order, the political economy of trade negotiations involved determining appropriate trade-offs between import-competing and export-oriented commercial interests. Indeed, much of the GATT's strength derived from its ingenious formula for harnessing the interests of export-oriented sectors to overcome the opposition to liberalization from import-competing sectors. The cumulative impact of this gradual, and thus politically acceptable, approach to trade liberalization has been a world in which virtually every productive sector of the economy accepts an open economy as a given; support for a liberal, rules-based multilateral trading system is now widespread among business interests. Opposition to trade agreements now comes from broader societal interests, fearful that liberal trade and international rules will erode the capacity and willingness of governments to address other societal problems. The new political economy of trade seeks to redefine the age-old conflict between allocative efficiency and distributive justice, between proponents of equality of opportunity and equality of results.

These competing perspectives are critical to understanding the emerging political economy of international trade. For corporate and related interests, the equality of opportunity perspective clearly dominates. While some business leaders may secretly harbour dreams of a truly open economy where markets determine all outcomes, most are quite happy to see governments play a role to protect the competitive process, to ensure fair play, or to establish basic standards. They know that the future of their firms lies in vigorously competing for market share – at home and abroad – on the basis of price, quality, design, delivery, and service within a framework of national and international rules that allows markets to work efficiently but fairly. Thus they are enthusiastic about the achievements of the regional and global trade agreements concluded between 1985 and 1994 and are prepared to consider further efforts at rule making to govern investment and competition policy. These agreements all share the objective of enhancing equality of opportunity by letting transnational markets work efficiently but fairly. Their concepts of efficiency are well grounded in neoclassical economics, and their concepts of fairness reflect Western concepts of law, order, and due process.

When it comes to concluding agreements on such issues as international fair labour standards or global environmental protection, however, business leaders become more sceptical. They are reluctant to extend to the international arena domestic rules and procedures that they have found of dubious value at the national level. Although not prepared to condemn the existence of national labour market regulations or of environmental protection laws, they would be prepared to live without many of them. At this stage, they see little value in extending them internationally.

Business leaders who attach great value to the convergence and even harmonization of regulatory regimes related to customs rules and procedures (e.g., classification, valuation, and rules of origin), product and process standards, the protection of intellectual property, or government procurement procedures, see little value in establishing global norms relating to labour market practices or environmental protection. Businesses at the forefront of calls to standardize the regulation of the telecommunications sector and to create more uniform approaches to controls over financial institutions are fully prepared to let markets alone determine the evolution of national approaches to the regulation of labour markets and the protection of the environment.

Over time, business leaders may reassess these policy attitudes, particularly as integration deepens and the cost of regulatory divergence increases. Equally, they may see the value of global rules that ensure basic standards but that constrain governments from pursuing discriminatory policies to restrict trade and investment with countries that exhibit social and other preferences at odds with prevailing attitudes in the importing or home country. In the meantime, business appears to have withdrawn from active engagement in delineating the contours of the new trade policy. Content with the achievements of the past fifty years and suspicious of many aspects of the emerging agenda, many business leaders refuse to be drawn into discussions on the merits of various proposals being advanced by governments.

Populist groups, on the other hand, tend to assess these issues differently.[3] Often attracted to a command-and-control perspective, they are uncomfortable with market outcomes and suspicious of a more integrated global economy. They see the trade regime as too committed to letting markets determine outcomes. Whether promoting the achievement of human rights, the protection of the environment, the social preferences of a particular polity, or the cultural values of indigenous peoples, they are convinced that only national governments can deliver what they seek. While their own vision and influence have been greatly enhanced by transnational networks, they are adamant that national borders have become too porous and that steps need to be taken to shield national economies from the debilitating effects of international or global competition. They criticize international trade agreements for undermining the will of the people. At the same time, on issues on which they are not making progress with voters at the national level, from environmental rules to human rights, they are eager to use international bodies to impose their policy preferences on democratically elected governments.

While generally still hostile to the lowering of tariffs, the elimination of nontariff barriers, and the convergence in or harmonization of standards and national regulatory regimes, some populist groups are determined to pursue human rights and environmental issues through the trading regime. Groups with this approach hope to harness the trade regime to ensure greater attention to the promotion of human rights and the protection of the environment. Committed to specific, measurable results, they see great utility in the coercive power of trade sanctions to achieve them. The discriminatory nature of some of these measures and the probability of ambiguous economic impacts are of little consequence to groups that view market outcomes with indifference or even repugnance.

Within pluralist democracies, the essence of governance involves finding the most politically persuasive balance between these elements, a quest that is constantly in flux as societal preferences and priorities respond to changing circumstances. In international economic rule making, the balance has traditionally tilted toward allocative efficiency, on the assumption that individual national governments can address the demands of distributive justice within their own jurisdictions. The globalization of production patterns and consumption choices, however, is straining the ability of governments to maintain this traditional line of demarcation. As a result, competing perspectives now complicate how governments approach issues in the international economy. In the coming years, as the process of international rule making intensifies, we are likely to see how these differing perspectives, when applied to specific issues, can become sources of conflict between governments and between governments and their electorates. In the words of the late Harvard scholar Ray Vernon, "The great sweep of technological change continues to link nations and their economies in a process that seems inexorable and irreversible ... Yet, the basic adjustments demanded by the globalization trend cannot take place without political struggle ... So the world is likely to be in for a long period of learning as nation-states grope for adequate responses to the problems of openness ... To shorten that struggle and reduce its costs will demand an extraordinary measure of imagination and restraint from leaders on both sides of the business-government divide."[4]

The global economy is rapidly becoming "denationalized," but governments continue to govern on the basis of national goals and frontiers. Over the decade 1985-94, governments quietly began to forge a new world order to accommodate the disjunction of a world in which political frontiers bore little resemblance to economic activity. They took a number of steps – some consciously, some less so – to create a post-cold-war order centred in the World Trade Organization. Making the new order effective will not be easy. Governments will need to develop consensus on a potentially difficult group of issues, many of which challenge traditional concepts of sovereignty. New negotiating tools and techniques may be required as well as even more robust institutions and approaches to the resolution of conflict. Efforts are likely to continue to consolidate and deepen governance of the global economy.

WORLD GOVERNMENT

Patrick Chappatte, "World Government." Chappatte, like many others, is suggesting that progress in establishing institutions of world governance appears to have slowed following establishment of the WTO.

Trade policy thus seems poised to become the focal point of a new, post-coldwar international relations system based on promoting sustainable economic growth and development. During and immediately after the Second World War, the Allies developed a set of institutions and rules to govern interstate behaviour aimed at preventing a repetition of the cataclysms of the previous thirty-five years: two world wars and a disastrous global depression. The hub of that system was the United Nations. Within it, economic development and similar matters were assigned to a range of specialized, functional agencies with a mandate to consider matters of low policy, i.e., the kinds of problems that require technical expertise and to which there are technical solutions. Matters of high policy, such as peace and security, requiring the attention of political leaders and their immediate advisors, were reserved for the Security Council.

The grand institutional design of the United Nations never worked as intended, but the cold war era did ensure that peace and security would be the crux of high policy and the main determinant of political relations among states. Economic welfare and other functional issues remained the focus of low policy, discussed among technicians. Politicians and their immediate advisors only became involved to provide broad direction. The end of the cold war in 1989, however, effectively ended this particular understanding of interstate relations. While at the level of detail, this perspective had already become more romantic than real, at the level of grand strategy it still commanded respect. Today, peace and security are more and more the work of a relatively small group of technicians dealing with issues such as peacekeeping and the gradual dismantling of the nuclear arsenal. By the late 1990s, the issues that dominated international meetings among political leaders and their immediate advisors were economic, whether meetings of the G7, bilateral summits, or regional summits in Latin America or Asia-Pacific. During the cold war, relations between the Soviet Union and the United States revolved around disarmament and the status of Berlin. By the beginning of the twenty-first century, the issues had become Russia's accession to the WTO and the IMF's latest loan guarantees.[5]

The trading system and its many constituent agreements organized on the principles first embodied in the GATT are steadily becoming the main rules of the game governing interstate relations. The protection of the environment and the promotion of human rights are among the leading issues about which polls show rising public concern. Individually, there might be a limit to what political leaders can do to satisfy such concerns. The reality of a global economy and of economic interdependence makes it more difficult for even the largest powers to act unilaterally. Collectively, however, governments are beginning to address these issues, and trade agreements might prove the most potent forums for doing that. Thus ministerial meetings of the WTO in Singapore, Geneva, Seattle, and Doha acted as lightning rods for dissatisfaction with the new regime. In keeping with this new reality, the meetings attracted not only ministers, officials, and media, but also a horde of nongovernmental organizations (NGOs) dedicated to the full range of issues potentially on the agenda. Many of these NGOs are ahead of governments and the media in reading the transformation in high policy. Many of them appeal to the same individuals who were at the forefront of the fight to ban the bomb or otherwise promote peaceful coexistence a generation ago; they now see the international agenda in terms of human rights and environmental protection. For them, the core of high policy has already shifted from peace and security to economic welfare and sustainable development.

Governments may eventually prove as successful in implementing and developing a WTO-based trade relations system as an earlier generation was in implementing and developing the GATT-based regime. To grasp this opportunity, however, governments must recognize that rule making for a global economy is fundamentally different from rule making for an international economy. They will have to adapt international negotiations to the radically different circumstances created by globalization. The new order may need to be built on the foundations of the old, but it is likely to focus on rules, institutions, and procedures that have more in common with existing domestic than past international regimes. It will be preoccupied less with liberalization and more with governance. The benefits from new rules, while real, may prove less direct and could require more difficult and protracted negotiations. For Canada, it will require further strategic thinking in the full knowledge of what has worked and what has not.

Choices and Opportunities for Canada

Canadians have a large stake in the success of efforts to define the new regime for governing interstate relations. Indeed, as a result of both economic and policy developments in the 1980s and 1990s, their stake has become significantly greater. Trade and related matters now loom larger than ever as determinants of Canadian prosperity (see table 15.2). Canadian capacity to contribute to the further evolution of rules and institutions to govern international trade has similarly grown. The lessons learned from more than a century and a half of trying to make the most of their geographic and demographic circumstances should serve Canadians well in the future.

Canadian ministers have begun to respond to the demands of the new political economy of trade, by committing the government to consultations with all sectors of society. Following the federal government's positive experience, in the Tokyo Round of GATT negotiations (1973-9), of consulting closely with the provinces and business interests, ministers developed a disposition to consult ever more widely before enunciating Canadian policies and priorities. They also became comfortable with a more transparent process of decision making, prepared to share a wide

Table 15.2

Trade and the Canadian economy, 1997-2000

Year	Value ($billions)			Share of GDP (%)	
	Exports	Imports	Total GDP	Exports	Imports
Total trade in goods and services					
1997	345	331	878	39.1	37.5
1998	371	359	902	41.2	39.8
1999	412	385	958	43.1	40.2
2000	474	426	1039	45.6	40.1
				Share of total (%)	
Trade in goods and services with the US				Exports	Imports
1997	282	223		81.8	67.5
1998	315	245		84.8	68.2
1999	358	259		86.8	67.3
2000	413	274		87.2	64.3

Source: Statistics Canada, *National Income and Expenditure Accounts* (Catalogue 13-001-PPB); and *Canada's Balance of International Payments* (Catalogue 67-00-XPB), 4th Quarter 2000.

range of previously restricted information and analysis. The advent of the Internet further allowed governments to shape and share information and analysis on the broadest possible basis. By the turn of the century, virtually every level of government routinely made material available that less than a generation earlier would have been considered sensitive and privileged.

At first confined to business and related interests, by the end of the 1990s consultations encompassed the full range of societal players. Ironically, as consultations expanded, they also became less effective. To recapture their earlier effectiveness, ministers may need to reconsider both the intent and process of consultations. As Denis Stairs has indicated, there are two kinds of consultations: political and bureaucratic.[6] The priority for ministers and parliamentarians is to determine whether Canada should negotiate and to what purpose. These are political questions on which only politicians can be fully engaged. Both before and after the government has determined its answer to these questions, a second level of consultations can come into play, focused on how, when, where, and what to negotiate. These are technical questions well suited to the skills and expertise of officials. Confusing the role of politicians and officials can lead to frustration on the part of both those consulted and those doing the consulting. Complexity requires expertise; democratic accountability requires political oversight. Effective consultations in an era of broad public participation and interest, therefore, require a partnership between politician and expert, each with important roles to fulfil.

In order for Canada to continue in the role that it played so effectively in the early postwar years, Canadian ministers and officials will need a renewed vision of Canada's place in the global economy and a new appreciation of the appropriate balance between domestic and international governance. Consultations may help to inform such a vision, but, more critically, it needs to emerge from a clear assessment of Canadian strengths, weaknesses, and interests. To date, Canadian governments – federal and provincial – have been tentative and defensive in their responses to the demands of a more integrated global economy, more prepared to follow than to lead. In the waning years of the twentieth century, energies appeared to be more focused on implementation and consolidation than on analysis and innovation.

In the opening years of the twenty-first century, even though little substantive progress was being made, governments were experimenting with a wide range of processes to test the scope of and demand for new negotiations. Canadian participation in the elaboration of a Free Trade Area of the Americas (FTAA), the agenda of Asia-Pacific Economic Cooperation (APEC), a new round of WTO negotiations, further Canada-US bilateral or NAFTA trilateral discussions, and bilateral free-trade discussions with newer trading partners may provide a basis for developing new ideas and proposals faithful to the achievements of the past but attuned to the demands of the future. Some of these initiatives, however, also illustrate well the emergence of trade policy as high policy: political factors frequently outweigh economic and commercial considerations.

For Canada, most of these experiments will prove of limited economic or commercial value. The FTAA discussions, for example, are symbolically important to the nations of the Americas, but they are unlikely to achieve the kind of agreement that early public discussions suggested. Successfully concluding and implementing an FTAA will require that all participants accept obligations that go well beyond their existing WTO obligations. That is a larger step than most of the countries of the region appear ready to take at this time. The absence of US fast-track negotiating authority throughout the preparation period and early negotiations invested discussions with a surreal quality, and the rivalry between competing US and Brazilian visions underlined their geopolitical nature. In any case, the discussions have been of considerable value in developing and deepening trade and political relations among the nations of the Americas, in providing the Caribbean, Central, and South American participants with a process to deepen their understanding of rules-based trade, and in enhancing their capacity to participate in such a system.

APEC similarly contributes to the intellectual capital and political momentum needed to move the international trade and investment agenda along. Like the FTAA process, discussions in APEC are in many ways the equivalent of discussions in the Commonwealth in earlier decades. They are characterized by a deep spirit of cooperation and a commitment to common objectives. To date, the results have been more modest than some of its more enthusiastic participants had hoped, but they have clearly been positive. Some of APEC's most important work has been to validate and complement the work of other forums. Over time, APEC's contribution is likely to continue to be constructive, adding to the forces leading to a more liberal, rules-based, better-functioning global economy.

For Canada, APEC and the FTAA are not likely to lead to significant breakthroughs in access to the markets of Asia and Latin America or in negotiating new trade and investment rules. Rather, they will contribute to ensuring that Canadian-based firms can take advantage of the access that exists, to identifying problems in access, and to proposing remedies, most of which will be addressed elsewhere. More importantly, both forums provide unique opportunities to strengthen ties with future trading partners that could contribute to future trade and investment opportunities and growth.

Developing and transitional economy countries may eventually become more important trading partners for Canada. Some will offer very large markets and a capacity to absorb more Canadian goods and services; others will provide Canadians with a range of attractive and competitive products. To get there, however, there need to be many more changes than we have seen to date. Most of these countries are now headed in the right direction; however, many do not have the wherewithal to complete the journey. Canada needs a robust and well-functioning global trade and investment regime. To remain viable, such a regime will require the active and constructive participation of developing and transitional countries. To that end,

Canada can usefully place itself at the forefront in helping them gain the capacity to meet this challenge.

Bilateral free-trade discussions with some of the emerging markets, including Chile, Costa Rica, the rest of Central America, Singapore, the remaining members of the European Free Trade Association (Norway, Switzerland, Liechtenstein, and Iceland), and others serve similar modest, long-term objectives. They expand the reach of freer, rules-based trade on the basis of, by-now, well-established patterns. They foster relationships with countries that offer interesting, if modest, new trade and investment opportunities. They strengthen geopolitical ties that might otherwise remain dormant. But they are largely peripheral to the mainstream of Canadian trade and investment interests. These are to be found, as they have for many years, in relations with the United States and in further elaboration of the multilateral trade and investment regime.

Members of the World Trade Organization held their fourth Ministerial Meeting in Doha, Qatar, in November 2001. Since the ill-fated Seattle meeting at the end of 1999, governments and their officials had worked to find the basis for renewed commitment and expanded horizons. Preliminary negotiations on agriculture and services, as required by the 1994 Marrakech agreements, helped to clear the way. At Doha, ministers agreed to launch a new round of multilateral negotiations. The ultimate shape and scope of these negotiations, however, remain obscure, suggesting that they will take many years to define and complete. As during the Uruguay Round, governments need to tackle some of the most difficult questions left over from previous rounds, particularly agriculture, and find ways and means to address some of the newer issues, from competition policy to environmental protection and labour regulation. In between, there is a full range of other thorny issues.

For Canada, WTO negotiations will serve a dual purpose. First and foremost, they will strengthen the systemic base for all of Canada's trade relations, including with the United States. Additionally, they will provide the best basis for pursuing stronger rules and better access commitments for trade with Europe, Japan, and the rest of the world. It is sometimes tempting to look to bilateral negotiations with the EU and Japan to effect change in these relationships, but experience has demonstrated that the degree of mutual interest in solving bilateral problems is not sufficient to overcome a host of complicating factors, including asymmetry in size and interest, sectoral sensitivities, concern about setting precedents for other relationships, and more. Multilateral negotiations are well suited to building coalitions and finding common cause to overcome some of these problems. Europe and Japan remain large and potentially important markets. They are now marginal trading partners, for reasons of both omission and commission, on Canada's part and theirs. There may be room for some modest initiatives to explore the scope for doing more, but the most important breakthroughs are likely to come through multilateral bargaining.

Canada's first priority remains the United States. That market represents some 85 percent of Canada's trade and economic relations. Canada's trade in goods and services with the United States adds up to about a third of its total economic activity and about a third of its total consumption. Canadians increasingly accept that living next door to the largest, most dynamic economy in the world is an asset to be nurtured and protected. This means that trade irritants, trade relations, trade promotion, and trade negotiations with the United States will remain at the top of Canada's agenda.

Together with the Mexicans, Canadians have a free-trade agreement with the United States. The reality, however, is that the three countries have reached a level of integration closer to that of a customs union, but without the institutions and rules to make sure that they are getting the full benefits of this level of integration. *New York Times* reporter Anthony DePalma posits the interesting thesis that, despite their disparate histories and characters, the three countries of North America have more in common than they think and NAFTA is drawing them ever closer together. Based on his experience as the *Times* bureau chief in Mexico City and Toronto, he concludes that "our border will not disappear, not any time soon. But what may fade away are the misunderstandings and ignorance that have plagued North America for so long."[7]

If nothing else, DePalma captured well an issue gaining increasing attention in Canada. Given developments in the global economy, the intensification of private-sector-led integration in North America, and the stresses created by diverging Canada-US economic performance, a growing number of analysts believe the time has come for Canada and the United States to consider jointly whether they can take steps to remove or constrain remaining barriers to cross-border trade and investment. The combined success of the FTA, NAFTA, and WTO negotiations has exposed policies and practices that do or might impede further growth in trade and investment. These policies and practices go beyond what can be resolved on a piecemeal, issue-by-issue basis and are of a type and nature unlikely to receive the attention they require in future WTO multilateral negotiations or ongoing regional FTAA or APEC discussions. They are most likely to be resolved on the basis of a comprehensive initiative that can capture the imagination of political leaders on both sides of the border and generate the level of support necessary to overcome narrowly focused opposition.

Such a comprehensive initiative is most likely to be considered initially on a bilateral Canada-US basis, without prejudice to the advisability or necessity of including Mexico or of incorporating the results of any discussions into the NAFTA framework. The two governments are likely to conclude that it is more important to define the issues and the feasibility of their resolution than to focus on their form or the institutional basis for administering the results of any new commitments. Similarly, they are likely to conclude that it is not necessary in the early stages to determine Mexico's role. That issue is more likely to be addressed later on the basis of the results of preliminary discussions and in light of Mexican interests and capacity.

Over the next decade, therefore, it will not be surprising to find Canada and the United States engaged in efforts to complete the work they started in the early 1980s to achieve a seamless market governed by a single set of rules, implemented and administered by the two governments to achieve their common interest in a well-functioning North American economy. Canadians will be asked to agree that such an initiative represents a prudent way for Canada to manage its deepening economic relations with its giant neighbour to the south. Americans will need to decide whether this is a good way for the United States to demonstrate to its other trading partners that it remains committed to rules-based internationalism and that it is prepared to adapt that system to the challenges and demands of deeper integration. For both, reducing the impact of the border may prove the best way to preserve Canada's status as an independent, reliable, and vibrant partner of the United States in the pursuit of common trade, economic, and security interests.

16 FROM A TRADING NATION
TO A NATION OF TRADERS

Canadians don't export; we permit others to import from us.

– JEAN-LUC PÉPIN, MINISTER OF INDUSTRY,
TRADE AND COMMERCE, 1969–72

Canada has always been a trading nation, but Canadians have not always been enthusiastic traders. From their earliest colonial days, Canadians have had to struggle with the reality of too much geography and too little demography. They found the answer in trade, but they were not always comfortable with the market determining what they would produce for themselves and what they would import from others. Canadians enthusiastically accepted the need to export their surplus resources, but they were less sanguine about importing a wide array of manufactures and other goods. Not surprisingly, the trade policy measures adopted by successive governments often suffered from a high level of internal conflict. Until well into the twentieth century, trade policy choices were further complicated by their need to serve both fiscal and economic development objectives.

Before Britain's full embrace of free trade in 1846, the trade policy that guided Canada's fiscal needs and economic development was a straightforward application of colonial and mercantilist ideas. After 1846, however, matters became more complicated. The economic mainstay of the colonies by that time was fishing, lumbering, and wheat – or corn – production. The export of these staples to Britain on preferential terms had provided the colonies with the necessary foreign exchange to buy luxuries, machinery, and other manufactured goods. To help get exports to market, the colonial legislature of the United Provinces had expended considerable funds on the building of the Laurentian canals.

The colonial response to the disaster threatened by Britain's repeal of the Corn Laws provides an early but classic example of Canadian policy making. It steered a middle course, seeking to enjoy the benefits of both trade and protection. US officials and legislators were persuaded to provide Canadian resource exports with free access to the US market on a reciprocal basis, paid for with fishing rights on the Grand Banks and navigation rights on the Great Lakes, rather than better, let alone free, access for American manufactured goods to the markets of the Canadian colonies. The Reciprocity Treaty lasted from 1854 until its abrogation by the US Congress in 1866, a time that coincided with growth and prosperity, leaving a legacy of positive feelings, particularly in the Maritime colonies. Not surprisingly, the search for reciprocity with the United States, at least on the favourable terms set out in the treaty, would remain a constant refrain in the politics of the newly confederated Canadian provinces for the next fifty years. Farmers and fishermen generally had mixed views about reciprocity, and merchants learned to like it, but manufacturers did not, and were not unhappy to see it end. To them, the colonial legislatures' need to raise revenue and their own desire for protection created a wonderful coincidence in interests, a coincidence that they learned to exploit with zeal and success.

Canadian trade policy had become clear by the time Sir John A. Macdonald's second government adopted a National Policy in 1879. Macdonald settled on this decidedly second-best option because of his inability to negotiate a successor to the Reciprocity Treaty, and because of the economic failure of Confederation. In announcing the National Policy, Macdonald emphasized that higher Canadian tariffs on the imports of US manufactured goods might dispose the United States to take a greater interest in reciprocity. More fundamentally, however, Macdonald was looking for a policy mix that would promote Canada's economic development by attracting both immigrants and industry. The National Policy was a classic import-substitution policy: high tariffs and subsidized infrastructure to attract industry and create employment, and immigration to increase population and create demand. Macdonald and his ministers opted for policies that would promote aggregate growth and a large, national economy, rather than individual welfare and high per capita incomes. This policy would, over time, create a growing business class and, for the century that followed, business leaders learned to draw a close connection between protection and Canadian nationhood.

In the long run, the National Policy did have its desired effect. It created a larger national economy by attracting immigrants and industry, albeit industry that proved critically dependent on high levels of protection. In the short run, however, the National Policy led to little but failure. Immigrants came, but even more people left for opportunities in the booming US economy. Industries came, but most were small and inefficient and created few new employment opportunities. The Canadian Pacific Railway united East and West and opened the Prairie frontier, but it took another generation before new strains of wheat made the Prairies economically viable. Not until the opening years of the twentieth century did the growth that Macdonald had sought begin to take hold.

By the end of the nineteenth century, a number of important features of Canadian trade policy had become clear: the sectoral tensions between East and West; the strong influence of events and decisions outside the country; the beginnings of

The National Policy.

anti-Americanism as an important justification for protection; a close identification between nationhood and protection; an emphasis on size rather than quality; and a strongly anti-intellectual, pragmatic bent to Canadian policy making. Canada's business leaders learned to exploit these characteristics in order to advance their immediate interests, and never so effectively as in 1911, when they succeeded in defeating the threat of renewed free trade with the United States.

In 1911, the Liberal government of Sir Wilfrid Laurier succeeded in renewing reciprocity with the Americans. The agreement provided Canada with free access for its resource and agriculture exports and harmonized tariff rates for manufactured products at the high levels then in vogue on both sides of the border. It would be hard to conceive of a policy more attuned to contemporary Canadian business and political interests. It solved the sectoral tensions created by the National Policy by gaining a reliable market for Western grains and Eastern lumber, pulp, fish, and mining products, and continued to protect emerging manufacturing interests in central Canada. Canada's business elite, however, determined that protection for manufacturers far outweighed the importance of markets for farmers, miners, and lumbermen. If US customers wanted and needed Canadian resources, they would buy them, reciprocity or not. But without the high tariffs by then firmly in place for manufactures, Canada's business leaders saw no future for Canadian industry.

Enough people agreed with this proposition to defeat the Laurier government in the 1911 election.

Canada's trade policy was now set for the next three generations. The government would promote the export of raw materials by negotiating access and supply contracts where it could, subsidize exports through infrastructure and other programs where necessary, and cosset the import-substitution sectors of eastern Canada with high tariffs and related policies where possible. It proved a politically popular mix. On the hustings, Conservatives insisted tariffs could go no lower and Liberals persisted that they could go no higher, but in office both maintained the pragmatic components of the National Policy, ensuring that any manufacturer who wanted protection could get it.

In making sure of that protection, Canadian officials earned a worldwide reputation for the inventive ways in which they could manipulate the tariff and related customs administration. Some of the provisions in the later GATT were put there to discipline such Canadian innovations and practices as antidumping duties, valuation manipulations, classification fiddles, and subsidies. Even after the GATT came into effect in 1948, Canadian officials retained their reputation for ingenuity. They may have been committed to progressive liberalization, but they appreciated that political and business support for a rules-based trading regime required the solution of short-term political problems, even if that sometimes entailed detours that stretched the letter and the spirit of the rules.

The 1911 episode reinforced a number of other, less attractive elements in Canada's trade policy: its anti-Americanism and its commitment to an economy based on world-class resource extraction and no-class manufacturing. It also reinforced the development of costly east-west distribution systems, ensured that the Canadian economy would continue to grow in aggregate, but doomed productivity growth to lag far behind that of the United States. Politicians and industrialists alike convinced themselves that being Canadian carried a price, an attitude that held sway as late as the 1980s.

The decades that followed the rejection of reciprocity were not kind to Canada, as war and depression roiled both the domestic and international landscapes. By the mid-1930s, however, Canada was ready to adopt changes with important long-term consequences. The professionalization of the public service placed trade policy making on a more stable foundation. A new reciprocity agreement with the United States and trade agreements with the United Kingdom and other Commonwealth countries provided Canadian exporters with more secure access to export markets. Canadian experience in negotiating agreements taught politicians and officials alike that small countries dependent on trade with larger countries have, at best, narrow scope for manoeuvre. They also learned that as long as other countries practised the same kind of mercantilism as Canada did, it was necessary to maintain a strong domestic economic base. The long-term solution to Canada's economic problems required a broad measure of cooperation from countries with larger markets.

These realities conditioned Canadian participation in the planning and negotiations that led to the General Agreement on Tariffs and Trade. At the initial GATT negotiations in Geneva in 1947, Canada opened its market substantially. By that time, Canada's large economic and military contributions to the Allied war effort had transformed the economy. In the years immediately after the war, Canadian generosity helped to stimulate the reconstruction of the United Kingdom and Europe. The Canadian economy adjusted swiftly to the demands of peacetime and grew at a rapid pace for most of the first three decades after the war. Much of that growth was fuelled by domestic demand as Canadians, tired of the deprivations of first depression and then war, sought and gained the benefits accruing to the second-most-productive economy in the world.

In the next four rounds of GATT negotiations, however, Canadian officials were among the sharpest negotiators, seeking much and giving little. They were quick to claim that others were not doing enough to justify better concessions from Canada. This habit of mind was so deeply ingrained by the time of the Kennedy Round (1964-7) that it could not be reversed. When the United States, EC, and others made significant concessions, Canadian officials convinced themselves and their ministers that Canada's manufacturing sector was too fragile to adjust to more competition. In 1948, Canadian tariffs were on average lower than those of the United States and many European countries. By the end of the Kennedy Round, they were among the highest in the industrialized world. The Canadian economy remained more sheltered than those of the United States and Europe. This strategy may have been good short-term politics, but proved to be poor long-term economics.

Thus, while the Canadian economy boomed, it did not become more outwardly oriented. For the first three postwar decades, the Canadian economy remained at roughly the same level of international integration. Foreign direct investment in Canada, largely by American firms, helped to ensure that most of the goods Canadians consumed were produced at home. Canadian exports continued to be heavily concentrated in the resource sector, although some progress was made in upgrading some of these resources in Canada before exporting them to world markets. Canadian trade policy contributed to this pattern. Through the first six rounds of GATT negotiations, Canada zealously sought market access for its resource-based exports, but maintained high levels of protection for its manufacturing sector. The result was an inwardly focused, foreign-dominated manufacturing sector and an outwardly focused, also foreign-dominated resource sector. Canadians' main source of manufactured goods remained the United States, and Americans became Canada's best customers. The United Kingdom's economic tailspin made it an increasingly unreliable trading partner, while the rest of Europe never developed into the market Canadians had optimistically expected. Similarly, Asian and Latin American markets turned out to be disappointing for all but a narrow range of resource products.

The GATT's rules-based system proved ideally suited to the requirements of a medium-sized country like Canada, heavily dependent on trade with larger countries.

To work, however, the GATT required that the larger countries with which Canada traded also adhere to the rules. The fact that respect for the rules did not always prevail undermined Canadian confidence in the system. Canadian officials learned to be wary of the degree of US commitment to the rules. The agricultural sector, for example, a critical component of Canada's export economy, was virtually taken out of the GATT at US insistence. Congressional ambivalence about the GATT further eroded confidence, as did US willingness to resort to power politics through voluntary export restraint agreements and other devices. The US rediscovery of trade remedies in the 1970s and their consolidation into the GATT codes in the Tokyo Round (1973-9) deepened the conviction that trade relations with the United States could not be managed solely on the basis of the GATT, and that conviction led to the negotiation of a bilateral free-trade agreement (FTA). Canada's most successful trade agreement with the United States prior to the FTA, the 1965 Auto Pact, had been negotiated outside the GATT and enjoyed at best an uneasy status under the GATT rules.

Canadian anxiety about the depth of commitment of its principal trading partners to the multilateral system of rules was further complicated by the emergence of the European Community and the decision by the United Kingdom to cast its lot with Europe rather than remain an independent player. Like the United States, the EC soon exhibited the ambivalence of a large player and was not averse to twisting the rules or helping to shape them to its purpose. Japan, once its economy fully recovered from wartime devastation, found even more ingenious ways to shelter its more vulnerable sectors from GATT-mandated international competition. Many developing countries practised a form of economic determinism that presaged a wait of many years before their economies might develop into reliable markets.

In these circumstances, it is not surprising that Canadian trade policy during the GATT's formative years involved a deft mix of rhetorical adherence to GATT theology and a hard-nosed determination to do what was politically necessary. Nevertheless, over the years, that theology had a continuing impact on Canadian attitudes, values, and even practices. Other countries similarly maintained the faith, even if they did not always practise it. Ultimately, the end of the Uruguay Round (1986-94) and the establishment of the World Trade Organization not only upheld that basic faith, but reinforced it with a much stronger, more detailed, and more extensive catechism.

By 1980, despite a reluctance to take full advantage of the GATT's opportunities, the value of Canada's merchandise exports had reached more than a quarter of Canada's GDP, including cars and parts traded under the terms of the 1965 Canada-US Auto Pact. In nominal terms, Canadian merchandise exports grew at a steady 14.9 percent over the period 1968 to 1981, or 4.9 percent in constant 1971 dollars, with motor vehicles and other end-products growing at more than 7 percent annually in real terms. An increasing number of firms and sectors were prepared to compete internationally by exporting to foreign markets. Even more firms, however, were finding that they had to compete at home, as tariff and other barriers reached levels that could no longer guarantee them the home market. The trade dependence of the Canadian economy was widening, and the need to adjust was more pressing. Trade policy needed to adapt to these new circumstances.

In response, the government took steps that significantly narrowed the gap between Canadian faith and practice. Upon accepting that there needed to be serious adjustments in the Canadian economy, governments and businesses cooperated in making Canada a more open and more competitive economy. They anchored this new orientation in the Canada-US Free Trade Agreement, which provided both the goad of greater competition at home and the reward of more open and secure access to a large market. The foundations laid over the previous three decades made this step both politically and economically less risky. The sure knowledge that a structure of rules and procedures guaranteed profitable returns in other markets if Canada opened its own market generated the assurance that was lacking in earlier years. It made Canadian trade practitioners less cautious and more willing to act on their faith. The benefits were also evident. Canada became better placed to compete in a global economy even if it continued to depend more and more on trade with its giant neighbour to the south.

The results exceeded all expectations. Over the course of the 1990s, Canada experienced one of the strongest periods of trade-led growth in its history. Merchandise exports to all sources more than doubled at market prices. Total trade – exports and imports, goods and services – hit $900 billion in 2000, rising from less than 50 to nearly 90 percent as a proportion of GNP. The United States accounted for the preponderance of this trade, as it had for most of the postwar years. In 2000, in nominal terms, two-way trade between Canada and the United States reached nearly $700 billion, the equivalent of almost 70 percent of Canadian GNP. Various factors contributed to this spurt in growth in the external sector, including the pull of the red-hot US economy and a favourable exchange rate, but the adjustments induced by freer trade in both production and consumption patterns played a significant role.

Behind these aggregate statistics lies the story of an economy becoming more outwardly oriented and diversified. Over the 1990s, Canada became steadily less dependent on exports of resources as knowledge-based sectors grew and chased markets in the United States and beyond. By the end of the decade, automotive products accounted for less than a quarter of total trade; resource-based products accounted for less than half. Industrial and agricultural machinery, aircraft and other transportation products, and consumer products accounted for nearly 30 percent of Canadian merchandise export sales. Additionally, sales of business services, software, and other knowledge-intensive products added billions to Canada's current account. As a further indication of Canada's growing integration into the North American economy and through that economy into the world economy, Canada has increased its foreign direct investment abroad, valued in 2000 at over

$779.3 billion, with foreign direct investment in Canada reaching a book value of $1,023 billion in 2000.[1]

Over the 1990s, Canadian participation in the global trade regime reached a new level of maturity. Canadians were more prepared to pursue opportunities and less reluctant to accept some of the risks of a more open economy. They successfully convinced the global community to adopt a stronger institutional basis for multilateral trade cooperation, and they were at the forefront in ensuring that the WTO evolved into a forum for the governance of a global economy. Nevertheless, for Canada, the trade relationship with the United States is and will remain the most important by a wide margin. A critical factor in any Canadian trade policy decision remains its impact on relations with the United States. Throughout the postwar years, multilateralism provided an efficient means for pursuing Canada's trade policy objectives, and not least for improving the Canada-US relationship. The importance of that relationship usually determined Canada's strategic choices: any policy

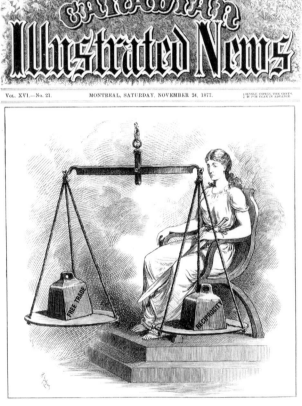

VOL. XVI.—No. 21.   MONTREAL, SATURDAY, NOVEMBER 24, 1877.   {SINGLE COPIES, TEN CENTS {$4 PER YEAR IN ADVANCE

Henry Julien, "This Looks Like Equality" 24 November 1877.

course or instrument that advanced Canadian interests in the US market and that strengthened Canada's capacity for managing the US relationship was worthy of pursuit, whether effected bilaterally, regionally, or multilaterally.

For Canadians, the need to be active in the future developments of the multilateral trading system cannot be overemphasized. Canada depends on and benefits from an effectively functioning trade and payments system. Its ability to play a constructive role is equally clear. But the capacity to ensure that Canadian values and priorities are reflected in the evolving regime requires that Canadians analyze the issues and make their contributions early in the process. As a relatively small player, that is when Canada is most likely to influence the content and course of a negotiation. In short, Canadians need to be quick, early, and creative. Canada's performance at the WTO suggests that this lesson has not been lost on those charged with this responsibility. Canada's continuing ability to meet this challenge will be an important determinant of our future economic welfare.

At the same time, the crucial role of the United States as an export market, as an investment partner, as the source of a wide range of competitive and attractive goods and services, and as the mainstay of our economic well-being ensures that relations with the United States are and will continue to be at the core of all Canadian trade policy choices. The FTA and NAFTA provided Canada and the United States with a strong institutional and legal basis for managing relations to their mutual benefit. Deepening integration suggests that further steps may be required to ensure the continued effectiveness of the North American regime.

Canada's painfully learned but increasingly effective tradecraft has taught Canadians well and prepared ministers and officials alike for the challenges of a much more integrated and more competitive global economy and for even deeper integration with the United States. The history of the past century and a half suggests that Canada-US trade and investment relations provide the dominant theme in Canada's economic development. It also suggests that Canadians – and Americans – have benefited from joint efforts to find mutually acceptable ways to best share the continent. That is likely to remain a theme and a lesson for the future as well.

NOTES

Chapter 1: Trade Policy and Economic Development

1   In a March 1999 Ekos poll, for example, most respondents felt either indifferent (25 percent) or positive and optimistic (52 percent) about globalization, and similarly about trade liberalization (more than 70 percent described themselves as either indifferent or optimistic and confident that liberalization will be rewarding for Canada). Nearly half of those polled believed that trade had contributed to Canadian technology development and innovation, and increased jobs, while fewer than a quarter expressed concerns about the impact of trade on cultural identity. Interestingly, although Canadians continue to believe that the government should not allow trade agreements to compromise social and environmental programs, only a quarter of respondents placed cultural and national identity issues near the top of their concerns (Ekos Research Associates, "Canadian Public Opinion: International Trade Issues 1999" [presented to a multistakeholder consultation hosted by the minister for international trade, 20 May 1999]). Another Ekos poll taken in spring 2001 indicated that while 58 percent of Canadians did not expect Canada to join the United States in the foreseeable future, only 22 percent did not anticipate the evolution of deeper North American economic integration over the same period (Tom Arnold, "Almost Half Foresee Canada, U.S. in Union within a Decade," *National Post*, 4 June 2001, A1). Liberal pollster Michael Marzolini told a Liberal caucus meeting in Edmonton that 85 percent of Canadians support closer trade and economic ties between Canada and the United States and 75 percent would support closer social and cultural connections. He cautioned, however, that Canadians continue to be allergic to such words as "integration" and "harmonization" (Juliet O'Neil, "'Integration' Talk with U.S. Risky: Pollster," *Ottawa Citizen*, 24 August 2001, A1). These findings were confirmed by a smaller National Post/COMPAS poll that found that 64 percent of Canadians want to see a freer flow of goods and services across the border (Joseph Brown, "64% Want Freer Border for Trade," *National Post*, 25 August 2001, A1). Polling as recent as August 2001 continues to confirm this assessment. A broader assessment of public attitudes to international trade and trade agreements can be found in Matthew Mendelsohn and Robert Wolfe, "Probing the Aftermyth of Seattle: Canada Public Opinion on International Trade 1980-2000" (paper prepared for the National Policy Research Conference, Ottawa, 1 December 2000).

2   David Henderson, *Innocence and Design: The Influence of Economic Ideas and Policy* (Oxford: Basil Blackwell, 1986), provides an excellent introduction to basic economic concepts and issues. An equally elegant, if more technically demanding, survey of popular misconceptions about international trade can be found in Jagdish Bhagwati, *Protectionism* (Cambridge: MIT Press, 1988). Bhagwati provides a more optimistic assessment than does Henderson of the ability of modern democratic governments to overcome the handicaps imposed by deeply engrained mercantilism. Patrick Luciani, *What Canadians Believe, but Shouldn't, about Their Economy* (Don Mills, ON: Addison-Wesley, 1993), provides a more general and easily read survey of basic economic concepts and the myths that surround them. Paul Krugman, the dean of modern trade economists, provides excellent rebuttals to current economic illiteracy in such books as *Pop Internationalism* (Cambridge: MIT Press, 1995) and *The Accidental Theorist and Other Dispatches from the Dismal Science* (Cambridge: MIT Press, 1998).

3   See Martin Wolf, "A European Perspective," in *Perspectives on a U.S.-Canadian Free Trade Agreement*, ed. Robert M. Stern, Philip H. Trezise, and John Whalley (Washington: Brookings Institution, 1987).

4 Judith Goldstein makes a persuasive case for the role of ideas and their implementation in laws and institutions in conditioning the choices available to future policy makers (*Ideas, Interests, and American Trade Policy* [Ithaca, NY: Cornell University Press, 1993]). Although set in the context of the evolution of US trade policy, her arguments for the "stickiness" of trade policy apply even more to conditions in Canada. Given the nature of Canada's parliamentary system and the large influence exercised by permanent officials, the policies adopted by Canadian politicians have had an even more precedential value than those pursued in the United States.

5 Richard Pomfret, *The Economic Development of Canada* (Toronto: Methuen, 1981), 1.

6 Goldstein, *Ideas, Interests, and Policy,* 238.

Chapter 2: The Old Mercantilism

1 In addition to the standard histories of early Canada and of Canadian economic development, a good and readable survey of the fishery and its contribution to early Canadian economic development can be found in Michael Bliss, *Northern Enterprise: Five Centuries of Canadian Business* (Toronto: McClelland and Stewart, 1987).

2 See Samuel Eliot Morison, *The European Discovery of America: The Northern Voyages A.D. 500-1600* (New York: Oxford, 1971), for a discussion of various claims and counterclaims involving the first European contacts with the North American continent. For Parkhurst, specifically, see pp. 478-9.

3 There are numerous early and detailed studies of the fur trade. Many of these have been found wanting by modern scholarship. For good and readable synopses of modern views, see Bliss, *Northern Enterprise,* and Kenneth Norrie and Douglas Owram, *A History of the Canadian Economy* (Toronto: Harcourt Brace Jovanovich, 1991).

4 In *A Social History of Canada* (Toronto: Penguin Books, 1988), George Woodcock provides a compelling portrait of the difficult life led by these early Canadian pioneers. See also Barry Gough, *First across the Continent: Sir Alexander Mackenzie* (Toronto: McClelland and Stewart, 1997), for a description of the motives and ambitions of some of the fur traders and the companies they founded.

5 For a full discussion of sixteenth- and seventeenth-century ideas of trade and trade policy, see Douglas A. Irwin, *Against the Tide: An Intellectual History of Free Trade* (Princeton: Princeton University Press, 1996), chapters 1-4.

6 Philip W. von Hornick, "Austria over All if She Only Will," reprinted in Arthur Eli Monroe, *Early Economic Thought* (Cambridge: Harvard University Press, 1925), 223-5.

7 Quoted in Klaus E. Knorr, *British Colonial Theories 1570-1870* (Toronto: University of Toronto Press, 1944), 85-6.

8 Contemporary theories justifying colonial development are reviewed in great detail ibid. See also Irwin, *Against the Tide.*

9 J. Steven Watson, *The Reign of George III* (Oxford: Clarendon Press, 1960), 14.

10 For an assessment of these problems within the context of British history, see ibid., 173ff.

11 This is the main thesis developed in Donald Creighton's classic study, *The Empire of the St. Lawrence* (Toronto: Macmillan, 1956).

12 Quoted in J.B. Brebner, *North Atlantic Triangle: The Interplay of Canada, the United States and Great Britain* (Toronto: Ryerson Press, 1945), 69.

13 See A.G. Kenwood and A.L. Lougheed, *The Growth of the International Economy, 1820-1980: An Introductory Text* (London: George Allen and Unwin, 1983), 21-37, for an account of the growth of an international economy in the nineteenth century.

14 Douglas Irwin points out that some of Smith's ideas had been advanced before, but Smith dealt with them comprehensively as part of a complete system, and it is Smith who is rightly credited with the establishment of modern economic analysis. See Irwin, *Against the Tide,* chapters 3-5.

15 Adam Smith, *An Inquiry into the Nature and Causes of the Wealth of Nations* (London: Methuen, 1961), vol. 2, 179.

16 Knorr, *British Colonial Theories,* 10ff.

17 Adam Smith, *The Wealth of Nations,* quoted in Samuel Hollander, *The Economics of Adam Smith* (Toronto: University of Toronto Press, 1973), 273.

18 John Kenneth Galbraith in his *Economics in Perspective: A Critical History* (Boston: Houghton Mifflin, 1987) explains the extent to which economic theories reflect prevailing practice and values and are not based on immutable laws of nature. By the turn of the century, *The Wealth of Nations* had gone through eight editions in Britain and had been translated into virtually every European language. Its ideas had come to dominate thinking about economic issues. See Paul Bairoch, *Economics and World History: Myths and Paradoxes* (Chicago: University of Chicago Press, 1993), 17.

19 Nathan Rosenberg and L.E. Birdzell, Jr., *How the West Grew Rich: The Economic Transformation of the Industrial World* (New York: Basic Books, 1986), provides a good introduction to the institutional and technological developments that were critical to the growth of industry and international trade. Similar arguments can be found in David S. Landes, *The Unbound Prometheus: Technological Change and Industrial Development in Western Europe from 1750 to the Present* (Cambridge: Cambridge University Press, 1972), as well as in his *The Wealth and Poverty of Nations: Why Some Are So Rich and Some So Poor* (New York: W.W. Norton, 1998).

20 See Craufurd D.W. Goodwin, *Canadian Economic Thought: The Political Economy of a Developing Nation 1814-1914* (Durham, NC: Duke University Press, 1961), and Robin Neill, *A History of Canadian Economic Thought* (London: Routledge, 1991), for discussions of early Canadian thinking on economic issues.

21 Judith Goldstein, in *Ideas, Interests, and American Trade Policy* (Ithaca, NY: Cornell University Press, 1993), traces the development of both free trade and protectionist ideas in the United States during the nineteenth century and details the influence of these ideas on US policy developments. Much of this thinking south of the border also influenced ideas and policy in Canada over the course of the nineteenth and early twentieth centuries.

22 Quoted in Peter Burroughs, *British Attitudes towards Canada, 1822-1849* (Scarborough, ON: Prentice-Hall, 1971), 11.

23 Quoted ibid., 12.

24 Orville J. McDiarmid, *Commercial Policy in the Canadian Economy* (Cambridge: Harvard University Press, 1946).

25 On Britain's conversion to free trade, see Kenwood and Lougheed, *Growth of the International Economy*, 73-80; and Paul Bairoch, "European Trade Policy 1815-1914," in Peter Mathias and Sidney Pollard, *The Cambridge Economic History of Europe* (Cambridge: Cambridge University Press, 1989).

26 Norrie and Owram, *History of the Canadian Economy*, 109.

27 These themes are explored in considerable detail in Ben Forster, *A Conjunction of Interests: Business, Politics and Tariffs 1825-1879* (Toronto: University of Toronto Press, 1986). See also J.M.S. Careless, *The Union of the Canadas: The Growth of Canadian Institutions 1841-1857* (Toronto: McClelland and Stewart, 1967).

28 For a classic statement of the staples theory, see W.A. Mackintosh, "Economic Factors in Canadian History," reproduced in *Approaches to Canadian History*, ed. Carl Berger (Toronto: University of Toronto Press, 1967). See also William L. Marr and Donald G. Paterson, *Canada: An Economic History* (Toronto: Macmillan, 1980), chapters 3 and 4; and Neill, *History of Canadian Economic Thought*, chapter 8.

29 On the early Canadian timber trade, see Bliss, *Northern Enterprise*, 130-40; Norrie and Owram, *History of the Canadian Economy*, 145-50; and Marr and Paterson, *Canada: An Economic History*, 61-73.

30 Douglas McCalla, "The Wheat Staple and Upper Canadian Development," in *Interpreting Canada's Past*, ed. J. M. Bumsted, vol. 1, *Before Confederation* (Toronto: Oxford University Press, 1986), 185-6.

31 On the Canadian wheat economy of the early nineteenth century, see Norrie and Owram, *History of the Canadian Economy*, 174-85; Marr and Paterson, *Canada: An Economic History*, 73-116; and McCalla, " Wheat Staple," 184-95.

32 The importance of the St. Lawrence water route is analyzed in Norrie and Owram, *History of the Canadian Economy*, 185-93.

33 See Donald C. Masters, *The Reciprocity Treaty of 1854* (Toronto: McClelland and Stewart, Carleton Library reprint, 1963); and Marr and Paterson, *Canada: An Economic History,* 117-48.
34 Quoted in Burroughs, *British Attitudes towards Canada,* 17.
35 Quoted in Forster, *Conjunction of Interests,* 14.
36 The detail of early colonial tariff making can be gleaned from McDiarmid, *Commercial Policy,* 34-60; and Forster, *Conjunction of Interests,* 13-32.
37 The British Possessions Act of 1842 was the last imperial act to set tariff levels for the colonies, mostly at sharply reduced levels from previous acts. The colonies added their own duties at differing rates, which varied from relatively low rates in PEI to higher rates in the United Provinces of Canada (see table 2.2). See McDiarmid, *Commercial Policy,* 51-2.

Chapter 3: Reciprocity and Preferences
1 John H. Young, *Canadian Commercial Policy* (Ottawa: Queen's Printer, 1957), 22.
2 See Richard Pomfret, *The Economic Development of Canada* (Toronto: Methuen, 1981), 69; and Ben Forster, *A Conjunction of Interests: Business, Politics and Tariffs 1825-1879* (Toronto: University of Toronto Press, 1986), 32-3.
3 Detailed discussions of the commercial policy issues of this period can be found in two minor classics of Canadian historiography: Donald C. Masters, *The Reciprocity Treaty of 1854* (Toronto: McClelland and Stewart, Carleton Library reprint, 1963); and Gilbert N. Tucker, *The Canadian Commercial Revolution 1845-1851* (Toronto: McClelland and Stewart, Carleton Library reprint, 1964). Also of interest but not as readily available is Charles C. Tansill, *The Canadian Reciprocity Treaty of 1854* (Baltimore: Johns Hopkins Press, 1922). Forster, *Conjunction of Interests,* contains a modern and very satisfactory treatment of the issues based on a detailed examination of contemporary records. M. Cross, ed., *Free Trade, Annexation and Reciprocity, 1846-1854* (Toronto: Holt, Rinehart and Winston, 1971) provides a collection of contemporary newspaper clippings.
4 Isaac Buchanan, for example, first pursued this option. See Forster, *Conjunction of Interests,* 22.
5 See ibid., 22-3; and Craufurd D.W. Goodwin, *Canadian Economic Thought: The Political Economy of a Developing Nation 1814-1914* (Durham, NC: Duke University Press, 1961), 59-68. Judith Goldstein, *Ideas, Interests, and American Trade Policy* (Ithaca, NY: Cornell University Press, 1993), provides a thorough and convincing account of the role of ideas in the development of American trade policy, setting out in considerable detail the interaction between early thinking about trade and related economic issues and the development of trade policy.
6 See Forster, *Conjunction of Interests,* 25-8; and Goodwin, *Canadian Economic Thought,* 43-59.
7 See Pomfret, *Economic Development of Canada,* 75-7; and Forster, *Conjunction of Interests,* 29.
8 See Pomfret, *Economic Development of Canada,* 72-3; and Forster, *Conjunction of Interests,* 31.
9 For a discussion of the early development of US trade policy, see Alfred E. Eckes, Jr., *Opening America's Market: U.S. Foreign Trade Policy Since 1776* (Chapel Hill: University of North Carolina Press, 1995), 1-27. The issues are also covered from a more analytical point of departure in Goldstein, *Ideas, Interests, and Policy,* 23-80. She concludes, "In the seventy-five years between the adoption of the Constitution and the Civil War, American commercial policy evolved from traditional mercantilism, to a quasi-liberal emphasis on free trade, and finally, following the war, to protectionism. This transformation did not result from objective shifts in America's national interest but, rather, reflected new beliefs about America's place in the world and altered perceptions about the efficacy of particular economic policies. In general, this period was characterized by the increasing legitimacy of protectionist ideas among the attentive public and government officials" (23).
10 See Paul Bairoch, *Economics and World History: Myths and Paradoxes* (Chicago: University of Chicago Press, 1993), 34-5.
11 Eckes, *Opening America's Market,* 26-7.
12 John M. Dobson, *Two Centuries of Tariffs: The Background and Emergence of the U.S. International Trade Commission* (Washington: United States International Trade Commission, 1976), 13.
13 Quoted in Eckes, *Opening America's Market,* 25.

14 The story of the negotiations can be found in Masters, *Reciprocity Treaty of 1854*, and Forster, *Conjunction of Interests*, 23-32. It is also told in amusing detail by Colin Robertson, "1854: Plus ça change, plus c'est la même chose," *bout de papier* 5, 2 (1987): 4-21.

15 The text of the agreement is reproduced in Masters, *Reciprocity Treaty of 1854*, 140-4.

16 Notes Ben Forster, "After a decade of tumult in the British North American political economy, a broad course had been decided upon. Markets for colonial raw or partly processed products seemingly had been retained or gained, and the protection that existed for colonial manufactures had not been lost" (*Conjunction of Interests*, 31).

17 See Eckes, *Opening America's Market*, 25-6 and 67, for a US perspective on the treaty. While Canadian exports had flourished, US exports had not, in part due to the disruptions of the Civil War; a substantial US merchandise trade surplus turned into a significant deficit during the years the agreement was in force.

18 See J.M.S. Careless, *The Union of the Canadas: The Growth of Canadian Institutions 1841-1857* (Toronto: McClelland and Stewart, 1967), for a general description of prosperity in the colonies during this period.

19 Careless, *Union of the Canadas*, chapter 8 provides a good account of the railway boom of the 1850s.

20 See L. Officer and L. Smith, "The Canadian-American Reciprocity Treaty of 1855 to 1866," *Journal of Economic History* 28 (December 1968): 598-623, for a generally sceptical assessment of the agreement's impact.

21 See Forster, *Conjunction of Interests*, 54.

22 Quoted in Edward Porritt, *Sixty Years of Protection in Canada* (London: Macmillan, 1906), 180-1.

23 Pomfret, *Economic Development of Canada*, 26.

24 Forster, *Conjunction of Interests*, 18-19.

25 Quoted ibid., 45-6.

26 Quoted ibid., 45.

27 Alfred Dubuc, "The Decline of Confederation and the New Nationalism," in *Nationalism in Canada*, ed. Peter Russell (Toronto: McGraw-Hill Ryerson, 1966), 17.

28 In July 1865, for example, at a convention of boards of trade in Detroit, American delegates expressed strong support for annexation (Forster, *Conjunction of Interests*, 57).

29 The 1890 US census identified a million US residents as Canadian-born, at a time that Canada itself had not yet attained a population of five million. Throughout the second half of the century, Canada had a net migration deficit virtually every year. See O.J. Firestone, *Canada's Economic Development, 1867-1952* (London: Bowes and Bowes, 1958), 240-1.

30 The various missions and the politicking behind them are described in Forster, *Conjunction of Interests*, 52-67.

31 For the Confederation debates and the important role of the Reciprocity Treaty, see Donald Creighton, *The Road to Confederation* (Toronto: Macmillan, 1964).

32 Forster, *Conjunction of Interests*, 80; and J.L. Granatstein and Norman Hillmer, *For Better or for Worse: Canada and the United States to the 1990s* (Toronto: Copp Clark Pitman, 1991), 9-13.

33 See Goodwin, *Canadian Economic Thought*, 63-4 and 116-20.

34 Forster, *Conjunction of Interests*, 130-3.

35 Quoted in Eckes, *Opening America's Market*, 30.

36 Quoted ibid. See also Goldstein, *Ideas, Interests, and Policy*, 73-8, for discussion of the development of protectionist ideas as the basis of Republican policy in the years immediately before and after the Civil War.

37 J.L. Morison, *The Eighth Earl of Elgin: A Chapter in Nineteenth-Century Diplomatic History* (London: Hodder and Stoughton, 1928), 157.

38 For a discussion of the retreat from free trade during the period 1870 to 1914, see Paul Bairoch, "European Trade Policy 1815-1914," *The Cambridge Economic History of Europe*, ed. Peter Mathias and Sidney Pollard (Cambridge: Cambridge University Press, 1989). Gerard Curzon, *Multilateral Commercial Diplomacy* (London: Michael Joseph, 1965), also places in perspective the fall and rise of nineteenth-century European protectionism.

39 Notes Paul Bairoch, "Around 1875, at the height of economic liberalism in Europe, whereas in Continental Europe the average level of duties on manufactured goods was 9-12% the rate in the United States was 40-50%. To these figures one must still add the natural protection resulting from geographical distance of European exporters" (*Economics and World History*, 35). By this time, US population and productive capacity placed it on a par with Britain, France, and other Continental powers. The infant industry argument of the early years of the century no longer had any basis in fact.

40 See Eckes, *Opening America's Market*, 28-99, for discussion of the consolidation of US protectionism in the years after the Civil War and the unsuccessful efforts to negotiate reciprocal trade agreements in the period leading up to the First World War. Eckes concludes that "from 1860 to 1932 Republicans preached and practiced a nationalistic trade policy that was intended to develop the American market and advance the commercial interests of domestic producers and workers" (31).

41 Some problems seem never to disappear. Canadian agricultural trade policy continues to be complicated by exactly the same conflict. Policies to protect Eastern dairy and poultry producers continue to undermine efforts to gain market access for Western grain and meat producers.

42 Forster, *Conjunction of Interests*, 80.

43 See Firestone, *Canada's Economic Development*, 140-70, for analysis of the prevailing economic conditions in Canada in the first thirty years of Confederation.

44 Firestone estimates that, in nominal terms, Canada's GNP increased by a factor of about 15 between 1870 and 1950 (ibid., table 88, 280). In constant dollars and on a per capita basis, the growth was in the order of 400 percent. Since then, Canada's output has more than tripled, indicating a growth in the size of the economy of about 5,000 percent, or a per capita increase in real terms of about 1,000 percent.

45 See John H. Dales, "Protection, Immigration and Canadian Nationalism," and R. Craig Brown, "The Nationalism of the National Policy," in *Nationalism in Canada*, ed. Russell, for a discussion of both the economics and nationalism of the National Policy.

46 In 1872, Macdonald wrote to T.C. Patteson, editor of the newly established Conservative *Toronto Mail*, "The paper must go in for a National Policy in Tariff matters, and while avoiding the word 'protection' must advocate a readjustment of the tariff in such a manner as incidentally to aid our manufacturing and industrial interest" (quoted in Brown, "National Policy," 156).

47 Forster, *Conjunction of Interests*, 68 ff.

48 Ibid., 68-77 and 80-5, provides the detail of tariff making during Macdonald's first government.

49 Comparing tariff rates over a period of more than a hundred years is not an easy task and can be somewhat misleading. Direct comparisons for a particular product would in most instances present an accurate picture, but aggregating tariffs introduces various distortions. The first involves conversion of specific rates to *ad valorem* rates in order to arrive at an arithmetic average. The average rate is usually considered to be the arithmetic average of all the rates, without taking any account of actual trade levels. Second, the overall incidence of the tariff reflects duties collected on all imports, taking into account any rebates and drawbacks. Finally, the rate can be expressed in terms of average duties collected on dutiable products. All of these averages are biased in one direction or the other. For example, should most rates be over 200 percent, very few duties will be collected since there is unlikely to be much trade. Should raw materials enter duty-free while manufactures enter at very high rates, it is likely that the overall incidence of the tariff will be very low, initially suggesting that all tariffs are low. Finally, tariff escalation, that is, higher rates at higher stages of processing, further distorts the picture. At the time of Confederation, when the tariff was not greatly differentiated, high average rates usually translated into a high overall incidence. As the tariff became a more sophisticated instrument of protection, however, drawing a general picture becomes increasingly complex. The Economic Council of Canada, in its 1975 study of free trade, produced an interesting chart comparing historical average tariffs, on a duty-collected basis, of the United States and Canada (*Looking Outward: A New Trade Strategy for Canada* [Ottawa: Supply and Services, 1975], 5).

50 See Eckes, *Opening America's Market*, 47.

51 The issue, however, had been debated for more than a generation. As early as the 1840s, Francis
    Hincks briefly toyed with the idea of a "national policy" based on a protective tariff, but aban-
    doned it as inconsistent with his strong free-trade principles. The leading champion of a pro-
    tectionist national policy throughout this period, Isaac Buchanan, newspaper editor and member
    of the legislature of the United Provinces, also favoured most of the elements of what became
    the National Policy. He was one of the earliest and most active members of the Association for
    the Promotion of Industry in Canada – the forerunner of the Canadian Manufacturers' Asso-
    ciation – and a tireless crusader for protection. In 1869, Finance Minister John Rose threatened
    a national policy if US politicians were not prepared to give serious consideration to renewed
    reciprocity. See Forster, *Conjunction of Interests,* 36-9 and 70ff; and Goodwin, *Canadian Eco-
    nomic Thought,* 49-51.
52 See Brown, "National Policy," and R. Craig Brown, *Canada's National Policy 1883-1900: A Study in
    Canadian-American Relations* (Princeton: Princeton University Press, 1964), for a discussion of
    the myth and reality of the National Policy.
53 See Granatstein and Hillmer, *For Better or for Worse,* 16-19; and Forster, *Conjunction of Interests,*
    201-6.
54 An *ad valorem* rate is calculated as a percentage of the customs value of the product whereas a
    specific rate is based on a specified charge for a given quantity of the product.
55 The nominal rate is that stated in the tariff schedule and collected by the customs officer. The
    effective rate of protection afforded by that tariff, however, depends on the price effect of the tariff,
    the degree of price elasticity of the product in question, and the levels of protection afforded to
    related products at earlier and later stages of production and their price elasticities. Thus a rela-
    tively low nominal rate on forged iron, in circumstances where iron ore and coking coal can be
    imported free of duty, may encourage the establishment of forging facilities and discourage the
    import of forged iron, exercising much more effective protection than suggested by the low nomi-
    nal rate.
56 House of Commons, *Debates,* vol. 1, 7 March 1878, 854 and 862.
57 Quoted in Earle Gray, *Free Trade, Free Canada: How Free Trade Will Make Canada Stronger*
    (Woodville, ON: Canadian Speeches, 1988), 11.
58 See Brown, *Canada's National Policy,* particularly chapters 5, 7, 8, and 12. The pattern in political
    positions has a parallel in the United States. Until recently, the Republicans favoured protection
    and the Democrats preferred open markets. In both countries, however, these historic positions
    have tended to reverse themselves in recent years, although populist wings in both parties have
    flirted with economic isolationism. The recent changes in orientation of the mainstream parties
    were in their attitudes to protection, not to business. In many ways it is the changing attitude of
    business and the changing nature of protection that have caused the politicians to alter their
    arguments. A century ago, progressive or reform politicians in Canada and the United States ar-
    gued that tariffs were regressive, harmed consumers, retarded competition, and gave manufactur-
    ers a privileged position at the expense of society as a whole. Today, as the tariff has ceased to be a
    major issue and the dominant barriers to trade have become subsidies and government regula-
    tions, politicians of the left argue that removing these barriers to trade will encourage too much
    competition at the expense of other values. A century ago manufacturers successfully convinced
    politicians in power that they had to have protection; today, business is successfully arguing that
    they want less protection and less regulation of business affairs.
59 Granatstein and Hillmer, *For Better or for Worse,* 19.
60 Firestone, *Canada's Economic Development,* 149.
61 Edward Blake, letter to the *Toronto Globe,* 6 March 1891, quoted in R.G. Brown and M.E. Prang,
    Canadian Historical Documents: Confederation to 1949 (Scarborough, ON: Prentice-Hall, 1966), 33.
62 See Brown, "National Policy," 158.
63 David J. Bercuson, "Canada's Historic Search for Secure Markets," in *Free Trade: The Real Story,* ed.
    John Crispo (Toronto: Gage, 1988), 11.
64 Eckes, *Opening America's Market,* 37.
65 Ibid., 70-4.

66   Quoted by Charles H. Tupper, House of Commons, *Debates,* 29 May 1891, 584.
67   See J.L. Granatstein, *Yankee Go Home? Canadians and Anti-Americanism* (Toronto: HarperCollins, 1996), chapter 2, for a discussion of anti-Americanism and the election of 1891.
68   McKinley sought a provision that would open "new markets for the products of our country, by granting concessions to the products of other lands that we need and can not produce ourselves, and which do not involve any loss of labor to our own people, but tend to increase their employment" (quoted in Eckes, *Opening America's Market,* 75). While these efforts at opening markets to US exports suggest the development of a more balanced appreciation of US trade interests and a more nuanced approach to policy, the record suggests otherwise. As Judith Goldstein argues, "This period witnessed a new consensus on the merits of protectionism, even though the economic rationale for such a policy vanished" (*Ideas, Interests, and Policy,* 82).
69   Eckes, *Opening America's Market,* 75. See also Goldstein, *Ideas, Interests, and Policy,* 101-27, for an analysis of the legislative history of US trade policy in the 1890s. Goldstein provides convincing evidence of the extent to which Blaine and other Republican administration officials had no interest in opening the US market to greater competition; they saw reciprocity purely as a device for opening the markets of other nations to American exports.
70   Eckes, *Opening America's Market,* 75-7.
71   See Orville J. McDiarmid, *Commercial Policy in the Canadian Economy* (Cambridge: Harvard University Press, 1946), table 9, 182; and Douglas Annett, *British Preference in Canadian Commercial Policy* (Toronto: Ryerson, 1948), table 7, 42.
72   House of Commons, *Debates,* 22 April 1897, column 1106.
73   The impact was so marginal that for the whole period of the Laurier government, the average incidence of the duty on imports from Britain was higher than on imports from the United States.
74   For a strong imperialist view of the search for preferences, see the speeches of the Honourable George Foster, Macdonald's last finance minister, Conservative trade and finance critic during the Laurier years, and minister of trade and commerce under Robert Borden. Some are collected in a volume edited by Arnold Winterbotham, *Canadian Addresses of the Hon. George E. Foster* (Toronto: Bell and Cockburn, 1914).
75   For Cartwright's role, as well as the early history and contribution of the Department of Trade and Commerce, see O. Mary Hill, *Canada's Salesman to the World: The Department of Trade and Commerce 1892-1939* (Montreal: McGill-Queen's University Press, 1977).
76   These objectives are discussed by Ken Taylor, a Finance official in the 1930s, in "The Commercial Policy of Canada," in *Canadian Marketing Problems,* ed. Hubert R. Kemp (a contemporary Trade and Commerce official) (Toronto: University of Toronto Press, 1939). They are also considered in the Rowell-Sirois report (Donald Smiley, ed., *Rowell/Sirois Report* [Toronto: McClelland and Stewart, 1963]). For a recent official statement of these objectives, see Department of External Affairs, *Canadian Trade Policy for the 1980s: A Discussion Paper* (Ottawa: Supply and Services, 1983).
77   Quoted in Gray, *Free Trade, Free Canada,* 13.
78   Quoted in Porritt, *Sixty Years of Protection in Canada,* 437.
79   Clifford Sifton to James Fleming, 13 March 1897, quoted in Brown and Prang, *Confederation to 1949,* 34.
80   Robert Bothwell, Ian Drummond, and John English, *Canada 1900-1945* (Toronto: University of Toronto Press, 1987), 73. Unlike most general histories of Canada, this study provides a solid appreciation of the economic dimensions of Canada's development and the important role of policy in shaping that development.
81   The document is reproduced in Department of External Affairs, *Documents on Canadian External Relations,* vol. 1 (Ottawa: Supply and Services, 1977), 758-63.
82   The 1910-11 reciprocity negotiations and subsequent federal election have been studied in painstaking detail by Canadian historians. The standard work is L. Ethan Ellis, *Reciprocity 1911: A Study in Canadian-American Relations, 1875-1911* (New York: Greenwood Press for the Carnegie Endowment, 1939). It is also given detailed treatment in Robert Craig Brown and Ramsay Cook, *Canada 1896-1921: A Nation Transformed* (Toronto: McClelland and Stewart, 1974). In addition to its treatment in Granatstein, *Yankee Go Home?* chapter 2 and McDiarmid, *Commercial Policy,* 228-38, further

light is cast on specific details by Bill Dymond, "Free Trade, 1911 and All of That," *bout de papier* 5, 2 (1987): 22-5; Paul Stevens, "Reciprocity 1911: The Canadian Perspective," in *Canadian-American Free Trade: Historical, Political and Economic Dimensions,* ed. A.R. Riggs and Tom Velk (Halifax: Institute for Research on Public Policy, 1987), 9-21; and Riggs and Velk, "Reciprocity 1911: Through American Eyes," in the same volume, 23-31. Paul Stevens has also edited a collection of studies on the election of 1911 which concludes that the Conservatives were much better organized and financed and that more than reciprocity was at stake: *The 1911 General Election: A Study in Canadian Politics* (Toronto: Copp Clark, 1970).

83 The exchange of letters, some of Fielding's reports, and other documents can be found in External Affairs, *Documents,* vol. 1, 756-98. See also Eckes, *Opening America's Market,* 84.

84 The exchange of letters between Fielding and Knox setting out the terms of the arrangement is in External Affairs, *Documents,* vol. 1, 792-5.

85 Quoted in Bruce Hutchison, *Mr. Prime Minister 1867-1964* (Don Mills, ON: Longmans, 1964), 141.

86 Indeed, Fielding's success prompted US free traders to complain that the United States had been snookered into a deal that might serve Canadian interests but did nothing for the United States. What Canada in fact exported to the United States would be free; what the United States in fact exported would not be free. Subsequent analysis by the US Tariff Commission confirmed this. See Riggs and Velk, "Reciprocity 1911," 25-6.

87 See Brown, "National Policy," 157.

88 Quoted in Dymond, "Free Trade, 1911," 24.

89 Ibid.

90 Quoted in Dymond, "Free Trade, 1911," 25.

91 The duplicity of Bourassa's position can be appreciated by perusing a series of articles he prepared in February 1911 for *Le Devoir,* of which he was editor, analyzing the agreement and the arguments for and against it. They make a masterful case in favour of the agreement. The articles were subsequently translated and published in pamphlet form for English-speaking readers under the title *The Reciprocity Agreement and Its Consequences As Viewed from the Nationalist Standpoint* (Montreal: Le Devoir [1911]).

92 Quoted in Hutchison, *Mr. Prime Minister,* 142.

93 Quoted in Stevens, ed., *The 1911 General Election,* 220.

94 James Bryce, *Modern Democracies* (1921), quoted in Frank Underhill, "Some Reflections on the Liberal Tradition in Canada," in *Approaches to Canadian History,* ed. Carl Berger (Toronto: University of Toronto Press, 1967), 34-5.

Chapter 4: War, Depression, and Revolution

1 See Glen Williams, *Not for Export: Toward a Political Economy of Canada's Arrested Industrialization* (Toronto: McClelland and Stewart, expanded ed. 1986). While I agree with much of Williams' analysis of the consequences of some of the policy choices exercised by Canadian governments in the late nineteenth and early twentieth centuries, I do not share his views on their motives and available alternatives. Policy choices in government are less conscious, more constrained by external and internal circumstances, and more conditioned by earlier policy choices than he and other social science analysts are prepared to admit.

2 O.D. Skelton's description of the strength and potential of the Canadian economy in 1912 – that is, after some fifteen years of steady growth – provides compelling insight into Canada's growing self-confidence as a separate and independent economic entity. See Skelton, "General Economic History, 1867-1912," in vol. 9 of *Canada and Its Provinces: A History of the Canadian People and Their Institutions,* ed. Adam Shortt and Arthur G. Doughty (Toronto: T. and A. Constable at the Edinburgh University Press for the Publishers' Association of Canada, 1914).

3 The Underwood Tariff of 1913 marked the only time in the period 1861-1934 when there was a conscious effort to roll back high tariffs and provide a basis for the United States to adopt a more outward-looking policy that recognized that trade was a two-way affair. As newly elected President Woodrow argued, "All trade is two-sided. You can't sell everything and buy nothing. You can't establish any commercial relationships that aren't two-sided. And if America is to insist upon

selling everything and buy nothing, she will find that the rest of the world stands very cold and indifferent to her enterprise" (quoted in David A. Lake, *Power, Protection, and Free Trade* [Ithaca, NY: Cornell University Press, 1988], 157). Some analysts have concluded that the new policy could have ushered in an era of growth under US leadership. Unfortunately, the eruption of war the following year disrupted markets and nullified the opportunities provided by the new policy. The return of the Republicans in 1921 led to the Fordney-McCumber Tariff of 1922 based on more traditional concepts of protectionism and US unilateralism. See ibid., 148-60; and Judith Goldstein, *Ideas, Interest and American Trade Policy* (Ithaca, NY: Cornell University Press, 1993), 123-6.

4 House of Commons, *Debates*, 6 April 1914, 2452. Orville J. McDiarmid, *Commercial Policy in the Canadian Economy* (Cambridge: Harvard University Press, 1948), 255, notes that during the immediate prewar period, the Underwood Tariff reduced US rates to about 26 percent, while Canadian rates on US imports averaged 15 percent. British goods, despite the one-third preference, included more luxuries and attracted an average rate of 19.5 percent during this period.

5 Table 8 in Douglas R. Annett, *British Preference in Canadian Commercial Policy* (Toronto: Ryerson Press, 1948), compares the duties collected on dutiable imports from the United Kingdom and the United States. Annett shows that with the exception of 1896-8, the difference was usually less than 1 percentage point and often less than 0.5 percentage points. More duty-free items among imports from the United States meant that the overall incidence of the tariff on all US imports could be as much as 6 percentage points lower than on UK imports during this period.

6 McDiarmid, *Commercial Policy*, 249-51 and 346-55, for example, analyzes prices on agricultural machinery in Canada and the United States and the role of the tariff.

7 O. Mary Hill, *Canada's Salesman to the World: The Department of Trade and Commerce, 1892-1939* (Montreal: McGill-Queen's University Press, 1977), 187-203 and 249-69, provides some of the detail. See also the *Canada Year Book* for a running account of some of this activity for the period 1914-29. The yearbook, published continuously since 1884 and first known as *The Statistical Year-Book for Canada*, was originally published by the Department of Agriculture and then from 1918 to 1971 by the Dominion Bureau of Statistics.

8 See J. Harvey Perry, *Taxes, Tariffs, & Subsidies: A History of Canadian Fiscal Development* (Toronto: University of Toronto Press, 1955), vol. 2, table 6, 624-7, for a breakdown of the sources of government revenue.

9 J.L. Granatstein, *How Britain's Weakness Forced Canada into the Arms of the United States* (Toronto: University of Toronto Press, 1989), 17-18.

10 C.P. Stacey, *Canada and the Age of Conflict*, vol. 1, *1867-1921* (Toronto: Macmillan, 1977).

11 Quoted in Robert Craig Brown and Ramsay Cook, *Canada 1896-1921: A Nation Transformed* (Toronto: McClelland and Stewart, 1974), 333.

12 The poet F.R. Scott captured the essence of King's talent for equivocation in his epitaph on King's long political career:

He skillfully avoided what was wrong
Without saying what was right.
And never let his on the one hand
Know what his on the other hand was doing.

Quoted in J.L. Granatstein and Norman Hillmer, *For Better or for Worse: Canada and the United States to the 1990s* (Toronto: Copp Clark Pitman, 1991), 79.

13 In terms of the development of Canadian trade policy, the whole period from 1921 to 1930 can be treated as one government, even though the Conservatives enjoyed a few months of office in mid-decade during the King-Byng constitutional crisis. Fielding had a stroke at the end of 1923 but did not retire until 1925, to be replaced first by James Robb and then Charles Dunning.

14 See C.P. Stacey, *Canada and the Age of Conflict*, vol. 2, *1921-1948: The Mackenzie King Era* (Toronto: University of Toronto Press, 1981); Ian Drummond, *British Economic Policy and the Empire 1919-1939* (London: George Allen and Unwin, 1972); and Max Beloff, *Imperial Sunset*, vol. 2, *Dream of Commonwealth 1921-42* (New York: Sheridan House, 1989), for descriptions of imperial policy and Canada's role and interests in the Empire.

15 See John F. Hilliker, *Canada's Department of External Affairs,* vol. 1, *The Early Years 1900-1946* (Montreal: McGill-Queen's University Press, 1990), for the establishment of the Department of External Affairs.

16 See Stacey, *Mackenzie King Era,* for an analysis of the development of Canadian foreign policy and its long-time Janus-like character. Most Canadians saw themselves as British subjects living in a self-governing dominion that was part of the British Empire. To Conservatives like Borden, benefits lay in emphasizing the British connection; to Liberals like King, more benefit was likely to be found in cultivating greater independence and self-government. The distance between these two seemingly incompatible poles, however, should not be exaggerated.

17 Granatstein and Hillmer, *For Better or for Worse,* 93-5.

18 For a discussion of the growth and importance of the wheat economy, see Kenneth Norrie and Douglas Owram, *A History of the Canadian Economy* (Toronto: Harcourt Brace Jovanovich, 1991), 321-33. Hill, *Canada's Salesman,* 187-204 and 249-70, discusses the interaction of wheat sales and trade policy during this period.

19 See Vernon C. Fowke, *Canadian Agricultural Policy: The Historical Pattern* (Toronto: University of Toronto Press, 1946); Vernon C. Fowke, *The National Policy and the Wheat Economy* (Toronto: University of Toronto Press, 1957); and Hill, *Canada's Salesman,* for some of the activities of the federal government in developing the Western grain trade.

20 See Paul Bairoch, "European Trade Policy 1815-1914," in Peter Mathias and Sidney Pollard, *The Cambridge Economic History of Europe* (Cambridge: Cambridge University Press, 1989), table 9, 76.

21 See Fowke, *Wheat Economy,* 72.

22 The figures are taken from Robert Bothwell, Ian Drummond, and John English, *Canada 1900-1945* (Toronto: University of Toronto Press, 1987), 217. See Norrie and Owram, *History of the Canadian Economy,* 441ff, for a more detailed description of the economic turbulence of this period.

23 See McDiarmid, *Commercial Policy,* 260ff, for the detail of Canadian trade and tariff policy in the 1920s.

24 See Bothwell, Drummond, and English, *Canada 1900-1945,* 225.

25 See Hill, *Canada's Salesman,* 271-91, for a description of these negotiating activities.

26 See below. Useful introductions to the growth of an international economy and the agreements that encouraged increased interdependence can be found in Richard Pomfret, *Unequal Trade: The Economics of Discriminatory Trade Policies* (Oxford: Basil Blackwell, 1988); and A.G. Kenwood and A.L. Lougheed, *The Growth of the International Economy, 1820-1980: An Introductory Text* (London: George Allen and Unwin, 1983).

27 The McKenna, Finance, and Key Industries Tariffs could all be justified on a basis other than protection, such as the requirements of war, the need to conserve shipping space, revenue needs, and national security, but the Safeguarding of Industries Act had no rationale but protection. Providing preferences to Empire goods further confirmed the fact that the United Kingdom had crossed the line. See Charles P. Kindleberger, "Commercial Policy between the Wars," in *Cambridge Economic History of Europe,* vol. 8, ed. Peter Mathias and Sidney Pollard (Cambridge: Cambridge University Press, 1989), 162.

28 An appreciation of the nature and depth of imperial feelings in Canada can be gleaned from the addresses to the Empire Club of Canada in Toronto, which from the beginning of the twentieth century has been a bastion of imperialism. The speeches are religiously transcribed and published every year in a handsome little red book.

29 Jan Tumlir, "Evolution of the Concept of International Economic Order 1914-1980," in *Changing Perceptions of Economic Policy,* ed. Frances Cairncross (London: Methuen, 1981).

30 A.J.P. Taylor, *English History 1914-1945* (Oxford: Clarendon Press, 1965), 321ff.

31 J.B. Condliffe, *The Reconstruction of World Trade* (New York: W.W. Norton, 1940), 145. See also the important lessons drawn from this experience by Charles P. Kindleberger in "Dominance and Leadership in the International Economy: Exploitation, Public Goods, and Free Rides," *International Studies Quarterly* 25, 2 (1981): 242-54, and expanded in *Power and Money: The Economics of International Politics and the Politics of International Economics* (New York: Basic Books, 1970).

32 J.M. Keynes, "National Self-Sufficiency," *The Yale Review,* June 1933, 758.

33 Jan Tumlir, *Protectionism: Trade Policy in Democratic Societies* (Washington: American Enterprise Institute, 1985), 20.

34 Gerard Curzon, *Multilateral Commercial Diplomacy* (London: Michael Joseph, 1965), 19. See also Bairoch, "European Trade Policy."

35 See Bairoch, "European Trade Policy"; and Kindleberger, "Commercial Policy between the Wars," for surveys of developments in European trade policy during this period.

36 On the League and Canadian policy toward it, see Richard Veatch, *Canada and the League of Nations* (Toronto: University of Toronto Press, 1975).

37 The work of the League is well summarized in League of Nations, *Commercial Policy in the Inter-war Period: International Proposals and National Policies* (Geneva: League of Nations, 1942). The findings were the result of solid analysis and greatly influenced those charged with planning for a new regime after the Second World War, both in terms of the direction in which the analysis pointed and of what it said about the impotence of League efforts.

38 Jan Tumlir concludes that "France's policy of commercial autonomy fatally compounded the problem that the American version of that policy [already] posed to Europe" (*Protectionism,* 24).

39 Notes Richard Pomfret, "Rather than marking a new dawn the late 1920s were a twilight phase in the 60-year trend towards discriminatory policies ... Between 1929 and 1939 government policies disrupted the flow of international trade, turned it increasingly into bilateral channels, and frequently determined which channels should be strengthened and which weakened" (*Unequal Trade,* 26 and 19).

40 Quoted in William Diebold Jr., *Bilateralism, Multilateralism and Canada* (New York: Council on Foreign Relations, 1988), 3-4.

41 Jacob Viner, "The Most-Favored-Nation Clause in American Commercial Treaties," reprinted in Viner, *International Economics* (Glencoe, IL: Free Press, 1954), 25.

42 Stephen Leacock, *Back to Prosperity: The Great Opportunity of the Empire Conference* (Toronto: Macmillan, 1932).

43 Jacob Viner, "The Tariff Question and the Economist," in Viner, *International Economics,* 117-18. Also reprinted in the same volume is a sympathetic treatment of the work of Frank Taussig: "Taussig's Contribution to the Theory of International Trade."

44 Viner, "The Tariff Question and the Economist," 109.

45 As Judith Goldstein, *Ideas, Interest and Policy,* demonstrates, respectable academic opinion in the United States had long been grounded in classic free-trade theory, with only a few universities and colleges maintaining any avowed protectionists in their economic departments. Nevertheless, the protectionist ideas of the nineteenth century had become so deeply institutionalized and engrained in American political discussion that it would take more than academic arguments to overcome them. What sparked the change were the disaster of the depression and the widely held conviction, in both political and academic circles, of the relationship between protectionism and depression. Further analysis of the development of US thinking about trade policy can be found in William B. Kelly, Jr., "Antecedents of Present Commercial Policy, 1922-1934," in *Studies in United States Commercial Policy,* ed. Kelly (Chapel Hill: University of North Carolina Press, 1963); and Edward S. Kaplan, *American Trade Policy, 1923-1995* (Westport, CT: Greenwood Press, 1996).

46 During the 1930s, especially after passage of the Statute of Westminster, the term Commonwealth began gradually to replace Empire, and imperial preferences gave way to Commonwealth or British preferences. In the Canadian tariff schedule, the official term was and remains British Preference, despite the fact that Britain itself, following entry into the Common Market, no longer enjoys the few remaining preferences. Only New Zealand and Australia now enjoy contractual rights to the preferences. For Commonwealth developing countries, the General Preferential Tariff often offers better terms of access. Most exports of the least developed members enter Canada duty-free.

47 The classic analysis of the events around the passage of the Smoot-Hawley Tariff Act is E.E. Schattschneider, *Politics, Pressures and the Tariff* (New York: Prentice-Hall, 1935).

48 Kaplan, *American Trade Policy,* 36.

49 J.L. Granatstein, "Free Trade between Canada and the United States: The Issue That Will Not Go Away," in *The Politics of Canada's Economic Relations with the United States*, ed. Denis Stairs and Gilbert R. Winham (Toronto: University of Toronto Press, 1985), 29.

50 McDiarmid, *Commercial Policy*, 273-4.

51 For Canada during the depression see A.E. Safarian, *The Canadian Economy in the Great Depression* (Toronto: University of Toronto Press, 1959). The evolution of Canadian trade policy can be traced in McDiarmid, *Commercial Policy*; Annett, *British Preference*; and W.A. Mackintosh, *The Economic Background of Dominion-Provincial Relations* (Toronto: McClelland and Stewart, 1964). Three departmental histories are also very useful: Hill, *Canada's Salesman*; Hilliker, *Department of External Affairs*; and Robert B. Bryce, *Maturing in Hard Times: Canada's Department of Finance through the Great Depression* (Montreal: McGill-Queen's University Press, 1986).

52 See Pomfret, *Unequal Trade*, table 2.1, 25.

53 See J.A. Stovel, *Canada in the World Economy* (Cambridge: Harvard University Press, 1959), 224ff; and McDiarmid, *Commercial Policy*, 306-21, for analyses of the protective effect of tariff administration in Canada during this period.

54 A good example of the rationale for comprehensive imperial preferences can be found in a booklet prepared by McGill economist and humorist Stephen Leacock. He had resolutely opposed reciprocity in 1911 and published *Back to Prosperity* in 1932 defending a comprehensive system of imperial preferences by using an artful mix of economic and political arguments.

55 The careers of Skelton, Robertson, McKinnon, Clark, Wilgress, and the other members of the remarkable group of public servants who founded the modern Canadian civil service are described in J.L. Granatstein, *The Ottawa Men: The Civil Service Mandarins 1935-1957* (Toronto: Oxford University Press, 1982).

56 For more detail on the conference, see Annett, *British Preference*; and Ian M. Drummond, *Imperial Economic Policy 1917-1939* (London: George Allen and Unwin, 1974).

57 Pomfret, *Unequal Trade*, 48.

58 Granatstein and Hillmer, *For Better or for Worse*, 86-91 and 110-13, analyze the changing place of the United States in popular Canadian attitudes and in the economy.

59 See Bothwell, Drummond, and English, *Canada 1900-1945*, 248ff; and Norrie and Owram, *History of the Canadian Economy*, 475-507, for an economic appreciation of Canada during the depression.

60 Senator Walsh of Massachusetts, the only Republican to vote against the act, quoted in Robert A. Pastor, *Congress and the Politics of U.S. Foreign Economic Policy, 1929-1976* (Berkeley: University of California Press, 1976), 80.

61 Industrialization had also led to a greater interest in exports and an orientation to more markets. In 1888, the United States shipped 52 percent of its exports to Britain. By 1912, this figure had declined to 26 percent, reflecting changing economic status and changes in product mix. In 1888, the two economies were still largely complementary; by 1912, the United States had industrialized and they were rivals. In 1889, 28.1 percent of US industry was moderately (5-10 percent of production) or highly (more than 10 percent of production) dependent on exports; by 1912 this proportion had risen to 57.6 percent. Foreign trade, however, remained less important to the US economy, at 14 percent of GNP, than it was to Britain (45 percent), France (50 percent), or Germany (30 percent). See Lake, *Power, Protection, and Free Trade*, 94, 121, 146.

62 The free list did not signify a commitment to free trade; originally, it represented those products, particularly industrial raw materials, that could not be supplied by US producers and needed to be imported. After 1890, it also represented part of an export strategy, offering free access to the exports of Latin American and other countries as an inducement to provide nondiscriminatory and preferably low-tariff access for US products. Failure to reciprocate would lead to penalty duties on products on the free list. The fact that a high proportion of total imports entered free of duty did not mean that the US economy was becoming more open; more likely it signified that tariff levels on dutiable goods were prohibitive, chilling trade in these products. Once US tariffs did come down from their prohibitive levels, the duty-free proportion of imports steadily declined, even as products were added to the free list, because imports could enter over low to medium duties. One of the benefits of the free list was that goods on the list not only entered free of duty

but also were exempted from some of the other provisions of the tariff legislation that provided additional protection. See ibid., 100ff; and Goldstein, *Ideas, Interests, and Policy,* 91ff.

63 In the period 1865-1934, while the tariff on dutiable goods was high, aggregate levels of protection did not march steadily upward; rather, each new tariff act adjusted tariff levels consonant with the political preferences of the congressional majority and in response to political pressures from producers and users. The McKinley Tariff (1890) represented a high point; the subsequent Wilson-Gorman Tariff (1894) generally lowered levels; the Dingley Tariff (1897) raised them again and stayed in force for twelve years; the Payne-Aldrich Tariff (1909) adjusted them; the Underwood Tariff (1913) substantially lowered them to levels not seen again until well into the 1950s; the Fordney-McCumber tariff (1922) raised them again, particularly on agricultural products, but not as high as the Dingley Tariff; the Smoot-Hawley Tariff made many changes, particularly in agriculture, but not with the intent of raising them to historic new levels. These came about as a result of the combined impact of the fall in prices and the large number of specific tariffs. Falling prices – as was also the case for a good part of the second half of the nineteenth century – raise the incidence of specific duties, while rising prices have the opposite effect. Consequently the aggregate impact of the act on dutiable imports unintentionally raised rates from around 42 percent at 1929 prices to nearly 60 percent at 1932 prices. See Eckes, *Opening America's Market,* 108.

64 John M. Letiche, *Reciprocal Trade Agreements in the World Economy* (New York: Columbia University Press, 1948), 2. Letiche provides a very readable overview of the development of US trade policy through the 1940s. The period after Letiche is well covered by Pastor, *U.S. Foreign Economic Policy;* and I.M. Destler, *American Trade Politics: System under Stress,* 3rd ed. (Washington: Institute for International Economics, 1995). A detailed survey of the rise of US protection, akin to McDiarmid's treatment of early Canadian trade policy *(Commercial Policy),* is F.W. Taussig, *Tariff History of the United States* (New York: Putnam, 1931). A more modern treatment can be found in John M. Dobson, *Two Centuries of Tariffs: The Background and Emergence of the United States International Trade Commission* (Washington: USITC, 1976). Detailed recent analyses can be found in Lake, *Power, Protection, and Free Trade;* Goldstein, *Ideas, Interests, and Policy;* and Eckes, *Opening America's Market.*

65 Quoted in Granatstein and Hillmer, *For Better or for Worse,* 94.

66 As J. Laurence Laughlin and H. Parker Willis wrote in 1903, reciprocity in the McKinley Act was a form of coercion, "since we offered not a differential advantage to the countries concerned, but ... only a differential disadvantage." *Reciprocity* (New York: Baker and Taylor, 1903), 112.

67 By March 1930, the State Department had negotiated commercial (Friendship, Commerce, and Navigation, or FCN) treaties with forty-three countries, twenty-one containing an unconditional MFN clause, but none containing any tariff concessions. Canada, Britain, and France, the United States' most important trading partners, were not among them. See Eckes, *Opening America's Market,* 92.

68 See Kindleberger, "Commercial Policy between the Wars," 170-3.

69 As Charles Kindleberger demonstrates, the Smoot-Hawley Tariff Act did not "cause" the depression. Its more immediate causes are to be found in fiscal and monetary policies and in economic policy responses to the issues of war debt and reparations. However, the failure of US policy leadership, of which Smoot-Hawley was the most visible symbol, certainly contributed to the depth and length of the depression. See Charles P. Kindleberger, *The World in Depression 1929-1939* (Berkeley: University of California Press, 1973). Viewed on its own merits, Smoot-Hawley was but the latest in a long series of US Tariff Acts passed by a protectionist Republican Congress. While it may have involved thousands of individual tariff changes, the aggregate level of protection it offered was not markedly different from that of many of its predecessors. Its notoriety thus rests not on what it did but on what it failed to do. The act became symbolic of the unwillingness of US Republican legislators to adopt policies in line with US economic capacity and importance. A more internationally sensitive Congress would have adopted policies that addressed the global problems of the 1920s and would have helped to ameliorate some of the worst problems of the depression that followed. Britain had exercised such leadership and responsibility – to its benefit – in the nineteenth century and the world had been better for it, but the demands of the First

World War had sapped its waning economic power and made it prey to a series of policy decisions that in retrospect look foolhardy and misguided. US failure to grasp the opportunity, however, proved equally foolhardy and misguided.

70 The Tariff Act of 1930 addressed much more than tariffs; it reformed all aspects of US trade policy and is still the basis of many of the trade laws in effect today.

71 Cordell Hull, *The Memoirs of Cordell Hull* (New York: Macmillan, 1948), vol. 1, 81-2.

72 After the passage of the Smoot-Hawley Tariff, country after country followed suit with increased tariffs, quotas, and exchange controls of their own. In consequence, by 1933 US exports fell to a quarter of their 1929 value, while world trade fell to a third of its 1929 value.

73 Hoover was also a strong believer in the flexible tariff, a notion introduced in the Payne-Aldrich Tariff of 1909 and also part of the Smoot-Hawley Tariff. It was an impractical notion aimed at removing the politics from tariff making by allowing an independent commission to adjust tariff rates so as to maintain rates just high enough to offset the cost disadvantages of domestic producers. As critics pointed out, not only was it wildly impractical, but it also removed the rationale for international trade. See Pastor, *U.S. Foreign Economic Policy*, 77-84. Wrote John Larkin, "Any tariff law framed upon the basis of the difference in cost of production has and can have but one object in view; that is, the granting of aid to domestic industry and totally ignoring whatever effect such action would have upon the Federal revenues ... [and] our international trade ... [These] are such important factors in our present economic life that they cannot be ignored without baneful results to our future welfare and prosperity" (*The President's Control of the Tariff* [Cambridge: Harvard University Press, 1936], 4-5).

74 John Kenneth Galbraith, *A Life in Our Times: Memoirs* (Boston: Houghton Mifflin, 1981), 273. Haberler succeeded Taussig as the dean of American classical trade theorists and was another of the influential economists of this period.

75 Some analysts, particularly those developing broad explanatory theories, are too quick to conclude or assume that the United States was a "free trader" after 1934. The reality is somewhat different. The United States adopted a policy in 1934 that provided for aggressive reciprocity, non-discrimination, bilateral negotiation, cooperative rule making, and more, which ultimately provided a framework of rules and procedures that would make it possible to make trade freer, more stable, and more predictable. It did not make trade "free." At the beginning of the Kennedy Round, that is, some thirty years after adoption of the reciprocal trade agreements program, exporters to the US market still faced a formidable series of hurdles from continued relatively high tariffs in some sectors to QRs to various other customs-based measures, particularly in agriculture. See chapter 7 for further detail on the breadth and depth of US protectionism. The United States did not become an open economy until after the Kennedy Round, and then only if we ignore the continuing high levels of standing protection in such industries as textiles and agriculture, and increasing resort to contingent protection for industries that considered themselves aggrieved by foreign competitors. Even as late as 1988, that is, before the Canada-US Free Trade Agreement entered into force, there remained significant barriers to trade between Canada and the United States. The protectionist barriers developed in the century before 1934 were high, broad, and deep and took more than two generations to undo. The act of 1934 laid the basis for a change in direction, that is, from a deep and abiding commitment that the US economy should be sheltered from foreign competition to a conviction that liberalization was the proper direction of policy, at least at the level of ideology if not always in practice.

76 Letiche, *Reciprocal Trade*, 19-20. The Reciprocal Trade Agreements Act was not a repudiation of protection or a desire to introduce US leadership into international trade; rather, it was an effort to restore export trade through reciprocal bargaining. It showed US willingness to trade moderate reductions in its high tariffs for major reductions in the tariffs of others. In procedural terms, the RTAA was an amendment to the Tariff Act of 1930, the rest of which remained in force; as a result, tariff levels did not return to Fordney-McCumber levels until 1939 nor to Underwood levels until well into the 1950s, that is, until after more than twenty years of reciprocal bargaining. See Lake, *Power, Protection, and Free Trade*, 204-5.

77 Wallace McClure of the State Department, for example, had suggested that State be provided authority to negotiate reciprocal tariff concessions and extend them through MFN, but the idea was firmly rejected by his political masters. A fellow Tennessean, McClure discussed this and other proposals in correspondence and otherwise with Hull. The two men worked to create the basis for what would become Hull's program in 1934. When Hull became secretary of state in 1933, he turned to McClure to chair an interagency group to prepare proposals for his consideration. William Culbertson, another State tariff specialist, had joined the Tariff Commission to try to move the United States to a more realistic position, including authority to negotiate tariff concessions on a reciprocal basis. See Eckes, *Opening America's Market,* 93-4.

78 Letiche, *Reciprocal Trade,* 24-35. Letiche provides a generally sympathetic contemporary account, as does Margaret S. Gordon, *Barriers to World Trade: A Study of Recent Commercial Policy* (New York: Macmillan, 1941). Grace Beckett, *The Reciprocal Trade Agreements Program* (New York: Columbia University Press, 1941), provides a more cautious assessment.

79 A general overview of the program is provided by Harry C. Hawkins and Janet L. Norwood, "The Legislative Basis of United States Commercial Policy," in *Studies in United States Commercial Policy,* ed. William B. Kelly Jr. (Chapel Hill: University of North Carolina Press, 1963). Hawkins was a member of Hull's team of negotiators. See also Destler, *American Trade Politics,* 11-38; and Kaplan, *American Trade Policy,* 43-63.

80 The United States possessed the economic capacity to exercise leadership well before the First World War. The Underwood Tariff and President Wilson's contributions to war and peace had indicated that administration policy makers understood this, as did Democratic political leaders. Republican politicians and their supporters, however, had remained wedded to an older vision of US interests and responsibilities. Their policy preferences in the 1920s indicated that the United States was not yet politically ready to assume leadership. As a result, the Smoot-Hawley Tariff Act came to symbolize the failure of US political leaders to rise to the occasion presented by the international problems of the 1920s and early 1930s. In the same vein, Hull's reciprocal trade agreements program came to symbolize the opposite; it indicated that US political leaders could rise above their traditional parochial focus and don the mantle of world leadership. For modern assessments of the RTAA and the change in the direction of US trade policy, see Kaplan, *American Trade Policy,* 43-52; and Stefanie Ann Lenway, *The Politics of U.S. International Trade: Protection, Expansion and Escape* (Boston: Pitman, 1985), 65-8.

81 Pomfret, *Unequal Trade,* 31.

82 Goldstein, *Ideas, Interests, and Policy,* 157-8.

83 See Richard N. Kottman, *Reciprocity and the North Atlantic Triangle 1932-38* (Ithaca, NY: Cornell University Press, 1968), 79-116, for the most detailed account of the negotiations.

84 The importance of the occasion was, however, not lost on President Roosevelt. He mustered the whole US cabinet to witness the signature to an agreement that marked the end of seventy years during which Canada and the United States extended each other *least-*favoured-nation treatment. See Granatstein and Hillmer, *For Better or for Worse,* 108.

85 See ibid., 107; and Kottman, *North Atlantic Triangle,* 110-11.

86 See Kottman, *North Atlantic Triangle,* 113-15.

87 The 1935 agreement is reproduced as No. 9 in the *Canada Treaty Series* (Ottawa: King's Printer, 1937) for 1936.

88 The 1937-8 trilateral negotiations are covered in considerable detail in Ian M. Drummond and Norman Hillmer, *Negotiating Freer Trade: The United Kingdom, the United States, Canada, and the Trade Agreements of 1938* (Waterloo, ON: Wilfrid Laurier University Press, 1989). While the research and detail are impressive, too much of the interpretation relies on British archival rather than Canadian and US material. The book fails to appreciate, for example, the tremendous importance of the reciprocal trade agreements program in providing a new basis for a better functioning world trading system and is too easily misled by the annoying habit of trade negotiators, particularly American negotiators, of getting hung up on issues that with the passage of time look distinctly unimportant. Trade negotiators know certain issues are unimportant, but are prepared

to play the game in order to get political approval of agreements that serve larger objectives. Economic historians should also appreciate this distinction.

89 The 1938 agreement is reproduced as No. 8 in the *Canada Treaty Series* (Ottawa: King's Printer, 1940) for 1939.

Chapter 5: Multilateral Dreams

1 The Commission on Dominion-Provincial Relations was chaired by Ontario chief justice Newton Rowell and, after he fell ill, Laval law professor Joseph Sirois, and hence is known as the Rowell-Sirois Commission. An abridged version of its 1940 report is available in the Carleton Library series, edited by Donald Smiley, *The Rowell-Sirois Report: An Abridgement of Book I of the Royal Commission Report on Dominion-Provincial Relations* (Toronto: McClelland and Stewart, 1963).

2 John Thompson and Allen Seager, *Canada 1922-1939: Decades of Discord* (Toronto: McClelland and Stewart, 1985), 330 and 332.

3 Quoted in J.L. Granatstein, *A Man of Influence: Norman A. Robertson and Canadian Statecraft 1929-68* (Toronto: Deneau, 1981), 74.

4 Smiley, ed., *Rowell-Sirois Report*, 161.

5 Kenneth Norrie and Douglas Owram, *A History of the Canadian Economy* (Toronto: Harcourt Brace Jovanovich, 1991), 509. Britain initially sought to conserve its dwindling supply of foreign exchange by curbing imports, but with the fall of France in 1940, all commercial considerations were subordinated to the requirements of war.

6 Ibid., 511-12.

7 Quoted in John H. Young, *Canadian Commercial Policy* (Ottawa: Queen's Printer, 1957), 48.

8 During these critical years, there was lively debate in Canadian foreign policy circles, involving, for example, the isolationist/nationalist views of undersecretary O.D. Skelton and his legal advisor Loring Christie, through the waning imperialism of first secretary Norman Robertson and the continentalism of necessity of finance deputy Clifford Clark. The point to be made, however, is that the preferences of various policy makers in Ottawa paled to insignificance when confronted with the tough problems of the war years and those immediately after. First and foremost, therefore, policy makers practised the art of the possible within circumstances that gave them very little room for manoeuvre. Among the realities they faced were Britain's weakness and the United States' strength and proximity. Churchill's, and Britain's, imperial hauteur in the prosecution of the war, when Churchill routinely felt able to speak for the dominions and commit their resources, men, and equipment, had a subtle but corrosive effect on future Canada-UK relations, while the ability to deal frequently and successfully with Roosevelt and his advisors had an equally important positive effect on relations with the United States. The war, rather than strengthening Canada-UK relations, weakened them. See C.P. Stacey, *Canada and the Age of Conflict*, vol. 2, *1921-1948: The Mackenzie King Era* (Toronto: University of Toronto Press, 1981), 321-3.

9 Jack Granatstein provides an amusing account of the financial and trade constraints within which Canadian governments operated. On three different occasions in 1917, 1944, and 1947, Canada sought US help on terms that strengthened Canada's ties to the United States and weakened those with the United Kingdom. On all three occasions, the United Kingdom's serious financial conditions prevented it from paying for imports from Canada, creating external financial problems for Canada. On all three occasions, the solution lay in US financial and commercial policy measures. See *How Britain's Weakness Forced Canada into the Arms of the United States* (Toronto: University of Toronto Press, 1989). The details of Canada-US wartime economic cooperation can be found in R. Warren James, *Wartime Economic Cooperation: A Study of Relations between Canada and the United States* (Toronto: Ryerson Press, 1949).

10 The detail of Canadian grants and loans to Britain to help finance British war efforts as well as imports from Canada can be gleaned from J.L. Granatstein, "Settling the Accounts: Anglo-Canadian War Finance, 1943-1945," *Queen's Quarterly* 83 (Summer 1976): 234-49; H.M. Mackenzie, "The Path to Temptation: The Negotiation of Canada's Reconstruction Loan to Britain in 1946," *Historical Papers/Communications historiques* (1982): 196-220; and H.M. Mackenzie, "Sinews of War and Peace: The Politics of Economic Aid to Britain, 1939-1945," *International Journal* 54, 4

(1999): 648-70. The British perspective is provided in L.S. Pressnel, *External Economic Policy Since the War*, vol. 1, *The Post-War Financial Settlement* (London: HMSO, 1986). All four accounts illustrate the extent to which trade considerations were complicated by inconvertible currencies and balance-of-payments problems that dwarfed what could be accomplished through trade policy measures.

11 See Stacey, *Mackenzie King Era*, 357-9.

12 Quoted in Mackenzie, "Path to Temptation," 197.

13 The year before, Roosevelt had struck a similar hard bargain in the destroyers-for-bases deal – fifty old US destroyers in return for long-term leases for bases in Newfoundland, Bermuda, and elsewhere.

14 Stacey, *Mackenzie King Era*, 311. The details of Anglo-American financial cooperation can be gleaned from Pressnel, *Post-War Financial Settlement*, particularly chapter 10.

15 Finance Minister Ilsley told the House on the third anniversary of the Hyde Park Declaration in 1944, "We never wished to ask the United States for lend-lease assistance – we always felt that, as a nation in a favoured position, free from the ravages of war, we were in duty bound to stand on our own two feet and indeed to share with the United States in assisting other less fortunate of our allies in carrying on the war against the common enemy" (House of Commons, *Debates*, 21 April 1944, 2227).

16 Wynne Plumptre points out that this was not a case of Canada's going hat in hand to the United States and seeking an exemption from US law or policy. When Congress passed the necessary provisions to put lend-lease into effect, it provided for a coordinated policy that would allow the Allies to make the best use of scarce resources. Similarly, the decision to procure some defence requirements in Canada made sense to both parties by strengthening the basis for cooperation. Having served its purpose, the agreement was terminated after two years. See *Three Decades of Decision: Canada and the World Monetary System, 1944-75* (Toronto: McClelland and Stewart, 1977), 82-5.

17 See Robert Bothwell and John English, "Canadian Trade Policy 1943-47," in *Canadian Foreign Policy: Historical Readings*, ed. J.L. Granatstein (Toronto: Copp Clark Pitman, 1986), 146.

18 Write Robert Bothwell, Ian Drummond, and John English, "The real Liberal plan, whether by accident or by design, was Howe's. It was based on optimism about the economy, and scepticism about the potentialities of planning. It would not be the economic abstraction of doctrinaire planners in Ottawa that would shape post-war Canada. That would be left to business's self-interest, guided, prodded, and shaped by incentives that businessmen could understand. Post-war Canada would be a free-enterprise society" (*Canada since 1945: Power, Politics and Provincialism* [Toronto: University of Toronto Press, 1981], 69). Some of the flavour of the discussions is captured by Mitchell Sharp in *Which Reminds Me ... A Memoir* (Toronto: University of Toronto Press, 1994), 16-32.

19 J. Harvey Perry, *Taxes, Tariffs & Subsidies: A History of Canadian Fiscal Development* (Toronto: University of Toronto Press, 1955), vol. 2, tables 2, 3, and 6, 620, 621, and 624-7.

20 See Bothwell, Drummond, and English, *Canada since 1945*, 79.

21 See John Deutsch, "Recent American Influence in Canada," in Hugh G.J. Aitken, John J. Deutsch, W.A. Mackintosh, et al., *The American Economic Impact on Canada* (Durham, NC: Duke University Press, 1959), 42.

22 As explained below, Mackenzie King also saw article 2 as an attractive, less threatening alternative to the proposed Canada-US free-trade agreement then under discussion.

23 See Escott Reid, "Canada and the Creation of the North Atlantic Alliance, 1948-1949," in Granatstein, *Canadian Foreign Policy*, 158-82.

24 See Bothwell and English, "Canadian Trade Policy," 147. The point is also illustrated by John Deutsch's analysis advocating the proposed Canada-US free-trade agreement, in Canada, *Documents on Canadian External Relations*, vol. 14: 1948 (Ottawa: Department of External Affairs, 1994), document 652, 1056-60.

25 Much of this section is drawn from a much more detailed study of the founding of the GATT and the failure of the ITO in Michael Hart, *Also Present at the Creation: Dana Wilgress and the United*

Nations Conference on Trade and Employment at Havana (Ottawa: Centre for Trade Policy and Law, 1995). It contains the full text of the report prepared by Wilgress, head of the Canadian delegation, as well as the text of the Havana Charter. A shorter version of the introductory analysis can be found in chapter 6 of Fen Hampson with Michael Hart, *Multilateral Negotiations: Lessons from Arms Control, Trade and the Environment* (Baltimore, MD: Johns Hopkins Press, 1995). See also Michael Hart, *Fifty Years of Canadian Tradecraft: Canada at the GATT 1947-1997* (Ottawa: Centre for Trade Policy and Law, 1998).

26 See Hart, *Also Present at the Creation*, 21-34, for a discussion of early Canadian involvement in the preparatory planning.

27 By this time, Canadian officials had developed the concept of "functionalism," that is, the idea that while Canada was obviously not a great power with interests across the full range of international issues, Canada did have interests and a contribution to make in areas in which its role was significant, such as trade, finance, aviation, and food and agriculture. By carefully deploying resources in areas where Canadian interests were most concentrated, Canadian officials were able to exercise considerable influence. See J.L. Granatstein and Norman Hillmer, *For Better or for Worse: Canada and the United States to the 1990s* (Toronto: Copp Clark Pitman, 1991), 175ff. I am not using the word "functionalism" here in its more restricted social science meaning.

28 Generally, see Department of External Affairs, *Canada and the United Nations: 1945-1975* (Ottawa: Supply and Services, 1977). On the founding of the financial institutions from a Canadian perspective, see Plumptre, *Three Decades of Decision*, 17-54.

29 On the founding of the GATT and efforts to found the ITO, see Hart, *Also Present at the Creation*. An eyewitness account can be found in Clair Wilcox, *A Charter for World Trade* (New York: Macmillan, 1949). Wilcox was the deputy head of the US delegation. See also Thomas W. Zeiler, *Free Trade, Free World: The Advent of GATT* (Chapel Hill: University of North Carolina Press, 1999); and Susan Ariel Aaranson, *Trade and the American Dream: A Social History of Postwar Trade Policy* (Lexington: University of Kentucky Press, 1996). Two older standard works on the postwar multilateral trade and financial negotiations are Richard N. Gardner, *Sterling-Dollar Diplomacy: The Origins and the Prospects of Our International Economic Order*, expanded ed. (New York: McGraw-Hill, 1969); and William Adams Brown, *The United States and the Restoration of World Trade* (Washington: Brookings Institution, 1950).

30 The difficulty of this task and the complexity of the negotiations can be gleaned from the diplomatic correspondence excerpted in Department of State Historical Office, Bureau of Public Affairs, *Foreign Relations of the United States,* 1947, vol. 1, Department of State Publication 8674 (Washington: United States Government Printing Office, 1973), 915ff. Of particular interest is the difficulty the United States had in meeting the request by Australia and New Zealand for a substantial cut in the wool tariff, without which there would be little of practical interest in the negotiations for them and the United States would be unable to gain their support for a major reduction in imperial preferences. The US preoccupation with the evil of these preferences is equally clear in this correspondence.

31 See John W. Evans, *The Kennedy Round in American Trade Policy: The Twilight of the GATT?* (Cambridge: Harvard University Press, 1971), 9-11; and John C. Campbell, *The United States in World Affairs 1947-1948* (New York: Harper and Brothers for the Council on Foreign Relations, 1948), 246-59.

32 There is some irony in this situation. One of Canada's motivations in pursuing multilateralism was to avoid being in a one-on-one, dependent relationship with the United States. In these multilateral negotiations, however, bilateral negotiations with the United States invariably proved the most productive, further deepening Canada's trade and economic ties to the United States.

33 Gerard Curzon, *Multilateral Commercial Diplomacy: The General Agreement on Tariffs and Trade and Its Impact on National Commercial Policies and Techniques* (London: Michael Joseph, 1965), 70.

34 John H. Jackson, *Restructuring the GATT System* (London: Pinter, 1990), 10-12.

35 The US delegation report on the conclusion of the Geneva negotiations, Department of State Historical Office, *Foreign Relations of the United States*, 1021-5, indicates that it was well satisfied with what had been achieved, particularly in concluding the General Agreement.

36 See, for example, King's diaries for 1947 (J.W. Pickersgill and Donald F. Forster, eds., *The Macken-zie King Record*, vol. 4, *1947-1948* [Toronto: University of Toronto Press, 1960-70], 90, 123-4) and his report to the House of Commons on 9 December (*Debates*, 9 December 1947 [vol. 1, 1948], 97-104). The details are also supplied by Robert A. Spencer, *Canada in World Affairs: From UN to NATO 1946-1949* (Toronto: Oxford University Press, 1959).

37 House of Commons, *Debates*, 9 December 1947 (vol. 1, 1948), 109. Bracken told the House of Commons, for example, "Under the terms of the treaties we lose all freedom of action in directing the course of our trade ... In no circumstances can we make special arrangements to buy from those who buy from us unless we offer the same privileges to all others."

38 For the problem of US Senate ratification, see William Diebold, Jr., *The End of the ITO*, Essays in International Finance No. 16 (Princeton: Princeton University Press, 1952); and Zeiler, *Free Trade, Free World*, chapter 9. Documentary material reflecting Canadian preoccupations can be found in Canada, *Documents on Canadian External Relations*, vols. 12, 13, and 14: 1946, 1947, and 1948 (Ottawa: Department of External Affairs, 1977, 1993, and 1994).

39 Clair Wilcox makes a frank assessment of these "beams in the American eye" in his analysis of the ITO charter: "The United States has championed active competition in open markets, but it has taken great pains to insure, in many cases, that competition will not be too active and that markets will not be opened too wide" (*Charter for World Trade*, 35).

40 The July 1945 election in Britain was the first in ten years. For many of those years, Churchill had headed a coalition National government created by the extraordinary demands of war, but he had never faced the people. When he did call an election in 1945, he lost to a Labour party that had campaigned on a domestic agenda. The return to normal politics illustrated the extent to which Churchill was not a typical Tory. The result reflected doubts about the Conservative party as much as about Churchill. See Kenneth O. Morgan, *The People's Peace: British History 1945-1989* (Oxford: Oxford University Press, 1990), 26-8.

41 Report of the Canadian delegation, para. 14, reproduced in Hart, *Also Present at the Creation*, 76.

42 See, in particular, King's musings in his diary regarding the Canada-US free-trade discussions, conveniently extracted in Canada, *Documents on Canadian External Relations*, vol. 14: 1948, documents 642 and 647, and John Deutsch's description and analysis of the negotiations, reproduced ibid. as document 652.

43 A detailed account of the 1947-8 negotiations can be found in Michael Hart, "Almost But Not Quite: The 1947-48 Bilateral Canada-U.S. Negotiations," *The American Review of Canadian Studies* 19, 1 (1989), 25-58. For other accounts, see Robert L. Cuff and J.L. Granatstein, "The Rise and Fall of Canadian-American Free Trade 1947-48," *Canadian Historical Review* 58, 4 (1977): 459-82; and Cuff and Granatstein, *American Dollars, Canadian Prosperity* (Toronto: Samuel-Stevens, 1978). A documentary account can be found in Canada, *Documents on Canadian External Relations*, vol. 14: 1948, documents 642 to 661.

44 See document 652 in Canada, *Documents on Canadian External Relations*, vol. 14: 1948.

45 Jack Granatstein argues in various publications that Canada's ability to benefit from Marshall Plan aid provides another example of Canadian exemptionalism, that is, Canada's successful effort to gain exemption from US laws that were inimical to Canadian interests. Wynne Plumptre in *Three Decades of Decision* (82-5) insists that the United Kingdom's ability to use Marshall Plan aid to make purchases in Canada was not something specifically sought by Canada, although it supported the legislation. Rather, it flowed from the US desire to avoid dislocating already disturbed trade patterns, including between Europe and Latin America.

46 See document 658 in Canada, *Documents on Canadian External Relations*, vol. 14: 1948.

47 Lester Pearson, for example, wrote Norman Robertson about King's decision and concluded, "I cannot help but feel that a very great opportunity has been missed. If only the Government had taken this matter actively in hand two or three months ago! It is not less than tragic that other things were allowed to interfere and that the moment has passed when immediate action could have been taken. It is a sad reflection on our comparative values that so much time has been spent on so many things during the last two or three months of infinitely less importance than these proposals. They now have to be suspended merely because of lack of time. Yet, if they could have

been accepted by the Government and converted into law by the present Parliament, they might have had a decisive strengthening effect on the whole economy of the country against the day when such strength is bound to be needed. I think that 'we missed the bus,' even if we have saved the time table!" (Canada, *Documents on Canadian External Relations*, vol. 14: 1948, document 654).

48 See Don Barry, "Eisenhower, St. Laurent and Free Trade, 1953," *International Perspectives* (March/April 1987): 8-11. When later in the decade Clarence Randall, chairman of the Randall Commission, urged Secretary of State Dulles to pursue free-trade negotiations with Canada, Dulles made clear that while the idea might have merit, it could in no way be pursued by Washington without the initiative being taken in Ottawa, a most unlikely prospect by this time. See John Herd Thompson and Stephen J. Randall, *Canada and the United States: Ambivalent Allies* (Montreal: McGill-Queen's University Press, 1994), 208-9.

Chapter 6: Continental Realities

1 Failure sufficiently to appreciate this reality explains much of the historiography of the period. Canadian nationalists who bemoan the increasing dominance of the United States in the Canadian economy and the decline in Canadian economic intercourse with the United Kingdom and the European continent should seek their explanations for this development as much in London, Paris, Bonn, and Washington as in Ottawa. Canada could obviously have opted for a trade and economic strategy that would have involved less integration into the international economy, but such a strategy would have required a much more interventionist government. It is not at all clear that such choices would have been tolerated by Canadians, particularly since it is questionable that such policy choices would have delivered the number-one priority for Canadians: a return to sustained prosperity. Whatever Canadian nationalist critics might find wanting in the policy choices of this period, they cannot deny that postwar governments delivered prosperity.

2 See Robert Bothwell, Ian Drummond, and John English, *Canada since 1945: Power, Politics and Provincialism* (Toronto: University of Toronto Press, 1981), 59-60.

3 See C.P. Stacey, *Canada and the Age of Conflict*, vol. 2, *1921-1948: The Mackenzie King Era* (Toronto: University of Toronto Press, 1981), 398ff. On the trade policy front, Canada threw cold water on UK suggestions during the GATT negotiations to form a Commonwealth free-trade area as a counter to US efforts to promote nondiscrimination. Canada preferred the latter to more discrimination.

4 John Deutsch, one of the architects of postwar Canadian trade policy, succinctly captured the dilemma he and others faced in the late 1940s and early 1950s in pursuing policies that resulted ultimately in dependence on the United States and a prosperity that appeared increasingly to be resented: "Policies of self-containment and self-sufficiency were policies of despair. Consequently the assurance and development of export markets on the widest possible basis was a primary objective of Canadian postwar policy. Immense difficulties stood in the way because of the ambivalence of the Canadian economy between the United States and Great Britain and because of the need for a triangular balancing of the external accounts." Later in the article, he notes, "Among the many tariff agreements which Canada negotiated in Geneva in 1947, only that with the United States achieved substantial results in reducing barriers to trade. The others were almost wholly nullified, as far as Canadian exports were concerned, by controls and currency restrictions. The preferences which continued to be accorded to Canada in other Commonwealth markets were also similarly nullified. The attempt to obtain a larger share of imports from Britain and Europe was frustrated by the claims for postwar reconstruction and by the persistence of inflationary conditions overseas" ("Recent American Influence in Canada," in Hugh G.J. Aitken, John J. Deutsch, W.A. Mackintosh, et al., *The American Economic Impact on Canada* [Durham, NC: Duke University Press, 1959], 41 and 47).

5 For a general discussion of postwar monetary problems, see W.S. Scammel, *The International Economy since 1945* (London: Macmillan, 1983), 19-38.

6 See Kenneth Norrie and Douglas Owram, *A History of the Canadian Economy* (Toronto: Harcourt Brace Jovanovich, 1991), 543.

7 John Deutsch captured the theme well in a 1947 dispatch from ongoing trade negotiations in Geneva: "We have the choice between two kinds of worlds – a relatively free enterprise world with the highest existing standard of living and a government-controlled world with a lower standard of living" (quoted in J.L. Granatstein and Norman Hillmer, *For Better or for Worse: Canada and the United States to the 1990s* [Toronto: Copp Clark Pitman, 1991], 171).

8 For a discussion of the long-term conflict between the liberalizing trade policy of the 1934 Reciprocal Trade Agreements Act and the protectionism of the 1933 Agricultural Adjustment Act, see Judith Goldstein, *Ideas, Interests, and American Trade Policy* (Ithaca, NY: Cornell University Press, 1993), chapter 4.

9 See Deutsch, "Recent American Influence," 44.

10 See J.L. Granatstein, *How Britain's Weakness Forced Canada into the Arms of the United States* (Toronto: University of Toronto Press, 1989).

11 Noted the official press release: "The purpose of the credit is to facilitate purchases by the United Kingdom of goods and services in Canada and to assist in making it possible for the United Kingdom to meet transitional post-war deficits in its current balance of payments, to maintain adequate reserves of gold and dollars and to assume the obligations of multilateral trade" (quoted in Stacey, *Mackenzie King Era*, 399). See H.M. Mackenzie, "The Path to Temptation: The Negotiation of Canada's Reconstruction Loan to Britain in 1946," *Historical Papers/Communications historiques* (1982): 196-220, for details of the negotiations.

12 See Stacey, *Mackenzie King Era*, 404.

13 In the end a deal was struck because Mackenzie King, despite reservations he shared with his ministers and senior officials on financial and commercial grounds, did not want to precipitate a breakdown of the Western alliance. See Mackenzie, "Path to Temptation," 217-19.

14 The story, as told here, reflects Canadian interests and preoccupations. It would not be difficult, in telling the story from a UK perspective, to emphasize how little room for manoeuvre British officials believed they had. See, for example, L.S. Pressnel, *External Economic Policy since the War*, vol. 1, *The Post-War Financial Settlement* (London: HMSO, 1986).

15 See Bruce W. Muirhead, *The Development of Postwar Canadian Trade Policy* (Montreal: McGill-Queen's University Press, 1992), 23-5.

16 The irony of the situation was not lost on some Canadians. McGill's Frank Scott, for example, noted that "we are in the curious position that the more we do to assist Great Britain ... the more we are obliged to co-operate with the United States ... We help Great Britain and therefore we must be more closely associated with the United States." Quoted in Granatstein and Hillmer, *For Better or for Worse*, 143-4.

17 The Marshall Plan was designed to help European countries expand production, reduce barriers to trade, and establish financial stability. US financial aid would complement measures taken by the European countries themselves, including cooperative efforts to create a unified market. For a contemporary view on the origins of the Marshall Plan, see John C. Campbell, *The United States in World Affairs 1947-1948* (New York: Harper and Brothers for the Council on Foreign Relations, 1948). The most complete recent analysis is provided by Alan S. Milward, *The Reconstruction of Western Europe: 1945-1951* (London: Methuen, 1984).

18 Quoted in Roy Jenkins, *Truman* (London: Collins, 1986), 107.

19 During its first two years of operation, Marshall Plan funds financed $1.155 billion in Canadian exports to the United Kingdom and Europe. See R.D. Cuff and J.L. Granatstein, *American Dollars – Canadian Prosperity: Canadian-American Economic Relations 1945-1950* (Toronto: Samuel-Stevens, 1978), 83-139, for the details of Canadian involvement in Marshall Plan discussions and disbursements.

20 Muirhead, *Postwar Canadian Trade Policy*, 27-8.

21 While it is true that Churchill was unstinting in his public praise of Canadian assistance during the war, British officials did not translate these public statements into decisions and actions that recognized Canadian aid. As is often the case with great powers, they had difficulty recognizing that smaller countries also have domestic political complexities that need to be addressed; smaller countries do not exist solely to satisfy the needs of great powers.

22 See Robert Bothwell and John English, "Canadian Trade Policy 1943-47," in *Canadian Foreign Policy: Historical Readings*, ed. J.L. Granatstein (Toronto: Copp Clark Pitman, 1986), 148-50.

23 See Kenneth Morgan, *The People's Peace: British History 1945-1989* (Oxford: Oxford University Press, 1990), 3-194, for an account of Britain's trials and tribulations during the postwar years.

24 See D.E. Moggridge, *Keynes* (London: The Macmillan Press, 1976), 140.

25 Muirhead, *Postwar Canadian Trade Policy*, 30-3.

26 Noted *The Economist*, "Britain's share of the European Recovery Programme [Marshall Plan] dollars [was] absentmindedly poured down the drain of Australia's high cost industrial boom" (quoted ibid., 87).

27 Quoted ibid., 82.

28 Quoted ibid., 104.

29 Ibid., 102.

30 See Philip Armstrong, Andrew Glyn, and John Harrison, *Capitalism since 1945* (Oxford: Basil Blackwell, 1991), 3-10, for an account of Europe's rapid recovery and reconstruction.

31 Milward, *Reconstruction of Western Europe*, particularly chapters 1, 3, 6, and 14.

32 For the story of European integration from a Canadian perspective, see Leolynn Dana Wilgress, *The Impact of European Integration on Canada* (Montreal: Private Planning Association of Canada, 1962).

33 Milward, *Reconstruction of Western Europe*, 478.

34 See Cuff and Granatstein, *American Dollars – Canadian Prosperity*, for discussion of the extent of early Canadian benefits under the Marshall Plan.

35 See Muirhead, *Postwar Canadian Trade Policy*, 110-12.

36 John Holmes has noted how Canadian generosity suffered from bad timing. In an unpublished paper he wrote, "It was Canada's bad luck that because of its earlier involvement in the war and in particular in the survival of Britain it provided help when it was most needed and least noticed, that is, during and immediately after the war. While the American administration coped with more refractory public attitudes and the division of powers, the Canadian Government was able to provide financial support to stave off a British collapse in 1946 and 1947 while Congress pondered. By the time the Marshall Plan was approved in 1948, Canada had virtually bankrupted itself ... The Marshall Plan is remembered by Europeans with gratitude and properly so, while the Canadian assistance is recalled, if at all, only by elderly ex-officials" (quoted in A.F.W. Plumptre, *Three Decades of Decision: Canada and the World Monetary System, 1944-75* [Toronto: McClelland and Stewart, 1977], 82).

37 See Muirhead, *Postwar Canadian Trade Policy*, 110.

38 See Michael Bliss, *Northern Enterprise: Five Centuries of Canadian Business* (Toronto: McClelland and Stewart, 1987), 445-77, for a discussion of Canadian business development during this period. Bliss's account indicates the extent to which the postwar boom was more than a matter of US investments. Canadian entrepreneurs were also deeply involved in the growth of Canadian business.

39 The escape clause allowed the United States to reintroduce protection if any tariff cut led to serious injury to US producers; the security exception stipulated that the president could not negotiate tariff cuts that imperilled US national security, while the peril-point required that the president not negotiate any reductions below the "peril point," a level determined by the US Tariff Commission in consultation with affected industries. All three had the effect of limiting the capacity of US negotiators to pursue creative new arrangements. See Howard S. Piquet, *The U.S. Trade Expansion Act of 1962: How Will It Affect Canadian-American Trade?* (Montreal: Private Planning Association of Canada, 1963), 4-5. A general overview of the program is provided by Harry C. Hawkins and Janet L. Norwood, "The Legislative Basis of United States Commercial Policy," and John M. Leddy and Janet L. Norwood, "The Escape Clause and Peril Points Under the Trade Agreements Program," in *Studies in United States Commercial Policy*, ed. William B. Kelly Jr. (Chapel Hill: University of North Carolina Press, 1963).

40 Robert A. Pastor, *Congress and the Politics of U.S. Foreign Economic Policy 1929-1976* (Berkeley: University of California Press, 1980), 100.

41 Ibid., 101. This decision also put paid to a Toronto round of GATT tariff negotiations in 1953, which had been planned at the end of the Torquay negotiations. The next GATT tariff conference would take place in Geneva in 1956.

42 As noted above (chapter 5, note 48), Randall was also a strong advocate of a Canada-US free-trade agreement, an idea that appealed to some US business interests but had by the mid-1950s become unacceptable in Ottawa with at best some support among academic economists. It would be another decade before Paul and Ronald Wonnacott would rekindle the issue at the academic level in their pioneering study that suggested the possibility of a 10 percent increase in Canadian GNP flowing from such an agreement. See *Free Trade between the United States and Canada: The Potential Economic Effects* (Cambridge: Harvard University Press, 1967).

43 Alfred E. Eckes, Jr., *Opening America's Market: U.S. Foreign Trade Policy since 1776* (Chapel Hill: University of North Carolina Press, 1995), 167-77, provides good insight into the conflict between narrow commercial policy considerations, as reflected in congressional logrolling, and the broader foreign policy priorities that animated the president and State Department. Similarly, Commerce Secretary Weeks and Treasury Secretary Humphrey were much less enthusiastic about further efforts to open the US market. Eckes suggests that Weeks and Humphrey were cast more in the mould of traditional Republicans than President Eisenhower.

44 Pastor, *U.S. Foreign Economic Policy*, 101.

45 In his diary, Eisenhower characterized calls for new import protection as "shortsightedness bordering upon tragic stupidity." He considered opening the US market to be a matter of "enlightened self-interest." See Eckes, *Opening America's Market*, 167. Eisenhower's personal views, however, rarely translated into bold or imaginative action, with the result that his administration markedly slowed the program of liberalization initiated by Hull.

46 Bothwell, Drummond, and English, *Canada since 1945*, 142.

47 In 1954, Congress passed Public Law 480 to provide for the surplus disposal of American agricultural products around the world, a nail in the coffin of multilateral agricultural discipline.

48 The United States had insisted in 1947 that GATT article XI provide it sufficient room to restrict agricultural imports in conjunction with limits on domestic production, a provision that Canada had vigorously opposed. The disciplines included in the article, however, proved too confining a policy for the United States. Congress wanted to restrict imports, not domestic production. Consequently, in 1955, the United States sought and received a waiver from this obligation so that agriculture restrictions could be imposed without this discipline. The rest of the world soon followed suit by removing any effective discipline on trade in agriculture. See Dana Wilgress, *Canada's Approach to Trade Negotiations* (Montreal: Private Planning Association of Canada, 1963), 20.

49 See Robert Bothwell, *Canada and the United States: The Politics of Partnership* (Toronto: University of Toronto Press, 1992), 64.

50 James Bovard, *The Farm Fiasco* (San Francisco: Institute for Contemporary Studies, 1989), provides a devastating account of the long-term impact of this rising tide of farm protectionism on both the US economy and on the legitimate interests of US trading partners.

51 See Bothwell, *Canada and the United States*, 64-5. US obtuseness on wheat sales did, however, have a silver lining. It stimulated the Canadian Wheat Board and the government to start looking to nontraditional markets, including Japan, the Soviet Union, and the People's Republic of China, the latter two markets rendered off-limits to US sales by anticommunist hysteria in the United States. In 1955, Secretary of State for External Affairs Lester Pearson led a mission to Moscow that included Trade and Commerce associate deputy Mitchell Sharp to talk wheat. The following year, the Soviet Union and Canada entered into the first of many wheat agreements. Within a few years, Alvin Hamilton would negotiate the first wheat sales to China to complement the already successful Japan trade. See William E. Morriss, *Chosen Instrument: A History of the Canadian Wheat Board, The McIvor Years* (Winnipeg: Reidmore Books for the Canadian Wheat Board, 1987), 229ff; and Mitchell Sharp, *Which Reminds Me ... A Memoir* (Toronto: University of Toronto Press, 1994), 57-8 and 66-7.

52 Francis Masson and J.B. Whitely, *Barriers to Trade between Canada and the United States* (Montreal: Canadian-American Committee, 1960), describe the extent of the barriers still in place by

the end of the 1950s. The nature of this protection on both sides of the border is discussed in more detail in chapter 7.

53 The difficulties with which GATT struggled during its first two decades are captured by Gardner Patterson, *Discrimination in International Trade: The Policy Issues 1945-1965* (Princeton: Princeton University Press, 1966).

54 In *The Development of Postwar Canadian Trade Policy,* chapter 2, Bruce Muirhead writes of the "failure" of the multilateral system and the impact of that failure in strengthening the continentalist option. It is more accurate to speak of the disappointment and limits of the multilateral option. In Geneva in 1947, the participating countries had set up a realistic but limited compromise that exhausted the negotiating mandates and room for manoeuvre of the major delegations. The conference at Havana stretched their mandates beyond the politically possible; the International Trade Organization (ITO) had thus collapsed. GATT was implemented and allowed to work because it was a limited agreement. Its early success, based on caution and conservatism, that is, on avoiding the mistakes of Havana and on harbouring what had been achieved instead of pushing matters too far and too fast, kept it alive and prepared it for the next leap forward at Geneva after the US Trade Expansion Act of 1962. Such an assessment cannot be gleaned solely from the archival record of memos and telexes, which are full of complaints and pessimism. Instead, it is to be found in the more reflective writings of officials of the period, such as John Deutsch and W.A. Mackintosh. See Michael Hart, *Also Present at the Creation: Dana Wilgress and the United Nations Conference on Trade and Employment at Havana* (Ottawa: Centre for Trade Policy and Law, 1995), for analysis contrasting the success of the GATT negotiations with the failure of the ITO negotiations.

55 Brian Tew, *The Evolution of the International Monetary System 1945-77* (London: Hutchinson, 1977) points out that post-Bretton Woods, monetary policy moved from a bilateral phase (1945-9) involving largely bilateral settlements of account, to a binary phase (1950-8) involving two parallel monetary systems (a sterling area and a dollar area) and settlement of accounts between them and, finally, following adoption of convertibility in 1958, a multilateral phase on the basis of the rules that had been negotiated at Bretton Woods in 1944. Along the way, governments relied on a variety of temporary expedients and regional arrangements, such as the Anglo-American and Anglo-Canadian loan agreements of 1946 and 1947, the Marshall Plan, the EPU, and the Organization for European Economic Cooperation. In effect, therefore, the system set up at Bretton Woods was not fully operational until 1959. The Bretton Woods system lasted only until 1971 when the United States abandoned the gold standard and ushered in a new crisis that was not resolved until the major members adopted a regime of floating exchange rates in 1973. See also Richard N. Cooper, *The Economics of Interdependence: Economic Policy in the Atlantic Community* (New York: Council on Foreign Relations, 1968), chapter 5.

56 While Canada did not resort to GATT article XXXV – GATT's nonapplication clause, allowing members not to apply GATT obligations to a new member – in its accession negotiations with Japan, it did negotiate an agreement that provided not only for the exchange of most-favoured-nation status but also for Canadian wheat sales and Japanese restraints on low-cost items that were likely to disrupt Canadian markets, such as cotton textiles and stainless-steel flatware. The fact that Canada enjoyed a ten-to-one advantage in trade did not deter Canada from practising this kind of realpolitik. See Sharp, *Which Reminds Me,* 66-7.

57 Canadian official Louis Couillard, from his vantage point as delegate to the OEEC in Paris, sighed that "the road to the once sacred objective of non-discriminatory multilateral trade [was] being detoured more and more in view of the continuing disequilibria and the growing maze of continuing artificial controls" (quoted in Muirhead, *Postwar Canadian Trade Policy,* 73).

58 I.M. Destler notes that it was not surprising that in response to Kennedy's request for a sweeping new authority, Congress concluded that the State Department would not be up to the challenge and created the new position of the Special Trade Representative, resident in the Executive Office but reporting to Congress (*American Trade Politics: System under Stress,* 3rd ed. [Washington: Institute for International Economics, 1995], 19-20).

59 See Pastor, *U.S. Foreign Economic Policy,* 97-8.

60 See Destler, *American Trade Politics*, 4-5. Judith Goldstein explores the continuing coexistence of both protectionist and liberalizing policies and institutions during the 1950s in *Ideas, Interests, and Policy*.

61 Robert E. Hudec, *The GATT Legal System and World Trade Diplomacy*, 2nd ed. (Salem, NH: Butterworth, 1990), 67-8.

62 See Gerard Curzon, *Multilateral Commercial Diplomacy: The General Agreement on Tariffs and Trade and Its Impact on National Commercial Policies and Techniques* (London: Michael Joseph, 1965), 87-93.

63 Mitchell Sharp recounts how, at the 1955 GATT session, the Australian chairman took the occasion to rub Canada's nose in its sanctimony by noting that unlike Canada, Australia came to the table prepared to acknowledge its sins. *Which Reminds Me*, 60-1.

64 See Wilgress, *Canada's Approach to Trade Negotiations*, 19; and Muirhead, *Postwar Canadian Trade Policy*, 69-70.

65 See Curzon, *Multilateral Commercial Diplomacy*, 108; and Hudec, *World Trade Diplomacy*, 70-1.

66 See Curzon, *Multilateral Commercial Diplomacy*, 127ff; and Hudec, *World Trade Diplomacy*, 72.

67 See Curzon, *Multilateral Commercial Diplomacy*, 94ff.

68 As late as 1971, John W. Evans could title his analysis of the Kennedy Round of negotiations (1963-7) *The Kennedy Round in American Trade Policy: The Twilight of the GATT?* (Cambridge: Harvard University Press, 1971).

69 See Robert E. Hudec, *Developing Countries in the GATT Legal System* (London: Harvester Wheatsheaf for the Trade Policy Research Centre, 1988). Jean Royer, deputy executive secretary of GATT for the first decade, suggested the extent to which GATT should be prepared to accommodate the special interests of developing countries, even where these were in fundamental conflict with GATT's basic principles, in "The Case for GATT: Reforming the Institutional Machinery of World Trade," in *New Directions for World Trade, Proceedings of a Chatham House Conference* (London: Oxford University Press, 1964), 139-60.

70 See Curzon, *Multilateral Commercial Diplomacy*, 81.

71 See Hudec, *World Trade Diplomacy*, 67-108, for a complete discussion of the evolution of dispute settlement procedures in the GATT.

Chapter 7: The Structure of Protection and Its Impact

1 See, for example, John H. Young, *Canadian Commercial Policy* (Ottawa: Queen's Printer, 1957); Francis Masson and J.B. Whitely, *Barriers to Trade between Canada and the United States* (Montreal: Private Planning Association for the Canadian-American Committee, 1960); H. Edward English, *Industrial Structure in Canada's International Competitive Position* (Montreal: Private Planning Association, 1964); M.G. Clark, *Canada and World Trade* (Ottawa: Queen's Printer, 1964); H.C. Eastman and S. Stykolt, *The Tariff and Competition in Canada* (Toronto: Macmillan, 1964); and B.W. Wilkinson, *Canada's International Trade: An Analysis of Recent Trends and Patterns* (Montreal: Private Planning Association, 1968).

2 Clark, *Canada and World Trade*, 1.

3 Ibid., 11.

4 Irving Brecher and S.S. Reisman, *Canada-United States Economic Relations* (Ottawa: Queen's Printer, 1957), 181.

5 F.H. Leacy, ed., *Historical Statistics of Canada*, 2nd ed. (Ottawa: Statistics Canada, 1983), series F109 and G479.

6 Ibid., series G482-7.

7 Constant Southworth and W.W. Buchanan, *Changes in Trade Restrictions between Canada and the United States* (Montreal: Private Planning Association for the Canadian-American Committee, 1960), 14.

8 US Bureau of the Census, *Statistical History of the United States, Colonial Times to 1957* (Washington, 1960), 539.

9   A useful comparative survey of Canadian and US tariff and trade policy making and administration as it stood in the mid-1960s can be found in K.C. Mackenzie, *Tariff-Making and Trade Policy in the U.S. and Canada* (New York: Praeger, 1968).
10 Masson and Whitely, *Barriers to Trade*, 19-20.
11 Ibid., 20-1.
12 Dana Wilgress, *Canada's Approach to Trade Negotiations* (Montreal: Private Planning Association, 1963), 57. Wilgress provides a scathing review of the status of Canadian tariff legislation and implementation at the end of the 1950s.
13 Testimony before Senate Standing Committee on Canadian Trade Relations, 6 March 1948, *Committee Proceedings*, 105-6.
14 For details on the structure of the Canadian and US tariffs at this time and the administration of tariff programs, see G.A. Elliott, *Tariff Procedures and Trade Barriers* (Toronto: University of Toronto Press for the Canadian Institute of International Affairs, 1955), 16-29 and 87-141.
15 Masson and Whitely, *Barriers to Trade*, 10.
16 Ibid., 10-13.
17 Ibid., 29, 32.
18 Randall Hinshaw, *The European Community and American Trade: A Study in Atlantic Economics and Trade* (New York: Council on Foreign Relations, 1964), 93-6.
19 Southworth and Buchanan, *Changes in Trade Restrictions*, 13.
20 Masson and Whitely, *Barriers to Trade*, 13.
21 Ibid., 14.
22 Emile Benoit, *Europe at Sixes and Sevens: The Common Market, the Free Trade Association, and the United States* (New York: Columbia University Press, 1961), 23. Dennis Swann, *The Economics of the Common Market* (London: Penguin, 1992), 102, provides slightly different averages of 0.1 percent for raw materials, 12.5 percent on capital goods, and 17.3 percent on industrial products.
23 Ryutaro Komiya and Motoshige Itoh, "Japan's International Trade and Trade Policy, 1955-1984," in Takashi Inoguchi and Daniel I. Okomoto, *The Political Economy of Japan*, vol. 2: *The Changing International Context* (Stanford: Stanford University Press, 1988), 173-224, provides an overview of the structure of Japanese protection and its evolution over the period 1955-84. See also Ippei Yamazawa, *Economic Development and International Trade: The Japanese Model* (Honolulu: East-West Center, 1990), 141-88.
24 Classification issues are discussed in Elliott, *Tariff Procedures and Trade Barriers*, 87-104, as well as in Masson and Whitely, *Barriers to Trade*, 48-52.
25 G.A. Elliott, the head of Canada's customs administration in the 1930s, noted that "this set of administrative provisions was Canada's distinctive contribution to the trade barriers of the great depression" (*Tariff Procedures and Trade Barriers*, 187).
26 See ibid., 190-1, for various examples.
27 Developments in valuation provisions are discussed ibid., 176-217, as well as in Masson and Whitely, *Barriers to Trade*, 52-6.
28 Elliott, *Tariff Procedures and Trade Barriers*, 110-14, and Masson and Whitely, *Barriers to Trade*, 49-50.
29 Elliott, *Tariff Procedures and Trade Barriers*, 114-16, and Masson and Whitely, *Barriers to Trade*, 48-9.
30 Elliott, *Tariff Procedures and Trade Barriers*, 142-70, and Masson and Whitely, *Barriers to Trade*, 27-30.
31 Southworth and Buchanan, *Changes in Trade Restrictions*, 14.
32 Masson and Whitely, *Barriers to Trade*, 1.
33 See Rodney de C. Grey, *The Development of the Canadian Anti-Dumping System* (Montreal: Private Planning Association, 1973) for a discussion of the Canadian antidumping system before the Kennedy Round reforms. Grey was a senior official in the Department of Finance. The system is also described in Masson and Whitely, *Barriers to Trade*, 52-6.
34 Elliott, *Tariff Procedures and Trade Barriers*, 171-5 and 215-17, provides a useful comparison of the Canadian and US antidumping systems as they operated in the 1950s.

35 Southworth and Buchanan, *Changes in Trade Restrictions*, 44.
36 Elliott, *Tariff Procedures and Trade Barriers*, 218-72, provides a good overview of the range of other restrictions applied by Canada and the United States. Briefer treatment can be found in Masson and Whitely, *Barriers to Trade*, 33-46 and 58-66.
37 Masson and Whitely, *Barriers to Trade*, 65-6. Masson, together with H. Edward English, prepared a further, more detailed study of nontariff barriers three years later and concluded that, if anything, these barriers had become even more prevalent as increasing overseas competition caused protectionist interests in both countries to delve deeper into the potential offered by these administrative devices (*Invisible Trade Barriers between Canada and the United States* [Montreal: Private Planning Association for the Canadian-American Committee, 1963] 3-4).
38 Masson and Whitely, *Barriers to Trade*, 3.
39 Paul and Ronald J. Wonnacott, *Free Trade Between the United States and Canada: The Potential Economic Effects* (Cambridge: Harvard University Press, 1967). A shorter version was published the following year by the Canadian-American Committee: *U.S.-Canadian Free Trade: The Potential Impact on the Canadian Economy* (Montreal: Private Planning Association, 1968). It again concluded that "the net benefits of free trade may be conservatively estimated at 10 per cent of Canadian income" (47).
40 Brecher and Reisman, *Canada-United States Economic Relations*, 146. By 1969, one of the most dedicated students of foreign investment and the behaviour of multinational enterprises concluded that the most important determinant of the behaviour of foreign-owned firms in Canada was not their ownership but the structure of protection in Canada. At an aggregate level there was little difference in the pattern of trade performance of foreign-owned and Canadian-owned firms. A.E. Safarian, *The Performance of Foreign-Owned Firms in Canada* (Montreal: Private Planning Association of Canada, 1969).
41 The Canadian-American Committee, for example, embarked on a systematic study of what would be required to increase Canada-US trade flows and strengthen the performance of the Canadian economy. In 1960 it published three studies examining the situation as it existed: Grant L. Reuber, *The Growth and Changing Composition of Trade between Canada and the United States* (Montreal: Private Planning Association for the Canadian-American Committee, 1960); Masson and Whitely, *Barriers to Trade;* and Southworth and Buchanan, *Changes in Trade Restrictions*. These were extensively discussed by CAC members, government, and other participants and led in 1963 to a further study, *A Canada-U.S. Free Trade Arrangement: Survey of Possible Characteristics* (Montreal: Private Planning Association, 1963), by Sperry Lea, as well as by two studies on nonmerchandise transactions: *Non-Merchandise Transactions between Canada and the United States,* by John W. Popkin (Montreal: Private Planning Association for the Canadian-American Committee, 1963) and Masson and English, *Invisible Trade Barriers*. Two years later, the staff of the CAC prepared a detailed report setting out *A Possible Plan for a Canada-U.S. Free Trade Area* (Montreal: Private Planning Association for the Canadian-American Committee, 1965). These and other CAC studies complemented ongoing analysis sponsored by the Canadian Trade Committee, such as English, *Industrial Structure;* and Wilkinson, *Canada's International Trade*. The cumulative effect of these studies was to provide a very detailed picture of the structure of the Canadian economy and of the role of trade and trade policy in its development to the mid-1960s. In 1966, the CAC finally issued *A New Trade Strategy for Canada and the United States*, signed by all its members, including union leaders on both sides of the border. It called for the two countries to consider proceeding to the negotiation of an Atlantic Free Trade Area among Canada, the United States, and the members of the European Free Trade Association as the basis for a broader free-trade area among all developed countries.
42 For the Canadian wheat economy and agriculture in general during the 1950s, see G.E. Britnell and Vernon C. Fowke, *Canadian Agriculture in War and Peace, 1935-50* (Stanford: Stanford University Press, 1962), and William E. Morriss, *Chosen Instrument: A History of the Canadian Wheat Board, The McIvor Years* (Edmonton: Reidmore Books for the Canadian Wheat Board, 1987).
43 V.W. Bladen, *An Introduction to Political Economy* (Toronto: University of Toronto Press, 1956), 168.
44 Ibid., 170.

45 T.K. Warley could write as late as 1976 that "partly because of this export orientation and partly because of [its] comparatively good farm structure, domestic agricultural policies in [Canada] historically have been limited in scale and modest in their objectives. They have been heavily oriented towards enhancement of bio-physical productivity; development of resources; the promotion of government or producer controlled statutory marketing boards; market development; and crop insurance programs" ("Western Trade in Agricultural Products," in *International Economic Relations of the Western World, 1959-1971*, ed. Andrew Shonfield [London: Oxford University Press, 1976], 323).

46 Some of the early difficulties with provincial and federal legislation are described in W.M. Drummond, "The Role of Marketing Boards in Canadian Food Marketing," in Canada, *Royal Commission on Price Spreads of Food Products* (Ottawa: Queen's Printer, 1960), vol. 3, 36-49.

47 Warley writes, "Such action leads to a situation in which the prices at which products are available in world markets bear little relationship to real costs and commercial demands, but are more a manifestation of the consequences of competition between national policies and treasuries" ("Western Trade in Agricultural Products," 296).

48 Masson and Whitely, *Barriers to Trade*, 17-18.

49 Ibid., 22-3.

50 See Timothy E. Josling, Stefan Tangermann, and T.K. Warley, *Agriculture in the GATT* (London: St. Martin's, 1996), for a thorough discussion of the difficulties encountered over the years in integrating agriculture into the GATT.

51 Letter signed by Pearson and prepared by H.O. Moran, head of the economic division, 15 January 1948, External Affairs Records, unpublished, author's files.

52 The story of the first five rounds of GATT negotiations is best told in Gerard Curzon, *Multilateral Commercial Diplomacy: The General Agreement on Tariffs and Trade and Its Impact on National Commercial Policies and Techniques* (London: Michael Joseph, 1965); and Kenneth W. Dam, *The GATT: Law and International Economic Organization* (Chicago: University of Chicago Press, 1970). Unlike some of the mandarins from this period, none of the trade policy veterans have as yet dictated their memoirs. Instead, the picture portrayed here is based on interviews and the folklore in the trade policy community of the 1970s and 1980s. During the 1985-7 Canada-US negotiations, for example, staff meetings with Simon Reisman sometimes turned into seminars on the early postwar development of Canadian trade policy, in which he had played a significant part.

53 Dana Wilgress did leave memoirs, but they are remarkably reticent about trade policy, devoting more time to his experiences in Russia. In any event, despite the fact that he chaired annual GATT sessions from 1948 to 1951, he did so outside the mainstream of trade policy formulation, spending that time as minister to Switzerland, and high commissioner to the United Kingdom. See his *Memoirs* (Toronto: Ryerson Press, 1967). More can be gleaned from his *Canada's Approach to Trade Negotiations*, prepared in 1963 for the Private Planning Association as background for the Kennedy Round negotiations.

54 Quoted in Gordon Blake, *Customs Administration in Canada* (Toronto: University of Toronto Press, 1957), 184.

55 Simon Reisman has told the author, for example, that he suggested to George Ball in the 1950s how the United States could use voluntary export restraints to address its worries about growing low-cost Japanese exports. Canada later adopted the same technique.

56 Department of State Historical Office, Bureau of Public Affairs, *Foreign Relations of the United States, 1952-1954*, vol. 6, part 2, W*estern Europe and Canada* (Washington: US Government Printing Office, 1986), no. 972, 2093. See also Robert A. Pastor, *Congress and the Politics of U.S. Foreign Economic Policy 1929-1976* (Berkeley: University of California Press, 1980), 99-104.

57 Robert A. Spencer, *Canada in World Affairs: From UN to NATO 1946-1949* (Toronto: Oxford University Press, 1959), 214.

58 Donald Creighton, *The Forked Road: Canada 1939-1957* (Toronto: McClelland and Stewart, 1976), 234-5.

59 Arnold Heeney, *The Things That Are Caesar's: Memoirs of a Canadian Public Servant* (Toronto: University of Toronto Press, 1972), 56-7.

60 It should be noted that the minister of finance well into the 1970s closely supervised any changes in the tariff, whether through negotiations or the budget. Each tariff change, of course, could call forth strong industry reaction and thus create political difficulties. But keeping close tabs on the details of tariff changes is not the same as staying on top of an increasingly complex trade policy that involved much more than the tariff.

61 In his memoirs, Mitchell Sharp provides a unique perspective on the efficacy of this form of bureaucratic government. First as an official (1942-58), then as a minister (1963-78), and again as an official (1978-86), his was a long and varied experience. In an essay explaining the proper relationship between mandarin and minister, Sharp extols the virtues of professional advice and administration under the political guidance of elected politicians (*Which Reminds Me ... A Memoir* [Toronto: University of Toronto Press, 1994], 79-84). Later he makes the point that his differences with Walter Gordon on economic nationalism reflected this dual ministerial and official experience, which taught him the limits of what governments can achieve in practice (145-9).

62 J.L. Granatstein, *The Ottawa Men: The Civil Service Mandarins 1935-1957* (Toronto: Oxford University Press, 1982), xi-xii.

63 For a discussion of Canadian nationalism and its origins, see Sylvia B. Bashevkin, *True Patriot Love: The Politics of Canadian Nationalism* (Toronto: Oxford University Press, 1991).

64 Polling in the mid-1950s showed that Canadians were generally satisfied with the US relationship. When asked if there was too much US influence on Canadian life, 63 percent said no. Asked whether it was good for Canada that Canadian economic development was US-financed, 69 percent said yes. Nevertheless, the US embassy periodically reported to Washington on Canadian nationalist complaints, that is, on growing anti-Americanism. See Bothwell, *Canada and the United States*, 61, 67 and 171.

65 Robert Bothwell, Ian Drummond, and John English, *Canada since 1945: Power, Politics and Provincialism* (Toronto: University of Toronto Press, 1981), 14.

66 Ibid., 154.

67 Pressed on cabinet by Lester Pearson, the establishment of the Gordon Commission was a decision not shared by the minister most affected, C.D. Howe. He regarded the commission as an enquiry into the mandate of his department by a man whose views he did not share. See Sharp, *Which Reminds Me*, 53-4.

68 Royal Commission on Canada's Economic Prospects, *Final Report* (Ottawa: Queen's Printer, 1957), 35 (Gordon Commission).

69 Brecher and Reisman, *Canada-United States Economic Relations;* Young, *Canadian Commercial Policy;* David W. Slater, *Canada's Imports;* and Roger V. Anderson, *The Future of Canada's Export Trade* (all Ottawa: Queen's Printer, 1957).

70 In *Globalization and the Meaning of Canadian Life* (Toronto: University of Toronto, 1998), William Watson gathers much evidence of the extent of the mythmaking of the 1960s and 1970s and its impact on later policy discussions and formulation. He also provides a compelling case that deepening economic integration between Canada and the United States has led to little erosion in Canada's ability to chart its own policy paths.

71 Hugh G.J. Aitken, John J. Deutsch, W.A. Mackintosh, et al., *The American Economic Impact on Canada* (Durham, NC: Duke University Press, 1959), 9 and 33.

72 Adding to the general problem of insufficient Canadian capital was the fact that Canadians liked to put their savings in the bank and in government and private bonds, while Americans were prepared to put it into equity stocks and bonds. Even though American investors proved time and again that investments in Canada paid good dividends, Canadian investors were less confident.

73 Already in 1948, John Deutsch weighed the impact of increased trade with the United States on Canadian sovereignty and political identity against other prospects for Canadian economic development and prosperity. He concluded that "free access to the United States would mean a permanently greater economic integration with the United States," while other alternatives might well "mean painful readjustments and a permanently lower standard of living" (Canada, *Documents on Canadian External Relations*, vol. 14: 1948 [Ottawa, Department of External Affairs, 1994], document 652).

74 Bothwell, Drummond, and English, *Canada since 1945*, 47-9.

Chapter 8: Professionalism and Nationalism

1 W.A. Mackintosh, "Economic Factors in Canadian History," *Canadian Historical Review* 4,1 (1923). Reprinted in *Approaches to Canadian History*, ed. Carl Berger (Toronto: University of Toronto Press, 1967), 8.

2 Canadian historiography for the period 1957-67 generally tends to be deficient in two respects. First, there is insufficient appreciation of the rather narrow margin for manoeuvre available to Canadian governments as they addressed circumstances beyond their control. More powerful states adopted policies that affected Canada directly or indirectly without any thought to Canadian needs or sensitivities. Governments – or at least their professional advisors – may be aware of more attractive options from a purely Canadian perspective, but they also know that the dictates of larger powers as well as other circumstances largely foreclose these options. Insisting on losing options may be great political theatre, but it tends to weaken Canada's ability to achieve second-best solutions and can lead to less attractive alternatives. What distinguishes the scene between 1957 and 1967 is the extent to which two Canadian nationalists – Diefenbaker and Gordon – tried to rise above these constraints and realize goals beyond Canada's reach. Canadian historians generally recognize that Diefenbaker's goals were fantastic, but are more reluctant to accept that Gordon's approach was as quixotic, albeit at the other end of the political spectrum. Many of those who write history find Gordon and his quest attractive but heap ridicule on Diefenbaker. Second, Canadian diplomatic and political historians of this period tend to be fascinated by security and political events and pay insufficient attention to the trade dimensions of Canada's international relations. Much has been written about the United Nations, the Commonwealth, and NATO, and not enough about GATT and the IMF. This may reflect the success of Canada's trade policy specialists in obscuring the issues, but it does not give a sufficiently rounded picture of what was important and what was not. Jack Granatstein's *Canada 1957-1967: The Years of Uncertainty and Innovation* (Toronto: McClelland and Stewart, 1986), for example, pays no attention to any of the GATT negotiations.

3 Basil Robinson in *Diefenbaker's World* (Toronto: University of Toronto Press, 1989) bends over backward to be fair and understanding of the man he served, but the portrait that emerges is of a man who would try the patience of Job.

4 See Granatstein, *Canada 1957-1967*, 44.

5 See John G. Diefenbaker, *One Canada: Memoirs of the Right Honourable John G. Diefenbaker*, vol. 2, *The Years of Achievement* (Toronto: Macmillan, 1976), 73-4. Diefenbaker also claims (53) that he fired Mitchell Sharp over an indiscretion related to this issue, a claim that appears to be as fantastic as the original boast. In his own memoirs Sharp notes that he left before the 1958 election to take up an attractive offer from the Brazilian Traction, Light, and Power Company. He admits disillusionment with Diefenbaker and his colleagues, but refers to a number of other issues. See *Which Reminds Me ... A Memoir* (Toronto: University of Toronto Press, 1994), 68-78. See also Robinson, *Diefenbaker's World*, 14, for another view from a close observer.

6 See Diefenbaker, *Years of Achievement*, 52-5.

7 See Gerard Curzon, *Multilateral Commercial Diplomacy: The General Agreement on Tariffs and Trade and Its Impact on National Commercial Policies and Techniques* (London: Michael Joseph, 1965), 280-1.

8 Notes Jeffrey Harrop, "The UK's ambivalent postwar relationship with the EC has something of a tragic farce about it" (*The Political Economy of Integration in the European Community* [Aldershot, UK: Edward Elgar, 1992], 21).

9 Dana Wilgress, *The Impact of European Integration on Canada* (Montreal: Private Planning Association, 1962), 5-6.

10 See, for example, the thirteen studies comprising the "Canada in the Atlantic Economy Series," sponsored at the end of the 1960s by the Private Planning Association under the direction of H. Edward English and published by the University of Toronto Press.

11 Wilgress, *Impact of European Integration*, 25-32, provides a sobering assessment of the extent to which Canada's immediate commercial interests would be compromised by British entry into the Common Market. He concludes, "The [United Kingdom] has become convinced of the imperative to join the European Economic Community. If it is successful in overcoming the very great obstacles that stand in the way of full membership, Canada will have to accept the challenge that this implies. This will involve many difficulties in making the adjustments that will be necessary. The stimulus afforded by this necessity may make Canada a stronger nation better fitted to achieve its destiny" (44). A contemporary and more upbeat US assessment can be found in Don D. Humphrey, "The United Kingdom, the Commonwealth, the Common Market, and the United States," in *Studies in United States Commercial Policy*, ed. William B. Kelly Jr. (Chapel Hill: University of North Carolina Press, 1963).

12 Granatstein, *Canada 1957-1967*, 55.

13 See Desmond Dinan, *Ever Closer Union? An Introduction to the European Union* (Boulder, CO: Lynne Riener, 1994), for a discussion of the trials of British entry and Gaullist opposition.

14 Notes historian Kenneth Morgan, "The mood when Britain joined was one of wary acceptance, since no obvious alternative could be found. It even appeared a kind of surrender, a recognition of the loss of Empire and the breakdown of an equal partnership with the Americans had left Britain as an enfeebled and divided offshore island with nowhere else to turn. It was not an invigorating mood in which to celebrate the ending of what Hugh Gaitskell had once termed 'a thousand years of history'. Indeed, 1 January 1973 came and went with little sense of historical change at all" (*The People's Peace: British History 1945-1989* [Oxford: Oxford University Press, 1990], 342-3).

15 Address at Dartmouth College, 7 September 1957, reprinted in *External Affairs* 9, 9 (1957): 275.

16 Quoted in Granatstein, *Canada 1957-1967*, 101.

17 Sharp, *Which Reminds Me*, 70-1.

18 Constant Southworth and W.W. Buchanan, *Changes in Trade Restrictions between Canada and the United States* (Montreal: Private Planning Association, 1960), 2.

19 Ronald Anderson, "Canadian Firms Claim Valuation Barriers Put up by U.S. Customs, Despite Pact," *Globe and Mail*, 31 October 1960, 29.

20 J. McLin, *Canada's Changing Defense Policy, 1957-1963* (Baltimore: Johns Hopkins Press, 1967), 176.

21 The Arrow made its maiden flight on 25 March 1958. Soon thereafter officials estimated that $300 million had been spent and that a further $871 million would be needed (Granatstein, *Canada 1957-1967*, 106-7). Total federal government expenditure in 1957 had been $7.6 billion.

22 Ibid., 107.

23 See John Kirton, "The Consequences of Integration: The Case of the Defence Production Sharing Agreements," in *Continental Community: Independence and Integration in North America*, ed. W. Andrew Axline et al. (Toronto: McClelland and Stewart, 1974), 118-19.

24 Robert Bothwell, Ian Drummond, and John English, *Canada 1900-1945* (Toronto: University of Toronto Press, 1987), 243.

25 The extent of Canada-US cooperation in the military field and the foundation it established for the DPSA can be gleaned from Danford W. Middlemiss, "Economic Defence Cooperation with the United States 1940-63," in *An Acceptance of Paradox: Essays in Honour of John W. Holmes*, ed. Kim Richard Nossal (Toronto: Canadian Institute of International Affairs, 1982), 86-109.

26 Kirton, "Consequences of Integration," 125.

27 Middlemiss, "Economic Defence Cooperation," details the arduous negotiations, which proceeded over the course of a number of years and gradually put the various elements of the DPSA together. Rather than a single agreement, the DPSA rests on a whole series of individual arrangements and understandings.

28 Kirton, "Consequences of Integration," 122. See also Richard A. Preston, *Canada in World Affairs 1959-1961* (Toronto: Oxford University Press for the Canadian Institute of International Affairs, 1965), 158-162.

29 B.W. Wilkinson, *Canada's International Trade: An Analysis of Recent Trends and Patterns* (Montreal: Private Planning Association, 1968), 72.

30   Charles Ritchie, *Storm Signals: More Undiplomatic Diaries, 1962-1971* (Toronto: Macmillan, 1983), 2.
31   The most detailed discussion of problems in Canada-US relations can be found in Knowlton Nash, *Kennedy and Diefenbaker: Fear and Loathing Across the Undefended Border* (Toronto: McClelland and Stewart, 1990). See also Lawrence Martin, *The Presidents and the Prime Ministers* (Toronto: Doubleday, 1982), 181-211; and the two volumes in the CIIA series: Preston, *Canada in World Affairs 1959-1961;* and Peyton Lyon, *Canada in World Affairs 1961-1963* (Toronto: Oxford University Press for the Canadian Institute of International Affairs, 1968).
32   J.-G. Castel, A.L.C. de Mestral, and W.C. Graham, *The Canadian Law and Practice of International Trade* (Toronto: Emond Montgomery, 1991), 302-4. See also J.I.W. Corcoran, "The Trading with the Enemy Act and the Controlled Canadian Corporation," *McGill Law Journal* 14, 2 (1968): 174.
33   The 9 July 1958 statement reads, "The Canadian and United States Governments have given consideration to situations where the export policies and laws of the two countries may not be in complete harmony. It has been agreed that in these cases there will be full consultation between the two governments with a view to finding through appropriate procedures satisfactory solutions to concrete problems as they arise" (quoted in Roger Frank Swanson, *Canadian-American Summit Diplomacy 1923-1973* [Toronto: McClelland and Stewart, 1975], 180-1).
34   Lyon, *Canada in World Affairs 1961-1963,* 411-20.
35   Address by Prime Minister Diefenbaker to the Governors' Conference, Glacier National Park, Montana, 27 June 1960, in Department of External Affairs, *Statements and Speeches,* no. 60/27.
36   Robert J. Samuelson, *The Good Life and Its Discontents: The American Dream in the Age of Entitlement 1945-1995* (New York: Random House, 1995), captures well the dilemma of the gap between expectations, fuelled by political promises, and the capacity of governments to manage the economy and satisfy these growing expectations. Although the book focuses on the United States, it applies equally well to Canada.
37   Kenneth Norrie and Douglas Owram, *A History of the Canadian Economy* (Toronto: Harcourt Brace Jovanovich, 1991), 569-71.
38   Mitchell Sharp notes wryly, "Exports increased when Hees was a flamboyant trade minister. They also increased and about as rapidly, when I was a less flamboyant trade minister" (*Which Reminds Me,* 117).
39   See Department of Trade and Commerce, *Annual Report* for 1960 and 1961 (Ottawa: Queen's Printer, 1961 and 1962).
40   Preston, *Canada in World Affairs 1959-1961,* 84-5, 97-9.
41   Ibid., 81, 93-5; and Granatstein, *Canada 1957-1967,* 62-5, 70-4.
42   Lyon, *Canada in World Affairs 1961-1963,* 328-48; and Granatstein, *Canada 1957-1967,* 86-8.
43   Granatstein, *Canada 1957-1967,* 62-100, provides a detailed overview of the economic muddle during the Diefenbaker years, including the problems surrounding James Coyne, the governor of the Bank of Canada.
44   "Breach of Contract," editorial, *Winnipeg Free Press,* 29 June 1962. The United Kingdom was the other country that provided Canada with standby credit.
45   Anson C. McKim, "How U.S. Customs Bureau Strangles Trade," *Saturday Night,* 26 November 1960, 22. McKim had just retired as president of Merck and Company.
46   Preston, *Canada in World Affairs 1959-1961,* 90-2, 95-7.
47   Ibid., 95.
48   Lyon, *Canada in World Affairs 1961-1963,* 343-7.
49   GATT, *Trends in International Trade: A Report by a Panel of Experts* (Geneva: GATT, 1958).
50   See Curzon, *Multilateral Commercial Diplomacy,* 98-101 and 178-80. Dillon became President Kennedy's treasury secretary in 1961.
51   Dana Wilgress, *Canada's Approach to Trade Negotiations* (Montreal: Private Planning Association, 1963), 21-3.
52   Lyon, *Canada in World Affairs 1961-63,* 351.
53   Gardner Patterson, *Discrimination in International Trade: The Policy Issues 1945-1965* (Princeton: Princeton University Press, 1966), 168-75.

54 Harry C. Hawkins and Janet L. Norwood, "The Legislative Basis of United States Commercial Policy," in *Studies in United States Commercial Policy*, ed. William B. Kelly Jr. (Chapel Hill: University of North Carolina Press, 1963), 112-14.

55 Curzon, *Multilateral Commercial Diplomacy*, 101.

56 See chapter 7, "The Tariff."

57 See John W. Evans, *The Kennedy Round in American Trade Policy: The Twilight of the GATT?* (Cambridge: Harvard University Press, 1971), 288; and Lyon, *Canada in World Affairs 1961-1963*, 350.

58 Patterson, *Discrimination in International Trade*, 174.

59 GATT, *Protocol to the General Agreement on Tariffs and Trade Embodying the Results of the 1960-61 Tariff Conference* (Geneva, 16 July 1962), Schedule V: Canada, 36-41.

60 "Tariff Conference Ends at Geneva," *External Affairs* 14, 8 (1962): 236. See also House of Commons, *Debates*, 7 March 1962, 1559, for the announcement by Finance Minister Fleming of the completion of Canada-US bilateral negotiations.

61 "General Agreement on Tariffs and Trade, Nineteenth Session, Geneva, 1961," *External Affairs* 14, 3 (1962): 86, and "General Agreement on Tariffs and Trade, Twentieth Session, Geneva, 1962," *External Affairs* 15, 1 (1963): 7-11. Trade and Commerce Assistant Deputy Minister Jake Warren was elected chairman of the contracting parties for 1962-3.

62 "General Agreement on Tariffs and Trade, Nineteenth Session, Geneva, 1961," *External Affairs* 14, 3 (1962): 86.

63 See Ernest H. Preeg, *Traders and Diplomats: An Analysis of the Kennedy Round of Negotiations under the General Agreement on Tariffs and Trade* (Washington: Brookings Institution, 1970), 46, 53.

64 Howard S. Piquet, *The U.S. Trade Expansion Act of 1962: How It Will Affect Canadian-American Trade* (Montreal: Private Planning Association for the Canadian-American Committee, 1963), 7-14; and Preeg, *Traders and Diplomats*, 47-9.

65 See Steve Dryden, *Trade Warriors: USTR and the American Crusade for Free Trade* (New York: Oxford University Press, 1995), 33-59, for a blow-by-blow account of the establishment of the STR.

66 Preeg, *Traders and Diplomats*, 53. See also Robert A. Pastor, *Congress and the Politics of U.S. Foreign Economic Policy 1929-1976* (Berkeley: University of California Press, 1980), 109-10.

67 On the development of a protectionist textile and clothing trade policy, see Michael M. Hart, *Canadian Economic Development and the International Trading System: Constraints and Opportunities* (Toronto: University of Toronto Press, 1985), 109-38.

68 Dryden, *Trade Warriors*, 61ff.

69 Lyon, *Canada in World Affairs 1961-1963*, 369.

70 William E. Morriss, *Chosen Instrument: A History of the Canadian Wheat Board, The McIvor Years* (Winnipeg: Reidmore Books for the Canadian Wheat Board, 1987), 221, 226-8.

71 Morriss, *Chosen Instrument*, 234-8; and Sharp, *Which Reminds Me*, 50-2, 55-8.

72 Mitchell Sharp makes the point that Hamilton had little to do with the sale; the credit should go to the Wheat Board. At the same time, he acknowledges that in politics, being in the right place at the right time is half the battle. He also does not shy away from taking credit for the wheat deals with Russia that followed (*Which Reminds Me*, 123-4).

73 Morriss, *Chosen Instrument*, 254; and Lyon, *Canada in World Affairs 1961-1963*, 420-9.

74 Preston, *Canada in World Affairs 1959-1961*, 86.

75 Morriss, *Chosen Instrument*, 254. The ruthlessness and intrigue of international grains marketing is well captured in Dan Morgan, *Merchants of Grain: The Power and Profits of the Giant Companies at the Center of the World's Food Supply* (New York: Viking Press, 1979).

76 Tom Kent, *A Public Purpose: An Experience of Liberal Opposition and Canadian Government* (Montreal: McGill-Queen's University Press, 1988), 223.

77 Denis Smith, *Gentle Patriot: A Political Biography of Walter Gordon* (Edmonton: Hurtig, 1973), 138ff.

Chapter 9: Nationalism and Pragmatism

1 Peter Newman, editorial, "Some of Our Best Friends Are Americans. Let's Keep It That Way during the Campaign," *Maclean's*, 9 March 1963, 4. Ironically, Newman would within a few years

become one of the founding members of the Committee for an Independent Canada, dedicated to a wholly different understanding of the American connection.

2   "Canada, the Exceptionally Favored: An American Perspective," in *Friends So Different: Essays on Canada and the United States in the 1980s*, ed. Lansing Lamont and J. Duncan Edmonds (Ottawa: University of Ottawa Press, 1989), 232.

3   Tom Kent, *A Public Purpose: An Experience of Liberal Opposition and Canadian Government* (Montreal: McGill-Queen's University Press, 1988), 207.

4   Lester Pearson, "The Recognition of Interdependence," in *The Four Faces of Peace and the International Outlook* (New York: Dodd, Mead, 1964), 237. In this speech, which anticipated discussion of the Third Option fifteen years later, Pearson identified the three options as continuing existing policy relying on GATT negotiations, seeking greater national self-sufficiency through higher tariffs and other interventionist policies, and consolidating economic interdependence through free-trade areas, preferably among members of the Atlantic alliance. In 1958, he clearly preferred the third course, even if it meant free trade with the Americans; he had, after all, supported free trade in 1948. He was least comfortable with the second approach of economic nationalism, although by 1963 he was prepared to give much more room to its supporters. As late as January 1963 in a speech in London, Ontario, he rhapsodized about a continental common market as a "dazzling" idea (Peyton Lyon, *Canada in World Affairs 1961-1963* [Toronto: Oxford University Press for the Canadian Institute of International Affairs, 1968], 403).

5   Tom Kent, for example, believed that "it is of the utmost importance to the world that the Canada-US relationship should be an example of how two free and independent countries can work together without the smaller having to sacrifice anything of its true identity or its real sovereignty" (*Public Purpose*, 309). The point is valid only as long as US interests are not harmed by Canadian actions; the moment they are, US interests dictate that Canada must adjust or suffer the consequences.

6   See J.L. Granatstein, *Yankee Go Home? Canadians and Anti-Americanism* (Toronto: HarperCollins, 1996), chapter 7, for a discussion of the Vietnam War and the spread of anti-Americanism. He discusses Diefenbaker's political use of anti-Americanism in chapter 5, and Walter Gordon's version of this quintessential Canadian sport in chapter 6.

7   J.L. Granatstein and Norman Hillmer, *For Better or for Worse: Canada and the United States to the 1990s* (Toronto: Copp Clark Pitman, 1991), 219.

8   Gordon's 1961 manifesto, *Troubled Canada: The Need for New Domestic Policies* (Toronto: McClelland and Stewart), set out his views in no uncertain terms, to the delight of his supporters and discomfort of his critics.

9   Charlotte S.M. Girard, *Canada in World Affairs 1963-1965* (Toronto: Canadian Institute of International Affairs, 1979), 99-114, provides a detailed account of the budget and reactions to it in Canada and abroad. Walter Gordon's own account, *A Political Memoir* (Toronto: McClelland and Stewart, 1977), 134-56, is largely a self-serving justification of his policies and behaviour.

10   House of Commons, *Debates*, 13 June 1963, 999. Gordon asserts in *Political Memoir*, 142, that this statement proves he was not a protectionist. His credentials as a protectionist, however, were already well established. During his chairmanship of the Gordon Commission, for example, he at first refused to have Jack Young's study, *Canadian Commercial Policy* (Ottawa: Queen's Printer, 1957), published because he thought it was both wrong and irresponsible. Told by other economists that its demonstration of the economic costs of the tariff was certainly not wrong and that failure to publish it could prove embarrassing, he acquiesced with a note that the commissioners "do not accept responsibility for or necessarily approve the statements and opinions which it contains" (interview with Simon Reisman, one of the directors of research for the Commission and under whose direction the study had been prepared). Mitchell Sharp minces no words, calling Gordon a protectionist in his own memoirs, *Which Reminds Me ... A Memoir* (Toronto: University of Toronto Press, 1994), 106, and calling Young's study "probably the best analysis ever made of the regional impact of Canadian tariff policy" (54).

11   See A.F.W. Plumptre, *Three Decades of Decision: Canada and the World Monetary System, 1944-75* (Toronto: McClelland and Stewart, 1977), 202-4, for a fair assessment of these three measures.

Plumptre was one of Gordon's senior officials at the time and one of those who warned him that the measures were both ill-advised and impractical.

12 The extent of Gordon's alienation from his senior officials is well captured by his biographer, Denis Smith, in *Gentle Patriot: A Political Biography of Walter Gordon* (Edmonton: Hurtig, 1973), 141-54. A more balanced portrait of Gordon's role is provided by Stephen Azzi, *Walter Gordon: The Rise of Canadian Nationalism* (Montreal: McGill-Queen's University Press, 1999).

13 See Plumptre, *Three Decades of Decision*, 204-11, for a discussion of the issues involved. Plumptre was one of the officials sent to Washington to negotiate the exemption. See generally Michael D. Mordo and Barry Eichengreen, eds., *A Retrospective on the Bretton Woods System* (Chicago: University of Chicago Press, 1993), for discussions of the broader issues at play in the decade leading to the collapse of the Bretton Woods system of fixed exchange rates.

14 Granatstein and Hillmer, *For Better or for Worse*, 222.

15 Robert Bothwell, Ian Drummond, and John English, *Canada since 1945: Power, Politics and Provincialism* (Toronto: University of Toronto Press, 1981), 272.

16 The issues are well described in Kent, *Public Purpose*, 315-22.

17 Conflicting accounts can be found in Gordon, *Political Memoir*, 266-76; and Sharp, *Which Reminds Me*, 143-5. See also Granatstein, *Yankee Go Home?*, 162-3.

18 Communiqué, "Canada-U.S. Economic Co-operation," *External Affairs* 15, 10 (1963): 349.

19 Communiqué, "Joint United States-Canadian Committee on Trade and Economic Affairs," *External Affairs* 16, 6 (1964): 276-7.

20 A.D.P. Heeney and Livingston T. Merchant, *Canada and the United States: Principles of Partnership* (Ottawa: Queen's Printer, 1965). Heeney provides a summary of the criticism generated by their report in *The Things That Are Caesar's: Memoirs of a Canadian Public Servant* (Toronto: University of Toronto Press, 1972), 194-8.

21 Quoted in Heeney, *Things That Are Caesar's*, 194. Interestingly, Walter Gordon was among the few members of cabinet who expressed reservations about the report, agreeing with populist critics that such an approach too often placed Canada in the position of supplicant.

22 See Plumptre, *Three Decades of Decision*, 211-31.

23 The pattern of production, protection, and trade in the Canadian automotive industry in the 1920s and 1930s is explained in Orville J. McDiarmid, *Commercial Policy in the Canadian Economy* (Cambridge: Harvard University Press, 1948), 354-70.

24 See Carl Beigie, *The Canada-U.S. Automotive Agreement: An Evaluation* (Montreal: Canadian-American Committee of the Private Planning Association, 1970), 11-16.

25 Ibid., table 3, 17.

26 Paul Wonnacott, *U.S. and Canadian Auto Policies in a Changing World Environment* (Toronto: C.D. Howe Institute, 1987), 3.

27 Beigie, *Automotive Agreement*, table 2, 13.

28 *Report of the Royal Commission on the Automobile Industry* (Ottawa: Queen's Printer, 1961). See also C.D. Arthur, *The Automotive Agreement in a Canada-United States Comprehensive Trade Arrangement*, a report prepared for the Department of External Affairs and International Trade, 6 November 1985. Arthur was on loan from the Department of Finance to provide Bladen with expert staff assistance. Bladen's report was subjected to a withering criticism by his former star pupil, Harry Johnson, in "The Bladen Plan for Increased Protection of the Canadian Automotive Industry," *Canadian Journal of Economics and Political Science* 29, 2 (1963): 212-38. Johnson characterized the plan as "fundamentally a scheme for increasing the amount, and the efficiency, of protection accorded to the automotive and especially the parts manufacturers, and extending such protection into the subsidization of exports" (212-13).

29 Beigie, *Automotive Agreement*, table 10, 62-3.

30 Ibid., 38-9.

31 See Communiqué, "Canada-U.S. Economic Co-operation," 349; and Communiqué, "Joint United States-Canadian Committee on Trade and Economic Affairs," 276-7.

32 On the Canadian side, the team included a pantheon of stars of the trade, economic, and foreign affairs bureaucracy, including Simon Reisman, Ed Ritchie, Jim Grandy, Bobby Latimer, Allan

Gotlieb, Bert Barrow, and Doug Arthur. The US team was headed by Phil Trezise, assistant secretary of state for economic affairs, and included officials from Treasury, Commerce, and the Office of the Special Trade Representative. US participant Julius Katz later recalled "that the thing about negotiating with the Canadians is that, at least in those days, you have two parties that are speaking the same language, I mean literally and figuratively. There are some minor cultural differences, but for the most part the negotiations are between people who think pretty much alike" (Georgetown University Library, Foreign Affairs Oral History Program, Canada Country Collection, Julius Katz interview, 1995).

33 Pearson provides amusing insight into life on the LBJ Ranch in his memoirs describing this trip, as well as into Canada's place in the US scheme of things. See *Mike: The Memoirs of the Right Honourable Lester B. Pearson,* vol. 3: 1957-1968 (Toronto: University of Toronto Press, 1975), 125-8.

34 See Gordon, *Political Memoir,* 163-72. In *Storm Signals: New Economic Policies for Canada* (Toronto: McClelland and Stewart, 1975) Gordon suggested that the solution to this problem was to force the patriation of the Canadian holdings of the automotive companies, along with the Canadian holdings of twenty-nine other major multinational enterprises. Where the capital for this fire sale would come from was never made clear.

35 Article I:b, *Agreement Concerning Automotive Products between the Government of Canada and the Government of the United States of America,* Canada Treaty Series 1966, no. 14, 16 January 1965.

36 The terms of the agreement are very succinctly summarized by Jon R. Johnson, "The Effect of the Canada-U.S. Free Trade Agreement on the Auto Pact," in *Driving Continentally: National Policies and the North American Auto Industry,* ed. Maureen Appel Molot (Ottawa: Carleton University Press, 1993), 255-60.

37 US officials initially turned a blind eye to the industry letters and only made them an issue well after the fact, when US politicians complained. US perceptions of and difficulties with the agreement are summarized in Wonnacott, *Auto Policies,* 11. It should be noted, however, that these problems were political; the industry was happy with the agreement and did not find the safeguards a major problem. If there had been substantive US concerns with the agreement, the United States could have used the threat of abrogation to bring Canada into line.

38 Strictly speaking, the safeguards continued to influence investment decisions because the right to source parts and vehicles from offshore suppliers on a duty-free basis was contingent on maintaining the required minimum level of production in Canada. With the exception of Chrysler during its difficulties in the early 1980s, however, the Big Three consistently exceeded their minimum production levels, suggesting that there were other factors responsible for the high levels of production maintained in Canada. Changes in the rules affecting trade in automotive products flowing from the FTA are explained in Johnson, "Effect of the Free Trade Agreement," 261-73. The final policy vestiges of the Auto Pact were removed in 2001 in response to a WTO panel finding in 2000 that they were discriminatory.

39 Kent, *Public Purpose,* 312.

40 The text of the waiver can be found in GATT, *Basic Instruments and Selected Documents* 14 (1966): 37-42.

41 Quoted in Lawrence Martin, *The Presidents and the Prime Ministers* (Toronto: Doubleday, 1982), 219.

42 See Arthur, *Automotive Agreement in a Trade Arrangement,* 11.

43 Reuther's principal concern was the differential in Canadian and US wages, but he was confident that as the industry in Canada grew, that wage differential would disappear. In addition, the labour adjustment provisions of the Trade Expansion Act of 1962 were available to deal with any short-term problems affecting US workers (interview with Doug Arthur). See also "Free Trade in Autos, Parts Studied by U.S. and Canada," *Christian Science Monitor,* 6 October 1964, 14; "Treaty Is Praised in Auto Industry – Union Joins Management in Hailing End of Tariffs," *New York Times,* 16 January 1965, 10.

44 Interview with Doug Arthur. See also "Big Part of Car Industry against Free Trade Plan," *Globe and Mail,* 23 October 1964, B1.

45 Robert Bothwell, *Canada and the United States: The Politics of Partnership* (Toronto: University of Toronto Press, 1992), 71.
46 Roger Smith, speech in Toronto, 16 January 1985, author's files.
47 Girard, *Canada in World Affairs 1963-1965*, 124-31, provides a detailed account of the first two years of Canadian participation in the Kennedy Round negotiations.
48 In his memoirs, Sharp characterizes Canada's position in the Kennedy Round as "astute bargaining ... and good politics." He admits, however, that Canada's position was not good economics. He notes, "It is a bit hypocritical for Canadian governments to argue ... that we were leaders in the movement for freer international trade when for a long time we lagged behind." Canada started out in 1948 with a tariff that was on average lower than that of the United States and many of the European countries. By the end of the Tokyo Round, the Canadian tariff was among the highest among industrialized countries, in large part because it did not participate fully in the Kennedy Round negotiations (Sharp, *Which Reminds Me*, 118).
49 Dana Wilgress, *Canada's Approach to Trade Negotiations* (Montreal: Private Planning Association, 1963), 47.
50 Girard, *Canada in World Affairs 1963-1965*, 129.
51 Quoted ibid., 125.
52 As Maurice Schwarzmann, one of Sharp's senior officials, explained to a Vancouver audience, "Since we import about ten times more manufactured goods than we export, a linear cut in Canadian tariffs to match a similar linear cut in the tariffs of our major trading partners would clearly be out of balance in terms of compensating benefits received and given by Canada, as well as being out of all proportion in terms of the degree of adjustment that would be required in Canadian industry as compared with the mass production industries of the U.S. and Europe" (quoted in J.L. Granatstein, *A Man of Influence: Norman A. Robertson and Canadian Statecraft 1929-68* [Toronto: Deneau, 1981], 365).
53 Sharp's concern that "Canada, with its limited domestic market, its patterns of production and trade and its relatively narrow range of exports" would not find "any single formula that would achieve the necessary balance of advantage" echoed almost word for word the same concerns expressed by his predecessor, George Hees, at the 1961 GATT ministerial meeting, suggesting that civil service briefing notes had not needed to adjust much to the change in the ministry (House of Commons, *Debates*, 24 May 1963, 232). For the text of Hees's remarks, see *External Affairs* 15, 3 (1962): 86. The text of the resolution adopted by ministers in May 1963 can be found in GATT, *Basic Instruments and Selected Documents* 12 (1964): 47-9.
54 On 6 May 1964, the second ministerial meeting of the round formally accepted Canada's special status, and extended a modified version to Australia and New Zealand, which claimed similar problems. Ernest H. Preeg, *Traders and Diplomats: An Analysis of the Kennedy Round of Negotiations under the General Agreement on Tariffs and Trade* (Washington: Brookings Institution, 1970), 10; and John W. Evans, *The Kennedy Round in American Trade Policy: The Twilight of the GATT?* (Cambridge: Harvard University Press, 1971), 254-6. The text of the resolution adopted by ministers can be found in GATT, *Basic Instruments and Selected Documents* 13 (1965): 109-12.
55 Granatstein, *Man of Influence*, 365.
56 Ibid.
57 Girard, *Canada in World Affairs 1963-1965*, 129.
58 It turned out to be a big, unwieldy, and quarrelsome group. Many would later regale their more junior colleagues in Ottawa with Kennedy Round war stories, most of which seemed to revolve around bars in the old town. The truth was that many of the members were too senior for the assignment and thus did not easily gel into a team. Each was jealous of his departmental prerogatives. Don McPhail was appointed the senior representative from External Affairs, charged with keeping Robertson informed and providing him with staff assistance as he got to work, leading discussions with Americans, holding hearings, and moulding the Canadian position in meetings of the delegation and with ministers (Granatstein, *Man of Influence*, 367). McPhail also went on to a distinguished career in External Affairs, including as assistant deputy minister for economic affairs and as ambassador to Geneva.

59   Ibid., 365.

60   Ibid., 369.

61   A brief biography of Pierce can be found in Michael Hart, *Also Present at the Creation* (Ottawa: Centre for Trade Policy and Law, 1995), 9. Robertson accepted a position as the first director of the Norman Paterson School of International Affairs at Carleton University. As his biographer points out, Robertson was ill-suited to this task but conscientious about trying anyway. He performed a series of more useful tasks for his old department, including a comprehensive review of Canadian foreign policy. He died 16 July 1968, having made a contribution to Canadian statecraft on a par with that of his mentor, O.D. Skelton (Granatstein, *Man of Influence*, 370ff).

62   In these negotiations, officials followed the philosophy first set out by Hector McKinnon that their job was to get as much as they could and give up as little as they could get away with. Officials at Trade and Commerce were responsible for getting as much as possible and officials at Finance for giving up as little as possible. Arthur Annis, the director of the tariffs division at Finance in the 1960s, applied this policy with a rigour that some could admire but many found difficult to accept. He was cautious to a fault and inculcated the same values in his staff. As late as the early 1980s, Canada still maintained tariffs on goods, such as silver buttonhooks, which last enjoyed a market during Queen Victoria's reign. Annis and his colleagues were of the view that such items could be useful at some point as payment for concessions Canada wanted.

63   The reports of Committee III dealing with developing countries are reproduced in GATT, *Basic Instruments and Selected Documents* 11 and 12 (1963 and 1964). The report of the special session is reproduced in the thirteenth supplement (1965).

64   Preeg, *Traders and Diplomats;* and Evans, *Kennedy Round.*

65   Andrew Shonfield, ed., *International Economic Relations of the Western World,* vol. 1, *Politics and Trade* (London: Oxford for the Royal Institute of International Affairs, 1976), 34.

66   The Final Act and Protocols are reproduced in GATT, *Basic Instruments and Selected Documents* 15 (1968).

67   See Timothy E. Josling, Stefan Tangermann, and T.K. Warley, *Agriculture in the GATT* (New York: St. Martin's, 1996), for a discussion of agriculture in the Kennedy Round.

68   Preeg, *Traders and Diplomats,* 253-5; and Evans, *Kennedy Round,* 289.

69   Preeg, *Traders and Diplomats,* 226-32; and Evans, *Kennedy Round,* 245-53. Evans is less willing than Preeg to concede that the developing countries gained little from the negotiations, noting the extent to which they were unprepared to participate and to which they benefited from MFN concessions.

70   Even though Canada had not agreed to participate in the formula cut, the extent of Canada's contribution is well illustrated by the number of items covered. At the end of the Dillon Round, changes in Canada's GATT schedule covered six pages; at the end of the Kennedy Round, Canada's tariff reductions and bindings covered 129 pages. GATT, *Legal Instruments Embodying the Results of the 1964-67 Trade Conference* (Geneva: GATT, 30 June 1967), vol. 1, Schedule V: Canada, 57-186.

71   "The Kennedy Round of Tariff Negotiations," *External Affairs* 19, 8 (August 1967): 306ff. As is common in reporting results, other countries, because of the importance of emphasizing gains and minimizing concessions, reported the conclusion of negotiations with Canada slightly differently. See Preeg, *Traders and Diplomats,* 186-8, and Evans, *Kennedy Round,* 287-8.

72   Anthony Westell, "Tariff Deal Will Cut Prices," *Globe and Mail,* 30 June 1967, A1.

73   "A Challenge for Traders," editorial, *Globe and Mail,* 3 July 1967, A6.

74   Evans, *Kennedy Round,* 255-6.

75   Rodney de C. Grey, *The Development of the Canadian Anti-dumping System* (Montreal: Private Planning Association of Canada, 1973), 29-59.

76   Victor Mackie, "Canada Still Protectionist," *Winnipeg Free Press,* 30 June 1967, 1.

77   Editorial, *Winnipeg Free Press,* 30 June 1967, 21.

78   See Evans, *Kennedy Round,* 299-327, for a pessimistic assessment of the post-Kennedy Round mood. Later commentators, such as I.M. Destler, *American Trade Politics: System under Stress,* 3rd ed. (Washington: Institute for International Economics, 1995), Judith Goldstein, *Ideas, Interests, and*

American Trade Policy (Ithaca, NY: Cornell University Press, 1993), and Edward S. Kaplan, *American Trade Policy, 1923-1995* (Westport, CT: Greenwood Press, 1996), place the ugly mood after the Kennedy Round into broader perspective.

79 Gerard and Victoria Curzon, "The Management of Trade Relations in the GATT," in *International Economic Relations of the Western World,* ed. Andrew Shonfield, vol. 1, *Politics and Trade* (London: Oxford for the Royal Institute of International Affairs, 1976), 147.

80 The growth in trade relations and the resources devoted to managing relations and nurturing new trading partners can be gleaned from the annual reports of the Department of External Affairs and the Department of Trade and Commerce.

81 Kenneth Norrie and Douglas Owram, *A History of the Canadian Economy* (Toronto: Harcourt Brace Jovanovich, 1991), 569-75.

82 Michael Bliss, *Northern Enterprise: Five Centuries of Canadian Business* (Toronto: McClelland and Stewart, 1987), 508, 511.

83 Kent, *Public Purpose,* 306.

84 Walter Gordon, *A Choice for Canada: Independence or Colonial Status* (Toronto: McClelland and Stewart, 1966).

85 See Smith, *Gentle Patriot,* for a detailed record of everyone's frustration, as well as Gordon, *Political Memoir,* chapter 16, and Sharp, *Which Reminds Me,* 148ff.

86 In the United States, Harvard scholar Raymond Vernon wrote a series of books, including *Sovereignty at Bay: The Multinational Spread of U.S. Enterprises* (New York: Basic Books, 1971) and *Storm over the Multinationals* (Cambridge: Harvard University Press, 1977) detailing the controversy. As graduate students, Watkins and Stephen Hymer, one of his colleagues on the task force, had worked with many of the scholars in the Boston area who contributed to the storm over the multinationals. See Dave Godfrey and Mel Watkins, eds., *Gordon to Watkins to You* (Toronto: New Press, 1970).

87 Task Force on the Structure of Canadian Industry, *Foreign Ownership and the Structure of Canadian Industry: Report of the Task Force on the Structure of Canadian Industry* (Ottawa: Privy Council Office, 1968). In 1967, Mel Watkins was a little known, 35-year-old professor at the University of Toronto with solid credentials as an MIT-trained neoclassical economist. He had already begun to have some doubts about his neoclassical training, but his work on what became known as the Watkins Report finished his reeducation. His favourable review of Gordon's *A Choice for Canada* for the *Canadian Forum* probably brought him to Gordon's attention. Working closely with political scientist Abe Rotstein and fellow economist Stephen Hymer, Watkins became convinced that the heavy presence of multinational firms posed a threat to Canada's economic independence. He soon joined others in the conviction that Canada's independence could only be guaranteed if it became a socialist state. Together with Jim Laxer and others, his next target became the NDP, the only party that he judged capable of realizing the establishment of an independent, socialist Canada. The NDP too, however, proved too bourgeois, and needed to be moved radically to the left. For an overview of evolving views of the costs and benefits of foreign direct investment, see Michael Hart, "A Multilateral Agreement on Foreign Direct Investment – Why Now?" in *Investment Rules for the Global Economy: Enhancing Access to Markets,* ed. Pierre Sauvé and Daniel Schwanen (Toronto: C.D. Howe Institute, 1996).

88 Richard N. Cooper, *The Economics of Interdependence: Economic Policy in the Atlantic Community* (New York: McGraw-Hill for the Council on Foreign Relations, 1968), 4-5. Emphasis in original.

Chapter 10: Reviews and Options

1 See Donald Macdonald, "The Trudeau Cabinet: A Memoir," in *Trudeau's Shadow: The Life and Legacy of Pierre Elliott Trudeau,* ed. Andrew Cohen and J.L. Granatstein (Toronto: Random House, 1998), for an insider's account of how the Trudeau cabinet operated. See also the opening pages of J.L. Granatstein and Robert Bothwell, *Pirouette: Pierre Trudeau and Canadian Foreign Policy* (Toronto: University of Toronto Press, 1990), for a telling portrayal of the difference between the Pearson and Trudeau styles.

2 See Colin Campbell, *Governments under Stress: Political Executives and Key Bureaucrats in Washington, London, and Ottawa* (Toronto: University of Toronto Press, 1983), for a discussion of the evolution of the Trudeau government's approach to decision making.

3 Canada, *Foreign Policy for Canadians* (Ottawa: Queen's Printer, 1970).

4 Peter C. Dobell, in *Canada's Search for New Roles: Foreign Policy in the Trudeau Era* (Toronto: Oxford University Press for the Royal Institute of International Affairs, 1972), provides a sympathetic analysis of the foreign policy review. His judgment, however, was not sustained by subsequent events or analysis. Granatstein and Bothwell, *Pirouette*, offers the most detailed and balanced assessment of Trudeau's foreign policy.

5 Interestingly, President Richard Nixon, in a similar review of US foreign policy in 1970-1, *US Foreign Policy for the 1970s*, also gave short shrift to US economic interests and ignored relations with Canada. See Granatstein and Bothwell, *Pirouette, 45.*

6 Trudeau's *Memoirs* (Toronto: McClelland and Stewart, 1993) do not offer much insight into his policies and their rationale. The next best thing is the volume he coedited with his last principal secretary, Tom Axworthy, *Towards a Just Society: The Trudeau Years* (Toronto: Viking, 1990), in which he and fourteen of his closest collaborators, political and bureaucratic, offer views on the most important policy themes pursued during the Trudeau years.

7 Trudeau was probably better versed on the ins and outs of economics as an academic discipline than most of his ministers, even if his practical understanding was perhaps underdeveloped. However, economic issues did not excite him in the same way as constitutional issues, leaving him content to let others provide the main direction in economic policy, even if some of those directions were at times bizarre and counterproductive.

8 A number of the research studies prepared for the Macdonald Royal Commission, edited by John Sargent, focused on Canada's postwar macroeconomic experience, particularly *Postwar Macroeconomic Developments* and *Fiscal and Monetary Policy* (all published Toronto: University of Toronto Press, 1986).

9 Keynesianism, derived from the economic ideas first developed by British economist John Maynard Keynes, emphasized that governments could stabilize the performance of an economy by stimulating demand through government spending at times of recession, and cutting back during times of growth, i.e., using the government's fiscal levers to counter the negative effect of the business cycle. Keynes's ideas stimulated the development of the study of macroeconomics and spawned a broader set of ideas about activist government management of the economy often referred to as the Keynesian consensus. See W.H. Hutt, *The Keynesian Episode: A Reassessment* (Indianapolis: Liberty Press, 1979).

10 For a balanced but generally sympathetic account of the difficulties experienced by the Trudeau government in implementing Keynesian demand management, see Ian A. Stewart, "Global Transformation and Economic Policy," in Axworthy and Trudeau, *Towards a Just Society.*

11 See Andrew Coyne, "Social Spending, Taxes, and the Debt: Trudeau's Just Society," in Cohen and Granatstein, *Trudeau's Shadow,* 231.

12 For readers prepared to look past the excessive ideological cant and eccentric interpretations offered by Stephen Clarkson and Christina McCall in *Trudeau and Our Times,* vol. 1, *The Magnificent Obsession,* and vol. 2, *The Heroic Delusion* (Toronto: McClelland and Stewart, 1990 and 1994), the authors do provide a wealth of detail on the economic difficulties the Trudeau government faced in the late 1970s and early 1980s; see particularly vol. 2, chapters 3 and 7.

13 The Science Council, established in the closing year of the Pearson government, dedicated itself to promoting interventionism and over the next twenty-six years published report after report extolling the virtues of activist government programs, often as an antidote to the reports of the Economic Council extolling the virtues of market-based policies. A typical example of its views on industrial policy can be found in its Report #37: *Canadian Industrial Development: Some Policy Directions* (Ottawa: Supply and Services, 1984). A concurrent example of the more mainstream analysis and prescriptions of the Economic Council on trade and industrial policy issues can be found in *The Bottom Line: Technology, Trade, and Income Growth* (Ottawa: Supply and Services, 1983).

14 Joel Bell, "Canadian Industrial Policy in a Changing World," in Axworthy and Trudeau, *Towards a Just Society*, 78.

15 Coyne, "Social Spending," 231.

16 Ibid., 225-7.

17 The most detailed account of US trade policies in this period can be found in Steve Dryden, *Trade Warriors: USTR and the American Crusade for Free Trade* (New York: Oxford University Press, 1995). See also Robert A. Pastor, *Congress and the Politics of U.S. Foreign Economic Policy 1929-1976* (Berkeley: University of California Press, 1980); John M. Dobson, *Two Centuries of Tariffs: The Background and Emergence of the United States International Trade Commission* (Washington: USITC, 1976); Alfred E. Eckes, Jr., *Opening America's Market: U.S. Foreign Trade Policy Since 1776* (Chapel Hill: University of North Carolina Press, 1995); I.M. Destler, *American Trade Politics: System under Stress*, 3rd ed. (Washington: Institute for International Economics, 1995); and Edward S. Kaplan, *American Trade Policy, 1923-1995* (Westport, CT: Greenwood Press, 1996).

18 For an overview of the macroeconomic problems and their effect on the monetary system, see Barry Eichengreen and Peter B. Kenen, "Managing the World Economy under the Bretton Woods System: An Overview," in *Managing the World Economy: Fifty Years after Bretton Woods*, ed. Kenen (Washington: Institute for International Economics, 1994).

19 The detail of the tension between administration and Congress is best captured in Dryden, *Trade Warriors*, chapters 5 through 9.

20 A fascinating case study of the interplay of macroeconomic, industrial, and trade policy interests and responses during this period is provided in Max Holland, *When the Machine Stopped: A Cautionary Tale from Industrial America* (Boston: Harvard Business School Press, 1989), which traces the troubles of the US machine tool industry in the face of Japanese competition.

21 See Destler, *American Trade Politics*, chapter 3.

22 See Dryden, *Trade Warriors*, 116-27; and Eckes, *Opening America's Market*, 210.

23 The extent to which this attitude still prevails in some quarters is well illustrated in Eckes, *Opening America's Market*. Eckes was appointed to the US International Trade Commission by President Reagan and from that perch researched the material for his book. The result is a strong endorsement of the view that the United States opened its market to a much greater extent than was prudent in the postwar years, resulting in many foreign governments taking advantage of US generosity. That is a view that still plays well with many members of Congress and was in full flower in the years immediately following the Kennedy Round.

24 These complexities are best captured in Destler's compelling analysis of what he calls the congressional penchant for "sigh and cry" irresponsibility (*American Trade Politics*).

25 Since issues between Canada and the United States usually involved trade matters, Kissinger found it difficult to take relations with Canada too seriously. During one call on him by Canada's patrician ambassador, Marcel Cadieux, he hoped the ambassador "didn't come here to talk to me about the sex life of the salmon" (quoted in Granatstein and Bothwell, *Pirouette*, 47). He appreciated that trade and similar low-policy issues were critical to Canada, but they were not important to him and to the United States in the broader realms of high strategy in which he dealt. Canada's problems were small matters and could be addressed by Washington's own technicians.

26 See Dryden, *Trade Warriors*, 129-49.

27 Commission on International Trade and Investment Policy, *United States International Economic Policy in an Interdependent World* (Washington: July 1971). The commission's report was accompanied by two thick volumes of papers submitted by various interests and analysts. See also Dryden, *Trade Warriors*, 155; and Eckes, *Opening America's Market*, 213-14.

28 See Destler, *American Trade Politics*, 41-63; and Dryden, *Trade Warriors*, 151-65. A detailed account of the deteriorating international and domestic monetary conditions that led to the Nixon measures can be found in Robert Solomon, *The International Monetary System 1945-1976: An Insider's View* (New York: Harper and Row, 1977).

29 Quoted in Robert Bothwell, *Canada and the United States: The Politics of Partnership* (Toronto: University of Toronto Press, 1992), 106.

30 See George P. Shultz and Kenneth W. Dam, *Economic Policy beyond the Headlines* (New York: W.W. Norton, 1977), particularly chapter 6, for the authors' appreciation of their effort to undo some of the damage done by the 15 August measures. Dam served as executive director of the Council on Economic Policy, which Shultz chaired.

31 See Robert D. Putnam and Nicholas Bayne, *Hanging Together: The Seven-Power Summits* (Cambridge: Harvard University Press, 1984), for an overview of the first cycle of economic summits.

32 Canada-US relations during this period are covered in Bothwell, *Canada and the United States;* and Granatstein and Bothwell, *Pirouette.* The Canadian domestic dimension is described best in Robert Bothwell, Ian Drummond, and John English, *Canada since 1945: Power, Politics and Provincialism* (Toronto: University of Toronto Press, 1981).

33 On Canadian economic anxieties after 1971, see Bothwell, Drummond, and English, *Canada since 1945,* 407-36.

34 On the contributions of various bilateral committees in the 1950s and 1960s, see Maureen Appel Molot, "The Role of Institutions in Canada-United States Relations: The Case of North American Financial Ties," in *Continental Community? Independence and Integration in North America,* ed. W. Andrew Axline et al. (Toronto: McClelland and Stewart, 1974).

35 Quoted in Dobell, *Canada's Search for New Roles,* 58-9.

36 See Robert Bothwell, "'Small Problems': Trudeau and the Americans," in *Trudeau's Shadow,* ed. Cohen and Granatstein.

37 Quoted in Bothwell, *Canada and the United States,* 102.

38 Quoted in Lawrence Martin, *The Presidents and the Prime Ministers* (Toronto: Doubleday, 1982), 251-2. It is not clear that Trudeau appreciated the nonsensical nature of this kind of demand.

39 Quoted in J.L. Granatstein and Norman Hillmer, *For Better or for Worse: Canada and the United States to the 1990s* (Toronto: Copp Clark Pitman, 1991), 250.

40 Mitchell Sharp, "Canada-US Relations: Options for the Future," *International Perspectives,* Special Issue (Autumn 1972).

41 *The Canadian Encyclopedia, Year 2000 Edition* (Toronto: McClelland and Stewart, 1999), 516.

42 The Waffle faction of the NDP, led by university professors Mel Watkins and James Laxer, called for the party to adopt a much more aggressive stance to establish an "independent and socialist" Canada, relying, for example, on public ownership to replace American private ownership.

43 Quoted in Martin, *Presidents and Prime Ministers,* 255.

44 Robert Bothwell, "Has Canada Made a Difference? The Case of Canada and the United States," in *Making a Difference? Canada's Foreign Policy in a Changing World Order,* ed. John English and Norman Hillmer (Toronto: Lester, 1992), 11.

45 Mitchell Sharp, *Which Reminds Me ... A Memoir* (Toronto: University of Toronto Press, 1994), 186.

46 See, for example, Rodney de C. Grey, *Trade Policy in the 1980s: An Agenda for Canada-U.S. Trade Relations* (Montreal: C.D. Howe Institute, 1981); Grey, *United States Trade Policy Legislation: A Canadian View* (Montreal: Institute for Research on Public Policy, 1982); and J. Michael Finger, ed., *Antidumping: How It Works and Who Gets Hurt* (Ann Arbor: University of Michigan Press, 1993).

47 Author's files. The author served at Canada's permanent mission in Geneva in 1976-8, and in various commercial policy assignments in Ottawa in 1975 and 1978-83.

48 Trudeau's performance at these events and his otherwise eloquent presence on the international stage stimulated Canada's international relations scholars to wax enthusiastically about Canada's role as a "middle," "foremost," or "minor great" power. See, for example, Norman Hillmer and Garth Stevenson, eds., *Foremost Nation: Canadian Foreign Policy and a Changing World* (Toronto: McClelland and Stewart, 1977).

49 The European Economic Community, the European Atomic Energy Community, and the European Coal and Steel Community were integrated in 1967 to become the European Community.

50 Developments in the EC are discussed in Desmond Dinan, *Ever Closer Union? An Introduction to the European Community* (Boulder, CO: Lynne Riener, 1994), 69-98; and Neill Nugent, *The Government and Politics of the European Union,* 4th ed. (Durham, NC: Duke University Press, 1999), chapters 1-3.

51 Most of the EFTA countries, while they were willing to forge closer economic relations with the EC, found its supranational institutions and noneconomic aspects too threatening to their status as neutrals. Norway, which unlike the rest was a member of NATO, had put the question of EC membership to its electorate. Norwegians demurred, fearing that membership would open its rich fishery to other member states and its energy resources to exploitation by energy-starved Continental countries. With the end of the cold war, these considerations waned and all but Norway, Switzerland, and Iceland joined the EC.

52 On British entry into the EC, see Dinan, *Ever Closer Union?* 75-81. Between 1968 and 1972, the Private Planning Association of Canada sponsored a series of thirteen studies by Canada's leading economists examining various dimensions of Atlantic free trade. See the concluding study, H. Edward English, Bruce W. Wilkinson, and H.C. Eastman, *Canada in a Wider Economic Community* (Toronto: University of Toronto Press, 1972). In the United States, the Council on Foreign Relations sponsored a series of similar studies by such eminent scholars as Henry Kissinger, Zbigniew Brzezinski, Stanley Hoffman, and Richard Cooper. See, for example, Richard N. Cooper, *The Economics of Interdependence: Economic Policy in the Atlantic Community* (New York: McGraw-Hill for the Council on Foreign Relations, 1968). See also *GATT Plus: A Proposal for Trade Reform*, Report of the Special Advisory Panel to the Trade Committee of the Atlantic Council (Washington: Atlantic Council, 1975), which recast Atlanticist sentiments into a broader proposal for a two-tiered GATT. These proposals waned after 1973, but seemed to gain new, if less credible, currency in the late 1990s among such proponents as Canadian newspaper baron Conrad Black and US senator Phil Gramm, both apparently oblivious to thirty years of institutional and economic developments.

53 See J.J. Servan-Schreiber, *Le Défi américain* (Paris: Denoël, 1967), for a passionate expression of concern about the influx of US capital, a concern shared by many Canadians and well captured by Raymond Vernon, *Storm over the Multinationals* (Cambridge: Harvard University Press, 1977). The seminal Canadian expression of anxiety about US foreign direct investment was Kari Levitt, *Silent Surrender: The Multinational Corporation in Canada* (New York: St. Martin's Press, 1970).

54 On US efforts to kindle EC interest in a new round in the early 1970s, see Dryden, *Trade Warriors*, chapters 7 and 8; and Gilbert R. Winham, *International Trade and the Tokyo Round Negotiation* (Princeton: Princeton University Press, 1986), chapter 2.

55 Following the publication of Chalmers Johnson's *MITI and the Japanese Miracle: The Growth of Industrial Policy, 1925-1975* (Stanford: Stanford University Press, 1982), US and European scholars produced a torrent of books and articles examining Japan's rise, and threat, as an industrial rival. An early look at the issues can be found in *Asia's New Giant: How the Japanese Economy Works*, ed. Hugh Patrick and Henry Rosovsky (Washington: Brookings Institution, 1976). For a recent summary, see Bradley Richardson, *Japanese Democracy: Power, Coordination, and Performance* (New Haven: Yale University Press, 1997), 200-39. Administrative guidance, one of the more inscrutable Japanese techniques, basically involved bureaucrats in the major ministries providing Japanese traders and manufacturers with advice on desirable behaviour and using licensing and other techniques to discipline those who failed to follow this advice.

56 On the challenges raised by these emerging East Asian economies, see Roy A. Matthews, *Canada and the "Little Dragons": An Analysis of Economic Developments in Hong Kong, Taiwan, and South Korea and the Challenge/Opportunity They Present for Canadian Interests in the 1980s* (Montreal: Institute for Research on Public Policy, 1983).

57 Two recent, popular considerations of the rise of the Asian newly industrialized countries can be found in Jim Rohwer, *Asia Rising: Why America Will Prosper As Asia's Economies Boom* (New York: Touchstone, 1995); and Christopher Lingle, *The Rise & Decline of the Asian Century: False Starts on the Path to the Global Millennium*, 3rd ed. (Hong Kong: Asia 2000, 1998).

58 Excerpted in Arthur E. Blanchette, ed., *Canadian Foreign Policy 1966-1976: Selected Speeches and Documents* (Ottawa: Gage in association with the Institute of Canadian Studies, Carleton University, 1980), 223.

59 See A.J. Easson, ed., *Canada and the European Communities: Selected Materials*, Canada-Europe Series No. 2/1979 (Kingston: Centre for International Relations, Queen's University, 1979), which reproduces dozens of press stories covering Canada-EC relations during this period.

60 On the negotiation of the contractual link, see Granatstein and Bothwell, *Pirouette,* 158-77; and Evan Potter, *Transatlantic Partners: Canadian Approaches to the European Union* (Montreal: McGill-Queen's University Press for Carleton University Press, 1999). The pages of *International Perspectives,* published by Department of External Affairs, provide some of the details of contemporary in-house policy thinking.

61 Hugh Winsor, "What Is Ottawa's EEC Agreement?" *Globe and Mail,* 10 June 1976.

62 Even Tom Axworthy had to admit that the government had bitten off more than it could chew: "The ability of government to redraw trading patterns was too limited to turn the diversification goal of the Third Option into a reality ... In defending its policy of autonomy, the Trudeau government opted for Canadian independence. It successfully withstood the protests of the US government, but it was less successful in persuading the Canadian business community of the wisdom of this course" ("'To Stand Not So High Perhaps but Always Alone': The Foreign Policy of Pierre Elliott Trudeau," in Axworthy and Trudeau, *Towards a Just Society,* 36, 38).

63 The CJBC was but one of a number of trans-Pacific consultative organizations established during this period. A few years earlier, Canadian and Japanese scholars were instrumental in the inauguration of the Pacific Trade and Development Conferences (PAFTAD), and later in the 1970s, Canadian and Japanese business leaders helped to set up the Pacific Basin Economic Council (PBEC) and the Pacific Economic Cooperation Council (PECC). Together with the CJBC, these private-sector and academic institutions ensured an increasingly lively dialogue involving Canadian and Japanese business, academic, and government specialists.

64 On the discussions with Japan, see Granatstein and Bothwell, *Pirouette,* 158-77. The broader context is provided in Klaus Pringsheim, *Neighbours across the Pacific: The Development of Economic and Political Relations Between Canada and Japan* (Westport, CT: Greenwood Press, 1983); and John Schultz and Kimitada Miwa, *Canada and Japan in the Twentieth Century* (Toronto: Oxford University Press, 1991).

65 Robert Bothwell, "'The Canadian Connection': Canada and Europe," in Hillmer and Stevenson, *Foremost Nation,* 35-6.

66 On the emergence of developing countries as a force in GATT and international affairs, see Robert E. Hudec, *Developing Countries in the GATT Legal System* (London: Harvester Wheatsheaf for the Trade Policy Research Centre, 1988); Joan Edelman Spero, *The Politics of International Economic Relations,* 4th ed. (New York: St. Martin's Press, 1990), part 3; and Michael J. Trebilcock and Robert Howse, *The Regulation of International Trade,* 2nd ed. (London: Routledge, 2000), chapter 14.

67 On the emergence of OPEC, see Spero, *The Politics of International Economic Relations,* 261-301.

68 For a reasonably balanced statement of Canadian hopes and actual experience during this period, see Economic Council of Canada, *For a Common Future: A Study of Canada's Relations with Developing Countries* (Ottawa: Supply and Services, 1978).

69 The term "Group of 77" refers to the seventy-seven developing countries who attended the first UN Conference on Trade and Development (UNCTAD) in Geneva in 1964 and who determined that they would maintain group solidarity throughout the conference. Over the years, their numbers grew, but the name remained the same.

70 On Canada and North-South relations, see Granatstein and Bothwell, *Pirouette,* 261-85. Ivan Head, Trudeau's principal advisor on foreign policy matters and the inspiration for much of his approach to developing countries, sets out his perspective in *On a Hinge of History: The Mutual Vulnerability of South and North* (Toronto: University of Toronto Press, 1991).

71 Statement by Mitchell Sharp, minister of finance, to the Canadian Society of New York, 4 November 1966, excerpted in Blanchette, *Canadian Foreign Policy,* 188.

72 Statement by the prime minister to a convocation ceremony marking the Diamond Jubilee of the University of Alberta, Edmonton, Alberta, 13 May 1968, excerpted ibid., 234-5. The exact nature of the threat Canadians might face is not clear, but, like so much of Trudeau's rhetoric, it sounded good at the time.

73 On trade in primary resources and the various UN and other efforts to address them, see Jere R. Behrman, *International Commodity Agreements: An Evaluation of the UNCTAD Integrated Commodity Programme* (Washington: Overseas Development Council, 1977); North-South Institute,

Commodity Trade: Test Case for a New Economic Order (Ottawa: North-South Institute, 1978); and Hugh Corbet, *Raw Materials: Beyond the Rhetoric of Commodity Power* (London: Trade Policy Research Centre, 1975).

74 Granatstein and Bothwell, *Pirouette.*

75 See, for example, Glen Williams, *Not for Export: Toward a Political Economy of Canada's Arrested Industrialization,* new ed. (Toronto: McClelland and Stewart, 1986).

76 A number of the research studies prepared for the Macdonald Royal Commission, edited by Donald G. McFetridge, focused on industrial policy, particularly *Canadian Industrial Policy in Action* (1985), *Economics of Industrial Policy and Strategy* (1986), *Canadian Industry in Transition* (1986), and *Technological Change in Canadian Industry* (1985). See also Michael Trebilcock, *The Political Economy of Economic Adjustment* (1986), Michael Hart, *Canadian Economic Development and the International Trading System: Constraints and Opportunities* (1985), and André Blais, ed., *Industrial Policy* (1986) (all published Toronto: University of Toronto Press).

77 Those who did take note often attributed these declining numbers to the "deindustrialization" of the country, insisting that a country's future economic prosperity could only be guaranteed by a growing manufacturing sector. The relatively smaller share of workers in Canada employed in manufacturing, explained by the relatively larger share of workers in the primary sector (agriculture, fishing, forestry, and mining), was often cited as evidence of Canada's "arrested" economic development. See, for example, Robert M. Laxer, ed., *(Canada) Ltd.: The Political Economy of Dependency* (Toronto: McClelland and Stewart, 1973).

78 See Christopher Green, *Canadian Industrial Organization and Policy* (Toronto: McGraw-Hill Ryerson, 1980), tables 1-1 to 1-4.

79 Noted Hugh Winsor in one of his *Globe and Mail* columns, "A view which has considerable currency in the Canadian government, especially in the East Block offices of the Prime Minister Pierre Trudeau, is that much of the Canadian business sector is akin to a herd of lumbering elephants that doesn't show much initiative or drive without prodding from the trainers" (11 June 1976).

80 Eric W. Kierans, *Challenge of Confidence: Kierans on Canada* (Toronto: McClelland and Stewart, 1967), 75-6.

81 Coyne, "Social Spending," 234-5.

82 Notes Coyne, Trudeau was "something of a policy magpie, as susceptible to persuasion by a neoclassical economist like Albert Breton as by the broad interventions prescribed by J.K. Galbraith" (ibid., 237). Trudeau was much animated by his conviction of the need for "counterweights," a concept that formed a powerful part of his approach to constitutional issues but also weighed heavily in his thinking on foreign and economic policy matters. He was impressed by the work of Canadian expatriate John Kenneth Galbraith, who had written a number of studies in the 1950s and 1960s extolling the virtues of government use of countervailing power to offset the growing power of large corporations.

83 Bell, "Canadian Industrial Policy," 102.

84 Canada, Task Force on Business-Government Interface, *How to Improve Business-Government Relations in Canada, A Report to the Minister of Industry, Trade and Commerce* (Ottawa, 1976).

85 Task Force on the Structure of Canadian Industry, *Foreign Ownership and the Structure of Canadian Industry: Report of the Task Force on the Structure of Canadian Industry* (Ottawa: Privy Council Office, 1968); House of Commons, Standing Committee on External Affairs and National Defence, *11th Report* (Ottawa: Queen's Printer, 1970); and Canada, *Foreign Direct Investment in Canada* (Ottawa: Information Canada, 1972).

86 Canada's leading student of foreign investment, A.E. Safarian, had already published two major studies suggesting the important contribution made to Canadian economic development by FDI: *Foreign Ownership of Canadian Industry* (Toronto: McGraw-Hill, 1966); and *The Performance of Foreign-Owned Firms in Canada* (Toronto: National Planning Association, 1969). See also his *Multinational Enterprise and Public Policy: A Study of the Industrial Countries* (Aldershot, UK: Edward Elgar, 1993), for a complete review of the issues.

87 Canada, *Foreign Investment Review Act: Final Annual Report 1984-85* (Ottawa: Supply and Services, 1985), table I: All Applications Outcome or Status – 9 April 1974 to 31 March 1985.

88 A good overview of FIRA's operations and industry experience is provided in Christopher Beckman, *The Foreign Investment Review Agency: Images and Realities* (Ottawa: Conference Board of Canada, 1984). See also Samuel Wex, *Instead of FIRA: Autonomy for Canadian Subsidiaries* (Montreal: Institute for Research on Public Policy, 1984).

89 In 1982, the US government raised a series of complaints about the trade impact of the administration of FIRA. In 1984, a GATT panel ruled that Canada was entitled to review foreign investment, but that the administration of these reviews needed to be brought into conformity with Canada's GATT obligations, particularly those regarding the purchase of goods in Canada and the export of goods from Canada. See GATT, *Basic Instruments and Selected Documents* 30 (1984): 140-68.

90 See Sylvia Ostry, *Governments and Corporations in a Shrinking World* (New York: Council on Foreign Relations, 1990), 58.

91 On Canadian agricultural policy in the 1970s, see J.D. Forbes, R.D. Hughes, and T.K. Warley, *Economic Intervention and Regulation in Canadian Agriculture*, A Study Prepared for the Economic Council of Canada and the Institute for Research on Public Policy (Ottawa: Supply and Services, 1982); R.E. Haack, D.R. Hughes, and R.G. Shapiro, *The Splintered Market: Barriers to Interprovincial Trade in Canadian Agriculture* (Ottawa: Canadian Institute for Economic Policy, 1981); Barry K. Wilson, *Farming the System: How Politicians and Producers Shape Canadian Agricultural Policy* (Saskatoon: Western Producer Prairie Books, 1990); Theodore Cohn, "Canada and the Ongoing Impasse over Agricultural Protectionism," in *Canadian Foreign Policy and International Economic Regimes*, ed. A. Claire Cutler and Mark W. Zacher (Vancouver: UBC Press, 1992); and J.C. Gilson, *World Agricultural Changes: Implications for Canada* (Toronto: C. D. Howe Institute, 1989). James Bovard, *The Farm Fiasco* (San Francisco: Institute for Contemporary Studies, 1989), provides a devastating portrait of the extent and impact of US agricultural protectionism on the United States and its trading partners.

92 Forbes, Hughes, and Warley, *Economic Intervention in Canadian Agriculture*, xiii.

93 See ibid., 29, table 3-5.

94 Farm fundamentalism involves a number of dogmas that can be summarized as follows:

   • Farming is more than just a business; it is essential to the social, political, and economic fabric of a country. It is not just a job but a way of life.
   • Costs of production should be calculated on the basis of those of the marginal, least productive farmer; productivity gains achieved through technology, management, and other improvements should not lead to lower prices; prices should only go up; governments owe farmers a fair price.
   • No farmer should ever fail; when a farm fails, part of the soul of the country dies with it.
   • Farmers have a rugged, self-reliant lifestyle, but every problem is a crisis requiring government help.

   For a discussion of farm fundamentalism, see Barry Wilson and Peter Finkle, "Is Agriculture Different? Another Round in the Battle between Theory and Practice," in Grace Skogstad and Andrew Cooper, *Agricultural Trade: Domestic Pressures and International Tensions* (Halifax: Institute for Research on Public Policy, 1990).

95 See Forbes, Hughes, and Warley, *Economic Intervention in Canadian Agriculture;* and Wilson, *Farming the System*, 171-8.

96 These same technological developments fuelled the conditions that led to the transatlantic chicken war between the EC and the United States. In the late 1950s, the United States quadrupled its exports of chicken to Europe, only to have these shipments blocked in the early 1960s by application of the EC Common Agricultural Policy. US chicken exports to the German market had skyrocketed from 4.9 million pounds in 1958 to 63.6 million pounds in 1960. See John W. Evans, *The Kennedy Round in American Trade Policy: The Twilight of the GATT?* (Cambridge: Harvard University Press, 1971), 174-80.

97 Wilson, *Farming the System*, 169.

Chapter 11: The GATT Shall Provide

1 Michael. M. Atkinson and William D. Coleman, *The State, Business, and Industrial Change in Canada* (Toronto: University of Toronto Press, 1987), 191.

2 See Joel Bell, "Canadian Industrial Policy in a Changing World," and Thomas S. Axworthy, "'To Stand Not So High Perhaps but Always Alone': The Foreign Policy of Pierre Elliott Trudeau," in *Towards a Just Society: The Trudeau Years*, ed. Axworthy and Pierre Elliott Trudeau (Toronto: Viking, 1990). See also J.L. Granatstein and Robert Bothwell, *Pirouette: Pierre Trudeau and Canadian Foreign Policy* (Toronto: University of Toronto Press, 1990), 170-1.

3 See, for example, Canada, Export Promotion [Hatch] Review Committee, *Strengthening Canada Abroad*, Final Report of the Export Promotion Review Committee, 30 November 1979; and Special [Parliamentary] Committee on a National Trading Corporation, *Canada's Trade Challenge*, Fourth Report (Ottawa: Supply and Services, 1981), for detailed discussions of the dream of involving the government much more actively and directly in exporting. A watered-down version of this dream was ultimately incorporated into the mandate of the Canadian Commercial Corporation.

4 A profile of the Canadian machinery industry as it existed in the early 1980s can be found in Department of External Affairs, *A Review of Canadian Trade Policy* (Ottawa: Supply and Services, 1983), 98-101. Chapter 3 of the *Review* provides a comprehensive snapshot of the state of Canadian industry at this time, a snapshot that belies the dire contemporary concerns about the deindustrialization of Canada.

5 On developments at the GATT in the years following the Kennedy Round, see Gilbert R. Winham, *International Trade and the Tokyo Round Negotiation* (Princeton: Princeton University Press, 1986); and Sidney Golt, *The GATT Negotiations 1973-75: A Guide to the Issues* (Montreal: C.D. Howe Institute – British-North American Committee, 1974).

6 See, for example, GATT, *Basic Instruments and Selected Documents* 17 (1970): 110-22, for reports on the work program on agriculture and on industrial products.

7 Interview with Percy Eastham, February 1998.

8 See Winham, *Tokyo Round Negotiation*, 140-1, and A.L.C. de Mestral, "The Impact of the GATT Agreement on Government Procurement in Canada," in *Non-Tariff Barriers after the Tokyo Round*, ed. John Quinn and Philip Slayton (Montreal: Institute for Research on Public Policy, 1982), 171-94.

9 OECD, *Policy Perspectives for International Trade and Economic Relations*, Report by the High Level Group on Trade Related Problems to the Secretary General of the OECD (Paris: OECD, 1972).

10 Upon retirement, Olivier Long wrote an important monograph, *Law and Its Limitations in the GATT Multilateral Trade System* (Dordrecht: Martinus Nijhoff, 1985). Chapter 3 describes the functioning of the GATT, including the role of the CG-18.

11 Quoted in W. Frank Stone, *Canada, the GATT and the International Trade System* (Montreal: Institute for Research on Public Policy, 1984), 176.

12 See Gerard and Victoria Curzon, "GATT: Trader's Club," in *The Anatomy of Influence*, ed. Robert Cox and Harold Jacobson (New Haven, CT: Yale University Press, 1973), 475.

13 See Robert E. Hudec, *Developing Countries in the GATT Legal System* (London: Harvester Wheatsheaf for the Trade Policy Research Centre, 1988); and Stone, *International Trade System*, chapters 10-12, for fuller discussions of the role of developing countries in the trading system.

14 On the role of the centrally planned economies in the GATT, see John Jackson, *The World Trading System: Law and Policy of International Economic Relations* (Cambridge: MIT Press, 1989), chapter 13; Leah A. Haus, *Globalizing the GATT: The Soviet Union's Successor States, Eastern Europe, and the International Trading System* (Washington: Brookings Institution, 1992); and Stone, *International Trade System*, chapter 14. For a discussion of early Canadian experience in trading with the centrally planned economies, see Ian M. Drummond, *Canada's Trade with the Communist Countries of Eastern Europe* (Montreal: Private Planning Association of Canada, 1966).

15 On the origins and evolution of the MFA, see Michael Hart, *Canadian Economic Development and the International Trading System: Constraints and Opportunities* (Toronto: University of Toronto Press, 1985), chapter 6; and Stone, *International Trade System*, chapter 9.

16 See Robert E. Hudec, *The GATT Legal System and World Trade Diplomacy*, 2nd ed. (Salem, NH: Butterworth, 1990); and Hudec, *Adjudication of International Trade Disputes* (London: Trade Policy Research Centre, 1978).

17 Hudec, *World Trade Diplomacy*, 287-97. The reports of all completed panels and working parties are reproduced in the annual series, GATT, *Basic Instruments and Selected Documents*.

18 GATT, *Basic Instruments and Selected Documents* 25 (1979): 42.

19 GATT, *Basic Instruments and Selected Documents* 23 (1977): 91.

20 See Robert E. Hudec, "Reforming the GATT Adjudication Procedures: The Lessons of the DISC Case," *Minnesota Law Review* 72, 6 (1988): 1443-509.

21 Ibid. The reports of the panel can be found in GATT, *Basic Instruments and Selected Documents* 23 (1977): 98-147.

22 See Robert E. Hudec, *Enforcing International Trade Law: The Evolution of the GATT Legal System* (Salem, NH: Butterworth, 1993), the second volume in his comprehensive overview of the evolution of the GATT legal system.

23 See Winham, *Tokyo Round Negotiation*, particularly chapter 2.

24 See I.M. Destler, *American Trade Politics: System under Stress*, 3rd ed. (Washington: Institute for International Economics, 1995), particularly 71-7, for a discussion of the relationship between the administration and Congress during the Tokyo Round. See also Winham, *Tokyo Round Negotiation*, 307-17.

25 See Winham, *Tokyo Round Negotiation*, 317-24, for a discussion of EC decision making during the Tokyo Round. A more detailed general description can be found in Neill Nugent, *The Government and Politics of the European Union*, 4th ed. (Durham, NC: University Press, 1999), part 2 and chapter 16.

26 See GATT, *Basic Instruments and Selected Documents* 20 (1974): 19-22; and GATT, *Activities in 1973* (Geneva: GATT, 1974). The *GATT Activities* series provides a handy annual overview of the principal developments in the GATT, including the Tokyo Round negotiations.

27 See Dryden, *Trade Warriors*, chapter 9; Winham, *Tokyo Round Negotiation*, 129-37; and George P. Shultz and Kenneth W. Dam, *Economic Policy beyond the Headlines* (New York: W.W. Norton, 1977), chapter 7.

28 Winham, *Tokyo Round Negotiation*, 76-84, and Golt, *GATT Negotiations 1973-75*.

29 Canadian interests are set out in Canada, *Multilateral Trade Negotiations 1973-1979, Background Documentation*, and in privately circulated memos by deputy chief negotiator Mel Clark at the conclusion of the round. Author's files provide further details.

30 See Caroline Pestieau, *The Sector Approach to Trade Negotiations: Canadian and U.S. Interests* (Montreal: C.D. Howe Institute, 1976), for a detailed description of the sector approach to tariff negotiations.

31 Quoted in Stone, *International Trade System*, 180.

32 See ibid. The Couillard Committee issued a report in August 1977, *Review of Developments in the GATT Multilateral Trade Negotiations in Geneva* (Ottawa: Canadian Trade and Tariffs Committee, 1977), which sets out a useful Canadian perspective on the negotiations.

33 GATT, *Basic Instruments and Selected Documents* 20 (1974): 21.

34 Winham, *Tokyo Round Negotiation*, chapter 3, provides a detailed overview of the issues, while the reports of the Rey Group and Williams Commission provide useful background information. See also Stone, *International Trade System*, chapter 15.

35 Winham, *Tokyo Round Negotiation*, 18.

36 The complexity and political difficulty of the agriculture negotiations are well captured in ibid., as well as in Timothy E. Josling, Stefan Tangermann, and T.K. Warley, *Agriculture in the GATT* (New York: St. Martin's, 1996), 72-100.

37 See Robert Middleton, *Negotiating on Non-Tariff Distortions of Trade: The EFTA Precedents* (London: Trade Policy Research Centre, 1975); and Stanley D. Metzger, *Lowering Nontariff Barriers: US*

Law, Practice, and Negotiating Objectives (Washington: Brookings Institution, 1974), for two important contemporary analyses setting out the issues.

38 See some of the individual chapters in Quinn and Slayton, *Non-Tariff Barriers after the Tokyo Round,* for a description of Canadian concerns related to NTBs pursued during the negotiations.

39 See Hart, *Canadian Economic Development,* chapter 5, for a more detailed examination of the safeguards issue.

40 See Hudec, *Developing Countries,* chapter 5, for a discussion of developing country negotiating interests.

41 See Josling, Tangermann, and Warley, *Agriculture in the GATT,* 83-4; and Winham, *Tokyo Round Negotiation,* 146-58.

42 The details of the gyrations in Geneva and elsewhere that cleared the way for serious negotiations are well set out in Winham, *Tokyo Round Negotiation,* chapters 4 and 5. See also Dryden, *Trade Warriors,* chapter 9. The following two chapters describe the range of other issues that preoccupied STR officials during this period and that added to the complications that needed to be addressed in the negotiations.

43 Winham, *Tokyo Round Negotiation,* 165-6.

44 Ibid., 200-5.

45 Stone, *International Trade System,* 181.

46 See Josling, Tangermann, and Warley, *Agriculture in the GATT,* 86-93.

47 Dryden, *Trade Warriors,* chapter 12, provides a blow-by-blow account of the final phases of the negotiations and references to the many individuals required to complete them.

48 See Winham, *Tokyo Round Negotiation,* 332-42, for a discussion of the political and bureaucratic organization of the negotiations in Ottawa and Geneva. See also Gilbert R. Winham, "Bureaucratic Politics and Canadian Trade Negotiations," *International Journal* 34 (Winter 1978-9): 64-90.

49 See Douglas M. Brown, "The Evolving Role of the Provinces in Canadian Trade Policy," in *Canadian Federalism: Meeting Global Economic Challenges?* ed. Brown and Murray G. Smith (Halifax: Institute for Research on Public Policy, 1991), 81-128.

50 Some of the detail is provided in Dryden, *Trade Warriors,* 231-9.

51 See Winham, *Tokyo Round Negotiation,* chapter 8, on the internal negotiations; and Dryden, *Trade Warriors,* 249-53.

52 See GATT, *The Tokyo Round of Multilateral Trade Negotiations, Report by the Director-General of GATT* (Geneva: GATT, April 1979); and Canada, *Multilateral Trade Negotiations.* Both documents include extensive descriptions of both the negotiations and the results.

53 See Josling, Tangermann, and Warley, *Agriculture in the GATT,* 98-100.

54 See Canada, *Multilateral Trade Negotiations;* and Mel Clark, "Canada and the Tokyo Round of Multilateral Negotiations," unpublished paper, for detailed analyses of Canada's gains. Clark's memo includes an annex setting out objectives virtually achieved, partly achieved, and not achieved.

55 Winham, *Tokyo Round Negotiation,* 286-93.

56 "The Demands of GATT," editorial, *Globe and Mail,* 13 July 1979, A6.

57 Wally Dennison, "Canadian Team Wins Top Grades in Trade Talks," *Winnipeg Free Press,* 20 April 1979, 17.

58 Richard Gwynn, "Foreign Trade – Canada's 'Noble Goal,'" *Montreal Star,* 17 July 1979, A7.

Chapter 12: The Twilight of the National Policy

1 Grattan O'Leary, *Recollections of People, Press, and Politics* (Toronto: Macmillan, 1977), 182-3.

2 Rodney Grey first suggested his concern in an article in the *Financial Post* in March 1980 but soon completed two books that outlined his concerns in considerable detail: *Trade Policy in the 1980s: An Agenda for Canada-U.S. Trade Relations* (Montreal: C.D. Howe Institute, 1981); and *United States Trade Policy Legislation: A Canadian View* (Montreal: Institute for Research on Public Policy, 1982).

3 Clark expressed his views in a series of papers circulated among former colleagues and in briefs prepared for private clients (author's files).

4 Canada, *The Results of the Tokyo Round of Multilateral Trade Negotiations* (Ottawa, 1979).

5 "MTN and the Legal Institutions of International Trade," memorandum prepared for the Committee on Finance, United States Senate, *MTN Studies* 4, June 1979, 96th Congress, 1st session, Committee Print, CP96-14 (Washington: US Government Printing Office, 1979).

6 It should be noted that Canada was not alone in this endeavour. As Daniel Verdier points out in chapter 12 of his *Democracy and International Trade: Britain, France, and the United States, 1860-1990* (Princeton: Princeton University Press, 1994), virtually every member of the OECD experimented with industrial strategies in response to the challenges created by deepening internationalization.

7 A good indication of the extent and expense of these programs was provided in 1984-5 during the comprehensive program review conducted under the auspices of Deputy Prime Minister Erik Nielsen. See, for example, Task Force on Program Review, *Services and Subsidies to Business: Giving with Both Hands; Natural Resources Program: From Crisis to Opportunity;* and *Agriculture: Study Team Reports to the Task Force on Program Review* (all Ottawa: Supply and Services, 1986).

8 See, for example, Abraham Rotstein, ed., *An Industrial Strategy for Canada* (Toronto: Canadian Forum, 1972); and Rotstein, *Rebuilding from Within: Remedies for Canada's Ailing Economy* (Toronto: James Lorimer for the Canadian Institute for Economic Policy Studies, 1984). In the dozen years between these two books, neither the diagnosis nor the prescription appeared to have altered in any material way. Both books paint exceedingly dismal pictures.

9 See Michael. M. Atkinson and William D. Coleman, *The State, Business, and Industrial Change in Canada* (Toronto: University of Toronto Press, 1987), for a full discussion of these two approaches to industrial policy.

10 For a more detailed examination and criticism of these claims, see Michael Hart, "The Chimera of Industrial Policy: Yesterday, Today and Tomorrow," *Canada-United States Law Journal* 19 (1993): 19-48.

11 For a full account of the NEP by the minister responsible, see Marc Lalonde, "Riding the Storm: Energy Policy 1968-1984," in Thomas L. Axworthy and Pierre Elliott Trudeau, *Towards a Just Society* (Toronto: Viking, 1990), 49-77. See also Bruce Doern and Glen Toner, *The Politics of Energy: the Development and Implementation of the NEP* (Toronto: Methuen, 1985).

12 *The Heroic Delusion* is the title of vol. 2 of Stephen Clarkson and Christina McCall's *Trudeau and Our Times* (Toronto: McClelland and Stewart, 1994).

13 Confidential document, author's files.

14 See, for example, Canadian Manufacturers' Association, *Trade-Offs: Some Crucial Economic Choices,* a discussion paper prepared by the Canadian Manufacturers' Association, February 1980. It summarized its views as: "The purpose of government economic policy is to create a framework for efficient allocation of resources, within the context of an incentive-oriented market system, compatible with social responsibility and political integrity of the country, and that preserves maximum personal freedom" (25).

15 Quoted in Clarkson and McCall, *Heroic Delusion*, 222. The story of Gray's frustrations is well told by Clarkson and McCall in chapter 7, but from a somewhat more sympathetic perspective than here. They conclude that "the nationalist Liberals had been routed by the prime minister's indifference, their own right-wing cabinet colleagues, and the manoeuvrings of their intractably continentalist economic bureaucrats" (223). As one of the bureaucrats interviewed for their study, I think it equally important to take account of the impracticality and expense of Gray's proposals, their lack of support in the business community, and the problems that they would have engendered in Canada's trade relations. The policy instincts of the federal government's most experienced officials and the political instincts of Trudeau's most experienced ministers all militated against the proposals.

16 Canada, *Economic Development for Canada in the 1980s* (Ottawa: Department of Finance, November 1981). The document called for the federal government to spend $42 billion over the next five years on economic development, along with $18.2 billion on energy development. The looming recession, plus the government's mounting fiscal woes, made these projections notional at best.

17 See I.M. Destler, *American Trade Politics: System under Stress*, 3rd ed. (Washington: Institute for International Economics, 1995), chapter 6, for a discussion of the ugly mood in Washington. See also Michael Hart with Bill Dymond and Colin Robertson, *Decision at Midnight: Inside the Canada-US Free Trade Negotiations* (Vancouver: UBC Press, 1994), chapter 3.

18 See Michael Hart, *Canadian Economic Development and the International Trading System: Constraints and Opportunities* (Toronto: University of Toronto Press, 1985).

19 The move prompted legal scholar Robert Hudec to note that "no adjudicatory process should be administered by officials whose supervisor is the chief government officer in charge of political relations with the business community. That is simply not a juridically valid way to adjudicate any issue" ("Dispute Resolution and the Domestic Setting," *Canada-United States Law Journal* 12 [1987]: 333). See Destler, *American Trade Politics*, 149-50, for the context for this decision.

20 Grey, *United States Trade Policy Legislation*, 95-100.

21 See Richard G. Lipsey and Murray G. Smith, *Global Imbalances and U.S. Responses: A Canadian Perspective* (Toronto: C.D. Howe Institute, 1987), for an analysis and discussion of this problem.

22 See Stephen L. Lande and Craig VanGrasstek, *The Trade and Tariff Act of 1984: Trade Policy in the Reagan Administration* (Lexington, MA: D.C. Heath, 1986); and Steve Dryden, *Trade Warriors: USTR and the American Crusade for Free Trade* (New York: Oxford University Press, 1985), chapter 13, for discussions of domestic trade and legislative activity in the first half of the 1980s.

23 Lande and VanGrasstek, *Trade and Tariff Act of 1984*, chapter 1.

24 A vast literature has developed analyzing the extent and impact of the more rigorous application of the trade remedy laws. A good overview can be found in Pietro S. Nivola, *Regulating Unfair Trade* (Washington: Brookings Institution, 1992).

25 Two contrasting descriptions and analyses of the deteriorating relationship can be found in Stephen Clarkson, *Canada and the Reagan Challenge*, updated ed. (Toronto: James Lorimer, 1985); and David Leyton-Brown, *Weathering the Storm: Canadian-US Relations, 1980-83* (Toronto: C.D. Howe Institute, 1985).

26 As part of the implementation of its Tokyo Round commitments, the Canadian government initiated a massive overhaul of its own trade remedy legislation. Subject to lengthy discussion and consultation, a revised Special Import Measures Act was finally passed in 1984. See, for example, Klaus Stegemann, *Report of the Policy Forum on Special Import Measures Legislation* (Kingston: John Deutsch Institute for the Study of Economic Policy, 1984). Canada initiated its first countervailing duty investigation in 1979 against baler twine from Brazil, Mexico, and Tanzania, and could thus no longer claim innocence on this front.

27 See, for example, Rodney Grey, "The General Agreement after the Tokyo Round," in *Non-Tariff Barriers after the Tokyo Round*, ed. John Quinn and Philip Slayton (Montreal: Institute for Research on Public Policy, 1982), 3-18; and Grey, "The Decay of the Trade Relations System," in *Issues in World Trade Policy: GATT at the Crossroads*, ed. R.H. Snape (New York: St. Martin's Press, 1986), 17-29.

28 William Cline, *Trade Policy in the 1980s* (Washington: Institute for International Economics, 1983).

29 The author participated in these negotiations. Generally, on developments at GATT, see the annual series, *GATT Activities*.

30 GATT, "Decision to Convene the Thirty-eighth Session at Ministerial Level," *Basic Instruments and Selected Documents* 28 (1982): 15.

31 See GATT, *Basic Instruments and Selected Documents* 29 (1983): 9-23.

32 For a very US-centric account of the GATT ministerial meeting and the problems besetting the multilateral trading system in the opening years of the 1980s, see Dryden, *Trade Warriors*, chapter 14. Dryden's journalistic history of the USTR, which is full of interesting details and insights, provides a disturbing hint of the lack of importance of Canada to US trade officials: there is virtually no coverage of Canada, despite its role as the United States' number-one trade and investment partner during this period.

33 On the Canada-US FTA negotiations, see chapter 13.

34 On developments in Europe, see Desmond Dinan, *Ever Closer Union? An Introduction to the European Community* (Boulder, CO: Lynne Riener, 1994), 69-98; and Neill Nugent, *The Government and Politics of the European Union,* 4th ed. (Durham, NC: Duke University Press, 1999), chapters 1-3.

35 See Robert E. Hudec, *The GATT Legal System and World Trade Diplomacy,* 2nd ed. (Salem, NH: Butterworth, 1990); and Hudec, *Enforcing International Trade Law: The Evolution of the Modern GATT Legal System* (Salem, NH: Butterworth, 1993), for a complete overview and analysis of GATT dispute settlement procedures and cases.

36 See Robert E. Hudec, "The Judicialization of GATT Dispute Settlement," in *In Whose Interest? Due Process and Transparency in International Trade,* ed. Michael Hart and Debra Steger (Ottawa: Centre for Trade Policy and Law, 1992).

37 This section provides a synopsis of a number of earlier articles and books, including Michael Hart, *What's Next: Canada, the Global Economy and the New Trade Policy* (Ottawa: Centre for Trade Policy and Law, 1994); Hart, "Searching for New Paradigms: Lessons from Recent and More Ancient History," in *Toward A North American Community,* ed. Don Barry (Boulder, CO: Westview Press, 1995), 33-49; Hart, "Coercion or Cooperation: Social Policy and Future Trade Negotiations," *Canada-United States Law Journal* 20 (1994): 351-90; and Hart, "The End of Trade Policy?" in *Global Jeopardy: Canada among Nations 1993-94,* ed. Christopher J. Maule and Fen Osler Hampson (Ottawa: Carleton, 1993), 85-105, which include notes on some of the literature analyzing the fundamental changes taking place in the Canadian and global economies.

38 While the GATT regime may have reflected these concepts, it was not built on them. Paul Krugman, in "Does the New Trade Theory Require a New Trade Policy?" *The World Economy* 15, 4 (1992): 423-41, convincingly demonstrates that the GATT system is based on an enlightened mercantilism that posits that countries have an individual incentive to be protectionist but can collectively benefit from rules-based free trade. "GATT-think," while popular with officials and politicians, makes little economic sense. Perversely, however, it can lead to economically sensible policy. GATT negotiations have successfully harnessed the producer biases of most national trade policies into a set of rules that lead generally to freer trade, in the process described by Martin Wolf as mercantilist bargaining. See his "A European Perspective," in *Perspectives on a U.S.-Canadian Free Trade Agreement,* ed. Robert M. Stern, Philip H. Trezise, and John Whalley (Washington: Brookings Institution, 1987).

39 Economists, geographers, and political scientists in Canada, the United States, and Europe have produced a torrent of literature describing and analyzing the complex and interrelated forces that began transforming the world economy in the 1970s. Some of the early interesting syntheses of this work include Robert Reich, *The Work of Nations* (New York: Alfred A. Knopf, 1991); Michael Porter, *The Competitive Advantage of Nations* (New York: Free Press, 1990); Kenichi Ohmae, *The Borderless World: Power and Strategy in the Interlinked World Economy* (New York: Harper Business, 1990); Sylvia Ostry, *Governments and Corporations in a Shrinking World* (New York: Council on Foreign Relations, 1990); and DeAnne Julius, *Global Companies and Public Policy: The Growing Challenge of Foreign Direct Investment* (London: Printer for the Royal Institute of International Affairs, 1990).

40 European Management Forum, *Report on Industrial Competitiveness* (Geneva: European Management Forum, annually since 1979).

41 Department of External Affairs, *A Review of Canadian Trade Policy* (Ottawa: Supply and Services, 1983); and Department of External Affairs, *Canadian Trade Policy for the 1980s: A Discussion Paper* (Ottawa: Supply and Services, 1983).

42 In the interest of full disclosure, it should be noted that the author was the "pen" of both *A Review of Canadian Trade Policy* and *Trade Policy for the 1980s.* As well, the author was actively engaged in the preparation of the Macdonald Commission's *Final Report.*

43 Letter from Klaus Goldschlag, then Canada's ambassador to the Federal Republic of Germany, to Robert Johnstone, 20 September 1982 (author's files). Goldschlag had been the principal author of the 1972 Third Option paper. His letter to Bob Johnstone, then serving as deputy minister for international trade, was among the many perceptive comments offered by those consulted. If the

review's authors had been prepared to go beyond Ottawa conventional thinking and incorporate more of these views into their analysis, the review might have raised some of the fundamental issues noted earlier. Neither the ministry nor the senior bureaucracy, however, appeared ready to colour the issues as boldly as outside commentators. It is hard for officials to review their performance and suggest anything more than incremental change.

44 See Michael Hart, *Some Thoughts on Canada-United States Sectoral Free Trade* (Halifax: Institute for Research on Public Policy, 1985), for a discussion of the sectoral initiative.

45 Standing Senate Committee on Foreign Affairs (chaired by Senator George C. van Roggen), vol. 1, *The Institutional Framework for the Relationship*, vol. 2, *Canada's Trade Relations with the United States*, and vol. 3, *Canada's Trade Relations with the United States* (Ottawa: Supply and Services, 1975, 1978, and 1982).

46 See Economic Council of Canada, *Looking Outward: A New Trade Strategy for Canada* (Ottawa: Supply and Services, 1975), as well as the various background studies cited in the report.

47 See, for example, John H. Young, *Canadian Commercial Policy* (Ottawa: Queen's Printer, 1957); Harry G. Johnson, *The Canadian Quandary: Economic Problems and Policies* (Toronto: McGraw-Hill, 1963); Paul and Ronald J. Wonnacott, *Free Trade between the United States and Canada: The Potential Economic Effects* (Cambridge: Harvard University Press, 1967); and H. Edward English, *Industrial Structure in Canada's International Competitive Position* (Montreal: Private Planning Association, 1964).

48 Young, *Canadian Commercial Policy*, 160.

49 Hart, Dymond, and Robertson, *Decision at Midnight*, 17-22.

50 Media reaction is detailed ibid., 21.

51 Ibid., 57-62.

Chapter 13: Full Circle

1 See Daniel Drache and Duncan Cameron, eds., *The Other Macdonald Report* (Toronto: James Lorimer, 1985).

2 In an interview with William Johnson, "Canada Must Act on Free Trade, Macdonald Says," *Globe and Mail*, 19 November 1984, A1.

3 Gilbert R. Winham, "Why Canada Acted," in *Bilateralism, Multilateralism and Canada*, ed. William Diebold Jr. (New York: Council on Foreign Relations, 1988), 40-1.

4 David Frum, "Free for All," *Saturday Night*, April 1988. His review article addressed a collection of essays by such luminaries as Margaret Atwood and Pierre Berton, assembled by Laurier LaPierre, *If You Love This Country* (Toronto: McClelland and Stewart, 1987). It and a similar collection edited by Keith Davey, *Canada Not for Sale* (Toronto: General Paperbacks, 1987), generated a response from Canadians who favoured the agreement: John Crispo, ed., *Free Trade: The Real Story* (Toronto: Gage, 1988); and Earle Gray, *Free Trade, Free Canada: How Free Trade Will Make Canada Stronger* (Woodville, ON: Canadian Speeches, 1988).

5 "The most portentous issue Prime Minister Brian Mulroney will deal with today when he meets President Ronald Reagan is that of free trade" (William Johnson, "Canada Tests Free Trade Waters," *Globe and Mail*, 25 September 1984, A1).

6 The material in this chapter is drawn from a much more detailed treatment of the negotiations I prepared in collaboration with my colleagues on the Canadian negotiating team, Bill Dymond and Colin Robertson, *Decision at Midnight: Inside the Canada-US Free Trade Negotiations* (Vancouver: UBC Press, 1994). Canadian deputy negotiator Gordon Ritchie, in addition to speeches and public testimony, has published various accounts of the negotiations from his perspective. His detailed testimony before the Senate Foreign Affairs Committee in the fall of 1987 and spring of 1988 provides the most accurate detail, while a more personal view can be found in *Wrestling with the Elephant: The Inside Story of the Canada-US Trade Wars* (Toronto: Macfarlane Walter and Ross, 1997).

7 Department of Finance, *A New Direction for Canada: An Agenda for Economic Renewal* (Ottawa, 1984), 33. Wilson had signalled his views as Tory trade critic some six months earlier. In an interview with the *Globe and Mail*'s Patrick Martin, he criticized the stalled sectoral initiative as "not

moving fast enough ... we must move more quickly to get a deal because the protectionist influences in the United States are moving quickly" ("Talks Not Fast Enough for Tory Spokesman," *Globe and Mail,* 16 March 1984, A14).

8   See, for example, Task Force on Program Review, *Services and Subsidies to Business: Giving with Both Hands; Natural Resources Program: From Crisis to Opportunity; and Agriculture: Study Team Reports to the Task Force on Program Review* (all Ottawa: Supply and Services, 1986).

9   Department of External Affairs, *How to Secure and Enhance Canadian Access to Export Markets* (Ottawa: External Affairs, 1985), 3.

10 Kelleher's report on his consultations is reproduced in Department of External Affairs, *Canadian Trade Negotiations: Introduction, Selected Documents, Further Reading* (Ottawa: Supply and Services, 1985), 15-18.

11 The Quebec Declaration is reproduced ibid., 13-14.

12 United States Trade Representative Bill Brock, who had guided preparatory work for the Quebec trade declaration on the US side, was appointed Secretary of Labor the day after it was signed. He was succeeded by Clayton Yeutter. The reports of Kelleher and Yeutter are reproduced ibid., 65-72.

13 See ibid., 57-64.

14 Special Joint Parliamentary Committee on Canada's International Relations, *Interim Report* (Ottawa: Supply and Services, 1985). For the conclusions and recommendations of the report, see External Affairs, *Canadian Trade Negotiations,* 43-8.

15 Royal Commission on the Economic Union and Development Prospects for Canada, *Final Report* (Ottawa: Supply and Services, 1985).

16 The text of the prime minister's statement in the House and the exchange of letters can be found in External Affairs, *Canadian Trade Negotiations,* 73-8.

17 An American account of the process leading up to Senate consideration of fast-track authority in April 1986 can be found in Raymond Vernon, Deborah L. Spar, and Glen Tobin, *Iron Triangles and Revolving Doors: Cases in U.S. Foreign Economic Policymaking* (New York: Praeger, 1991), 21-53.

18 Under the terms of the US fast-track procedures, the president had to notify Congress of his intent to enter into the agreement at least ninety days before the authority expired on 3 January 1988. The imprecision of US legal drafting created much confusion during the negotiations, but it was widely accepted that the negotiations would need to conclude no later than 4 October 1987.

19 In addition to the writings of private-sector analysts and advocates of freer trade with the United States, the government's 1982-3 trade policy review and the final report of the Macdonald Royal Commission were particularly important in shaping Canadian objectives. See Department of External Affairs, *A Review of Canadian Trade Policy* (Ottawa: Supply and Services, 1983); and Royal Commission on the Economic Union, *Final Report.* A handy overview of official attitudes at the beginning of the negotiations is provided by External Affairs, *Canadian Trade Negotiations.*

20 The FTA and the debate preceding and during the negotiations generated a lively literature in Canada. Among early commentaries on the agreement and its implications, see Murray G. Smith and Frank Stone, eds., *Assessing the Canada-U.S. Free Trade Agreement* (Halifax: The Institute for Research on Public Policy, 1987); Jeffrey J. Schott and Murray G. Smith, eds., *The Canada-United States Free Trade Agreement: The Global Impact* (Ottawa: Institute for Research on Public Policy and Institute for International Economics, 1988); William Diebold, Jr., ed., *Bilateralism, Multilateralism and Canada in US Trade Policy* (New York: Council on Foreign Relations, 1988); Richard G. Lipsey and Robert C. York, *Evaluating the Free Trade Deal: A Guided Tour through the Canada-U.S. Agreement* (Toronto: C.D. Howe Institute, 1988); Donald M. McRae and Debra P. Steger, eds., *Understanding the Free Trade Agreement* (Halifax: Institute for Research on Public Policy, 1988); and Richard Dearden, Michael Hart, and Debra Steger, eds., *Living with Free Trade: Canada, the Free Trade Agreement and the GATT* (Ottawa: Centre for Trade Policy and Law and Institute for Research on Public Policy, 1989).

21 For example: article 104 of the FTA provides a general affirmation of GATT rights and obligations, as well as any other preexisting rights and obligations under other agreements, such as the Auto Pact; articles 407, 409, 902, and 904 clarify existing GATT rights and obligations under GATT

articles I, II, XI, XIII, and XX with respect to import and export restrictions and prohibitions; article 501 incorporates article III of the GATT respecting national treatment rights and obligations; article 602 affirms rights and obligations under the GATT Agreement on Technical Barriers; article 710 affirms GATT rights with respect to supply management measures; article 1201 incorporates the exceptions clauses of GATT article XX; chapter 13 builds on the GATT Agreement on Government Procurement; article 1801 affirms the right of the two parties to solve disputes arising under either the GATT or the FTA in either forum, for example in regard to FTA article 501/GATT article III; article 2010 is a modernized version of GATT article XVII regarding state-trading practices; and article 2011 incorporates parts of GATT article XXIII.

22 Allan Gotlieb, *"I'll Be with You in a Minute, Mr. Ambassador": The Education of a Canadian Diplomat in Washington* (Toronto: University of Toronto Press, 1991), 56-7.

23 Derek Burney, Donald W. Campbell Lecture in International Trade, Wilfrid Laurier University Chancellor's Symposium, Toronto, 14 June 1995.

24 G. Bruce Doern and Brian W. Tomlin, *Faith and Fear: The Free Trade Story* (Toronto: Stoddart, 1991), 206.

25 See ibid., 205-42, for a discussion of the election.

26 Given the important role played by third parties in Canadian politics, few parties ever command more than half the popular vote, a fact that has not hampered Canada's governance. Indeed, some of Canada's most advanced social legislation was passed by the minority Pearson (1963-7) and Trudeau (1972-4) governments.

27 Judith H. Bello and Alan F. Holmer, *Guide to the U.S. Canada Free-Trade Agreement: Text, Commentary, Source Materials* (Englewood Cliffs, NJ: Prentice-Hall, 1990), chapters 3-7, provides a detailed discussion of the US legislative process from various perspectives.

28 Royal Bank of Canada, "Two Cheers for the FTA: Tenth-Year Review of the Canada-U.S. Free Trade Agreement," *Econoscope* 23, 6 (1998), reprinted in *Policy Options* 20, 5 (1999): 6-11.

29 Shenje Chen and Prakash Sharma, "Accounting for Canadian Export Growth: 1983-1997," Trade and Economic Policy Paper No. 98-01, December 1998, at <http://www.dfait-maeci.gc.ca> (December 2001).

30 Daniel Schwanen, *Trading Up: The Impact of Increased Continental Integration on Trade, Investment, and Jobs in Canada*, Commentary no. 89 (Toronto: C.D. Howe Institute, 1997), his third report. See also his *Were the Optimists Wrong on Free Trade? A Canadian Perspective*, Commentary no. 37 (Toronto: C.D. Howe Institute, 1992) and *A Growing Success: Canada's Performance under Free Trade*, Commentary no. 52 (Toronto: C.D. Howe Institute, 1993). See also Marcel Côté, "Le Libre-échange dix ans après: dix ans plus tard, le bilan est positif," *Cité libre*, April/May 1998, 51-64; and Peter Morici, "Assessing the Canada-U.S. Free Trade Agreement," *American Review of Canadian Studies* 26, 4 (1997): 491-7.

31 Controversy about productivity numbers created considerable confusion among Canadians. Studies by Daniel Trefler at the University of Toronto ("The Long and Short of the Canada-U.S. Free Trade Agreement," mimeo) clearly suggest, however, that productivity improvements in Canada in sectors liberalized by the FTA, after an initial adjustment lag, outpaced those in the United States by the end of the decade.

32 See Mahmood Iqbal, *Are We Losing Our Minds? Trends, Determinants and the Role of Taxation in Brain Drain to the United States* (Ottawa: Conference Board of Canada, 1999), 9.

33 For a discussion of the issues raised for Canada, the United States, and Mexico of extending the FTA to Mexico, see Michael Hart, *A North American Free Trade Agreement: The Strategic Implications for Canada* (Ottawa: Centre for Trade Policy and Law, 1990). See also Gary Clyde Hufbauer and Jeffrey J. Schott, *North American Free Trade: Issues and Recommendations* (Washington: Institute for International Economics, 1992).

34 Various commentators had suggested that the United States, if successful in negotiating a series of free-trade agreements with Latin American partners, would become the only country with free access to all the countries of the hemisphere while the rest enjoyed free access only to the United States, like spokes in a wheel dominated by the United States at its hub. See, for example, Richard G. Lipsey, *Canada at the U.S.-Mexico Free Trade Dance: Wallflower or Partner*, Commentary no. 20

(Toronto: C.D. Howe Institute, 1990); and Ronald J. Wonnacott, *U.S. Hub-and-Spoke Bilaterals and the Multilateral Trading System,* Commentary no. 23 (Toronto: C.D. Howe Institute, 1990).

35   All three ministers provide their personal perspectives on the negotiations in L. Ian MacDonald, ed., *Free Trade: Risks and Rewards* (Montreal: McGill-Queen's University Press, 2000).

36   A number of recent books fill this need, including Brian Tomlin and Max Cameron, *Negotiating NAFTA: How the Deal Was Done* (Ithaca, NY: Cornell University Press, 2000); Frederick W. Mayer, *Interpreting NAFTA: The Science and Art of Political Analysis* (New York: Columbia University Press, 1998); William A. Orme, Jr., *Understanding NAFTA: Mexico, Free Trade and the New North America* (Austin: University of Texas Press, 1996); and Maryse Robert, *Negotiating NAFTA: Explaining the Outcome in Culture, Textiles, Autos, and Pharmaceuticals* (Toronto: University of Toronto Press, 2000).

37   On the results of the negotiations, see Canada, *NAFTA: What's It All About?* (Ottawa: Supply and Services, 1992); Gary Clyde Hufbauer and Jeffrey J. Schott, *NAFTA: An Assessment* (Washington: Institute for International Economics, 1993); and Jon R. Johnson, *The North American Free Trade Agreement: A Comprehensive Assessment* (Aurora, ON: Canada Law Book, 1994).

38   Tomlin and Cameron, *Negotiating NAFTA,* 179ff.

39   Ibid., 203.

40   Ibid., 201ff.

Chapter 14: The New Multilateralism

1   This chapter is a revised and shortened version of chapters 7 and 8 of Fen Hampson with Michael Hart, *Multilateral Negotiations: Lessons from Arms Control, Trade and the Environment* (Baltimore, MD: Johns Hopkins Press, 1995), which contain extensive notes. See also chapters 10 and 11 of Hart, *Fifty Years of Canadian Tradecraft: Canada at the GATT 1947-1997* (Ottawa: Centre for Trade Policy and Law, 1998).

2   See, for example, Lester C. Thurow, "GATT Is Dead," *Inside Guide* (February 1991), 27-30; and Clyde Prestowitz, Alan Tonelson, and Robert W. Jerome, "The Last Gasp of GATTism," *Harvard Business Review* (March-April 1991), 130-8.

3   The ambivalence of the US approach is well captured by C. Michael Aho and Jonathan D. Aronson, *Trade Talks: America Better Listen!* (New York: Council on Foreign Relations, 1985).

4   On the EC and the multilateral trading system in the late 1980s, see Michael Smith and Stephen Woolcock, *Redefining the US-EC Relationship* (London: Royal Institute of International Affairs, 1993); Gary C. Hufbauer, ed., *Europe 1992: An American Perspective* (Washington: Brookings Institution, 1990); and Ernest Wistrich, *After 1992: The United States of Europe* (London: Routledge, 1991).

5   Among the many interesting books written on the emergence of Japan as a major global competitor but hesitant and less-than-effective player on the multilateral stage, see Karel van Wolferen, *The Enigma of Japanese Power: People and Politics in a Stateless Nation* (London: Papermac, 1990); and Mayumi Itoh, *Globalization of Japan: Japanese Sakoku Mentality and United States Efforts to Open Japan* (New York: St. Martin's Press, 1998).

6   Fritz Leutwiler et al., *Trade Policies for a Better Future: Proposals for Action* (Geneva: GATT, 1985).

7   The period 1980-6 at GATT is well covered by Patrick Low, *Trading Free: The GATT and US Trade Policy* (New York: Twentieth Century Fund, 1993), 189-207.

8   Alan Oxley, *The Challenge of Free Trade* (London: Harvester Wheatsheaf, 1990), 100-10 discusses LDC participation in GATT during the lead-up to the Punta del Este meeting.

9   See ibid., 84-7, on evolving EC attitudes toward the round.

10   GATT, *Basic Instruments and Selected Documents* 32 (Geneva: GATT, 1986): 9-10.

11   Oxley, *Challenge of Free Trade,* 133-4; and GATT, *Activities 1986: An Annual Review of the Work of the GATT* (Geneva: GATT, 1987), 7.

12   Gilbert R. Winham, "The Prenegotiation Phase of the Uruguay Round," *International Journal* 44 (Spring 1989): 280-303.

13 Oxley, *Challenge of Free Trade*, 138-40.
14 The Punta del Este Declaration is reproduced in GATT, *Basic Instruments and Selected Documents* 33 (Geneva: GATT, 1987): 19-28.
15 For a detailed discussion of the issues in the round, see Gary C. Hufbauer and Jeffrey J. Schott, *Trading for Growth: The Next Round of Trade Negotiations* (Institute for International Economics, 1985). On the issues raised by the services negotiations, see Rodney de C. Grey, *Concepts of Trade Diplomacy and Trade in Services* (London: Harvester Wheatsheaf for the Trade Policy Research Centre, 1990).
16 The decision of 28 January 1987 can be found in GATT, *Basic Instruments and Selected Documents* 33: 31-52. See also John Croome, *Reshaping the World Trading System* (Geneva: World Trade Organization, 1995), chapter 3.
17 Complaints were launched by the United States against Japan (various agricultural products), the Nordics (apples and pears), EC (apples), Canada (ice cream and yoghurt), Korea (beef), and Thailand (cigarettes). The details of all these cases can be gleaned from the panel reports reproduced in GATT, *Basic Instruments and Selected Documents* 35 through 37 (Geneva: GATT, 1989, 1990, 1991), and in GATT, *GATT Activities 1987* and *GATT Activities 1988* (Geneva: GATT, 1988 and 1989). See also Ingrid Nordgren, "The GATT Panels During the Uruguay Round: A Joker in the Negotiating Game," *Journal of World Trade* 25, 4 (1991): 57-72.
18 See Robert E. Hudec, *Enforcing International Trade Law: The Evolution of the Modern GATT Legal System* (Salem, NH: Butterworth, 1993), for a complete discussion of the final set of GATT dispute settlement cases.
19 GATT, *Activities 1988*, 19. Oxley's point spoke more directly to the smaller than the larger countries and was more a professional than a political sentiment.
20 See I.M. Destler, *American Trade Politics: System under Stress*, 3rd ed. (Washington: Institute for International Economics, 1995), 164-6.
21 GATT, *Activities 1988*, 22.
22 Oxley, *Challenge of Free Trade*, 158-9.
23 At both the Venice (1987) and Toronto (1988) summits, the leaders of the seven summit countries underlined the importance of making progress on agriculture and at Venice went so far as to commit their delegations to table detailed proposals before the end of the year (ibid., 161-2).
24 GATT, *Activities 1988*, 22-3.
25 Ibid., 24-5. The texts adopted are reproduced on 138-67.
26 The TPRM decision is reproduced in GATT, *Basic Instruments and Selected Documents* 36 (Geneva: GATT, 1990): 403-9, and the streamlined dispute settlement procedures on 61-7. For a critical examination of the TPRM, see Gary Banks, "Transparency, Surveillance and the GATT System," in *In Whose Interest? Due Process and Transparency in International Trade*, ed. Michael Hart and Debra Steger (Ottawa: Centre for Trade Policy and Law, 1992), 55-85. William J. Davey, "GATT Dispute Settlement: The 1988 Montreal Reforms," in *Living with Free Trade: Canada, the Free Trade Agreement and the GATT*, ed. Richard Dearden, Michael Hart, and Debra Steger (Ottawa: Centre for Trade Policy and Law and Institute for Research on Public Policy, 1989), 167-85, provides a critical overview of the dispute settlement reforms.
27 Detailed descriptions of the issues in the negotiations and progress on them can be found in GATT, *GATT Activities 1989* (Geneva: GATT, 1990), 37-75, and GATT, *GATT Activities 1990* (Geneva: GATT, 1991), 27-54. For an analysis of many of the critical issues, see Jeffrey J. Schott, ed., *Completing the Uruguay Round: A Results-Oriented Approach to the GATT Trade Negotiations* (Washington: Institute for International Economics, 1990); and Croome, *Reshaping the World Trading System*.
28 Jackson had developed his views on the constitutional shortcomings of the GATT and proposals for reform in John H. Jackson, *Restructuring the GATT System* (London: Royal Institute of International Affairs, 1990).
29 GATT, *Activities 1990*, 22. For an explanation of the fast-track procedures, see Destler, *American Trade Politics*, 71-7.

30 GATT, *Activities 1990*, 22-3.

31 Ibid., 26-7.

32 Since the draft text of the Final Act was still unfinished and the all-important negotiations on market access were far from complete, it may be somewhat disingenuous to speak of a "package." Nevertheless, the negotiators under Dunkel's direction had made the judgment that the contours of the agreements being developed in each of the groups, plus the market access elements that they anticipated, did constitute a useful package. See Schott, *Completing the Uruguay Round*, and Croome, *Reshaping the World Trading System*, chapter 7, for assessments of that package.

33 Progress reports on the work pursued in each of the seven groups are outlined in GATT, *GATT Activities 1991* (Geneva: GATT, 1992), 22-47. See also Croome, *Reshaping the World Trading System*.

34 "Draft Final Act Embodying the Results of the Uruguay Round of Multilateral Trade Negotiations," MTN.TNC/W/FA, 20 December 1991 (the "Dunkel Text"). The text is described in some detail in GATT press release NUR 055 of 3 December 1992.

35 Statement by Arthur Dunkel to the TNC as quoted in GATT, *Activities 1991*, 5.

36 The ups and downs during the closing stages of the negotiations are captured well in the reporting of *The Economist*, which over the final year frequently devoted a leader to the issue. See, for example, "GATT's Trade Talks – Final Sprint or Stumble?" 18 January 1992; "Endgame" and "The Fairest Trader of Them All," 14 November 1992; "The Uruguay Round: Coup de Grace, Coup de Foudre," 28 November 1992; "Uruguay Round Unraveling," 26 December 1992; and "The Uruguay Round ... and Round," 23 January 1993.

37 The profiles of the new director-general set out in the media all stressed these characteristics. See, for example, *Times* (London), 17 July 1993; *Financial Times* (London), 8 October 1993; and *European*, 23 December 1993.

38 Summit veteran and former chief negotiator for Canada Sylvia Ostry noted, "All the delays in the GATT negotiations were getting to be a serious political embarrassment. So what could the G-7 leaders do to give a positive signal? They chose what was most feasible, most workable and most politically easy – market access" (Barbara Wickens, "A Kick Start for Trade," *Maclean's*, 19 July 1993, 12-13).

39 Newspaper clippings for the period from mid-June to mid-July are a study in the art of media manipulation. While little of substance had in fact been agreed in Tokyo, briefings – on and off the record – had carefully built and resolved crises that served the purpose of restoring momentum to the negotiations. All this flim-flammery is well captured in *Economist*, 10 July 1993; and Frances Williams, "General Agreement to End All the Talk," *Financial Post* (London), 9 July 1993.

40 See Samuel Brittan, "Where GATT's $200bn Really Comes From," *Financial Post* (London), 4 October 1993; and Frances Williams, "General in the War for Free Trade," *Financial Post* (London), 8 October 1993.

41 See "The Eleventh Hour Has Arrived," *Financial Post* (London), 24 September 1993; and "Endgame in the GATT," *Financial Post* (London), 29 September 1993.

42 See, for example, reports in the *Financial Post* and the *Times* of London as well as the *Wall Street Journal* in the second half of September 1993 for some of the ongoing jockeying within the EC.

43 Annex 1A to the GATT 1994 lists twelve separate codes covering trade in agriculture, sanitary and phytosanitary measures, textiles and clothing, technical barriers to trade, trade-related investment measures, antidumping measures, customs valuation, preshipment inspection, rules of origin, import licensing procedures, subsidies and countervailing measures, and safeguards. Understandings were reached on the interpretation of articles II:1(b), XVII, XXIV, XXV, XXVIII, and XXXV as well as on dispute settlement and the trade policy review mechanism. A total of twelve "decisions" further clarify or amplify various aspects of the agreements and understandings.

44 For a full discussion of the results of the round, see Jeffrey J. Schott, *The Uruguay Round: An Assessment* (Washington: Institute for International Economics, 1995); Bernard Hoekman and Michel Kostecki, *The Political Economy of the World Trading System* (Oxford: Oxford University Press, 1995); and Croome, *Reshaping the World Trading System*.

45 "GATT Deal a Reason to Celebrate," *Montreal Gazette*, 16 December 1993, B2.
46 Editorial, "The Protection Racket Loses Its Grip," *Globe and Mail*, 7 December 1993, A24.
47 For example, editorial, *Winnipeg Free Press*, 17 December 1993, A6.
48 David Crane, "Canada Gains in GATT Deal," *Toronto Star*, 15 April 1994, B1.

Chapter 15: Canada in a Globally Integrated Economy

1 A 1996 WTO report concluded that more than a century of evidence suggests a strong correlation between international policy efforts to keep markets open and the growth of world trade and investment and, subsequently, integration and prosperity. The period 1860 to 1914 was marked by an increasing level of internationalization as European countries followed the example of the Cobden-Chevalier Treaty between France and England and entered into a set of interlocking most-favoured-nation treaties that lowered barriers and created institutional reinforcements to keep them low. Although the momentum of liberalization was lost by the early 1880s, markets were kept relatively open as a result of these institutional factors. These international MFN treaties did not survive the disintegration of international relations during the First World War. As a result, the period 1914 to 1947 was characterized by a high degree of instability as barriers were raised and frequently adjusted. In the absence of institutions to prevent country after country from adopting protectionist and discriminatory policies, world trade levels plummeted. The integration achieved before the turn of the century had therefore been largely lost even before the catastrophe of the depression of the 1930s. The period after 1948 was again one of steady integration, underwritten by a set of liberalizing rules and institutions. By the middle of the 1970s, the ground lost in the period 1914 to 1947 had been largely regained, and since the 1980s, integration has widened and accelerated considerably as more countries have increased participation in the global economy by becoming more open economies and adopting more liberal trade policies. See WTO, *International Trade Trends and Statistics* (Geneva: WTO, 1996).
2 See William A. Dymond, "The MAI: A Sad and Melancholy Story," in *A Big League Player? Canada among Nations 1999*, ed. Fen Hampson, Michael Hart, and Martin Rudner (Toronto: Oxford University Press, 1999).
3 See, for example, Jerry Mander and Edward Goldsmith, eds., *The Case against the Global Economy* (San Francisco: Sierra Club, 1996).
4 Raymond Vernon, *In the Hurricane's Eye: The Troubled Prospects of Multinational Enterprises* (Cambridge: Harvard University Press, 1998), 219.
5 The tragic events of 11 September 2001 and the consequent war on terrorism have added new, complicating factors in the evolution of a new world order. Government focus on security-related issues has sharpened, but on a basis fundamentally different from during the cold war. The new security challenge is deeply intertwined with globalization and economic well-being and being pursued at a global level.
6 See Denis Stairs, "Foreign Policy Consultations in a Globalizing World: The Case of Canada, the WTO, and the Shenanigans in Seattle," *IRPP Policy Matters* 1, 8 (2000).
7 Anthony DePalma, *Here: The Biography of the North American Continent* (New York: Public Affairs, 2000), 354.

Chapter 16: From a Trading Nation to a Nation of Traders

1 These figures are extracted from Department of Foreign Affairs and International Trade, *Trade Update 2001: Second Annual Report on Canada's State of Trade*, available at <http://www.dfait-maeci.gc.ca> (January 2002).

CHRONOLOGY

1497	John Cabot and his sons stake claim for England to Grand Banks and Newfoundland.
1535	Jacques Cartier makes first of two voyages up St. Lawrence River and claims new territories for France.
1600s	Samuel de Champlain founds first settlement in North America at Annapolis on Bay of Fundy (1604), but moves settlement a few years later to Quebec (1608) and establishes French suzerainty over St. Lawrence drainage basin.
–	Growing conflict between French fur traders and missionaries and English settlers creates tensions that are swept up in European dynastic struggles. Widely different patterns of trade and economic development in southern and northern colonies add to tensions.
1610s	Various English settlements along Atlantic seaboard, starting at Jamestown, Virginia (1607), and Plymouth, Massachusetts (1620), lay foundation for a series of English colonies with growing populations and thriving economies.
1700s	Tensions between colonies and different economic interests mount, as Britain, France, and other metropolitan states develop full-fledged mercantilist trade and industrial policies to govern their overseas economic interests.
1759	Victory of British general Wolfe over French general Montcalm at Quebec signals end of French control of St. Lawrence drainage basin.
1763	Treaty of Paris cedes all French territories east of the Mississippi, except islands of St. Pierre and Miquelon, to British crown. Britain now exercises control over some twenty-five separate colonial possessions in North America and Caribbean. Britain tightens mercantilist administration of its possessions.
1774	Quebec Act restores administration of St. Lawrence drainage basin to British governor at Quebec, to delight of Montreal merchants and frustration of New England colonists.
1776	Adam Smith publishes *The Wealth of Nations*, a major and influential criticism of mercantilism supporting free trade and other market-based economic policies.
–	Thirteen American colonies revolt against increasingly unpopular mercantilist administration of colonies, seeking greater economic and political freedom. Northern colonies decline invitation to join, citing lack of grievance with British administration and satisfaction with economic and political conditions.
1778	British Declaratory Act establishes that proceeds of imperial customs tariff collected in colonies can be used in colonies to pay for their own administration.
1783	American colonists succeed in their revolution and establish new nation, United States of America. Many of those who remain loyal to King George III migrate to northern colonies. These swell population of Canadian colonies, providing them with a more sustainable population base for economic development.
1787-9	United States adopts Constitution providing greater power to federal government, and elects first president, General George Washington. Congress, assigned responsibility for trade policy, passes first Tariff Act in order to raise needed revenues but also sets new nation on mildly, but ultimately, protectionist course.
1791	British Constitutional Act divides Quebec into Upper and Lower Canada, and gives colonial assemblies right to impose additional duties to raise revenue for their own administrative needs.

–	US treasury secretary Alexander Hamilton sends Congress his *Report on Manufactures*, the first fully articulated response to ideas of Adam Smith, developing in detail a case for infant industry protection. US Congress adopts report and, in subsequent years, becomes increasingly enamoured of protection.
1800s	With influx of United Empire Loyalists into Canadian colonies, economic development of Upper and Lower Canada and Maritime colonies takes off. Immigration from Ireland and Scotland further swells size of colonies.
1815	Congress of Vienna restores peace in Europe and ushers in century of British hegemony and prosperity.
–	Canadian Corn Law creates preference for Canadian wheat in the United Kingdom. Similar provisions are enacted for Canadian timber.
1821	Montreal-based North West Company, mainstay of the St. Lawrence fur trade, collapses, its remaining rights assumed by Hudson's Bay Company.
1820s	Increasing impact of industrial revolution on British economy, attitudes, and interests spells end of mercantilism and steady march toward freer trade; by 1849, all vestiges of old mercantilist regime have disappeared.
–	Canadian economic development by now firmly tied to exports of staples such as lumber, potash, fish, and corn (wheat) to British markets on preferential terms, in return for British manufactures and other necessities.
1832	Rebellions in Upper and Lower Canada lead eventually to greater self-government for Canadian colonies, providing colonial legislatures with greater responsibility, including in raising revenue and setting trade policy.
1840s	United Provinces of Upper and Lower Canada embark on an ambitious program of canal-building to stimulate economic development by facilitating export of wheat and flour, in competition with Erie Canal in New York.
1846	Britain repeals its Corn Laws and ends preferences enjoyed by Canadian producers in British market.
1849	A US annexationist movement briefly flourishes in Montreal.
1850s	United Provinces of Upper and Lower Canada begin an extensive – and expensive – program of railway-building to stimulate economic activity.
1854	Governor General Lord Elgin successfully negotiates Elgin-Marcy Reciprocity Treaty between Canadian colonies and United States, providing for free trade in commodities of export interest to Canadians.
1858-9	Tariff legislation introduced by Cayley and Galt raises tariffs in Upper and Lower Canada to new levels, necessary to pay for debts incurred by Laurentian canals and railroads. Tariff is restructured in 1859 to afford more protection.
1860	Cobden-Chevalier Treaty between Britain and France ushers in period of interlocking and liberalizing MFN agreements in Europe. Canada and United States do not participate in this system of treaties.
1861-5	US Civil War leads to triumph of Northern Republicans, committed to protectionism, and decline of Southern, free-trade Democrats.
1866	US Congress abrogates Elgin-Marcy Treaty, claiming it favoured Canadian interests. Northern dominance of post-Civil War Congress and British support to South also factors in decision.
1866-71	Sir John A. Macdonald tries, unsuccessfully, to negotiate successor reciprocity agreement with United States.
1867	On 1 July, Ontario, Quebec, New Brunswick, and Nova Scotia form a new Confederation, in part to ease trade among themselves and to offset negative effects of increased barriers to US market. Parliament adopts first Canadian tariff legislation, based on moderate levels in Upper and Lower Canada, and raising protection in Maritime colonies.
1874	New Liberal prime minister Alexander Mackenzie negotiates a new reciprocity agreement with United States that fails in US Senate.

1879	Conservatives under Macdonald adopt National Policy of higher tariffs, increased immigration, and a railroad to the West in order to forge stronger economic union, but only after further futile attempt at negotiating US reciprocity agreement.
1880s	Liberals introduce concept of unrestricted reciprocity to political debate in Canada.
1890	McKinley Tariff raises US tariff rates to new, protectionist levels; average rates on dutiable imports reach 48 percent.
1891	Macdonald successfully campaigns against reciprocity in 1891 election, but only after checking in Washington that Americans are as unreceptive to the idea as ever.
1892	Conservative minister of trade and commerce, Richard Cartwright, establishes Trade Commissioner Service aimed at promoting Canadian exports, finding new export markets, negotiating trade agreements, and providing services to Canadian exporters.
1896	Election of Liberal government, under Sir Wilfrid Laurier, pledged to reciprocity. Early overtures to Americans, however, are rejected in most jingoistic and certain terms; as alternative, government introduces preferences on British goods and, unsuccessfully, invites Britain to reciprocate.
1900s	After nearly a quarter-century of disappointing economic development, Canadian economy finally experiences sustained and broadly based growth.
1904	Finance Minister W.S. Fielding, as part of further adjustments to now relatively high Canadian tariff, introduces concept of antidumping duties. Together with other innovations, including bounties, grants, and creative use of valuation provisions, Fielding succeeds in raising protection without raising tariff rates.
1907	Fielding introduces three-tier tariff: general, MFN, and preferential.
1909	US Payne-Aldrich Tariff pushes US tariffs further in protectionist direction, but adds penalty tariffs on goods from countries that discriminate against United States, including Canada.
1910	Fielding and Laurier successfully negotiate exemption from US penalty tariffs, and kindle US interest in full reciprocity agreement.
1911	Laurier and Fielding successfully negotiate reciprocity agreement with Taft administration in United States, only to be defeated in subsequent election.
1912	Conservatives, under Sir Robert Borden, intensify efforts to expand imperial preferences, and introduce, for first time, concept of "bound" margins of preference in trade agreement with West Indies.
1913	Underwood Tariff in United States lowers many US tariffs on imports from Canada to level of aborted reciprocity agreement of 1911.
1914-18	First World War disrupts normal trade relations. Revenues needed to prosecute war dispose governments to look to an increasingly diverse range of taxes.
1917	Canada and United States both introduce modest income tax, gradually beginning to decouple revenue needs from protection and industrial policy.
1922	US Fordney-McCumber Tariff restores high levels of protection favoured by Republican Congress.
1930	US Congress adopts Smoot-Hawley Tariff Act, marking height of US protectionism and zenith of congressional responsibility for US trade policy making. Other countries respond with retaliatory tariffs, setting off spiral of competitive beggar-your-neighbour policies, including quantitative restrictions, tariff preferences, and currency manipulation. World trade plummets, establishing strong ideological link between depression and protectionism.
–	Canada reacts to punitive impact of Smoot-Hawley Tariff Act by raising some tariffs and increasing discrimination. Conservatives under R.B. Bennett are elected on platform dedicated to raising tariffs and discrimination even more.
1932	United Kingdom completes retreat from long-held (since 1846) unilateral free trade and establishes full-scale tariff protection; United Kingdom and Commonwealth dominions (Canada, Australia, New Zealand, and South Africa) adopt

comprehensive system of bilateral preferences at Imperial Economic Conference in Ottawa.

1934   US Congress adopts Reciprocal Trade Agreements Act (RTAA), for first time delegating tariff-negotiating authority to president. Under leadership of Cordell Hull, US State Department over next eight years negotiates some thirty reciprocal trade agreements with twenty-eight countries, reducing US tariff by nearly 50 percent for countries participating in program.

1935   Canada and United States successfully negotiate agreement under RTA program, ushering in more free trade than under any previous agreement.

1937-8   United States, United Kingdom, and Commonwealth dominions negotiate trilaterally to reduce tariffs and margins of preference, providing broader base for efforts to cushion impact of protectionism. Canada and United States negotiate a more comprehensive reciprocal trade agreement.

1939-45   Second World War. Trade policy plays subordinate role to broader strategic and security concerns. During course of war, United States, United Kingdom, and Canada work closely together in planning roles and structure of a series of postwar political and economic multilateral institutions, including institutions to address international trade and monetary problems.

1941   Atlantic Charter, agreed between US president Franklin Roosevelt and UK prime minister Winston Churchill, lays foundation for postwar trade and economic institutions based on principle of nondiscrimination.

1944   Successful negotiation at Bretton Woods, New Hampshire, of charters of International Monetary Fund (IMF) and International Bank for Reconstruction and Development (IBRD or World Bank).

1945   Founding of United Nations in San Francisco, and establishment of various UN specialized agencies, including FAO and ICAO.

–   United States, with reluctant UK acquiescence, issues *Proposals for International Trade Organization* based on principles first enunciated in Atlantic Charter: rules to promote nondiscrimination and freer trade among market-based economies. Following year, subsequent to consultation with Britain, Canada, and others, United States issues draft ITO charter.

1946   UN invites eighteen countries to form a preparatory committee to prepare draft ITO charter for consideration at Conference on Trade and Employment. Preparatory committee holds first session in London. At end of session, agrees to hold second session in Geneva. Simultaneously with work of preparatory committee, five countries join in Geneva to negotiate series of tariff-cutting agreements.

1947   Preparatory committee holds second session in Geneva from May through October and completes draft charter for ITO; Canada, the United States, Britain, and twenty other countries concurrently conclude 123 bilateral tariff-cutting agreements and annex these to interim General Agreement on Tariffs and Trade (GATT).

1947-8   Canada and United States initiate, but do not conclude, negotiations toward a bilateral free-trade agreement (FTA). The United States promotes, indirectly, necessary amendments to include FTAs in ITO – and GATT – provisions governing regional agreements.

1948   GATT is brought into force by Canada, the United States, Britain, and five others on 1 January on basis of Protocol of Provisional Application. Its extensive grandfather provisions allow members to bring GATT into force without seeking specific enabling legislation.

–   UN Conference on Trade and Employment concludes in Havana and adopts Havana Charter for an International Trade Organization. Draft charter is signed at level of heads of delegation by fifty-three of fifty-six participating countries. Charter receives lukewarm-to-hostile reception in capitals.

1949	GATT holds second tariff negotiating conference in Annecy, France, expanding membership beyond original twenty-three signatories.
–	US administration withdraws ITO from congressional consideration. Informed opinion agrees that ITO is dead. GATT, framed and implemented as executive RTA agreement, begins to take on more permanent shape.
–	US introduces Marshall Plan to address serious reconstruction problems in Europe and sponsors establishment of OEEC and EPU to stimulate and facilitate intra-European economic cooperation.
1950s	Relative openness of US market and continuing difficulty in accessing UK, European, and other markets due to currency restrictions, balance-of-payments measures, and other forms of protection lead to growth of ever-deeper Canada-US trade and investment links.
1950-1	GATT holds third tariff negotiating conference in Torquay, England, expanding membership to thirty-three. Canada invites members to hold next round in Toronto the following year. Toronto Round never held due to failure of US administration to gain negotiating authority.
1951	France, Germany, Italy, and Benelux countries agree to establish European Coal and Steel Community (ECSC) to help address problems of trade and industrialization among participants. UK Labour government's nationalization of steel industry disposes it to stay out of ECSC.
1955	United States successfully engineers open-ended waiver from its GATT obligations for its quota and other restrictions covering most of its agricultural sector. Result sets precedent that makes it increasingly difficult to introduce discipline on world trade in agriculture. Canada is one of few countries that vigorously protest this development.
1956	GATT holds fourth tariff negotiating conference, consolidating schedules of by now thirty-five members, including Germany and Japan. At subsequent Review Session of Contracting Parties, GATT is placed on more permanent footing by agreement that tariff bindings will no longer be time-bound.
1957	France, Germany, Italy, and Benelux countries sign Treaty of Rome establishing European Economic Community (EEC). United Kingdom decides to stay out, convinced its future lies more with Commonwealth and United States than with Continental trading partners.
–	Royal Commission on Canada's Economic Prospects, chaired by Walter Gordon, warns of Canada's increasing dependence on US foreign investment. John Young's study for commission points out the high cost of protection to Canadian economy.
–	Election of Conservative government led by John Diefenbaker ends twenty-two years of Liberal hegemony. Diefenbaker intimates desire to shift trade from United States to United Kingdom and Commonwealth, but fails to take any concrete measures to bring this about.
1958	Treaty of Rome enters into force, and EEC members begin process of dismantling tariff and other barriers and replacing them with Common External Tariff, Common Commercial Policy, and Common Agricultural Policy.
1959	Haberler Report, the work of international group of eminent academic economists, provides intellectual basis for series of GATT initiatives, recognizing that GATT has reached the end of postwar reconstruction – currencies are by now convertible. It is time to address three major problems within the trading system: 1) organization of a new round with mandate to tackle tariffs seriously on horizontal rather than item-by-item basis; 2) mounting problem of trade in agriculture; and 3) emerging problem of developing countries.
–	Diefenbaker government kills Avro Arrow and enters into Defence Production Sharing Arrangements (DPSA) with United States to meet both Canadian defence and industrial objectives.

1959-60	United Kingdom organizes conference among non-EEC European countries to explore prospect for free-trade agreement. Resulting 1960 Treaty of Stockholm establishes European Free Trade Association (EFTA) among Britain, Norway, Sweden, Denmark, Portugal, Switzerland, and Austria.
1950s-60s	Various other experiments in regional cooperation and integration introduced in Africa and Latin America, pursuant to GATT article XXIV, prove much less successful than European experiments. Most are conceived as efforts to reinforce import-substitution development strategies among members rather than as trade-competing development strategies.
–	After a decade of being among most enthusiastic supporters of GATT, and being disappointed in results, Canada begins to exhibit more subtle approach to demands of GATT membership on its own policy formation.
1960s	Anxiety grows in Canadian academic and policy circles about close trade and investment ties between Canada and United States, leading to proposals to diversify Canadian trade and industrial patterns.
1960	OEEC reorganized into Organization for Economic Cooperation and Development (OECD), with membership drawn from Europe, North America, Japan, and Australasia. Gradually evolves into think tank of industrialized countries, providing forum for research and consultation on range of common public policy issues.
1960-1	GATT holds its fifth tariff negotiating conference (Dillon Round). First half is devoted to negotiations to settle claims arising under GATT article XXIV:6 against new EEC, as well as examination of EEC and EFTA for conformity with requirements of article XXIV.
1961	GATT members establish Short-term Arrangement on Trade in Cotton Textiles, providing for temporary derogation from nondiscrimination provisions of article XIX to address problem of market disruption in trade in cotton textiles and clothing. Arrangement becomes Long-term Arrangement Regarding International Trade in Cotton Textiles the following year.
1962	US president John F. Kennedy recaptures leadership and imagination of earlier Democratic presidents and asks Congress for sweeping new negotiating authority in Trade Expansion Act aimed at forging stronger ties with Europe and newly emerging LDCs.
1963	United Kingdom changes its mind about membership in EEC but France vetoes application.
1964-7	GATT's sixth or Kennedy Round of negotiations seeks not only to reduce tariffs by a significant margin, but also to begin to harmonize trade policies of leading members by addressing nontariff barriers, such as valuation and antidumping procedures. Canada participates, but less enthusiastically than during earlier rounds.
1964	Independence of Europe's former colonial possessions prompts negotiation of Yaoundé Convention, providing them with mixture of aid and trade concessions maintaining their ties to Europe. Association agreements are also negotiated with Mediterranean countries. Europe thus continues two-track trade policy: multilateral and regional.
–	Developing countries, frustrated by lack of attention to their aspirations in GATT negotiations, launch new UN-based organization, UN Conference on Trade and Development (UNCTAD), to pursue their agenda. GATT responds by adopting Part IV – a set of nonbinding obligations related to economic development – and establishing Committee on Trade and Development.
–	Canada and United States step outside GATT framework to solve major problem in trade in automotive products by negotiating Canada-US Automotive Products Agreement (the Auto Pact), providing quasi-free trade (i.e., managed free trade)

	for automotive products and allowing development of integrated North American auto industry. Treaty signed and entered into force in 1965.
1965	EEC, ECSC, and Euratom (European Atomic Energy Community) agree to meld under single institutional umbrella of European Community (EC) in 1967, with executive (Council and Commission) and bureaucratic seat in Brussels, Parliament in Strasbourg, and Court in Luxembourg.
1967	After prolonged discussion and negotiations, GATT approves Protocol of Accession for Poland, the first nonmarket economy to accede to GATT.
–	Long-term Agreement on Cotton Textiles is extended for three years.
–	United Kingdom again applies to join EC and is again vetoed by France.
–	Paul and Ron Wonnacott publish their pioneering study of benefits of free trade between Canada and United States.
1967-8	US Congress fails to adopt nontariff aspects of Kennedy Round results; instead threatens to pass, and almost succeeds, a number of bills clearly at odds with US GATT obligations, indicating new era in US attitudes to international economic cooperation.
1968	Pierre Elliott Trudeau succeeds Lester Pearson as Liberal leader and prime minister and ushers in era of "rational" rather than "mandarin" government.
–	Olivier Long of Switzerland becomes GATT's second director general, succeeding Eric Wyndham White, who served in that capacity during GATT's first twenty years.
1970	Long-term Agreement on Cotton Textiles is extended for three years.
–	United Kingdom successfully sues for entry into the EC.
1971	GATT approves General System of Preferences, first developed and advocated in UNCTAD, allowing industrialized members to adopt one-way tariff preferences in favour of developing countries. Waiver is made more general and permanent in 1979 with adoption of so-called Enabling Clause adopted at end of Tokyo Round, which allows industrialized countries to implement measures extending "differential and more favourable treatment" to developing countries.
–	US president Richard Nixon, faced with rising congressional protectionist sentiments and deteriorating US balance-of-payments position, adopts series of tough trade and monetary measures that bring an end to Bretton Woods monetary arrangements, shake international faith in continued US leadership of trade arrangements, and undermine Canadian faith in "special relationship" between Canada and United States.
1972	Rey Group of twelve eminent policy and political officials, organized by OECD, provides international support for new round of trade negotiations.
1973	United Kingdom, Denmark, and Ireland accede to EC, bringing membership to nine. The six remaining EFTA members negotiate bilateral FTAs with EC.
–	In reaction to 1971 Nixon measures, Canada adopts "Third Option," involving a mix of both domestic and trade and foreign policy initiatives, including trade initiatives with EC and Japan, establishment of the Foreign Investment Review Agency (FIRA), and various industrial policy initiatives.
–	GATT launches new, ambitious round of trade negotiations at ministerial conference in Tokyo.
1974	Cotton textile agreement extended for further three years and its coverage expanded to include wool and synthetics. Now becomes popularly known as Multi-fibre Agreement (MFA).
–	US Congress provides president with sweeping new negotiating authority to participate in Tokyo Round of GATT negotiations, including both tariff-cutting and nontariff barrier authority, on basis satisfactory to other participants.
1975	EC negotiates Lomé Convention as successor to earlier Yaoundé Convention, but this time on more comprehensive basis, including former British dependencies.

–	Economic Council of Canada releases report calling for Canada and United States to negotiate bilateral free-trade agreement.
–	Canada establishes Foreign Investment Review Agency (FIRA) to screen foreign investment proposals and determine whether they meet "net benefit" test. FIRA is part of more interventionist approach by federal government to Canadian trade and industrial policy.
1976	Canada concludes Framework Agreement on Commercial and Economic Cooperation with EC and Framework for Economic Cooperation with Japan, both aimed at providing base for diversifying trade relations.
–	UNCTAD IV in Nairobi proves high point of UNCTAD experiment. Coupled with number of special sessions of UN General Assembly, as well as special conferences such as Conference on International Economic Cooperation in Paris, it provides renewed political urgency to demands of developing countries and adopts ambitious program to address problem of trade in primary commodities.
1979	Election of Conservatives under Joe Clark ends sixteen years of Liberal government, and begins effort to reduce government role in economy.
–	After difficult and protracted negotiations, more than 100 participating countries bring Tokyo Round of GATT negotiations to successful conclusion.
1980	Return of Liberals under Pierre Trudeau leads to further efforts to strengthen industrial policy, including establishment of a National Energy Policy.
–	Arthur Dunkel, another Swiss official, succeeds Olivier Long to become GATT's third director general.
–	Greece joins EC.
1981-2	Global recession hits Canada particularly hard and leads to a broad reevaluation of interventionist economic and industrial policies.
1982	GATT meets at ministerial level for first time since launch of Tokyo Round in 1973, but fails to adopt work program that meets aspirations of major participants.
–	Government establishes a royal commission chaired by former finance minister Donald Macdonald to examine Canada's economic prospects.
1982-3	Canadian business community organizes committee under chairmanship of David Braide to lobby government to improve trade relations with United States; provincial governments echo sentiments.
1983	Federal government releases *A Review of Canadian Trade Policy* and announces plan to negotiate sectoral free-trade agreements with United States.
1984	United States ends its long distaste for regional agreements by signing FTA with Israel.
–	Election of Conservative government led by Brian Mulroney leads to more market-oriented trade and economic policies, including dismantling of various earlier interventionist experiments such as FIRA and NEP.
1985	Leutwiler Report, prepared by group of eminent persons appointed by GATT Director General Dunkel, provides intellectual and public policy support for new negotiating round focused on mix of traditional, new, and systemic issues.
–	Macdonald Royal Commission issues *Final Report* containing strong recommendation that Canada and United States negotiate a bilateral free-trade agreement.
–	Canada and United States agree in principle to negotiate bilateral FTA.
–	EC adopts Single European Act to address challenges raised by deepening economic integration with plan to complete common market by beginning of 1992.
1986	Spain and Portugal join EC to make it twelve countries.
–	Canada and United States launch free-trade negotiations.
–	United States and its allies finally succeed in launching new round of GATT negotiations at Punta del Este in Uruguay.
1987	Canada and United States successfully conclude free-trade negotiations with broad-based agreement (FTA) covering not only trade in goods, but also trade in services and investment. FTA enters into force January 1989.

1988	Midterm review of Uruguay Round meets in Montreal and seeks to gather early harvest of agreements but instead demonstrates difficulty of negotiating broad-based agreement among more than 100 participants with wide range of objectives. It formally concludes at level of senior officials April 1989.
1989	Implosion of Soviet Union and COMECON, symbolized by fall of Berlin Wall, removes many of geopolitical underpinnings of postwar trade and payments system, and after some drift, provides basis for new developments more closely attuned to the commercial and economic challenges posed by globalization.
1990	Concluding ministerial conference of Uruguay Round fails to reach agreement. MIT economist Lester Thurow announces that GATT is dead at annual gathering of business and government leaders in Davos, Switzerland, capturing widely held opinion that GATT was instrument suited to earlier era, but not to emerging, post-cold-war commercial rivalry among Europe, North America, and East Asia.
1991	Brazil, Argentina, Uruguay, and Paraguay sign Treaty of Asunción, committing themselves to development of Common Market of Southern Cone by 1995 (Mercosur).
1991-2	Failure of efforts to conclude Uruguay Round seems to confirm new pessimism about future of multilateral trading system.
1993	United States and Canada expand their free-trade agreement to include Mexico in new, more ambitious North American Free Trade Agreement (NAFTA), confirming fears of those convinced world is breaking up into three competing trading blocs.
–	Peter Sutherland succeeds Arthur Dunkel as GATT's fourth director general.
–	Upon ratification of Maastricht Treaty, EC is transformed into European Union (EU).
1993-4	Despite growing scepticism of media and intellectuals, GATT members succeed in bringing Uruguay Round to successful conclusion at end of 1993, agreeing to transform interim GATT into definitive World Trade Organization. Some 129 countries sign Marrakech Protocol, formally bringing Uruguay Round to conclusion on 15 April 1994. WTO is accepted as "single undertaking," requiring signatories to accept all its elements.
1994	NAFTA, first free-trade agreement between developed and developing countries, successfully enters into force following protracted ratification procedures in the United States and Canada.
1995	WTO enters into force. Renato Ruggiero, former Italian trade minister, chosen as WTO's first director general.
–	Government leaders of members of Asia Pacific Economic Cooperation (APEC), including United States, Canada, Japan, Australia, and members of Association of South East Asian Nations (ASEAN) agree to work toward process of coordinated unilateral trade liberalization with goal of achieving tariff-free trade for industrialized participants by year 2010 and for developing participants by 2020.
–	Leaders representing every western hemisphere government except Cuba adopt decision to work toward Free Trade Area for Americas (FTAA), with goal of tariff-free trade by year 2005.
–	Sweden, Austria, and Finland join EU, to make fifteen member states. Switzerland and Norway stay out as result of referenda. EFTA now down to Iceland, Switzerland, and Norway.
–	OECD organizes negotiation of a multilateral agreement on investment (MAI) among its members, in hope of concluding a "quality" agreement that will provide a model for wider acceptance at a later stage.
1996	Singapore hosts first WTO ministerial meeting in December, with more than 100 ministers in attendance, membership of 128 countries, and a further 29 countries

	having indicated their formal intent to accede, including China, Saudi Arabia, Vietnam, Russia, and most other USSR successor states.
–	Canada concludes FTAs with Chile and Israel.
1997	GATT celebrates its fiftieth anniversary, finally within fold of a multilateral organization, WTO.
–	Canada hosts APEC summit at which members pledge renewed commitment to process of concerted, unilateral steps toward freer trade.
–	Canada and the United States conclude Open Skies agreement, providing for much more open, market-based regime for reciprocal air services.
1998	WTO holds its second ministerial meeting in Geneva.
–	French withdrawal from OECD's MAI negotiations provides coup de grace to failed negotiating process.
1999	Mike Moore, former New Zealand trade minister, accepts appointment of reduced three-year term as second director general of WTO, following protracted campaign that suggests alternative visions for the world trade regime.
–	Third ministerial meeting of WTO ends in disarray in Seattle, Washington, besieged by thousands of antiglobalization protestors. Weak US leadership and lack of consensus on emerging agenda of new and old issues broadly cited as contributing to failure.
2000	US president Bill Clinton concludes two terms in office without gaining trade negotiating authority from Congress, the first president since Roosevelt to fail in this quest; widely interpreted as indicative of hardening attitudes in the United States to liberalization and multilateralism.
–	Canada hosts third Summit of Americas, at which thirty-four democratically elected heads of state pledge once again to conclude a Free Trade Area of Americas by year 2005.
–	WTO members begin prenegotiations to further liberalize trade in services and agriculture, as provided in "built-in" agenda adopted at conclusion of Uruguay Round. Little progress, however, is expected until members find basis for launching a new round of negotiations.
–	Canada and Singapore agree to explore the prospect for a free-trade agreement.
–	Canada and four countries in Central America – Guatemala, El Salvador, Honduras, and Nicaragua – agree to explore the prospect for a free-trade agreement.
2001	Canada concludes FTA with Costa Rica.
–	Fourth ministerial meeting of WTO held in Doha, Qatar, largely to reduce scope for antiglobalization protests. Ministers succeed in launching new round of multilateral trade negotiations.

GLOSSARY OF TRADE AND RELATED TERMS

accession. The process of becoming a contracting party to a multilateral agreement such as the WTO. Negotiations with established WTO members, for example, determine the trade liberalizing concessions or other specific obligations a nonmember country must undertake before it is entitled to the full benefits of WTO membership.

adjustment. The ongoing process by which an economy declines or renews and adjusts to changing circumstances. Among the factors that influence the scope and pace of adjustment are changes in technology and productivity, trade liberalization, consumer taste, resource exhaustion, and the changing composition of the labour force.

adjustment assistance. Financial, training, technical, and other assistance to workers, firms, and industries to help them cope with adjustment difficulties arising from increased international competition and other factors.

ad valorem **tariff.** A tariff calculated as a percentage of the value of goods cleared through customs, e.g., 15 percent *ad valorem* means 15 percent of the value. *See also* **specific duty or tariff.**

antidumping code. A code of conduct first negotiated under the auspices of the GATT and now administered by the WTO that establishes both substantive and procedural standards for national antidumping proceedings. *See also* **codes of conduct** and **dumping.**

antidumping duty. A special duty imposed to offset the price effect of dumping that has been determined to cause or threaten material injury to domestic producers. Under article VI of GATT, antidumping duties may be imposed against dumped goods equal to the difference between their export price and their normal value in the exporting country. *See also* **contingency protection, dumping,** and **injury.**

antidumping tribunal. See **Canadian International Trade Tribunal.**

autarky. See **economic nationalism.**

Auto Pact. A sectoral trade agreement (The Canada-US Automotive Products Agreement) entered into by the United States and Canada in 1965 in order to encourage the rationalization and growth of the North American auto industry. It provided for duty-free movement between the two countries of new automobiles and original equipment parts. In the case of Canada, only producers were allowed to import duty-free.

balance of payments. A tabulation of a country's credit and debit transactions with other countries and international institutions. These transactions are divided into two broad groups: current account and capital account. The current account includes exports and imports of goods, services (including investment income), and unilateral transfers. The capital account includes financial flows related to international direct investment, investment in government and private securities, international bank transactions, and changes in official gold holdings and foreign exchange reserves. An imbalance in the balance of payments requires adjustment in a country's macroeconomic polices, often effected through changes in the exchange rate. Trade measures may also be deployed as a temporary measure to safeguard the balance of payments.

balance of trade. A component of the balance of payments; the surplus or deficit that results from comparing a country's expenditures on merchandise imports with receipts derived from its merchandise exports.

binding. Agreeing to maintain a particular tariff level or other trade restriction, i.e., binding it against increase or change. In trade negotiations, binding a tariff is considered equivalent to a significant reduction in the level. The industrialized countries have bound virtually all their tariffs on industrial products in eight rounds of GATT negotiations, while the NAFTA binds all

Canadian, US, and Mexican tariffs at free at the end of the transition period. Margins of preference may also be bound.

binding arbitration. Concept in dispute settlement by which the parties to the dispute agree at the outset to abide by the results of the settlement procedures.

bound tariff. *See* **binding.**

bounty. *See* **subsidy.**

Bretton Woods. The place in New Hampshire, USA, where the International Monetary Fund and International Bank for Reconstruction and Development were negotiated in 1944. These two agreements are often referred to as the Bretton Woods institutions or Bretton Woods monetary arrangements.

buy-national. Discriminatory government procurement policies, such as Buy America or Buy Canadian, which provide a margin of preference for local suppliers over foreign suppliers. The GATT does not require nondiscrimination by governments in their purchasing policies. A modest code agreed during the Tokyo Round provides for nondiscriminatory purchasing practices by specified government entities. FTA chapter 23 provides a modest extension of the coverage of the GATT code. *See also* **government procurement.**

Canadian International Trade Tribunal (CITT). A body responsible under Canadian legislation for findings of injury in antidumping and countervailing duty cases, the adjudication of government procurement appeals, and the provision of advice to the government on other import issues. It was created by the Special Import Measures Act and replaced the Antidumping Tribunal established in 1968. In 1988, it also assumed the responsibilities of the Tariff Board, created in 1931.

CAP. *See* **Common Agriculture Policy.**

certificate of origin. *See* **rules of origin.**

CET. *See* **Common External Tariff.**

CIF. Cost plus insurance and freight charges. Abbreviation used to indicate the terms upon which goods are sold for export. *See also* **FOB.**

CIT. *See* **US Court of International Trade.**

CITT. *See* **Canadian International Trade Tribunal.**

classification. *See* **customs classification.**

codes of conduct. International instruments that indicate standards of behaviour by nation-states or multinational corporations. *See also* **antidumping code** and **subsidies code.**

commercial presence. In trade in services, the presence that a national of one country must have in another in order to complete a service transaction, such as a branch office staffed by local staff. Commercial presence falls short of **establishment.**

Common Agriculture Policy (CAP). The series of policies and measures related to the agricultural sector that were adopted by the original six members of the European Common Market (ECM) and subsequently by the European Community (EC) and the European Union (EU).

Common External Tariff (CET). The tariff provisions of the European Union and its precursors, including the European Common Market (ECM) and the European Community (EC).

common market. A more integrative version of a **customs union** in which the member countries agree to common policy measures affecting the internal operation of the market in order to promote the free movement of goods, capital, services, and people.

comparative advantage. A central concept in international trade theory that holds that a country or a region should specialize in the production and export of those goods and services that it can produce relatively more efficiently than other goods and services, and import those goods and services that it can produce relatively less efficiently.

compensation. Concept that withdrawal or amendment of a previously negotiated or bound concession, such as a tariff increase, change in quota level, or temporary surtax, requires a new and equivalent concession.

competition policy. Set of policy measures adopted to protect the effective operation of the economy based on the premise that generally a market system will give better results in terms of economic and industrial performance than any alternative system of industrial organization. Canada's competition policy is founded in the Competition Act.

conditional MFN. *See* **most-favoured-nation treatment.**

continentalism. Policies and programs that facilitate and encourage Canada-US trade and investment ties, as opposed to policies that encourage either domestic east-west patterns of trade and investment or multilateral trade and investment relations. *See also* **multilateralism.**

contingency protection. Collective term referring to trade remedies that may be imposed by a government contingent upon certain criteria being met, such as the importation of dumped or subsidized goods that cause material injury to domestic producers. *See also* **antidumping duty, countervailing duty, injury,** and **safeguards.**

convertible currency. Currency that can be converted into other major currencies with few, if any, restrictions. Some countries maintain foreign-exchange controls and restrict the convertibility of their currency to essential needs, such as the financing of approved imports.

countervailing duty. An additional duty imposed by an importing country to offset government subsidies in an exporting country, when the subsidized imports cause material injury to domestic industry in the importing country. *See also* **contingency protection** and **injury.**

cultural identity programs. Programs and policies, such as subsidies, content regulations, and ownership restrictions, aimed at providing domestic providers of cultural products with support and protection, in order to strengthen national identity.

Customs Act. Canadian legislation that provides the basic framework for customs procedures in Canada.

customs classification. The particular category in a tariff nomenclature in which a product is classified for tariff purposes, or the procedure by which a country determines that category, used for the classification, coding, and description of internationally traded goods. Most important trading nations have agreed to use a common classification system known eventually as the Harmonized Commodity Coding and Description System (HS). During its early development, it was referred to as the Harmonized System of Tariff Nomenclature (HS).

customs duties. *See* **tariff.**

Customs Tariff Act. Canadian legislation that provides the legal framework for the collection of customs duties in Canada, including rules related to **drawbacks,** duty **remission,** and **customs valuation.**

customs union. A group of nations that have eliminated trade barriers among themselves and imposed a common customs regime on all goods imported from all other countries.

customs valuation. The appraisal of the value of imported goods by customs officials for the purpose of determining the amount of duty payable in the importing country. The WTO Customs Valuation Code obligates governments to use the "transaction value" of imported goods – the price actually paid or payable for them – as the principal basis for valuing the goods for customs purposes.

Defence Production Sharing Arrangements (DPSA). A set of administrative arrangements between the United States and Canada dating back to the 1941 Hyde Park arrangement, providing for free trade in defence materiel and encouraging shared production of such materiel.

deficiency payments. Government payments to compensate farmers for all or part of the difference between domestic market price levels for a commodity and a higher target price. *See also* **variable levy.**

developing countries (LDCs). Countries at an early state of economic development, evident from such factors as low levels of per capita income, low levels of education, health, and other social factors, and the absence of sophisticated and widespread infrastructure and industry. Developing countries are eligible for special and differential treatment under many trade agreements, including preferential tariff treatment. *See also* **least developed countries** and **general preferential tariff.**

Dillon Round. The fifth in the series of GATT multilateral trade negotiations (1960-1), named in honour of US assistant secretary of state (later treasury secretary), Douglas Dillon, who first proposed that GATT members initiate a new round of tariff negotiations.

dispute settlement mechanism. Those institutional provisions in a trade agreement that provide the means by which differences of view between the parties can be settled.

Dispute Settlement Understanding (DSU). The WTO agreement that sets out the procedures by which members settle disputes relating to the implementation of the other WTO agreements.

domestic content requirements. A requirement that firms selling a particular product within a particular country must use, as a certain percentage of their inputs, goods produced within that country.

DPSA. *See* **Defence Production Sharing Arrangements.**

drawback. Import duties or taxes repaid by a government, in whole or in part, when the imported goods are reexported or used in the manufacture of exported goods.

DSU. *See* **Dispute Settlement Understanding.**

dumping. The export of a commodity at a price lower than that at which it is sold within the exporting country. Dumping is considered an actionable trade practice when it disrupts markets and injures producers of competitive products in the importing country. Article VI of GATT permits the imposition of special antidumping duties against dumped goods equal to the difference between their export price and their normal value in the exporting country. *See also* **antidumping code, antidumping duty,** and **injury.**

duty. *See* **tariff.**

duty remission. Import duties or taxes repaid by a government, in whole or in part, to a particular company or industry contingent upon exports, manufacture in the importing country, or similar performance requirements, usually on imports of components, parts, or products to complete a product line.

EC. *See* **European Community.**

ECM. European Common Market. *See* **European Community.**

economic nationalism. The desire to make a nation as self-sufficient as possible in terms of trade, so that it requires few imports or exports for its economic well-being; also known as autarky or national self-sufficiency.

EEA. *See* **European Economic Area.**

EEC. European Economic Community. *See* **European Community.**

EFTA. *See* **European Free Trade Association.**

emergency restrictions. *See* **escape clause** and **safeguards.**

end-use tariff item. Tariff classification according to which the rate of duty depends upon the use to which the imported product is put, e.g., cotton sheeting for medical use taxed at a lower rate than all other cotton sheeting.

escape clause. A provision in a bilateral or multilateral commercial agreement permitting a signatory nation to suspend tariff or other concessions when imports threaten serious harm to the producers of competitive domestic goods. GATT article XIX and FTA chapter 11 sanction such "safeguard" provisions to help firms and workers adversely affected by a relatively sudden surge of imports adjust to the rising level of import competition. *See also* **injury** and **safeguards.**

establishment. One of the basic principles that comprise national treatment for investors. Right of establishment provides foreign investors the right to establish new businesses on the same basis as nationals. *See also* **national treatment.**

European Common Market (ECM). *See* **European Community.**

European Community (EC). The common market established by the Treaty of Rome in 1958, and also its subsequent evolution, also known before 1967 as the European Economic Community (EEC) or European Common Market (ECM). By 1986, the EC included Belgium, Denmark, France, Germany, Greece, Ireland, Italy, Luxembourg, Netherlands, Portugal, Spain, and the United Kingdom. In 1994, it evolved into the European Union (EU) and now also includes Sweden, Finland, and Austria.

European Economic Area (EEA). The term used to describe the end result of a series of negotiations between the EC and the EFTA countries aimed at creating greater market integration between the two groups.

European Free Trade Association (EFTA). Originally comprised Austria, Finland, Norway, Portugal, Sweden, Switzerland, and the United Kingdom. Iceland and Liechtenstein joined later. It is now comprised of Iceland, Norway, Switzerland, and Liechtenstein.

EU. European Union. *See* **European Community.**

European Union (EU). *See* **European Community.**

exceptions. Provisions in a trade agreement that deal with special circumstances, such as import or export controls for security reasons. GATT articles XX and XXI provide for the basic exceptions to the GATT. FTA chapters 12 and 20 provide similar exceptions.

exchange controls. Measures restricting the quantity of foreign currency a company or individual may purchase or use at any one time.

exchange rate. The price (or rate) at which one currency is exchanged for another currency, for gold, or for **special drawing rights (SDRs).**

exemptions. Provisions that exempt particular products or situations from a general rule, e.g., in a free-trade area eliminating all tariffs, agriculture might be exempted.

Export and Import Permits Act. Canadian legislation that provides the mechanism (licensing) by which exports from Canada and imports into Canada can be controlled. Three basic controlling lists are prescribed under the act: an Import Control List, an Export Control List, and an Area Control List. Any product listed on the first two lists or any exports to a country on the third list requires a permit, the conditions for which may be prescribed by Order-in-Council.

export quotas. Specific restrictions or ceilings imposed by an exporting country on the value or volume of certain exports, designed, for example, to protect domestic producers and consumers from temporary shortages of the goods affected or to bolster their prices in world markets. Some international commodity agreements explicitly indicate when producers should apply such restraints. Export quotas are also often applied in orderly marketing agreements and voluntary restraint agreements, in order to promote domestic processing of raw materials in countries that produce them.

export restraints. Quantitative restrictions imposed by an exporting country to limit exports to specified foreign markets, usually pursuant to a formal or informal agreement concluded at the request of the importing country.

export subsidies. Government payments or other financially quantifiable benefits provided to domestic producers or exporters contingent on the export of their goods or services.

extraterritoriality. The application of national laws, policies, and practices beyond the frontier. The United States actively practises the extraterritorial application of its laws, e.g., in the area of antitrust and strategic export controls through its jurisdiction over the head offices of US-owned multinational enterprises.

fair trade. *See* **unfair trade.**

fast-track procedures. US legislative procedures stipulating that once the president formally submits to Congress a bill implementing an agreement negotiated under the authority of a trade act, both houses must vote on the bill within ninety days. No amendments are permitted. The purpose of these procedures is to assure foreign governments that Congress will act expeditiously on an agreement they negotiate with the US government.

FIRA. Foreign Investment Review Agency. *See* **Investment Canada.**

FOB. Free on board. Abbreviation used to indicate the terms upon which goods are sold for export, i.e., the price does not include insurance and freight charges. *See also* **CIF.**

Foreign Investment Review Agency (FIRA). *See* **Investment Canada.**

formula approach. A technique used in tariff negotiations, whereby participants agree to reduce tariffs on the basis of an agreed formula, for example a 10 percent reduction for tariffs over 10 percent and a 5 percent reduction for tariffs under 10 percent. The Kennedy, Tokyo, and Uruguay Rounds of GATT negotiations all used complicated formula approaches to reduce tariffs. A linear approach involves a formula based on a straight reduction from existing tariffs. Given the wide range of tariff structures and interests, most formulas have tended to be more complicated.

free trade. In economics, trade unfettered by government-imposed trade restrictions; also used as a general term to denote the end result of a process of trade liberalization. Freer trade is the comparative term used to denote circumstances between current practice and the achievement of free trade.

free-trade area. An arrangement among two or more nations that removes substantially all tariff and nontariff barriers to trade between them, while each maintains its differing schedule of tariff and other barriers applying to all other nations. GATT article XXIV provides a framework of rules for the negotiation of free-trade areas such as the Canada-US FTA.

Free Trade Area of the Americas (FTAA). An initiative among the thirty-four democratically elected governments of the Americas aimed at negotiating a free-trade area covering all of the Americas by the year 2005.

free-trade zone. An area within a country (a seaport, airport, warehouse, or any designated area) regarded as being outside its customs territory. Importers may therefore bring goods of foreign origin into such an area without paying customs duties and taxes, pending their eventual processing, transshipment or reexportation. Free-trade zones may also be known as "free ports," "free warehouses," or "foreign trade zones."

FTA. Free Trade Agreement. In North America, the abbreviation usually refers to the Canada-US Free Trade Agreement that entered into force on 1 January 1989.

FTAA. *See* **Free Trade Area of the Americas.**

G7. Group of seven most important industrialized countries (Canada, France, Germany, Italy, Japan, the United Kingdom, and the United States) that meet annually at a summit to discuss economic and, increasingly, political issues of common concern. In 2000, Russia was invited to participate, converting the group into the G8.

GATS. *See* **General Agreement on Trade in Services.**

GATT. *See* **General Agreement on Tariffs and Trade.**

GDE/GNE. *See* **Gross Domestic/National Expenditure.**

GDP/GNP. *See* **Gross Domestic/National Product.**

General Agreement on Tariffs and Trade (GATT). A multilateral treaty that delineates rules for international trade in goods, originally negotiated in 1947 and, since 1995, part of the World Trade Organization Agreement. The primary objective of the GATT is to liberalize world trade and place it on a secure basis, thereby contributing to global economic growth and development.

General Agreement on Trade in Services (GATS). A multilateral treaty modelled on the GATT negotiated during the Uruguay Round of GATT negotiations (1986-94), applying to trade in services. The GATS forms part of the World Trade Organization Agreement. The primary objective of the GATS is to liberalize world trade in services and to place it on a secure basis, thereby contributing to global economic growth and development.

general preferential tariff (GPT). The tariff treatment applied by most industrialized countries, on a noncontractual basis, to goods originating in developing countries. This preference is covered under a GATT (now WTO) decision allowing industrialized members to discriminate in favour of developing countries. Canada's GPT has been in effect since 1974. *See also* **developing countries.**

general system of preferences (GSP). *See* **general preferential tariff.**

government procurement. Purchases of goods and services by official government agencies. Procurement preferences refer to discriminatory purchases from domestic suppliers, even when imported goods are more competitive; procurement preferences are a major nontariff barrier to trade. *See* also **buy-national.**

GPT. *See* **general preferential tariff.**

grandfather clause. A GATT provision that allowed the original contracting parties to accept various GATT obligations despite the fact that some existing domestic legislation was otherwise inconsistent with GATT provisions. More generally, any clause in an agreement which provides that certain existing programs, practices, and policies are exempt from an obligation. *See also* **Protocol of Provisional Application.**

Gross Domestic/National Expenditure. The total of all domestic purchases by corporations, individuals, and governments.

Gross Domestic/National Product. The total of goods and services produced by a country.

GSP. General system of preferences. *See* **general preferential tariff.**

Harmonized Commodity Coding and Description System (HS), or Harmonized System of Tariff Nomenclature. *See* **customs classification.**

IBRD. International Bank for Reconstruction and Development. *See* **World Bank.**

IMF. *See* **International Monetary Fund.**

imperial preferences. Preferences extended first by Canada to goods from Britain and gradually extended to goods from elsewhere in the British Empire. The other dominions and eventually the United Kingdom also introduced imperial preferences into their trade policies.

import substitution. An attempt by a country to reduce imports (and hence foreign exchange expenditures) by encouraging the development of domestic industries.

import quota. *See* **quantitative restriction.**

inconvertible currency. *See* **convertible currency.**

industrial policy. Governmental actions affecting, or seeking to affect, the sectoral composition of the economy by influencing the development of particular industries.

injury. In international commerce, describes the effect on domestic producers of a decline in output, lost sales, decline in market share, reduced profits and return on investment, reduced capacity utilization, and so on, as a result of import competition. A distinction is often made between serious injury (required for emergency safeguard measures) and material injury (required for antidumping and countervailing duties). *See also* **antidumping duty, countervailing duty,** and **safeguards.**

intellectual property. A collective term for new ideas, inventions, designs, writings, films, and the like, protected by copyright, patent, trademark, and similar laws.

International Monetary Fund (IMF). Established at Bretton Woods in 1944, in order to restore and promote monetary and economic stability. Its headquarters are in Washington. All OECD and most developing countries are members.

International Trade Administration (ITA). The branch of the US Department of Commerce responsible for investigating and determining the existence of dumping or subsidization in US trade remedy cases.

International Trade Advisory Committee (ITAC). A committee of private-sector leaders that advises the Canadian government on trade negotiations. *See also* **Sectoral Advisory Groups on International Trade.**

International Trade Commission. *See* **US International Trade Commission.**

International Trade Organization (ITO). The stillborn organization that was to do for trade what the IMF had done for the management of international monetary issues. GATT, the commercial policy chapter of the Havana Charter for an ITO, implemented on a "provisional" basis in 1948, gradually gained organizational status and ultimately performed this function. GATT was superseded by the WTO in 1995.

Investment Canada. Agency established by the Canadian federal government in 1984 to promote and monitor incoming foreign direct investment with a view to ensuring that Canada benefits to the greatest extent possible from such investment. It replaced the Foreign Investment Review Agency (FIRA), which had a mandate to screen foreign direct investment and determine the extent to which each proposed investment would be of net benefit to Canada.

investment performance requirements. Special conditions imposed on direct foreign investors by host governments, sometimes requiring commitments to export a certain percentage of the output, to purchase given supplies locally, or to ensure the employment of a specified percentage of local labour and management.

invisibles. The nonmerchandise part of a country's current account in its balance of payments, including receipts and payments for services, investments, and royalty payments.

ITA. *See* **International Trade Administration.**

ITAC. *See* **International Trade Advisory Committee.**

ITC. *See* US International Trade Commission.

ITO. *See* International Trade Organization.

Kennedy Round. The sixth in the series of GATT multilateral trade negotiations (1963-7), named in honour of US president John F. Kennedy, who first proposed that GATT members initiate a major new round of tariff negotiations.

LDCs. *See* developing countries.

least developed countries (LLDCs). Those developing countries that are at the earliest stage of economic development, often indicated by annual per capita income levels below US$1,000. The United Nations maintains a list of countries so designated. *See also* developing countries.

liberalization. Reductions in tariff and other measures that restrict world trade, unilaterally, bilaterally, or multilaterally. Trade liberalization has been the objective of all GATT trade negotiations as well as of the FTA and NAFTA negotiations.

linear approach. *See* formula approach.

LLDCs. *See* least developed countries.

margin of preference. The difference between the MFN tariff rate and a preferential rate, such as the general preferential tariff or a free-trade area rate.

market access. Availability of a national market to exporting countries, indicative of a government's willingness to permit imports to compete relatively unimpeded with similar domestically produced goods.

mercantilism. A prominent economic philosophy in the sixteenth and seventeenth centuries that equated the accumulation and possession of gold and other international monetary assets, such as foreign currency reserves, with national wealth. Although this point of view is generally discredited among modern economists and trade policy experts, some contemporary politicians still favour policies designed to create trade "surpluses," such as import substitution and tariff protection for domestic industries, and consider such policies essential to national economic strength.

MFA. *See* Multifibre Agreement.

most-favoured-nation (MFN) treatment. A commitment that a country will extend to another country the treatment it extends to its "most-favoured" trading partner, i.e., the lowest tariff rates it applies to any third country. The MFN principle has provided the foundation for the world trading system since the end of the Second World War. All members of the WTO apply MFN treatment to one another under article I of GATT and article I of GATS. Exceptions to this basic rule are allowed in the formation of regional trading arrangements, provided certain strict criteria are met. The modern form of MFN is generally "unconditional," i.e., a country that is entitled to MFN treatment automatically benefits from any new benefits extended to a third country. Until 1922, the United States practised the "conditional" variety, i.e., new benefits extended to one country would only be applied to other countries entitled to MFN treatment if they agreed to make equivalent concessions. *See also* national treatment.

MTN. *See* multilateral trade negotiations.

Multifibre Agreement (MFA). A sectoral derogation from the GATT (1974-94) that allowed countries to reach discriminatory agreements or to impose quantitative restrictions restricting trade in low-cost textile and clothing products. It was preceded by similar arrangements limited to cotton textiles (The Short- and Long-term Cotton Textile Arrangements, 1961-73), and succeeded by the WTO Agreement on Textiles, which seeks to phase out all QRs by the end of 2004.

multilateral agreement. An international compact involving three or more parties, such as the GATT.

multilateralism. The conviction that widely shared agreements are superior to bilateral or smaller agreements. *See also* continentalism.

multilateral trade negotiations (MTN). Eight rounds of multilateral trade negotiations have been held under the auspices of GATT since 1947. Each round represents a discrete and lengthy series of interacting bargaining sessions among the participating countries in search of mutually beneficial agreements looking toward the reduction of barriers to world trade. The agreement reached at the conclusion of each round constitutes new GATT commitments and thus amounts to an important step in the evolution of the world trading system. *See also* **round of trade negotiations.**

NAFTA. *See* **North American Free Trade Agreement.**

National Policy. A policy adopted by the Conservative government of Sir John A. Macdonald in 1879, involving increased tariff protection aimed at encouraging establishment of import-substitution industries, with the additional goal of convincing the US government to negotiate a new reciprocity agreement. Over time, other nation-building elements were added, including transportation policies to knit the country together, and immigration policies to provide Canada with the necessary population base to reward import-substitution industries. The economic effects of the National Policy cast a long shadow, well into the twentieth century.

national self-sufficiency. *See* **economic nationalism.**

national treatment. Extension to imported goods (and services and investment) of treatment no less favourable than that accorded to domestic goods (and services and investment) with respect to internal taxes, laws, regulations, and requirements. WTO members are obliged to accord to one another national treatment with respect to internal measures that can affect trade in goods (GATT article III) and, on a more limited basis resulting from negotiated commitments, services (GATS article XVII). *See also* **most-favoured-nation treatment.**

New Deal. Popular name for the various policies advanced by US president Franklin D. Roosevelt to fight the depression in his country, most based on a much higher level of government involvement in the economy than had been considered politically acceptable by earlier administrations. The New Deal provided the base in the United States for the modern welfare state.

nontariff barriers or **measures.** Government measures or policies other than tariffs that restrict or distort international trade. Examples include import quotas, discriminatory government procurement practices, and measures to protect intellectual property. Such measures have become relatively more conspicuous impediments to trade as tariffs have been reduced during the period since the Second World War.

North American Free Trade Agreement (NAFTA). Involving Canada, the United States, and Mexico, which entered into force on 1 January 1994.

OECD. *See* **Organization for Economic Cooperation and Development.**

OEEC. Organization for European Economic Cooperation, established in 1954 to promote intra-European economic cooperation. Evolved in 1960 into the OECD.

Organization for Economic Cooperation and Development (OECD). Paris-based organization of industrialized countries responsible for study of and cooperation on a broad range of economic, trade, scientific and educational issues. Membership includes Canada, Australia, Austria, Belgium, Denmark, Finland, France, Germany, Greece, Iceland, Ireland, Italy, Japan, Luxembourg, Netherlands, New Zealand, Norway, Portugal, Spain, Sweden, Switzerland, Turkey, the United Kingdom, and the United States.

overall approach. The term adopted by the EC to describe its approach to the Tokyo Round of GATT negotiations, intended in part to balance the fully articulated US position set out in the Trade Act of 1974.

peril point. A concept adopted in US trade legislation in the 1940s and 1950s to describe the point at which further reductions in tariff protection would create economic difficulties for the protected industry. US legislation required the US Tariff Commission to report to the administration prior to negotiations at what point an individual tariff level would "imperil" US industry. The concept was based on political, rather than economic, considerations, and was similar to earlier efforts to develop a "scientific" or "flexible" tariff, i.e., a tariff calculated to equalize the price difference between domestic and imported goods.

PPA. *See* **Protocol of Provisional Application.**

predatory pricing. Business practice that involves deliberately charging prices low enough to drive a competitor out of business or deter entry by new competitors. It is usually directed toward competitors at the same level of production or distribution as the offender. Both Canadian and US laws on competition consider predatory pricing an offence.

preferences. More favourable tariff or other treatment extended to goods from one country than those from another. Canada historically extended preferences to goods from countries in the British Empire and, throughout its early history, sought preferences for its exports in the UK market.

price discrimination. Business practice that involves charging different customers different prices for the same product by differentiating between groups of customers. It may be used to benefit the seller or the buyer of the product. Both Canadian and US laws on competition consider certain types of price discrimination as offences. Dumping is a form of international price discrimination.

productivity. A way of expressing changes in the value of economic activity; labour productivity measures the amount of production per unit of effort; capital productivity measures the amount of production per unit of capital; total factor productivity measures the amount of production obtained from combined units of effort, capital, and technology. For economists, growth in productivity is an important indicator that an economy is making the best use of available factors of production. Sustained increases in total factor productivity are an important determinant for a rising standard of living.

protectionism. The deliberate use or encouragement of restrictions on imports to enable relatively inefficient domestic producers to compete successfully with foreign producers.

Protocol of Provisional Application (PPA). The device that allowed eight countries to implement the GATT on an "interim" or "provisional" basis in 1948, by agreeing that they would implement much of the agreement only insofar as it did not conflict with existing legislation. In the event, the PPA lasted until 1994 and was part of the foundation of pragmatism that allowed GATT members to implement their obligations gradually on a politically acceptable basis.

Public Law 480. US legislation adopted in 1954 to allow the United States to dispose of surplus agricultural production as food aid.

quantitative restriction (QR). Explicit limits, or quotas, on the amounts of particular products that can be imported or exported during a specified time period, usually measured by volume but sometimes by value. The quota may be applied on a "selective" basis, with varying limits set according to the country of origin, or on a global basis that only specifies the total limit and thus tends to benefit more efficient suppliers. Quotas are frequently administered through a system of licensing.

quasi-judicial procedures. Procedures through which decisions are made by regulatory agencies applying general statutes to specific cases. On trade, procedures administered by the Canadian International Trade Tribunal (CITT) and the Canada Customs and Revenue Agency determine the eligibility of petitioners for import relief under safeguards, countervailing duty, antidumping, and other trade rules.

quota. *See* **quantitative restriction.**

reciprocity. The practice by which governments extend similar concessions to each other, as when one government lowers its tariffs or other barriers impeding its imports in exchange for equivalent concessions from a trading partner on barriers affecting its exports (a "balance of concessions"). Reciprocity was traditionally a principal objective of negotiators in GATT negotiations. Reciprocity is also termed "mutuality of benefits," "quid pro quo," and "equivalence of advantages."

reciprocity agreements. Historical term referring to trade agreements between Canada and the United States providing for reciprocal trade concessions, including the 1854 Elgin-Marcy Treaty and the aborted 1911 agreement.

remission. A tariff measure that allows domestic industries to claim a refund on import duties paid in defined circumstances, e.g., establishing production in a particular location, or using particular inputs. Unlike **drawback,** which is a general program based on widely defined circumstances, remission orders are often plant- or product-specific and tied to specific industrial policy objectives.

retaliation. Action taken by a country to restrain its imports from a country that has increased a tariff or imposed other measures that adversely affect exports in a manner inconsistent with the GATT. The GATT and the FTA permit such reprisal in certain circumstances, although this has very rarely been practised. The value of trade affected by such retaliatory measures should, in theory, approximately equal the value affected by the initial import restriction.

right of establishment. *See* **establishment.**

round of trade negotiations. A cycle of multilateral trade negotiations under the aegis of GATT (now WTO) leading to simultaneous trade agreements among participating countries to reduce tariff and nontariff barriers to trade. Eight rounds have been completed thus far: Geneva, 1947-8; Annecy, France, 1949; Torquay, England, 1950-51; Geneva, 1956; Geneva, 1960-1 (the Dillon Round); Geneva, 1963-7 (the Kennedy Round); Geneva, 1973-9 (the Tokyo Round); and Geneva, 1986-94 (the Uruguay Round). *See also* **multilateral trade negotiations.**

rules of origin. The set of measures used to differentiate among goods originating in different countries for the purpose of the application of trade measures such as tariffs. For example, goods made up of components originating in various countries whose assembly adds 50 percent to their overall value may be considered to be goods originating in one country, whereas the addition of 25 percent in value would not qualify. Such rules are very important for countries that are members of a free-trade area. Under the FTA, all exported goods require a certificate of origin to demonstrate to customs authorities that they qualify for FTA treatment.

safeguards. Emergency actions in the form of additional duties or import quotas applied to fairly traded imports that nevertheless cause or threaten serious injury to domestic producers. *See also* **contingency protection, escape clause, injury,** and **surcharge.**

SAGITs. *See* **Sectoral Advisory Groups on International Trade.**

SDRs. *See* **special drawing rights.**

Section 301. Provision in US law that enables the president to withdraw concessions or restrict imports from countries that discriminate against US exports, subsidize their own exports to the United States, or engage in other unjustifiable or unreasonable practices that burden or discriminate against US trade. Canada enacted similar legislation in the Special Import Measures Act of 1984.

Section 337. A provision in US trade law to address unfair methods of competition, most often used in patent infringement cases and leading to exclusion orders.

Sectoral Advisory Groups on International Trade (SAGITs). Established in 1986 to provide the Canadian federal government with advice on trade negotiations from a sectoral perspective. *See also* **International Trade Advisory Committee.**

services. Economic activities that provide something other than tangible goods, including such diverse activities as transportation, communications, insurance, banking, advertising, consulting, distribution, engineering, medicine, and education. The services sector is the fastest-growing area of economic activity in Canada, and employs more than two-thirds of working Canadians. Trade in services takes place when a service is exported from a supplier nation to another nation, such as an international air flight, the extension of credit, or the design of a bridge.

special drawing rights (SDRs). A reserve asset created by the IMF to replace gold and US dollars as the basic monetary unit in the management of the international monetary system.

Special Import Measures Act (SIMA). Canadian legislation adopted in 1984, following four years of study and debate, incorporating Canadian rights and obligations flowing from the Tokyo Round in the area of antidumping and countervailing duties and safeguards procedures. It provides for antidumping and countervailing procedures basically similar to one another, including separate investigations of the existence of dumping and subsidization and their margin by the Canada Customs and Revenue Agency and investigations of injury by the Canadian International Trade Tribunal.

special trade representative (STR). *See* **US Trade Representative.**

specific duty or **tariff.** An import tax set at a fixed amount per unit or per unit of measure regardless of the value of the item imported. *See also* ***ad valorem*** **tariff.**

standards. As defined by the GATT Agreement on Technical Barriers to Trade (Standards Code), a standard specifies technical characteristics of a product such as levels of quality, performance, safety, or dimensions. It may include, or deal exclusively with, terminology, symbols, testing and test methods, packaging, marking, or labelling requirements as they apply to a product.

sterling bloc. Those countries that in the 1930s, 1940s, and 1950s cast their economic lot with Britain by tying their currency to the British pound, which remained inconvertible for most of this period. As a result, members of the bloc traded largely among themselves, since trade with other countries could only take place under more restrictive conditions.

subsidies code. A set of rules first negotiated under the auspices of GATT during the Tokyo Round that expanded on GATT articles VI, XVI, and XXIII by establishing both substantive and procedural standards for national countervailing duty proceedings as well as obligations regarding notification and dispute settlement in the area of subsidy practices. The Subsidies Code was substantially revised and expanded during the Uruguay Round to become the WTO Agreement on Subsidies and Countervailing Duties. *See also* **codes of conduct** and **subsidy.**

subsidy. An economic benefit granted by a government to producers of goods or services, often to strengthen their competitive position. The subsidy may be direct (a cash grant) or indirect (low-interest export credits guaranteed by a government agency, for example). Subsidies that cause harm to competing producers in other countries may give rise to claims for remedies, such as countervailing duties. *See also* **subsidies code.**

supply management. The measures used by Canada to protect the dairy and poultry industries, controlling both production within Canada and imports from other suppliers. Canada defended supply management with quotas pursuant to GATT article XI until 1995. Pursuant to the WTO Agreement on Agriculture, Canada now uses tariff rate quotas.

surcharge or **surtax.** A tariff or tax on imports in addition to the existing tariff, often used as a safeguard measure. *See also* **safeguards.**

tariff. A duty (or tax) levied upon goods transported from one customs area to another. Tariffs raise the prices of imported goods, thus making them less competitive within the market of the importing country. After eight rounds of GATT trade negotiations that focused heavily on tariff reductions, tariffs are less important measures of protection than they used to be. The term "tariff" often refers to a comprehensive list or schedule of merchandise with the rate of duty to be paid to the government for importing products itemized. The tariff rate is the rate at which imported goods are taxed. Within a free-trade area or customs union, tariffs are eliminated on goods that qualify for duty-free treatment. *See also* **tariff schedule.**

Tariff Board, Canada. *See* **Canadian International Trade Tribunal.**

Tariff Commission, US. *See* **US International Trade Commission.**

tariff escalation. A situation in which tariffs on manufactured goods are relatively high, tariffs on semi-processed goods are moderate, and tariffs on raw materials are nonexistent or very low. Such escalation, which exists in the tariff schedules of most developed countries, is said to discourage the development of manufacturing industries in resource-rich countries.

tariff rate quota. Tariff rates that take effect only after a certain quantity has been imported, commonly used in agriculture following the Uruguay Round. For example, the tariff on a product may be 10 percent for the first 10,000 tonnes imported in any given year, and 100 percent for all subsequent imports.

tariff schedule. A comprehensive list of the goods that a country imports and the import duties applicable to each product. Annex 401.2 to the FTA sets out the tariff schedules of the United States and Canada and the timetable for the elimination of tariffs.

tariffication. The process agreed on during the Uruguay Round to convert all forms of nontariff protection in the agriculture sector, including quotas and variable levies, to ordinary tariffs, or **tariff rate quota**s.

terms of trade. The volume of exports that can be traded for a given volume of imports. Changes in the terms of trade are generally measured by comparing changes in the ratio of export prices to import prices. The terms of trade are considered to have improved when a given volume of exports can be exchanged for a larger volume of imports.

Third Option. Policy adopted by the federal government in the mid-1970s that sought to develop a more independent Canadian economy by strengthening economic ties to Europe and Japan, promoting Canadian ownership, and decreasing ties to the US economy.

Tokyo Round. The seventh in the series of multilateral trade negotiations held under the auspices of GATT, launched at a ministerial meeting in Tokyo in 1973 and concluded in Geneva in 1979.

Trade Commissioner Service. A quasi-diplomatic service introduced by Canada in 1892, dedicated to finding new markets for Canadian products and servicing the needs of Canadian exporters.

trade diversion. A shift in the source of imports that occurs as a result of altering a country's import policies or practices, without regard for any increase in importation of the items involved. For example, the establishment of a customs union will cause countries participating in the new economic unit to import goods from other countries in the union that previously were imported from countries outside the union.

trade liberalization. Generally, the gradual process of removing tariff and nontariff barriers. Eight rounds of negotiations under GATT since 1947 have resulted in a large measure of trade liberalization among industrialized countries.

TPRM. *See* **trade policy review mechanism.**

trade policy review mechanism (TPRM). The process adopted during the Uruguay Round negotiations, and now part of the WTO, to review the trade policies of all member states. The largest four trading entities – the United States, the EU, Japan, and Canada – are reviewed every other year. Other members are reviewed less frequently, depending on the extent of their international trade, but all members must be reviewed every ten years. The TPRM is based on the premise that greater transparency in the practice of members' trade policies will have a liberalizing effect and promote better trading conditions.

Trade-Related Intellectual Property Rights (TRIPs) Agreement. One of the agreements negotiated during the Uruguay Round, and now part of the WTO, setting out members' obligations related to the protection of **intellectual property** rights.

Trade-Related Investment Measures (TRIMs) Agreement. One of the agreements negotiated during the Uruguay Round, and now part of the WTO. It sets out various obligations members undertake in the trade-related aspects of their investment policies, for example, not to require certain performance requirements from foreign investors.

trade remedies. The various recourses available to governments to provide relief to producers that may be harmed by either the quantity or the nature of imports, including **safeguard** measures and **antidumping** and **countervailing duties.**

transfer of technology. The movement of modern or scientific methods of production or distribution from one enterprise, institution, or country to another, as through foreign investment, international trade licensing of patent rights, technical assistance, or training.

transitional measures. Those measures in place for a limited period of time during which a new trade agreement is gradually implemented. The FTA tariff cuts, for example, were phased in over a period of ten years. Other transitional measures could include, for example, the right to temporary safeguards or adjustment assistance measures.

transparency. Visibility and clarity of laws and regulations. Some of the codes of conduct negotiated during the Tokyo Round sought to increase the transparency of nontariff barriers that impede trade. Much of the FTA is predicated on the idea of improving transparency.

TRIMs Agreement. *See* **Trade-Related Investment Measures Agreement.**

TRIPs Agreement. *See* **Trade-Related Intellectual Property Rights Agreement.**

unconditional MFN. *See* **most-favoured-nation treatment.**

UNCTAD. *See* **United Nations Conference on Trade and Development.**

unfair trade. An American term used to describe trade in dumped, subsidized, or counterfeit goods; the application of the term has steadily widened as US trade remedy laws have defined new practices that are considered to harm the export and import interests of US companies.

United Nations Conference on Trade and Development (UNCTAD). Launched at a meeting in Geneva in 1964, UNCTAD inaugurated a program of meetings and initiatives to promote special and differential treatment in favour of LDCs. Ministerial meetings in New Delhi, Santiago,

Nairobi, and Manila sought to promote a range of policies and measures, which, except for some limited achievements, such as the general system of preferences, remained largely at a rhetorical level. By the time of UNCTAD VI in Belgrade, its programmatic elements were in retreat. It lives on today as a source of analysis, research, and ideas on the problems of LDCs.

unrestricted reciprocity. A version of reciprocity introduced by the Liberal party in the 1880s, calling for the extension of free trade to a much larger share of goods than the earlier commitment to reciprocity in "natural" or resource products.

Uruguay Round. The eighth in a series of multilateral trade negotiations held under the auspices of GATT. This round was launched at a ministerial meeting in Punta del Este, Uruguay, in September 1986 and concluded with a ministerial meeting at Marrakech, Morocco, in April 1994.

US Court of International Trade (CIT). Special court set up to hear appeals from administrative and quasi-judicial trade decisions, e.g., from decisions of the USITC or ITA.

USITC. *See* **US International Trade Commission.**

US International Trade Commission (USITC). Originally established as the US Tariff Commission in 1916, it became the USITC, with a broader mandate, as a result of the Trade Act of 1974. An independent US fact-finding and regulatory agency whose six members make determinations of injury and recommendations for relief for industries or workers seeking relief from increasing import competition. In addition, upon the request of Congress or the president, or on its own initiative, the Commission conducts comprehensive studies of specific industries and trade problems, and the probable impact on specific US industries of proposed reductions in US tariffs and nontariff trade barriers.

USTR. *See* **US Trade Representative.**

US Trade Representative (USTR). An official in the Executive Office of the President, with cabinet-level and ambassadorial rank, charged with advising the president and with leading and coordinating US government policy on international trade negotiations and the development of trade policy. (USTR also designates the White House office that the representative heads.) Originally designated the Special Trade Representative (STR), both the person and the office have been referred to as USTR since 1979.

valuation. *See* **customs valuation.**

variable levy. A tariff subject to alterations as world market prices change, the alterations being designed to assure that the import price after payment of duty will equal a predetermined "gate" price. The variable levy of the European Community, the best known example, equals the difference between the target price for domestic agricultural producers and lowest offers for imported commodities on a **CIF** basis. The amount of the levy is adjusted for changes in the world market situation, daily in the case of grains, fortnightly for dairy products, and quarterly for pork. *See also* **deficiency payments.**

voluntary export restraint (VER). An agreement by an exporting country to limit its exports to another country, often in response to a threat from the importing country to take restrictive action.

World Bank. International Bank for Reconstruction and Development, established, together with the International Monetary Fund, at the Bretton Woods Conference in 1944. Its original purpose was to help countries to reconstruct their economies after the damage inflicted by the war, but it is now devoted to helping developing countries grow and strengthen their economies. Its headquarters are in Washington.

World Trade Organization (WTO). Organization established in 1994 at the conclusion of the Uruguay Round of multilateral trade negotiations to administer the various agreements resulting from these negotiations, including the GATT, GATS, TRIPs, TPRM, and DSU. By the end of 2001, 144 countries were members of the WTO.

CREDITS

A reasonable attempt has been made to secure permission to reproduce all material used. If there are errors or omissions they are wholly unintentional and the publisher would be grateful to learn of them.

Illustrations

385 Prime Minister Brian Mulroney meets with key members of his free-trade team: Gordon Ritchie, Derek Burney, and Simon Reisman, 1988. Author's photo.

403 Dale Cummings, "Roll out the GATT Barrel," *Financial Post* [Winnipeg *Free Press*, 18 December 1993].

422 Brian Gable, "GATT and the Marketing Boards," *Globe and Mail*, 15 December 1993.

426 John S. Pritchett, "The Global Economy, the Deep, Dark Woods," courtesy Pritchett Cartoons, www.pritchettcartoons.com.

435 Patrick Chappatte, "World Government," © Chappatte, globecartoon.com.

445 The National Policy, NAC C17233.

450 Henry Julien, "This Looks Like Equality," *Canadian Illustrated News*, 24 November 1877, NAC C66165.

Tables

2.1, 2.2, 3.1, 3.2, 3.6   O.J. McDiarmid, *Commercial Policy in the Canadian Economy* (Cambridge, MA: Harvard University Press, 1946), 40, 116-17, 76, 148. Reproduced with permission of Harvard University Press.

3.3   *Journal of Economic History* 28, 4 (December 1968): 598-623. Reproduced with permission of Cambridge University Press.

3.4   D.F. Barnett, "The Galt Tariff: Incidental or Effective Protection," *Canadian Journal of Economics* 9, 3 (August 1976): 393-5, tables 1-4. Reproduced with permission of Blackwell Publishing.

3.5   J.H. Perry, *Taxes, Tariffs and Subsidies*, vol. 1 (Toronto: University of Toronto Press, 1955), 31, 72, 107. Reproduced with permission of the University of Toronto Press.

3.9, 4.2, 4.11   Hugh McA. Pinchin, *The Regional Impact of the Canadian Tariff*, prepared for the Economic Council of Canada (Minister of Supply and Services, 1979). The findings of this Study are the personal responsibility of the author and, as such, have not been endorsed by Members of the Economic Council of Canada. Courtesy Industry Canada. Reproduced with the permission of the Minister of Public Works and Government Services Canada, 2001.

3.10   A.E. Safarian, *The Canadian Economy in the Great Depression* (Toronto: University of Toronto Press), table 1, 22. Reproduced with permission of the University of Toronto Press.

4.9   Richard Pomfret, *Unequal Trade: The Economics of Discriminatory Trade Policies* (Oxford: Basil Blackwell, 1988), table 3.3. From Blackwell Publishing.

6.3, 8.2, 9.2, 11.2, 14.1, 15.1   Reproduced with permission of the World Trade Organization.

7.2   Randall Hinshaw, *The European Community and American Trade: A Study in Atlantic Economics and Trade* (New York: Council on Foreign Relations, 1964), 90. Reproduced with permission of the Council on Foreign Relations.

7.3   Grant. L. Reuber, *The Growth and Changing Composition of Trade between Canada and the United States* (Montreal: Private Planning Association for the Canadian-American Committee, 1960), 38. Reproduced with permission of the C.D. Howe Institute.

12.3, 12.5   Richard G. Lipsey and Murray G. Smith, *Taking the Initiative: Canada's Trade Options in a Turbulent World* (Toronto: C.D. Howe Institute, 1985), 47, 15. Reproduced with permission of the C.D. Howe Institute.

Text

119   Quotation from Judith Goldstein, *Ideas, Interests, and American Trade Policy*, © 1993 Cornell University. Used by permission of the publisher, Cornell University Press.

195   Donald Creighton, *The Forked Road: Canada 1939-1957* (Toronto: McClelland and Stewart, 1976), 234-5. Courtesy the Estate of Donald Creighton.

200   Hugh G.J. Aitken, John J. Deutsch, W.A. Mackintosh, et al., *The American Economic Impact on Canada* (Durham, NC: Duke University Press, 1959), 9 and 33.

24   Phillip W. Von Hornick, *Austria over All If Only She Will*. Reprinted by permission of the publisher from *Early Economic Thought* by Arthur Eli Monroe, pp. 223-5, Cambridge, Mass.: Harvard University Press, Copyright © 1924 by the President and Fellows of Harvard College.

197   J.L. Granatstein, *The Ottawa Men* (Toronto: Oxford University Press, 1982), xii. Reproduced with permission of Professor Granatstein.

INDEX

Note: All references to Canada unless otherwise stated; "f" indicates a figure, "m" a map, "t" a table; WWI indicates the First World War, WWII the Second World War.

Canada and International Relations
Kim Richard Nossal, Brian L. Job, and Mark W. Zacher, General Editors

The Canada and International Relations series explores issues in contemporary world politics and international affairs. The volumes cover a wide range of topics on Canada's external relations, particularly international trade and foreign economic policy.

Printed and bound in Canada by Friesens
Set in Minion, Cheltenham, and Akzidenz Grotesk
  by Artegraphica Design Co. Ltd.
Copy editor: Sarah Wight
Proofreader: Gail Copeland
Indexer: Patricia Buchanan
Cartographer: Eric Leinberger